EDITORIAL COMMITTEE

José María Casciaro, General Editor
Gonzalo Aranda, Santiago Ausín
Tomás Belda, Klaus Limburg,
Gonzalo Landáburu, Secretary

FOR THE ENGLISH EDITION
James Gavigan, Brian McCarthy
Thomas McGovern

VOLUMES IN THIS SERIES

Standard Edition
NEW TESTAMENT
St Matthew's Gospel
St Mark's Gospel
St Luke's Gospel
St John's Gospel
Acts of the Apostles
Romans and Galatians
Corinthians
Captivity Letters
Thessalonians and Pastoral Letters
Hebrews
Catholic Letters
Revelation

OLD TESTAMENT
The Pentateuch
Joshua–Kings [Historical Books 1]
Chronicles–Maccabees [Historical Books 2]
The Psalms and the Song of Solomon
Wisdom Books
Major Prophets
Minor Prophets

Reader's (Omnibus) Edition
The Gospels and Acts
The Letters of St Paul
Revelation, Hebrews and Catholic Letters

Single-volume, large-format New Testament

THE NAVARRE BIBLE

Revelation, Hebrews & Catholic Letters

in the Revised Standard Version and New Vulgate
with a commentary by members of the
Faculty of Theology of the University of Navarre

READER'S EDITION

FOUR COURTS PRESS • DUBLIN
SCEPTER PUBLISHERS • NEW YORK

Typeset by Carrigboy Typesetting Services for
FOUR COURTS PRESS LTD
7 Malpas Street, Dublin 8, Ireland
www.fourcourtspress.ie
Distributed in North America by
SCEPTER PUBLISHERS, INC.
P.O. Box 211, New York, NY 10018–0004
www.scepterpublishers.org

© Text of the biblical books in English: The translation used in this book is the Revised Standard Version, Catholic Edition, copyrighted 1965 and 1966 by the Division of Christian Education of the National Council of the Churches of Christ in the U.S.A. and used by permission.

© Other material (origination and selection): Ediciones Universidad de Navarra, SA 1984
Original title: [Part of] *Sagrada Biblia*.
© Translation and typography: Michael Adams 2006

The translation of introductions and commentary was made by Michael Adams.

Nihil obstat: Stephen J. Greene, *censor deputatus*
Imprimi potest: Desmond, Archbishop of Dublin, various dates

A catalogue record for this title is available from the British Library.

ISBN 978–1–85182–998–9 (Four Courts Press)
ISBN 978–1–59417–038–6 (Scepter Publishers)

First printing 2006; reprinted 2012, 2018.

Library of Congress Cataloging-in-Publication Data [for first volume in this series]

Bible. O.T. English. Revised Standard. 1999.
    The Navarre Bible. – North American ed.
        p.   cm
    "The Books of Genesis, Exodus, Leviticus, Numbers, Deuteronomy in the Revised Standard Version and New Vulgate with a commentary by members of the Faculty of Theology of the University of Navarre."
    Includes bibliographical references.
    Contents: [1] The Pentateuch.
    ISBN 1–889334–21–9 (hardback: alk. paper)
I. Title.
BS891.A1   1999.P75   99–23033
221.7'7—dc21   CIP

The title "Navarre Bible" is © Four Courts Press 2003.

ACKNOWLEDGMENTS

Quotations from Vatican II documents are based on the translation in *Vatican Council II: The Conciliar and Post Conciliar Documents*, ed. A. Flannery, OP (Dublin 1981).

The New Vulgate text of the Bible can be accessed via
http://www.vatican.va.archive/bible/index.htm

Printed and bound in England by TJ International, Padstow, Cornwall.

Contents

Map	8
Preface and Preliminary Notes	9
Abbreviations	11

REVELATION (APOCALYPSE)

Introduction	13
Last book of the Bible	13
Authorship and canonicity	13
Place and date of composition	15
Immediate readership	16
Literary form	17
Style and language	18
Interpreting the book of Revelation	19
Historical background	20
Structure and content	21
Teachings contained in the book of Revelation	23
The Revelation to John: English version, with notes	29

HEBREWS

Introduction	127
Canonicity	127
Author, and place and date of composition	128
Immediate readership	129
Structure	130
Language and style of argument	132
Interpretation of the Old Testament	133
Theology	135
The Letter to the Hebrews: English version, with notes	141

Contents

CATHOLIC LETTERS

General Introduction	267
Canonicity	267
Common features	268
Introduction to the Letter of St James	269
The author	269
Canonicity	270
Date of composition	271
Immediate readership	271
Content	272
Doctrinal and moral questions	274
The Letter of James: English version, with notes	277
Introduction to the First Letter of St Peter	311
St Peter the Apostle	311
The author	313
Immediate readership and date of composition	315
Content	315
Trials	316
Baptism	317
Other doctrinal aspects	319
The First Letter of Peter: English version, with notes	321
Introduction to the Second Letter of St Peter	349
The author	349
Immediate readership	350
Links between 2 Peter and the Letter of St Jude	351
Content	351
The final coming of the Lord	352
The false teachers	352
Moral conduct	353
The Second Letter of Peter: English version, with notes	355
Introduction to the First Letter of St John	375
Immediate readership	376
Date of composition	377
The reason for the letter	377
Content	378
Teaching	379

Contents

The First Letter of John: English version, with notes	385
Introduction to the Second and Third Letters of St John	421
The author	421
Special introduction to 2 John	424
The Second Letter of John: English version, with notes	425
Special introduction to 3 John	431
The Third Letter of John: English version, with notes	433
Introduction to the Letter of St Jude	439
The author	439
Authenticity	440
Canonicity	440
Immediate readership	441
Background and purpose	441
Plan and content	442
The Letter of Jude: English version, with notes	443
New Vulgate Text	455
Explanatory Notes	481
Headings added to the Biblical Text	485
Sources quoted in the Commentary	489
Subject Index to the New Testament	495

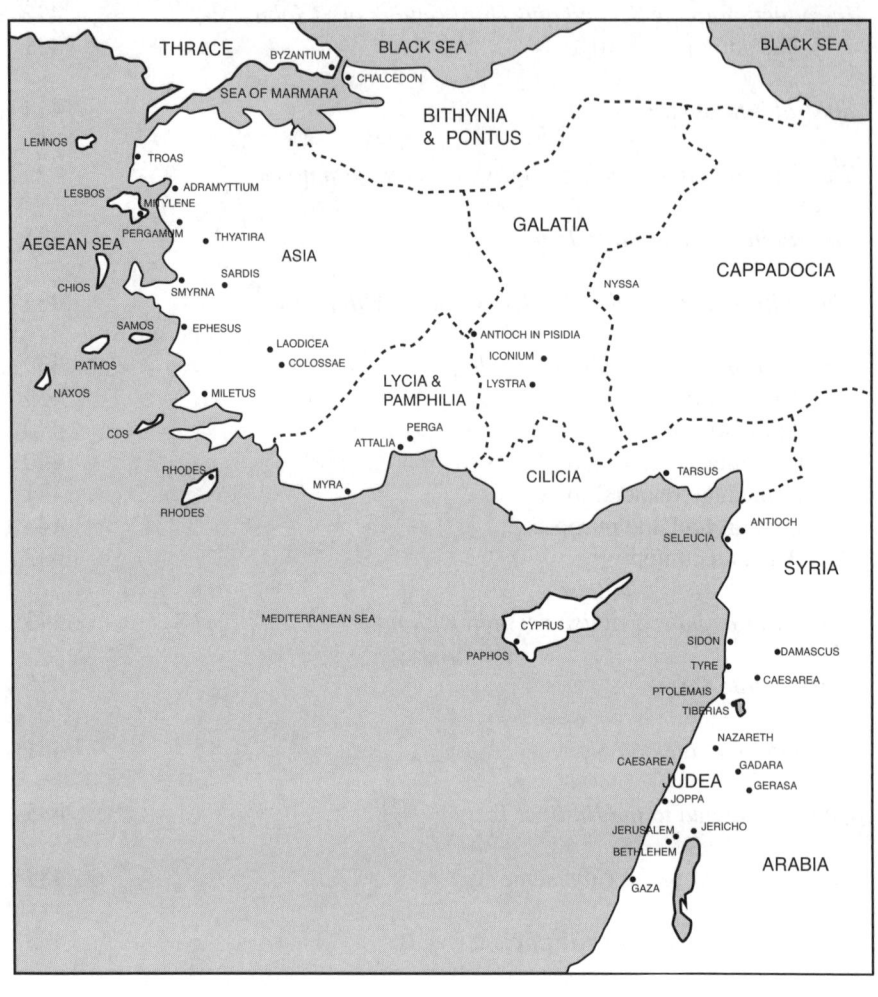

The Eastern Mediterranean in the first century AD

Preface and Preliminary Notes

The Commentary
The distinguishing feature of the *Navarre Bible* is its commentary on the biblical text. Compiled by members of the Theology faculty of the University of Navarre, Pamplona, Spain, this commentary draws on writings of the Fathers, texts of the Magisterium of the Church, and works of spiritual writers, including St Josemaría Escrivá, the founder of Opus Dei; it was he who in the late 1960s entrusted the faculty at Navarre with the project of making a translation of the Bible and adding to it a commentary of the type found here.

The commentary, which is not particularly technical, is designed to explain the biblical text and to identify its main points, the message God wants to get across through the sacred writers. It also deals with doctrinal and practical matters connected with the text.

The first volume of the *Navarre Bible* (the English edition) came out in 1985—first, twelve volumes covering the New Testament; then seven volumes covering the Old Testament. Many reprints and revised editions have appeared over the past twenty years. All the various volumes are currently in print.

The Revised Standard Version
The English translation of the Bible used in the *Navarre Bible* is the Revised Standard Version (RSV) which is, as its preface states, "an authorized revision of the American Standard Version, published in 1901, which was a revision of the King James Version [the "Authorized Version"], published in 1611".

The RSV of the entire Bible was published in 1952; its Catholic edition (RSVCE) appeared in 1966. The differences between the RSV and the RSVCE New Testament texts are listed in the "Explanatory Notes" in the end-matter of this volume. Whereas the Spanish editors of what is called in English the "Navarrre Bible" made a new translation of the Bible, for the English edition the RSV has proved to be a very appropriate choice of translation. The publishers of the *Navarre Bible* wish to thank the Division of Christian Education of the National Council of the Churches of Christ in the USA for permission to use that text.

The Latin Text
This volume also carries the official Latin version of the New Testament in the *editio typica altera* of the New Vulgate (Vatican City, 1986).

Preface

PRELIMINARY NOTES

The headings within the biblical text have been provided by the editors (they are not taken from the RSV). A full list of these headings, giving an overview of the New Testament, can be found at the back of the volume.

An asterisk *inside the biblical text* signals an RSVCE 'Explanatory Note' at the end of the volume.

References in the biblical text indicate parallel texts in other biblical books. All these marginal references come from the *Navarre Bible* editors, not the RSV.

Abbreviations

1. BOOKS OF HOLY SCRIPTURE

Acts	Acts of the Apostles	1 Kings	1 Kings
Amos	Amos	2 Kings	2 Kings
Bar	Baruch	Lam	Lamentations
1 Chron	1 Chronicles	Lev	Leviticus
2 Chron	2 Chronicles	Lk	Luke
Col	Colossians	1 Mac	1 Maccabees
1 Cor	1 Corinthians	2 Mac	2 Maccabees
2 Cor	2 Corinthians	Mal	Malachi
Dan	Daniel	Mic	Micah
Deut	Deuteronomy	Mk	Mark
Eccles	Ecclesiastes (Qoheleth)	Mt	Matthew
Esther	Esther	Nah	Nahum
Eph	Ephesians	Neh	Nehemiah
Ex	Exodus	Num	Numbers
Ezek	Ezekiel	Obad	Obadiah
Ezra	Ezra	1 Pet	1 Peter
Gal	Galatians	2 Pet	2 Peter
Gen	Genesis	Phil	Philippians
Hab	Habakkuk	Philem	Philemon
Hag	Haggai	Ps	Psalms
Heb	Hebrews	Prov	Proverbs
Hos	Hosea	Rev	Revelation (Apocalypse)
Is	Isaiah	Rom	Romans
Jas	James	Ruth	Ruth
Jer	Jeremiah	1 Sam	1 Samuel
Jn	John	2 Sam	2 Samuel
1 Jn	1 John	Sir	Sirach (Ecclesiasticus)
2 Jn	2 John	Song	Song of Solomon
3 Jn	3 John	1 Thess	1 Thessalonians
Job	Job	2 Thess	2 Thessalonians
Joel	Joel	1 Tim	1 Timothy
Jon	Jonah	2 Tim	2 Timothy
Josh	Joshua	Tit	Titus
Jud	Judith	Wis	Wisdom
Jude	Jude	Zech	Zechariah
Judg	Judges	Zeph	Zephaniah

Abbreviations

2. OTHER ABBREVIATIONS

ad loc.	*ad locum*, commentary on this passage	f	and following (*pl.* ff)
AAS	*Acta Apostolicae Sedis*	ibid.	*ibidem*, in the same place
Apost.	Apostolic	in loc.	*in locum,* commentary on this passage
can.	canon	loc.	*locum*, place or passage
chap.	chapter	par.	parallel passages
cf.	*confer*, compare	Past.	Pastoral
Const.	Constitution	RSV	Revised Standard Version
Decl.	Declaration	RSVCE	Revised Standard Version, Catholic Edition
Dz-Sch	Denzinger-Schönmetzer, *Enchiridion Biblicum* (4th edition, Naples & Rome, 1961)	SCDF	Sacred Congregation for the Doctrine of the Faith
Enc.	Encyclical	sess.	session
Exhort.	Exhortation	v.	verse (*pl.* vv.)

"Sources quoted in the Commentary", which appears at the end of this book, explains other abbreviations used.

Introduction to the Book of Revelation

LAST BOOK OF THE BIBLE

The Apocalypse or book of Revelation is the last book of Holy Scripture and is the only prophetical book in the New Testament. The Church makes frequent use of it, particularly in the Liturgy, to sing the praises of the risen Christ and the splendour of the heavenly Jerusalem which symbolizes the Church in the glory of heaven.

A certain parallel can be seen between the book of Revelation and Genesis, the first of the sacred books. Genesis describes the beginning of the world through the creative action of God. Using similar symbolism, the Apocalypse speaks at length of the new creation (cf. Rev 21:1, 5) initiated by the Redemption brought about by Christ which will reach its climax when he comes again at the end of the world. The last chapters of Revelation specifically mention the river that watered paradise (cf. Gen 2:6; Rev 22:1) and the tree of life (cf. Gen 2:8; Rev 22:14).

The Apocalypse is a book at once difficult and profound, and yet it focuses intense light on the figure of Christ in glory and builds up our hope of attaining eternal life.

AUTHORSHIP AND CANONICITY

The Apocalypse is one of the "deuterocanonical" books, that is, one of those which at one time were not accepted as sacred by all Christian communities. Its authenticity was suspect in parts of the Church, particularly in the east, probably because it was widely used by some early heretical sects in support of their teachings.

However, the earliest testimonies we have, which go back to the second century, are unanimous in recognizing the apostle John as the author of the book. St Justin refers to "a man named John, one of the apostles of Christ", as having received the revelations contained in the Apocalypse.[1] This is a particularly valuable testimony in view of the fact that Justin was converted to Christianity in Ephesus in the year 135, only a few decades after John wrote the book to the seven churches of Asia, the foremost of which was Ephesus.

---

1. *Dialogue with Trypho*, 81, 3.

Introduction to the Book of Revelation

Contemporary with Justin's text is the commentary on the book of Revelation written by St Melito, bishop of Sardis, another of the churches mentioned at the start of the book. The bishop's commentary is not extant but it is referred to by Eusebius of Caesarea in his *Ecclesiastical History*.[2] Other second-century writers who support Johannine authorship of the book of Revelation are Papias, bishop of Hierapolis,[3] and St Irenaeus, who frequently quotes from it.[4] The Muratorian Fragment, which dates from the end of the century, includes the Apocalypse in its list of sacred books.

An outstanding third-century testimony is that of Origen of Alexandria: he says that the author of the book was the man who wrote the Fourth Gospel and had the good fortune to rest his head on Jesus' breast.[5] In the West, Tertullian also attributes the book of Revelation to St John.[6] However, other views were being expressed around the same time as Tertullian: a Roman priest named Caius thought the Apocalypse was written by Cerinthus, a prominent Gnostic contemporary of John.[7] Other writers of the same period, called *álogoi* because they rejected the *Logos* of St John, refused to accept the authenticity of the Apocalypse.[8] Dionysius of Alexandria denied its canonicity because millenarianists were using it to support their arguments. To show that St John was not the author despite clear church tradition, Dionysius put forward arguments (not compelling ones) based on differences between the Apocalypse and the Fourth Gospel.[9]

In the fourth century, St Athanasius, bishop of Alexandria, recognized the Apocalypse as canonical and used it in his controversy with the Arians.[10] St Basil and St Gregory of Nyssa, for their part, accepted the tradition in favour of authenticity. However, the school of Antioch generally denied both the authenticity and the canonicity of the book; St Cyril of Jerusalem, St John Chrysostom, Theodoret and others do not use it.[11] This lack of conviction among some writers of the Eastern Church must be set against the unanimity of the Latin Church, which always accepted the Apocalypse as part of the canon of inspired books and as written by St John.

From the sixth to the sixteenth century the authenticity of the book was undisputed. Doubts which arose in Spain in the early seventh century were dispelled by the first Council of Toledo.[12] Once the danger from millenarianism was over, the Eastern Church came round again to accepting the Apocalypse as inspired.

In the sixteenth century Erasmus[13] expressed some doubts about its authenticity and canonicity, but his views were rejected and censored by the University of Paris. Luther[14] initially argued against authenticity but later

2. *Ecclesiastical History*, 4, 26, 2. **3.** Cf. Andrew of Caesarea, *Comment in Apoc.*, prologue. **4.** Cf. *Against Heresies*, 4, 20. **5.** Cf. *In Ioann. comm.*, 1, 14. **6.** Cf. *Against Marcion*, 3, 14; *De resurrectione carnis*, 25. **7.** Cf. *Ecclesiastical History*, 3, 28, 2. **8.** Cf. St Epiphanius, *Haer.*, 51, 1–35. **9.** Cf. Dionysius of Alexandria, *Ex libro de promission.*, 3–7. **10.** Cf. *Oratio II contra Arianos*, 23. **11.** Cf *Ecclesiastical History*, 3, 25, 2. **12.** Cf. Mansi, 10, 624. **13.** Cf. Erasmus, *In Apoc.*, 22, 21. **14.** Cf. Luther, *Praef. in Apoc.*

changed his view. In the eighteenth century rationalists (who rejected prophecy out of hand) naturally had no place for the book of Revelation: rationalist arguments were based on internal evidence (the same kind of arguments as put forward earlier by Dionysius of Alexandria). On the basis of a passage in Eusebius' *History*, rationalists attributed the Apocalypse to a personage called John the Presbyter; but these arguments are weak; what Eusebius says is far from clear, and his thinking was coloured by the danger posed by millenarianism.

At the present time there is a certain amount of disagreement among scholars. Some, Protestants for the most part, are of the opinion that the Apocalypse could not have been written by the author of the Fourth Gospel, given the differences in style and language. Others, Catholics mainly, accept that it is a Johannine text, given the antiquity of Tradition to this effect and the fact that the difference in subject matter between the two books can account for the differences in style.

The Magisterium has on different occasions pronounced on the authenticity and canonicity of the Apocalypse—for example, at the councils of Hippo (in 393), Carthage (397) and Toledo (633).[15] This teaching was confirmed later by the ecumenical councils of Florence and Trent.[16] However, whereas the Church has dogmatically defined the book as canonical, it has not pronounced as strongly on who wrote it or how it was redacted.

PLACE AND DATE OF COMPOSITION

At the beginning of the book, we are told of how the hagiographer received this divine revelation: "I John, your brother, who share with you in Jesus the tribulation and the kingdom and the patient endurance, was on the island called Patmos on account of the word of God and the testimony of Jesus. I was in the Spirit on the Lord's day, and I heard behind me a voice like a trumpet ..." (1:9–10). Patmos is a small island in the Aegean Sea, one of a group of islands known as the Dodecanese. It was a Sunday, the Lord's day, the day that ever since the beginning of the Church Christians had dedicated to divine worship in place of the Jewish sabbath; the *Didaché* and St Ignatius of Antioch testify to this Christian practice. An ancient tradition, witnessed to by Tertullian, mentions that St John, the beloved disciple, was exiled on Patmos because of his preaching and apostolic ministry. The author of the Apocalypse seems to confirm this by saying at the outset that he shares the affliction, pain and patience experienced by those he is addressing.

St Irenaeus thinks that the book was written towards the end of the reign of Domitian, around the year 96.[17] Writing in the third century or towards the end

---

15. Cf. *EB* 17 and 34. **16.** Cf. *EB* 47 and 59. **17.** Cf. *Against Heresies*, 5, 30.

of the second, Victorinus says that Domitian sent St John into exile, interning him on the island of Patmos.[18] St Jerome[19] and Eusebius[20] say the same.

Information contained in the book itself confirms this date. We know in fact from the Acts of the Apostle (20:7) that the Christians met together on the "first day of the week", which Revelation 1:10 describes as "Dies Domini", "the Lord's Day" (our Sunday). Also, the life of the Christian communities of Asia Minor as reflected in the book of Revelation clearly indicates they were at a more mature stage than the churches referred to in other New Testament texts. All this means that the year 95, given by tradition, is realistic and acceptable.

IMMEDIATE READERSHIP

The book is addressed to "the seven churches that are in Asia" (1:4)—Ephesus, Smyrna, Pergamum, Thyatira, Sardis, Philadelphia and Laodicea (cf. 1:11). Commentators are agreed that this number is symbolic and that the book is in fact addressed to the entire Church. The second-century Muratorian Canon puts it this way: "John in the Apocalypse, although writing to seven churches, is however addressing all churches."[21] An early commentator called Primasius states that what the Lord says to his servant is addressed to the whole Church, "uni Ecclesiae septiforme", a single Church of which these seven are a symbol.[22]

Various things in the text confirm this world-wide reference—for example, when it says (without being specific), "Blessed is he who reads aloud the words of the prophecy, and blessed are those who hear, and who keep what is written therein (1:3)"; or its repeated warning, "he who has an ear, let him hear what the Spirit says to the churches" (2:7, 11, 17, 29; 3:6; etc.).

The book seeks to alert Christians to the grave dangers which threaten faith, while consoling and encouraging those who are suffering tribulation, particularly due to the fierce and long-drawn-out persecution mounted by Domitian. The very earliest heresies were already wreaking havoc among the Christian communities: the Nicolaitans were arguing in favour of some degree of compromise with idolatry and pagan lifestyles (cf. 2:7, 14) and there was evidence of a loss of early fervour (2:4) and a slackening of charity (3:2).

Persecution was coming from both Jews and pagans. Jewish persecutors are described as false Jews, "a synagogue of Satan" (2:9–10); pagan persecution had begun with the first great persecution (instigated by Nero), the memory of which was still fresh thirty years on (cf. 6:9–11; 17:6). The empire would repeatedly persecute Christians up to the fourth century, when the advent of Constantine brought peace. Some emperors, Domitian for example,

---

18. Cf. *In Apoc.*, 10, 11 and 17, 10. **19.** Cf. *Of Famous Men*, 9. **20.** Cf. *Ecclesiastical History*, 3, 18, 4. **21.** Cf. *EB* 4. **22.** Cf. *Commentarium super Apoc.* 1, 1.

required idolatrous worship of their person, giving themselves the title of "our Lord and God". Christians refused, thereby incurring their wrath. However, as Tertullian put it, the blood of martyrs would prove to be the seed of Christians. St John seeks to console Christians experiencing such cruel injustice and harassment, and strives to keep alive their hope in the ultimate victory of Christ and of all who stay true to him even to death if necessary (cf. 2:10).

LITERARY FORM

In line with the teaching of Pius XII,[23] the Second Vatican Council reminds us that to understand what sacred writers had in mind one need to take into account, among other things, the literary forms they use, that is, the genre in which they are writing—historical narrative, prophecy, poetry, etc.—and the patterns of language prevailing in their time and culture.[24]

This principle needs to be particularly borne in mind in the case of the book of Revelation, given its special characteristics and language, so remote from our own experience. In fact, during the two centuries before and after Christ there was quite a crop of Jewish and Christian writings entitled Apocalypse (Revelation), with a content and style of a type now called "apocalyptic writing"—for example, the *Book of Enoch*, the *Apocalypse of Moses* (which heretics attributed to St Paul) and others, including the Apocrypha of the Old and the New Testaments.

These books all had two basic features: (a) they dealt with the subject of the last age of the world, when good would triumph and evil be annihilated; (b) they made much use of symbolism taken from the animal kingdom, astrology, numbers and so forth, to depict past and present history and to prophesy the future. From the point of view of content and style these writings are a kind of late extension of prophetical literature, for the Prophets already spoke of the "day of Yahweh"[25] and used symbolism to convey their message.[26] Some Old Testament passages in fact have a markedly apocalyptic ring about them—for example, Isaiah 24–27, Zechariah 9–14 and, particularly, the book of Daniel, which is clearly a precursor of apocalyptic literature. That literature, in turn, is influenced by wisdom literature; its visions are interwoven with moral exhortations, invitations to reflection and promises of future beatitude or retribution.

Compared with the prophets, authors of apocalypses have distinct features of their own: a) they write under pseudonyms, using the names of celebrated figures who might have received divine revelations—men like Enoch who

---

23. Cf. Pius XII, *Divino afflante Spiritu*, EB 558. **24.** Cf. Vatican II, *Dei Verbum*, 12. **25.** Cf. Amos 5:18–20; Is 2:6–21; Jer 30:5–7; Joel 2:1–17; etc. **26.** Cf. Amos 7:1–8:3; Hos 13:7–8; Joel 2:10–11; Ezek 1–2, etc.

Genesis 5:24 tells us was taken to heaven at the end of his life; b) in general, they conceive this world as being in the power of Satan and incapable of regeneration, and therefore they place their hopes in a new world to be created by God: the most that man can contribute is prayer; c) they exhibit a marked tendency towards determinism; everything that has to be said is contained in these books, and very little room is left for freedom and personal conversion.

Although St John's work is entitled Apocalypse (Revelation), its key features are more akin to the books of the prophets than to those of "apocalyptic writers". He in fact describes his book as "prophecy" (1:3; cf. 22:7, 10, 18, 19; 22:9), and although for the most part he uses language and symbolism akin to Jewish apocalyptic writing, his historical perspective is quite different, namely, that which human history acquires under the lordship of Christ, which is acknowledged and extolled in the Church, the new people of God, who like their Lord suffer in this present world at the hands of the forces of evil. However, the final outcome has already been revealed by the resurrection and ascension of Christ, and the ground is being laid for it all through the course of history by the holiness, good works and suffering of the just. Christ's definitive victory will come at the end and the Church will be raised on high in a new world where there will be no more mourning or pain (cf. 21:4) and where there will be room for all those who choose to repent (cf. 16:11).

The Revelation to John constitutes a strong call to conversion; it urges people to commit themselves to good and put their trust in God; in this it is like the oracles spoken by the prophets. Like other "apocalypses" it is a book of consolation written at a time of exceptional stress; but it also provides encouragement to holiness and fidelity in all ages. Those parts of the book which have epistolary features (at the beginning and end: 1:1—3:22; 22:21) and indeed to a lesser degree the whole text are in the tradition of didactical wisdom writing.

STYLE AND LANGUAGE

Symbolism is of the essence of apocalyptic literature: its lofty, supernatural message calls for the use of analogies and similes which will bring the reader not so much to understand its exact meaning as to grasp it intuitively.

The symbols used are in some cases physical objects, such as the seven-branched golden lampstand (cf. 1:12; Zech 4:2, 10), the book with the seven seals (cf. 5:1; Ezek 2:9), the two olive trees (cf. 11:4; Zech 4:2, 14). At other times the symbols are actions—the sealing of the foreheads of the elect (cf. 7:3; Ezek 9:4), the eating of the prophetical scroll (cf. 10:8–11; Ezek 2:8), the measurement of the temple (cf. 11:1; Ezek 40–41). Certain cities are also used as symbols—Zion, Jerusalem, Babylon and Armageddon.[27] Numbers also

---

27. Cf. Rev 14:1; 3:12; 21:2; 14:8; 18:2; 16:14, 16; etc.

have a symbolic purpose: the number three refers to things supernatural and divine, four to created things; seven and twelve imply completion, fullness. Colours are used in similar way; white stands for victory and purity, red for violence, black for death.

Another feature of apocalyptic writing is what we might call the "law of anticipation", that is, its tendency to refer briefly to some event which will be dealt with fully later on. And sometimes the narrative is interrupted to include a passage designed to provide consolation to the just.

INTERPRETING THE BOOK OF REVELATION

Due to the wealth of symbolism in the book it has been interpreted in many different ways over the centuries. The four main interpretations are as follows:

a) The book is a history of the Church, proclaiming the main events and epochs of the Church, past and future. Seven periods are identified, the last being the reign of a thousand years which Christ and his followers will establish before the end of the world, if Revelation 20:1–7 is taken literally. This interpretation was widespread in the early centuries of the Church and in the Middle Ages; it is also popular in our own days among certain sects which have made a number of (mistaken) predictions of the date of the end of the world.

b) The Apocalypse has to do solely with events in St John's own time—persecutions and trials of the Church, for the most part the result of the actions of outsiders. This interpretation, first proposed in the sixteenth century, is still held by many scholars in the rationalist tradition. It sees the book as merely a symbolic description of first-century events.

c) The content of the Apocalypse is exclusively a proclamation and premonition of the last days: it refers to the eschatological era. This interpretation was very much in vogue in the eighteenth century and still has its followers today.

d) The Apocalypse is a theological vision of the entire panorama of history, a vision which underlines its transcendental and religious dimension. According to this interpretation (favoured by most Fathers of the Church) St John is describing the situation of the Church in his own time and he is also surveying the panorama of the last times; but for him these last times have already begun: they began with the entry into the world of Jesus Christ, the Son of God made man. This idea is very much in line with the Fourth Gospel, which also conceives the last era of the world, and eternal life, as having already in some way begun and as developing towards ultimate and total fullness. It provides a special perspective on events in history and is involved with expectation of final victory. The book does depict the cosmic struggle between good and evil, but it takes for granted Christ's ultimate triumph. This is, in our view, the most valid interpretation of the book and therefore it is the one we follow in the commentary provided.

HISTORICAL BACKGROUND

It is helpful to bear in mind the background against which the Apocalypse was written. The evangelization of Asia Minor began very early on and may well have been initiated by those Jews from Asia Minor who witnessed the events of Pentecost in Jerusalem (cf. Acts 2:9). When St Paul arrived in Ephesus he found followers of Christ there already (cf. Acts 19:1). However, until the period 53–56 and St Paul's missionary work, there were no Christian communities in these regions which could properly be called local churches. These now began to develop, and very soon there were signs of cockle growing up among the young wheat; persecution, too, was becoming part of the picture.

This period also saw the final break with the synagogue, and some Jews began to sow confusion (cf. 2:9; 3:9). There was, moreover, the threat of syncretism, as a result of the influence of oriental religions in the Roman empire. Phrygia, the centre of the cults of Cybele and Attis, was quite close to the churches mentioned in the Apocalypse; the sins denounced in the book reflect to some extent the mystery-rites of those pagan religions (cf. 13:11–13; 2:14; 2:20ff).

Another feature of the historical background is the persecution of Christianity by Rome. The more emperor-worship increased, the more difficult it was for Christians to stay loyal to their faith. With Domitian (81–96) the situation worsened, because those who refused him divine honours became liable to the death penalty.

From five of the seven cities to whose churches St John writes we have positive evidence of emperor-worship: Thyatira and Laodicea are the exceptions. Additionally, Ephesus had its famous temple dedicated to the goddess Artemis (cf. Acts 19:28). In Smyrna, St Polycarp would later suffer martyrdom (*c.* 156) for refusing to acknowledge Caesar as *Kyrios*, Lord. Pergamum saw the martyrdom of Antipas, "my witness, my faithful one" (cf. 2:13). As time went on, Christianity continued to spread, but opposition and violence towards Christians also increased. This grieves St John and, enlightened by the Holy Spirit, he tries to make the faithful see that Jesus Christ, the Lamb of God, will ultimately triumph over his enemies. In the meantime, however, the great struggle must go on, a struggle which involves

Introduction to the Book of Revelation

Christians in every epoch of history. The enemy often gains the upper hand, but his victory is merely temporary and apparent. In fact things are quite the reverse of what they seem: martyrdom and suffering may appear to overwhelm Christians but really that experience guarantees their victory.

STRUCTURE AND CONTENT

It is difficult to divide the book into parts which clarify its meaning; this is particularly so from chapter 4 onwards, when the author begins to describe his vision of the last times. For example, certain themes seem to be dealt with more than once—the scourges prior to the End (cf. 6:1–15; 8:6—9:21; 16:1–21), the victory of the elect (cf. 7:9–17; 14:1–5; 19:1–10), the fall of Babylon (cf. 14:6–11; 18:1–3), etc. Sometimes the rhythm of the narrative seems to break abruptly (cf. 8:2; 10:1; 12:1); it is broken, for example, by the episode of the two witnesses (cf. 11:1–13) and by that of the woman in heaven (cf. 12:1–17). This has led some scholars to suggest that the text of the Apocalypse in the form that has come down to us may be a fusion of two earlier works of St John on the same subject.

This is only a theory, however, besides, there is enough thematic development in the book to give it a strong basic unity. From chapter 4 onwards, everything is tending towards the final outcome of a dramatic battle between Christ and the powers of evil, a battle which reaches its climax in the last chapters (cf. 19:11—22:5). But it is true that we are already given the result of the last battle long before the detailed narrative of that event. As he describes each vision, the author seems to repeat his entire message: he feels under no restraint to deal with events or subjects in a tidy, systematic or chronological way; apocalyptic writing is different from other genres in this respect.

By using a series of literary devices he manages to keep the reader's interest alive right to the end. For example, he uses the number seven as a device of this kind: after the seven letters to the seven churches (cf. 1:4—3:22) the writer sees a scroll sealed with seven seals (cf. 5:1—8:1), hears the seven trumpets (cf. 8:2—11:15) and sees the seven plagues being poured out of the seven bowls (15:1—16:17). The seven letters seem to form a section of their own but all the other symbolic sevens appear to be connected with one another: the seventh seal introduces the vision of the seven angels with the seven trumpets (cf. 8:1–2), and once the seventh trumpet has been blown the author sees God's temple from which the seven angels with the seven plagues emerge (cf. 11:19; 15:5). After the seventh bowl has been poured, the author is shown, in detail, the various adversaries, the last battles, and the glorification of the Church (cf. chaps. 17–22). To maintain the reader's interest and attention, the gap between the sixth and seventh events is sometimes extended by the introduction of a new vision (cf. 7:1–17; 10:1—11:14) or the appearance of the next set of seven (cf. 12:1—15:5) is delayed, so that when he thinks he is nearing the end the reader finds that preliminary episodes are still being introduced.

The number seven is so frequently used that some scholars have opted for dividing the book into seven acts, with seven scenes in each. But the text refuses to submit to this rigid scheme: the author writes with total freedom of style, though he clearly uses the "seven" device to help shape the book. However, after the seventh trumpet is sounded (11:15), this device becomes less prominent and the symbols of the woman, the beasts, the Lamb and the city occupy centre stage.

Given the way the various themes are developed and the literary aspects of the work, the following division is probably generally acceptable:

PROLOGUE: The book and its author are introduced (1:1–3).

PART ONE: LETTERS TO THE SEVEN CHURCHES OF ASIA (1:4—3:22).

Formal address and greeting (1:4–8)

Introduction: Christ in glory commissions John to write the book (1:9–20)

Letters: to the churches of Ephesus (2:1–7), Smyrna (2:8–11), Pergamum (2:12–17), Thyatira (2:18–29), Sardis (3:1–6), Philadelphia (3:7–13) and Laodicea (3:14–22).

PART TWO: ESCHATOLOGICAL VISIONS (4:1—22:15)

1. INTRODUCTORY VISION. The author is taken up into heaven, where he sees God in majesty directing the destinies of the world and the Church. Only Christ can reveal what those destinies are, for only he can open the seven seals (chaps. 4–5).

2. FIRST SECTION. Events prior to the final outcome. A series of visions before the last trumpet is sounded (6:1—11:14):

Christ opens the first six seals. The great day of God's wrath has arrived (6:1–17).

The great multitude of the saved (7:1–17).

The opening of the seventh seal and the vision of the seven angels bearing seven trumpets (8:1–6).

The sounding of the first trumpets. They herald the coming of God and cause catastrophes which stir people to repent (8:7—9:21).

Introduction to the Book of Revelation

The author is given the little scroll to eat. What must still remain hidden and what is going to be prophetically revealed (10:1–11).

The death and resurrection of the two witnesses (11:1–14).

3. SECOND SECTION. Christ's victory over the powers of evil, and the glorification of the Church (11:15—22:15).

The sounding of the seventh trumpet: the advent of the Kingdom of Christ (11:15–19).

The woman pursued by the dragon: the Church (12:1–17).

The beasts given authority by the dragon (13:1–18).

The Lamb and his companions (14:1–5).

Proclamation and symbols of the Judgment; the harvest and the vintage (14:6–20).

The hymn of the saved: the song of Moses and the song of the Lamb (15:1–4).

The seven bowls of plagues: the last chance for conversion (15:5—16:21).

Description of the powers of evil: the harlot, Babylon and the beast (17:1–18).

The fall of Babylon proclaimed: joy and lamentation (18:1–24).

Songs of victory in heaven (19:1–10).

The first battle: the beast is destroyed (19:11–21).

The thousand-year reign of Christ and his people (20:1–6).

The second battle: Satan is overthrown (20:7–10).

The Last Judgment of the living and the dead (20:11–15).

A new world comes into being: the messianic Jerusalem is described (21:1—22:15).

CONCLUSION: A dialogue between Jesus and the Church. Warnings to the reader and words of farewell (22:16–21).

TEACHINGS CONTAINED IN THE BOOK OF REVELATION

The core of the teaching contained in the book concerns the second coming of our Lord—the Parousia—and the definitive establishment of his Kingdom at the end of time. Various elements go to make up this teaching.

Introduction to the Book of Revelation

1. *God the almighty.* God is described as "the Alpha and the Omega, the beginning and the end" (1:8; 22:13), words which teach the sublimity and absolute authority of God. Alpha is the first letter of the Greek alphabet and Omega the last; the sacred author chooses this graphic method to explain that God is the source from which all created things derive their being: he wills that what did not exist should come to be (cf. 4:11); he is also the end or goal to which everything is directed and where it finds its fulfilment.

In another passage God is defined as he "who is and who was and who is to come" (1:4), a form of words also found in Jewish literature as an explanation of the name Yahweh, "I AM WHO I AM", revealed to Moses (Ex 3:14). This teaches that God is he who existed in the past (he is eternal); he who is (he is active in the world since its creation); and he who is to come (that is, his dynamic and saving presence will never cease).

Echoing the book of Daniel, the Apocalypse teaches that God "lives for ever and ever" (4:9–10; cf. Dan 4:34). He is also called the "living God", an expression often met in the Old Testament, which underlines the essential difference between Yahweh (the living God) and idols, "the work of men's hands. They have mouths, but do not speak; eyes but do not see" (Ps 115:4–5). God is, then, eternal and immortal; he has no beginning or end. He is also the *Pantocrator*, the Almighty; his power is unique and all-embracing (cf. 1:8; 4:3). God is the Lord of history; nothing falls outside his providence; he is the just Father whose word is true, who will bestow himself on the victor as he promised: "I will be his God and he shall be my son" (21:7). Finally, God's creative power and unbounded love will lead him to restore all things and create a new world (cf. 21:5).

God is also presented as the universal Judge, against whose verdict there is no appeal; none can evade his judgment (cf. 20:12). However, at the end of time his infinite love will prevail and will cause all things to be made new (cf. 21:5), and night shall be no more, for the Lord will shine on them forever (cf. 22:5), nor shall there be any pain or tears, for the old world shall have passed away.

2. *Jesus Christ.* At the start of the book the figure of the suffering Christ is evoked by reference to "every one who pierced him" (1:7), and later on it speaks of the great city "where their Lord was crucified" (11:8). Elsewhere there is further reference to the saving blood of Christ (cf. 7:14; 12:11), particulary in connexion with the impressive yet humble figure of the lamb, often depicted as "slain" (cf. 5:12; 22:14), the victim of the greatest of all sacrifices. However, our Lord is usually depicted in the glory of heaven under the tender symbol of the Lamb enthroned on Mount Zion, with the river of the water of life flowing from his throne (cf. 14:1; 5:6; 22:3; 22:1). He will shepherd and guide his people (7:17). His enemies will make war on him, but he will emerge victorious (cf. 17:14). He is worthy to receive power and glory and to be worshipped by all creation (cf. 5:12; 7:1; 13:8).

Introduction to the Book of Revelation

Jesus Christ is also given the title of "Son of man", destined to receive power and dominion over all nations and languages (cf. Dan 7:13–14; Rev 1:13–16). He is "Lord of lords and King of kings" (cf. 17:14; 19:12–16); he is above the angels, who are his emissaries, and unlike them he is rendered the worship due to God alone (cf. 1:1; 22:6; 19:10; 22:8–9). In other passages Christ is given divine titles and attributes (cf. 1:18; 3:7; 5:13; 22:1–3). He is also depicted as the Word of God: this is in line with the Fourth Gospel and clearly teaches that he is divine (cf. 19:13; Jn 1:1–14; 1 Jn 1:1).

3. *The Holy Spirit.* There are a number of passages which indirectly refer to the Holy Spirit—for example, when the book speaks of the seven spirits who are before the throne, or the seven torches of fire (1:4; 4:5). It also explicitly teaches that it is the Holy Spirit who is speaking to the churches (2:7, 11, 17; etc.). And, at the end, the voice of the Spirit joins with that of the Bride to make entreaty for the coming of Christ. This passage is reminiscent of St Paul's teaching about how the Holy Spirit prays by interceding for us with sighs too deep for words (cf. Rom 8:26). In the book of Revelation, the Holy Spirit is presented in relation to the Church: he nourishes the Church with his word and moves it interiorly to pray earnestly for the coming of the Lord.

4. *The Church.* In a more or less explicit way the Church is present throughout the book of Revelation. It teaches that the Church, which is one and universal, is the Bride of Christ, insistently making supplication for the Lord's coming (cf. 22:17, 20). But the Church is also depicted as Christian communities located in various cities of proconsular Asia (cf. chaps. 2–3). These communities do not constitute a Church distinct from the Church as such; rather, we can begin to perceive here the idea that all communities, taken together, make up the universal Church: the Church becomes present in these believing communities which are "parts" of the one Church of Christ.[28]

The apocalyptic vision of the woman in heaven (cf. chap. 12) has been interpreted in many different ways, particularly as referring to the Church. This interpretation sees her as the Church undergoing severe affliction. Her crown of twelve stars is taken as symbolizing both the twelve tribes of Israel and the twelve apostles, the pillars of the new Church. The passage is reminiscent of what the prophet Isaiah says when he compares the suffering of the people to those of a woman in labour.

The Apocalypse also uses a variety of symbols designed to convey the beauty and grandeur of the Church. Thus, it speaks of the holy city, the new Jerusalem, where God dwells; it is also the "beloved city" (cf. 3:12; 21:2, 10; 20:9). Its glory and splendour are described with a wealth of detail, ranging from the richness of its walls to the fruitfulness of its waters (cf. 21:16–27;

---

28. Cf. Vatican II, *Christus Dominus*, 68.

22:1–2). It is called the "temple of God", whose pillars are those who have won the victory; in it stands the Ark of the Covenant and there the countless multitudes of the elect render worship to God (cf. 3:12; 7:15; 11:19).

The text implies that in both its earthly stage and its heavenly stage, the Church is the chosen people of God. Thus, the voice from heaven warns the elect who live in Babylon, "Come out of her, my people, lest you take part in her sins, lest you share in her plagues" (18:4); and towards the end of the book we are reminded that God will dwell in the midst of his people (cf. 21:3): the Church is depicted as the new Israel, increasing in number, and at a future time preserved from all evil by the seal of God (cf. 7:4–8).

The image of the Kingdom also reveals the nature of the Church. John depicts it, now as sharing in tribulation and the Kingdom (cf. 1:9), now as singing the praises of Jesus Christ: he has "made us a kingdom", a royal line, "priests to his God and Father" (1:6).

One of the most important and revealing things the Bible tells us about the Church is God's love for his people as symbolized by the beloved Bride. The Apocalypse frequently speaks in these terms, focusing attention on the marriage of the Lamb, whose wife is decked out as a new bride (cf. 19:7; 21:9), eagerly calling for her beloved (cf. 22:17). One of the most significant moments described is the wedding of the Lamb, an occasion for great joy and exultation (cf. 19:7). The book also alludes to the Bride when it says, "Blessed are those who are invited to the marriage supper of the Lamb" (19:9).

5. *The angels.* Throughout the book angels are very much in evidence. Etymologically, the word "angel" means "messenger"; this role of theirs in bringing God's messages to men is stressed continually. At the start of the book it is through an angel that John is given to know the things that are to come, and at the end it will also be an angel who shows him the final visions of the heavenly Jerusalem (cf. 1:1; 22:6, 16). At certain points an angel passes his message on to other angels (cf. 7:2; 8:2—11:15), or proclaims the Gospel to all mankind and makes known God's dire warnings and punishments (cf. 14:6–19; 16:17; 19:17).

The angels are also depicted as man's protectors. We see them standing at the four corners of the earth, holding back the winds to prevent their harming men (cf. 7:1), and standing as sentinels at the gates of the holy city (cf. 21:12). The angels of the churches (cf. 1:20; 2:1, 8, 12, 18; 3:1, 7, 14) are interpreted by some commentators as symbolizing the bishops of these churches, for the main mission of bishops is to watch over their flocks. However, these angels can also be seen as divine messengers who are given things by the Lord to communicate to the churches, whom they also have a mission to protect and govern.

On occasions the angels are deputed to carry out God's punishment (cf. 9:15; 14:18; etc.). With the archangel St Michael as their leader, they fight the great cosmic battle of Good and Evil (cf. 12:7ff) against the dragon, "that ancient serpent, who is called the Devil and Satan, the deceiver of the whole world" (12:9). But this is a war which goes on throughout history: thus, the demons, also called angels of Satan, are often shown as coming from the abyss, temporarily released to roam the earth, causing war and confusion (cf. 20:7–8); in the end, however, they will be cast down into hell where they will suffer everlasting torment (cf. 12:9; 20:10).

In addition to their important and varied mission on earth, the angels are also in heaven, in the presence of God, interceding on mankind's behalf, offering "upon the golden altar before the throne" the prayers of the saints, which reach God via the angels (cf. 8:4). Special emphasis is also put on the unceasing worship offered by the angels to God and to the Lamb (cf. 5:11; 7:11; etc.)

6. *The Virgin Mary.* The woman clothed with the sun, crowned with stars, and with the moon under her feet is undoubtedly a symbol of the Church. However, from very early on many Fathers also saw her as representing the Blessed Virgin. It is true that Mary suffered no birth-pangs when her Son was born, and had no children other than him to be "the rest of her offspring" (12:17). However, this vision does evoke the Genesis account, which speaks of enmity between the serpent and the woman. The Son who is caught up to God and to his throne is Jesus Christ (cf. 12:5). As in the case of the parables, not everything in the imagery necessarily happens in real life; and the same image can refer to one or more things—particularly when they are closely connected, as the Blessed Virgin and the Church are. So, the fact that this passage is interpreted as referring to the Church does not exclude its referring also to Mary. More than once, the Church's Magisterium has given it a Marian interpretation. For example, St Pius X says: "Everyone knows that this woman was the image of the Virgin Mary, who, in giving birth to our head, remained inviolate. 'And being with child,' the Apostle continues, 'she cried out in her travail and was there in the anguish of delivery' […]. It was the birth of all of us who, while being exiles here below, are not yet brought forth into the perfect love of God and eternal happiness. The fact that the heavenly Virgin labours in childbirth shows her loving desire to watch over us and through unceasing prayer complete the number of the elect."[29]

John Paul II adopted this interpretation in a sermon at the shrine of Allötting: "Mary […] carries the *features of that woman* whom the Apocalypse describes […]. The woman, who stands *at the end* of the history of creation and salvation, corresponds evidently to the one about whom it is said *in the first pages* of the Bible that she 'is going to crush the head of the serpent'. Between

---

29. Cf. *Ad Diem illum*, 15.

this promising beginning and the apocalyptic end Mary *has brought to light a son* 'who is to rule all nations with an iron sceptre' (Rev 12:5) [...]. She it is with whom the *apocalyptic* dragon makes war, for being the mother of the redeemed, she is the image of the Church whom we likewise call mother."[30]

---

30. *Homily*, 18 November 1980.

THE REVELATION TO JOHN

The Revised Standard Version, with notes

Prologue

1 ¹The revelation of Jesus Christ, which God gave him to show to his servants what must soon take place; and he made it known by sending his angel to his servant John, ²who bore witness to the word of God and to the testimony of Jesus Christ, even to all that he saw. ³Blessed is he who reads aloud the words

Dan 2:28
Rev 22:6
Rev 6:9
1 Jn 1:1–3
Rev 22:7, 18

1:1–20. After a brief prologue (vv. 1–3) and a letter-style greeting (vv. 4–8), St John describes a vision which acts as an introduction to the entire book; in it the risen Christ is depicted with features identifying his divinity and his position as Lord and Saviour of the churches. In the course of the book Jesus Christ will also appear as God's envoy, sent to teach Christians of the time, and subsequent generations (chaps. 2–3), and to console them in the midst of persecution by proclaiming God's design for the future of the world and of the Church (chaps. 4–22).

1:1–3. Despite its brevity this prologue conveys the scope of the book, its authority and the effect it hopes to have on its readers.

The *content* of the letter is a revelation made by Jesus Christ about contemporary and future events (cf. 1:19; 4:1). Its author, John, gives it its *authority*: Christ's revelation has been communicated to him in a supernatural manner, and he bears faithful witness to everything revealed to him. The book's *purpose* is to have the reader prepare for his or her definitive encounter with Christ by obeying what is written in the book: blessed are those who read it and take it to heart and do what it says.

God made known his salvific purpose through everything Jesus did and said. However, after his resurrection Christ continues to speak to his Church by means of revelations such as that contained in this book and those made to St Paul (cf. Gal 1:15–16; etc.). These bring the Christian revelation to completion and apply the saving action of Jesus to concrete situations in the life of the Church. When revelations reach us through an inspired writer they have universal validity, that is, they are "public" revelation and are part and parcel of the message of salvation entrusted by Christ to his apostles to proclaim to all nations (cf. Mt 28:18–20 and par.; Jn 17:18; 20:21). Public divine Revelation ceased with the death of the last apostle (cf. Vatican II, *Dei Verbum*, 4).

1:1. "The revelation of Jesus Christ": The word in Greek is *apocalypsis*, hence the name often given to this book of Holy Scripture. Revelation always implies the unveiling of something previously hidden —in this case, future events. The future is known to God the Father (the Greek text uses the definite article, "the God", which is how the New Testament usually refers to God the Father); and Jesus Christ, being the Son, shares in this knowledge which is being communicated to the author of the book. It speaks of "the revelation of Jesus Christ" not only because it has come to John from Christ but also because our Lord is the main subject, the beginning and end, of this revelation: he occupies the central position in all these great visions in which the veils concealing the future are torn to allow Light (Jesus Christ himself: cf. Rev 21:23; 22:5) to dispel the darkness.

"Soon": as regards how imminent or not all those events are, one needs to

of the prophecy, and blessed are those who hear, and who keep what is written therein; for the time is near.

PART ONE

Letters to the seven churches

Address and greeting

Ex 3:14
Is 11:2ff; 41:4

⁴John to the seven churches that are in Asia:*
Grace to you and peace from him who is and who was and who is to come, and from the seven spirits who are before his throne,

---

remember that the notion of time in Holy Scripture, particularly in the Apocalypse, is not quite the same as ours: it is more qualitative than quantitative. Here indeed "with the Lord one day is as a thousand years, and a thousand years as one day" (2 Pet 3:8). So, when Scripture says that something is about to happen it is not necessarily referring to a date in the near future: it is simply saying that it will happen and even in some sense is happening already. Finally, one needs to bear in mind that if events are proclaimed as being imminent, this would have a desired effect of fortifying those who are experiencing persecution, and would give them hope and consolation.

1:3. The book of Revelation is a pressing call to commitment in fidelity to everything our Lord has chosen to reveal to us in the New Testament, in this instance from the pen of St John.

The book seems to be designed for liturgical assemblies, where someone reads it aloud and the others listen. This is the preferential place for Holy Scripture, as Vatican II indicates: "The Church has always venerated the divine Scriptures as she venerated the Body of the Lord, in so far as she never ceases, particularly in the sacred liturgy, to partake of the bread of life and to offer it to the faithful from the one table of the Word of God and the Body of Christ" (*Dei Verbum*, 21).

"Sacred Scripture is of the greatest importance in the celebration of the liturgy. For it is from it that lessons are read and explained in the homily, and psalms are sung. It is from the scriptures that the prayers, collects, and hymns draw their inspiration and their force, and that actions and signs derive their meaning" (Vatican II, *Sacrosanctum Concilium*, 24).

The situation when St John was writing called for just the sort of exhortations and warnings this text contains. Its words call for a prompt, committed response which leaves no room for any kind of doubt or hesitation. They are also a dire warning to those who try to hinder the progress of the Kingdom of God, a Kingdom which must inexorably come about and which in some way is already with us.

1:4–8. Following the prologue (vv. 1–3), a short reflection (vv. 4–8) introduces the series of seven letters which form the first part of the book (1:4—3:22). This introduction begins with a salutation to the seven churches of Asia Minor, located in

Revelation 1:6

⁵and from Jesus Christ the faithful witness, the first-born of the dead, and the ruler of kings on earth. To him who loves us and has freed us from our sins by his blood ⁶and made us a kingdom, priests to his God and Father, to

Ps 89:28, 38
Col 1:18
Rev 19:16
Ex 19:6; 1 Pet 2:9; Rom 16:27
Is 61:6

---

the west of the region known at the time as "proconsular Asia", the capital of which was Ephesus.

The salutation is in the usual New Testament style: it sends good wishes of grace and peace on behalf of God and Jesus Christ (vv. 4–5, cf. 1 Thess 1:1; 2 Thess 1:2; etc.); it depicts our Lord and his work of salvation (vv. 5–8) and projects that work onto the panorama of world history.

1:4. Even though there were other churches in Asia Minor, John addresses only seven, a number which stands for "totality", as an early ecclesiatical writer, Primasius, explains: "He writes to the seven churches, that is, to the one and only Church symbolized by these seven" (*Commentariorum super Apoc.*, 1, 1).

Grace and peace are the outstanding gifts of the messianic era (cf. Rom 1:7). This form of salutation embodies the normal forms of greeting used by Greeks (*jaire*, grace) and Jews (*shalom*, peace); but here the words mean the grace, forgiveness and peace extended to men by the redemptive action of Jesus Christ. Thus, St John is wishing these gifts on behalf of God, the seven spirits and Jesus Christ.

The description of God as he "who is and who was and who is to come" is an elaboration of the name of "Yahweh" ("I AM WHO I AM") which was revealed to Moses (cf. Ex 3:14), and underlines the fact that God is the Lord of history, of the past, the present and the future, and that he is at all times acting to effect salvation.

The "seven spirits" stand for God's power and omniscience and intervention in the events of history. In Zechariah 4:10 divine power is symbolized by the seven "eyes of the Lord, which range the whole earth". Further on in the Apocalypse (5:6), St John tells us that the seven spirits of God sent out into all the earth are the seven eyes of the Lamb, that is, Christ. This symbolism (also found in the Old Testament: cf. Is 11:2ff) is used to show that God the Father acts through his Spirit and that this Spirit has been communicated to Christ and by him to mankind. So, when St John wishes grace and peace from the seven spirits of God it is the same as saying "from the Holy Spirit", who is sent to the Church after the death and resurrection of Christ. Patristic tradition has in fact interpreted the seven spirits as meaning the septiform Spirit with his seven gifts as described in Isaiah 11:1–2 in St Jerome's translation, the Vulgate.

1:5–6. Three messianic titles taken from Psalm 89:28–38 are given a new meaning in the light of fulfilment of Christian faith and applied to Jesus Christ. He is "the faithful witness" of the fulfilment of God's Old Testament promises of a Saviour, a son of David (cf. 2 Sam 7:14; Rev 5:5;), for it is Christ who has in fact brought about salvation. That is why, later on in the book, St John calls Jesus Christ "the Amen" (Rev 3:4)–which is like saying that through what Christ did God has ratified and kept his word; St John also calls him "Faithful and True" (Rev 19:11), because God's fidelity and the truth of his promises have been manifested in Jesus. This is to be seen in the Resurrection, which made Jesus "the first-born from the

Revelation 1:7

Dan 7:13
Zech 12:10, 14
Jn 19:37
Mt 24:30

him be glory and dominion for ever and ever. Amen. ⁷Behold, he is coming with the clouds, and every eye will see him, every one who pierced him; and all tribes of the earth will wail on account of him. Even so. Amen.

---

dead", in the sense that the Resurrection constituted a victory in which all who abide in him share (cf. Col 1:18). Christ is also "the ruler of kings on earth" because he is Lord of the world: this will be clearly seen when he comes a second time, but his dominion is already making itself felt because he has begun to conquer the power of sin and death.

The second part of v. 5 and all v. 6 are a kind of paean in praise of Christ recalling his great love for us as expressed in his words, "Greater love has no man than this, that a man lay down his life for his friends" (Jn 15:13). Christ's love for us knows no bounds: his generosity led him to sacrifice his life by the shedding of his blood, which redeemed us from our sins. There was nothing we could have done to redeem ourselves. "All were held captive by the devil", St Augustine comments, "and were in the thrall of demons; but they have been rescued from that captivity. The Redeemer came and paid the ransom: he shed his blood and with it purchased the entire orb of the earth" (*Enarrationes in Psalmos*, 95, 5).

Not content with setting us free from our sins, our Lord gave us a share in his kingship and priesthood. "Christ the Lord, high priest taken from among men (cf. Heb 5:1–5), made the new people 'a kingdom of priests to his God and Father' (Rev 1:6; cf. 5:9–10). The baptized, by regeneration and the anointing of the Holy Spirit, are consecrated to be a spiritual house and a holy priesthood, that through all the works of Christian men and women they may offer spiritual sacrifices and proclaim the perfection of him who has called them out of darkness into his marvellous light (cf. 1 Pet 2:4–10)" (Vatican II, *Lumen gentium*, 10).

1:7. Christ's work is not finished. He has assembled his holy people on earth to bring them enduring salvation, and he will be revealed in all his glory to the whole world at the end of time. Although the text speaks in the present tense—"he is coming with the clouds"—this should be understood as referring to the future: the prophet was seeing future events as if they were actually happening (cf. Dan 7:13). This will be the day of final victory, when those who crucified Jesus, "every one who pierced him" (cf. Zech 12:10; Jn 19:37), will be astonished by the grandeur and glory of the crucified One. "The Holy Scriptures inform us that there are two comings of the Son of God—one when he assumed human flesh for our salvation in the womb of a virgin; the other when he shall come at the end of the world to judge all mankind [...]; and if, from the beginning of the world that day of the Lord, on which he was clothed with our flesh, was sighed for by all as the foundation of their hope of deliverance; so also, after the death and ascension of the Son of God, we should make that other day of the Lord the object of our most earnest desires, 'awaiting our blessed hope, the appearing of the glory of our great God' (Tit 2:13)" (*St Pius V Catechism*, 1, 8, 2).

Commenting on this passage of the Apocalypse, St Bede says: "He who at his first coming came in a hidden way and in order to be judged (by men) will then come in a manifest way. (John)

Revelation 1:10

⁸"I am the Alpha and the Omega," says the Lord God, who is and who was and who is to come, the Almighty. Rev 1:4; 21:6

Reason for writing
⁹I John, your brother, who share with you in Jesus the tribulation and the kingdom and the patient endurance, was on the island called Patmos on account of the word of God and the testimony of Jesus. ¹⁰I was in the Spirit on the Lord's day, and I heard behind Rom 3:26

Rev 4:1

---

recalls these truths in order to help the Church bear its suffering: now it is being persecuted by its enemies, later it will reign at Christ's side" (*Explanatio Apocalypsis*, 1, 1).

The joy of those who put their hope in this glorious manifestation of Christ will contrast with the pains of those who reject God's love and mercy to the very end. "Then all the tribes of the earth will mourn, and they will see the Son of man coming in the clouds of heaven with power and great glory" (Mt 24:30).

1:8. The coming of the Lord in glory, the climax of his dominion, is guaranteed by the power of God, the absolute master of the world and its destiny. Alpha and Omega are the first and last letters of the Greek alphabet; here they are used to proclaim that God is the beginning and end of all things, of the world and of history; he is present at all times—times past, present and future.

1:9–20. After greeting the churches (vv. 4–8) the author explains his reason for writing: he has been commanded to do so by his glorious Lord, in a vision of the risen Christ concerning his Church.

In Holy Scripture God's messages are frequently communicated to prophets in the form of a vision (cf. Is 6; Ezek 1:4—3:15; etc.; Zech 1:7—2:9; etc.). Accounts of divine visions are particularly found in "books of revelation" or apocalypses, such as Daniel 8–12, and also in other Jewish and Christian writings of the time immediately before and after Christ's life on earth: although not included in the canon of the Bible, these writings were designed to keep up Christians' morale in times of persecution. In a genuinely prophetic vision God elevates the prophet's mind to enable him to understand what God desires to tell him (cf. *Summa theologiae*, 2–2, 173, 3). In the Apocalypse, when St John reports his vision he is making known the message given him by the risen Christ: Christ is continuing to speak to his Church in a number of ways, including the exhortations and teachings contained in this book.

1:9–11. Like other prophets and apostles (cf. Ezek 3:12; Acts 10:10; 22:17; 2 Cor 12:2–3), John feels himself caught up by a divine force; in an ecstasy he hears the voice of our Lord; its power and strength he describes as a trumpet.

Some scholars think that the seven churches listed here were chosen because of their particular situation at the time. They stand for the entire Church universal, and therefore what is said in the seven letters is addressed to all Christians who, in one way or another, find themselves in situations similar to that of these churches of proconsular Asia.

The apostles' vigilant care of the Church is discernible in many of the

Revelation 1:11

me a loud voice like a trumpet ¹¹saying, "Write what you see in a book and send it to the seven churches, to Ephesus and to Smyrna and to Pergamum and to Thyatira and to Sardis and to Philadelphia and to Laodicea."

Rev 1:4, 20
Dan 7:13; 10:5

¹²Then I turned to see the voice that was speaking to me, and on turning I saw seven golden lampstands, ¹³and in the midst of

---

letters they addressed to their communities. Like St Paul (cf. 2 Cor 11:28; 1 Thess 2:2), the other apostles felt anxiety for all the churches. St Peter, for example, wrote to elders telling them to be good shepherds of the flock God gave into their care, tending it "not by constraint but willingly, as God would have you, not for shameful gain but eagerly, not as domineering over those in your charge but being examples to the flock" (1 Pet 5:2–3).

This pastoral solicitude leads St John to show solidarity with the joy and affliction of Christians of his day. His consoling words come from someone who well knows (because he has learned it from Jesus and later from his own experience) that fidelity to the Gospel calls for self-denial and even martyrdom. Communion and solidarity are wonderful features of the mystical body of Christ: they stem from the fact that all Christians are united to each other and to Jesus Christ, the head of that body which is the Church (cf. Col 1:18; Eph 4:16; etc.). The visionary of Patmos clearly has tremendous love for Christ and for the Church. We should remember that "charity more than any other virtue, unites us closely with Christ, and it is the heavenly ardour of this love which has caused so many sons and daughters of the Church to rejoice in suffering contumely for his sake, joyfully to meet and overcome the severest trials, and even to shed their blood and die for him" (Plus XII, *Mystici corporis*, 33).

From the very start of his public ministry our Lord foretold how much his followers would have to suffer for his sake. For example, in the Sermon on the Mount, he said, "Blessed are you when men revile you and persecute you and utter all kinds of evil against you falsely on my account. Rejoice and be glad, for your reward is great in heaven, for so men persecuted the prophets who were before you" (Mt 5:11–12).

"The Lord's day": the *dies Dominica*, Sunday, the day which the Church, ever since the apostolic age, keeps as its weekly holy day in place of the Jewish sabbath, because it is the day on which Jesus rose from the dead: "on this day Christ's faithful are bound to come together into one place. They should listen to the word of God and take part in the Eucharist, thus calling to mind the passion, resurrection, and glory of the Lord Jesus, and giving thanks to God by whom they have been begotten 'anew through the resurrection of Christ from the dead, unto a living hope' (1 Pet 1:3)" (Vatican II, *Sacrosanctum Concilium*, 106). This day should be sanctified by attending Mass and also by giving time to other devotions, rest, and activities which help build up friendship with others, especially in the family circle.

1:12–16. The lampstands in this first vision symbolize the churches at prayer; they remind us of the seven-branched candlestick (the *menoráh*) which used to burn in the temple of Jerusalem and which is described in detail in Exodus 25:31–40. In the midst of the candlestick, as if guarding and governing the

the lampstands one like a son of man,* clothed with a long robe and with a golden girdle round his breast; ¹⁴his head and his hair were white as white wool, white as snow; his eyes were like a flame of fire, ¹⁵his feet were like burnished bronze, refined as in a furnace, and his voice was like the sound of many waters; ¹⁶in his right hand he held seven stars, from his mouth issued a sharp two-edged sword, and his face was like the sun shining in full strength.

¹⁷When I saw him, I fell at his feet as though dead. But he laid his right hand upon me, saying, "Fear not, I am the first and the

Dan 7:9; 10:6
Rev 2:18; 19:12
Ezk 1:24; 43:2
Mt 17:2; Judg 5:31; Rev 2:12
Dan 8:18; 10:5–19; Is 41:4; 44:6 48:12

churches, a mysterious figure appears, in the form of a man. The expression "son of man" originates in Daniel 7:14 where, as here, it refers to someone depicted as Judge at the end of time. The various symbols used indicate his importance. His "long robe" shows his priesthood (cf. Ex 28:4; Zech 3:4); the golden girdle, his kingship (cf. 1 Mac 10:89); his white hair, his eternity (cf. Dan 7:9); his eyes "like a flame of fire" symbolize his divine wisdom (cf. Rev 2:23), and his bronze feet his strength and stability.

The seven stars stand for the angels of the seven churches (cf. v. 20), and our Lord's holding them in his hand is a sign of his power and providence. Finally, the splendour of his face recalls the Old Testament theophanies or apparitions, and the sword coming from his mouth shows the power of his word (cf. Heb 4:12).

It is interesting to note that our Lord used the title "son of man" to refer to himself (cf., e.g., Mt 9:6; Mk 10:45; Lk 6:22); it is always used in St John's Gospel to indicate Christ's divinity and transcendence (cf., e.g., Jn 1:51; 3:14; 9:35; 12:23).

"Burnished bronze": Latin versions transliterate the original as "orichalc", a shining alloy of bronze and gold.

1:17–19. When the glory of Christ, or the glory of God, is manifested, man becomes so conscious of his insignifi-

cance and unworthiness that he is unable to remain standing in his presence. This happened to the Israelites at Sinai (cf. Ex 19:16–24) and to the apostles on Mount Tabor (cf. Mk 9:2–8 and par.). A person who experiences the divine presence in a vision reacts in the same way (cf. Ezek 1:29f; Dan 8:18; etc.), and in the case of the Apocalypse it happens when Christ is seen in glory surrounded by his Church. However, the risen Christ's first word to his followers was one of peace and assurance (cf., e.g., Mt 28:5, 10), and here he places his right hand on the seer's head in a gesture of protection.

The risen Christ is depicted as reassuring the Christian, who sees him as having absolute dominion over all things (he is the first and the last) though he shared man's mortal nature. By his death and resurrection Christ has overcome death; he has dominion over death and over the mysterious world beyond the grave—Hades, the place of the dead (cf. Num 16:33). "Christ is alive. This is the great truth which fills our faith with meaning. Jesus, who died on the cross, has risen. He has triumphed over death; he has overcome sorrow, anguish and the power of darkness" (St Josemaría Escrivá, *Christ Is Passing By*, 102).

The vision St John is given is meant for the benefit of the whole Church, as can be seen from the fact that he is told to write down what he sees; it is connected

Revelation 1:18

last, ¹⁸and the living one; I died, and behold I am alive for evermore, and I have the keys of Death and Hades. ¹⁹Now write what you see, what is and what is to take place hereafter. ²⁰As for the mystery of the seven stars which you saw in my right hand, and the seven golden lampstands, the seven stars are the angels of the seven churches and the seven lampstands are the seven churches.

Heb 7:25; Mt 16:18
Rev 1:11, 12, 16

Letter to the church of Ephesus

Ps 36:5; Mic 2:1; Rev 1:13, 16, 20

2 ¹To the angel of the church in Ephesus write: 'The words of him who holds the seven stars in his right hand, who walks among the seven golden lampstands.

---

with contemporary events and with the future. The immediate context of the vision is the salvation of the churches mentioned and the glory of Christ who is caring for them (chaps. 2–3); the future has to do with the afflictions the Church must undergo and the full establishment of Christ's kingdom: his second coming will mean definitive victory over the powers of evil (cf. chaps. 4–22).

1:20. To understand the meaning of the revelation made to St John, which he is transmitting in this book, one needs to know the mysterious, hidden meaning behind the images which appear in the vision. When John says that Jesus Christ himself revealed this to him, he is saying that this is the true interpretation and he is inviting us to interpret the book's symbolism by using this key to its meaning; no parallel explanation is given of the other visions when he comes to describe them.

The angels of the seven churches may stand for the bishops in charge of them, or else the guardian angels who watch over them, or even the churches themselves insofar as they have a heavenly dimension and stand in God's presence as angels do. Whichever is the case, the best thing is to see the angels of the churches, to whom the letters are addressed, as meaning those who rule and protect each church in Christ's name. He is the only Lord, which is why he is shown holding the stars (angels) in his right hand. In the Old Testament the "angel of Yahweh" is the one charged to guide the people of Israel (cf. Ex 14:19; 23:20; etc.); and in the Apocalypse itself angels are given the mission of ruling the material world (cf. Rev 7:1; 14:18; 16:5). So, Christ exercises his loving care and government of each Church through the mediation of "angels", but it is difficult to say whether this means angels as such, or bishops, or both.

Lampstands may be used as a symbol because the Church is being seen in liturgical terms: it is, from that point of view, like a lamp burning constantly and giving light in praise of Christ. The symbol is reminiscent of the seven-branched candlestick which used to burn continually in the presence of Yahweh (cf. Ex 27:20; Lev 24:2f) and which Zechariah saw in his visions (cf. Zech 4:1f). The lamps are a very good symbol, given that the churches are the light of the world (cf. Mt 5:14; Phil 2:15; etc.).

2:1–3:22. These chapters, which form the first part of the book, contain seven

²"'I know your works, your toil and your patient endurance, and how you cannot bear evil men but have tested those who call themselves apostles but are not, and found them to be false; ³I

2 Cor 11:13
1 Jn 4:1

letters to the churches already mentioned (cf. 1:11), each represented by an angel to whom the letter is addressed. In these letters Christ (who is referred to in various ways) and the Holy Spirit speak: hence the warning at the end of each, "he who has an ear, let him hear what the Spirit says to the churches." The first part of that formula is reminiscent of things our Lord said in the Gospels (cf., e.g., Mt 11:15; 13:9, 43; Mk 9:23), while the second part underlines the influence of the Holy Spirit on the churches: one needs to belong to the Church, to "feel with" the Church, if one is to understand what the Spirit says and what is being committed to writing in this book. The book, therefore, must be taken as the true word of God. All Scripture needs to be approached in this way: "Since all that the inspired authors, or sacred writers, affirm should be regarded as affirmed by the Holy Spirit, we must acknowledge that the books of Scripture, firmly, faithfully and without error, teach that truth which God, for the sake of our salvation, wished to see confided to the sacred Scriptures. Thus 'all scripture is inspired by God, and profitable for teaching, for reproof, for correction and for training in righteousness, so that the man of God may be complete, equipped for every good work' (2 Tim 3:16–17)" (Vatican II, *Dei Verbum*, 11).

Although the letters are different from one another, they all have the same basic structure: there is reference to the past, which is contrasted with the present; various warnings are given and promises made; then there is an exhortation to repentance and conversion, a reminder that the end, and Christ's definitive victory, will soon come.

2:1. Ephesus, with its great harbour and commercial importance, was the leading city of Asia Minor at the time. It was also the centre of the cult of the goddess Artemis or Diana (cf. Acts 19:23ff).

St Paul spent three years preaching in Ephesus and had considerable success there: St Luke tells us that "the word of the Lord grew (there) and prevailed mightily" (Acts 19:20). In ancient times it was the most important Christian city in the whole region, especially after the fall of Jerusalem in the year 70. St John spent the last years of his life in Ephesus, where his burial place is still venerated.

In these letters in the book of Revelation, Christ is depicted with attributes connected in some way with the circumstances of each church at the time. In the case of Ephesus symbols described in the vision in 1:12, 16 appear again. The seven stars in his right hand signify his dominion over the whole Church, for he is the one who has power to instruct the angels who rule the various communities. His walking among the lampstands shows his loving care and vigilance for the churches (the lampstand symbolizing their prayer and liturgical life). Because the Church in Ephesus was the foremost of the seven, Christ is depicted to it as Lord of all the churches.

2:2–3. In these verses the church of Ephesus is praised for its endurance and for the resistance it has shown to false apostles. These two attributes—endurance or constancy, and holy intransigence—are basic virtues every Christian should have. Endurance means doggedly pursuing good and holding one's ground against evil influences; this virtue makes

Revelation 2:4

1 Tim 5:12
Rev 2:16, 22;
3:3, 19

know you are enduring patiently and bearing up for my name's sake, and you have not grown weary. ⁴But I have this against you, that you have abandoned the love you had at first. ⁵Remember then from what you have fallen, repent and do the works you did

---

Christians "perfect and complete, lacking in nothing" (Jas 1:4). Indeed, St Paul asserts, "we rejoice in our sufferings, knowing that suffering produces endurance, and endurance produces character, and character produces hope" (Rom 5:3–4). In the Letter to the Hebrews we read, "For you have need of endurance, so that you may do the will of God and receive what is promised" (10:36). Endurance, patience, is also the first mark of charity identified by St Paul (cf. 1 Cor 13:4) and one of the features of the true apostle (cf. 2 Cor 6:4; 12:12). Our Lord has told us that by endurance we will gain our lives, will save our souls (cf. Lk 21:19). As St Cyprian puts it, patience "is what gives our faith its firmest basis; it enables our hope to grow to the greatest heights; it guides our actions so as to enable us to stay on Christ's path and make progress with his help; it makes us persevere as children of God" (*De bone patientiae*, 20).

Another virtue of the church of Ephesus (mentioned again in v. 6) is firm rejection of false apostles. We know from other New Testament writings, especially those of St Paul (cf. 2 Cor 3:1; Gal 1:7; Col 2:8; etc.) and St John (cf. 1 Jn 2:19; etc.), that some people were falsifying the Christian message by distorting its meaning and yet seeming to be very devout and concerned about the poor. Reference is made here to the Nicolaitans, a heretical sect difficult to identify. However, the main thing to notice is the resolute way the Christians of Ephesus rejected that error. If one fails to act in this energetic way, one falls into a false kind of tolerance, "a sure sign of not possessing the truth. When a man gives way in matters of ideals, of honour or of faith, that man is a man without ideals, without honour and without faith" (St Josemaría Escrivá, *The Way*, 394).

2:4. "He does not say that he was without charity, but only that it was not such as in the beginning; that is, that it was not now prompt, fervent, growing in love, or fruitful: as we are wont to say of him who from being bright, cheerful and blithe, becomes sad, heavy and sullen, that he is not now the same man he was" (St Francis de Sales, *Treatise on the Love of God*, 4, 2). This is why our Lord complains that their early love has grown cold.

To avoid this danger, to which all of us are prone, we need to be watchful and correct ourselves every day and return again and again to God our Father. Love of God, charity, should never be allowed to die down; it should always be kept ardent; it should always be growing.

2:5. This is a call to repentance, to a change of heart which involves three stages. The first is recognizing that one is at fault—having the humility to admit one is a poor sinner: "To acknowledge one's sin, indeed—penetrating still more deeply into the consideration of one's own personhood—to recognize oneself as being a sinner, capable of sin and inclined to commit sin, is the essential first step in returning to God" (John Paul II, *Reconciliatio et paenitentia*, 13). Then comes "love-sorrow" or contrition, which leads us to mend our ways. This is followed by acts of penance which

at first. If not, I will come to you and remove your lampstand from its place, unless you repent. ⁶Yet this you have, you hate the works of the Nicolaitans, which I also hate. ⁷He who has an ear, let him hear what the Spirit says to the churches. To him who conquers I will grant to eat of the tree of life, which is in the paradise of God.'

<small>Rev 2:15
Ps 139:21

Gen 2:9
Rev 22:2</small>

Letter to the church of Smyrna

⁸"And to the angel of the church in Smyrna write: 'The words of the first and the last, who died and came to life.

<small>Is 44;6; 48:12
Rev 1:17; Jas 2:5</small>

⁹"'I know your tribulation and your poverty (but you are rich) and the slander of those who say that they are Jews and are not,

<small>2 Cor 11:14, 15
Rev 3:9</small>

---

enable us to draw closer to God and live in intimacy with him.

Evangelization is always calling us to repent. "To evoke conversion and penance in man's heart and to offer him the gift of reconciliation is the specific mission of the Church as she continues the redemptive work of her divine Founder" (ibid., 23). The church of Ephesus is given a warning that if it does not change its course it will lose its leading position and possibly disappear altogether.

2:6. On the Nicolaitans, see the note on 2:14–16.

2:7. The image of the tree of life (cf. also Rev 22:2) is a reference to Genesis 2:9 and 3:22, where we find that tree in the middle of Paradise outside the reach of man; it is a symbol of immortality. The fruit of the tree is now to be found in Christ, and he promises to grant it to those who are victorious. This promise of a happiness that will last forever, rather than any threat of punishment, is what spurs us on to strive day in, day out, not knowing whether today's battle, no matter how small it is, may not be our last: "We cannot take it easy. Our Lord wants us to strive harder, on a broader front, more intensely each day. We have an obligation to outdo ourselves, for in this competition the only goal is to reach the glory of heaven. If we do not get there, the whole thing will have been useless" (St Josemaría Escrivá, *Christ Is Passing By*, 77).

2:8. Smyrna was a port some 60 kilometres (35 miles) north of Ephesus; one of the main cities of the region, it was renowned for its loyalty to Rome and its ritual worship of the emperor. Christ is depicted to this church as truly God, "the first and the last" (cf. 1:8), that is, he who has had no beginning and will have no end. Despite the vigorous emperor worship which was a feature of Smyrna, its Christians were very assiduous in the practice of their faith in Christ as the only true God and Lord, as verified especially by his glorious resurrection. That is why we are reminded that Christ died and then rose again: the words used emphasize that Christ's death was something quite transitory, whereas his return to life is something permanent and irreversible (cf. 1:18).

2:9. The Christians of Smyrna had to endure persecution and deprivation, due no doubt to the fact that they refused to take part in ceremonies connected with emperor worship. Their poverty can become something of great value, for

Revelation 2:10

<small>Dan 1:12, 14
Mt 10:28
1 Cor 9:25</small>

but are a synagogue of Satan. ¹⁰Do not fear what you are about to suffer. Behold, the devil is about to throw some of you into prison, that you may be tested, and for ten days* you will have

---

God has high regard for the poor and despised (cf. 1 Cor 1:27–28; Jas 2:5). As an ancient Christian writer puts it, "They say that most of us are poor. That is nothing to be ashamed of; rather, we glory in it, because man's soul is demeaned by easy living and strengthened by frugality. Besides, can a person be poor who is in need of nothing, who does not covet the goods of others, who is rich in the eyes of God? That person is truly poor who has much and yet desires to have more [...]. Just as the wayfarer is happier the less he has to carry, so in this journey of life the poor person who is unencumbered is happier than the well-to-do person burdened with riches" (Minucius Felix, *Octavius*, 36, 3–6).

In addition to poverty, the Christians of Smyrna had to bear with the lies spread by certain Jews, who were accusing them of being agitators against the civil authorities and against pagans in general. Jews were quite influential in the empire: for example, the *Martyrdom of St Polycarp* tells of how, fifty years after the Apocalypse was written, the saintly bishop Polycarp of Smyrna was martyred because the Jews of that city incited the people to clamour for his death.

Because they were collaborating in this way with idolatry instead of defending worshippers of the true God, these people did not deserve the honourable title of "Jews": "ministers of Satan", God's adversary, was a better label for them. In opposing Christians, they were adopting the same attitude as those who opposed Jesus Christ, an attitude which earned them the title of children of the devil (cf. Jn 8:44). Although they bore the name of Jews, they were not really members of the people of God, because, as St Paul teaches, "Not all who are descended from Israel belong to Israel, and not all are children of Abraham because they are his descendants [...]. This means that it is not the children of the flesh who are the children of God, but the children of the promise are reckoned as descendants" (Rom 9:6–8). The new Israel, the true Israel, is the Church of Jesus Christ who "acknowledges that in God's plan of salvation the beginning of her faith and election is to be found in the patriarchs, Moses and the prophets. She professes that all Christ's faithful, who as men of faith are sons of Abraham (cf. Gal 3:7), are included in the same patriarch's call" (Vatican II, *Nostra aetate*, 4).

The harsh accusation made in this passage of the book refers to those Jews who at that time were denouncing Christians in Smyrna: it should not be applied to Jews in general; similarly, "even though the Jewish authorities and those who followed their lead pressed for the death of Christ (cf. Jn 19:6), neither all Jews indiscriminately at that time, nor Jews today, can be charged with the crimes committed during his passion. It is true that the Church is the new people of God, yet the Jews should not be spoken of as rejected or accursed as if this followed from Holy Scripture" (ibid., 4).

2:10. The church of Smyrna receives no words of reproach from our Lord, only encouragement: God has foreseen the situation it finds itself in, and things will get even worse for a while—"ten days" (cf. Dan 1:12). He therefore exhorts them to stay true to the very end, even to death, so as to win the crown of victory (cf. 1

tribulation. Be faithful unto death, and I will give you the crown of life. ⁱⁱHe who has an ear, let him hear what the Spirit says to the churches. He who conquers shall not be hurt by the second death.'

Rev 20:14; 21:8

Letter to the church of Pergamum

¹²"And to the angel of the church in Pergamum write: 'The words of him who has the sharp two-edged sword.

Rev 1:16; 19:15
Is 49:2; Heb 4:12

¹³"'I know where you dwell, where Satan's throne is; you hold fast my name and you did not deny my faith even in the days of Antipas my witness, my faithful one, who was killed among you,

Rev 3:8; 14:12

Cor 9:25; Phil 3:14; 1 Pet 5:4). The simile of the crown comes from athletic contests of the time, in which victors received a crown of laurels or a floral wreath—a symbol of enduring glory, but in fact something very perishable.

This passage, in fact, provides us with an entire programme for living—faithfulness to commitments, enduring loyalty to the love of Christ. If we want to be saved we need to persevere to the very end; as St Teresa of Avila puts it, "by making an earnest and most determined resolve not to halt until the goal [eternal life] is reached, whatever may come, whatever may happen, however much effort one needs to make, whoever may complain about one, whether one dies on the road or has no heart to face the trials one meets, even if the ground gives away under one's feet" (*Way of Perfection*, 21, 2). "It is easy", John Paul II has reminded us, "to stay true to the faith for a day or for a few days. The difficult thing, the important thing, is to do so right through life. It is easy to keep the faith when things are going well, and difficult to do so when obstacles are met. Consistent behaviour which lasts one's whole life is the only kind which deserves to be called 'fidelity'" (*Homily*, 27 January 1979).

2:11. "Second death": a reference to irreversible, enduring, condemnation. Further on, the book is more specific about what this involves, and who will suffer it (cf. 20:6, 14; 21:8).

2:12–13. Pergamum, some 70 kilometres (40 miles) to the north of Smyrna, was renowned for its temples, among other things. It was the first city in Asia Minor to erect a temple to the "divine Augustus" and "divine Rome" (in the year 29 BC). The temple had a huge altar, of the whitest marble, dedicated to Zeus. The city was also a place of pilgrimage where sick people flooded to the temple of Aesculapius, the god of health and miracles. For all these reasons it is described as the place where Satan has his throne. Pergamum was also noted for its great library and for its manufacture of parchment.

Christ is portrayed to this church as a judge, that is, one whose word distinguishes good from evil, and who distributes rewards and punishments (cf. Rev 1:16; 19:15, 21; Heb 4:12)—the reason being that the church at Pergamum is a mix of truth and error, with some people holding on to sound teaching and others supporting the Nicolaitans (cf. v. 15).

The letter begins by praising the fidelity of this church despite the per-

Revelation 2:14

Num 25:1, 2; 31:16
2 Pet 2:15
Jude 11
Rev 2:6

where Satan dwells. ¹⁴But I have a few things against you: you have some there who hold the teaching of Balaam, who taught Balak to put a stumbling block before the sons of Israel, that they might eat food sacrificed to idols and practise immorality. ¹⁵So you also have some who hold the teaching of the Nicolaitans.

secution which has led to the death of Antipas. We do not know for sure who Antipas was; some traditions refer to his undergoing ordeal by fire in the reign of Domitian. The emperors of the time insisted on being acknowledged as *Kyrios* (Lord), which amounted to divine honours: this implied a form of idolatry, to which no Christian could subscribe. Tertullian says that there was nothing against acknowledging the emperor as *Kyrios*, if the title referred to his temporal power, but he could not be given it if it had a different, religious, meaning—"ut dominum dei vice dicam", as if it meant treating him as a god (cf. *Apologeticum*, 34).

The title given to this Christian who died for the faith—"my witness, my faithful one"—was and is an outstanding title of honour for a believer, applied as it is to one who has kept faith with Christ even at the cost of life itself. In the early times of the Church (a time of unique persecution), many Christians followed the example of the first martyr, St Stephen (cf. Acts 7:55–60) and bore heroic witness to the faith by shedding their blood. Their deaths, marked as they were by serenity and hope, played an important part in the spread of Christianity, so much so that, as Tertullian put it, the blood of the martyrs was the seed from which Christians grew (cf. *Apologeticum*, 197). St Justin also notes that the more martyrs there were, the more Christians increased in number; the same is true of the vine when it is pruned: the branches which are pruned put out many more shoots (cf. *Dialogue with Trypho*, 110, 4).

2:14–16. After being praised for their fidelity, the Christians of Pergamum are told where they are going wrong; some of them are compromising their faith by taking part in pagan ritual banquets and "sacred fornication" rites. A comparison is drawn with Balaam, who encouraged the Moabite women to marry Israelites and draw them to worship the god of Moab (cf. Num 31:16). As regards the Nicolaitans, some early authors suggest that this was a heresy started by Nicholas, one of the first seven deacons (cf. Acts 6:5); but their view is not well founded. It is easy to understand how this aberration could have arisen in a society where Christians were living cheek by jowl with pagans who went in for sacred banquets in honour of idols, and rites of an erotic character. It was a situation which arose more than once (cf., e.g., Rom 14:2, 15; 1 Cor 8:10; 2 Cor 2:16).

As in v. 5, there is a new call to conversion, and the same pattern is found in the subsequent letters. John Paul II states that "in all periods of history this invitation constitutes the very basis of the Church's mission" (*Address*, 28 February 1982). Elsewhere, he points out where conversion begins: "Authentic knowledge of the God of mercy, the God of tender love, is a constant and inexhaustible source of conversion, not only as a momentary interior act but also as a permanent attitude, as a state of mind. Those who come to know God in this way, who 'see' him in this way, can live only in a state of being continually converted to him. They live, therefore, *in statu conversionis*; and

¹⁶Repent then. If not, I will come to you soon and war against them with the sword of my mouth. ¹⁷He who has an ear, let him hear what the Spirit says to the churches. To him who conquers I will give some of the hidden manna, and I will give him a white stone, with a new name written on the stone which no one knows except him who receives it.'

Rev 1:16; 2:5
Is 62:2; 65:15
Rev 3:12; 19:12
Ps 78:24

Letter to the church of Thyatira

¹⁸"And to the angel of the church in Thyatira write: 'The words of the Son of God, who has eyes like a flame of fire, and whose feet are like burnished bronze.

Rev 1:14, 15
Dan 10:6

it is this state of conversion which marks out the most profound element of the pilgrimage of every man and woman on earth *in statu viatoris*" (*Dives in misericordia*, 13).

2:17. The promise of the hidden manna to the victors can be seen as a counter to the sin of indulging in idolatrous meals. St Paul also contrasts sacrifices to idols with the eucharistic sacrifice; and tells the Corinthians that they cannot "drink the cup of the Lord and the cup of demons [...], cannot partake of the table of the Lord and the table of demons" (1 Cor 10:21). Elsewhere, St John tells us of our Lord's referring to manna when speaking about the Eucharist (cf. Jn 6:31–33). The nourishment which Yahweh gave his people in the desert was described as "bread from heaven" (cf. Ex 16:4) and "the bread of the angels" (Ps 78:25), kept in the Ark of the Covenant to be revered by the people (cf. Heb 9:4). Here it is described as "hidden" manna, a reference to the supernatural, divine, character of the reward of heavenly beatitude; we share in this in Holy Communion, to a degree; in eternal life it is partaken of fully.

The "white stone" is a reference to the custom of showing a little stone, with some appropriate mark on it, to gain entrance to a feast or banquet. The name inscribed on the stone referred to here shows that the Christian has a right to partake of the good things which the Lord reserves for those who win the victory,

The fact that only the recipient knows what is written on the stone points to the personal, intimate relationship between God (who issues the invitation) and the invited guest. "Go over, calmly, that divine admonition which fills the soul with disquiet and which at the same time tastes as sweet as honey from the comb: *redemi te, et vocavi te, nomine tuo: meus es tu* (Is 43:1); I have redeemed you, I have called you by your name, you are mine" (St Josemaría Escrivá, *Friends of God*, 312).

2:18. Thyatira, located some 75 kilometres (48 miles) to the south-east of Pergamum, was the least important of the seven churches mentioned; the city was noted for smelting, weaving and dyeing. Acts 16:13–15 gives an account of the conversion of a native of Thyatira, a dealer in purple called Lydia. The city had many craft guilds which organized festivities in honour of the gods. This involved danger for Christians, because they felt obliged to take part.

Jesus Christ is depicted explicitly as "the Son of God". This is the only time he is given this title in the Apocalypse,

Revelation 2:19

Rev 2:14
2 Kings 9:22

¹⁹"'I know your works, your love and faith and service and patient endurance, and that your latter works exceed the first. ²⁰But I have this against you, that you tolerate the woman Jezebel, who calls herself a prophetess and is teaching and beguiling my servants to practise immorality* and to eat food sacrificed to idols. ²¹I gave her time to repent, but she refuses to repent of her immorality.* ²²Behold, I will throw her on a sickbed, and those who commit adultery with her I will throw into great tribulation, unless they repent of her doings; ²³and I will strike her children dead. And all the churches shall know that I am he who searches mind and heart, and I will give to each of you as your works

Ps 7:10; 62:13
Jer 11:20;
17:10

---

but it is implicit in the many references to God as his Father (cf. 1:6; 3:5, 21; 14:1). As Son of God, Christ appears clothed in the attributes proper to the Godhead—divine knowledge, which enables him to search man's soul (cf. v. 23) and divine power (cf. note on 1:14–15). These attributes are revealed particularly by the way he deals with the church of Thyatira.

2:19. The letter begins with praise of the good works of this Church, the most outstanding of which is its service (*diakonia*) to the poor (cf. Acts 11:28; Rom 15:25, 31; 1 Cor 16:15; 1 Pet 4:10; etc.). Unlike Ephesus, its "latter works" are more perfect than its earlier works; in other words, it is making progress in virtue.

2:20–23. Our Lord again inveighs against those Christians who are compromising themselves by taking part in pagan worship, involving, as it does, idolatry and moral aberration. The letter seems to refer to the same (Nicolaitan) heresy, here symbolized by Jezebel, the wife of King Ahab, who led many of the people of Israel into the sin of idolatry (cf. 1 Kings 16:31; 2 Kings 9:22). This may be a reference to a real person (described here symbolically by this biblical name) who projected herself as a prophetess and led many people astray by getting them to take part in idolatrous rites and banquets. When wrong is being done and one fails to point it out, one's silence is really a form of complicity.

The passage reveals how patient God is: he has waited for these people to mend their ways and only at a later stage condemned them for not doing so. This is a warning which those who persist in evil must bear in mind, for "the more we postpone getting out of sin and turning to God", the Curé of Ars warns us, "the greater the danger we run of dying with our sins on us, for the simple reason that bad habits become more and more difficult to shed. Every time we despise a grace, our Lord is going further away from us, and we are growing weaker, and the devil gets more control of us. So, my conclusion is that the longer we remain in sin, the greater the risk we run of never being converted" (*Selected Sermons*, 4th Sunday in Lent).

The punishment meted out to Jezebel is quite frightening: she will be afflicted with a grievous illness (cf. Ex 21:18; Jud 8:3; 1 Mac 1:5). The same will happen to her followers: they are warned to this effect, in the hope that this will cause them to repent. In other words, our Lord still has hopes of their conversion, and even uses the threat of punishment to move people to think again and repent.

deserve. ²⁴But to the rest of you in Thyatira, who do not hold this teaching, who have not learned what some call the deep things of Satan,* to you I say, I do not lay upon you any other burden; ²⁵only hold fast what you have, until I come. ²⁶He who conquers and who keeps my works until the end, I will give him power over the nations, ²⁷and he shall rule them with a rod of iron, as when earthen pots are broken in pieces, even as I myself have received power from my Father; ²⁸and I will give him the morning star.* ²⁹He who has an ear, let him hear what the Spirit says to the churches.'

Rev 3:11
Ps 2:8
Rev 12:5; 19:15
2 Pet 1:19
Is 14:12

Letter to the church of Sardis

3 ¹"And to the angel of the church in Sardis write: 'The words of him who has the seven spirits of God and the seven stars.

Rev 1:16

2:24–28. Knowledge of the "deep things of Satan" was another aspect of the Nicolaitan heresy, which claimed to possess secrets leading to salvation. Some scholars link this kind of arcane knowledge with Gnosticism, which was making headway in the East at the time.

The promise made to the victors (taken from Psalm 2:9) involves sharing in Christ's sovereignty and power because one is in full communion with him. The "morning star" is an expression also applied to Christ in Revelation 22:16. It may refer to the perfect communion with the Lord enjoyed by those who persevere to the end: the symbolism of the power given to the victors (vv. 26–27) is followed in v. 28 by reference to sharing in the resurrection and glory of Christ, expressed by the image of the "morning star", which heralds the day, that is, rebirth, resurrection.

3:1. Sardis, about 50 kilometres (30 miles) south-east of Thyatira, was an important hub in the highway system; it was also famous for its acropolis, which was located in an unassailable position. Herodotus describes its inhabitants as immoral, licentious people (cf. *History*, 1, 55). The Christians of the city were probably somewhat infected by the general atmosphere.

Christ is now depicted as possessing the fullness of the Spirit, with the power to effect radical change by sanctifying the churches from within (cf. note on 1:4). He is also portrayed as the sovereign Lord of the universal Church (cf. note on 2:1), ever ready to imbue it with new life.

The church of Sardis is accused of seeming to be alive but in fact being dead: in other words, although its external practice of religion makes it look Christian, most of its members (not all: cf. v. 4) are estranged from Christ, devoid of interior life, in a sinful condition. Anyone who lives like that is dead. Our Lord himself described the situation of the prodigal son as being a kind of death: "my son was dead, and is alive again", the father exclaims in the parable (Lk 15:24); and St Paul invites Christians to offer themselves to God "as men who have been brought from death to life" (Rom 6:13). Now, in this passage of Revelation, we are told that the cause of this spiritual, but real, death is the fact that the works of this church are imperfect in the sight of God (v. 2); they were works which led

Revelation 3:2

Ezek 34:4
1 Thess 5:2
Mt 24:43
Jude 23
Rev 4:4; 20:12
Mt 10:32; Ex 32:32; Ps 69:29

"'I know your works; you have the name of being alive, and you are dead. ²Awake, and strengthen what remains and is on the point of death, for I have not found your works perfect in the sight of my God. ³Remember then what you received and heard; keep that, and repent. If you will not awake, I will come like a thief, and you will not know at what hour I will come upon you. ⁴Yet you have still a few names in Sardis, people who have not soiled their garments; and they shall walk with me in white, for they are worthy. ⁵He who conquers shall be clad thus in white garments,

---

to spiritual death, that is, what we would term mortal sins. "With the whole tradition of the Church", John Paul II says, "we call *mortal sin* the act by which man freely and consciously rejects God, his law, the covenant of love that God offers, preferring to turn in on himself or to some created and finite reality, something contrary to the divine will (*conversio ad creaturam*) [...]. Man perceives that this disobedience to God destroys the bond that unites him with his life-principle: it is a mortal sin, that is, an act which gravely offends God and ends in turning against man himself with a dark and powerful force of destruction" (*Reconciliatio et paenitentia*, 17).

3:2–3. Vigilance is always necessary, particularly in certain situations like that of Sardis where there was a number of people who had not fallen victim to sin. In this kind of peril, Christians need to be alerted and confirmed in the faith. They need to remember what they learned at the beginning, when they were instructed in the faith, and try to bring their lives into line with that teaching. And so they are not simply exhorted to conversion but told how to go about it—by comparing their lives with the Word of God and making the necessary changes: "no one is safe if he ceases to strive against himself. Nobody can save himself by his own efforts. Everyone in the Church needs specific means to strengthen himself—humility, which disposes us to accept help and advice; mortifications, which temper the heart and allow Christ to reign in it; the study of abiding, sound doctrine, which leads us to conserve and spread our faith" (St Josemaría Escrivá, *Christ Is Passing By*, 81).

"I will come like a thief': an image also found elsewhere in the New Testament (cf. Mt 24:42–51; Mk 13:36; Lk 12:39ff; 1 Thess 5:2; 2 Pet 3:10). This does not mean that our Lord is lying in wait, ready to pounce on man when he is unawares, like a hunter waiting for his prey. It is simply a warning to us to live in the grace of God and be ready to render our account to him. If we do that we will not run the risk of being found empty-handed at the moment of death. "That day will come for us. It will be our last day, but we are not afraid of it. Trusting firmly in God's grace, we are ready from this very moment to be generous and courageous, and take loving care of little things: we are ready to go and meet our Lord, with our lamps burning brightly. For the feast of feasts awaits us in heaven" (St Josemaría Escrivá, *Friends of God*, 40).

3:4–5. Despite the corrupt environment in which they were living, there were some Christians who had not been contaminated by the immoral cults and lifestyles of the pagans: their loyalty is symbolized by white garments. When

and I will not blot his name out of the book of life; I will confess his name before my Father and before his angels. ⁶He who has an ear, let him hear what the Spirit says to the churches.'

Letter to the church of Philadelphia
⁷"And to the angel of the church in Philadelphia write: 'The words of the holy one, the true one, who has the key of David, who opens and no one shall shut, who shuts and no one opens.

Rev 1:18
Is 6:3; 22:22

---

narrating his visions St John mentions white garments a number of times (cf. 7:9, 13; 15:6; 19:14); this colour symbolizes purity and also the joy of victory.

The symbol of the "book of life", which occurs often in the Apocalypse (cf. 13:8; 17:8; 20:12, 15; 21:27; etc.), is taken from the Old Testament, where those who belong to the people of Israel are described as enrolled in the "book of the living", which is also referred to as the book of the Lord (cf. Ps 69:28; Ex 32:32ff). Those whose names are in the book will share in the promises of salvation (cf. Is 4:3), whereas those who are unfaithful to the Law will be excluded from the people of God and their names blotted out of the "book of the living". Other New Testament texts use the same image (cf., e.g., Lk 10:20; Phil 4:3).

The names of the victors will stay in the "book of life" which lists those who have proved loyal to Christ, as well as those who belonged to the people of Israel.

Finally, on Judgment Day, those Christians who have kept the faith, will be spoken for by Christ (cf. Mt 10:32; Lk 12:8).

3:7. Philadelphia, in the province of Lydia, was about 45 kilometres (25 miles) south-east of Sardis. Its geographical location made it a gateway to all of Phrygia —hence the sacred writer's reference to its having an open door (the same turn of phrase is used by St Paul to refer to scope for apostolate: cf. 1 Cor 16:9; 2 Cor 2:12; Col 4:3).

Philadelphia had suffered an earthquake around the year AD 17: there is a possible allusion to this in the promise to make it a supportive pillar in God's temple (v. 12). When the city was rebuilt, it was given the new name of Neocaesarea, but that name soon fell into disuse. Here, however, it is promised another new name (v. 12), the name of God and the name New Jerusalem, and this name will endure forever. There was quite a sizeable and influential Jewish community in Philadelphia (cf. v. 9), many of whom will later become converts and recognize the Church, the beloved Bride of Jesus Christ.

The titles given to Jesus in this letter clearly indicate his divinity: "the holy one" is proper to Yahweh, as can be seen frequently in the Old Testament (cf. Lev 11:44; Josh 24:19; Is 6:3; 12:6; Job 6:10; etc.). The title of "the true one" (also used by St John in his Gospel: cf., e.g., Jn 1:9; 4:23; 7:28; 15:1; 17:3) conveys the idea of the complete reliability and faithfulness of the Lord with regard to keeping his promises (cf. Ps 86:15; 116; 135). And the words "who has the key of David" and the power to open and shut signify the absolute sovereignty of Christ in the messianic Kingdom. Our Lord used this metaphor when he confirmed St Peter in the primacy (cf. Mt 16:19) and when he passed on his own powers to the college of apostles (cf. Mt 18:18).

Revelation 3:8

^{Acts 14:27}
^{1 Cor 16:9}

^{Rev 2:9}
^{Is 43:4; 45:14; 49:23; 60:14}

^{2 Pet 2:9}
^{2 Thess 2:12}

^{Rev 2:25}
^{1 Cor 9:25}
^{Rev 21:2}
^{Gal 2:9}
^{Ezek 48:35}
^{Is 62:2; 65:15}

⁸"'I know your works. Behold, I have set before you an open door, which no one is able to shut; I know that you have but little power, and yet you have kept my word and have not denied my name. ⁹Behold, I will make those of the synagogue of Satan who say that they are Jews and are not, but lie—behold, I will make them come and bow down before your feet, and learn that I have loved you. ¹⁰Because you have kept my word of patient endurance, I will keep you from the hour of trial which is coming on the whole world, to try those who dwell upon the earth. ¹¹I am coming soon; hold fast what you have, so that no one may seize your crown. ¹²He who conquers, I will make him a pillar in the temple of my God; never shall he go out of it, and I will write on him the name of my God, and the name of the city of my God, the new Jerusalem which comes down from my God out of heaven, and my own new name.* ¹³He who has an ear, let him hear what the Spirit says to the churches.'

Letter to the church of Laodicea

^{Ps 89:38}
^{2 Cor 1:20}

¹⁴"And to the angel of the church in Laodicea write: 'The words of the Amen, the faithful and true witness, the beginning of God's creation.

3:8–12. The fidelity of these Christians is praised despite their limitations. As a reward they are given an open door which no enemy can shut—an assurance of evangelical success, despite opposition and perhaps also a promise of unimpeded access to the Kingdom.

On the "synagogue of Satan", see the note on Revelation 2:9. The promise that their enemies will admit defeat and do obeisance to the victor is reminiscent of Isaiah 49:23 and 60:14, which contain a prediction that the nations will do homage to the chosen people. Before that happens, however, the entire world will experience tribulation, as described later on in the book (cf. Rev 8–9 and 16); but those who stay faithful will be protected. As to the imminence of these predicted events, see what is said in the note on Revelation 1:1 about the whole matter of timing (cf. also 22:12, 20). When all is over, the strife and the victory, the conquering church will be a pillar of the temple, that is, it will have a place of honour (cf. Gal 2:9).

When it says that despite their weakness they have not denied Christ's name (v. 8), this implies that the strength which enables them to win victory is something given them by God, who often acts and triumphs amidst man's weakness and shortcomings. St Paul says as much to the faithful of Corinth: "Consider your call, brethren; not many of you were wise according to worldly standards, not many were powerful, not many were of noble birth; but God chose what is foolish in the world to shame the wise, God chose what is weak in the world to shame the strong. God chose what is low and despised in the world, even things that are not, to bring to nothing things that are, so that no human being might boast in the presence of God" (1 Cor 1:26–29).

3:14. Laodicea was a city on the border of Phrygia, about 75 kilometres (45 miles)

15"'I know your works: you are neither cold nor hot. Would that you were cold or hot! **16**So, because you are lukewarm, and neither cold nor hot, I will spew you out of my mouth. **17**For you say, I am rich, I have prospered, and I need nothing; not knowing

Col 1:15
Jn 1:3

Hos 12:9
1 Cor 4:8

south-west of Philadelphia. It is also mentioned by St Paul when he suggests to the Colossians that they exchange his letter to them for the one he sent the Laodiceans (cf. Col 4:16).

Jesus Christ is given the title of "the Amen"; a similar description is applied to Christ in 2 Corinthians 1:20. Both texts are instances of a divine name being applied to Christ, thereby asserting his divinity. "Amen", so be it, is an assertion of truth and veracity and connects with the title of "the true one" in the previous letter. It highlights the fact that our Lord is strong, dependable and unchangeable; the words that follow, "faithful and true witness", spell out the full meaning of the "Amen" title (cf. 1:5).

The most satisfactory interpretation of the phrase "the beginning of God's creation" is in terms of Jesus Christ's role in creation: for "all things were made through him" (Jn 1:3) and therefore he, along with the Father and the Holy Spirit, is the Creator of heaven and earth.

3:15–16. The prosperity Laodicea enjoyed may have contributed to the laxity and lukewarmness the church is accused of here (Israel tended to take the same direction when living was easy: the people would become forgetful of Yahweh and adopt an easy-going lifestyle: cf., e.g., Deut 31:20; 32:15; Hos 13:6; Jer 5:7).

The presence of hot springs close to the city explains the language used in this passage, which amounts to a severe indictment of lukewarmness. It shows God's repugnance for mediocrity and bourgeois living. As observed by Cassian, one of the founders of Western monasticism, lukewarmness is something that needs to be nipped in the bud: "No one should attribute his going astray to any sudden collapse, but rather [...] to his having moved away from virtue little by little, through prolonged mental laziness. That is the way bad habits gain ground without one's even noticing it, and eventually lead to a sudden collapse. 'Pride goes before destruction, and a haughty spirit before a fall' (Prov 16:18). The same thing happens with a house: it collapses one fine day due to some ancient defect in its foundation or long neglect by the occupiers" (*Collationes*, 6, 17).

Spiritual lukewarmness and mediocrity are very closely related: neither is the route Christian life should take. As St Josemaría Escrivá: puts it, "'In medio virtus'.... Virtue is to be found in the middle, so the saying goes, warning us against extremism. But do not make the mistake of turning that advice into a euphemism to disguise your own comfort, calculation, lukewarmness, easy-going-ness, lack of idealism and mediocrity. Meditate on these words of Sacred Scripture: 'Would that you were cold or hot. So, because you are lukewarm, and neither cold nor hot, I will spew you out of my mouth'" (*Furrow*, 541).

3:17–19. The Christians of Laodicea did not realize how precarious their spiritual situation was. The city's flourishing trade and industry, and the fact that the church was not being persecuted in any way, made them feel prosperous and content: they were proud as well as lukewarm.

Revelation 3:18

_{1 Pet 1:7}
_{Rev 4:4; 16:15}

_{Prov 3:12}
_{1 Cor 11:32}
_{Heb 12:6}

that you are wretched, pitiable, poor, blind, and naked. [18]Therefore I counsel you to buy from me gold refined by fire, that you may be rich, and white garments to clothe you and to keep the shame of your nakedness from being seen, and salve to anoint your eyes, that you may see. [19]Those whom I love, I reprove and chasten; so be zealous and repent. [20]Behold, I stand at the door and knock; if

---

They had fallen victim to that self-conceit the wealthy are always inclined to feel and which moved our Lord to say that rich people enter heaven only with difficulty (cf. Mt 19:23); he often pointed to the dangers of becoming attached to material things (cf. Lk 1:53; 6:24; 12:21; 16:19–31; 18:23–25). The Laodiceans had become proud in their prosperity and did not see the need for divine grace (which is worth more than all the wealth in the world). As St Paul says in one of his letters: "Whatever gain I had, I counted as loss for the sake of Christ. Indeed I count everything as loss because of the surpassing worth of knowing Christ Jesus my Lord. For his sake I have suffered the loss of all things, and count them as refuse, in order that I may gain Christ" (Phil 3:7–8).

There was an important textile industry in Laodicea which specialized in the manufacture of black woollen cloth. Instead of wearing that material, the Laodiceans must dress in garments which only our Lord can provide and which are the mark of the elect (cf., e.g., Mt 17:2 and par; Rev 3:4–5; 7:9). The city was also famous for its oculists, like Zeuxis and Philetos, who had developed a very effective ointment for the eyes. Jesus offers an even better ointment—one which will show them the dangerous state they are in. This dire warning comes from God's love, not his anger: it is his affection that leads him to reprove and correct his people: "the Lord reproves whom he loves, as a father the son in whom he delights" (Prov 3:12). After quoting these same words the Epistle to the Hebrews adds: "It is for discipline that you have to endure. God is treating you as sons; for what son is there whom his father does not discipline? If you are left without discipline, in which all have participated, then you are illegitimate children and not sons" (12:7–8).

"Be zealous": stop being lukewarm and enter the fervour of charity, have an ardent zeal for the glory of God.

3:20–21. Christ knocking on the door is one of the most touching images in the Bible. It is reminiscent of the Song of Songs, where the bridegroom says, "Open to me, my sister, my dove, my perfect one; for my head is wet with dew, my locks with the drops of the night" (Song 5:2). It is a way of describing God's love for us, inviting us to greater intimacy with him, as happens in a thousand ways in the course of our life. We should be listening for his knock, ready to open the door to Christ. A writer from the Golden Age of Spanish literature evokes this scene in poetry: "How many times the angel spoke to me:/'Look out of your window now,/you'll see how lovingly he calls and calls.'/ Yet, sovereign beauty, how often/I replied, 'We'll open for you tomorrow',/to reply the same when the morrow came" (Lope de Vega, *Rimas sacras*, Sonnet 18).

Our Lord awaits our response to his call, and when we make the effort to revive our interior life we experience the indescribable joy of intimacy with him. "At first it will be a bit difficult. You must

any one hears my voice and opens the door, I will come in to him and eat with him, and he with me. ²¹He who conquers, I will grant him to sit with me on my throne, as I myself conquered and sat down with my Father on his throne. ²²He who has an ear, let him hear what the Spirit says to the churches.'"

Jn 14:23
Mt 19:28
Rev 20:4

PART TWO

Eschatological visions

1. INTRODUCTORY VISION

God in majesty

4 ¹After this I looked, and lo, in heaven an open door! And the first voice, which I had heard speaking to me like a trumpet, said, "Come up hither, and I will show you what must take place

Ex 19:16, 24
Dan 2:29; Rev 1:10, 19; Rev 1:10; Ezek 1:26
Is 6:1; Ps 47:9

---

make an effort to seek out the Lord, to thank him for his fatherly and practical concern for us. Although it is not really a matter of feeling, little by little the love of God makes itself felt like a rustle in the soul. It is Christ who pursues us lovingly: 'Behold, I stand at the door and knock' (Rev 3:20). How is your life of prayer going? At times during the day don't you feel the impulse to have a longer talk with him? Don't you then whisper to him that you will tell him about it later, in a heart-to-heart conversation [...]. Prayer then becomes continuous, like the beating of our heart, like our pulse. Without this presence of God, there is no contemplative life; and without contemplative life, our working for Christ is worth very little, for vain is the builder's toil if the house is not of the Lord's building (cf. Ps 126:1)" (St J. Escrivá, *Christ Is Passing By*, 8).

Jesus promises that those who conquer will sit beside him on his throne. He gave a similar promise to St Peter about how the Apostles would sit on twelve thrones to judge the twelve tribes of Israel (cf. Mt 19:28; 20:20ff). The "throne" is a reference to the sovereign authority Christ has received from the Father. Therefore, the promise of a seat beside him is a way of saying that those who stay faithful will share in Christ's victory and kingship (cf. 1 Cor 6:2–3).

4:1. The second part of the Apocalypse begins at this point and extends to the start of the Epilogue. The author describes visions concerning the future of mankind, particularly the ultimate outcome of history when our Lord Jesus Christ will obtain the final victory at his second coming. It begins with a formal introduction (chaps. 4–5); this is followed by a first section as it were (6:11—11:14) covering the visions of the seven seals and the first six trumpets, which describes the event prior to the final battle. The war begins with the sound of the seventh trumpet and it goes on (this is the second section

Revelation 4:2

Ezek 1:26;
10:1f; Is 6:1
Is 24:23
Rev 3:4

after this." ²At once I was in the Spirit, and lo, a throne stood in heaven, with one seated on the throne! ³And he who sat there appeared like jasper and carnelian, and round the throne was a rainbow that looked like an emerald.* ⁴Round the throne were

11:15—22:5) until the beast is completely routed and the Kingdom of God is definitively established in the heavenly Jerusalem.

This introductory vision (chaps. 4–5) begins with God in heaven in all his glory being worshipped and celebrated by all creation (chap. 4). He alone controls the destiny of the world and the Church.

Only Jesus knows God's salvific plans, and he, through his death and resurrection, reveals them to us. All this is expressed in chapter 4 by the image of the Lamb who is able to open the scroll and its seven seals.

4:1–3. The risen and glorified Christ, who spoke to St John previously (cf. 1:10–13), now invites him, in a new vision, to go up into heaven to be told God's plan for the world. "I looked," "I was in the Spirit," "I went up to heaven" all describe the same phenomenon—God revealing something to the writer. Because the things he is being told are things man could not possibly discover for himself, the writer speaks about going up to heaven: this enables him to contemplate heavenly things, that is, God. Going up to heaven is the same as being in ecstasy, "being in the Spirit", being taken over by the Holy Spirit so as to be able to understand what God wants to reveal to him (cf. note on 1:10).

He is going to be shown "what must take place after this"; it is something which has already begun to happen in the writer's own time but it will not reach its climax until the end of the world. The revelation he is given shows him the ultimate meaning of contemporary events, the outcome of which is guaranteed by the authority of the revealer, Jesus Christ.

The description given here of heaven stresses the majesty and power of God. Heaven is depicted with a throne at its centre, an image taken from Isaiah (cf. Is 6:1) and Ezekiel (cf. Ezek 1:26–28; 10:1). God's appearance is described in terms of the vivid colouring of precious stones; this avoids the danger of defining God in human terms (an inversion of values). The rainbow round the throne further emphasizes the sublimity of God and is also a reminder (cf. Gen 9:12–17) of God's merciful promise never to destroy mankind.

4:4. God's sovereignty over the world—as symbolized by the throne—is shared in by others whom the vision also portrays as seated on thrones. They are symbolically described as twenty-four elders who act as a kind of heavenly council or senate. These elders appear frequently in the course of the book, always positioned beside God, rendering him tribute of glory and worship (cf. 4:10; 5:9; 19:4), offering him the prayers of the faithful (cf. 5:8) or explaining events to the seer (cf. 5:5; 7:13). It is not clear whether they stand for angels or saints; the Fathers and recent commentators offer both interpretations.

The symbolic number (twenty-four) and the way they are described suggest that they stand for saints in the glory of heaven. They are twenty-four—twelve plus twelve, that is, the number of the tribes of Israel plus that of the apostles. Our Lord in fact promised the latter that they would sit on thrones (cf. Mt 19:28).

twenty-four thrones, and seated on the thrones were twenty-four elders,* clad in white garments, with golden crowns upon their heads. ⁵From the throne issue flashes of lightning, and voices and peals of thunder, and before the throne burn seven torches of fire, which are the seven spirits of God; ⁶and before the throne there is as it were a sea of glass, like crystal.

Ex 19:16
Ezek 1:13
Rev 8:5; 11:9;
16:18 Zech 4:2
Ezek 1:5–26;
10:1f

The twenty-four elders, then, would represent the heavenly Church, which includes the old and the new Israel and which, in heaven, renders God the tribute of perfect praise and intercedes for the Church on earth. The number twenty-four has also been seen as reflecting the twenty-four priestly classes of Judaism, thereby emphasizing the liturgical dimension of heaven (cf. 1 Chron 24:7–18; 25:1, 9–13). Whichever is the case, the white garments indicate that they have achieved everlasting salvation (cf. 3:5); and the golden crowns stand for the reward they have earned (cf. 2:10), or their prominence among Christians, who have been promised that, if they come out victorious, they will sit on Christ's throne (cf. 3:21).

Through these visions laden with symbolism the Apocalypse shows the solidarity that exists between the Church triumphant and the Church militant—specifically, the connexion between the praise that is rendered God in heaven and that which we offer him on earth, in the liturgy. The Second Vatican Council refers to this: "In the earthly liturgy we take part in the foretaste of that heavenly liturgy which is celebrated in the Holy City of Jerusalem toward which we journey as pilgrims, where Christ is sitting at the right hand of God [...]. With all the warriors of the heavenly army we sing a hymn of glory to the Lord; venerating the memory of the saints, we hope for some part and fellowship with them; we eagerly await the Saviour, our Lord Jesus Christ, until he, our life, shall appear and we too will appear with him in glory" (*Sancrosanctum Concilium*, 8).

4:5. This vision is similar to the Old Testament theophanies, especially that of Sinai. There too the Lord's presence was revealed with thunder and lightning (cf. Ex 19:16). Storms are often used to symbolize the salvific power and majesty of God at the moment of revelation (cf. Ps 18:14; 50:3; etc.). Further on, the author will describe, in more detail, the signs accompanying God's self-revealing; this gives the book a sense of on-going revelation with an increasing tempo (cf. Rev 8:5; 11:19; 16:18; etc.). It is generally accepted practice to interpret fire as a manifestation of the Spirit of God. On the seven spirits, see the note on 1:4.

4:6–7. To describe the majesty of God, John uses symbols which are sometimes quite difficult to interpret. This is the case with the sea as transparent as glass, and the four living creatures round the throne and on each side of it. The scene may be a kind of heavenly replica of the arrangements in Solomon's temple where there stood in front of the Holy of Holies a huge water container called the "molten sea" supported by figures of oxen, twelve in number (cf. 1 Kings 7:23–26; 2 Chron 4:2–5). This similarity between heaven and the temple would be a a way of expressing the connexion between liturgy on earth and worship of God in heaven.

The crystal sea may also be an allusion to God's absolute dominion over all forms of authority on earth. In biblical tradition the sea is often used as a

Revelation 4:7

<small>Ezek 1:10;
10:14</small>

And round the throne, on each side of the throne, are four living creatures,* full of eyes in front and behind: ⁷the first living creature like a lion, the second living creature like an ox, the third living creature with the face of a man, and the fourth living creature like a flying eagle. ⁸And the four living creatures, each of them with six wings, are full of eyes all round and within, and day and night they never cease to sing,

<small>Is 6:2, 3; Ezek
1:18; 10:12
Ex 3:14</small>

"Holy, holy, holy,* is the Lord God Almighty,
who was and is and is to come!"

---

symbol for the powers of darkness (cf. Rev 13:1; 21:1). To God, however, the sea is crystal-clear, that is, he is its master; cf. the way the spirit of God moved over the surface of the waters in Genesis 1:2.

Elsewhere in the Apocalypse (15:2) it speaks of the sea of glass supporting the blessed while they praise God: just as the Israelites passed through the Red Sea, so those who have conquered the beast will cross this solid sea to make their way to God.

The author of the book of Revelation avails of images used by the prophets to describe the glory of Yahweh. The four living creatures are very like those in the prophet Ezekiel's vision of the chariot of the Lord drawn by four angels representing intelligence, nobility, strength and agility (cf. Ezek 1:10; 10:12; Is 6:2).

Christian tradition going back as far as St Irenaeus has interpreted these four creatures as standing for the four evangelists because they "carry" Jesus Christ to men. The one with the face of a man is St Matthew, who starts his book with the human genealogy of Christ; the lion stands for St Mark: his Gospel begins with the voice crying in the wilderness (which is where the lion's roar can be heard); the ox is a reference to the sacrifices in the temple of Jerusalem, which is where St Luke begins his account of Christ's life, and the eagle represents St John, who soars to the heights to contemplate the divinity of the Word.

4:8–11. The chant of the four living creatures is virtually the same as that which the prophet Isaiah heard the six-winged seraphim sing in his vision of God in the temple of Jerusalem (cf. Is 6:1–3). St John changes the ending by bringing in the new name of God which is an elaboration of the name "Yahweh" (cf. note on Rev 1:4). The four creatures (who, because there are four of them, stand for government of the entire universe) take the lead in worshipping and praising God; but they are joined by all the people of God, as represented by the twenty-four elders, that is, the Church victorious in heaven. They throw down their crowns to show that they realize their victory is due to God, and that all power belongs to him. Essentially what they are praising here is God as creator. By reporting this vision the author of the Apocalypse is inviting the pilgrim Church on earth to associate with the worship and praise offered God the creator in heaven.

The Church uses these words of praise in its eucharistic liturgy: at the end of the Preface, it chants the angelic *Sanctus* in preparation for the Canon. This angelic chant, performed as it is in heaven and on earth, reminds us of the sublimity of the Mass, where the worship of God crosses the frontiers of time and space and has a positive influence on the entire world, for, "through the communion of the saints, all Christians receive grace from every Mass that is celebrated, regardless of whether

⁹And whenever the living creatures give glory and honour and thanks to him who is seated on the throne, who lives for ever and ever, ¹⁰the twenty-four elders fall down before him who is seated on the throne and worship him who lives for ever and ever; they cast their crowns before the throne, singing,

¹¹ "Worthy art thou, our Lord and God,
   to receive glory and honour and power,
   for thou didst create all things,
   and by thy will they existed and were created."

Is 6:1; Ps 47:9
Dan 4:31
Rev 5:14
Rom 4:17
Rev 14:7

The sealed scroll and the Lamb

5 ¹And I saw in the right hand of him who was seated on the throne a scroll* written within and on the back, sealed with seven seals; ²and I saw a strong angel proclaiming with a loud

Is 29:11
Ezek 2:9, 10
Dan 12:4, 9
Rev 4:2

---

there is an attendance of thousands or whether it is only a boy with his mind on other things who is there to serve. In either case, heaven and earth join with the angels of the Lord to sing: *Sanctus, Sanctus, Sanctus ...*" (St Josemaría Escrivá, *Christ Is Passing By*, 88). The saintly Curé of Ars refers to this intercommunion of praise and thanksgiving, of grace and forgiveness: "The Holy Mass is a source of joy to all the heavenly court; it alleviates the poor souls in purgatory; it draws down to earth all kinds of blessings; and it gives more glory to God than all the sufferings of all the martyrs taken together, than all the penances of all the hermits, than all the tears shed for them [the holy souls] since time began and all that will be shed from now till the end of time" (*Selected Sermons*, 2nd Sunday after Pentecost).

5:1–5. The sealed scroll contains God's mysterious plans for the salvation of mankind; no one on earth can disclose them (v. 3). Only the risen Christ can take the scroll and make its contents known (vv. 6–7). On this account he is praised by the four living creatures, by the elders (vv. 8–10), by a whole host of angels (vv. 11–12) and by all creation (vv. 13–14).

The image of a scroll (or book) containing God's hidden plans for mankind was used before, particularly by the prophet Daniel (cf. Dan 12:4–9; also Is 29:11), who refers to a prophecy remaining sealed until the end of time. St John uses this image to make the point that the End Time, the Last Days, have already begun with Christ, so now he can reveal God's plans. The fact that there are seven seals stresses the hidden nature of the scroll's contents; and its being written on both sides shows its richness.

The author of the book of Revelation, and everyone in fact, really does need to know what is written on the scroll; for, if he knows God's plans he will be able to discover the meaning of life and cease to be anxious about events past, present and future. Yet no one is able to open the scroll: that is why the author weeps so bitterly.

The scroll is sealed: the Revelation of the salvation of mankind and the consolation of the Church is being delayed. Soon, however, the seer ceases to weep, for he learns that Christ (here called "the Lion of the tribe of Judah" and "the

Revelation 5:3

_{Gen 49:9f}
_{Is 11:1, 10}
_{Rom 15:12}

voice, "Who is worthy to open the scroll and break its seals?" ³And no one in heaven or on earth or under the earth was able to open the scroll or to look into it, ⁴and I wept much that no one was found worthy to open the scroll or to look into it. ⁵Then one of the elders said to me, "Weep not; lo, the Lion of the tribe of Judah, the Root of David, has conquered, so that he can open the scroll and its seven seals."

_{Is 53:7; 11:2}
_{Jn 1:29}
_{Rev 4:5}
_{Zech 3:9; 4:6}

⁶And between the throne and the four living creatures and among the elders, I saw a Lamb standing, as though it had been slain, with seven horns and with seven eyes,* which are the seven spirits of God sent out into all the earth; ⁷and he went and took the

---

Root" or descendant of David: cf. Gen 49:9; Is 11:1, 10) has conquered and therefore is able to break the seven seals.

The Church contemplates Christ's victory when it "believes that Christ, who died and was raised for the sake of all, can show man the way and strengthen him through the Spirit in order to be worthy of his destiny [...]. The Church likewise believes that the key, the centre and the purpose of the whole of man's history is to be found in its Lord and Master" (Vatican II, *Gaudium et spes*, 10). "In fact," the Council adds, "it is only in the mystery of the Word made flesh that the mystery of man truly becomes clear. For Adam, the first man, was a type of him who was to come (cf. Rom 5:14). Christ the Lord, Christ the new Adam, in the very revelation of the mystery of the Father and of his love, fully reveals man to himself and brings to light his most high calling" (ibid., 22).

5:6–7. Christ is able to open the scroll on account of his death and resurrection—an event symbolized by the Lamb standing upright and victorious and at the same time looking as though it had been immolated. In the Fourth Gospel, John the Baptist calls Christ "the Lamb of God" (Jn 1:29, 36); in the Apocalypse this expression is the one most often used to refer to him: he is the Lamb raised to the very height of God's throne and has dominion over the entire cosmos (cf. 5:8, 12–13; 6:1, 16; 7:9–10; 13:8; 15:3; etc.). This Christological title, which is a feature of St John's writings, has great theological depth; the Church much reveres it, often using it in the liturgy—particularly in the Mass, after the kiss of peace when the Lamb of God is invoked three times; also, just before Holy Communion is distributed the host is shown to the faithful as him who takes away the sin of the world and those who are called to his marriage supper are described as "happy" (cf. Rev 19:9).

The image of the Lamb reminds us of the passover lamb, whose blood was smeared on the door frames of houses as a sign to the avenging angel not to inflict on Israelites the divine punishment being dealt out to the Egyptians (cf. Ex 12:7, 13). St Paul refers to the Lamb in one of his letters: "Christ, our paschal lamb, has been sacrificed" (1 Cor 5:7). At a high point in Old Testament prophecy Isaiah portrays the Messiah as the suffering Servant of Yahweh, "a lamb that is led to the slaughter" (Is 53:7). St Peter, on the basis of that text, states that our Lord "bore our sins in his body on the tree, that we might die to sin and live to righteousness" (1 Pet 2:24).

scroll from the right hand of him who was seated on the throne. ⁸And when he had taken the scroll, the four living creatures and the twenty-four elders fell down before the Lamb, each holding a harp, and with golden bowls full of incense, which are the prayers of the saints; ⁹and they sang a new song, saying,

Rev 14:2
Ps 141:2

Rev 14:3, 4
Rom 3:24

The Lamb is a sacrifice for sin, but the Apocalypse also focuses attention on the victorious power of the risen Lamb by showing him standing on the throne, in the centre of the vision; the horns symbolize his power and the eyes his knowledge, both of which he has to the fullest degree as indicated by the number seven. The seven spirits of Christ also indicate the fullness of the Spirit with which Christ is endowed and which he passes on to his Church (cf. notes on Rev 1:4 and 4:5). This completes the description of the risen Christ, who through his victory reveals the mystery of God.

5:8–10. The greatness of Christ the Lamb is duly acknowledged and proclaimed through the worship rendered him, firstly, from the four living creatures and the twenty-four elders, then from all the angels and finally from the whole of creation (vv. 11–13). St John selects these three points to highlight the praise rendered by the heavenly Church, with which the pilgrim Church on earth joins through its own prayer (symbolized by the image of the golden bowls). Later on (15:7ff), seven bowls appear again, this time filled with God's wrath, which is caused by the complaint of the righteous who are being cruelly tormented by the agents of evil.

All this shows the value of the prayers of those who stay loyal to God: "the prayer of a righteous man has great power in its effects" (Jas 5:16), for "the prayer of the humble pierces the clouds, and he will not be consoled until it reaches the Lord" (Sir 35:17).

The "new song" proclaims that Christ alone decides the destinies of the world and of mankind; this is a consequence of himself being offered in sacrifice as the atoning victim *par excellence*. By shedding his blood Christ has won for himself an immense people from every nation under heaven; in them a holy people, his chosen ones, that people which was originally assembled in the Sinai desert (cf. Ex 19:6; 1 Pet 2:9f) has come to full maturity. When it says that they have been ransomed from every tribe and nation, it is pointing out that God's salvific plans extend to the whole human race: he "desires all men to be saved and to come to the knowledge of the truth" (1 Tim 2:4). This does not exempt us from making an effort to merit salvation, for, as St Augustine teaches, "God who created you without your cooperation will not save you without your cooperation" (*Sermon*, 169, 11). Here is how another early writer puts it: "we know that God will give to each individual the opportunity to be saved—to some in one way, to others in another. But whether we respond eagerly or listlessly depends on ourselves" (Cassian, *Collationes*, 3, 12).

"Didst ransom men for God": in many important Greek manuscripts this reads, "you ransomed us for God", and some even change the reading of the following verse: "you made us a kingdom. ... and we will reign". The earlier Latin translation, the Vulgate, chose that reading, which emphasizes that those who are intoning the chant are men, that is, members of the Church triumphant in heaven. The New Vulgate, follows what it

Revelation 5:10

<blockquote>
"Worthy art thou to take the scroll and to open its seals, for thou wast slain and by thy blood didst ransom men for God from every tribe and tongue and people and nation, ¹⁰ and hast made them a kingdom and priests to our God, and they shall reign on earth."

¹¹Then I looked, and I heard around the throne and the living creatures and the elders the voice of many angels, numbering myriads of myriads and thousands of thousands, ¹²saying with a loud voice, "Worthy is the Lamb who was slain, to receive power and wealth and wisdom and might and honour and glory and blessing!" ¹³And I heard every creature in heaven and on earth and under the earth and in the sea, and all therein, saying, "To him who sits upon the throne and to the Lamb be blessing and honour and glory and
</blockquote>

Margin references:
Ex 19:6; Is 61:6; Rev 1:6; 20:6; 22:5
Dan 7:10
Is 53:7
1 Chron 29:11
Phil 2:9
Phil 2:10
1 Tim 1:17

---

considers to be the most reliable Greek text. But the meaning does not really change.

5:11–14. The host of angels around the throne act as a kind of guard of honour proclaiming the sublime perfection of Christ the Lamb (v. 12), they list seven attributes which all point to the fact that he has everything that belongs to the Godhead.

After the song of the spiritual, invisible, creation, there follows the hymn of the material, visible, world. This hymn (v. 14) differs from the previous one in that it is also addressed to him who sits upon the throne. It thereby puts on the same level God and the Lamb, whose Godhead is being proclaimed. This marks the climax of the universal, cosmic praise that is rendered the Lamb. The emphatic "Amen!" of the four living creatures, and the worship offered by the elders bring this introductory vision to a close.

As in other passages of the book, mention is made of the role of the angels in heaven, particularly the worship and praise they offer God before his throne (cf. Rev 7:11), their role in putting God's plans into operation (cf. 11:15; 16:17; 22:6, etc.) and their intercession with God on behalf of mankind (cf. 8:4).

The Church has always encouraged special devotion to the angels (cf. *Lumen gentium*, 50). Holy Scripture and the teaching of the Church clearly tells us about the existence of angels and about their mission to guide and protect us; cf. Exodus 23:20: "Behold, I send an angel before you, to guard you on the way and to bring you to the place which I have prepared. Give heed to him and harken to his voice." Echoing these words the *Catechism of St Pius V* states that "by God's providence angels have been entrusted with the office of guarding the human race and of accompanying every human being [...]. (God) not only deputes angels on particular and private occasions, but also appoints them to take care of us from our very births. He furthermore appoints them to watch over the salvation of every member of the human race" (4, 9). Devotion to one's guardian angel, a part of ordinary Christian practice, is something we learn as children and should keep up during our adult lives: "Have confidence in your guardian Angel. Treat him as a lifelong friend—that is what he is—and he will

might for ever and ever!" ¹⁴And the four living creatures said, "Amen!" and the elders fell down and worshipped.

2. EVENTS PRIOR TO THE FINAL OUTCOME

Christ opens the first six seals. Vision of the four horsemen

6 *¹Now I saw when the Lamb opened one of the seven seals, and I heard one of the four living creatures say, as with a voice of thunder, "Come!" ²And I saw, and behold, a white horse, and its rider had a bow; and a crown was given to him, and he went out conquering and to conquer.

Rev 5:1, 2; 4:6; 5:6, 8

Zech 1:8–10; 6:1–3

---

render you a thousand services in the ordinary affairs of each day" (St Josemaría Escrivá, *The Way*, 562).

6:1—11:14. After describing his vision of heaven, especially the risen Christ empowered to reveal God's hidden plans (chaps. 4–5), the author now begins to disclose that revelation little by little as each of the seven seals is opened (chaps. 6–7). When he comes to the seventh seal, the main one, a new series of visions or revelations begins. These are symbolized by the blowing of the seven trumpets in turn; when the seventh is sounded (cf. 11:15) the description begins of the last battles fought by Christ and his followers against the powers of evil, the beast and its followers. The sound of the seventh trumpet marks the fulfilment of "the mystery of God" (cf. 10:7).

In its description of the opening of the first six seals, this section covers, firstly, the arrival of the day of the wrath of God (cf. 6:17), which is heralded by natural calamities and social upheaval (a foretaste of God's judgment on mankind). This gives the author the opportunity to jump ahead and describe a vision of the saved in heaven (chap. 7)—putting human history into its proper perspective: all its tragedies and untoward events are a kind of forewarning of the punishment that lies in wait for the evildoer.

The vision then describes another series of catastrophes akin to the plagues of Egypt; preceded by the blowing of the trumpets, they herald the coming of God. Like the earlier disasters they are designed to provoke men to a change of heart; because they fail to have any effect, these people will incur God's wrath and will each be judged by him in due course (cf. 9:20–21; 11:18).

At the end of this section, as a kind of transition to the next, the author stresses the prophetic character of his words: evil seems to have come out winning (as symbolized by the death of the two witnesses: cf. 11:1–13), but this is only apparently so, for Christ, who has already won the victory by his death and resurrection, will be seen to triumph at his second coming. The Lamb will confront the beast and overwhelm it. Until that moment, there is still time for conversion, for opting for or against God. There is no middle course.

6:1–8. The first four seals have various things in common: as they are opened horsemen appear, each of a different colour; and it is always one of the four living creatures that calls up the horsemen.

Revelation 6:3

Ezek 21:14–16

³When he opened the second seal, I heard the second living creature say, "Come!" ⁴And out came another horse, bright red; its rider was permitted to take peace from the earth, so that men should slay one another; and he was given a great sword.

The last three horsemen are easy to identify: the second carries a sword, which stands for war; the third a balance, here a symbol of famine, to do with the measuring out of rations; and the fourth represents plague, as indicated by the colour of his horse. All three are forms of divine punishment already predicted in the Old Testament: "I will send famine and wild beasts against you, and they will rob you of your children; pestilence and blood shall pass through you; and I will bring the sword upon you. I, the Lord, have spoken" (Ezek 5:17). Jesus used similar language in his eschatological discourse: "And when you hear of wars and tumults, do not be terrified [...]; there will be great earthquakes, and in various places famines and pestilence" (Lk 21:9, 11).

The first rider is, however, difficult to interpret: his features suggest that he is some type of power in the service of God. The colour white is symbolic of belonging to the heavenly sphere and of having won victory with God's help (cf., e.g., Rev 3:4, 5, 18; 14:14; 20:11). The crown he is given and the words "he went out conquering and to conquer" would refer to the victory of good over evil (cf. 2:7, 11, 17, 28; 3:5, 12; etc.); and the bow indicates the connexion between this horse and the other three: these latter will be as it were arrows loosed from a distance to implement God's plans.

This first rider, who goes forth "conquering and to conquer", refers to Christ's victory in his passion and resurrection, as St John has already mentioned (cf. 5:5), and also announces the final victory of the Word of God which first will come about later (cf. 19:11). The horseman is a kind of key which provides a specifically Christian meaning for all the terrifying scenes described in the book. Apropos of this figure, Pius XII wrote: "He is Jesus Christ. The inspired evangelist not only saw the devastation brought about by sin, war, hunger and death; he also saw, in the first place, the victory of Christ. It is certainly true that the course the Church takes down through the centuries is a *via crucis*, a way of the cross, but it is also a victory march. It is the Church of Christ, men and women of Christian faith and love, who are always bringing light, redemption and peace to a mankind without hope. 'Jesus Christ, the same yesterday and today and for ever' (Heb 13:8)" (*Address*, 15 November 1946).

6:4. The sword carried by the rider on the red horse stands for war (cf. Mt 10:34), referring to the wars being waged at the time in the Roman empire, but also to war in general, the scourge of mankind, which at the time of the End will be a signal of the imminent destruction of the world (cf. Mt 24:6 and par.).

The Church has had much to say about war in recent times. Thus, the Second Vatican Council says that "insofar as men are sinners, the threat of war hangs over them and will so continue until the coming of Christ; but insofar as they can vanquish sin by coming together in charity, violence itself will be vanquished and they will make these words come true: 'They shall beat their swords into ploughshares, and their spears into pruning hooks; nation shall not lift up

⁵When he opened the third seal, I heard the third living creature say, "Come!" And I saw, and behold, a black horse, and its rider had a balance* in his hand; ⁶and I heard what seemed to be a voice in the midst of the four living creatures saying, "A quart of wheat for a denarius,ᵃ and three quarts of barley for a denarius;ᵃ but do not harm oil and wine!"

⁷When he opened the fourth seal, I heard the voice of the fourth living creature say, "Come!" ⁸And I saw, and behold, a pale horse, and its rider's name was Death, and Hades followed him; and they were given power over a fourth of the earth, to kill with sword and with famine and with pestilence and by wild beasts of the earth.

⁹When he opened the fifth seal, I saw under the altar the souls of those who had been slain for the word of God and for the witness they had borne; ¹⁰they cried out with a loud voice, "O Sovereign Lord, holy and true, how long before thou wilt judge and avenge our blood on those who dwell upon the earth?" ¹¹Then

Ezek 4:16f
1 Kings 6:25f

Hos 13:14
Ezek 5:12; 14:21
Jer 14:12

Rev 20:4
Rev 3:7; Zech 1:12; Ps 79:5
Deut 32:43;
Gen 4:10
Lk 18:7

---

sword against nation, neither shall they learn war any more' (Is 2:4)" (*Gaudium et spes*, 78).

6:5–6. A sudden (perhaps tenfold) rise in the price of wheat and barley, part of the staple diet at the time, signals a period of famine. If we bear in mind that a "quart" (Greek: *choinix*) was about one kilo or 30 ounces and a denarius a day's wage for a labourer (cf. Mt 20:13), these are clearly very high prices.

Famine and hunger are ultimately a consequence of sin and therefore can be interpreted as a "punishment". The Church reminds us all that we have a strict duty to help alleviate the needs of others, for this is a way of combatting evil. "The Council asks individuals and governments to remember the saying of the Fathers: 'Feed the man dying of hunger, because if you do not feed him you are killing him' (Gratian, *Decretum*, 21, 86) and it urges them according to their ability to share and dispose of their goods to help others, above all by giving them aid which will enable them to help and develop themselves" (*Gaudium et spes*, 69).

6:8. "Pale horse": the fourth horse has a strange colour, which some translate as greenish or ashen; it probably means a death-like colour. Death is personified by the horse's sinister rider; this symbol is reinforced by his companion *Hades* or *Sheol*, the dark abode of the dead (cf. Rev 1:18). All this is meant to show that in the midst of all the terrible chastisement God has pity on mankind: most (three quarters, that is) will manage to survive the test.

6:9–11. Here St John sees all who gave their lives for God. The vision takes in the Old Testament martyrs from Abel down to Zechariah (cf. Mt 23:35–37; Heb 11:35–40), and Christian martyrs of all eras; St John sees them under the altar of holocausts where victims were sacrificed in honour of God and their blood collected beneath. Here we see a heavenly copy of that altar, meaning that the

---

a. The denarius was a day's wage for a labourer

Revelation 6:12

Is 13:10
Ezek 32:7, 8
Joel 3:3, 4
Mt 24:29

Is 34:4

Rev 16:20; 20:11
Ps 2:2; Is 2:10; 24:21; Jer 4:29

Hos 10:8; Lk 23:30; Ps 47:9
Joel 2:11; 3:4
Rom 2:5; Mal 3:2; Zeph 1:14

they were each given a white robe and told to rest a little longer, until the number of their fellow servants and their brethren should be complete, who were to be killed as they themselves had been. ¹²When he opened the sixth seal, I looked, and behold, there was a great earthquake; and the sun became black as sackcloth, the full moon became like blood, ¹³and the stars of the sky fell to the earth as the fig tree sheds its winter fruit when shaken by a gale; ¹⁴the sky vanished like a scroll that is rolled up, and every mountain and island was removed from its place. ¹⁵Then the kings of the earth and the great men and the generals and the rich and the strong, and every one, slave and free, hid in the caves and among the rocks of the mountains, ¹⁶calling to the mountains and rocks, "Fall on us and hide us from the face of him who is seated on the throne, and from the wrath of the Lamb; ¹⁷for the great day of their wrath has come, and who can stand before it?"

---

martyrs are very close to God and that their death has been a most acceptable offering to him (cf. Phil 2:17; 2 Tim 4:6).

The presence of the martyrs in heaven shows that when man dies his soul receives its reward or punishment immediately. God's judgment of each soul begins to take effect the moment he dies, although it is not until the resurrection of all the dead that it will have its full effect, on body as well as soul.

The martyrs' song is a clamour for justice: our Lord refers to it in the Gospel (cf. Lk 18:7) and it echoes the aboriginal lament raised at Abel's death (cf. Gen 4:10). What the martyrs say seems to be at odds with Christ's prayer on the cross (cf. Lk 23:24) and Stephen's on the eve of his martyrdom (cf. Acts 7:60), but there is really no contradiction. "This prayer of the martyrs", St Thomas says, "is nothing other than their desire to obtain resurrection of the body and to share in the inheritance of those who will be saved, and their recognition of God's justice in punishing evildoers" (*Summa theologiae*, 3, 72, 3, ad. 1).

It is, thus, a prayer for the establishment of the Kingdom of God and his justice, which causes his divine holiness and fidelity to shine forth.

6:12–17. This passage predicts the events which will occur just before the second coming of our Lord Jesus Christ. It does not refer to the very End, but to the fact that it is imminent. The terrifying symbols used to indicate these events derive from literary style and language used in the Old Testament (cf., e.g., Amos 8:9; Is 13:98f; 34:4; 50:3; Job 3:4). This was the prophets' way of warning the people—and of consoling them by telling them that Christ's definitive victory would soon come. Jesus speaks in the same way to the grieving women of Jerusalem whom he meets on his way to Calvary (cf. Lk 23:30).

In v. 15 there is a reference to seven social groups embracing all mankind, ranging from the highest to the lowest. Nothing escapes God's judgment and there is no appeal against it. The *Dies Irae* has come, the day of the Lamb's wrath. The Lamb symbolizes the innocence and immolation of the Messiah; but it also stands for messianic royalty, symbolized here by his fury.

The great multitude of the saved

7 ¹After this I saw four angels standing at the four corners of the earth, holding back the four winds of the earth, that no wind might blow on earth or sea or against any tree. ²Then I saw another angel ascend from the rising of the sun, with the seal of the living God, and he called with a loud voice to the four angels who had been given power to harm earth and sea, ³saying, "Do not harm the earth or the sea or the trees, till we have sealed the servants of our God upon their foreheads." ⁴And I heard the number of the sealed, a hundred and forty-four thousand* sealed, out of every tribe of the sons of Israel, ⁵twelve thousand sealed out of the tribe of Judah, twelve thousand of the tribe of Reuben, twelve thousand of the tribe of Gad, ⁶twelve thousand of the tribe of Asher, twelve thousand of the tribe of Naphtali, twelve thousand of the tribe of Manasseh, ⁷twelve thousand of the tribe of Simeon, twelve thousand of the tribe of Levi, twelve thousand

Jer 49:36
Ezek 7:2; 37:9
Dan 7:2
Zech 6:5
Mt 24:31

Ezek 9:4, 6
Rev 9:6

Rev 14:1, 3

Num 1:21–43

7:1–17. This chapter consists of two visions designed to illustrate God's protection of Christians and the happy circumstances of the martyrs. The victory of the Church is depicted—of the entire Church, made up of people from the four points of the compass (vv. 9–12). What is not so clear, however, is who the 144,000 are, drawn from the twelve tribes of Israel and marked with the seal of the living God (vv. 1–8). Some commentators interpret them as all being Christians of Jewish background (Judaeo-Christians). Others say that they are those who make up the new Israel which St Paul speaks about in Galatians 6:17; that is, all the baptized viewed first as still engaged in their battle (vv. 1–8) and then after they have won victory (vv. 9–17). The most plausible interpretation is that the 144,000 stand for the Jews converted to Christianity (as distinct from those not converted)—the "remnant of Israel" (cf. Is 4:2–4; Ezek 9; etc.). St Paul says that they prove the irrevocable nature of God's election (cf. Rom 11:1–5) and are the first-fruits of the restoration which will come about at the End (cf. Rom 11:25–32).

The 144,000 are included in the second vision; they would be part of the great multitude "from all tribes and people and tongues". Thus, the vision in vv. 9–17 takes in the entire Church without any distinctions, whereas the vision in vv. 1–8 can refer only to a part of the Church—those Jews who, by becoming Christians, made up the original nucleus of the Church. The Church admits these on the same basis as all those who become Christians later without having had to pass through any stage of Jewish observance.

7:1–8. In Jewish tradition angels were divided into two groups—angels of the Presence and sanctification, and those charged with controlling the forces of nature. Both kinds appear there.

According to the custom of the time, when something bore the mark of a seal or brand that meant that it belonged to the seal's owner. This passage is saying that the 144,000 belong to God and therefore will be protected by him as his property. This fulfils what Ezekiel prophesied about the inhabitants of Jerusalem

of the tribe of Issachar, ⁸twelve thousand of the tribe of Zebulun, twelve thousand of the tribe of Joseph, twelve thousand sealed out of the tribe of Benjamin.

⁹After this I looked, and behold, a great multitude which no man could number, from every nation, from all tribes and peoples and tongues, standing before the throne and before the Lamb, clothed in white robes, with palm branches in their hands, ¹⁰and crying out with a loud voice, "Salvation belongs to our God who sits upon the throne, and to the Lamb!" ¹¹And all the angels stood round the throne and round the elders and the four living creatures, and they fell on their faces before the throne and worshipped God, ¹²saying, "Amen! Blessing and glory and wisdom and thanksgiving and honour and power and might be to our God for ever and ever! Amen."

¹³Then one of the elders addressed me, saying, "Who are these, clothed in white robes, and whence have they come?" ¹⁴I said to

Margin references:
Rev 15:2–5; Gen 15:5
Rev 19:1; Ps 47:9
Rev 5:11; 11:16
Rev 22:14; Dan 12:1

(cf. Ezek 9:1–7): some would be sealed on the forehead with a *tau* (the last letter of the Hebrew alphabet) and would therefore escape the punishment to be inflicted on all the rest: this shows the special way God makes provision for those who are his not only because he created them but also by a new title.

The Fathers of the Church saw this mark as symbolizing the character that Baptism impresses on the souls of the faithful to show that they are destined for eternal life. Thus, the persons preserved from harm are the Jews who were converts to Christianity: their Baptism marked them out from those Jews who rejected Christ and were not baptized.

The list of tribes is somewhat different from the usual list which keeps the order of Genesis 29. The name of Judah is put first because the Messiah came from that tribe, as St John recently mentioned (cf. 5:5); and there is no mention of the tribe of Dan, presumably because it fell into idolatry (cf. Judg 17–18) and eventually disappeared. To make up the tally of twelve, the tribe of Joseph is mentioned twice—as that of Joseph and as that of Manasseh, his first-born.

The number of those sealed (12 x 12 x 1000) symbolizes completeness, totality—in this instance, a huge multitude, depicted as the new Israel. Included in this number are the descendants of Jacob who receive Baptism, irrespective of when they do. Obviously this number is not meant to be taken literally, as if only 144,000 people will attain salvation. In this scene all those of Gentile background who become Christians over the course of history are explicitly not included. They will appear in the vision which follows.

7:9–17. Pope John Paul II has commented on this passage as follows: "The people dressed in white robes whom John sees with his prophetic eye are the redeemed, and they form a 'great multitude', which no one could count and which is made up of people of the most varied backgrounds. The blood of the Lamb, who has been offered in sacrifice for all, has exercised its universal and most effective

him, "Sir, you know." And he said to me, "These are they who have come out of the great tribulation;* they have washed their robes and made them white in the blood of the Lamb.

¹⁵ Therefore are they before the throne of God,
and serve him day and night within his temple;
and he who sits upon the throne will shelter them with his presence.
¹⁶ They shall hunger no more, neither thirst any more;
the sun shall not strike them, nor any scorching heat.
¹⁷ For the Lamb in the midst of the throne will be their shepherd,
and he will guide them to springs of living water;
and God will wipe away every tear from their eyes."

Cross references: Mt 24:21; Gen 49:11; Is 6:1; Rev 15:5; Is 49:10; Ps 121:6; Ps 23:2; Is 25:8; 49:10; Rev 21:4

---

redemptive power in every corner of the earth, extending grace and salvation to that 'great multitude'. After undergoing the trials and being purified in the blood of Christ, they—the redeemed—are now safe in the Kingdom of God, whom they praise and bless for ever and ever" (*Homily*, 1 November 1981). This great crowd includes all the saved and not just the martyrs, for it says that they washed their robes in the blood of the Lamb, not in their own blood.

Everyone has to become associated with Christ's passion through suffering, as St Augustine explains, not without a certain humour: "Many are martyrs in their beds. The Christian is lying on his couch, tormented by pain. He prays and his prayers are not heard, or perhaps they are heard but he is being put to the test ... so that he may be received as a son. He becomes a martyr through illness and is crowned by him who hung upon the Cross" (*Sermon* 286, 8).

It is consoling and encouraging to know that those who attain heaven constitute a huge multitude. The passages of Matthew 7:14 and Luke 13:24 which seem to imply that very few will be saved should be interpreted in the light of this vision, which shows that the infinite value of Christ's blood makes God's will be done: "(God) desires all men to be saved and to come to the knowledge of the truth" (1 Tim 2:4).

In vv. 14–17 we see the blessed in two different situations—first, before the resurrection of the body (v. 14) and, then, after it, when body and soul have been reunited (vv. 15–17). In this second situation the nature of risen bodies is highlighted: they cannot suffer pain or inconvenience of any kind: they are out of harm's reach; they have the gift of "impassibility" (cf. *St Pius V Catechism*, 1, 12, 13).

This consoling scene is included in the vision to encourage believers to imitate those Christians who were like us and now find themselves in heaven because they have come through victorious. The Church invites us to pray along similar lines: "Father, you sanctified the Church of Rome with the blood of its first martyrs. May we find strength from their courage and rejoice in their triumph" (*Roman Missal*, Feast of the First Martyrs of the Church of Rome, opening prayer).

Revelation 8:1

The opening of the seventh seal

Zech 2:17
Hab 2:20
Mt 24:31
Tob 12:15

Rev 5:8
Ps 141:2

Lev 16:12
Ezek 10:2
Rev 4:5
Ex 19:16

8 ¹When the Lamb opened the seventh seal, there was silence in heaven for about half an hour. ²Then I saw the seven angels who stand before God, and seven trumpets were given to them. ³And another angel came and stood at the altar with a golden censer; and he was given much incense to mingle with the prayers of all the saints upon the golden altar before the throne; ⁴and the smoke of the incense rose with the prayers of the saints from the hand of the angel before God. ⁵Then the angel took the censer and filled it with fire from the altar and threw it on the earth;* and there were peals of thunder, voices, flashes of lightning, and an earthquake.

8:1–2. The silence signals that the End has come: it expresses the Lord's patient waiting—as if he were putting off the day of judgment, to the chagrin of the faithful. However, "the Lord is not slow about his promise as some count slowness, but is forbearing toward you, not wishing that any should perish, but that all should reach repentance" (2 Pet 3:9).

The opening of the seventh seal leads to another "seven", the seven trumpets; and the last of these leads to the seven bowls (cf. Rev 11:15). But first we are told what happens when the first six trumpets are blown (chaps. 8–9) and God's judgments are visited on the earth. There is a certain parallel here with the plagues of Egypt (cf. Ex 7:14—12:34). Before the seventh trumpet is sounded, there is a sort of interlude (cf. 10:1—11:14).

Trumpets were used by the Israelites not only in battle (cf. Josh 6:5) but also in the temple liturgy, where they proclaimed the presence of Yahweh (cf. Ps 47:6). In accounts of our Lord's second coming we find references to trumpets being sounded to signal that divine intervention is imminent (cf., e.g., Mt 24:31; 1 Cor 15:52; 1 Thess 4:15).

8:3–5. The prayers of the saints, previously identified by bowls of incense (cf. 5:8), are now mingled with the aromatic incense rising from the golden censer. All this is a reference to the fact that the saints in heaven intercede with God on our behalf. The Second Vatican Council reminds us that "the Church has always believed that the apostles and Christ's martyrs, who gave the supreme witness of faith and charity by the shedding of their blood, are closely united with us in Christ; she has always venerated them, together with the Blessed Virgin Mary and the holy angels, with a special love, and has asked piously for the help of their intercession" (*Lumen gentium*, 50). The Council of Trent recommends that the faithful be taught how profitable it is to have recourse to the intercession of the saints: "it is a good and useful thing to invoke the saints humbly and to have recourse to their prayers" (*De sacris imaginibus*).

The usefulness of intercessory prayer is something we learn about first in the Old Testament. For example, we are told how Moses, with his hands raised to heaven, pleaded successfully for Israelite victory over the Amalekites (cf. Ex 17:8f). Also, the references here to the altar of incense recall elements of Jewish worship (cf. Ex 29:13; Lev 21:6; Ps 141:2; etc.), which was a prefiguration of the

⁶Now the seven angels who had the seven trumpets made ready to blow them.

The first six trumpet calls. The three woes
⁷The first angel blew his trumpet, and there followed hail and fire, mixed with blood, which fell on the earth; and a third of the earth was burnt up, and a third of the trees were burnt up, and all green grass was burnt up.

⁸The second angel blew his trumpet, and something like a great mountain, burning with fire, was thrown into the sea; ⁹and a third of the sea became blood, a third of the living creatures in the sea died, and a third of the ships were destroyed.

¹⁰The third angel blew his trumpet, and a great star fell from heaven, blazing like a torch, and it fell on a third of the rivers and on the fountains of water. ¹¹The name of the star is Wormwood. A third of the waters became wormwood, and many men died of the water, because it was made bitter.

¹²The fourth angel blew his trumpet, and a third of the sun was struck, and a third of the moon, and a third of the stars, so that a third of their light was darkened; a third of the day was kept from shining, and likewise a third of the night.

Joel 2:1
Joel 3:3
Ex 9:23–26
Ezek 38:22
Rev 16:2
Jer 51:25
Ex 7:20f
Rev 16:4
Dan 8:10
Is 14:12
Jer 9:14
Ex 10:21
Rev 6:12; 16:8

---

worship "in spirit and truth" (Jn 4:23) announced by Jesus.

In response to the prayers of the saints, the Lord once again manifests his presence in the way he did at Sinai (cf. note on 4:5). The angel's action is reminiscent of Ezekiel 10:2, where the angel fills his hands with burning coals and scatters them over Jerusalem. This rain of fire now signals the start of God's fury on the world and on mankind, which is described here in stages marked by trumpet blasts.

8:6–12. The blowing of the first four trumpets is separated from that of the following ones by a vision (v. 13); the same pattern applied to the seven seals. The punishments the trumpet calls herald are reminiscent of the plagues of Egypt. No necessary historical sequence of events is being described here; the order is more logical than historical. Each successive divine intervention is simply a further manifestation of God's power and justice. The devastation which the trumpets introduce is greater than that produced by the opening of the first four seals: a third of the earth is affected, not just a quarter (cf. 6:8). Divine mercy, however, still controls the range of the punishment and prevents total annihilation.

Following the logical order which classifies the cosmos into land, sea and sky, the blowing of the first trumpet affects the vegetation (v. 7); the description is parallel to the account of the seventh plague in Exodus 9:13–35.

The blowing of the two next trumpets affects seas and rivers (vv. 10–11). Many perish as a result of the pollution of the waters. Both these calamities are connected with the first plague of Egypt (cf. Ex 7:19–21).

After this contamination of land and sea, the heavens are affected by the

Revelation 8:13

^{Rev 14:6; 9:12; 11:14}

¹³Then I looked, and I heard an eagle crying with a loud voice, as it flew in midheaven, "Woe, woe, woe to those who dwell on the earth, at the blasts of the other trumpets which the three angels are about to blow!"

^{Rev 8:10; 20:1
Is 14:12
Gen 19:28
Ex 19:18
Joel 2:10}

9 ¹And the fifth angel blew his trumpet, and I saw a star* fallen from heaven to earth, and he was given the key of the shaft of the bottomless pit; ²he opened the shaft of the bottomless pit, and from the shaft rose smoke like the smoke of a great furnace, and the sun and the air were darkened with the smoke from the shaft.

^{Ex 10:12, 15
Wis 16:9}

³Then from the smoke came locusts on the earth, and they were

---

fourth trumpet. The sun and the heavenly bodies are darkened, so that their power is reduced by a third: these effects are reminiscent to some degree of Exodus 10:21–29.

8:13. This passage is a short break before the last three trumpet calls. The lament of the eagle, which may stand for an angel, can be heard all over the world. Its "woe, woe, woe" expresses horror and compassion at the events which follow. This cannot fail to impress the reader; it creates an atmosphere of foreboding.

"Those who dwell on earth": a reference to idolaters (cf. Rev 3:10), who are persecuting Christians. It does not refer to the faithful but only to those who have let themselves be led astray by Christ's enemies (cf. Rev 6:10; 11:10; 13:8, 12, 14; 17:2–8).

9:1—11:19. The next two trumpets will impact directly on mankind, producing more horrific effects, in a kind of crescendo. These trumpets follow one after the other (9:1–21), whereas there is a delay before the blowing of the seventh (11:15–19), during which a number of visions occur (10:1—11:14) which anticipate later events narrated in chapters 12–22.

9:1–2. The commonest interpretation of the star fallen from heaven to earth is that it stands for one of the fallen angels, most likely Satan himself, of whom Christ said, "I saw Satan fall like lightning from heaven" (Lk 10:18) and whom the present text later describes as being thrown down to the earth (cf. note on 12:13). Behind this lies the notion that the demons are incarcerated in the bowels of the earth. The writer is trying to convey the idea that, when the fifth trumpet is blown, God is going to let demoniacal forces loose to wreak havoc on those of mankind who refuse to recognize God (cf. v. 4). They will be free to operate only for a limited period and to a limited degree and will have to obey "the angel of the bottomless pit" (v. 11), who would be the same angel as received the key of the shafts of the abyss (v. 9), the prince of the demons. Very near the end of the Apocalypse the writer sees the other side of the coin, as it were—Satan and his followers being shut up once more in the pit, after Christ's victory (cf. 20:1–3).

9:3–6. In order to describe the demons and the havoc they create, St John evokes the eighth plague of Egypt, the plague of locusts (cf. Ex 10:14f), making it clear, however, that this plague is much more horrific and on another level altogether. It will do such grievous harm to men that they will wish they were dead, but they

given power like the power of scorpions of the earth; ⁴they were told not to harm the grass of the earth or any green growth or any tree, but only those of mankind who have not the seal of God upon their foreheads; ⁵they were allowed to torture them for five months, but not to kill them, and their torture was like the torture of a scorpion, when it stings a man. ⁶And in those days men will seek death and will not find it; they will long to die, and death will fly from them.

⁷In appearance the locusts were like horses arrayed for battle; on their heads were what looked like crowns of gold; their faces were like human faces, ⁸their hair like women's hair, and their teeth like lions' teeth; ⁹they had scales like iron breastplates, and the noise of their wings was like the noise of many chariots with horses rushing into battle. ¹⁰They have tails like scorpions, and stings, and their power of hurting men for five months lies in their tails. ¹¹They have as king over them the angel of the bottomless pit; his name in Hebrew is Abaddon, and in Greek he is called Apollyon.ᵇ

¹²The first woe has passed; behold, two woes are still to come.

¹³Then the sixth angel blew his trumpet, and I heard a voice from the four horns of the golden altar before God, ¹⁴saying to the

Rev 7:3
Ezek 9:4, 6

Job 3:21
Lk 23:30

Joel 2:4

Joel 1:6
Joel 2:5

Rev 9:19

Rev 9:1

Rev 8:13
Ex 30:1–3
Rev 16:12

---

will have to endure it for a fixed amount of time: the "five months", the life-time of the locust, conveys the idea that these afflictions will last for a limited time.

9:7–12. The description of the locusts is designed to show how terrifying demons are; cf. the prophet Joel's description of the invading army (Joel 1:2—2:17). The crowns of gold identify them as conquerors; their faces, as creatures with intelligence; their hairiness and lions' teeth symbolize ferocity; their iron breastplates show them to be fully armed warriors; and the noise they create and their scorpion tails show their extreme cruelty. They obey a leader, Satan, whose name (Abaddon, Apollyon) denotes destruction and extermination. His name contrasts with that of Jesus, which means "Yahweh saves".

9:13–19. As before, God permits the angels of evil to have their way; he uses them to inflict just punishment and offer the rest of mankind a chance to repent of their sins (vv. 20–21). The golden altar standing before the throne of God is shaped like the altar of the temple of Jerusalem (cf. Ex 37:26; Amos 3:14), with its four prominent corners and four horns; from the midst of the horns comes the voice which sets these punishments in motion.

The inspired writer now describes a new and dreadful vision. The vast size of the cavalry shows the scale of the evil in the world. The river Euphrates (in a sense the frontier of the world of the Bible) was the direction from which invasions of Israel usually came (cf. Is 7:20; Jer 46:10; etc.). At the time of writing it was the region from which the Parthians

b. Or *Destroyer*

Revelation 9:15

Rev 8:7–12

sixth angel who had the trumpet, "Release the four angels who are bound at the great river Euphrates."* ¹⁵So the four angels were released, who had been held ready for the hour, the day, the month, and the year, to kill a third of mankind. ¹⁶The number of the troops of cavalry was twice ten thousand times ten thousand; I heard their number. ¹⁷And this was how I saw the horses in my vision: the riders wore breastplates the colour of fire and of sapphire[c] and of sulphur, and the heads of the horses were like lions' heads, and fire and smoke and sulphur issued from their mouths. ¹⁸By these three plagues a third of mankind was killed, by the fire and smoke and sulphur issuing from their mouths. ¹⁹For the power of the horses is in their mouths and in their tails; their tails are like serpents, with heads, and by means of them they wound.

Rev 9:10

Is 2:8, 20; 17:8
Dam 5:4, 23
Ps 115:4;
135:15
1 Cor 10:20

²⁰The rest of mankind, who were not killed by these plagues, did not repent of the works of their hands nor give up worshipping demons and idols of gold and silver and bronze and stone and wood, which cannot either see or hear or walk; ²¹nor did they repent of their murders or their sorceries or their immorality* or their thefts.

---

mounted their threat to the Roman empire.

Some of the details of the vision are reminiscent of other descriptions of ruin and desolation (cf. Gen 19:24–28) and of monstrous animals (cf. Job 41:11). Fire, smoke and sulphur all indicate that this army of monsters originates in hell.

9:20–21. In the last analysis, as shown here, all the punishments described in the Book of Revelation are designed to move people to repentance. That was also the thrust of the letters to the seven churches (cf. Rev 2:5, 16, 21; 3:3; etc.). But the author shows that people persist in turning away from God to worship idols, which are really only scarecrows compared with Yahweh, the living God (cf., e.g., Ps 113; Jer 10:3–5).

In the last analysis idolatry is the root of all other sins: by turning his back on God man comes under the control of the forces of evil (forces within him as well as outside him) which push him to commit all kinds of sins and perversions. St Paul deals with the same idea in his Letter to the Romans where he says that by cutting themselves off from God men are given over to their own passions and commit most abominable sins (cf. Rom 1:18–32).

God inflicts punishment in order to bring about the conversion of sinners. Sometimes, however, the end result is that they become more obdurate. That was the case with Pharaoh; when the plagues struck Egypt, far from repenting, he persecuted the Israelites more bitterly than ever. Divine punishment, then, has a medicinal and exemplary purpose and is good for everyone without exception. In the Gospel Jesus tells us that the Galileans whom Pilate put to death, and the people who perished when the tower collapsed on them in Siloam, were not

---

c. Greek *hyacinth*

The seer is given a little scroll to eat

10 ¹Then I saw another mighty angel coming down from heaven, wrapped in a cloud, with a rainbow over his head, and his face was like the sun, and his legs like pillars of fire. ²He had a little scroll open in his hand. And he set his right foot on the sea, and his left foot on the land, ³and called out with a loud voice, like a lion roaring; when he called out, the seven thunders

Rev 5:2; 4:3

Hos 11:10
Amos 1:2, 3:8
Ps 29:3–9
Jer 25:30

---

more blameworthy than other people, and therefore we too will perish unless we repent (cf. Lk 13:1–5).

10:1. After the events following the sixth trumpet call (cf. 9: 13–21) and before the seventh (cf. 11:15), we are shown a new vision (as an aside, as it were). The seer is once again back on earth, as he was when the seven letters were being despatched (cf. 10:4; 1:4—3:22), whereas he sees the "trumpet" visions from the vantage point of heaven (chaps. 4–9 and 12). This shows that we are dealing here with an aside which is designed to prepare the reader for the seventh and final trumpet blast.

In this "out of sequence" vision St John reminds us of his prophetic role by bringing in the symbolic action of eating a little scroll (cf. 10:8–11) and recalling the testimony of the ancient prophets, who are represented by the two witnesses (cf. 11:1–13).

Although the angel is not named, he may be Gabriel: he is described as "mighty" (*geber*, in Hebrew), and Gabriel (*gabri'el*, in Hebrew) means "strength of God" or "man of God" (cf. Dan 8:15) or "God shows his strength". Be that as it may, Gabriel is the name given to the angel charged with explaining the messianic prophecies to Daniel and with communicating divine messages to Zechariah (cf. Lk 1:19) and to the Blessed Virgin (cf. Lk 1:26). He performed a function parallel to that of the angel who appears in 8:3–5 and who is usually identified as St Michael. The way he is described emphasizes his heavenly character and his strength.

10:2. The open scroll carried by the angel is different from the sealed scroll in the vision recounted in Revelation 5:2. It is more like the scroll described by the prophet Ezekiel (cf. Ezek 2:9—3:1) which was also meant to be eaten by the seer. The fact that it is open indicates that its content is not secret. The eating of the scroll symbolizes that what the prophet has to say after he eats it is really the word of God. It also indicates that God speaks through the medium of a written text. So, this imagery helps to strengthen people's faith in the divine inspiration of sacred writings, that is, the Bible, and to recognize them for what they are—holy books because they are the very word of God which reaches the Church in written form via inspired authors: by reading these books publicly the Church is in fact proclaiming their divine inspiration.

We are not told what this little scroll contains; so, the only reason the writer brings in this symbol is to make it clear that he is a prophet. He wants people to be in no doubt about the fact that his prophecies apply to all creation—both heaven and earth (v. 6).

10:3–7. Like the voice of God in the Old Testament, the angel's voice is here compared to the roar of a lion (cf. Hos 11:10; Amos 1:2; 3:8) and to thunder (cf. Is 29:6) which strikes fear into men.

Revelation 10:4

sounded. ⁴And when the seven thunders had sounded, I was about to write, but I heard a voice from heaven saying, "Seal up what the seven thunders have said, and do not write it down." ⁵And the angel whom I saw standing on sea and land lifted up his right hand to heaven ⁶and swore by him who lives for ever and ever, who created heaven and what is in it, the earth and what is in it, and the sea and what is in it, that there should be no more delay, ⁷but that in the days of the trumpet call to be sounded by the seventh angel, the mystery of God,* as he announced to his servants the prophets, should be fulfilled.

⁸Then the voice which I had heard from heaven spoke to me again, saying, "Go, take the scroll which is open in the hand of the

Marginal references:
Dan 8:26; 12:4, 9; Rev 22:10
Deut 32:40
Dan 12:7
Neh 9:6
Ex 20:11
Rev 6:11
Acts 3:21
Amos 3:7
Dan 9:10
Rom 16:25
Rev 10:2

According to the text each peal of thunder carries a message of its own; and the fact of there being seven means that they carry everything God wishes to reveal. However, the content of this revelation is not to be communicated further and will only be made known at the end of time. The sealing of the scroll shows that this revelation is to be kept secret and that there is no point in anyone trying to discover it. It is part of the mystery which God chooses to keep hidden—in the same way as we do not know when our Lord's second coming and the end of the world will be (cf. Mt 24:36).

The angel's gesture and solemn oath assured the seer that the definitive establishment of the Kingdom of God will come about when there will be "no more delay", no more time, for the world in its present form. However, as to the timing, all that is said is that it will happen when the mystery of God (his plan of salvation) has reached its final climax, when the harvest-time has come (cf. Mt 13:24–30) and good and evil—wheat and weeds—will be clear for all to see (cf. 2 Thess 2:6ff).

In the Apocalypse, the end of time is signalled by the blowing of the seventh trumpet (described later: cf. 11:15) which signals that the "three woes" are over (cf. 8:13; 9:13). The point being made here is that this outcome is certain—which is a motive of hope for the Church and a call to conversion for all mankind: "But do not ignore this one fact, beloved, that with the Lord one day is as a thousand years, and a thousand years as one day. The Lord is not slow about his promise as some count slowness, but is forbearing toward you, not wishing that any should perish, but that all should reach repentance" (2 Pet 3:8–9).

10:8–11. Cf. note on 10:2. The book described by Ezekiel 2:8—3:3 was sweet as honey when eaten; but when Ezekiel began to prophesy, his heart was filled with bitterness (cf. Ezek 3:14). The same symbolism of the two kinds of taste is used here—no doubt to indicate that the prophecy contains grace and blessing, and also judgment and condemnation. The sweetness can also be interpreted as reflecting the triumph of the Church, and the bitterness its afflictions.

Although nothing is said about what is written on the scroll John is given to eat, it is reasonable to suppose that it has to do with the passage about the two witnesses which now follows, before the blowing of the seventh trumpet; this would make it a prophetic oracle, brought

angel who is standing on the sea and on the land." ⁹So I went to the angel and told him to give me the little scroll; and he said to me, "Take it and eat; it will be bitter to your stomach, but sweet* as honey in your mouth." ¹⁰And I took the little scroll from the hand of the angel and ate it; it was sweet as honey in my mouth, but when I had eaten it my stomach was made bitter. ¹¹And I was told, "You must again prophesy about many peoples and nations and tongues and kings."

Ezek 2:8; 3:1

Ezek 3:3

Dan 3:4

Death and resurrection of the two witnesses

11 *¹Then I was given a measuring rod like a staff, and I was told: "Rise and measure the temple of God and the altar and those who worship there, ²but do not measure the court outside the temple; leave that out, for it is given over to the nations, and they

Ezek 40:3; Zech 2:5; Is 63:18; Ps 79:1 Dan 7:25; 8:14 Lk 21:24; Rev 12:6, 14; 13:5

---

in here as a preview of the final eschatological battles, to show that evil apparently triumphs on earth.

11:1–13. The prophecy connected with what is on the scroll (11:1–13) acts as a preamble to the events that follow the blowing of the seventh and last trumpet (11:15ff). It has to do with the tribulation suffered by the Church (the Church is symbolized by the temple of Jerusalem and its altar). The ultimate cause of this suffering is the forces of evil, that is, the beast (antichrist) which makes its appearance in the Holy City (cf. 11:7). In the course of a limited period, that is, the history of mankind, there are moments when the forces of evil prevail and many people transgress God's law. The witnesses of the true God come forward to preach penance (11:3–6) and are martyred to the great delight of their adversaries (cf. 11:7–10). But God intervenes on behalf of these martyrs, taking them up into heaven and decimating their foes; the terrified survivors submit to God (cf. 11:11–13).

This prophetic teaching echoes what we are told in the Second Letter to the Thessalonians: "Let no one deceive you in any way; for that day will not come, unless the rebellion comes first, and the man of lawlessness is revealed, the son of perdition, who opposes and exalts himself against every so-called god or object of worship, so that he takes his seat in the temple of God, proclaiming himself to be God" (2 Thess 2:3–4). Using Old Testament imagery and language the author of Revelation is pointing out, as Jesus did (cf. Mk 13:14–32), that the destruction of Jerusalem and the catastrophes which accompany it are a sign and symbol of the end of the world and a warning to everyone (particularly the Jewish people) who are called as the Jews are, to share in the salvation brought by Christ (cf. Rom 11:25–26).

11:1–2. The image of the measuring rod is taken from the prophet Ezekiel but it is used in a different way: it shows God is going to preserve part of the Holy City from the destructive power of the Gentiles. This part stands for the Church, the community of those who worship God in spirit and in truth (cf. Jn 4:23).

Jerusalem was trampled under foot by the Gentiles in the time of Antiochus Epiphanes, who profaned the temple and

Revelation 11:3

will trample over the holy city for forty-two months.* ³And I will grant my two witnesses* power to prophesy for one thousand two hundred and sixty days, clothed in sackcloth."

Zech 4:3, 11–14
2 Kings 1:10
Jer 5:14; Lk 9:54f; 2 Sam 22:9; 1 Kings 17:1; Ex 7:17
Jas 5:17

⁴These are the two olive trees and the two lampstands which stand before the Lord of the earth. ⁵And if any one would harm them, fire pours out from their mouth and consumes their foes; if any one would harm them, thus he is doomed to be killed. ⁶They have power to shut the sky, that no rain may fall during the days of their prophesying, and they have power over the waters to turn

---

installed in it a statue of Zeus Olympus (cf. 1 Mac 1:54); worse destruction still was done by the Romans, who destroyed both temple and city, leaving not a stone upon a stone (Mt 24:21; Mk 13:14–23; Lk 21:20–24). Taking his cue from these events, St John prophesies that the Church will never suffer the same fate, for God protects it from the power of its enemies (cf. Mt 16:16–18). Christians may suffer persecution in one way or another, but physical or moral violence cannot overpower the Church, because God protects it. "The Church, 'like a stranger in a foreign land, presses forward amid the persecutions of the world and the consolations of God' (St Augustine, *The City of God*, 18, 51), announcing the cross and death of the Lord until he comes (cf. 1 Cor 11:26). But by the power of the risen Lord it is given strength to overcome, in patience and in love, its sorrows and its difficulties, both those that are from within and those that are from without, so that it may reveal in the world, faithfully, however darkly, the mystery of its Lord until, in the consummation, it shall be manifested in full light" (Vatican II, *Lumen gentium*, 8).

The forty-two months established as the period during which the Gentiles will trample on the Holy City stand for the length of the persecution. This is a symbolic number equivalent to three and a half years or "a time, times and half a time" (12:13), that is, "a half week of years"—half seven—which stands for an incomplete, that is, limited, period of time. Perfect, complete time is symbolized by the figure seven (cf. Gen 1:2—2:3) or by seventy (cf. Dan 9:24). The prophet Daniel uses the same symbolism to indicate the duration of persecution (cf. Dan 7:25; 12:7); the author of the Apocalypse puts it to the same purpose here and in the next verse, where the same period is expressed in terms of days (1,260): the period stands for the duration of the Church's sufferings in the course of history (cf. Rev 12:6, 14; 13:5): this period is of limited duration, merely a prelude to the definitive victory of Christ and his Church.

11:3–6. The period of tribulation coincides with the length of time the two witnesses prophesy. They call people to penance (symbolized by their use of sackcloth). God protects them in a very special way; and yet he does not spare them death or suffering; in the end, however, they will be glorified in heaven. In the Apocalypse the identity of the two witnesses is not given; they are referred to as "olive trees"—the same language as used of Zerubbabel, a prince of the line of David, and Joshua, the high priest (cf. Zech 3:3–14). But they are assigned features of Elijah, who brought about a drought (cf. 1 Kings 17:1–3; 18:1), and Moses, who

them into blood, and to smite the earth with every plague, as often as they desire. ⁷And when they have finished their testimony, the beast that ascends from the bottomless pit will make war upon them and conquer them and kill them, ⁸and their dead bodies will lie in the street of the great city* which is allegorically^d called Sodom and Egypt, where their Lord was crucified. ⁹For three days

Dan 7:3, 7, 21
Rev 13:1, 7

turned the Nile to blood (cf. Ex 7:14–16). The enemies of Elijah and Moses were also devoured by fire from heaven (cf. 2 Kings 1:10; Num 16:35). However, because the two witnesses testify to Jesus Christ and die martyrs, tradition identifies them with St Peter and St Paul, who suffered martyrdom in Rome, the city which the book of Revelation later mentions symbolically. Some early commentators (e.g. Ticonius and St Bede) saw the two witnesses as standing for the Old and New Testaments; but this interpretation has had little following. St Jerome (*Epist.*, 59) says that they are Elijah and Enoch, and St Gregory the Great and others give that interpretation (*Moralia*, 9, 4).

What St John is doing is using a theme which occurs fairly frequently in apocalyptic writings where Elijah and Enoch or other combinations of prominent figures are portrayed as opponents of antichrist. His two witnesses do have features of Elijah and Moses, both of whom bore witness to Christ at the transfiguration (cf. Mt 17:1–8 and par.). However, the duration of the trial they undergo, and the entire context of the passage, point rather to them standing for the prophetic witness of the Church, symbolized by certain more outstanding witnesses, who were present at the death of Christ, which took place in Jerusalem, and who were also witnesses of his glorious resurrection. However, it is the entire Church, right through the course of its history, that has been given the prophetic role of calling men to repentance in the midst of harassment and hostility: "The holy People of God shares also in Christ's prophetic office: it spreads a broad and living witness to him, especially by a life of faith and love and by offering to God a sacrifice of praise, the fruit of lips praising his name (cf. Heb 13:15)" (Vatican II, *Lumen gentium*, 12). "The Church announces the good tidings of salvation [...], so that all men may believe the one true God and Jesus Christ whom he has sent and may be converted from their ways, doing penance (cf. Jn 17:3; Lk 24:27; Acts 2:38)" (Vatican II, *Sacrosanctum Concilium*, 9).

11:7–10. The prophet Daniel used four beasts to symbolize the empires of the world as enemies of the people of Israel. In the Apocalypse the beast stands for the enemy of the Church and the enemy of God. Further on it will develop this theme and link the beasts to the dragon or Satan (cf. 13:2), and describe their defeat by Christ, the Lamb of God (cf. 14:1; 19:19–21).

The symbol of the beast is brought forward in this passage to show that there will be a point, or various points, before the End when the forces of evil will apparently win victory. Martyrdom silences the voices of the witnesses of Jesus Christ who preach repentance; many will rejoice over this and even deride those whose words or actions they

d. Greek *spiritually*

Revelation 11:10

and a half men from the peoples and tribes and tongues and nations gaze at their dead bodies and refuse to let them be placed in a tomb, ¹⁰and those who dwell on the earth will rejoice over them and make merry and exchange presents, because these two prophets had been a torment to those who dwell on the earth.

Ezek 35:5, 10 ¹¹But after the three and a half days a breath of life from God entered them, and they stood up on their feet, and great fear fell on
2 kings 2:11 those who saw them. ¹²Then they heard a loud voice from heaven

---

find uncomfortable, despite the fact that when a Christian bears witness to the salvation that comes from Jesus he is motivated purely by love. "Since Jesus, the Son of God, showed his love by laying down his life for us, no one has greater love than he who lays down his life for him and for his brothers (cf. 1 Jn 3:16; Jn 15:13). Some Christians have been called from the beginning, and will always be called, to give this greatest testimony of love to all, especially to persecutors. Martyrdom makes the disciple like his Master, who willingly accepted death for the salvation of the world, and through it he is conformed to Him by the shedding of blood. Therefore the Church considers it the highest gift and supreme test of love. And while it is given to few, all however must be prepared to confess Christ before men and to follow him along the way of the cross amidst the persecutions which the Church never lacks" (*Lumen gentium*, 42).

"The great city", whose name is not given, seems to be Jerusalem, which in Isaiah 1:10 is called Sodom because it has turned its back on God. However, when the writer tells us that it is "allegorically called Sodom and Egypt, where their Lord was crucified" (v. 8), we may take Jerusalem here to stand for any city or even any nation where perversity holds sway (cf. Wis 19:14–17, which alludes to Sodom and Egypt) and where Christians are persecuted and hunted down (cf. Acts 9:5). Thus, St Jerome (*Epist.* 17) interpreted the names of Sodom and Egypt as having a mystical or figurative meaning, referring to the entire world seen as the city of the devil and of evildoers. Further on, St John will identify the Rome of his time with this "great city" (cf. 17:9).

Evil will triumph for only a limited period. Its reign is fixed to last "three days and a half", to show its brevity and temporary character as compared with the 1,260 days (three years and a half) for which the prophetic witness endures (cf. note on 11:1–2).

11:11–13. Those who have given their lives to bear witness to Jesus will also, through the power of the Holy Spirit, share in his resurrection and ascension into heaven. The writer describes this by various references to the Old Testament, references rich in meaning. The breath of life which causes the witnesses to stand up, that is, to be resurrected, reveals the power of the Spirit of God, which is also described by the prophet Ezekiel in his vision of the dry bones which become living warriors (cf. Ezek 37:1–14). The voice which calls them up to heaven reminds us of what happened to Elijah at the end of his life (cf. 2 Kings 2:11), and to certain other Old Testament saints like Enoch (cf. Gen 5:24; Sir 44:16); according to certain Jewish traditions (cf. Flavius Josephus, *Jewish Antiquities*, 4, 8, 48), all of these men were carried up into heaven at the end of their days on earth.

saying to them, "Come up hither!" And in the sight of their foes they went up to heaven in a cloud. [13]And at that hour there was a great earthquake, and a tenth of the city fell; seven thousand people were killed in the earthquake, and the rest were terrified and gave glory to the God of heaven. _{Ezek 38:19, 20}

[14]The second woe has passed; behold, the third woe is soon to come. _{Rev 8:13; 9:12}

3. CHRIST'S VICTORY OVER THE POWERS OF EVIL. THE CHURCH IN GLORY

The seventh trumpet call
[15]Then the seventh angel blew his trumpet, and there were loud voices in heaven, saying, "The kingdom of the world has become the kingdom of our Lord and of his Christ, and he shall reign for _{Dan 2:44; 7:14, 27; Zech 14:9 Ezek 15:18 Ps 2:2; 22:9}

The exaltation of the witnesses is in sharp contrast with the punishment meted out to their enemies, a punishment designed to move men to conversion. The earthquake indicates that the chastisement is sudden and unexpected; the number of those who die symbolizes a great crowd (thousands) embracing all types (seven).

The prophecy of the two witnesses is a call to the Christian to bear witness to Christ in the midst of persecution, even to the point of martyrdom. It makes it quite clear that God does not abandon those who boldly take his side. If the prophets of the Old Testament suffered martyrdom, the same will happen in the new, only more so: the messianic times have begun, persecution will grow in strength, but the end of the world is approaching.

11:14. The tribulations connected with the blowing of the last three trumpets are thrown into sharp and terrible relief by the three "woes" announced from heaven (cf. 8:13), which are a kind of loud lamentation. The second "woe" is described as something that has already taken place, and the third one is announced. Thus, after the parenthesis of 10:1—11:13, the thread of the narrative (following the successive trumpet blasts) is taken up again, and our attention is drawn to the importance of what follows.

11:15. The seventh trumpet opens a new section which will tell us, first, about the climax of the confrontation between Satan and the powers of evil, and Christ and the Church (cf. 12:1—16:16), and then go on to describe the last battles; with Christ triumphing as Lord of all for ever (cf. 16:17—22:5). All this is prefaced by an introduction which tells us that his kingdom will come and will endure forever (cf. 11:15–19).

The description of the confrontation between Christ and Satan begins with the war between the dragon and the beasts, on the one hand, and the Messiah, the woman and her children, on the other (cf. 12:1—13:18). Then the Lamb appears, Christ in glory, and the moment of judgment is announced (cf. 14:1–20). This is depicted by the seven bowls or plagues (cf. 15:1—16:16); when the

Revelation 11:16

Rev 4:10; 7:11

ever and ever." ⁱ⁶And the twenty-four elders who sit on their thrones before God fell on their faces and worshipped God, ¹⁷saying,

Ez 3:14
Rev 1:4; 4:8; 19:6

"We give thanks to thee, Lord God Almighty, who art and who wast,
that thou hast taken thy great power and begun to reign.

Ps 2:1, 5; 46:7; 99:1; 115:13
Amos 3:7

¹⁸ The nations raged, but thy wrath came,
and the time for the dead to be judged,
for rewarding thy servants, the prophets and saints,
and those who fear thy name, both small and great,
and for destroying the destroyers of the earth."

---

seventh plague is released, the contenders are introduced again, and the account of the last battles follows (cf. 16:17).

As announced earlier (cf. 10:17), the blowing of the seventh trumpet means that God's mysterious design has been fully implemented. The voices from heaven (11:15) proclaim the revelation of this mystery: that divine design which makes Christ reign forever has taken effect. As elsewhere in the New Testament (cf. Acts 4:25–28), this passage of the Apocalypse also teaches that Christ's complete dominion fulfils the prophetic words of Psalm 2. The climax of human history is the full installation of Christ's Kingdom; the Apocalypse, given its perspective, views this as a present event. It thereby offers Christians a great message of hope and consolation, for the Church "is on earth the seed and the beginning of that kingdom. While it slowly grows to maturity, the Church longs for the completed kingdom and, with all its strength, hopes and desires to be united in glory with its king" (Vatican II, *Lumen gentium*, 5).

Jesus himself teaches us to pray constantly to the Father, "Thy Kingdom come."

11:16–18. In response to this revelation from God, his people (represented by the twenty-four elders: cf. 4:4) hasten to adore him and thank him. Although all this is set in a celestial context, it also represents the Church's response to its Redeemer's victorious struggle, which will culminate in his second coming. At that point almighty God will establish his absolute sovereignty; that period will come to an end in which God in his infinite patience permitted man to rebel against him; and all men who ever existed will be judged. This is the faith the Church professes when it proclaims its belief in Jesus Christ, "who will come again in glory to judge the living and the dead" (*Nicene-Constantinopolitan Creed*).

The author of the Apocalypse carries us forward to that final moment when God's action in human history reaches its climax. That is why it no longer speaks of God with reference to the future (as it previously did)—he "who is and who was and who is to come": cf. Rev 1:4, 8; 4:8—but rather in relation to the present and the past—"who art and who wast" (v. 17).

At this final point in history God's justice is fully revealed. Insofar as it involves the condemnation of those who oppose him it is referred to as his "anger" or "wrath" (cf. Rom 1:18). Only God has the power to establish enduring justice or righteousness, as Psalms 96 and 98 tell us.

Revelation 11:19

¹⁹Then God's temple in heaven was opened, and the ark of his covenant was seen within his temple; and there were flashes of lightning, voices, peals of thunder, an earthquake, and heavy hail.

Ez 19:16; 25:8–10
Rev 15:5; 4:5
2 Mac 2:5–8

Mankind is divided into two groups —those who are rewarded and those who are destroyed; cf. how our Lord describes the Last Judgment in Matthew 25:31–46. The first group consists of those who, down the centuries (in the times of both the Old and the New Covenants) have borne witness to Christ (the prophets), those who have been sanctified by Baptism and have striven for holiness (the saints), and all people great and small who have sought God with sincerity of heart. The second group consists of those who have not kept the law of God (impressed on Creation itself) and who by their sins have helped to corrupt the world by serving the powers of evil (cf. Rev 19:2). When it says that God will destroy them that does not mean that he will annihilate them but rather that he will make them incapable of doing any more evil and will punish them as they deserve. On the Last Judgment, see the notes on Matthew 25:31–46.

11:19. The seer introduces the heavenly temple (the location *par excellence* of God' s presence), paralleling the earlier mention of the temple of Jerusalem (cf. 11:1–2). The opening of the temple and the sight of the Ark of the Covenant show that the messianic era has come to an end and God's work of salvation has been completed. The ark was the symbol of Israel's election and salvation and of God's presence in the midst of his people. According to a Jewish tradition, reported in 2 Maccabees 2:4–8, Jeremiah placed the ark in a secret hiding place prior to the destruction of Jerusalem, and it would be seen again when the Messiah came. The author of the Apocalypse uses this to assure us that God has not forgotten his covenant: he has sealed it definitively in heaven, where the ark is located.

Many early commentators interpreted the ark as a reference to Christ's sacred humanity, and St Bede explains that just as the manna was kept in the original ark, so Christ's divinity lies hidden in his sacred body (cf. *Explanatio Apocalypsis*, 11, 19).

The heavenly covenant is the new and eternal one made by Jesus Christ (cf. Mt 26:26–29 and par.) which will be revealed to all at his second coming when the Church will triumph, as the Apocalypse goes on to describe. The presence of the ark in the heavenly temple symbolizes the sublimity of the messianic kingdom, which exceeds anything man could create. "The vigilant and active expectation of the coming of the Kingdom is also the expectation of a finally perfect justice for the living and the dead, for people of all times and places, a justice which Jesus Christ, installed as supreme Judge, will establish (cf. Mt 24:29–44, 46; Acts 10:42; 2 Cor 5:10). This promise, which surpasses all human possibilities, directly concerns our life in this world. For true justice must include everyone; it must explain the immense load of suffering borne by all generations. In fact, without the resurrection of the dead and the Lord's judgment, there is no justice in the full sense of the term. The promise of the resurrection is freely made to meet the desire for true justice dwelling in the human heart" (SCDF, *Libertatis conscientia*, 60).

The thunder and lightning which accompany the appearance of the ark are reminiscent of the way God made his

Revelation 12:1

The woman pursued by the dragon

Gen 37:9

Gen 3:15, 16

12 *¹And a great portent appeared in heaven, a woman clothed with the sun, with the moon under her feet, and on her head a crown of twelve stars; ²she was with child and she cried out in

---

presence felt on Sinai; they reveal God's mighty intervention (cf. Rev 4:5; 8:5) which is now accompanied by the chastisement of the wicked, symbolized by the earthquake and hailstones (cf. Ex 9:13–35).

12:1–17. We are now introduced to the contenders in the eschatological battles which mark the final confrontation between God and his adversary, the devil. The author uses three portents to describe the leading figures involved, and the war itself. The first is the woman and her offspring, including the Messiah (12:1–2); the second is the dragon, who will later transfer his power to the beasts (12:3); the third, the seven angels with the seven bowls (15:1).

Three successive confrontations with the dragon are described—1) that of the Messiah to whom the woman gives birth (12:1–6); 2) that of St Michael and his angels (12:7–12); and 3) that of the woman and the rest of her offspring (12:13–17). These confrontations should not be seen as being in chronological order. They are more like three distinct pictures placed side by side because they are closely connected: in each the same enemy, the devil, does battle with God's plans and with those whom God uses to carry them out.

12:1–2. The mysterious figure of the woman has been interpreted ever since the time of the Fathers of the Church as referring to the ancient people of Israel, or the Church of Jesus Christ, or the Blessed Virgin. The text supports all of these interpretations but in none do all the details fit. The woman can stand for the people of Israel, for it is from that people that the Messiah comes, and Isaiah compares Israel to "a woman with child, who writhes and cries out in her pangs, when she is near her time" (Is 26:17).

She can also stand for the Church, whose children strive to overcome evil and to bear witness to Jesus Christ (cf. v. 17). Following this interpretation St Gregory wrote: "The sun stands for the light of truth, and the moon for the transitoriness of temporal things; the holy Church is clothed like the sun because she is protected by the splendour of supernatural truth, and she has the moon under her feet because she is above all earthly things" (*Moralia*, 34, 12).

The passage can also refer to the Virgin Mary because it was she who truly and historically gave birth to the Messiah, Jesus Christ our Lord (cf. v. 5). St Bernard comments: "The sun contains permanent colour and splendour; whereas the moon's brightness is unpredictable and changeable, for it never stays the same. It is quite right, then, for Mary to be depicted as clothed with the sun, for she entered the profundity of divine wisdom much much further than one can possibly conceive" (*De B. Virgine*, 2).

In his account of the Annunciation, St Luke sees Mary as representing the faithful remnant of Israel; the angel greets her with the greeting given in Zephaniah 3:15 to the daughter of Zion (cf. notes on Lk 1:26–31). St Paul in Galatians 4:4 sees a woman as the symbol of the Church, our mother; and non-canonical Jewish literature contemporary with the book of Revelation quite often

her pangs of birth, in anguish for delivery. ³And another portent appeared in heaven; behold, a great red dragon, with seven heads and ten horns, and seven diadems upon his heads. ⁴His tail swept

Is 66:7
Mic 4:10
Dan 7:7
Dan 8:10

personifies the community as a woman. So, the inspired text of the Apocalypse is open to interpreting this woman as a direct reference to the Blessed Virgin who, as mother, shares in the pain of Calvary (cf. Lk 2:35) and who was earlier prophesied in Isaiah 7:14 as a "sign" (cf. Mt 1:22–23). At the same time the woman can be interpreted as standing for the people of God, the Church, whom the figure of Mary represents.

The Second Vatican Council has solemnly taught that Mary is a "type" or symbol of the Church, for "in the mystery of the Church, which is itself rightly called mother and virgin, the Blessed Virgin stands out in eminent and singular fashion as exemplar both of virgin and mother. Through her faith and obedience she gave birth on earth to the very Son of the Father, not through the knowledge of man but by the overshadowing of the Holy Spirit, in the manner of a new Eve who placed her faith, not in the serpent of old but in God's messenger, without wavering in doubt. The Son whom she brought forth is he whom God placed as the first-born among many brethren (cf. Rom 8:29), that is, the faithful, in whose generation and formation she cooperates with a mother's love" (Vatican II, *Lumen gentium*, 63).

The description of the woman indicates her heavenly glory, and the twelve stars of her victorious crown symbolize the people of God—the twelve patriarchs (cf. Gen 37:9) and the twelve apostles. And so, independently of the chronological aspects of the text, the Church sees in this heavenly woman the Blessed Virgin, "taken up body and soul into heavenly glory, when her earthly life was over, and exalted by the Lord as Queen over all things, that she might be the more fully conformed to her Son, the Lord of lords (cf. Rev 19:16) and conqueror of sin and death" (*Lumen gentium*, 59). The Blessed Virgin is indeed the great sign, for, as St Bonaventure says, "God could have made none greater. He could have made a greater world and a greater heaven; but not a woman greater than his own mother" (*Speculum*, 8).

12:3–4. In his description of the devil (cf. v. 9), St John uses symbols taken from the Old Testament. The dragon or serpent comes from Genesis 3:1–24, a passage which underlies all the latter half of this book. Its red colour and seven heads with seven diadems show that it is bringing its full force to bear to wage this war. The ten horns in Daniel 7:7 stand for the kings who are Israel's enemies; in Daniel a horn is also mentioned to refer to Antiochus IV Epiphanes, of whom Daniel also says (to emphasize the greatness of Antiochus' victories) that it cast stars down from heaven onto the earth (cf. Dan 8:10). Satan drags other angels along with him, as the text later recounts (Rev 12:9). All these symbols, then, are designed to convey the enormous power of Satan. "The devil is described as a serpent", St Cyprian writes, "because he moves silently and seems peaceable and comes by easy ways and is so astute and so deceptive [...] that he tries to have night taken for day, poison taken for medicine. So, by deceptions of this kind, he tries to destroy truth by cunning. That is why he passes himself off as an angel of light" (*De unitate Ecclesiae*, 1–3).

After the fall of our first parents war broke out between the serpent and his

Revelation 12:5

down a third of the stars of heaven, and cast them to the earth. And the dragon stood before the woman who was about to bear a child, that he might devour her child when she brought it forth; ⁵she brought forth a male child, one who is to rule all the nations with a rod of iron, but her child was caught up to God and to his throne, ⁶and the woman fled into the wilderness, where she has a place prepared by God, in which to be nourished for one thousand two hundred and sixty days. ⁷Now war arose in heaven, Michael and his angels fighting against the dragon; and the dragon and his angels fought, ⁸but they

Is 66:7
Ps 2:9
Rev 2:27
Hos 2:16
Dan 10:31, 21; 12:1
Jn 12:31

---

seed and the woman and hers: "I will put enmity between you and the woman, between your seed and her seed; he shall bruise your head, and you shall bruise his heel" (Gen 3:15). Jesus Christ is the woman's descendant who will obtain victory over the devil (cf. Mk 1:23–26; Lk 4:31–37; etc.). That is why the power of evil concentrates all his energy on destroying Christ (cf. Mt 2:13–18) or deflecting him from his mission (cf. Mt 4: 1–11 and par.). By relating this enmity to the beginnings of the human race St John paints a very vivid picture.

12:5. The birth of Jesus Christ brings into operation the divine plan announced by the prophets (cf. Is 66:7) and by the Psalms (cf. Ps 2:9), and marks the first step in ultimate victory over the devil. Jesus' life on earth, culminating in his passion, resurrection and ascension into heaven, was the key factor in achieving this victory. St John emphasises the triumph of Christ as victor, who, as the Church confesses, "sits at the right hand of the Father" (*Nicene-Constantinopolitan Creed*).

12:6. The figure of the woman reminds us of the Church, the people of God. Israel took refuge in the wilderness to escape from Pharaoh, and the Church does the same after the victory of Christ. The wilderness stands for solitude and intimate union with God. In the wilderness God took personal care of his people, setting them free from their enemies (cf. Ex 17:8–16) and nourishing them with quail and manna (cf. Ex 16:1–36). The Church is given similar protection against the powers of hell (cf. Mt 16:18) and Christ nourishes it with his body and his word all the while it makes its pilgrimage through the ages; it has a hard time (like Israel in the wilderness) but there will be an end to it: it will take 1,260 days (cf. notes on 113).

Although the woman, in this verse, seems to refer directly to the Church, she also in some way stands for the particular woman who gave birth to the Messiah, the Blessed Virgin. As no other creature has done, Mary has enjoyed a very unique type of union with God and very special protection from the powers of evil, death included. Thus, as the Second Vatican Council teaches, "in the meantime [while the Church makes its pilgrim way on earth], the Mother of Jesus in the glory which she possesses in body and soul in heaven is the image and beginning of the Church as it is to be perfected in the world to come. Likewise she shines forth on earth, until the day of the Lord shall come (cf. 2 Pet 3:10), a sign of certain hope and comfort to the pilgrim people of God" (*Lumen gentium*, 68).

12:7–9. The war between the dragon with his angels, and Michael and his, and the defeat of the former, are depicted as

were defeated and there was no longer any place for them in heaven. ⁹And the great dragon was thrown down, that ancient serpent, who is called the Devil and Satan, the deceiver of the whole world—he was thrown down to the earth, and his angels were thrown down with him. ¹⁰And I heard a loud voice in heaven, saying, "Now the salvation and the power and the kingdom

Lk 10:18
Gen 3:1, 14
Rev 20:2
Job 1:11
Lk 22:31
Mt 28:18
Rev 11:15

---

being closely connected with the death and glorification of Christ (cf. vv. 5, 11). The reference to Michael and the "ancient" serpent, and also the result of the battle (being cast down from heaven), reminds us of the origin of the devil. Once a most exalted creature, according to certain Jewish traditions (cf. *Latin Life of Adam and Eve*, 12–16) he became a devil because when God created man in his own image and likeness (cf. Gen 1:26; 2:7), he refused to acknowledge the dignity granted to man: Michael obeyed, but the devil and some other angels rebelled against God because they regarded man as beneath them. As a result the devil and his angelic followers were cast down to earth to be imprisoned in hell, which is why they ceaselessly tempt man, trying to make him sin so as to deprive him of the glory of God.

In the light of this tradition, the book of Revelation emphasizes that Christ, the new Adam, true God and true man, through his glorification merits and receives the worship that is his due— which spells the total rout of the devil. God's design embraces both creation and redemption. Christ, "the image of the invisible God, the first-born of all creation; for in him all things were created" (Col 1:15–16), defeats the devil in a war which extends throughout human history; but the key stage in that war was the incarnation, death and glorification of our Lord: "Now is the judgment of this world," Jesus says, referring to those events; "now shall the ruler of this world be cast out; and I, when I am lifted up from earth, will draw all men to myself" (Jn 12:31–33). And, when his disciples come to him to tell him that demons were subject to his name, he exclaimed, "I saw Satan fall like lightning from heaven" (Lk 10:18).

In Daniel 10:13 and 12:1 we are told that it is the archangel Michael who defends the chosen people on God's behalf. His name means "Who like God?" and his mission is to guard the rights of God against those who would usurp them, be they human tyrants or Satan himself, who tried to make off with the body of Moses according to the Letter of St Jude (v. 9). This explains why St Michael appears in the Apocalypse as the one who confronts Satan, the ancient serpent, although the victory and punishment is decided by God or Christ. The Church, therefore, invokes St Michael as its guardian in adversity and its protector against the snares of the devil (cf. *Divine Office*, 29 September, office of readings).

The Fathers of the Church interpret these verses of the Apocalypse as a reference to the battle between Michael and the devil at the dawn of history, a battle which stemmed from the test which angelic spirits had to undergo. And, in the light of the Apocalypse, they interpret as referring to that climactic moment the words which the prophet Isaiah uttered against the king of Babylon: "How you are fallen from heaven, O Day Star, son of Dawn! How you are cut down to the ground, you who laid the nations low!"

of our God and the authority of his Christ have come, for the accuser of our brethren has been thrown down, who accuses them day and night before our God. ¹¹And they have conquered him by the blood of the Lamb and by the word of their testimony, for they loved not their lives even unto death. ¹²Rejoice then, O heaven and you that dwell therein! But woe to you, O earth and sea, for the devil has come down to you in great wrath, because he knows that his time is short!"

Rev 7:14
Jn 12:25

Is 44:23

(Is 14:12). They also see this passage of the Apocalypse as referring to the war Satan wages against the Church throughout history, a war which will take on its most dreadful form at the end of time: "Heaven is the Church," St Gregory writes, "which in the night of this present life, the while it possesses in itself the countless virtues of the saints, shines like the radiant heavenly stars; but the dragon's tail sweeps the stars down to the earth [...]. The stars which fall from heaven are those who have lost hope in heavenly things and covet, under the devil's guidance, the sphere of earthly glory" (*Moralia*, 32, 13).

12:10–12. With the ascension of Christ into heaven the Kingdom of God is established and so all those who dwell in heaven break out into a song of joy. The devil has been deprived of his power over man in the sense that the redemptive action of Christ and man's faith enable man to escape from the world of sin. The text expresses this joyful truth by saying that there is now no place for the accuser, Satan, whose name means and whom the Old Testament teaches to be the accuser of men before God (cf. Job 1:6–12; 2:1–10). Given what God meant creation to be, Satan could claim as his victory anyone who, through sinning, disfigured the image and likeness of God that was in him. However, once the Redemption has taken place, Satan no longer has power to do this, for, as St John writes, "if any one does sin, we have an advocate with the Father, Jesus Christ the righteous; and he is the expiation for our sins, and not for ours only but also for the sins of the whole world" (Jn 2:1–2). Also, on ascending into heaven, Christ sent us the Holy Spirit as "Intercessor and Advocate, especially when men, that is, mankind, find themselves before the judgment of condemnation by that 'accuser' about whom the Book of Revelation says that 'he accuses them day and night before our God'" (John Paul II, *Dominum et Vivificantem*, 67).

Although Satan has lost this power to act in the world, he still has time left, between the resurrection of our Lord and the end of history, to put obstacles in man's way and frustrate Christ's action. And so he works ever more frenetically, as he sees time run out, in his effort to distance everyone and society itself from the plans and commandments of God.

The author of the book of Revelation uses this celestial chant to warn the Church of the onset of danger as the End approaches.

12:13–17. In these verses the dragon's onslaught is seen in terms of the Church which suffers it. The woman who gives birth to a male child is an image of the Mother of the Messiah, the Blessed Virgin, and of the Church, who "faithfully fulfilling the Father's will, by

¹³And when the dragon saw that he had been thrown down to the earth, he pursued the woman who had borne the male child. ¹⁴But the woman was given the two wings of the great eagle that she might fly from the serpent into the wilderness, to the place where she is to be nourished for a time, and times, and half a time.* ¹⁵The serpent poured water like a river out of his mouth after the woman, to sweep her away with the flood. ¹⁶But the earth came to the help of the woman, and the earth opened its mouth and swallowed the river which the dragon had poured from his mouth. ¹⁷Then the dragon was angry with the woman,* and went

Gen 3:15

Ex 19:4
Dan 7:25
Is 40:31

Num 16:32

Gen 3:15
1 Jn 5:10

---

receiving the word of God in faith becomes herself a mother" (*Lumen gentium*, 64). By means of the Church men become members of Christ and contribute to the growth of his body (cf. note on Eph 4:13). It is in this sense that we can speak of the Church as the woman who gives birth to Christ.

The struggle the Church maintains against the powers of evil is described here in terms of the Exodus (another time of great peril for the people of Israel). God brought the Israelites into the wilderness "on eagle's wings" (Ex 19:4), that is, by ways no man could devise. When the prophet Isaiah announces the liberation from captivity in Babylon he also says that "they shall mount up with wings like eagles" (Is 40:31). Throughout the course of history, the Church enjoys this same divine protection which enables her to have that intimacy with God symbolized by the wilderness. The period of "a time, and times and half a time", that is, three and a half years, is regarded as the conventional duration of any persecution, at least from Daniel 7:25 onwards.

The river of water symbolizes the destructive forces of evil unleashed by the devil. Just as in the wilderness of Sinai the earth swallowed up those who rebelled against God (cf. Num 16:30–34), so will these forces be frustrated in their attack on the Church, for, as our Lord promised, "the powers of death [hell] shall not prevail against it" (Mt 16:18). "This is nothing new," St Josemaría Escrivá comments. "Since Jesus Christ our Lord founded the Church, this Mother of ours has suffered constant persecution. In times past the attacks were delivered openly. Now, in many cases, persecution is disguised. But today, as yesterday, the Church continues to be buffeted from many sides" (*In Love with the Church*, 18).

The Church is holy, but those who make it up—Christians, "the rest of her offspring"—suffer the onslaught of the Evil One, who is unrelenting in his efforts to seduce them. That is why "the Christian is certainly bound both by need and by duty to struggle with evil through many afflictions and to suffer death; but, as one who has been made a partner in the paschal mystery, and as one who has been configured to the death of Christ he will go forward, strengthened by hope, to the resurrection" (Vatican II, *Gaudium et spes*, 22).

12:18. Most Greek manuscripts, but not the most important ones, give this verse in the first person singular: "And I stood" (cf. RSV note below), referring to the seer. The New Vulgate, however, prefers the third person, in which case the phrase

Revelation 13:1

off to make war on the rest of her offspring, on those who keep the commandments of God and bear testimony to Jesus. And he stood[e] on the sand of the sea.

The beasts given authority by the dragon

Rev 11:7; 17:3, 9, 12; Dan 7:3, 7
Dan 7:4–6

13 ¹And I saw a beast* rising out of the sea, with ten horns and seven heads, with ten diadems upon its horns and a blasphemous name upon its heads. ²And the beast that I saw was like a leopard, its feet were like a bear's, and its mouth was like a lion's mouth. And to it the dragon gave his power and his throne and great authority. ³One of its heads seemed to have a mortal wound, but its mortal wound was healed, and the whole earth followed the beast with wonder. ⁴Men worshipped the dragon, for

Rev 17:8
Rev 12:7
2 Thess 2:4

---

refers to the dragon, who is thus depicted as causing the powers of evil (in the form of the beasts: 13:1) to emerge.

13:1–18. Satan, the ancient serpent, launches his attack via the beasts, whom he endows with his power (cf. vv. 2, 12). The beasts stand for those who in the course of history have embodied the powers of evil in one way or another. The first beast (vv. 1–10) symbolizes political power taken to such an extreme that it supplants God; the second (vv. 11–12), those forces of evil who defend, justify and propagate that deification of power by giving it an acceptable face. These beasts are, first, a reference to the Roman empire, but that empire is seen in turn as being the tool of a diabolical power which forever hovers over mankind and will become more virulent as the End approaches.

In his war against the woman's children, the devil in addition to himself attacking them one by one also avails of socio-political and cultural factors which usurp the position of the one true God: "Unfortunately, the resistance to the Holy Spirit which St Paul emphasizes in the *interior and subjective dimension* as tension, struggle and rebellion taking place in the human heart finds in every period and especially in the modern era its *external dimension*, which takes concrete form as the content of culture and civilization, as *a philosophical system, an ideology, a programme* for action and for the shaping of human behaviour. It reaches its clearest expression in materialism, both in its theoretical form—as a system of thought—and in its practical form—as a method of interpreting and evaluating facts, and likewise as a programme of corresponding conduct. The system which has developed most and carried to its extreme practical consequences this form of thought, ideology and praxis is dialectical and historical materialism, which is still recognized as the essential core of Marxism" (John Paul II, *Dominum et Vivificantem*, 56).

13:1–4. In his description of the first beast St John employs symbols used by the prophet Daniel to describe the various empires which overran Israel, particularly the successors of Alexander the Great (notably Antiochus Epiphanes); they are

---

e. Other ancient authorities read *And I stood*, connecting the sentence with 13:1

he had given his authority to the beast, and they worshipped the beast, saying, "Who is like the beast, and who can fight against it?" ⁵And the beast was given a mouth uttering haughty and blasphemous words, and it was allowed to exercise authority for forty-two months; ⁶it opened its mouth to utter blasphemies against God, blaspheming his name and his dwelling, that is, those who dwell in heaven. ⁷Also it was allowed to make war on the saints and to conquer them.ᶠ And authority was given it over every tribe and

Dan 7:8, 11, 25
Rev 11:2

Rev 11:7
Dan 7:21

---

symbolized in the fourth beast of the prophet's vision (cf. Dan 7:7–8). In Jewish and Christian circles at the time when the Apocalypse was written, the fourth beast in the book of Daniel was already being reinterpreted as the Roman empire; and the author of the book of Revelation himself does this more explicitly when he says later that the seven heads and ten horns are so many other emperors and kings (cf. Rev 17:9–12).

The wound on one of the heads may be a reference to some particular political crisis, like the assassination of Julius Caesar or the disturbances which followed the death of Nero and in the event came to nothing. The majority of the Fathers see the beast as representing antichrist; St Irenaeus, for example, writes: "The beast that rises up is the epitome of evil and falsehood, so that the full force of apostasy which it embodies can be cast into the fiery furnace" (*Against Heresies*, 5, 29).

In any event, the sacred text is denouncing the sin of idolizing political authority, as if it had divine attributes. The exclamation "Who is like the beast?" is a kind of rejoinder to the meaning of the archangel Michael's name, "Who like God?" It makes sense, then, that the description of the head of the beast is the same as that of the serpent (cf. 12:3), showing they are undoubtedly connected with one another. "Idolatry is an extreme form of disorder produced by sin. The replacement of adoration of the living God by worship of created things falsifies the relationships between individuals and brings with it various kinds of oppression" (SCDF, *Libertatis conscientia*, 39).

13:5–8. The beast's blasphemous language and acts of violence show that his power derives from Satan. He is active throughout the course of history—forty-two months or three and a half years—and is present the world over. Only those who by the grace of God acknowledge and follow Christ can avoid worshipping the beast, that is, can resist political absolutism which has no place for God or his law.

Christian faith is the great guarantor of true freedom: "The reality of the depth of freedom has always been known to the Church, above all through the lives of a multitude of the faithful, especially among the little ones and the poor. In their faith, these latter know that they are the object of God's infinite love. Each of them can say: 'I live by faith in the Son of God, who loved me and gave himself for me' (Gal 2:20b). Such is the dignity which none of the powerful can take away from them: such is the liberating joy present in them" (SCDF, *Libertatis conscientia*, 21). And so it is that the Church, in the socio-political context, is "the sign and the safeguard of the transcendental dimension of the human person" (Vatican II, *Gaudium et spes*, 76).

---

f. Other ancient authorities omit this sentence

Revelation 13:8

<small>Ps 69:29
Is 53:7
Rev 3:5

Mt 13:9

Jer 15:2
Mt 26:52
Rev 14:12</small>

people and tongue and nation, ⁸and all who dwell on earth will worship it, every one whose name has not been written before the foundation of the world in the book of life of the Lamb that was slain. ⁹If any one has an ear, let him hear:
  ¹⁰ If any one is to be taken captive,
    to captivity he goes;
  if any one slays with the sword,
    with the sword must he be slain.
Here is a call for the endurance and faith of the saints.

The beast rising from out of the earth

<small>Mt 7:15
Rev 16:13
Rev 13:3

Mt 24:24
2 Thess 2:9–10</small>

¹¹Then I saw another beast* which rose out of the earth; it had two horns like a lamb and it spoke like a dragon. ¹²It exercises all the authority of the first beast in its presence, and makes the earth and its inhabitants worship the first beast, whose mortal wound was healed. ¹³It works great signs, even making fire come down from

---

13:9–10. Here, in an aside, St John addresses the reader directly, inviting him to recognize the contemporary truth of what he is revealing at God's command. The people to whom the book was originally addressed could see for themselves what happened when Satan's power was unleashed against the Church (it was the time of Domitian's persecution: AD 95–96). However, his invitation is addressed to everyone who reads the book, irrespective of what period of history they live in. We well know that "our age has seen the birth of totalitarian systems and forms of tyranny which would not have been possible in the time before the technological leap forward. On the one hand, technical expertise has been applied to acts of genocide. On the other, various minorities try to hold in thrall whole nations by the practice of terrorism. Today control can penetrate into the innermost life of individuals, and even the forms of dependence created by early-warning systems can represent potential threats of oppression" (SCDF, *Libertatis conscientia*, 14).

The book of Revelation, using the words which Jeremiah addressed to evil-doers (cf. Jer 15:2; 43:11), applies them to the last times. St John thereby exhorts Christians to stiffen their resistance despite what persecution brings—to call on their resources of faith. "Suffering", says John Paul II commenting on Romans 5:3, "as it were contains a special *call to the virtue* which man must exercise on his own part. And this is the virtue of perseverance in bearing whatever disturbs and causes harm. In doing this, the individual unleashes hope, which maintains in him the conviction that suffering will not get the better of him, that it will not deprive him of his dignity as a human being" (*Salvifici doloris*, 23).

13:11–17. Further on (cf. 16:13; 19:20 and notes), this second beast is identified with the false prophet because his role consists in leading men astray, getting them to worship the first beast. Because he has real (but evil) power he is able to work wonders similar to those performed by the prophets (for example, Elijah, who brought fire down from heaven: cf. 1 Kings 18:38) and can even seem to vie with the power of the life-giving Spirit by

heaven to earth in the sight of men; ¹⁴and by the signs which it is allowed to work in the presence of the beast, it deceives those who dwell on earth, bidding them make an image for the beast which was wounded by the sword and yet lived; ¹⁵and it was allowed to give breath to the image of the beast so that the image of the beast should even speak, and to cause those who would not worship the image of the beast to be slain. ¹⁶Also it causes all, both small and great, both rich and poor, both free and slave, to be marked on the right hand or the forehead, ¹⁷so that no one can buy or sell unless he has the mark, that is, the name of the beast or the number of its name. ¹⁸This calls for wisdom: let him who has understanding reckon the number of the beast, for it is a human number, its number is six hundred and sixty-six.ᵍ*

Deut 13:2–4
Rev 19:20

Dan 3:5f

Rev 16:2; 14:9, 11; 19:20; 20:4

Rev 17:9

---

breathing life into the images of the beast. He is despotic in the extreme, depriving people of subsistence unless they submit to him and bear his mark. "The beast that rises from the earth stands for pride in earthly glory; and the fact that it has two horns like a lamb means that its hypocritical sanctity makes it appear to have wisdom, whereas only the Lord has true wisdom" (St Gregory the Great, *Moralia*, 33, 20).

We do not know if the author is referring to a specific individual (such as the Asiarch who was charged with the fostering of emperor worship in Asia Minor) or a group (such as the pagan priests who exercised and propagated that cult). There is little doubt but that this beast is introduced in order to draw attention to the political-religious implications of emperor worship and its consequences for Christians. Basically the beast is a symbol for regimes which reject God and put man on a pedestal. Nowadays emperor worship is seldom a problem but militant atheism has been a modern parallel whether in the form of atheistic secularism or of dialectic materialism. St Hippolytus describes the mark and seal of the beast in these words: "I reject the Creator of heaven and earth; I reject Baptism; I refuse to worship God. To you [Beast] I adhere; in you I believe" (*De consummat.*).

Materialism works in the same deceptive way as the beast does, for although "it sometimes also speaks of the 'spirit' and of 'questions of the spirit', as for example in the fields of culture or morality, it does so only insofar as it considers certain facts as derived from matter (*epiphenomena*), since according to this system matter is the one and only form of being. It follows, according to this interpretation, that religion can only be understood as a kind of 'idealistic illusion', to be fought with the most suitable means and methods according to circumstances of time and place, in order to eliminate it from society and from man's very heart" (John Paul II, *Dominum et Vivificantem*, 56).

13:18. The author of the Apocalypse here uses a method (called *gematria* in Greek) to reveal the name of the beast in a numerical form. In both Hebrew and Latin letters of the alphabet were also used as numbers. The figure 666 fits with the name Caesar Nero in Hebrew. Some

---

g. Other ancient authorities read *six hundred and sixteen*

Revelation 14:1

The Lamb and his entourage

^{Ezek 9:4; Joel 3:5; Rev 7:4–5}
^{Ezek 1:24; 43:2; Rev 1:15}
^{Ps 33:3; 40:4; 98:1; 144–9; 149:1}

14 ¹Then I looked, and lo, on Mount Zion stood the Lamb, and with him a hundred and forty-four thousand who had his name and his Father's name written on their foreheads. ²And I heard a voice from heaven like the sound of many waters and like the sound of loud thunder; the voice I heard was like the sound of harpers playing on their harps, ³and they sing a new song before the throne and before the four living creatures and before the

---

manuscripts gave the number as 616, which fits Caesar Nero in Greek. However, Tradition does not provide an exact interpretation and various other names have in fact been suggested.

14:1–16:21. The book now turns to the Lamb and to divine judgment (anticipating the victory of the Lamb). It stays with this theme up to chapter 17, at which point the powers of evil appear again (in various symbolic forms) and are subjected to the judgment of God. First we are shown the Lamb and his entourage (cf. 14:1–5); immediately after this the Last Judgment is proclaimed and a preliminary description given (14:6–20); the glory of the Lamb is again extolled (cf. 15:1–4) and the unleashing of the wrath of God is further described in terms of the pouring out of the seven bowls (cf. 15:5—16:21).

In opposition to the powers of evil and the active hostility to God and the Church caused by the machinations of Satan stand the risen Christ and his followers, who sing in praise of his glory and triumph. These followers are those who have attained redemption; the salvation will reach its climax when the Kingdom of God is fully established (the marriage of the Lamb, and the heavenly Jerusalem: chaps. 21–22). In the meantime, although the Church has to do battle with the forces of evil, it can contemplate Christ "as an innocent lamb (who) merited life for us by his blood

which he freely shed. In him God reconciled us to himself and to one another, freeing us from the bondage of the devil and of sin, so that each one of us could say with the Apostle: the Son of God 'loved me and gave himself for me' (Gal 2:20)" (Vatican II, *Gaudium et spes*, 22).

14:1–3. It is highly significant that the Lamb stands on Mount Zion, in Jerusalem, which was where God dwelt among men according to the Old Testament (cf. Ps 74:1; 132:14; etc.) and where, according to certain Jewish traditions, the Messiah would appear, to join all his followers. The assembly, then, is an idealization of the Church, protected by Christ and gathered about him. It includes all those who belong to Christ and to the Father and who therefore bear their mark, which shows them to be children of God. They are so many that it is impossible to count them, but their number is complete: they are given a symbolic number which is 12 (the tribes of Israel) by 12 (the Apostles) by 1,000 (a number indicating a huge scale): cf. Rev 7:3ff.

The 144,000 are not yet in heaven (for the loud noise comes from heaven); they are on earth, but they have been rescued from the power of the beast (cf. 13:13–14). The voice from heaven symbolizes the strength and power of God; and the heavenly voice speaks with the gentleness of liturgical music. It is a new song, for it now sings of the salvation

Revelation 14:6

elders. No one could learn that song except the hundred and forty-four thousand who had been redeemed from the earth. ⁴It is these who have not defiled themselves with women, for they are chaste;ʰ* it is these who follow the Lamb wherever he goes; these have been redeemed from mankind as first fruits for God and the Lamb, ⁵and in their mouth no lie was found, for they are spotless.

Is 42:10
Rev 5:9
Jas 1:18
1 Cor 7:24
Rev 5:9
Ps 32:2
Is 53:9
Zeph 3:13

Proclamation and symbols of the Judgment
⁶Then I saw another angel flying in midheaven, with an eternal gospel to proclaim to those who dwell on earth, to every nation

Rev 8:13

---

wrought by Christ (cf. 15:3–4) in the same style as the Old Testament chants the praises of God (cf., e.g., Ps 33:3; 40:2; 96:1). Only those who belong to Christ can join in this song and be associated with the heavenly liturgy: "It is especially in the sacred liturgy that our union with the heavenly Church is best realized; in the liturgy, through the sacramental signs, the power of the Holy Spirit acts on us, and with community rejoicing we celebrate together the praise of the divine majesty; when all those of every tribe and tongue and people and nation (cf. Rev 5:9) who have been redeemed by the blood of Christ and gathered together into one Church glorify, in one common song of praise, the one and triune God" (*Lumen gentium*, 50).

14:4–5. The text refers to those who are properly disposed to take part in the marriage supper of the Lamb (cf. 19:9; 21:2) because they have not been stained by idolatry but have kept themselves undefiled for him. St Paul compares every Christian to a chaste virgin (cf. 2 Cor 11:2) and describes the Church as the spouse of Christ (cf. Eph 5:21–32). The author of the Apocalypse is referring to all the members of the Church insofar as they are holy, that is, called to holiness; but the symbolism he uses also draws attention to the fact that virginity and celibacy for the sake of the Kingdom of heaven is a special expression and clear sign of the Church as Bride of Christ. Referring to the chastity practised by religious, the Second Vatican Council teaches that in this way they "recall that wonderful marriage made by God, which will be fully manifested in the future age, and in which the Church has Christ for her only spouse" (*Perfectae caritatis* 12).

The 144,000 are also those who have identified themselves fully with Christ, dead and risen, by denying themselves and devoting all their energies to apostolate (cf. Mt 10:38). They also stand for those whom Christ, by the shedding of his blood, has made his own and his Father's property (like Israel, the first fruits of Yahweh: cf. Jer 2:3), that is, those who constitute a holy people like that remnant of Israel described in Zephaniah 3:13: "they shall do no wrong and utter no lies, nor shall there be found in their mouth a deceitful tongue." The prophet's words refer to people who have not invoked false gods, but the Apocalypse applies them to those who are fully committed to Christ.

14:6–20. Christ comes in victory at the end of time (the Parousia) to judge all mankind. In this passage, which is a

---

h. Greek *virgins*

Revelation 14:7

Ex 20:11
Mt 10:28

and tribe and tongue and people; ⁷and he said with a loud voice, "Fear God and give him glory, for the hour of his judgment has come; and worship him who made heaven and earth, the sea and the fountains of water."

Dan 4:27; Jer 51:7, 8; Is 21:9
Rev 18:2–3

⁸Another angel, a second, followed, saying, "Fallen, fallen is Babylon* the great, she who made all nations drink the wine of her impure passion."

Rev 13:15–17

⁹And another angel, a third, followed them, saying with a loud voice, "If any one worships the beast and its image, and receives a mark on his forehead or on his hand, ¹⁰he also shall drink the wine of God's wrath, poured unmixed into the cup of his anger, and he shall

Is 51:17; Ps 75:9; Gen 19:24
Ezek 38:22; Jer

---

general call to conversion, that judgment is solemnly announced in a scenario in which seven personages appear—three angels who proclaim the judgment (cf. vv. 6, 8, 9), the Son of man who delivers it (v. 14), and three more angels charged with implementing it (vv. 15, 17, 19): God's decision is final and it affects all mankind.

The Church warns us that "since we know neither the day nor the hour, we should follow the advice of the Lord and watch constantly so that, when the single course of our earthly life is completed (cf. Heb 9:27), we may merit to enter with him into the marriage feast and be numbered among the blessed (cf. Mt 25:31–46) [...]. Before we reign with Christ in glory we must all appear 'before the judgment seat of Christ, so that each one may receive good or evil, according to what he has done in the body' (2 Cor 5:10), and at the end of the world 'they will come forth, those who have done good, to the resurrection of life, and those who have done evil, to the resurrection of judgment' (Jn 5:29; cf. Mt 25:46)" (*Lumen gentium*, 48).

14:6–7. "Another angel": this tells us that this angel is not one of those who blew the trumpets (cf. 11:15), and yet is one of the same series of divine messengers that will be sent at the last times. He delivers his message from "midheaven" so that it can be heard by all who dwell on earth. It is a call to acknowledge and worship God as Creator of all things; this presupposes, therefore, that man can "know and love his creator" (*Gaudium et spes*, 12). And the proclamation is described as "an eternal Gospel" because man's acknowledgment of God will be ratified and rewarded on the Day of Judgment and will therefore be valid for ever (cf. Acts 14:15ff; 1 Thess 1:9).

14:8. Viewed from the perspective of the end of time, the downfall of the Church's enemy is seen as an accomplished fact. Absolutist and pagan Rome insisted on everyone worshipping the emperor; those who conformed earned God's anger. Rome is called "Babylon the great" because ever since the deportation of the Jews to that ancient city in 587 BC it had symbolized pagan power hostile to the people of God.

14:9–11. This passage predicts and describes the punishment to be inflicted on those who worship the beast, that is, those who submit to false gods. The "fire and brimstone", deriving from Genesis 19:24, indicates the horrific nature of the punishment: it will be like that suffered

be tormented with fire and sulphur in the presence of the holy angels and in the presence of the Lamb. ¹¹And the smoke of their torment goes up for ever and ever; and they have no rest, day or night, these worshippers of the beast and its image, and whoever receives the mark of its name." 25:15; Rev 16:19; 19:20
Is 34:9–10
Rev 19:3; 13:16

¹²Here is a call for the endurance of the saints, those who keep the commandments of God and the faith of Jesus. Rev 12:17

¹³And I heard a voice from heaven saying, "Write this: Blessed are the dead who die in the Lord henceforth." "Blessed indeed," says the Spirit, "that they may rest from their labours, for their deeds follow them!" Is 57:2
Heb 4:10
Mt 11:28–29

---

by Sodom and Gomorrah but it will be everlasting and will take place in the presence of the Lamb and his angels.

Eternal punishment of the damned and eternal reward of the elect is a dogma of faith, solemnly defined by the Magisterium in the Fourth Lateran Council: "[Christ] will come at the end of the world; he will judge the living and the dead; and he will reward all, both the damned and the elect, according to their works. And all these will rise from their own bodies which they now have so that they may receive according to their works, whether good or bad; the wicked, a perpetual punishment with the devil; the good, eternal glory with Christ" (*De fide catholica*, chap. 1).

The punishment suffered in hell will be both spiritual (permanent unhappiness) and physical (pain), because man is made up of spirit and matter. We do not know what form hell takes; however, from what the book of Revelation says here and from other passages of Holy Scripture (cf., e.g., Mt 25:41) we can deduce that it involves both pain of loss (of God and eternal happiness) and physical suffering.

14:12. As in Revelation 13:10, the faithful are exhorted to stand firm in the midst of tribulation, confident in the hope that God will reward each according to his merits. Patience of that type does not mean that one should retreat before the powers of evil or fail to try to secure and guarantee "the conditions needed for the exercise of an authentic Christian freedom" (SCDF, *Libertatis conscientia*, 31). In this connexion the Second Vatican Council teaches: "Far from diminishing our concern to develop this earth, the expectancy of a new earth should spur us on, for it is here that the body of a new human family grows, foreshadowing in some way the age which is to come" (*Gaudium et spes*, 39).

In this passage of the book Christians are told that, in their efforts to deal with the particular persecution which was going on at the time, they should never answer with violence. This teaching always applies where the kind of liberation one is claiming is a temporal one: "Christ has commanded us to love our enemies (cf. Mt 5:44; Lk 6:27–28, 35). Liberation in the spirit of the Gospel is therefore incompatible with hatred of others, taken individually or collectively, and this includes hatred of one's enemy" (SCDF, *Libertatis conscientia*, 77).

14:13. God's blessing proclaims the joy of those who stay true to Christ to death. Jewish rabbis taught that "when a man

Revelation 14:14

The harvest and the vintage

Dan 7:13; 10:16
Mt 13:39, 41

Joel 4:13
Mk 4:29
Jn 4:35

¹⁴Then I looked, and lo, a white cloud, and seated on the cloud one like a son of man, with a golden crown on his head, and a sharp sickle in his hand. ¹⁵And another angel came out of the temple, calling with a loud voice to him who sat upon the cloud, "Put in your sickle, and reap, for the hour to reap has come, for the harvest of the earth is fully ripe." ¹⁶So he who sat upon the cloud swung his sickle on the earth, and the earth was reaped.

¹⁷And another angel came out of the temple in heaven, and he too had a sharp sickle. ¹⁸Then another angel came out from the altar, the angel who has power over fire, and he called with a loud voice to

Rev 6:9; 8:3–5
Joel 4:13

---

dies, neither silver nor gold, neither precious stones nor pearls, follow him, but rather the law and good works" (*Pirqe Abhoth*, 6, 9). It is not simply that the righteous are rewarded for their works but that these works (in some way) stay with them; as the Church teaches, "when we have spread on earth the fruits of our nature and our enterprise—human dignity, brotherly communion, and freedom—according to the command of the Lord and in his Spirit, we will find them once again, cleansed this time from the stain of sin, illuminated and transfigured, when Christ presents to his Father an eternal and universal kingdom of truth and life, a kingdom of holiness and grace, a kingdom of justice, love and peace" (*Gaudium et spes*, 39).

Death, understood in this way, is not the end but rather a transition, a step; St Bernard compares it to Easter: "The unfortunate unbelievers call it death—this step into life—but how can believers call it anything other than Easter? For one dies to the world in order to live completely for God. One enters the precinct of the marvellous tabernacle, the house of God" (*Divini amoris*, chap. 15).

14:14–20. This preliminary description of the Last Judgment is given in two scenes—the harvest (cf. 14:14–16) and the vintage (cf. 14:17–20)—no doubt following the prophecy of Joel about how God will judge nations hostile to Israel: "Let the nations bestir themselves, and come up to the valley of Jehoshaphat; for there I shall sit to judge all the nations round about. Put in the sickle, for the harvest is ripe. Go in, tread, for the wine press is full" (Joel 3:12–13).

In the first scene Christ himself appears, described as "son of man" (cf. Dan 7:13); it is he who will deliver the judgment (symbolized by the harvest), as in the parable of the wheat and the weeds (cf. Mt 13:24–30). In the second it is an angel sent by God who gathers the grapes and puts them in the press to be trodden on either by God (in keeping with the prophecy of Isaiah 63:3, which says, "I have trodden the wine press alone") or by Christ (as we are told later in Revelation 19:15). In either case we are being told that Jesus Christ, true God and true man, has been empowered to perform the General Judgment which, according to Jewish tradition, will take place at the gates of Jerusalem (cf., e.g., Zech 14:4) and which involves a huge bloodbath (cf. Rev 14:20).

In both scenes, an angel has the prominent role of giving the order (cf. vv. 15, 18). The fact that he comes out from the temple and the altar shows that the

him who had the sharp sickle, "Put in your sickle, and gather the clusters of the vine of the earth, for its grapes are ripe." ¹⁹So the angel swung his sickle on the earth and gathered the vintage of the earth, and threw it into the great wine press of the wrath of God; ²⁰and the wine press was trodden outside the city, and blood flowed from the wine press, as high as a horse's bridle, for one thousand six hundred stadia.ⁱ

Rev 19:15

Is 63:3

The hymn of the saved

15 ¹Then I saw another portent in heaven, great and wonderful, seven angels with seven plagues, which are the last, for with them the wrath of God is ended.

²And I saw what appeared to be a sea of glass mingled with fire, and those who had conquered the beast and its image and the number of its name, standing beside the sea of glass with harps of God in their hands. ³And they sing the song of Moses,* the servant of God, and the song of the Lamb, saying,

Lev 26:21
Rev 16:17

Rev 13:15, 18

Deut 32:4;
Ex 15:1, 11;
Ps 92:6; 111:2;
145:17;
Rev 14:3

---

outcome is linked to the prayers of the saints and martyrs, which stir Christ to take action (cf. Rev 8:3–4). So it is that the moment Christ is made present on the altar through the consecration of the bread and wine the Church calls for him to come again—calls for his second coming, the Parousia, which will make his victory complete: "When we eat this bread and drink this cup, we proclaim your death, Lord Jesus, until you come in glory" (*Roman Missal*, eucharistic acclamation) .

15:1. The third portent (cf. the first two in 12:1, 3) is of special significance—it is "great and wonderful"—for it heralds the final outcome of the contention between the beasts and the followers of the Lamb, between the powers of evil and the Church of Jesus Christ. That this is the denouement is shown by the use of the figure seven for a third time, after the seven seals (5:1) and the seven trumpets (cf. Rev 8:2). This is the last word: "the wrath of God is ended."

As in the case of the two earlier groups of seven, the author first announces the sevenfold nature of the sign. It consists of seven plagues—which immediately recall the punishments God inflicted on Pharaoh in Egypt prior to the Exodus. Then follows a very liturgical type of scene (15:2–8) which as it were encourages and calls for the divine judgments which follow (cf. 16:1–17). The last of these plagues acts as an introduction to the account of the last battles and total victory of the church (cf. chaps. 17–22).

15:2–4. The image of the sea of glass mixed with fire is somewhat reminiscent of the passage of the Red Sea during the Exodus. On that occasion, according to the book of Wisdom (cf. Wis 19:6–22), natural elements were changed to enable the Israelites to walk on water: the water became as hard as glass for the Israelites whereas for the Egyptians it was unable to protect them from the fire sent to punish them. The sea of glass may also be evocative of the molten sea (used for

---

i. About two hundred miles

Revelation 15:4

"Great and wonderful are thy deeds,
O Lord God the Almighty!
Just and true are thy ways,
O King of the ages!^j
⁴Who shall not fear and glorify thy name, O Lord?
For thou alone art holy.
All nations shall come and worship thee,
for thy judgments have been revealed."

Jer 10:6, 7
Ps 86:9
Rev 14:17

The seven bowls of plagues

Ex 25:21
Lev 26:21
Rev 19:8

⁵After this I looked, and the temple of the tent of witness in heaven was opened, ⁶and out of the temple came the seven angels with the seven plagues, robed in pure bright linen, and their

---

the cleansing of those going to take part in temple rites) which was positioned in front of the Holy of Holies (cf. note on Rev 4:6–7). In any event, the author depicts the saved as giving thanks and praising God while entoning a hymn which fuses the salvation of the Israelites with the Redemption wrought by Christ. The latter is the full realization of the former, and God's plan is seen to embrace all men and all nations (cf. v. 4; Eph 3:4–7). For this reason some early Christian writers (Primasius, for example) interpret the sea of glass as a symbol of Baptism (prefigured in the Red Sea) which makes Christians pure and transparent. The reference to fire signifies the gift of the Holy Spirit (cf. *Commentariorum super Apoc.*, 15, 2).

Every saving action of God has ultimately a supernatural purpose, even though it may include noble human aims, for when "God rescues his people from hard economic, political and cultural slavery, he does so in order to make them, through the Covenant on Sinai, 'a kingdom of priests and a holy nation' (Ex 19:6). God wishes to be adored by people who are free. All the subsequent liberations of the people of Israel help to lead them to this full liberty that they can only find in communion with their God" (SCDF, *Libertatis conscientia*, 44).

15:5–8. The text now goes on to describe the divine intervention which is as it were a response to this hymn of praise; its language is very similar to that used in connexion with the blowing of the seventh trumpet (cf. 11:19). This helps to link up the two passages. The difference is that the tent of witness now takes the place of the Ark of the Covenant. Both tent and ark were supposed to remain hidden until the advent of the messianic times (cf. 2 Mac 2:4–8); once they were rediscovered, the glory of God would make itself manifest again, as happened when the temple of Solomon was dedicated. The cloud of smoke (a symbol of the glory of the Lord) meant that the priests were unable to perform their ministry (cf. 1 Kings 8:10–11).

The appearing of the tent signals that God's design is about to be fully realized. The author is telling us that the Parousia is imminent; he will describe it further on.

Because the seven golden bowls are used to cast the plagues on the earth, they are said to be full of the wrath of God: in

j. Other ancient authorities read *the nations*

breasts girded with golden girdles. ⁷And one of the four living creatures gave the seven angels seven golden bowls full of the wrath of God who lives for ever and ever; ⁸and the temple was filled with smoke from the glory of God and from his power, and no one could enter the temple until the seven plagues of the seven angels were ended.

16 ¹Then I heard a loud voice from the temple telling the seven angels, "Go and pour out on the earth the seven bowls of the wrath of God."

Rev 14:10
Ex 40:34
1 Kings 8:10
Is 6:4
Ez 44:4

Is 66:6
Ps 69:25
Jer 10:25
Rev 8:6–12

---

other words, they are filled with divine justice, as will now be made manifest to all. The bowls, then, symbolize both the prayers of the saints (which have caused God to intervene: cf. note on 5:8) and the effects of those prayers—the victory of good and the punishment of evil. Strictly speaking the *bowls* symbolize the prayers of the saints; their *content* is not the plagues as such but the outcome of prayer —action on God's part which serves to console the righteous (the perfume of incense) and punish the followers of the beast, those who work iniquity (the wrath of God).

16:1. The events which result from the pouring out of the seven bowls of the wrath of God are depicted in the same kind of system as used in connexion with the seven trumpet blasts. In both cases the imagery is inspired by the plagues of Egypt; the first four actions have to do with the elements of nature (cf. 16:2–9, paralleling 8:6–12), the fifth and sixth with historical forces (cf. 16:10–16 and 9:1–21), and the seventh with the final climax. The main difference lies in the fact that whereas previously only a third of everything was affected, here it is everything— signifying that divine intervention is on the increase right up to the End.

The fury of God's anger expresses itself in various evils which overtake mankind; God is not their direct cause; he allows them to occur, in the hope that men will turn back to him. These evils are the result of sin, and God's wrath expresses itself in fact by his allowing men to follow the desires of their idolatrous hearts (as St Paul explains in Romans 1:18–32). As history advances, the signs are that sin is on the increase; sin is the ultimate cause of the new plagues which can be seen in the world today. "It must be added", John Paul II writes, "that on the horizon of contemporary civilization—especially in the form that is most developed in the technical and scientific sense—the signs and symptoms of death have become particularly present and frequent. One has only to think of the arms race and of its inherent danger of nuclear self-destruction. Moreover, everyone has become more and more aware of the grave situation of vast areas of our planet, marked by death-dealing poverty and famine. It is a question of problems that are not only economic but also and above all ethical. But on the horizon of our era there are gathering ever darker 'signs of death': a custom has become widely established—in some places it threatens to become almost an institution—of taking the lives of human beings even before they are born, or before they reach the natural point of death" (*Dominum et Vivificantem*, 57).

Revelation 16:2

Ex 9:10–11
Deut 28:35
Rev 13:15–17

²So the first angel went and poured his bowl on the earth, and foul and evil sores came upon the men who bore the mark of the beast and worshipped its image.

Ex 7:19–24
Rev 8:8

³The second angel poured his bowl into the sea, and it became like the blood of a dead man, and every living thing died that was in the sea.

Rev 8:10
Ps 78:44

⁴The third angel poured his bowl into the rivers and the fountains of water, and they became blood. ⁵And I heard the angel of water say,

Ps 119:137;
145:17; Ex 3:14

"Just art thou in these thy judgments,
thou who art and wast, O Holy One.

Ps 79:3
Rev 18:24

⁶For men have shed the blood of saints and prophets,
and thou hast given them blood to drink.
It is their due!"

Ps 19:10;
119:137
Rev 19:2

⁷And I heard the altar cry,
"Yea, Lord God the Almighty,
true and just are thy judgments!"

Rev 9:20–21
Amos 4:11

⁸The fourth angel poured his bowl on the sun, and it was allowed to scorch men with fire; ⁹men were scorched by the fierce heat, and they cursed the name of God who had power over these plagues, and they did not repent and give him glory.

Ex 10:21
Is 8:21–22

¹⁰The fifth angel poured his bowl on the throne of the beast, and its kingdom was in darkness; men gnawed their tongues in anguish

---

16:2–9. The author uses the plagues of Egypt writ large to show how terrifying are the evils which will overtake mankind because of its failure to turn to God. Creation itself, through the words of the angel, acknowledges the justice of this punishment, as do the true worshippers of God symbolized by the altar (cf. vv. 5–7).

The whole scenario shows how nature turns against man to threaten him with total destruction. Although the imagery and language used here seem somewhat strange to us, the text does act as a warning for all generations, including our own. Thus, as John Paul II points out, the "second half of our century, in its turn, brings with it—*as though in proportion to the mistakes and transgressions* of our contemporary civilization—such a horrible threat of nuclear war that we cannot think of this period except in terms of *an incomparable accumulation of sufferings*, even to the possible self-destruction of humanity" (*Salvifici doloris*, 8).

The book of Revelation views these events from the vantage-point of the end of time: God has already intervened radically, making himself manifest once and for all (this is why he is called "thou who art and wast"), performing prodigious actions and giving men the opportunity of conversion. The panorama provides no room for superficial optimism; it gives a stark warning of what will happen to those who are unfaithful and who fail to respond to grace (cf. v. 9).

16:10–11. The beast is the same "star fallen from heaven to earth" and now shut up in the depths of the abyss as first

¹¹and cursed the God of heaven for their pain and sores, and did not repent of their deeds.

¹²The sixth angel poured his bowl on the great river Euphrates, and its water was dried up, to prepare the way for the kings from the east. ¹³And I saw, issuing from the mouth of the dragon and from the mouth of the beast and from the mouth of the false prophet, three foul spirits like frogs; ¹⁴for they are demonic spirits, performing signs, who go abroad to the kings of the whole world, to assemble them for battle on the great day* of God the Almighty. ¹⁵("Lo, I am coming like a thief! Blessed is he who is awake, keeping his garments that he may not go naked and be seen exposed!") ¹⁶And they assembled them at the place which is called in Hebrew Armageddon.*

Gen 15:18
Deut 1:7; Josh 1:4; Rev 9:14
Ex 8:3; Rev 12:9; 13:1, 11
Rev 13:13; 19:19
1 Thess 5:2
Rev 3:3, 18
2 Kings 23:29
Zech 12:11

---

appeared at the blowing of the fifth trumpet (cf. note on Rev 9:1–2). The meaning of human life which the beast proposes, the savagery with which it vents its fury on the Church, is now exposed as total meaninglessness which leads man to despair. As time goes on, it becomes clearer and clearer that when "man wishes to free himself from the moral law and become independent of God, far from gaining his freedom he destroys it. Escaping the measuring rod of truth, he falls prey to the arbitrary; fraternal relations between people are abolished and give place to terror, hatred and fear" (SCDF, *Libertatis conscientia*, 19).

16:12–16. The kings from the east, the Parthians, were the great threat to the Roman empire in John's time; here, paralleling the description of the sixth trumpet blast (cf. Rev 9:14) they stand for immense, terrifying power. Joining forces with the kings the world over, they will be marshalled by the powers of evil which derive from Satan (the dragon), the beast and the false prophet. These "three foul spirits" (v. 13) constitute a kind of blasphemous counterpoint to the Blessed Trinity.

The assembling of the kings of the whole world marks the climax of the final victory of Christ, which will take place when the seventh bowl is poured out; at that point his enemies will be routed in reverse order—first the kings (cf. 19:18), then the beast and the false prophet (cf. 19:20), and finally the Devil (cf. 20:10). Then the words of Psalm 2 will find their complete fulfilment: "The kings of the earth set themselves, and the rulers take counsel together, against the Lord and his anointed [...]. You shall break them with a rod of iron, and dash them to pieces like a potter's vessel" (Ps 2:3, 9). "That is a strong promise, and it is God who makes it. We cannot tone it down. Not for nothing is Christ the Redeemer of the world; he rules as sovereign, at the right hand of the Father. It is a terrifying announcement of what awaits each man when life is over—for over it will be. When history comes to an end, it will be the lot of all those whose hearts have been hardened by evil and despair" (St Josemaría Escrivá, *Christ Is Passing By*, 186).

In the middle of the prophecy the author breaks off into an exhortation to vigilance and faithfulness (v. 15), as he did in 3:1–3, 18, for "God, although he can conquer, prefers to convince people" (*Christ Is Passing By*, 186), as can be

Revelation 16:17

^{Is 66:6}
^{Rev 21:6}
^{Ex 19:16}
^{Dan 12:1}
^{Mk 13:19}
^{Jer 25:15}
^{Rev 14:8–10}
^{Rev 6:14}
^{Ex 9:23}

^{17}The seventh angel poured his bowl into the air, and a loud voice came out of the temple, from the throne, saying, "It is done!" ^{18}And there were flashes of lightning, voices, peals of thunder, and a great earthquake such as had never been since men were on the earth, so great was that earthquake. ^{19}The great city was split into three parts, and the cities of the nations fell, and God remembered great Babylon, to make her drain the cup of the fury of his wrath. ^{20}And every island fled away, and no mountains were to be found; ^{21}and great hailstones, heavy as a hundredweight, dropped on men from heaven, till men cursed God for the plague of the hail, so fearful was that plague.

---

seen from what Psalm 2 itself says: "Therefore, O kings, be wise; be warned, O rulers of the earth ..." (Ps 2:10).

The name Armageddon means "the mountain of Megiddo", the place where King Josiah suffered defeat (cf. 2 Kings 23:21f) and which now symbolizes defeat for the assembled armies (cf. 12:11).

16:17. The symbolic action of pouring the seventh and last bowl into the air means that it affects the entire world. What is now happening is final and irreversible: this is proclaimed by the heavenly voice which, coming as it does from the temple and the centre of heaven, makes it plain that God is Lord of all, that the prayers of the saints have been answered and that nothing can reverse God's intervention in human history.

The episode of the seventh bowl introduces the final scene of the book, in which are described the last battles, the victory of Christ and the absolute establishment of his kingship. The scene is a triptych: first we are shown the harlot (*porne*), or Babylon (cf. 16:19; 17:5; 18:8, 10, 25), already mentioned (cf. 14:8), and her trial, condemnation and destruction by fire (cf. chaps. 17–18). Then, in the centre, comes the victory of Christ, the Lamb, "Lord of lords and King of kings" (17:14), and his battles are described and lauded (cf. chaps. 19–20). The third part of the triptych shows the exaltation of the Bride (*nymphe*) and spouse of the Lamb (cf. 19:7), the Church or heavenly Jerusalem (cf chaps. 21–22).

16:18–21. God's intervention is described in terms of a great storm, as in the theophany on Sinai (cf. Ex 19:16) and earlier passages of the Apocalypse (cf. 4:5; 8:5; 11:9). In this instance the storm is compounded by an earthquake, its unique character underlined by words of the prophet Daniel: there had never been the like before (cf. Dan 12:1). This is designed to show that God's intervention has reached its climax; sea as well as land suffers upheaval. The enormous hailstones recall the seventh plague of Egypt (cf. Ex 9:24) and show how drastic the punishment is. The great city, Rome, whose ruin has already been decreed, is singled out for special treatment.

These events are the last call to conversion—a useless call, for, instead of turning to God, men in their fury curse his name.

17:1—19:10. This first section of the final scene begins with the depiction of the city of Rome (described as the great harlot, the great city, great Babylon), its punishment, and its connexion with the

The great harlot and the beast

17 ¹Then one of the seven angels who had the seven bowls came and said to me, "Come, I will show you the judgment of the great harlot* who is seated upon many waters, ²with whom the kings of the earth have committed fornication, and with the wine of whose fornication* the dwellers on earth have become drunk." ³And he carried me away in the Spirit into a wilderness, and I saw a woman sitting on a scarlet beast which was full of blasphemous names, and it had seven heads and ten horns. ⁴The woman was arrayed in purple and scarlet, and bedecked with gold and jewels and pearls, holding in her hand a golden cup full of abominations and the impurities of her fornication; ⁵and on her forehead was written a name of mystery: "Babylon the great, mother of harlots and of earth's abominations." ⁶And I saw the woman, drunk with the blood of the saints and the blood of the martyrs of Jesus.

Jer 51:13
Ezek 16

Is 23:27
Nahum 3:4

Dan 7:7; Is 21:1f; Rev 13:1

Jer 51:7

2 Thess 2:7
Rev 14:8

Rev 18:24

---

beast (the symbol of absolutist antichristian power personified by certain emperors: cf. 13:18). This takes up chapter 17. The vision then goes on to depict the fall of Rome as an accomplished fact, followed on the one hand by lamentation (cf. chap. 18) and on the other by hymns of praise sung by the righteous (cf. chap. 19).

17:1–6. An angel joins the seer to explain the vision to him. Again the imagery used is very evocative of the Old Testament: the great harlot recalls the cities of Tyre and Nineveh, which Isaiah and Nahum described as harlots (cf. Is 23:16–17; Nah 3:4). As explained in 17:15, the "many waters" are the peoples ruled by the great harlot. Some commentators have interpreted this as a reference to their ultimate downfall, which would precipate the collapse of the ancient world.

The metaphor of prostitution is used in the Old Testament to refer to idolatry and also alliances with foreign powers (cf. Ezek 16:15, 23–24; 23:1–20). In the present case, the power and influence of Rome was practically universal, given the extent of the empire. It is called Babylon because Babylon was the prototype of cities hostile to God (cf. v. 5; Is 21:9; Jer 51:1–19). It is characterized by its wealth, its immoral influence (v. 4) and its horrendous crimes against the Christian martyrs (cf. v. 6), who, according to the Roman historian Tacitus, "were abused in various ways: they were covered with hides to be set upon by dogs, or nailed to crosses, or burned alive and used as torches to light up the darkness" (*Annals*, 15, 44).

The figure of the great harlot, and the influence she wields, is also interpreted as referring to impurity; St John of the Cross, for example, explains the passage as follows: "This phrase 'have become drunk' should be noted. For, however little a man may drink of the wine of this rejoicing, it at once takes hold of the heart, as wine does to those who have been corrupted by it. So, if some antidote is not at once taken against this poison, to expel it quickly, the life of the soul is put in jeopardy" (*Ascent of Mount Carmel*, 3, 22).

When I saw her I marveled greatly. ⁷But the angel said to me, "Why marvel? I will tell you the mystery of the woman, and of the beast with seven heads and ten horns that carries her. ⁸The beast that you saw was, and is not, and is to ascend from the bottomless pit and go to perdition; and the dwellers on earth whose names have not been written in the book of life from the foundation of the world, will marvel to behold the beast, because it was and is not and is to come. ⁹This calls for a mind with wisdom: the seven heads are seven hills on which the woman is seated; ¹⁰they are also seven kings, five of whom have fallen, one is, the other has not yet come, and when he comes he must remain only a little while. ¹¹As for the beast that was and is not, it is an eighth but it belongs to the seven, and it goes to perdition. ¹²And the ten horns that you saw are ten kings who have not yet received royal power, but they are to receive authority as kings for one hour, together with the beast. ¹³These are of one mind and give over their power and authority

Rev 13:1–5

Rev 13:18

Rev 17:8; 19:20
Dan 7:20, 24
Rev 13:1

17:7–8. The angel explains the meaning of the beast (v. 8), its seven heads (v. 9) and its ten horns (v. 12), and then reveals the identity of the great harlot (v. 18). However, what he says is still enigmatic, in keeping with the style of apocalyptic texts, which are written in a kind of code to protect the writer from being sought out and punished.

The phrase "was, and is not" (v. 8) is a kind of counter and parody of "him who is and was and is to come" (Rev 1:4). It identifies the antichrist who is headed for perdition (v. 11); St Paul also calls him "the son of perdition" (2 Thess 2:3). When it speaks of the beast reappearing ("is to come"), this refers, according to some commentators, to the legend about Nero returning at the head of the Parthians to avenge himself on his enemies in Rome. However, what the sacred writer really means is that the beast, which had disappeared, will return to wage war on Christians (cf. Rev 11:7; 13:1ff).

17:9–15. In v. 9 St John warns the reader that what he is writing has a deeper, hidden meaning, rich in wisdom. He is inviting the reader to interpret what he is reading, to discern an implicit, concealed meaning: the harlot is the city of Rome (cf. 13:18 on the name of the emperor), as is fairly plain from the reference to the seven hills on which the harlot is seated. Pliny the Elder describes Rome as "complexa septem montes" (*Historia naturalis*, 3, 9), nestling on seven hills.

The beast's seven heads (cf. 17:3) also stand for seven kings. From what the author says we can deduce that he is referring to seven emperors. The sixth, alive when St John is writing, would be Domitian, and the first five would be Caligula (37–41), Claudius (41–54), Nero (54–68), Vespasian (69–78) and Titus (79–81); with Nerva (96–98) as the seventh. The beast is number eight, though it can also be taken as one of the seven, for it will be as cruel as one of them—Nero. The ten kings (v. 12) stand for those whom Rome established as kings in the nations it conquered, rulers subject to the emperor.

The description of Christ as the Lamb (cf. 5:6) forms a contrast here with the beast. Through his death and resur-

to the beast; ¹⁴they will make war on the Lamb, and the Lamb will conquer them, for he is Lord of lords and King of kings, and those with him are called and chosen and faithful."

¹⁵And he said to me, "The waters that you saw, where the harlot is seated, are peoples and multitudes and nations and tongues. ¹⁶And the ten horns that you saw, they and the beast will hate the harlot; they will make her desolate and naked, and devour her flesh and burn her up with fire, ¹⁷for God has put it into their hearts to carry out his purpose by being of one mind and giving over their royal power to the beast, until the words of God shall be fulfilled. ¹⁸And the woman that you saw is the great city which has dominion over the kings of the earth."

Deut 10:17
Dan 2:47
Rev 19:14, 16, 19; 1 Tim 6:15
Jer 51:13
Rev 18:8
Ezek 16:39–41
Ps 2:2
Rev 11:8

The fall of Babylon announced

18 ¹After this I saw another angel coming down from heaven, having great authority; and the earth was made bright with his splendour. ²And he called out with a mighty voice,

Ezek 43:2
Rev 14:8
Is 13:21; 21:9; 34:11, 14

---

rection, this humble figure has been made King and Lord of the entire universe (cf. Acts 2:32–36) and already truly reigns in the hearts of Christians. Therefore his victory over the powers of evil, no matter how strong they be, is assured. As Pius XI rightly put it, "it has long been a common custom to give Christ the metaphorical title of 'king', because of the high degree of perfection whereby he excels all creatures [...]. He is king of our hearts, too, by reason of his charity 'which surpasses knowledge' (Eph 3:19) and his mercy and kindness, which draw all men to him; for there never was, nor ever will be a man loved so much and so universally as Jesus Christ" (*Quas primas*, 6).

17:16–18. With words taken from Ezekiel's prophecy of the destruction of Jerusalem (by the very kingdoms with which Judah had made idolatrous alliances instead of trusting in Yahweh: cf. 16:30–41; 23:25–29), St John now predicts the punishment which will befall Rome, at the hands too of those nations which, like Rome and under her influence, serve the beast, that is, have fallen into idolatrous absolutism, which prevents the exercise of freedom of conscience. God makes use of the forces of evil to punish those very people who follow evil ways.

18:1–3. These verses about the downfall of Rome follow the prophetical style of foretelling a future event by reporting it as something that has already happened. First the fall of the city is proclaimed (vv. 1–3). Then the people of God are exhorted to leave the city and escape the terrible punishment soon to befall it (vv. 4–8). This is followed by the lament of the kings who were allied to Rome (vv. 9–10), of the merchants who prospered by trading with her (v. 11–17a) and of the sailors (17b–19). Finally we are shown the joy of those who suffered under her yoke and now see justice done.

In words reminiscent of Old Testament passages foretelling the destruction of hostile cities (cf. Is 13:21–22; 21:9; Jer 50:30; Ezek 43:3–5), St John describes the fate of Rome in the last days before its desolation. Among the sins which have

Revelation 18:3

Jer 50:39; 51:8	"Fallen, fallen is Babylon the great!
	It has become a dwelling place of demons,
	a haunt of every foul spirit,
	a haunt of every foul and hateful bird;
Jer 25:15; 51:7 Nahum 3:4	³for all nations have drunk[k] the wine of her impure passion,
	and the kings of the earth have committed fornication with her,
	and the merchants of the earth have grown rich with the
Is 48:20; 52:11	wealth of her wantonness."
Jer 50:8; 51:6, 9, 45 2 Cor 6:17	⁴Then I heard another voice from heaven saying,
	"Come out of her, my people,
	lest you take part in her sins,
	lest you share in her plagues;
Gen 18:20–21 Jer 51:9	⁵for her sins are heaped high as heaven,
	and God has remembered her iniquities.
Ps 137:8 Jer 50:15, 29 2 Thess 1:6	⁶Render to her as she herself has rendered,
	and repay her double for her deeds;
	mix a double draught for her in the cup she mixed.
Jer 50:29 Is 47:8	⁷As she glorified herself and played the wanton,
	so give her a like measure of torment and mourning.

brought about its ruin is unbridled sexual indulgence (cf. also vv. 7 and 12–14). Such behaviour leads to the degradation and self-destruction of a society, as witness the history of civilization and contemporary experience. Consumerism, self-indulgence and greed for possessions, clearly features of our time, were denounced by Pius XI when he said that "the disease of the modern age, and the main source of the evils we all deplore, is that lack of reflection, that continuous and quite feverish pursuit of external things, that immoderate desire for wealth and pleasure, which gradually causes the heart to lose sight of its nobler ideals, drowning them in a sea of impermanent, earthly things, and preventing them from contemplating higher, eternal things" (*Mens nostra*, 5).

18:4–8. St John is inserting here the scene in which Jeremiah prophesies the punishment of Babylon and God protects his people by ordering them to leave the city before it falls (cf. Jer 51:6, 45). The verses also echo the flight of Lot from Sodom (cf. Gen 19:12ff) and the advice Jesus gave his followers on what to do when the fall of Jerusalem came (cf. Mt 24:16ff).

The idea of the sins heaped as high as heaven (cf. Gen 18:20) is a way of saying that sin is something very grave because it is above all an offence to the Godhead, and so "is linked to the *sense* of God, since it derives from man's conscious relationship with God as his Creator, Lord and Father" (John Paul II, *Reconciliatio et paenitentia*, 18). When one's perception of the greatness of God becomes vague one loses the sense of sin; as John Paul II adds, "my predecessor Pius XII one day declared, in words that have almost become proverbial, that 'the sin of the century is the loss of the sense of sin'" (ibid.).

k. Other ancient authorities read *fallen by*

Since in her heart she says, 'A queen I sit,
I am no widow, mourning I shall never see,'
⁸ so shall her plagues come in a single day,
pestilence and mourning and famine,
and she shall be burned with fire;
for mighty is the Lord God who judges her."

⁹And the kings of the earth, who committed fornication and were wanton with her, will weep and wail over her when they see the smoke of her burning; ¹⁰they will stand far off, in fear of her torment, and say,

"Alas! alas! thou great city,
thou mighty city, Babylon!
In one hour has thy judgment come."

¹¹*And the merchants of the earth weep and mourn for her, since no one buys their cargo any more, ¹²cargo of gold, silver, jewels and pearls, fine linen, purple, silk and scarlet, all kinds of scented wood, all articles of ivory, all articles of costly wood, bronze, iron and marble, ¹³cinnamon, spice, incense, myrrh, frankincense, wine, oil, fine flour and wheat, cattle and sheep, horses and chariots, and slaves, that is, human souls.

¹⁴"The fruit for which thy soul longed has gone from thee,
and all thy dainties and thy splendour are lost to thee,
never to be found again!"

¹⁵The merchants of these wares, who gained wealth from her, will stand far off, in fear of her torment, weeping and mourning aloud,

¹⁶"Alas, alas, for the great city
that was clothed in fine linen, in purple and scarlet,
bedecked with gold, with jewels, and with pearls!
¹⁷ In one hour all this wealth has been laid waste."

Cross references: Is 47:9; Rev 17:16; Ezek 26:16; 27:30, 33, 35; Is 23:17; Ezek 26:17; Rev 18:17; Ezek 37:36; Ezek 27:12, 13, 22; Rev 18:3; Rev 17:4; Ezek 27:27–29

The punishment ordained by God and carried out by his agents is related to the scale of the offence; the word "double" does not refer to any particular amount but to the severity of the punishment (as in Is 40:2; Jer 16:18; etc.).

Using this passage as his basis, St John of Avila teaches that in order to overcome strong temptation it is very helpful to reflect on the love we should have for God; but "if that does not get rid of the temptation, turn your thoughts to hell and see how ferociously that fire burns" (*Audi, filia*, 10).

18:9–19. To describe the punishment inflicted on Rome, the author of the book of Revelation seems to be borrowing from the oracles of Ezekiel about the fall of Tyre. In both cases we have the lament of the kings (cf. Ezek 26:15–18) and the complaint of merchants and sailors, who see it as meaning financial ruin (cf. Ezek 27:9–36). Each of these three groups, from different standpoints of time, will lament over the city—the kings in the future (cf. v. 10), the merchants in the present (cf. v. 11) and the sailors in the past (v. 18). This style of writing makes for a very vivid narrative

Revelation 18:18

<small>Ezek 27:32
Is 34:10</small>

And all shipmasters and seafaring men, sailors and all whose trade is on the sea, stood far off ¹⁸and cried out as they saw the smoke of her burning,
"What city was like the great city?"

<small>Ezek 27:30–34</small>

¹⁹And they threw dust on their heads, as they wept and mourned, crying out,
"Alas, alas, for the great city
where all who had ships at sea grew rich by her wealth!
In one hour she has been laid waste.

<small>Deut 32:43
Is 44:23
Rev 19:1–2</small>

²⁰ Rejoice over her, O heaven,
O saints and apostles and prophets,
for God has given judgment for you against her!"

<small>Jer 51:63–64
Ezek 26:21</small>

²¹Then a mighty angel took up a stone like a great millstone and threw it into the sea, saying,
"So shall Babylon the great city be thrown down with violence,
and shall be found no more;

<small>Is 24:8
Ezek 26:13
Jer 25:10</small>

²² and the sound of harpers and minstrels, of flute players and trumpeters,
shall be heard in thee no more;
and a craftsman of any craft
shall be found in thee no more;
and the sound of the millstone
shall be heard in thee no more;

<small>Jer 25:10; 7:34; 16:9
Is 23:8; 47:9</small>

²³ and the light of a lamp
shall shine in thee no more;
and the voice of bridegroom and bride
shall be heard in thee no more;

---

and depicts the punishment as both forthcoming and already executed.

18:20–24. In sharp contrast with the previous lamentation is this invitation to rejoice—the reply to which comes in 19:1–8, where we are told that the elect joyfully intone songs in praise of God almighty. The throwing of the millstone into the sea is an instance of "prophetic action"; it comes from Jeremiah 51:60–64, which uses this device to prophesy the total downfall of Babylon. The millstone also appears in Luke 17:2 and par. as a symbol of disgrace and shame.

The sepulchral silence and darkness of the city are described in detail. The reason for this terrible punishment was its opulence, its idolatry and the fact that it was where the Christian martyrs were tortured and put to death. Like Jerusalem it is called "city of blood" (cf. Ezek 24:6), and just as the ancient capital of Israel was accused by Jesus of murdering the prophets and messengers of God and was told that all the blood it had spilt would come back upon it (cf. Mt 23:35), so will Rome be punished for martyring the saints.

for thy merchants were the great men of the earth,
and all nations were deceived by thy sorcery.
²⁴ And in her was found the blood of prophets and of saints,
and of all who have been slain on earth."

Mt 23:35–37
Jer 51–49
Rev 6:10; 17:6; 19:2

Songs of victory in heaven

19 ¹After this I heard what seemed to be the mighty voice of a great multitude in heaven, crying,

"Hallelujah! Salvation and glory and power belong
to our God,
²for his judgments are true and just;
he has judged the great harlot who corrupted the earth
with her fornication,
and he has avenged on her the blood of his servants."
³Once more they cried,
"Hallelujah! The smoke from her goes up for ever
and ever."
⁴And the twenty-four elders and the four living creatures fell down and worshipped God who is seated on the throne, saying, "Amen. Hallelujah!" ⁵And from the throne came a voice crying,
"Praise our God, all you his servants,
you who fear him, small and great."
⁶Then I heard what seemed to be the voice of a great multitude, like the sound of many waters and like the sound of mighty thunderpeals, crying,

Rev 7:10

Ps 19:10
Rev 16:7; 11:18
Deut 32–43
2 Kings 9:7

Is 34:10
Rev 14:11

Rev 4:6, 10

Ps 115:13; 134:1

Ezek 1:24; 43:2
Ps 93:1; 97:1; 99:1
Rev 11:17

19:1–4. The righteous rejoice to see their enemy overwhelmed; the praises they sing of God end in three loud "Hallelujahs". In the following passage (vv. 6–8), they welcome the establishment of the Kingdom of God and the imminent marriage of the Lamb.

This is the first and only time the word "Hallelujah" appears in the New Testament. It is a Hebrew term (*hallelu-yah*) meaning "Praise Yahweh" used especially in the psalms (cf., e.g., Ps 111; 114; 115). The Church uses it, unchanged, usually to express to God its joy and praise at the resurrection of Christ. It is used particularly at Eastertide and also on many other days, both in the divine office and in the celebration of the Eucharist.

These shouts of praise are motivated by the salvation which comes from God and by the rightness of his judgments as evidenced by the punishment inflicted on the great harlot who is turned into a fire which burns forever.

19:5–8. This further invitation to praise God is very reminiscent of the Psalms; in fact it contains some direct quotations from them (cf. Ps 93:1; 97:1; 115:2; 135:1, 20). The response is on a grand scale, like a choral symphony involving all the elect. This particular chant praises not only the destruction and defeat of evil but the definitive establishment of the Kingdom of God; his is a Kingdom of love, as symbolized by a marriage feast.

Revelation 19:7

<small>Ps 118:24
Rev 21:2, 9</small>

<small>Is 61:10
Ps 45:14–15</small>

<small>Rev 1:3
Mt 22:1–14</small>

<small>Acts 10:25–26
Rev 22:8–9</small>

"Hallelujah! For the Lord our God the Almighty reigns. ⁷Let us rejoice and exult and give him the glory, for the marriage of the Lamb* has come, and his Bride has made herself ready; ⁸it was granted her to be clothed with fine linen, bright and pure"— for the fine linen is the righteous deeds of the saints. ⁹And the angel said¹ to me, "Write this: Blessed are those who are invited to the marriage supper of the Lamb." And he said to me, "These are true words of God." ¹⁰Then I fell down at his feet to worship him, but he said to me, "You must not do that! I am a fellow servant with you and your brethren who hold the testimony of Jesus. Worship God." For the testimony of Jesus is the spirit of prophecy.

In the Old Testament Yahweh was sometimes likened to a bridegroom (cf., e.g., Is 54:6; Jer 2:2; Ezek 16:7–8; Hos 2:16) and in the New Testament the Church is depicted as the Bride of Christ (cf. Eph 5:22–23). Thus, the Second Vatican Council says that the Church "is described as the spotless spouse of the spotless lamb (Rev 19:7; 21:2, 9; 22:17). It is she whom Christ 'loved and for whom he delivered himself up that he might sanctify her' (Eph 5:26). It is she whom he unites to himself by an unbreakable alliance, and whom he constantly 'nourishes and cherishes' (Eph 5:29). It is she whom, once purified, he willed to be joined to himself, subject in love and fidelity (cf. Eph 5:24), and whom, finally, he filled with heavenly gifts for all eternity" (*Lumen gentium*, 6). And so, John Paul II teaches, *"redemptive love* is transformed, I might say, into *spousal love*. Christ, on giving himself to the Church, by that very act of redemption has made himself one with her for ever, as husband and wife" (*Address*, 18 July 1982).

This singing of the praises of the marriage of the Lamb from the vantage-point of the end of time also depicts the Church down the ages; it shows us, too, the destiny that awaits every Christian and the form his or her every day should take—weaving the wedding garment by doing good works, by praising God and by living a holy life, so as to be ready to attend the marriage feast. Those who live well away from idolatry, unbridled sensuality and all the sins of the "great city" can already celebrate their victory by joining in the praises sung by the choirs of heaven. Here again we can see the intimate connexion between the heavenly and earthly liturgies. By taking part in the liturgy of the Church, especially the Mass, we are already entering the sphere of things divine. And so the Second Vatican Council tells us that "the liturgy is the summit toward which the activity of the Church is directed; it is also the fount from which all her power flows. For the goal of apostolic endeavour is that all who are made children of God by faith and Baptism should come together to praise God in the midst of his Church, to take part in the Sacrifice and to eat the Lord's Supper" (*Sacrosanctum Concilium*, 10). For his part, John Paul II exhorts us:

---

l. Greek *he said*

The first battle—the beast is destroyed

¹¹Then I saw heaven opened, and behold, a white horse! He who sat upon it is called Faithful and True, and in righteousness he judges and makes war. ¹²His eyes are like a flame of fire, and on his head are many diadems; and he has a name inscribed which no one knows but himself. ¹³He is clad in a robe dipped in^m blood, and the name by which he is called is The Word of God. ¹⁴And the

Is 11:4–5
2 Mac 3:25
Rev 1:5; 3:7, 14
Rev 1:14; 2:18; 19:16
Is 63:1f
Jn 1:1

"Nourish yourselves with this eucharistic Bread, which will enable you to make your way through the paths of the world ever united in the faith of your fathers, always faithful to God and his Church, ever active in building the kingdom of God, and feeling privileged if at any time the Lord should allow your faith to be put severely to the test. Only he who perseveres will be worthy to share in the marriage supper of the Lamb" (*Radio message*, 22 July 1984).

19:9. On the instructions of the angel who is explaining the vision to him (cf. 17:1), St John tells Christians to count themselves blessed (v. 9); God guarantees the truth of this assurance. At Mass the priest makes a similar proclamation just before distributing Holy Communion: "Happy are those who are called to his [the Lord's] supper." This shows that the Eucharist truly is "a pledge of future glory".

19:10. The angel apparently leaves at this point and St John again reminds Christians that they have a prophetic mission—to bear witness to Jesus by spreading his teaching by word and deed.

19:11—20:15. The prophetic narrative (given in the form of a proclamation) of the fall of Babylon (Rome) is now followed by a depiction of Christ as endowed with power (vv. 11–16) permanently and decisively to conquer the forces of evil which sustained the great city. Their defeat is narrated in reverse order to that given earlier in the book: the first to be conquered are the kings of the earth (who first allied themselves with the great city and then rebelled against it: vv. 17–18) and the beast and the false prophet to whom the kings gave over their royal power (vv. 20–21; cf. 17:16–17). Then, in a second eschatological battle, Christ defeats the ancient serpent, Satan, the one who originally gave power to the beast (cf. 20:1–10; 13:2). Not until this happens will the general judgment take place (20:11–15).

The Apocalypse in this way points to the origin of evil and its later manifestations. The most immediate manifestation of evil, and the first to be destroyed, is the world of opulence, unbridled sexuality and power, and idolatry—that society which persecuted and martyred the Christians. Pagan Rome, the symbol of that world, draws its strength from absolutist divinized forces intolerant of human freedom and dignity (and especially hostile to religion), and from atheistic and materialistic ideologies which make for absolutism. These forces are the beast and the false prophet. However, at a deeper and more mysterious level lies the ultimate source of these sociological phenomena—Satan (symbolized by the dragon or ancient serpent). The message of Revelation is that Christ towers above all these forces, and his victory (which began with his death and resurrection) will reach its

---

m. Other ancient authorities read *sprinkled with*

Revelation 19:15

^{Rev 17:14}
^{Is 63:3; Ps 2:9}
^{Rev 1:16; 2:27; 14:19}
^{Deut 10:7}
^{1 Tim 6:15}
^{Rev 17:14}

armies of heaven, arrayed in fine linen, white and pure, followed him on white horses. ¹⁵From his mouth issues a sharp sword with which to smite the nations, and he will rule them with a rod of iron; he will tread the wine press of the fury of the wrath of God the Almighty. ¹⁶On his robe and on his thigh he has a name inscribed, King of kings and Lord of lords.

^{Ezek 39:17–20}
^{Ps 2:2}
^{Rev 17:12–14; 16:14, 16}

¹⁷Then I saw an angel standing in the sun, and with a loud voice he called to all the birds that fly in midheaven, "Come, gather for the great supper of God, ¹⁸to eat the flesh of kings, the flesh of captains, the flesh of mighty men, the flesh of horses and their riders, and the flesh of all men, both free and slave, both small and great." ¹⁹And I saw the beast and the kings of the earth

---

climax at the end of time, although it will be manifested to a degree over the course of history by the holiness of the Church.

19:11–16. This vision of the glorious and conquering Christ is similar to the way he is portrayed at the start of the book: by focusing attention on parts of his body (though not in any systematic way: cf. Rev 1:5, 12–16), he seems to be the same person as the rider on the white horse mentioned when the first seal was broken (cf. 6:2). White is the symbol of victory, and the narrative is now going to describe that victory. Christ is portrayed first in a "static" fashion (vv. 11–14) and then in a "dynamic" one, in terms of his actions (vv. 15–16).

The two titles "Faithful" and "True" are closely connected. In the Old Testament Yahweh is frequently described as "faithful" (cf. Deut 32:4; Ps 145:13; Ps 117:2). When this title is applied to Christ in the New Testament it suggests his divinity (cf. 1 Thess 5:24; Rev 1:5; 3:14) and shows that, through Christ, God has been faithful to the promises he made in the Old Testament. The name "which no one knows but himself" (v. 12) is an allusion to his divinity, which is something sublime, mysterious and beyond man's grasp.

Another title is "The Word of God". St John is the only one to use this name (cf. Jn 1:1–18), which is a reference to Jesus as the Revealer, the Word of the Father (cf. Jn 1:18). Regarding the titles "King of Kings" and "Lord of lords", see the note on Revelation 17:14. The "thigh" may well mean "standard", because both words are similar in Hebrew, or else it refers to that part of his tunic which covered his thigh.

The blood on the Victor's robe refers not to his passion but to his victory over his enemies, whom he treads as in a wine press. This imagery is used by the Old Testament prophets (cf., e.g., Is 63:1–6; Joel 4:13). The sword coming out of his mouth is a reference to the word of God (cf. Heb 4:12). It is a way of referring to divine omnipotence and judgment.

19:17–21. After describing Christ and his army, the text deals with preparations for the last battle, and its outcome. The angel's call to the birds is reminiscent of the passage in Ezekiel (39:17–20) which tells who the vanquished will be. Here they include people of every type and description who followed the beast and the false prophet, that is, who served the forces of evil they represent.

The lake of fire and brimstone, which will appear again in 20:10, 14 as the final

with their armies gathered to make war against him who sits upon the horse and against his army. ²⁰And the beast was captured, and with it the false prophet who in its presence had worked the signs by which he deceived those who had received the mark of the beast and those who worshipped its image. These two were thrown alive into the lake of fire that burns with sulphur. ²¹And the rest were slain by the sword of him who sits upon the horse, the sword that issues from his mouth; and all the birds were gorged with their flesh.

Dan 7:11, 26
Rev 13:1, 13–17; 20:10, 14

Ezek 39:17, 20

The thousand-year reign of Christ and his people

20 ¹Then I saw an angel coming down from heaven, holding in his hand the key of the bottomless pit and a great chain. ²And he seized the dragon, that ancient serpent, who is the Devil and Satan, and bound him for a thousand years, ³and threw him into the pit, and shut it and sealed it over him, that he should deceive the nations no more, till the thousand years were ended. *After that he must be loosed for a little while.

Jude 6
Gen 3:1
Rev 12:9
2 Thess 2:8

---

destination of the powers of evil, is hell, called *gehenna* elsewhere in the New Testament (cf., e.g., Mt 5:22; 10:28; Mk 9:42; Lk 12:5). It is also where those men will end up who earn damnation in the eyes of God (cf. Rev 20:15), although now the writer focuses attention only on the physical death their punishment involves (v. 21; cf. Mt 10:28 and note).

The fact that they are thrown alive into the fire emphasizes the horrific nature of their punishment. This physical torment is a terrible one, but far more painful is the eternal loss of God, which is what hell essentially involves. As St John Chrysostom puts it, "the pain of hell is indeed insufferable. But even if one were to imagine ten thousand hells, this suffering would be nothing compared to the pain caused by the loss of heaven and by being rejected by Christ" (*Hom. on St Matthew*, 28).

20:1–3. The victory of the Lamb is manifested by the fact that Rome, the great harlot, has been destroyed (chap. 18); then the beast and its prophet are overcome (chap. 19); there remains the dragon whom we saw in chapter 12 and whose defeat marks the final outcome of the war referred to in that chapter.

The battle between Satan and God is described in two scenes; the first tells of how Satan is brought under control and deprived of his power for a time (vv. 1–3); the second describes his last assault on the Church and what happens to him in the end (vv. 7–10). Between these two scenes comes the reign of Christ and his followers for a thousand years (vv. 4–6). At the end of the second scene comes the General Judgment, with the reprobate being damned (vv. 11–18) and a new world coming into being (21:1–8).

The bottomless pit, or abyss, refers to a mysterious place, different from the lake of fire, or hell. Satan is also called the "ancient serpent" because it was he who seduced our first parents at the dawn of history (cf. Gen 3:1–19).

Revelation 20:4

^{Dan 7:9, 22, 27}
^{1 Cor 6:9}
^{Rev 5:10;}
^{13:16}

⁴Then I saw thrones, and seated on them were those to whom judgment was committed. Also I saw the souls of those who had been beheaded for their testimony to Jesus and for the word of God, and who had not worshipped the beast or its image and had not received its mark on their foreheads or their hands. They came to life, and reigned with Christ a thousand years. ⁵The rest of the dead did not come to life until the thousand years were ended. This is the first resurrection. ⁶Blessed and holy is he who shares in the first resurrection! Over such the second death has no power, but they shall be priests of God and of Christ, and they shall reign with him a thousand years.

1 Cor 15:21–27

Is 61:6
Rev 5:10; 1:3

The second battle—Satan is overthrown

Ezek 7:2; 38:2, 9, 15

⁷And when the thousand years are ended, Satan will be loosed from his prison ⁸and will come out to deceive the nations which are at the four corners of the earth, that is, Gog and Magog, to gather them for battle; their number is like the sand of the sea.

The period during which Satan is held captive coincides with the reign of Christ and his saints—one thousand years (cf. v. 4)—and contrasts with the "little while" during which he is given further scope to act. This contrast is very significant and it may simply be a symbolic way of showing that Christ's power is vastly greater than Satan's and that the devil's power is doomed to perish even though on occasions it may emerge with unsuspected force.

20:4–6. The power to judge belongs to Jesus Christ in his own right because he has been given it by the Father (cf., e.g., Jn 5:22; 9:39; Acts 10:42). However, our Lord gives a share in his power to the apostles, whom he promised would sit on twelve thrones judging the tribes of Israel (cf. Mt 19:28). All other Christians will also share in Christ's power (cf: 1 Cor 6:2–3).

Various interpretations have been offered for this "thousand years". The "millenarian" interpretation, supported by some early writers, takes the passage literally and says that after the resurrection of the dead Christ will reign on earth for a thousand years; the Church has never accepted this interpretation. Like the other numbers mentioned in the book of Revelation, the number of one thousand should be taken as more symbolic than arithmetic. It may be a reference to the period that runs from the incarnation of Christ to the end of time. It is also possible to see this millenium as a reference to a world of the future after the second coming of Christ; or simply as a symbolically long time contrasting with the "little while". It could also be that the author is fusing two notions current in Judaism in his time—one which saw the end of time as a messianic kingdom on earth, and the other which saw that End as a future which transcends this world, when a new heaven and a new earth would appear.

Our Lord Jesus Christ depicts the establishment of the messianic Kingdom as happening in two stages—his first

⁹And they marched up over the broad earth and surrounded the camp of the saints and the beloved city; but fire came down from heaven[n] and consumed them, ¹⁰and the devil who had deceived them was thrown into the lake of fire and sulphur where the beast and the false prophet were, and they will be tormented day and night for ever and ever.

Ps 78:68
2 Kings 1:10
Gen 19:24
Lk 21:24

Ezek 38:22
Rev 19:20

---

coming, in which he demonstrates his power over the devil and inaugurates the Kingdom of God; and his second coming at the end of time, when that kingdom will be established in its full, finished form. That is why we see St Augustine's explanation of the millenium as the most satisfactory. According to him, this millenium covers the time between the incarnation of the Son of God and his coming at the end of the world. During this period the activity of the devil is to some degree restricted; he is in some way enchained. Christ reigns fully in the Church triumphant and he reigns in the Church militant in an incomplete way. The power of the devil is no longer sovereign, which means that man is able to elude him. So, although "he desires to do us harm, he cannot do so because his power is subject to another's power [...]. He who gives him the ability to tempt, also gives his mercy to the one who is tempted. He has restricted the devil's ability to tempt people" (St Augustine, *De Serm. Dom. in monte*, 2, 9, 34). In fact, the Curé of Ars used to say, "the devil is a big dog on a chain, who threatens and makes a lot of noise but who only bites those who go too near him" (*Selected Sermons*, 1st Sunday of Lent).

According to this interpretation, the "first resurrection" should be understood in a spiritual sense; it is Baptism, which regenerates man and gives him new life by freeing him from sin and making him a son of God. The second resurrection is the one which will take place at the end of time, when the body is brought back to life and the human being, body and soul, enters into everlasting joy. The "rest of the dead" are those who did not receive Baptism. They too will rise again on the last day, to be judged according to their deeds.

On the priesthood referred to in v. 6, see the note on 1:6.

20:7–10. God will give the devil a particularly free rein during the last days. Our Lord also said that they would be marked by great tribulation the like of which had never been seen (cf. Mt 24:21–22). And St Paul refers to "the man of lawlessness" who will take his seat in the temple and proclaim himself to be God (cf. 2 Thess 2:3–8).

The writer once again draws on Ezekiel (chaps. 38–39) to describe the final eschatological battle. Gog and Magog are names connected with the nations of the north near the Black Sea, whose invasion of Israel was so devastating that it became the prototype of the worst kind of invasion. Ezekiel describes how they advance through the plain of Esdraelon, scene of so many battles, till they reach the mountains of Judea, on one of whose hills Jerusalem sits, the symbol of the beloved city, the Church. However, the progress of this destructive force is suddenly brought to a halt by the overwhelming might of God.

Once the devil is thrown into the lake of fire and brimstone evil ceases to act in

---

n. Other ancient authorities read *from God, out of heaven*, or *out of heaven from God*

Revelation 20:11

The Last Judgment of the living and the dead

Dan 7:9; Ps 114:3; Mt 25:31-46 2 Pet 3:7, 10, 13 Rev 21:1; Ps 62:13; Jer 17:10; Dan 7:10 Rev 3:5; 13:8 Jn 5:28-29

¹¹Then I saw a great white throne and him who sat upon it; from his presence earth and sky fled away, and no place was found for them. ¹²And I saw the dead, great and small, standing before the throne, and books were opened. Also another book was opened, which is the book of life. And the dead were judged by what was written in the books, by what they had done. ¹³And the sea gave up the dead in it, Death and Hades gave up the dead in them, and

---

the world. In that fire the ungodly, along with the beast and the false prophet, will suffer eternal torment. Scripture's teaching on the everlasting duration of divine punishment is yet again confirmed (cf., e.g., Mt 18:8; 25:41, 46; Mk 4:43, 48).

20:11-15. Now that the devil, the root of all evil, is removed from the scene, we are shown (as we were after the previous battle) the resurrection of the dead and the General Judgment. The white throne symbolizes the power of God, who judges the living and the dead. Other New Testament texts tell us that the supreme Judge is Christ, who has been charged with this task by the Father (cf., e.g., Mt 16:27; 25:31-46; Acts 17:31; 2 Cor 5:10). The "flight of earth and sky" mean that they disappear (for even non-rational created things have been contaminated by sin: cf. Rom 8:19ff) to make way for a new heaven and a new earth (21:1; cf. 2 Pet 3:13; Rom 8:23).

The author then turns his attention to the resurrection, when all men will be judged according to their works. He describes this by using the metaphor of two books. One of these records the actions of men (as in Daniel 7:10 and other passages of the Old Testament, cf., e.g., Is 65:6; Jer 22:30). The second book contains the names of those predestined to eternal life (an idea inspired by Daniel 12:1; cf. also, e.g., Ex 32:32). This is a way of showing that man cannot attain salvation by his own efforts alone: it is God who saves him; however, he needs to act in such a way that he responds to the destiny God has marked out for him; if he fails to do that he runs the risk of having his name blotted out of the book of life (cf. Rev 3:5), that is, of being damned. By using this metaphor, the author of Revelation is teaching us two truths which are always mysteriously connected—1) that we are free and 2) that there is a grace of predestination.

Regarding Hades or hell, it should be pointed out that this does not refer to hell in the strict sense, but to *sheol*, the name the Jews gave to the gloomy abode of the dead.

The Last Judgment is a truth of faith concerning which Paul VI says: "He ascended to heaven, and he will come again, this time in glory, to judge the living and the dead—each according to his merits; those who have responded to the love and compassion of God going to eternal life, those who have refused them to the end going to the fire that is not extinguished [...]. We believe in the life eternal. We believe that the souls of all those who die in the grace of Christ, whether they must still be purified in purgatory, or whether from the moment they leave their bodies Jesus takes them to paradise as he did for the Good Thief, are the people of God in the eternity beyond death, which will be finally conquered on the day of the Resurrection when these souls will be reunited with their bodies" (*Creed of the People of God*, 12 and 28).

all were judged by what they had done. ¹⁴Then Death and Hades were thrown into the lake of fire. This is the second death, the lake of fire; ¹⁵and if any one's name was not found written in the book of life, he was thrown into the lake of fire.

Ref: 1 Cor 15:26, 54; Rev 14:10; 2:11; Ps 69:29

A new world comes into being. The new Jerusalem

21 ¹Then I saw a new heaven and a new earth; for the first heaven and the first earth had passed away, and the sea was no more.* ²And I saw the holy city, new Jerusalem, coming down out of heaven from God, prepared as a bride adorned for her husband; ³and I heard a loud voice from the throne saying, "Behold, the dwelling of God is with men. He will dwell with them, and they shall be his people,⁰ and God himself will be with them;ᵖ ⁴he will wipe away every tear from their eyes, and death shall be no more, neither shall there be mourning nor crying nor pain any more, for the former things have passed away."

Refs: Is 65:17; 68:22; 2 Pet 3:13; Rom 8:19–23; Rom 20:11; Is 52:1; 61:10; Gal 4:26; Heb 11:10, 16; Rev 19:7, 8; Is 7:14; Ezek 37:37; 2 Chron 6:18; Jn 1:14; Zech 8:8; Rev 7:17; Is 25:8; 35:10; 65:17, 19

21:1—22:15. Now that all the forces of evil, including death, have been vanquished the author turns to contemplate the establishment of the Kingdom of God in all its fullness. Thus, the climax of the book shows a new world inhabited by a new race—the new Jerusalem (cf. 21:1–4); a world guaranteed by the eternal and almighty Word of God to last forever (cf. 21:5–8).

The focus of attention now becomes the people of God; the new Jerusalem is portrayed as the Bride of the Lamb; a detailed description shows it to be a wonderful city of great beauty ruled over by God the Father and Christ (21:9—22:6). The contrast between this and the pilgrim Church in its present circumstances is so great that the new city can be discerned only if one puts one's faith in what God's messengers reveal (cf. 22:6–9). Faith is also an effective stimulus to the Christian to continue to strive for holiness and the reward of eternal life (cf. 22:10–15).

21:1–4. The prophet Isaiah depicted the messianic times as a radical change in the fortunes of the people of Israel—so radical that, as he put it, God was going to create new heavens and a new earth, a new Jerusalem full of joy, where the sound of weeping would never more be heard, where God would make himself plain for all to see and where everything would be as it was in paradise before sin (cf. Is 65:12–25). The author of the Apocalypse uses this same format to describe the future Kingdom of God. The imagery of a new heaven and a new earth (taken in a physical sense) was very much in vogue in Jewish writing around the time of the Apocalypse (cf. 1 Enoch 72:1; 91:16), and is probably reflected also in 2 Peter 3:10–13 and Matthew 19:28. Scripture nowhere indicates what form the new heaven and the new earth will take. However, what is clear is that there will be a radical "renewal" of the present cosmos, contaminated as it is by the sin of man and the powers of evil (cf. Gen 2:8—3:24; Rom 8:9–13); through this renewal all creation will be "recapitulated" in Christ (cf. Eph 1:10; Col 1:16–20). No reference is made to the

---

o. Other ancient authorities read *peoples* **p.** Other ancient authorities add *and be their God*

Revelation 21:5

⁵And he who sat upon the throne said, "Behold, I make all things new." Also he said, "Write this, for these words are trustworthy and true." ⁶And he said to me, "It is done! I am the Alpha and the Omega, the beginning and the end. To the thirsty I will give from the fountain of the water of life without payment. ⁷He who conquers shall have this heritage, and I will be his God and he shall be my son. ⁸But as for the cowardly, the faithless, the polluted, as for murderers, fornicators, sorcerers, idolaters, and all

Marginal references: 2 Cor 5:17; Is 43:19; Is 55:1; Zech 14:8; Rev 1:8; 22:17; 2 Sam 7:14; Ps 89:27; Rev 22:15

---

sea, probably because in Jewish literature it symbolized the abyss, the abode of demonic powers hostile to God.

Those who will inhabit this new world (symbolized by the Holy City, the new Jerusalem) are the entire assembly of the saved, the entire people of God (cf. vv. 12–14)—a holy people disposed to live in loving communion with God (as reflected by the image of the adorned bride: cf. vv. 2, 9). The promise of a new covenant (Ezek 37:27) will be fulfilled to the letter: God will see to it that none of the evil, suffering or pain found in this world will find its way into the new world.

This passage of the book of Revelation strengthens the faith and hope of the Church—not only St John's own generation but all generations down the ages for as long as the Church makes its way through this valley of tears. The Second Vatican Council says: "We know neither the moment of the consummation of the earth and of man nor the way the universe will be transformed. The form of this world, distorted by sin, is passing away and we are taught that God is preparing a new dwelling and a new earth in which righteousness dwells, whose happiness will fill and surpass all the desires of peace arising in the hearts of men. Then with death conquered the children of God will be raised in Christ and what was sown in weakness and dishonour will put on the imperishable: charity and its works will remain, and all of creation, which God made for man, will be set free from its bondage to decay" (*Gaudium et spes*, 39).

21:5–8. For the first and only time in the book God himself speaks. He does so as absolute Lord of all, to ratify what has just been expounded. While the author and his readers are still in this world of suffering, God affirms that he—even now—is creating a new world. There is, then, a connexion between present human suffering and the future world which is taking shape thanks to the mercy of God.

Although that new world will emerge in its complete form on the last day, the renewal of all things has already begun; it began with the life, death and resurrection of Christ. "The kingdom of life has begun," St Gregory of Nyssa teaches, "and the empire of death has been undone. Another generation, another life, another way of loving has made its appearance: our very nature is being transformed. What type of generation am I referring to? A generation which results not from blood or carnal love or human love, but from God. Are you wondering how that can be? I shall explain it in a few words. This new creature is begotten by faith; the regeneration of Baptism brings it to birth; the Church, its nurse, weans it by her teaching and institutions and nourishes it with her heavenly bread. This new creature matures through holiness of life; its marriage is marriage with

liars, their lot shall be in the lake that burns with fire and sulphur, which is the second death."*

⁹Then came one of the seven angels who had the seven bowls full of the seven last plagues, and spoke to me, saying, "Come, I will show you the Bride, the wife of the Lamb." ¹⁰And in the Spirit he

Rev 15:1, 6, 7; 19:7
Mt 4:8; Ezek 40:2; Rev 21:2

Wisdom; its children, hope; its home, the Kingdom; its inheritance and its riches, the delights of paradise; its final destiny is not death, but eternal and joyful life in the dwelling-place of the saints" (*Oratio I in Christi resurrectionem*). We should remember that "the Kingdom is mysteriously present here on earth; when the Lord comes it will enter into its perfection" (*Gaudium et spes*, 39).

The promise of a world to come is so sure that although that world has not achieved its full perfection, it can be categorically stated that it is a promise *already kept*—"It is done": God himself, the Lord of history guarantees it (cf. note on Rev 1:8).

"To the thirsty": being thirsty refers to the desire man should have for the good things of the Kingdom, which God's loving kindness grants him. The idea of thirst (taken from Isaiah 55:1) here points to that yearning for God and the infinite which can only be satisfied by the grace of Christ, by the Holy Spirit within us (symbolized by St John in the water of life, cf., e.g., Jn 4:10; 7:38).

A Christian who has the grace of Christ and the gifts of the Holy Spirit can consider himself a conqueror, a sharer in our Lord's victory over sin and the powers of evil, and a sharer therefore in the dignity of a son or daughter of God in Christ. And so the title "son of God" (which in 2 Samuel 7:14 is applied, almost with the very same words as here, to the successor of David, and in Psalm 2:7 to the Messiah) is extended by St John to cover all Christians, called as they are to share in Christ's victory.

Contrasting with the beatitudes is the proclamation of the rejection of those who will have no part in the future Kingdom because they are damned for ever due to their persistence in sin. Therefore, we should be vigilant, as St Augustine taught: "Everyone fears physical death; but few fear the death of the soul [...]. Mortal man strives not to die; so, should not the man destined to live eternally strive not to sin?" (*In Ioann. Evang.*, 49, 2).

21:9–21. In contrast with the punishment visited on the evil city, Babylon, the harlot (cf. 17:1), we are now shown the Holy City, the new Jerusalem, the spouse, coming down from heaven. There is a significant parallel between 17:1ff and 21:9ff.

The author writes with a truly remarkable mastery of language: after the introduction (v. 9), he describes the Holy City using three literary devices which, after giving the measurements of the city, he repeats in more or less reverse order. The description is like the impressions a traveller has as he approaches: first, from afar, he sees its radiance—the city as a whole and the glory of God (vv. 10–11); as he comes closer he can distinguish walls and gates (vv. 12–13), and when closer still its foundation stones (v. 14). Once inside, he realizes its sheer scale (vv. 15–16) and is able to assess the size and richness of its walls (vv. 17–18) and foundation stones and gates (vv. 19–21); and he is spellbound by the brightness that shines from the glory of God (21:22—22:5).

Revelation 21:11

Rev 21:23
Is 58:8; 60:1, 2, 19

Ezek 48:31–35
Rev 7:1–8

Eph 2:20

Ezek 40:3, 5

Ezek 43:16; 48:16f

carried me away to a great, high mountain, and showed me the holy city Jerusalem coming down out of heaven from God, [11]having the glory of God, its radiance like a most rare jewel, like a jasper, clear as crystal. [12]It had a great, high wall, with twelve gates, and at the gates twelve angels, and on the gates the names of the twelve tribes of the sons of Israel were inscribed; [13]on the east three gates, on the north three gates, on the south three gates, and on the west three gates. [14]And the wall of the city had twelve foundations, and on them the twelve names of the twelve apostles of the Lamb.

[15]And he who talked to me had a measuring rod of gold to measure the city and its gates and walls. [16]The city lies foursquare, its length the same as its breadth; and he measured the city with his rod, twelve thousand stadia;[q] its length and breadth and height are equal. [17]He also measured its wall, a hundred and forty-four cubits by a

---

The city is given the titles of Bride and Wife (Spouse) which are normally used to designate the Church (cf. 19:7). This is easy to understand in the context of the imagery used: the city represents the Church, the community of the elect viewed in its complete, indissoluble union with the Lamb.

21:10–14. This vision is rather like the one the prophet Ezekiel had when he saw the New Jerusalem and the temple of the future (cf. Ezek 40–42). However, St John stresses (cf. also 21:2) that the city comes down from heaven: this shows that the full establishment (so long desired) of the messianic kingdom will be brought about by the power of God and in line with his will.

The description of the Holy City begins with the view from outside. This is the first thing that is seen and it is what makes it strong and unassailable. He speaks of pitfalls and gates and foundations. The names of the tribes of Israel and the twelve apostles show the continuity between the ancient chosen people and the Church of Christ; and yet the point is made that the Church is something quite new which rests on the twelve apostles of the Lord (cf. Eph 2:20). The arrangement of the gates, in threes facing the four points of the compass, indicates that the Church is universal: all nations must come to it to gain salvation. This is what St Augustine means when he says that "outside the catholic Church one can find everything except salvation" (*Sermo ad Cassar.*, 6).

21:15–17. The proportions, purely symbolic, convey the idea of the city's solidity and stability: it is depicted as a cube, as high as it is broad and long.

The Holy of Holies (described in 1 Kings 6:19f) was also cubic in form. The numbers are also symbolic: the 12,000 stadia signify the chosen people with its twelve tribes and also the multitude of nations which make up the new people. The one hundred and forty-four cubits (also a multiple of twelve), the height of the wall, are nothing compared with the towering height of the city; this is making the point that the walls are ornamental rather than defensive. Its enemies have been overthrown and it has no need of fortifications.

---

q. About fifteen hundred miles

man's measure, that is, an angel's. ¹⁸The wall was built of jasper, while the city was pure gold, clear as glass. ¹⁹The foundations of the wall of the city were adorned with every jewel; the first was jasper, the second sapphire, the third agate, the fourth emerald, ²⁰the fifth onyx, the sixth carnelian, the seventh chrysolite, the eighth beryl, the ninth topaz, the tenth chrysoprase, the eleventh jacinth, the twelfth amethyst. ²¹And the twelve gates were twelve pearls, each of the gates made of a single pearl, and the street of the city was pure gold, transparent as glass.

Is 54:11–12
Tob 13:17

The point is made that the measurements are human ones, despite the fact that it is an angel that does the measuring. In any case they are measures which indicate that the heavenly Jerusalem is vast and rich.

21:18–21. These descriptions recall those of Ezekiel, but they are much more colourful and beautiful. Each one of the precious foundation stones reveals the richness of the Holy City, as do the huge pearls which form its gates. Some Fathers of the Church have seen these descriptions as a reference to all the divine gifts present in some way in the soul in the state of grace.

As usual in the book, the message draws on the Old Testament: Tobit 13:17 speaks of the rebuilding of Jerusalem with precious stones such as sapphires and emeralds, which in turn are reminiscent of the ornamentation on the high priest's breastplate (cf. Ex 28:17–20) and the raiment of the prince of Tyre (Ezek 28:13). Thus, the precious stones identify the priestly and royal features of the City.

21:21b–27. After taking us up to the walls and through the gates of the City, the author brings us right inside, to its very centre; this also is amazingly rich. However, surprisingly, there is no temple. This makes it different from the Jerusalem described by Ezekiel, for the centre of that city was the temple (cf. Ezek 40–42). The temple in Jerusalem and the tent of the tabernacle in the wilderness symbolized the fact that God dwelt there; it was the visible sign of divine presence (*shekinah* in Hebrew), a presence revealed by the descent of the cloud of the glory of God.

In the heavenly Jerusalem there is no longer any need for God to have a dwelling-place, because God the Father himself and the Lamb are always present. The Godhead does not need to be brought to mind by the temple (the symbol of his invisible presence), because the blessed will always see God face to face. This sight of God is what causes the righteous to be forever happy. "There are no words to explain the blessedness which the soul enjoys, the gain which he obtains once his true nature has been restored to him and he is able henceforth to contemplate his Lord" (Chrysostom, *Ad Theodorum lapsum*, 1, 13).

In the Old Testament theophanies of Yahweh, a splendid brightness revealed the divine glory. And so, the presence of God will fill the heavenly Jerusalem with such a brightness of light that there is no need of sun or moon. Beside God the Father, with equal rank and dignity, is the Lamb, whose glory will also shine out, revealing his divinity.

This light will illuminate all those who worship the Lord, thereby fulfilling

Revelation 21:22

²²And I saw no temple in the city, for its temple is the Lord God the Almighty and the Lamb. ²³And the city has no need of sun or moon to shine upon it, for the glory of God is its light, and its lamp is the Lamb. ²⁴By its light shall the nations walk; and the kings of the earth shall bring their glory into it, ²⁵and its gates shall never be shut by day—and there shall be no night there; ²⁶they shall bring into it the glory and the honour of the nations. ²⁷But nothing unclean shall enter it, nor any one who practises abomination or falsehood, but only those who are written in the Lamb's book of life.

Cross-references: Jn 2:19–21; Is 24:23; 60:1, 19; Rev 22:5; Is 60:3, 5; Is 60:11; Rev 22:5; Is 60:11; Is 52:1; 2 Pet 3:13; Zech 13:1–2

22 ¹Then he showed me the river of the water of life, bright as crystal, flowing from the throne of God and of the Lamb ²through the middle of the street of the city; also, on either side of the river, the tree of life^r with its twelve kinds of fruit, yielding its fruit each month; and the leaves of the tree were for the healing of the nations. ³There shall no more be anything accursed, but the throne of God and of the Lamb shall be in it, and his servants shall worship him; ⁴they shall see his face, and his name shall be on their foreheads. ⁵And night shall be no more; they need no light of lamp or sun, for the Lord God will be their light, and they shall reign for ever and ever.

Cross-references: Ezek 47:1, 7; Zech 14:8; Ezek 47:12; Gen 2:9; Zech 14:11; Rev 7:15; 1 Jn 3:2; 1 Cor 13:12; Ps 17:15; 42–3; Rev 21:25; 5:10; Is 60:19; Dan 7:18, 27

---

the messianic prophecies of Isaiah (cf. Is 60:3, 5, 11; 65–66).

The gates of the Holy City will stay open by day, that is, always, because there will be no more night, nor anything unclean: the saints will be the only ones to enter.

22:1–5. Since the water of life is a symbol of the Holy Spirit (cf. 21:6), some Fathers and modern commentators have, justifiably, read a trinitarian meaning into this passage—interpreting the river that flows from the throne of God and of the Lamb as representing the Holy Spirit who proceeds from the Father and the Son.

The trees whose leaves never fade (cf. Ps 1:3), with their fruit and medicinal foliage, symbolize the joy of eternal life (cf. Ezek 47:1–12; Ps 46:5).

The passage also takes up the prophecy in Zechariah 14:11 that nothing will be accursed—a reference to the terrible practice of anathema (Hebrew *herem*) which marked the Israelite conquest of Canaan: to avoid being tainted by idolatrous pagans, the Israelites laid cities and fields waste, putting them to torch and killing inhabitants and livestock. Peace and security will now reign supreme. And the dream of every man will come true—to see God (something impossible to attain on earth). Now all the blessed will see God (cf. 1 Cor 13:12); and because they see him they shall be like him (cf. 1 Jn 3:2). The name of God on their foreheads shows that they belong to God (cf. Rev 13:16–17).

---

r. Or *the Lamb. In the midst of the street of the city, and on either side of the river, was the tree of life*, etc.

The visions come to an end

⁶And he said to me, "These words are trustworthy and true. And the Lord, the God of the spirits of the prophets, has sent his angel to show his servants what must soon take place. ⁷And behold, I am coming soon."

Blessed is he who keeps the words of the prophecy of this book.

⁸I John am he who heard and saw these things. And when I heard and saw them, I fell down to worship at the feet of the angel who showed them to me; ⁹but he said to me, "You must not do that! I am a fellow servant with you and your brethren the prophets, and with those who keep the words of this book. Worship God."

¹⁰And he said to me, "Do not seal up the words of the prophecy of this book, for the time is near. ¹¹Let the evildoer still do evil, and the filthy still be filthy, and the righteous still do right, and the holy still be holy."

22:6–9. The author concludes his account of his visions by reaffirming that everything he has written is true (vv. 5–9) and by issuing a solemn warning: it will all come to pass and people will either be blessed or rejected (vv. 10–15).

The truth of what the book says is grounded on God, who is truth itself. This is St John's usual way of referring to the authority and reliability of his teaching (cf. Rev 1:1, 9; Jn 19:35; 1 Jn 1:1ff). He is acutely conscious of having written in the same manner as the prophets spoke—inspired by "the God of the spirits of the prophets". That is why he presents his book as "prophecy".

He also insists on the fact that the Lord's coming is imminent: he says this no less than three times in this chapter (vv. 7, 12 and 20): this is designed to make it quite clear that the Lord will come, and to create a climate of vigilance and hope (cf. note on Rev 1:1, on the imminence of the second coming).

Because this is a genuine book of prophecy, those who read it and tell others its message are described as "blessed". This is the attitude which Jesus required people to have towards the word of God and towards his own words: when a woman proclaims his Mother "blessed", our Lord replies, "Blessed rather are those who hear the word of God and keep it" (Lk 11:28), and he promises that a person who listens to his word and keeps it is like someone who builds on solid foundations (cf. Mt 7:24). St James gives a similar warning: "be doers of the word, and not hearers only, deceiving yourselves" (Jas 1:22).

22:10–15. Unlike other revelations (cf. Rev 10:4; Dan 8:26), God makes it plain that he wants everyone to know the things St John has just written; Christians needed to be consoled and strengthened in the trials that lay ahead. They must keep pressing on, for the end is near (v. 11); these words are somewhat ironic, ridiculing as they do those who are bent on continuing to live a depraved life, unwilling to admit their sin and unwilling to mend their ways in time. The passage makes it quite clear that there will be a judgment made by Christ when he comes again; when he exercises this judicial authority

Revelation 22:12

Ps 28:4; 62:13
Jer 17:10; Is 40:10; Is 44:6; 48:12; Heb 13:8
Rev 1:17, 8

¹²"Behold, I am coming soon, bringing my recompense, to repay every one for what he has done. ¹³I am the Alpha and the Omega, the first and the last, the beginning and the end."

Gen 2:9; 3:22
Rev 7:14

¹⁴Blessed are those who wash their robes,ˢ that they may have the right to the tree of life and that they may enter the city by the gates.

Rev 21:8; 27

¹⁵Outside are the dogs and sorcerers and fornicators and murderers and idolaters, and every one who loves and practises falsehood.

4. EPILOGUE

Rev 1:1; 2:28
Is 11:1, 10; 14:12; Lk 1:78
Num 24:17

¹⁶"I Jesus have sent my angel to you with this testimony for the churches. I am the root and the offspring of David, the bright morning star."

Zech 14:8
Jn 7:37
Is 55:1
Rev 21:6

Prayer of the Spirit and the Bride. Words of warning and farewell
¹⁷The Spirit and the Bride say, "Come." And let him who hears say, "Come." And let him who is thirsty come, let him who desires take the water of life without price.

---

which belongs to God alone, he appears with divine attributes (cf. note on Rev 1:8). The message contained in these verses should be reassuring for the Christian. As St Teresa of Avila says, "May His Majesty be pleased to grant us to experience this before he takes us from this life, for it will be a great thing at the hour of death to realize that we shall be judged by One whom we have loved above all things. Once our debts have been paid we shall be able to walk in safety. We shall not be going into a foreign land, but into our own country, for it belongs to him whom we have loved so truly and who himself loves us" (*Way of Perfection*, 40).

The robes washed in the blood of the Lamb (cf. note on Rev 7: 14) are a reference to the fact that the righteous have been cleansed by having applied to them the merits of the passion, death and resurrection of Christ.

22:16. In a formal, solemn manner Jesus Christ addresses believers and confirms the genuineness of the prophetic content of the book. This marks the start of the epilogue, which records the testimony of the Church (v. 17) and the writer (vv. 18–19) and once again, before the words of farewell, Christ's own confirmation (v. 20).

The titles applied to Jesus focus on his Hebrew and Davidic ancestry, without which he could not be the Messiah. Instead of the word "root", other passages speak of his being a young, vigorous shoot which grows out of the ancient trunk of Jesse (cf. Is 11:1). The morning star is another metaphor designating the Messiah (cf. Num 24:17).

22:17. The Bride is the Church who, in reply to Christ's promise (cf. 22:12), ardently desires and prays for his coming.

---

s. Other ancient authorities read *do his commandments*

Revelation 22:20

¹⁸I warn every one who hears the words of the prophecy of this Deut 4:2; 13:1
book: if any one adds to them, God will add to him the plagues
described in this book, ¹⁹and if any one takes away from the words
of the book of this prophecy, God will take away his share in the Rev 21:10–22:2
tree of life and in the holy city, which are described in this book.
²⁰He who testifies to these things says, "Surely I am coming 1 Cor 16:22
soon." Amen. Come, Lord Jesus!

The prayer of the Church is inspired by the Holy Spirit, the voices of both Church and Spirit fusing in a single cry. Every Christian is invited to join in this prayer and discover in the Church the gift of the Spirit, symbolized by the water of life (cf. 21:6); this gift allows the Christian to taste in anticipation the good things of the Kingdom. The language of this verse reminds us of the liturgical dimension of the Church with its prayer and celebration of the sacraments.

22:18–19. Using language similar to Deuteronomy 4:2 (cf. also Deut 13:1; Prov 30:6), the author warns that nothing in this book may be altered, for the very good reason that it is a revelation from God. No one may tamper with it, no one may add or subtract anything, or if he does God will call him to account. What St John says here is applicable to all divine Revelation. That is why St Paul told the Galatians that anyone—even an angel—would be accursed, excommunicated, who dared to change the Gospel, the message of received faith (cf. Gal 1:8).

The Revelation made by Christ has been entrusted to the Church, who guards it faithfully with the aid of the Holy Spirit. As St Vincent of Lerins teaches, "in the catholic Church the greatest care must be taken to keep what has been believed everywhere, always and by all […]. The very nature of religion demands that everything be passed on to children as faithfully as it has been received by parents" (*Commonitorium*, 2 and 6). The deposit of faith is so inviolable that "true ecumenical activity means openness, drawing closer, availability for dialogue, and a shared investigation of the truth in the full evangelical and Christian sense; but in no way does it or can it mean giving up or in any way diminishing the treasures of divine truth that the Church has constantly confessed and taught" (John Paul II, *Redemptor hominis*, 6).

22:20. Christ himself replies to the supplication of the Church and the Spirit: "I am coming soon." This idea occurs seven times in the course of the book (cf. 2:16; 3:11; 16:15; 22:7, 12, 17, 20), showing that this is a promise which will certainly be kept. On the basis of this passage, John Paul II makes this exhortation: "Therefore, let Christ be your sure point of reference, let him be the basis of a confidence which knows no vacillation. Let the passionate invocation of the Church, 'Come, Lord Jesus' become the spontaneous sigh of your heart, a heart never content with the present because it always tends towards the 'not yet' of promised fulfilment" (*Homily*, 18 May 1980).

This invocation—"Come, Lord Jesus"—was so often on the lips and in the hearts of the first Christians that it was even expressed in Aramaic, the language which Jesus and the apostles spoke: *Marana-tha* (cf. 1 Cor 16:22; *Didache*, 10, 6). Today, translated into

Revelation 22:21

1 Cor 16:23   ²¹The grace of the Lord Jesus be with all the saints.ᵗ Amen.

---

the vernacular, it is used as an acclamation at Mass, after the elevation. And so "the earthly liturgy harmonizes with that of heaven. And now, as in every Mass, there reaches our heart, which is so much in need of consolation, that reassuring reply: 'He who testifies to these things says, "Surely I am coming soon [...]".' Strengthened by this certainty, let us set out again along the ways of the earth, feeling greater unity and solidarity with one another, and at the same time bearing in our heart the desire that has become more eager to make known to our brothers and sisters, still enveloped by the clouds of doubt and depression, the 'joyful proclamation' that there has risen over the horizon of their lives 'the bright morning star' (Rev 22:16), the Redeemer of man, Christ the Lord" (John Paul II, *Homily*, 18 May 1980).

---

t. Other ancient authorities omit *all*; others omit *the saints*

Introduction to the Letter to the Hebrews

The content of the Letter to the Hebrews makes it one of the most imposing and important books in the New Testament. It is very accurately reflected in its title, even though that title probably only goes back to the second century. It is very likely that the "Hebrews" to whom this letter was addressed were in the first instance Christians of Jewish background who were very familiar both with the Greek language and with Hebraic culture, particularly the ceremonies of Mosaic worship.

The Epistle to the Hebrews is of a type which falls between a letter and a written address or sermon (cf. 13:22, where it is described as a "word of consolation"). Its structure and presentation are reminiscent of a short theological treatise. This is perhaps why some scholars have described it as a "literary letter", although the literary letter proper is addressed to a fictitious reader, which is not the case here. By using the letter form, the writer was able to produce a text which would appeal to a wider readership than an essay would.

Historically and doctrinally this epistle is connected, via its content, with the corpus of Pauline letters, for it faithfully echoes the preaching of St Paul. And yet it has characteristic features of its own which point to its obvious originality.

The main purpose of the letter is to show the superiority of Christianity over the Old Covenant; yet its style and purpose are not polemical. It is designed to show that the New law is the perfection, the fulfilment, of the Old law, which it supersedes. To do this, it focuses on the idea that Christ's priesthood and sacrifice are superior to those of the Levitical priesthood. The writer uses this teaching as the basis for exhorting his readers to persevere in the faith: this pastoral purpose is also a primordial aim of the letter.

CANONICITY

Hebrews forms part of the canon of the Bible and therefore it must be taken as divinely inspired: certain early councils—for example, the Council of Carthage in 397—put it in this category, as did all the Fathers of the Church.

The Letter to the Hebrews was solemnly pronounced to be canonical by the Councils of Florence (1442) and Trent (Session IV, 1546).[1]

---

1. *Reply* of the Pontifical Biblical Commission, 24 June 1914, *Dz-Sch* 2176.

Introduction to the Letter to the Hebrews

AUTHOR, AND PLACE AND DATE OF COMPOSITION

Many Christian writers of the East regarded the Letter to the Hebrews as having been written by St Paul himself. These included, for example, St John Chrysostom, a great admirer of the writings of the Teacher of the Gentiles and one deeply versed in them.

If St Paul did write this letter, it would mean that there is a total of fourteen letters in the canon written by the Apostle. However, the tradition of the western Church is not quite unanimous on this point. "Ambrosiaster", the anonymous author of the first complete Latin commentary on St Paul, does not include this letter in his work. St Jerome himself touches on the question and expresses some doubts, as does St Augustine from 409 onwards. However, as to whether it can be directly attributed to St Paul, both Augustine and Jerome (later on and under the influence of tradition) came to accept not only that this is an inspired letter—which was never in doubt—but also that it is by Paul. Thus St Jerome, for example, quoting a passage from Hebrews, writes: "thus speaks St Paul in his letter, the letter he writes to the Hebrews, although many Latin authors doubt (his authorship)" (*In Mt,* 4, 26). The Muratorian Fragment or "Muratorian Canon", a Roman papyrus of the end of the second century containing an official listing of inspired books, does not explicitly include this letter among the Pauline writings, whereas the others are listed in detail. Some Renaissance theologians, among them Erasmus and Cajetan, also held the view that St Paul was not the author of this letter—and this is the opinion of most twentieth-century exegetes. According to these scholars, the main arguments against St Paul's authorship are—the absence of his name at the heading of the letter; the absence also of St Paul's usual form of signing-off and other typical features of Pauline letters; the marked difference in syntax and other aspects of literary style between this and the other Pauline letters; the diversity of doctrinal themes; and the letter's particular way of quoting the Old Testament.

The sacred writer and his personality stay very much in the background (cf. 13:18b), as if he were deliberately hiding behind the sublimity of his subject-matter. At the same time it is quite clear that he was an educated Christian, deeply versed in Holy Scripture and very familiar with the main theological issues of the day. The person who actually wrote the letter must have been someone very close to St Paul, familiar with his thinking and with his apostolic work. The content of the letter clearly shows the writer to have been someone of Hellenist culture and a person with much pastoral zeal, who had a deep knowledge of the religious life of the Jews and of the religious worship conducted in the temple of Jerusalem.

Origen, in the second century, spoke of the possibility of an "editor" of Paul's ideas being the direct author of the letter. "The ideas of the epistle", the Alexandrian exegete writes, "certainly belong to the Apostle; however, the

Introduction to the Letter to the Hebrews

language and composition seem to belong to someone else, who wished to record Paul's thinking, writing down the words of the Master."

Origen's theory has been widely followed in the tradition of the Church and has been indirectly supported by the Pontifical Biblical Commission in its reply of 24 June 1914.[2] However, attempts are still made to identify the author-editor, and among the names put forward are those of St Barnabas, St Luke, St Clement of Rome and the disciple Apollos (cf. Acts 18:24f). However, all these suggestions are pure conjecture.

Most of the Fathers and early commentators were of the opinion that the letter was written in Rome or in some part of Italy—given the reference in Hebrews 13:24, "Those who come from Italy send you greetings." However, that sentence could also be taken as a greeting from a group of Italian Christians now living in some other (unidentified) place from which the letter is being sent. In fact, one manuscript gives Athens as its place of composition; others say it was written in Rome or in Italy; basically we do not know for sure where it was written.

It is less difficult to establish the approximate time of writing. Hebrews 1:3–13 appears as a quotation in chapter 36, 2–5 of St Clement of Rome's *Letter to the Corinthians*, which was written around the year 95. If the letter was already quite widely known by that date, then it could not have been written later than the start of the 90s.

The internal evidence of the letter allows us to push the date back much further and to say that there is every likelihood that it was written prior to the destruction of Jerusalem in the year 70. At no point is there any reference to the fall of the city; whereas many references clearly imply that the temple and Mosaic worship are still active (cf. 8:4; 9:7, 13, 25).

Moreover, the text refers repeatedly (cf. 10:25; 10:37; 12:26f; 13:13) to difficult times for the Jews. This might suggest that we are on the eve of the Jewish-Roman war, which was declared in the year 67. Quite a number of scholars opt for 67 as the date of composition.

IMMEDIATE READERSHIP

The content of the letter allows us to state that it was undoubtedly addressed to converts from Judaism, that is, Christians of Jewish origin. They seem to be people well-known to the writer, for he confidently asks them to pray for him and tells them to expect him soon (cf. 13:18–19, 23). They are Christians who are familiar with the sacred books, especially the book of Exodus and the Psalms, and they are very familiar with standard Jewish interpretation. They know the temple well and are familiar with the details of divine worship as

---

2. Cf. *Dz-Sch* 2178.

performed there; they have attended the ceremonies of the great "Day of Atonement", and the daily sacrifices (cf. 8:1–10, 18) and understand the terminology connected with those rites.

Furthermore, they are not recent converts. The letter refers to their having already received initiation catechesis (cf. 5:12); and they may have been teachers, because they were converted a long time back (cf. 10:32) and saw for themselves the miracles and supernatural gifts which accompanied the early preaching of the apostles (cf. 6:4–5; 10:26). They may even have heard the preaching of Stephen (cf. 2:4; Acts 6:8). However, in addition to this, they have earned merit by their service to the saints (cf. 6:10) and have bravely and patiently borne overt persecution involving public opprobrium, confiscation of property, imprisonment and, in some cases, even capital punishment (cf. 10:32–34; 12:4).

The central purpose of the epistle is to encourage these brethren to stay loyal in the face of persecution—because they were showing signs of weakening (cf. 10:25; 12:25; 13:10)—and ultimately to protect them from the danger of apostasy. This explains the way in which the sacred writer prudently combines warm encouragement with straight talk (cf. 6:4–6; 10:26–31; 12:15–29).

From early on, commentators have asked whether the author of Hebrews was addressing a specific local church, as in the case of the letters to the Romans, Corinthians, Galatians etc.; or whether he was writing to a small group of people within a wider Christian community—what we might call a "domestic church" or perhaps a group of faithful who used to meet in the house of some particular family. The writer seems to be addressing a group of people who are cut off from their background—perhaps refugees or exiles.

Certainly, the specialized subject and focus of the letter suggest that the sacred writer is addressing a definite group that forms part of a wider Christian community. Some scholars even think that it is addressed to former Levitical priests, converts to the Gospel, who, harassed by persecutions, feel tempted to revert to Judaism (cf. Acts 6:7; Heb 3:12–14; 6:4–6; 10:39; 12:12–13; 13:5–6).

STRUCTURE

The literary structure of Hebrews has been the subject of detailed study; nevertheless, it is difficult to come to grips with, for various reasons. Firstly, the rules of rhetoric in the ancient Greek and Latin world did not require a rigorously developed composition, with paragraphs of more or less equal length: the writer was free to digress, develop, go back, anticipate himself, etc. Secondly, although the literary form chosen by the writer, that of a letter, approaches that of a sermon or theological essay, it does not really lend itself to a very systematic exposition; and thirdly, the writer's Semitic mind is not

Introduction to the Letter to the Hebrews

concerned with the harmonious arranging of parts (of the letter) but rather focuses on certain basic ideas. All this helps to explain why, throughout his exposition, he is constantly changing from a doctrinal vein to an exhortative one and back again. He purposely mixes moral and dogmatic elements, presenting the truths of faith as the basis for the line of conduct he is recommending. From this point of view the letter is a very good example of the unity that should obtain between doctrine and life, a unity which is so proper to the New Testament; it is a model for the best sort of Christian religious writing.

Hebrews does not, therefore, contain a doctrinal section followed by a moral section. Its doctrinal content is spread throughout the letter and liable to appear at any moment. Drawing on earlier exegetical tradition, St Thomas Aquinas rightly says that the central theme of the epistle is Christ; in which case it can be divided into four sections. The first three would aim at showing Christ's superiority over the most prominent figures in the Old Testament—angels, Moses and the priests of the Levitical order. The fourth and last section would be mainly moral and exhortative in character. Hugh of St-Cher proposes a similar division of the letter: 1) Christ's superiority over all creation; 2) the superiority of Christ's priesthood over the priesthood of the Old Testament; 3) an exhortation to faith, which brings us closer to Christ; and 4) moral teaching.

Modern scholarship proposes a division into five parts (individual scholars may offer minor variations on this). Obviously there is nothing hard and fast about this division; it is essentially tentative.

It is fairly easy to identify five doctrinal sections in the letter:

1. Christ's pre-existence, his divine condition and his activity as Creator (1:1–4).
2. Christ's superiority over angels (1:5—2:18).
3. His superiority over Moses (3:1—4:13).
4. Christ's priesthood is on a higher level than the Levitical priesthood (4:14—7:28).
5. Christ's sacrifice is greater than all the sacrifices of the Old Law (8:1—10:18).

The ascetic, exhortatory and moral content of the letter, which is interlayered with the theological parts, deals with the following themes:

- to attain salvation it is essential to follow Jesus (2:1–4);
- to enter God's "rest" one must imitate those faithful souls who accepted Revelation (3:7—4:13);
- the prospect of everlasting joy; criteria for Christian living (5:11—6:20);

- reasons why a believer should persevere in the faith despite difficulties; and the good example set by those who have gone before (10:19—12:19);
- final advice (13:1–19).

Verses 7–17 of chapter 13 seem to summarize the main themes of the epistle and contain a concluding exhortation to that right living and spiritual vitality which should characterize Christian life.

LANGUAGE AND STYLE OF ARGUMENT

The language of the Letter to the Hebrews is notable for its singular clarity; this gives it an important place in literature and it also makes it a well argued theological treatise. Its majestic flow and the sublimity of its subject-matter explain why the Church uses it so extensively in the Liturgy.

The author, who must have had a good Hellenist education, writes very correct and elegant Greek; his vocabulary is rich, and he manages to express his thought very graphically by employing many stylistic devices, such as contrasts, comparisons, parallelisms, and use of quotations and examples from Scripture. He is particularly good at linking phrases and clauses to form elaborate, formal sentences, in line with the style of the best writers of Hellenist Greek prose. The letter does not have the limpid, transparent and agile Greek of St Luke, but from a literary point of view it undoubtedly comes next in line in the New Testament after Luke.

We might refer in particular to how, in the midst of the generally precise and sober style of the letter, certain passages stand out for their deep religious emotion—for example, its evocation of Christ's agony in Gethesemane (cf. 5:7–8), his passion and death on the cross (cf. 6:6; 12:2; 13:22), and the faith and steadfastness of the Patriarchs (cf. 11:1–40).

The author, who was deeply versed in Holy Scripture, uses for the most part the Greek translation (the "Septuagint"), which was what all the apostles used in their preaching. When he quotes a passage of the Old Testament he does so with an introductory formula which shows his conviction that the Bible is divinely inspired: the passage being quoted is seen as something said directly by God the Father or by the Son, or, in some instances, by the Holy Spirit (cf. 3:7; 10:15). Also, the author of Hebrews almost always interprets Scripture in its literal sense, that is, he focuses on what the text seems to be saying directly. A distinguishing feature of Hebrews is the way it "actualizes" the Old Testament texts by applying them to Christ. In the Psalms and the Prophets it is God the Father who is addressing his Son, or God the Son speaking to his Father.

Introduction to the Letter to the Hebrews

INTERPRETATION OF THE OLD TESTAMENT

To understand the way the author of Hebrews uses Holy Scripture, it is useful to bear in mind that in many instances he is applying rabbinical rules of biblical interpretation. This type of exegesis is called *derash* in Hebrew (deriving from the verb meaning "to seek", "to interpret").[3]

Derash is to be found in many documents—translations of biblical texts with short explanations built into them; ascetical or moral commentaries; and lists of rules and regulations derived from the Law (for example, marriage rites, regulations about the celebration of feasts, etc.).[4] It is essentially a form of exegesis that sticks to the letter of the text and uses certain procedures from logic—analogies, reflections on the text, parallel passages, moving from the general to the particular, etc. However, in the course of its development this type of exegesis tended more and more to become a search for a religious meaning that went beyond the obvious or immediate meaning, towards "actualization" of the texts, in other words, applying it to new situations in history. *Derash* gradually liberated itself from purely literal and linguistic explanations and tended to take on the main features of spiritual or allegorical interpretation.

An example might show more clearly what we mean. Hebrews 1:5-14 quotes a number of Old Testament texts to show the superiority of Christ, the Son of God, over the angels (cf. 2 Sam 7:14; Deut 32:43; Ps 45:7-8; 97:7; 102:256ff; 104:4; 110:1); in addition to the number of references given, the interesting thing to note is that some of the Psalms are read as words of God the Father addressed to his Son, even though in their original context these psalms were addressed to God in praise of his omnipotence (cf. Ps 97:7;

---

3. In Jewish culture we find three main types of biblical interpretation. The first is *derash*; used in the synagogue, this uses a series of seven fixed criteria, laid down—as tradition has it—by Rabbi Hillel; the second is the form of exegesis known as *pesher* (= explanation), widely used in the Qumran community on the shores of the Dead Sea in the period from the second century BC to the first century AD and found in the famous Dead Sea Scrolls; the third is exegesis of an allegorical-moral type popularized by the famous Jewish scholar Alexander of Philo (d. AD 40). **4.** Particularly the *targumim*, the *midrashim*, the *Mishnah* and the *Talmud*. The targums are translations of the Hebrew Old Testament into Aramaic, with explanatory notes. These are of great importance, on account both of their antiquity (they go back to the first century B.C., but use material of an earlier date) and of their content; and they reflect common rabbinical interpretation of difficult passages. The *midrashim* (from *midrash* = research, search) are explanations of the Bible, of an exhortatory or edifying character, sourced in synagogal preaching, that is, in the homilies of rabbis. The *Mishnah* (= repetition) is a collection of short legal and ethical treatises based on rabbinical sayings and decisions. It began to be compiled as a text in the second century AD and was finished around the fifth century AD. It reflects the Law or Torah and the interpretations of numerous oral prescriptions. Its exegesis is called *halakic* (from *halak* = walking, in both the physical and moral sense); it is legal and ethical in character and has to do with providing answers to particular questions and situations. The *Talmud* (= teaching) is a commentary on the Mishnah in line with traditional Jewish religious teaching. It has only a distant connexion with Scripture but it does provide information useful to understanding Jewish customs during the period of our Lord's life on earth.

Introduction to the Letter to the Hebrews

102:26; 104:4) or, in some instances, were prayers or petitions to the Messiah King (cf. Ps 45:7–8; 110:1).

What the author of Hebrews, under divine inspiration, has done is to "actualize" the psalm by interpreting it as referring to Jesus Christ (whom he implicitly sees as Author of creation and true King of the chosen people).

There are many other examples[5] that might be given of the same type of exegesis. One very important one has to do with the figure of Melchizedek, without father, mother or genealogy; another concerns the sprinkling of the tablets of the Law with the blood and ashes of a cow, using a swab of scarlet wool: they are important because they refer to the priesthood and sacrifice, respectively, of Christ.

The compilation of sequences of scriptural passages and the application of texts to current situations were methods frequently used in derashic interpretation. There is every reason, therefore, for saying that Hebrews was written by a Jew steeped in rabbinical ways, a qualified "doctor of the Law" or scribe, or perhaps a rabbi. The intellectual or cultural background, then, of the writer, is that of a rabbi, a Pharisee; whereas its literary form is appropriate to a Hellenist Jew of Alexandrian background. This is compatible with seeing St Paul as responsible for the ideas of the letter: Paul was a Pharisee, a zealous upholder of the Law, a member of the tribe of Benjamin, proud of his background, in his youth a student of Gamaliel.[6]

The *derash* of the Letter of the Hebrews, however, parts company with rabbinical exegesis on one fundamental point: it is centred on Jesus, the climax of the Law. In this respect it is very different from rabbinical exegesis, which confined itself to explaining obscure or difficult points and which attended only to Mosaic precepts.

In Hebrews the Old Testament is not quoted to "prove" the excellence and superiority of Jesus; rather, the truths concerning Jesus throw light on and enable us to understand what the Old Testament is all about. The Old Testament is not used to interpret the new: on the contrary, the opposite is the case. The Old Testament text is "actualized" in the light of the New, or, as the Fathers often put it, the New Testament is to be found latent in the Old, and the Old is made manifest in the New. In line with this approach, the first Christians delved in the Old Testament to discover predictions about Christs birth and his role. As they saw it, it was not possible to understand the Old Testament without reference to the New; however, using the Old Testament as a basis, they felt they could demonstrate that everything to do with Christ occurred in line with a pre-ordained divine plan.

---

5. Other examples of "actualization" are to be found in the case of Ps 40:7 and 95:8, applied to the situation of Christians or to the sacrifice of the cross. **6.** Cf. Phil 3:5–6; Acts 8:13; 21:40; 22:3; 23:6; Rom 9:3–5; 10:1–2; 2 Cor 11:22.

Introduction to the Letter to the Hebrews

THEOLOGY

The theological teaching contained in the Letter to the Hebrews is essentially Christological. Its view of Christ, God and man and High Priest of the New Law, provides the structure of the letter, linking all its parts together and giving the whole letter a remarkable cohesion.

In connexion with this Christological purpose, the letter has extremely important things to say on the relationship between Judaism and Christianity, on faith and revelation, on the last things, and on Christian life in the world as the way to eternal life.

a) *Judaism and Christianity.* The relationship between the two religions—Judaism and Christianity—which contain supernatural Revelation, being, respectively, the foundation and the culmination of God's saving designs, is not viewed only from the standpoint of defence of the Christian faith. In a non-polemical spirit and with a serenity befitting one who is writing with a vision of eternity and in the presence of God, the sacred author shows that the objective superiority of Christianity is the key factor in salvation history. The thrust of the letter is not designed to discredit the Jewish religion but rather to assign it its proper place as a preparatory stage in God's plan of salvation.

The central idea of the letter is that the Mosaic Law is incapable of saving mankind which finds itself in a fallen state because of Adam's sin. In line with this it proclaims the religious impermanence of the Old Law, which Christ has abolished and replaced with the Law of the Gospel, which is the law of grace, freedom and interior challenge. This is in fact a basic principle in the thinking that imbues the letters of the Apostle of the Gentiles. This was the great dogmatic point clarified by the Council of Jerusalem. As recounted in Acts 15, that first assembly laid down that it is not necessary for salvation to observe the rites of the Mosaic Law, and that therefore people of Gentile background who become Christians are not obliged to observe those regulations. The letter is very mindful of this teaching and in a sense develops it.

The superiority of the New Testament over the Old—which comes across clearly not only from the letter's teaching about Christ but also from what it has to say about the sacraments and about sacrifice, and from the unvarying testimony of the apostles—does not, however, affect the *unity*, the continuum, of the two Testaments. The letter evidences this unity, about which the Second Vatican Council solemnly reminded the Church;[7] it does this mainly by its use of Old Testament figures or "types". All the key figures in the Old Covenant look forward to Christ and place their hope in him. Moses and Melchizedek are, respectively, "types" of the Messiah and High Priest of the New Law.

---

7. Cf. *Dei Verbum*, 16.

Introduction to the Letter to the Hebrews

Christianity is therefore the culmination of Judaism, with the result that the Mosaic religion cannot be understood without reference to the Gospel. Logically, the dogmatic principle enunciated here has many implications for properly understanding the history of salvation and Judaism; and it also is very relevant to the life of the converts to whom the letter seems to be addressed.

b) *Faith and Revelation.* The Letter to the Hebrews is a "word of exhortation" (13:22) to steadfastness in the faith. The letter frequently makes reference to this virtue, but Hebrews 11:1 offers a particularly rich and concise definition of faith, one which has become classical in the commentaries of the Fathers and Doctors of the Church. St Thomas Aquinas studies it at length in his treatise on faith and says that it meets all the conditions necessary to make it an exact and adequate definition. In as many words, he defines faith as "that habit of mind whereby we attain to an initial grasp of eternal life, leading the understanding to assent to things unseen."[8] Faith, as described in the epistle, is seen as a habit,[9] a disposition which moves a person to adhere firmly to what God has revealed. The characters and situations of the Old Testament whom the epistle refer to are always cited in connexion with fidelity to God's promises. But the content of these promises was Jesus Christ himself and the benefits he would provide to men through his redemptive sacrifice. Faith, therefore, is anchored in Jesus, "the pioneer and perfecter of our faith" (12:2): he is the cause of our faith, and it is him that we believe in the first instance. He it is, as author of grace, who infuses this virtue into us. We start out from faith in Jesus, and in our ultimate homeland we shall see him face to face. In heaven, faith is transformed into glory—hence its close connexion with hope. Faith in Christ, in his sacrifice, in his resurrection and glorification, is the foundation of Christian hope. Christ has entered into heaven, thereby opening the way for all mankind. That is why suffering makes sense, that is why it is worth the effort to endure affliction (cf. 10:19ff).

But faith in Christ is faith in Revelation, because Christ is the fullness of the revelation of the Father. God has made himself manifest to us in his own Son, the perfect Word of the Father spoken to mankind.[10] Faith in Christ requires, therefore, that we should not only believe in him, in his person, but also believe in his precepts and teachings. Hence the letter's numerous exhortations to Christian living interwoven with its dogmatic teaching: these exhortations are consequences that arise from faith in the Son of God and in what he has revealed to us.

c) *Christology.* The teaching about Jesus Christ which is the predominant feature of the letter is extremely rich and at the same time has a remarkable

---

8. *Summa theologiae*, 2, q. 4, a. 1. **9.** Faith as an act is dealt with particularly in Romans 4, when St Paul comments on the faith of Abraham who "believed against (all) hope" (Rom 4:18). **10.** Cf. Heb 1:1–2; *Dei Verbum*, 4.

simplicity and directness. The subject of Christ's priesthood, tying in naturally with discussion of the Mosaic Law and the Levitical priesthood, is central to the letter.

The sacred author explores the subject of the universal Redemption brought about by Christ the mediator through the sacrifice of the cross and the shedding of his blood. Christ is at one and the same time the perfect Victim atoning for all the sins of mankind and the true High Priest offering to God the Father a worship that is acceptable and everlasting; this is another basic idea of Pauline theology. However, prior to dealing with the subject of Redemption and priesthood, in its opening verses the letter gives a brief but solemn proclamation of the eternal pre-existence of the Word, his role as creator and his equality with the Father (cf. 1:1–3)—verses which are reminiscent of what the prologue to St John's Gospel reveals about the Word.

The letter's teaching about Christ is given against the backdrop of the fact that Christ is true God and true man—as he must be if he is to bring about Redemption. It never juxtaposes the divine and the human: these are inseparable dimensions of our Lord's being. What alone appears is the unique person of the Word Incarnate, the Son of God: everything he does on earth reveals who he is—God made man.

In line with the general subject of the letter, which is the salvation wrought by Christ, the sacred writer concentrates on our Lord's priesthood, which makes him higher than the angels, superior to the lawgiver of the Old Law and to the Levitical priesthood, and superabundantly fitted to redeem mankind. The Redemption wrought by Christ is a universal remedy for a universal need.

Christ alone is the true High Priest, and his is the only true priesthood, that is, the mediation of his priesthood alone is capable of blotting out men's sins. From now on, no one can be a true priest unless he be called by and receive priestly anointing from Jesus. The priesthood cannot result from inheritance or birth into a particular tribe; it stems from a vocation, a call, from our Lord, who is the only Priest of the New Testament.

Christ's sacrifice, which does not consist—as Old Testament sacrifices did—in ritual shedding of the blood of animals, is something unrepeatable; its saving effects have been produced once for all, for it is infinite in its effectiveness. What happens in the Mass is that the sacrifice of the cross is made present in an unbloody manner: Jesus Christ "renews" the offering he made to the Father "once for all".

The intercession of Christ the Priest on our behalf is effective, definitive and enduring. What redeemed man must do is to apply to himself, through faith, the effects of Christ's sacrifice and grow in that charity which saves him.

Jesus Christ manifests who he is and his priestly function both in his self-abasement and in his glorification. Both were necessary to the performance of his priestly and redemptive role. Christ's self-abasement and humiliation demonstrate his absolute obedience to the Father's will; they also show the

Introduction to the Letter to the Hebrews

strength of the temptations experienced by his human nature, and the extraordinary sufferings he underwent in the mortal flesh he chose to assume (cf. 5:7).

The sacred writer's reflections, which are so full of emotion and pathos, come to a head in the statement that is the very core of the letter: "we have such a high priest, one who is seated at the right hand of the throne of the Majesty in heaven" (8:1). This central truth of Christian dogma is also, as the letter makes clear, a moving exhortation to hope.

In addition to showing Jesus and his work from the viewpoint of his eternal priesthood and exploring what flows from his being Priest and Mediator, the epistle applies to Christ four main titles—Son, Messiah, Jesus and Lord. Each of these reveals different aspects of Christ. The letter also refers to him elsewhere as Sanctifier, Heir, Mediator, Shepherd and Apostle (this being the only place in the New Testament where he is described as Apostle).

Thus, the sacred writer emphasizes the fact that Christ is always, for each and every Christian, his or her Priest and Mediator: "Jesus Christ is the same yesterday and today and forever" (13:8).

d) *Eschatology.* The letter's teaching on the subject of the last things takes an apparently secondary place in the sense that it occurs apropos of other themes. Eschatology, however, imbues the entire letter. It provides the key to interpreting the relationship between the provisional covenant of Judaism and the definitive covenant of Christianity. Judaism was a preparation for Christianity, and Christianity is the perfection of the Mosaic religion. At the same time, Christianity has two dimensions: it is something that begins here on earth but it will find its full expression only in heaven. It is true that the land promised to Abraham was Palestine; but it was much more than that. It was the grace of Christ, which guarantees heaven. The promised land, which we are all called to enter, is heaven. In this sense the exodus whereby Moses led the people to take possession of the promised land, is a prefigurement of Christian life: Jesus, the new Moses, will lead his people into the definitive Fatherland. And so the exhortation addressed to the followers of Moses, "Today, when you hear his voice, do not harden your hearts" (3:7; 4:7), means a number of things: it is an invitation to make an act of faith, similar to Abraham's, that is, to enjoy, through faith, the peace which grace brings; but it also is an invitation to stay faithful until the last moment of our life, and so enter into eternal rest. This focus on the future life runs right through the letter. It is a way of presenting the Christian life as a journey from the salvation which has already been brought about but which has yet to take its final form, towards the Kingdom of the future city, whose builder is God (cf. 11:10; 12:8) and whose head is Christ.

The letter speaks often of the second coming of Christ, the Parousia, when he will judge the living and the dead (cf. 10:25). It also announces the future judgment (cf. 10:27; Acts 24:25) and refers to the final re-creation of the world (cf. 12:26–28).

e) *The Christian's life on earth.* The letter sees Christian life in the world as a pilgrimage to the heavenly Fatherland, where one will "rest" in God. In keeping with this perspective, it frequently emphasizes the virtues of faith and hope, virtues necessary to pilgrim man. Despite the difficulties and obstacles encountered, he will reach the end of the journey if he has Christ as his guide. This is in fact an "exodus" theology, seen from a Christian or New Testament perspective. Christians are engaged in a new exodus, leaving Judaism and sin behind them, and they are convinced and fully assured of reaching the true promised land (cf. 4:11; 9:11; 11:8–10; 13:13).

THE LETTER TO THE HEBREWS

The Revised Standard Version, with notes

The greatness of the incarnate Son of God

1 ¹In many and various ways God spoke of old to our fathers by the prophets; ²but in these last days he has spoken to us by a

<small>Lk 1:55
Heb 2:3; Ps 2:8
Mt 21:38f; Jn 1:3</small>

1:1–4. The first four verses are a kind of prologue to the letter, which does not carry the greetings and words of thanksgiving to God normally found in letters of St Paul. Like the prologue of John's Gospel, the letter moves immediately into its main subject—the divinity of Jesus Christ, our Redeemer. It speaks of Christ as a Son whose sonship is eternal, prior to the creation of the world and to his Incarnation; it speaks also of Christ's mission to save all men, a mission appropriate to the Word who created all things. This exposition culminates in the affirmation of Christ's absolute superiority over angels, a theme dealt with, in different ways, up to the end of the second chapter.

The entire letter in fact develops the subject entered upon in the prologue—the sublimity of Christ, the natural and eternal Son of God, the universal Mediator, the eternal Priest. This is why St Thomas Aquinas says that the subject matter of this letter is the "excellence" of Christ. In this respect the Letter to the Hebrews is different from the other letters in the Pauline corpus: in some (the "Great Epistles" and the Captivity Letters) the Apostle deals with the grace which imbues the entire mystical body of the Church; others (the Pastoral Letters) deal with the grace bestowed on certain members of the Church (such as Timothy and Titus); whereas the Letter to the Hebrews looks at grace as it is found in the Head of the mystical body, Christ. This "excellence" of Christ, the Angelic Doctor adds, is examined by St Paul from four points of view: the first is that of Christ's origin, which the sacred writer identifies by calling him the true (natural, metaphysical) Son of God, when he says that God has spoken to us by a Son; the second is that of his power, for he depicts him as being made the heir of all things; the third is that of his activity, when he affirms that he created the world; the fourth, his sublime dignity, when he says that Christ reflects the glory of God (cf. *Commentary on Heb*, prologue and 1:1).

Christ is thus presented as the pinnacle and fullness of salvific Revelation, as the Second Vatican Council reminds us: "After God had spoken many times and in various ways through the prophets 'in these last days he has spoken to us by a Son' (Heb 1:1–2). For he sent his Son, the eternal Word who enlightens all men, to dwell among men and to tell them about the inner life of God […]. He did this by the total fact of his presence and self-manifestation—by words and works, signs and miracles, but above all by his death and glorious resurrection from the dead, and finally by sending the Spirit of truth. He revealed that God was with us, to deliver us from the darkness of sin and death, and to raise us up to eternal life" (*Dei Verbum*, 4).

1:1. Divine Revelation, which is rightly called "the Word of God", develops in stages in the course of the Old and New Testaments. "By this Revelation," Vatican II teaches, "the invisible God (cf. Col 1:15; 1 Tim 1:17), from the fullness of his love, addresses men as his friends (cf. Ex 33:11; Jn 15:14–15), and moves among men (cf. Bar 3:38), in order to invite and receive them into his own company. This economy of Revelation is realized by deeds and words, which are intrinsically bound up with each other. As a result, the works performed by God in the history of salvation show forth and bear out the doctrine and realities signified by the words; the words, for their part, proclaim the works, and bring to light the mystery they contain" (*Dei Verbum*, 3). Revelation is, then, a gradual opening up of God's mysteries whereby little by little, like a wise teacher, it makes known who he is and what his plans are concerning the salvation of all mankind. For, although there is only one God and one way of salvation, man needs to be educated by means of many precepts and to progress by stages on his way to God and so advance in faith towards complete salvation in Christ. God in his mercy reveals his mysteries to man in this way in order that the whole world, experiencing "this saving proclamation, on hearing it should believe, on believing it hope, on hoping in it love" (St Augustine, *De catechizandis rudibus*, 4, 8).

When speaking of Revelation, the First Vatican Council recalled that although "God, the origin and end of all things, can be known with certainty by the natural light of human reason from the things that he created, [...] it was, nevertheless, the good pleasure of his wisdom and goodness to reveal himself and the eternal decrees of his will to the human race in another and supernatural way" (*Dei Filius*, chap. 2). This supernatural revelation, as it says (reaffirming the teaching of the Council of Trent), is contained in books and in oral traditions which the apostles received from Christ or from the Holy Spirit and passed on to us. Christ's Gospel had earlier been promised by the prophets and, more generally, by the entire Old Testament. The letter refers to this when it says that God spoke in the past through the mouth of the prophets "in many ways", that is, at various stages in the history of the chosen people, and "in various ways", that is, by means of visions, words, actions and historical events.

1:2. "The most intimate truth that this revelation gives us about God and the salvation of man shines forth in Christ, who is himself both the mediator and the sum total of Revelation" (*Dei Verbum*, 2).

St John of the Cross comments on this passage in a very beautiful and profound way: "And this is as if he had said: That which God spoke of old in the prophets to our fathers in sundry ways and divers manners, he has now, at last, in these days, spoken to us once and for all in the Son. Herein the Apostle declares that God has become, as it were, dumb, and has no more to say, since that which he spoke before, in part, to the prophets, he has now spoken altogether in him, giving us the All, which is his Son.

"And so he who would now enquire of God, or seek any vision or revelation, would not only be acting foolishly, but would be committing an offence against God, by not setting his eyes altogether upon Christ, and seeking no new thing or aught beside. And God might answer him after this manner, saying: 'If I have spoken all things to you in my Word, which is my Son, and I have no other word, what answer can I now make to you, or what can I reveal to you which is greater than this? Set your eyes on him alone, for in him I have spoken and revealed to you all things'" (*Ascent of Mount Carmel*, book 2, chap. 22).

The "last days" refer to the period of time between the first coming of Christ and the second coming, or Parousia. These days have begun because the definitive "Word" of God, Jesus Christ, can be seen and heard. Mankind already finds itself in the "last age", in the "end

Hebrews 1:3

Son, whom he appointed the heir of all things, through whom also he created the world. ³He reflects the glory of God and bears the

Col 1:15–17
Wis 7:25
Heb 9:14, 26

of the ages" (cf. 1 Cor 10:11; Gal 4:4; Eph 1:10).

By speaking to us through his Son, God reveals to us his saving will from the moment of the Incarnation onwards, for the second person of the Blessed Trinity has come into the world to redeem us by dying for us and to open for us the way to heaven by his glorification. Therefore, Jesus Christ is the "prophet" *par excellence* (cf. note on Jn 7:40–43), for he perfects and completes God's merciful revelation. The Incarnation and the subsequent events of our Lord's life are, like his teaching, a source of salvation.

It was appropriate that the Son who perfectly revealed God the Father should also be the divine Word, the Creator of the world (cf. Jn 1:3). The creative action of the divine *Logos* or Word is not contradicted by the statement that Creation is the work of God the Father, for everything done by God outside himself (*ad extra*) is an action common to the three divine persons; nor is it correct to see the Word as merely an instrument used by the Father, for he is one in substance with him.

"It is the good Father's own, unique Word who has ordered this universe. Being the good Word he has arranged the order of all things […]. He was with God as Wisdom; as Word he contemplated the Father and created the universe, giving it substance, order and beauty" (St Athanasius, *Oratio contra gentes*, 40 and 46). Not only did the Word make the Father manifest by creation; he, together with the Father and the Holy Spirit, acted in the revelation of the Old Testament: in fact, many patristic writers attributed to the Son—as "angel" or "messenger of Yahweh"—the divine epiphanies witnessed by Moses and the prophets. St Irenaeus writes, for example, that Christ prefigured and proclaimed future events through his "patriarchs and prophets", thereby acting in his role as Teacher, promulgating the divine commandments and rules and training his people to obey God the Father (cf. *Against Heresies*, 14, 21). A profound harmony links God's revelation in Creation, in the Old Testament and in the New Testament: in each case it is the same God who is manifesting himself and the Word is ever actively involved. This activity of the Word is hidden and happens through the prophets in the Old Testament; whereas in the New the Word becomes flesh and acts directly. This passage in Hebrews combines the revelation of Jesus Christ as Mediator and maker of the universe (cf. Col 1:15–18; 1 Cor 8:6) with the idea that God has at last spoken to us in his Son, who "is in the bosom of the Father", and has made known to us the invisible mysteries of the Godhead (cf. Jn 1:18).

1:3a. These words, which describe Christ's divinity and eternity, recall the passage in the book of Wisdom which reads, "For she is a reflection of eternal light, a spotless mirror of the working of God" (Wis 7:26). What the Old Testament described as an attribute of God is now revealed as a personal being, the second person of the Trinity, the incarnate Word, Jesus Christ.

Using three images, the text teaches that Jesus Christ is perfect God, identical to the Father. By saying that he "reflects" the glory of the Father it means that he and the Father share the same nature—which is what we profess in the Creed when we say that Jesus Christ, the only-begotten Son of God, is "light from light,

Hebrews 1:3

true God from true God" (Nicene-Constantinopolitan Creed). "The author means", St John Chrysostom writes, "that Christ has this glory in his own right; it can suffer no eclipse nor can it either increase or diminish" (*Hom. on Heb*, 2).

The Son is also "stamped" with the nature of the Father; "stamp" is a translation of the Greek word *character*, which means the mark left by a tool used to engrave or seal (for example, the impression of a seal on wax, or the seal affixed to a document, or the brand used to identify livestock). This word indicates two things—first, the perfect equality between the mark and the seal which makes it, and second, the permanence of the mark.

"Upholding the universe by his word of power": the Son, through whom all things have been created, is also maintaining them in existence. God the Father not only creates but, through the Son, maintains a continual, direct influence on his creation; if he did not do so, as St Thomas Aquinas explains, the world would revert into non-being: "If the divine power ceased to operate, existence would cease, the being and subsistence of every created thing would end: (the Word) therefore upholds all things in respect of their existence, and he sustains them also by virtue of being the first cause of everything he has created" (*Commentary on Heb*, 1, 2). It makes sense that God the Father should wish to keep the world in existence by means of the same Word by whom he created it.

1:3b. This is the central message of the Letter to the Hebrews: Christ, the consubstantial Son of the Father, the perfect reflection of his substance, who created all things and maintains them in existence, by becoming man brought about purification for sins and by his sacrifice was glorified and put at the right hand of the Father, receiving "the name which is above every name" (cf. Phil 2:6–11; Jn 1:1, 3, 14). The actions of Jesus Christ are a continuum of mercy and salvation which extends from the creation of the world and mankind to the point where he is seated in heaven at the right hand of the Father. Creation and Redemption are mysteries intimately linked to each other. The Son, the divine Word, is both Creator and Redeemer. "It is appropriate to speak in the first instance", St Athanasius writes, "of the creation of the universe and of God its Creator, in order correctly to appreciate the fact that the new creation of this universe has been brought about by the Word who originally created it. For there is no contradiction in the Father's effecting the salvation of creatures by him through whom they were created" (*De Incarnatione contra arianos*, 1). This is why the tradition of the Church, echoing certain references in the New Testament (cf. Gal 6:15; 2 Cor 5:17; Eph 4:24; Col 3:10), describes the Redemption as a "new creation".

To "sit down at the right hand of the Majesty" is equivalent to saying to "have the status of God": "Majesty" is a term of reverence used to refer to God without naming him; thus, Jewish rabbis would refer to God as "Lord", "the most High", "the Power", "Glory", etc. Sitting in the presence of God was a prerogative of the Davidic kings (cf. 2 Sam 7:18; Ezek 44:3), and the person at the right hand was seen as occupying the place of honour (cf. Ps 45:10). Psalm 110 proclaims that God will have the Messiah sit at his right hand, and at various times Christ referred to that prophecy to affirm that he was the Messiah and God (cf. Mt 22:44; 26:63–65;

very stamp of his nature, upholding the universe by his word of power. When he had made purification for sins, he sat down at the right hand of the Majesty on high, ⁴having become as much superior to angels as the name he has obtained is more excellent than theirs.*

Mk 16:19
Ps 110:1
Phil 2:9; Eph 1:20f; 1 Pet 3:22; Ps 113:5

Jn 5:17–18; 10:30–33). The exaltation of the Son to the right hand of the Father was a constant theme of apostolic preaching (cf. Acts 2:33; Rom 8:34; 1 Pet 3:22; Rev 3:21; Eph 1:20). As St John Chrysostom comments, when St Paul says that the Son sat down at the right hand of the Majesty he means principally to refer to the status of the Son as equal to that of the Father. And when he says that he is on high, in heaven, far from meaning to confine God within spatial limits, he wants us to see God the Son, as Lord of the universe, raised up to the very throne of his Father (cf. *Hom. on Heb*, 2).

1:4. The prologue ends with a very important statement, which introduces the theme of the rest of the first chapter: Christ is superior to the angels. To understand this comparison of Christ with the angels, one needs to bear in mind the outlook of the Jews at the time. The period immediately prior to the New Testament had seen a considerable development of devotion to angels among the ordinary religious Jews; with the result that this was the danger of Jesus, because he was a man, in some way being seen as on a lower level than angels, who, created beings though they are, are pure spirits. In the Acts of the Apostles (cf. Act 23:9), we find the Pharisees in the Sanhedrin surmising that St Paul's preaching may result from revelation given him by an angel; and belief in the existence of angels was a point of contention between Pharisees and Sadducees (cf. Acts 23:7). For this reason the author of Hebrews wants to make it quite clear to Christians of Jewish origin that Jesus is much more than an angelic being.

Christ is superior to angels, the inspired writer says, because he has the title of Son, which is his by natural right. This name demonstrates his divine nature, a nature superior to that of any visible or invisible created being, whether material or spiritual, whether earthly or angelic: something's name describes its essence and, particularly in Holy Scripture, name and essence are at times one and the same. Thus, for example, the phrase "in the name of" (cf. Mt 28:19; Acts 3:6; 4:7; 4:12; etc.) refers not just to the authority or power of the person named, but to the person himself. Jesus Christ, because he is the very Son of God, is superior to angels by virtue of the glory due to his eternal oneness with the Father. As eternal Son of God, to him belonged, by right of inheritance, the title of Son and Lord. Moreover, after his passion and resurrection he has "become" superior to angels by a new title through his exaltation on high (cf. 1 Cor 15:24–27; Phil 2:9–11). This passage refers primarily to Jesus' glorification as man; for the words "having become as much superior to angels ..." cannot refer, St John Chrysostom points out, to his divine essence: by virtue of his divinity the Son is equal to the Father and cannot be subject to change, cannot "become" anything: he is eternally what he is by generation from the Father: "Eternal Word by nature, he did not receive his divine essence by way of inheritance. These words, which manifest his superiority over the angels, can only refer to the human nature with which he

PART ONE

Excellence of the religion revealed by Christ

1. CHRIST IS GREATER THAN THE ANGELS

Ps 2:7, LXX
2 Sam 7:14
Acts 13:33

Proof from Holy Scripture

⁵ For to what angel did God ever say,
"Thou art my Son,
today I have begotten thee"?

---

has been clothed: for it is that nature that is a created one" (*Hom. on Heb*, 1).

On the essence of angels and what they are, see the note on Lk 1:11.

1:5. Ancient Hebrew exegesis of this verse of Psalm 2 took it in a messianic sense: the Messiah or Anointed would be king of Israel and would enjoy God's special protection. Therefore he merited being called "Son of God", in the same kind of way, though more eminently, as other kings and just men of Israel deserved the title. But in Hebrews 1:5 the verse is given a much more profound interpretation: the Messiah, Jesus Christ, is the eternal Son of God, begotten "today", that is, in the continuous present of the eternal Godhead. It is affirming the generation of the Son by the Father in the bosom of the Trinity, whereby the Son proceeds eternally from the Father and is his mirror image. This form of generation is radically different from physical generation, whereby one living being physically begets another like unto himself; and it is also quite different from Creation, whereby God makes everything out of nothing. It is different from physical generation because, in the Holy Trinity, Father and Son co-exist eternally and are one and the same and only God, not two gods. It is different from Creation because the Son has not been made from nothing but proceeds eternally from the Father.

God created angels in the context of time, as the Fourth Lateran Council says in its profession of faith: "We firmly believe and profess without qualification that there is only one true God [...], Creator of all things visible and invisible, spiritual and corporeal, who, by his almighty power, from the very beginning of time, has created both orders of creatures in the same way out of nothing, the spiritual or angelic world and the corporeal or visible universe. And afterwards he formed the creature man, who in a way belongs to both orders, as he is composed of spirit and matter" (*De fide catholica*, chap. 1).

The Son, on the other hand, proceeds from the Father eternally as light rays come constantly from the sun or as water forms one single thing with the spring from which it flows.

"These words have never been addressed to an angel," St Thomas Aquinas comments, "but to Christ alone. In them three things may be observed. First, the mode of origin, expressed in the word 'say'. It refers to a type of

Or again,
"I will be to him a father,
and he shall be to me a son"?
⁶And again, when he brings the first-born into the world, he says,
"Let all God's angels worship him."

Deut 32:43, LXX
1 Chron 17:13
Ps 97:7; Rom
8:29; Col 1:18

---

generation which is not of the flesh but rather of a spiritual and intellectual kind. Second, this generation has an altogether singular character, for he says, 'Thou art my Son', as if saying that although many others are called sons, being [God's] natural son is proper to Him alone; others are called sons of God because they partake of the Word of God. Third, this is not a temporal but an eternal generation" (*Commentary on Heb*, 1, 3).

The quotation from Psalm 2 is completed by Nathan's prophecy to David (2 Sam 7:14: "I will be his father, and he shall be my son"), which announces that a descendant of David will be the Messiah and will ever enjoy God's favour. But the Hebrews text also makes it much clearer that the Messiah is the Son of God in the proper sense of the word—a son by nature, and not by adoption (cf. Lk 1:32–33). In Christ, therefore, two things combine: he is the Son of God and he is the Messiah King.

1:6. Here the words of Deuteronomy 32:43, identical with those of Psalm 97:7 as given in the Septuagint, are used to convey, as a divine commandment addressed to spiritual beings, a directive to adore the Son. This is a further proof of Christ's superiority: the angels are to worship him. "This adoration shows his absolute superiority over angels: it is the superiority of the master over his servants and his slaves. When Jesus Christ left the bosom of his Father to enter this world, God required his angels to worship him. This is what a monarch does when he brings some great personage into his palace and wishes to have him honoured: he orders his dignitaries to bow in his presence" (*Hom. on Heb*, 3).

This reference to "bringing the first-born into the world" is consistently interpreted by the Fathers of the Church and by ancient writers as a reference to the Incarnation. Some authors also see this verse as referring to the second coming of Christ, when the world to come, unlike the present world, will be totally subject to the Redeemer. This interpretation connected with the end of time may explain why the text of Deuteronomy 32:43 is used: that passage is followed by reference to the last judgment by God.

Christ's human nature should be worshipped now and always by angels and men alike, for by doing so they adore Jesus, who is one person—which is divine—with two natures, one divine and one human; he is worshipped as one: his divinity and his humanity are worshipped at one and the same time.

This worship due to Christ over every created being is reminiscent of what St Paul says in Philippians 2:10: "at the name of Jesus every knee should bow, in heaven and on earth and under the earth", referring to the glorified human nature of Christ. "It is fitting that the sacred humanity of Christ should receive the homage, praise and adoration of all the hierarchies of the angels and of all the legions of the blessed in heaven" (St Josemaría Escrivá, *Holy Rosary*, second glorious mystery).

Hebrews 1:7

Ps 104:4, LXX ⁷Of the angels he says,
"Who makes his angels winds,
and his servants flames of fire."
Ps 45:7f, LXX ⁸But of the Son he says,
"Thy throne, O God,ᵃ is for ever and ever,
the righteous sceptre is the sceptre of thyᵇ kingdom.
⁹Thou hast loved righteousness and hated lawlessness;
therefore God, thy God, has anointed thee
with the oil of gladness beyond thy comrades."

1:7–8. Unlike the Son, who is divinely unchangeable like the Father, angels are on a lower level of being, although a spiritual one; words of Psalm 104:4 used here convey this idea: winds often change direction and flames constantly change shape. St Thomas Aquinas says that this double comparison fits in very well with what angels are: they are messengers and ministers. "The air can receive light and in a similar way any image perfectly reflects what it receives and it moves with speed. These are qualities which a good messenger should also have [...] and they are very appropriate to angels because angels receive divine illuminations perfectly, for they are the purest of mirrors [...]. Similarly they are excellent transmitters of what is said to them [...] and are also very swift [...]. As ministers they are flames of fire, for of all the elements fire is the most active and most effective. Therefore in Psalm 104 where it says that angels are ministers of God it adds that he makes his ministers 'fire and flame'" (*Commentary on Heb*, 1, 3).

V. 8 of Psalm 45 is taken in Hebrews 1:8 as words spoken by God the Father to his Son, whose throne is established for ever and ever. The term "God" is expressly applied to Jesus Christ. Although the New Testament normally uses "Lord" when referring to the divinity of the Son, it does not systematically refrain from calling him "God" (cf. Jn 1:1; 20:28; Rom 9:5; Tit 2:13; 2 Pet 1:1); but it usually keeps that word for the person of the Father. The "throne" is Christ's and expresses his majesty, because, as St Thomas comments, a throne is a royal seat but it is also a teacher's chair and a judgment seat, all of which are very appropriate to Christ, who is our King by virtue of his Godhead, and also, as man, he has merited the kingship by virtue of his passion, victory and resurrection (cf. *Commentary on Heb*, 1, 4). It is stressed that this throne will remain for ever, in keeping with Nathan's prophecy (cf. note on Heb 1:5) and the announcement made to the Blessed Virgin (cf. Lk 1:33) and another prophecy in the book of Daniel: "their kingdom shall be an everlasting kingdom, and all dominions shall serve and obey them" (Dan 7:27).

1:9. Through the author of Hebrews God himself is revealing to us the deeper meaning of this psalm. The psalmist, who was also divinely inspired, addresses the people's king on his wedding-day; he extols him and praises him, emphasizing his beauty, the fact that he is fully endowed with spiritual gifts, virtues and power. Praise on this scale goes far beyond what any human being could deserve. It shows the king of Israel as an eternal king, a king of righteousness who

---

a. Or *God is thy throne* **b.** Other ancient authorities read *his*

Hebrews 1:11

¹⁰And,   Ps 102:26–28,
"Thou, Lord, didst found the earth in the beginning,   LXX
and the heavens are the work of thy hands;
¹¹ they will perish, but thou remainest;

---

hates lawlessness, and it says that he has not been anointed just with ordinary oil but the oil "of gladness", a distinction not given to other princes and kings. All these prerogatives, particulary joy and gladness, are proper to the advent of the Messiah (cf. Ps 21:6; 72:1–7; Song 5:10–16; Is 44:23; 51:1; 52:9; 54:1; etc.). The Messiah King, therefore, as portrayed in the Old Testament and definitively confirmed by Hebrews, has divine authority. He is Christ who, through the anointing he has received, has been put over all his "comrades", that is, over all creatures, whose "comrade" or fellow he has become through the Incarnation: by becoming man, the eternal Son of the Father has, as man, the fullness of grace and divine gifts; and thanks to him everyone can obtain these graces and gifts, but not to the same, full, extent. Some Fathers were of the view that this anointing refers directly to the eternal generation of the Word; others applied it to the Incarnation. Certainly, Christ's exaltation is entirely due to his being God; however, because anointing is here linked with love of righteousness and hatred of evil-doing, it seems more likely that it refers to the divine favour shown to Jesus throughout his life, especially at his baptism (cf. Lk 4:18; Acts 10:38) and in his glorification after the Resurrection (cf. 1 Tim 3:16). Of course, the very name "Christ", meaning "anointed", refers to the fact that he had the fullness of the Holy Spirit. "These words", St Thomas writes, "refer to the spiritual anointing which makes Christ full of the Holy Spirit" (*Commentary on Heb*, 1, 4). St John says as much when he describes the Word as being "full of grace and truth" (Jn 1:14). "To the name *Jesus* is added that of *Christ*, which signifies *the anointed*. [...] Jesus Christ was anointed for the discharge of these functions, not by mortal hand or with earthly ointment, but by the power of his heavenly Father and with a spiritual oil; for the plenitude of the Holy Spirit and a more copious effusion of all gifts than any other created being is capable of receiving were poured into his soul. This the Prophet clearly indicates when he addresses the Redeemer in these words: 'You love justice, and hate iniquity. Therefore God, your God, has anointed you with the oil of gladness above your fellows'" (*St Pius V Catechism*, 1, 3, 7).

1:10–12. To the arguments previously given (vv. 5–9) in support of Christ's superiority over angels, a further factor is now added—his power to create the world; 1:10 links up with 1:2 (cf. *Commentary on Heb*, 1, 5). This passage is taken from Psalm 102:25–27, a psalm of lamentation in which a just man in affliction confidently asks God to hear his prayer because God is forever, whereas all created things are transitory. This is an idea which occurs very often in the Old Testament and is very much part of Jewish piety (cf., e.g., Ps 119:88–90; Is 40:8; 51:6–8; Sir 43:26–32). All these passages stress the everlasting nature of God's "Word" in contrast with the changeability of created things. In Hebrews 1:10–12 the words of Psalm 102:25–27, which were addressed to Yahweh, are applied to Christ: that is, he is regarded as being God, the Father's equal.

Hebrews 1:12

^{Rev 6:14}

¹² they will all grow old like a garment,
like a mantle thou wilt roll them up,
and they will be changed.^c
But thou art the same,
and thy years will never end."

^{Ps 110:1, LXX}
^{Mt 22:44}

¹³ But to what angel has he ever said,
"Sit at my right hand,
till I make thy enemies
a stool for thy feet"?

^{Mt 4:11; 18:10f}
^{Dan 7:10}
^{Ps 91:11}

¹⁴Are they not all ministering spirits sent forth to serve, for the sake of those who are to obtain salvation?

1:12. To show the difference between Creator and creature the epistle uses the words of Psalm 102, mentioning two attributes of the Creator: he is eternal, and he is unchanging. The visible world, on the contrary, had a beginning and it will come to an end. The comparison with a mantle and a garment reminds us that the material world will ultimately disintegrate; it is a passing thing despite its beauty and apparent solidity.

This basic truth of revelation is directly at odds with the notion that the universe is eternal and the world and matter are in some way divine. The Magisterium of the Church has often rejected theories which say that "God is identical with nature [...], God is actually in the process of becoming, in man and in the world; all things are God and have the very substance of God himself; God and the world are one and the same thing" (Pius IX, *Syllabus of Errors*, 1). As Christians understand it, the created universe not only will not retain its present form but at the end of time will undergo a transformation which will turn it into "a new heaven and a new earth" (Rev 21:1; cf. Rom 8:19; Is 65:17; 2 Pet 3:13). Only God is eternal.

1:14. "Ministering spirits sent to serve" is a very accurate definition of angels: they are spiritual creatures whose role is to serve and worship God. In the New Testament the angels, good and bad, are given various names such as "powers", "principalities", "thrones", "dominions" (cf. Rom 8:38; 1 Cor 15:24; Eph 1:21; Col 1:16). In the Old Testament angels served God by bearing messages to men (cf. Gen 16:7f; Judg 2:1; 6:11; 1 Kings 13:18; 40:3; Dan 8:16–26; 9:21–27; etc.), by protecting them and on occasions by imposing divine punishment on them. From the time of Christ's coming, angels "ministered" to him on earth (cf. Mt 4:11; Lk 22:43) and they helped the early Church to develop (cf. Acts 5:19; 12:7–10). Hebrews 1:14 underlines the role of angels in the salvation of men; in the Gospel we are told that children have angels of their own in heaven (cf. Mt 18:10); and indeed everyone has a guardian angel (cf. Acts 12:15). This ministerial role of angels is a consequence of their state of blessedness, because, as St Thomas Aquinas explains, there is no difference between angels who contemplate God and angels who have service functions, for "all are ministers or administrators, in that the higher ones convey the will of God to those in the middle rank; and the latter to those of lower rank, and these last-mentioned

c. Other ancient authorities add *like a garment*

An appeal for faith

2 ¹Therefore we must pay the closer attention to what we have heard, lest we drift away from it. ²For if the message declared

Acts 7:38, 53
Gal 3:19
Heb 10:28f

---

to us" (*Commentary on Heb*, 1, 6). Ministerial angels have the specific task of helping us to reach heaven; "by God's providence angels have been entrusted with the office of guarding the human race and of accompanying every human being so as to preserve him from any serious danger. Just as parents, whose children are about to travel a dangerous and infested road, appoint guardians and helpers for them, so also in the journey we are making towards our heavenly country our heavenly Father has placed over each of us an angel under whose protection and vigilance we may be enabled to escape the snares secretly prepared by our enemy [...] and thus be secure against all false steps which the wiles of the evil one might cause us to make in order to draw us aside from the path that leads to heaven" (*St Pius V Catechism*, 14, 9, 4). In addition to giving personal help to every human being, the Church teaches that angels echo the prayer of the faithful and carry their petitions to God. Origen, a very early ecclesiastical writer and in this matter a faithful representative of orthodox teaching, says in this connexion: "We say that the angels ascend to bear men's prayers to the purest parts of the world, that is, the heavenly regions [...]. And from there they descend in turn to bear to everyone, according to his merits, such benefits as God entrusts to them [...]. Given that they have this role, we have learned to call them angels or messengers" (*Against Celsus*, 5, 4). Devotion to angels and to one's own guardian angel is an important and ancient teaching: "You are amazed that your guardian Angel has done you such obvious favours. And you should not be amazed: that's why our Lord has placed him beside you" (St Josemaría Escrivá, *The Way*, 565).

2:1–4. At this point the letter makes an earnest appeal for prudence and fidelity. The direct style and confident tone of personal exhortation which runs right through the letter indicates that the author knew his readers very well, as they did him. He has no inhibitions about showing that he is somewhat worried that some of them may not appreciate the wonderful gift they have received. They should all remember that apostasy can come about not only through a conscious, clear rejection of faith but also through continuous neglect of God's teaching. This exhortation reminds us of 2 Corinthians 6:1: "We entreat you not to accept the grace of God in vain". Christians should absorb God's word as much as possible and strive to put it into practice, thereby becoming ever holier. Also, the practice of Christian life is the best way to obtain a deeper understanding of the faith.

2:2–3. "The Apostle has previously explained, in various ways, Christ's superiority over angels. Here he concludes by stating that greater obedience is due to Christ's teaching, that is, to the New Testament, than to the Old Testament [...]. Thus, by obeying the command of the angel through whom the Law was given, they obtained entry into the promised land (Ex 23:20–22). Therefore, it is said in Matthew 19:17, 'If you would enter life, keep the commandments.' So, if it was necessary to obey the commandments of Moses, now it is even more necessary to obey the commandments of

by angels* was valid and every transgression or disobedience received a just retribution, ³how shall we escape if we neglect such a great salvation? It was declared at first by the Lord, and it was attested to us by those who heard him, ⁴while God also bore witness by signs and wonders and various miracles and by gifts of the Holy Spirit distributed according to his own will.

Acts 10:37
2 Cor 12:12
1 Cor 12:4, 11
Mk 16:20

Him who is higher than the angels by whom the Law was promulgated" (St Thomas, *Commentary on Heb*, 2, 1).

The Law of Moses is not being viewed as something at odds with the redemption and grace won by Christ, but as a first stage on the way of salvation and a kind of foretaste of eternal beatitude. The Law also is a manifestation of God's mercy. "This Law", Tertullian writes, "was not promulgated out of the severity of its author but out of that supreme generosity which decided to teach a rebellious people and to make easier (by stipulating with exact duties) a faith which they were as yet unable to obey" (*Against Marcion*, 2, 19).

In the Old Covenant God backed up his word by imposing just punishment for prevarication and disobedience—as happened, for example, in the case of Dathan, Korah, Abiram (cf. Num 16:1–35), Moses' sister Miriam (cf. Num 12:1–9) and later Saul (1 Sam 15:9–23) and unfaithful kings of Judah and Israel. We should, therefore, have a holy fear of being unfaithful to the New Covenant established in Jesus Christ, for the divine word of salvation which Jesus promulgated is infinitely precious. It is the greatest gift a human being can be given, because it equips one to know and to praise God and at the same time attain one's own temporal and eternal happiness.

"It was attested to us by those who heard him": an explicit reference to the preaching of the apostles, which confirms and transmits the proclamation of salvation initiated by Christ's preaching (cf. 1 Cor 11:23; 15:3).

2:2. The *a fortiori* kind of argument used here was very popular in rabbinical exegesis at that time. The argument is this: if transgression of the Old Covenant commandments promulgated by angels was severely punished, so much more respect is due to the commandments of the New Testament, established by the Son of God. The same form of argument is used in Heb 7:21–22; 9:13–14; 10:28–29 and 12:25.

The "message declared by angels" is the Mosaic Law. According to some Jewish traditions, the Law was given to Moses on Mount Sinai by an angel or by a number of angels. The New Testament reflects this tradition in Acts 7:38, 53 and Gal 3:19.

2:4. "Signs", "wonders" and "miracles" are to a certain extent all the same— things which bear witness to supernatural Revelation. "Signs" may be natural events which, occurring as they do at a special time, carry a supernatural meaning and manifest God's power. "Wonders" and "miracles", on the other hand, exceed in various degrees, the possibilities of nature; "wonders" seems to refer to signs in the heavens (cf. Acts 2:19), whereas miracles are any type of special demonstration of divine power, like the sudden cure of paralysis or the raising of a person from the dead.

The miracles Jesus worked help us see him as bringing God's salvation to men. They are, as it were, credentials the Father gives the Son (Acts 2:22; Jn 3:2). From the start, signs and wonders also

Jesus, man's brother, was crowned with glory and honour above the angels

⁵For it was not to angels that God subjected the world to come, of which we are speaking. ⁶It has been testified somewhere,   Ps 8:5–7, LXX
> "What is man that thou art mindful of him,
> or the son of man, that thou carest for him?

---

accompanied apostolic preaching to attest to its divine origin (cf. Mk 16:20; Acts 2:43; 4:30; 5:12; etc.). Thus, we are told that Stephen "did great wonders and signs among the people" (Acts 6:8) and that St Paul's preaching was confirmed by signs and miracles (cf. Acts 14:3; Rom 15:19; 2 Cor 12:12).

St John Chrysostom asked: "Could it happen that those who made out they were God's witnesses were nothing but imposters? No!, St Paul replies. This revelation was not the invention of the human mind. If men had thought up these truths and these mysteries, how could God's omnipotence have supported this lie with supernatural actions? So, God intervenes, through the wonders worked by the apostles, to support the testimony they bear [...]. He supports it not by speech (which would have been enough, for God is trustworthy) but by 'various miracles', the greatest type of testimony he can provide. The Apostle speaks of diverse miracles to show the greater abundance of spiritual gifts given Christians as compared with the ancient Jewish people who were given few wonders and less marvellous signs" (*Hom. on Heb*, 3).

The early years of the Church were indeed marked by an exceptional number of miracles and signs of the Holy Spirit (cf. Acts 4:31; 10:44; 1 Cor 12:4–11). Once apostolic preaching became consolidated, the incidence of signs diminished but there remained and still remains the greatest of these signs, charity (cf. 1 Cor 13:1).

2:5–9. The saving dimension of the Incarnation is being explored here with the help of quotations from Psalm 2 and other psalms. Christians should stay true to Christ, because in addition to his being the cause and beginning of salvation he has been made Lord of the universe; everything is subject to him. God the Father, in other words, has established Christ—not the angels—as Lord of "the world to come".

God has put everything under Christ *as man*. The words of Psalm 8 are quoted as applying to Christ as man, for he is the perfection of manhood, the perfect man, and he merited being crowned with glory and honour because of his obedience, humility, and passion and death (cf. Phil 2:6–11; 1 Pet 2:21–25); even death itself has become subject to him (cf. 1 Cor 15:22–28). His enemies have been made his footstool (cf. Ps 8:6; 110:1; Mt 22:44); he will channel everything back to God, and God will be all in all.

2:5. "The world to come" was a term the Jews used to refer to the period immediately following the coming of the Messiah. The rabbis distinguished three periods in the history of the world—the "present world", the time when they were waiting for the Messiah; the "day of the Messiah", the point at which his kingdom would be established; and the "world to come", which would begin with the resurrection of the dead and the judging of the nations. Many teachers of the Law tended to confuse the "world to come" in some way with the "day of the Messiah", which was its initial stage.

Hebrews 2:7

> [1 Cor 15:25–27
> Eph 1:20–23
> Phil 3:21]
>
> ⁷Thou didst make him for a little while lower than the angels,
> thou hast crowned him with glory and honour,ᵈ
> ⁸putting everything in subjection under his feet."
> Now in putting everything in subjection to him, he left nothing outside his control. As it is, we do not yet see everything in

The author of the epistle seems to be saying that the government of the present world is entrusted by God to angels (cf. Deut 32:8; Dan 10:13f), but that in the world to come—that is, in the definitive Kingdom—God the Creator's original plan will be implemented: Christ, true God and true man, with his glorified manhood, will be the King of Creation and the holy angels and the blessed will reign with him. The "world to come", although it has begun with the resurrection and glorification of Jesus, will not reach its fullness until the second coming of Christ and the resurrection of the dead. Until then, there exists a tension between "this world" and the "world to come": the former has received a mortal wound but it is still alive; the latter has begun to exist but it has not yet attained its final full expression.

2:6. Psalm 8 is a hymn praising God for creating all things; particularly man, whom he has made master of all creation. The words of the Psalm quoted here are those which praise God's caring love, as shown by his making man, despite his limitations, lord of Creation.

However, the text of the epistle shows us that the words of the Psalm have a deeper meaning: they refer to Jesus (cf. 1 Cor 15:27; Eph 1:22) and particularly to his degradation. "Although these words can be applied to every man," St John Chrysostom comments "they do however most properly apply to Christ. For the words 'thou hast put everything in subjection under his feet' (v. 8) are more suitable to him than to us, for the Son of God visited us who were of no account and having taken and loved our condition, he became higher than us all" (*Hom. on Heb*, 4).

The author of Hebrews uses Psalm 8 to demonstrate Christ's superiority over angels by giving it a deeply messianic interpretation. Thus, the man "crowned with glory and honour" is the risen Christ, now seated at the right hand of the Father; and the one to whom everything has been subjected is also the same Christ (cf. 1:13), as St Paul proclaims in 1 Cor 15:27; Eph 1:22; Phil 3:21.

2:8. In line with its application to Christ of the words of Psalm 8:4–6, the epistle says that God the Father has subjected everything to him. This does not mean that there is inequality or difference in power or nature between Father and Son, as if the Son himself were subject to the Father, and the Father had given him, as he would a subordinate, authority over the world. "Arius argued in this way," writes St Thomas: "the Father subjected everything to the Son; therefore, the Son is less than the Father. I reply that it is true that the Father subjected everything to the Son according to his human nature, in respect of which he is less than the Father, as St John says, 'the Father is greater than I' (14:28). But according to his divine nature, Christ himself subjected all things to himself" (*Commentary on Heb*, 2, 2).

Christ's dominion over the universe is something which men cannot see and it

---

d. Other ancient authorities insert *and didst set him over the works of thy hands*

subjection to him. ⁹But we see Jesus, who for a little while was made lower than the angels, crowned with glory and honour because of the suffering of death, so that by the grace of God he might taste death for every one.

Phil 2:6–11

---

will not become manifest until his second coming as Lord and Judge of the living and the dead. "Christ, true God and true man, lives and reigns. He is the Lord of the universe. Everything that lives is kept in existence only through him. Why, then, does he not appear to us in all his glory? Because his kingdom is 'not of this world' (Jn 18:36), though it is *in* this world [...]. Those who expected the Messiah to have visible temporal power were mistaken. [...] When Christ began to preach on earth he did not put forward a political programme. He said, 'Repent, for the kingdom of God is at hand' (Mt 3:2; 4:17). He commissioned his disciples to proclaim this good news (cf. Lk 10:9) and he taught them to pray for the coming of the Kingdom (cf. Mt 6:10)" (St Josemaría Escrivá, *Christ Is Passing By*, 180).

2:9. The words "who for a little while was made lower than the angels" refer to Jesus in the crisis of his passion and death, when he freely humbled himself and lowered himself to suffer punishment and death—sufferings to which angels are not subject.

"For a little while" is a translation of the Greek word which the New Vulgate renders as "*paulo minus*" (a little less than), and which also occurs in Hebrews 2:7 in the quotation from Psalm 8. The RSV translation in both instances is "for a little while".

Every human creature, including Christ as man, can be seen in some sense as lower than the angels. This inferiority basically has to do with the fact that human knowledge is inferior to that of angels because it is dependent on sense experience, and also because angels cannot experience suffering and death. "The angels cannot suffer and are immortal by nature, so that when Christ deigned to submit to his passion and death he made himself lower than them, not because he lost his sublimity or in any way was diminished, but because he took on our weakness. He made himself lower than the angels, not as far as his divinity or his soul were concerned but only in respect of his body" (*Commentary on Heb*, 2, 2).

Christ's self-abasement is a permanent example to us to strive to respond to his love. St John Chrysostom suggests that we draw from it this practical lesson: "If he whom the angels worship consented, out of love for us, to become for a time lower than them, you for your part should endure everything out of love for him" (*Hom. on Heb*, 4).

One of the results of Christ's passion was his exaltation and glorification. Because Christ attained victory on the cross, to the benefit of all mankind, the cross is the only route to heaven: "The holy cross is shining upon us", the Church says. "In the cross is victory, in the cross is power. By the cross every sin is overcome" (*Divine Office*, Exaltation of the Cross, morning prayer, Ant. 3). By virtue of Christ's passion, the cross is no longer an ignominious scaffold; it is a glorious throne. Tradition attributes to St Andrew the apostle these words in praise of the cross on which he was going to die: "O goodly cross, glorified by the limbs of our Lord, O cross so long desired, so ardently loved, so tirelessly

Hebrews 2:10

Rom 11:36
Heb 5:8f

¹⁰For it was fitting that he, for whom and by whom all things exist, in bringing many sons to glory, should make the pioneer of

---

sought and now offered to me: take me to my Master so that he who redeemed me through thee, may welcome me through thee" (*Ex passione S. Andreae*, reading).

Through his death, Christ has been crowned with glory and honour; moreover he has died on our behalf. His death and glorification are the cause and model of our salvation and glorification. Sacrifice, atonement and merit are indissolubly linked to the redemptive work of Christ and constitute a "grace of God", that is, a gratuitous gift from God. St Thomas Aquinas explains that "the passion of Christ is here alluded to in three ways. Firstly, its cause is referred to, for the text says 'by the grace of God'; then, its usefullness, when it says 'for every one'; thirdly, its outcome, when it says 'might taste'" (*Commentary on Heb*, 2, 3): Jesus did indeed, by the will of the Father, experience or "taste" death. His death is described as being like a bitter drink which he chose to take in sips, as if savouring it. The "cup" or chalice of the agony in the garden comes immediately to mind (cf. Mt 26:39; Mk 14:26; Lk 22:42; Jn 18:11; cf. also Mt 20:22f and Mk 10:38f).

Christian tradition has seen these words about "tasting death" as underlining that Christ underwent a most severe passion voluntarily, accepting it to atone for all the sins of mankind. These words also show that he accepted death without ceasing to be Lord of life: "This expression", St John Chrysostom states, "is very precise. It does not say 'that by the grace of God he might die', for the Lord once he tasted death delayed there only for a moment and immediately rose [...]. All men fear death; therefore, to enable us to take death in our stride, he tasted death even though it was not necessary for him to do so" (*Hom. on Heb*, 4).

2:10. After pointing to the results of Christ's death, the text stresses how appropriate it was that he should be abased in this way: he had to make himself in every way like his brethren in order to help them.

God the Father, who is the beginning and end of all things, desired to bring men to glory by means of his Son. Christ was to be the author of their salvation, and therefore it was fitting that he should be made perfect through suffering. The Father made his Son "perfect" in the sense that by becoming man and therefore being able to suffer and die, he was fully equipped to be mankind's representative. "God has acted in a manner in keeping with his kindness towards us: he has clothed his first-born in a glory greater than that of all mankind and made him outstanding as a champion. Suffering is, therefore, a way to attain perfection and a source of salvation" (*Hom. on Heb*, 4). By perfectly obeying his Father, offering his life and especially his passion and death, Christ offers a perfect and superabundant sacrifice for the forgiveness of the sins of mankind and makes full atonement to the Father. As a reward for his obedience, Christ, as man, is made Head of the Church and King of the universe. It is in that sense that he is made "perfect" by the Father.

Ever since the Redemption, human suffering has become a way to perfection: it acts as expiation for personal sins, it spurs man to assert his spiritual and transcendental dimension, it makes for solidarity with others and links man to Christ's sacrifice. "Suffering must serve for conversion, that is, for the rebuilding of goodness in the subject, who can recognize the divine mercy in this call to repentance [...]. But in order to perceive

their salvation perfect through suffering.* ¹¹For he who sanctifies and those who are sanctified have all one origin. That is why he is not ashamed to call them brethren, ¹²saying,

Jn 17:19

Ps 22:23, LXX

---

the true answer to the 'why' of suffering, we must look to the revelation of divine love, the ultimate source of the meaning of everything that exists [...]. Christ causes us to enter into the mystery and to discover the 'why' of suffering, as far as we are capable of grasping the sublimity of divine love" (John Paul II, *Salvifici doloris*, 12–13).

2:11. To accomplish the salvation of men Christ needed to be one of them—to share, with them, a human nature. This is why Christ is the only "true sanctifier", the priest who performs rites and sacrifices, taking things stained by sin and making them pure and pleasing to God, that is, holy. Our Lord said something similar in the Gospel: "For their sake I consecrate myself, that they also may be consecrated in truth" (Jn 17:19).

"Have all one origin". Various interpretations have been given to these words. Most have to do with the parallelism between the first man and Christ (cf. Acts 17:26; Rom 5:15–19), seeing this "origin" as Adam—in which case the text would mean that Christ and other men are children of Adam. A more usual interpretation sees the "one" origin as being God, thus stressing that Christ's holy humanity and the humanity of men both stem from the one Creator and derive from the first man. In either case, Christ and the rest of men can rightly be called "brethren". "As to his divine generation he has no brethren or co-heirs, being the only-begotten Son of the Father, while we mortals are the work of his hands. But if we consider his birth as man, he not only calls many by the name of brethren, but treats them as such, since he admits them to share with him the glory of his paternal inheritance" (*St Pius V Catechism*, 1, 3, 10).

2:12. Psalm 22, which begins with the words, "My God, my God, why has thou forsaken me?", speaks of the sufferings and exaltation of the Messiah, as perfect Servant of Yahweh. Christ prayed this psalm on the cross, applying it to himself and thereby revealing it to be a prophecy of his passion (cf. Mt 27:35, 46; Mk 15:34). For this reason it is a psalm which is highly revered and much used by Christian tradition. It had a special place in divine services in the synagogue and is used by the Church in the liturgical ceremonies of Holy Thursday and Good Friday.

The Servant of Yahweh, after being freed by God from the suffering and abuse inflicted on him, expresses his gratitude to his liberator. That is why he wishes to "proclaim", that is, extol the name of Yahweh before the faithful who meet in the congregation and whom he calls "brethren". The evangelists see this psalm as being fulfilled in our Lord's passion (cf. Mt 27:35 and Jn 19:23–24 compared with Ps 22:18). But in Hebrews 2:12 other words of the same psalm (Ps 22:23) are applied not so much to our Lord's passion as to Christ's revelation of the Father: he proclaims the name of the true God, that is, his inner life, his mercy and power. This passage of Hebrews echoes the words of Jesus in John 17:6, 26: "I have manifested thy name to the men whom thou gavest me out of the world; thine they are, and thou gavest them to me, and they have kept thy word [...]. I have made known to them thy name, and I will make it known, that the

"I will proclaim thy name to my brethren,
in the midst of the congregation I will praise thee."

Is 8:17f
2 Sam 22:3

¹³And again,
"I will put my trust in him."
And again,
"Here am I, and the children God has given me."

Rom 8:3
Mt 16:17

¹⁴Since therefore the children share in flesh and blood, he himself likewise partook of the same nature, that through death he

---

love with which thou hast loved me may be in them, and I in them."

2:13. Two verses from Isaiah are now quoted, revealing their messianic meaning: what the prophet said centuries earlier anticipated the sentiments of Christ. Isaiah 8:17 shows his trust in God despite the threat of an Assyrian invasion and the unfaithfulness of the people of Israel, who had resorted to superstition and magic instead of turning to God. The same words express Christ's confidence in God the Father.

In Isaiah 8:18 the children of the prophet, whose names symbolize the divine plan of salvation, stand for the Christian people whom the Father has entrusted to Christ, the Saviour and Sanctifier (cf. Jn 6:37, 39; 17:6, 12).

2:14. As in the prologue of St John's Gospel (Jn 1:12–13), "flesh" and "blood" apply to human nature in its weakened condition. Jesus has assumed man's nature: "He has taken it on without sin but with all its capacity to suffer pain, given that he took a flesh similar to sinful flesh; he 'shared therefore in flesh and blood', that is, he took on a nature in which he could suffer and die—which could not occur in a divine nature" (St Thomas, *Commentary on Heb*, 2, 4).

Christ chose to submit to death, which is a consequence of sin, in order to destroy death and the power of the devil. The Council of Trent teaches that, as a result of original sin, man "incurred the wrath and indignation of God, and consequently incurred death [...] and, together with death, bondage in the power of him who from that time had the empire of death" (*De peccato originali*, can. 3; cf. Rom 5:12; 6:12–14; 7:5; etc.). To explain this power of the devil, St Thomas comments: "A judge has one kind of power of death: he can punish people with death; a criminal has a different kind of power of death—a power he usurps by killing another [...]. God has the first kind of dominion over death; the devil has the second kind, for he seduces man to sin and leads him to death" (*Commentary on Heb*, 2, 4).

Addressing Christ and his cross, the Church sings, "O altar of our victim raised, / O glorious passion ever praised, / by which our Life to death was rendered, / that death to life might thence be mended" (Hymn *Vexilla Regis*). The death of Christ, the only one who could atone for man's sin, wipes out sin and makes death a way to God. "Jesus destroyed the demon", St Alphonsus writes; "that is, he destroyed his power, for the demon had been lord of death on account of sin, that is, he had power to cause temporal and eternal death to all the children of Adam infected by sin. And this was the victory of the cross— that Jesus, the author of life, by dying obtained Life for us through that death" (*Reflections on the Passion*, chap. 5, 1).

might destroy him who has the power of death, that is, the devil, ¹⁵and deliver all those who through fear of death were subject to lifelong bondage. ¹⁶For surely it is not with angels that he is concerned but with the descendants of Abraham. ¹⁷Therefore he had to be made like his brethren in every respect, so that he might

1 Cor 15:56; Rev 12:10; Is 41:8f

Rom 8:3; 1 Sam 2:35; Ex 4:16; 1 Jn 2:2

2:15. Christ has freed men not from physical but from spiritual death and therefore from fear of death, because he has given us certainty of future resurrection. Man's natural fear of death is easily explained by his fear of the unknown and his instinctive aversion to what death involves; but it can also be a sign of excessive attachment to this life. "Because it does not want to renounce its desires, the soul fears death, it fears being separated from the body" (St Athanasius, *Oratio contra gentes*, 3).

The fear of death which some people in the Old Testament had can be explained by their not knowing what fate awaited them, and by the possibility of being completely cut off from God. But physical death is not something to be feared by those who sincerely seek God: "To me to live is Christ, and to die is gain," St Paul explains (Phil 1:21). "Don't be afraid of death. Accept it from now on, generously ... when God wills it, where God wills it, as God wills it. Don't doubt what I say: it will come in the moment, in the place and in the way that are best: sent by your Father-God. Welcome be our sister death!" (St Josemaría Escrivá, *The Way*, 739).

2:16. "It is not with angels that he is concerned": the original text says literally "he did not take angels with his hand", "did not catch hold of", "did not take [the nature of angels]"; meaning that Christ took to himself a human nature, not an angelic nature. St John Chrysostom explains the text in this way: "What does he mean by 'take with his hand'; why does he not say 'took on/assumed' but instead uses the expression 'took with his hand'? The reason is this: this verb has to do with those who are in pursuit of their enemies and are doing all they can to catch those who are in flight from them and to seize those who resist. In other words, humankind had fled from him and fled very far, for it says 'we were very far from God and were almost without God in the world' (Eph 2:12). That is why he came in pursuit of us and 'seized us for himself'. The Apostle makes it clear that he did all this entirely out of love for men, in his charity and solicitude for us" (*Hom. on Heb*, 2).

"This single reflection, that he who is true and perfect God became man, supplies sufficient proof of the exalted dignity conferred on the human race by the divine bounty; since we may now glory that the Son of God is bone of our bone, and flesh of our flesh, a privilege not given to angels" (*St Pius V Catechism*, 1, 4, 11).

2:17. This is the first mention of the central theme of the letter, the priesthood of Christ. Because he is God and man, Jesus is the only Mediator between God and men, who have lost God's friendship and divine life on account of sin; he exercises this mediation as High Priest; his Love saves men by bridging the abyss which separates the sinful stock of Adam from God whom it has outraged.

It first refers clearly to our Lord's human nature: he is in no way different from men (except that he is not guilty of sin: cf. Heb 4:15). "These words mean that Christ was reared and educated and grew up and suffered all he had to suffer

Hebrews 2:18

Heb 4:15
Mt 4:1–11

become a merciful and faithful high priest in the service of God, to make expiation for the sins of the people. ¹⁸For because he himself has suffered and been tempted, he is able to help those who are tempted.

---

and finally died" (Chrysostom, *Hom. on Heb*, 5). "He partook of the same food as we do," writes Theodoret of Cyrus, "and he endured work; he experienced sadness in his soul and shed tears; he underwent death" (*Interpretatio Ep. ad Haebr.*, 2).

Christ the Priest is able perfectly to understand the sinner and make satisfaction to divine Justice. "In a judge what one most desires is mercy," St Thomas writes, "in an advocate, reliability. The Apostle implies that both things were found in Christ by virtue of his passion. Mankind desires mercy of him as judge, and reliability of him as advocate" (*Commentary on Heb*, 2, 4).

Christ's priesthood consists in making expiation by a sacrifice of atonement and a peace-offering for the sins of men: he takes our place and atones on our behalf: "Christ merited justification for us [...] and made satisfaction for us to God the Father" (Council of Trent, *De iustificatione*, chap. 7).

2:18. Suffering can link a person to Christ in a special and mysterious way. "The Redeemer suffered in place of man and for man. Every man has *his own share in the Redemption*. Each one is also *called to share in that suffering* through which the Redemption was accomplished. He is called to share in that suffering through which all human suffering has also been redeemed. In bringing about the Redemption through suffering, Christ *has* also *raised human suffering to the level of the Redemption*. Thus each man, in his suffering, can also become a sharer in the redemptive suffering of Christ" (John Paul II, *Salvifici doloris*, 19).

Christ's main purpose in undergoing his passion was the Redemption of mankind, but he also suffered in order to strengthen us and give us an example. "By taking our weaknesses upon himself Christ has obtained for us the strength to overcome our natural infirmity. On the night before his passion, by choosing to suffer fear, anguish and sorrow in the garden of Gethsemane he won for us strength to resist harassment by those who seek our downfall; he obtained for us strength to overcome the fatigue we experience in prayer, in mortification and in other acts of devotion, and, finally, the fortitude to bear adversity with peace and joy" (St Alphonsus, *Reflections on the Passion*, 9, 1).

A person who suffers, and even more so a person who does penance, should realize that he is understood by Christ. Christ will then console him and help him bear affliction: "You too some day may feel the loneliness of our Lord on the Cross. If so, seek the support of him who died and rose again. Find yourself a shelter in the wounds in his hands, in his feet, in his side. And your willingness to start again will revive, and you will take up your journey again with greater determination and effectiveness" (St Josemaría Escrivá, *The Way of the Cross*, XII, 2).

Chaps. 2 and 3. This chapter and the following one are a further "word of exhortation". After professing faith in Christ's divinity and showing his superiority over angels, the writer now shows our Lord's superiority over Moses, whom all Jews regarded as the true founder, liberator and lawgiver of the chosen

2. CHRIST IS GREATER THAN MOSES

Moses' ministry and that of Christ compared

3 ¹Therefore, holy brethren, who share in a heavenly call, consider Jesus, the apostle and high priest of our confession.

Heb 4:14; 9:15
Eph 1:18
Phil 3:14

---

people. This comparing of Christ and Moses is not done in a polemical sort of way: the language is careful and restrained. Conscious that he is addressing Christians of Jewish background, the sacred writer does not try to diminish or gloss over the importance of the first lawgiver and foremost prophet of the Old Testament. His sole purpose is to show the incomparable excellence of Jesus Christ. Our Lord in fact introduced himself as a "new Moses" and that was how those who witnessed his words and actions perceived him (cf. Mt 2:4, recalling Ex 7:11; Mt 2:15, quoting Hos 11:1; Mt 5:21, 27, 31, 33; etc.).

St John Chrysostom points out that the comparison being made here is between Moses and Christ as men, and particularly with Christ as priest, for priesthood in Israel went back to Moses and all the Jews saw Moses as someone of singular importance. By approaching the subject in this way, the sacred writer shows great sensitivity to Christians of Jewish origin: "He starts by laying the foundations of Christ's superiority, beginning with his Incarnation so as to come back later to his divinity; but at that point comparison [of Moses with Christ] is not possible. So he begins by putting them, as *men*, on the same level [...]. He does not, to begin with, show Jesus' total superiority, because he was afraid his listeners would rebel and block their ears. Since these people had been devout Jews, the memory of Moses was deeply etched in their hearts" (*Hom. on Heb*, 5).

For the Jews, Moses stands for the entire Law, and for Christians he is a figure of Christ, the new lawgiver. For this reason, tradition has pointed to a certain parallelism between this chapter of the letter and the episode of the Transfiguration, when our Lord appeared with Moses and Elijah at his side (cf. Mt 17:2–3 and par.). St Ambrose comments that today also Christians can see Moses with Jesus, can see the Law as part of the Gospel; in the Church Moses continues to teach; indeed, there he is given greater prominence than he had in the Old Testament (cf. *Expositio Evangelii sec. Lucam*, 7, 10–11). The glory which caused Moses' face to shine now shines from the face of Christ (cf. 2 Cor 3:7–18).

3:1. "Holy brethren": the faithful are here described as holy because, by virtue of baptismal grace and the sanctification by Jesus which Baptism involves, this is a correct term for them, and one which reminds them of the spiritual perfection they are invited to share in (cf. Rom 1:7 and note; 16:2; 1 Cor 1:2; 2 Cor 1:1; etc.).

Christians have always been conscious of this high calling: "We are not just a people", St Justin writes, "we are a holy people [...]. We are not, then, some despicable or barbarous tribe, or nation of [...] Phrygians; we have been chosen by God: to us who did not ask about him, he manifested himself" (St Justin, *Dialogue with Trypho*, 119, 3).

The Christian vocation, here described as a "heavenly call" because it comes from heaven and leads towards heaven, is a personal call from God to follow Jesus in the Church: "This is a heavenly call in

Num 12:7, LXX ²He was faithful to him who appointed him, just as Moses also
2 Cor 3:7ff   was faithful in^e God's house. ³Yet Jesus has been counted worthy

two senses—because Christians are called not to an earthly kingdom but to a heavenly one; and because the call does not have its source in our merits or any human event: it derives solely from divine grace" (St Thomas, *Commentary on Heb*, ad loc.).

The titles of "apostle" and "high priest", applied here to Christ, convey a very accurate sense of the Son's mission in the world. As "apostle" Jesus is the messenger or envoy of God to men. As "high priest" he is the representative of men before God. Jewish rabbis gave the high priest, in the ceremonies on the Day of Atonement, the title of "Messenger of Justice", that is, God's apostle sent to effect justification. However, Jesus Christ is the only one to whom can be applied the two titles of "apostle" and "high priest". "Christ is called messenger and apostle", St Justin writes, "because he proclaims what must be made known and is sent to reveal what the Father has to tell us. The Lord himself gave us to understand this when he said, 'he who hears me, hears him who sent me'" (*First Apology*, 63, 5).

3:2–6. For the Jews the great prophet and mediator of the Sinai Covenant was vested with such glory that some rabbis ranked him higher than the angels.

Moses can be regarded not only as the founder of the people of Israel and of the Hebrew nation but also as their first prophet. In his religious office, which stemmed from his divine call to be "a servant" of God (v. 5), Moses worked as a priest, teacher and lawgiver, which made him a "type" of Christ. However, Jesus Christ brought to perfection and fulfilment the divine plan of salvation sketched out in the words and actions of Moses, the mediator of the Old Covenant.

The writer of the letter starts out from the faithfulness of Moses and, pre-eminently, of Jesus; he shows the superiority of the latter by using the simile of a house in the sense, sometimes, of a building and, at other times, of a family. Just as the architect is more important than the house he builds, just as God is greater than the universe he created, so Christ is superior to Moses. Similarly, the son or master of a house is on a higher level than its manager; so, although Moses served the house well, Christ is greater than he because he is the Son of God, the master of the house.

3:2. When it says that "he was faithful to him who appointed him", this refers to Christ's faithfulness to the Father, who made him the apostle and high priest, the mediator between God and men (cf. Chrysostom, *Hom. on Heb*, 5).

"Moses also was faithful in all God's house": the people of Israel were sometimes described as God's house, and Moses was faithful in "all" God's house because the Lord chose to give him alone the task of governing it and rejected those who tried to put themselves on his level (Num 12:1–9). But Israel, God's house in the Old Testament, has now become the new people of God, the Church, the house of Christ, in the New Testament, as Vatican II says: "Often, too, the Church is called the 'building' of God (1 Cor 3:9). The Lord compared himself to the stone which the builders rejected, but which was made into the cornerstone (Mt 21:42). On this foundation the Church is

e. Other ancient authorities insert *all*

of as much more glory than Moses as the builder of a house has more honour than the house. ⁴(For every house is built by some one, but the builder of all things is God.) ⁵Now Moses was faithful in all God's house as a servant, to testify to the things that were to be spoken later, ⁶but Christ was faithful over God's[f] house as a son. And we are his house if we hold fast our confidence and pride in our hope.[g]

Eph 2:19
1 Cor 3:9
Heb 4:16; 10:23

built by the Apostles and from it the Church receives solidity and unity. This edifice has many names to describe it—the house of God in which his family dwells (1 Tim 3:15); the household of God in the Spirit (Eph 2:19, 22); the dwellingplace of God among men (Rev 21:3), and, especially, the holy temple" (*Lumen gentium*, 6).

3:3–4. The comparison between Christ and Moses begins by noting that both were faithful to God (v. 2). God himself described Moses as faithful (cf. Num 12:7) and Christ showed his faithfulness, St Thomas comments, firstly by attributing his preaching not to himself but to the Father who sent him (cf. Jn 5:41; 7:18); secondly, because he sought the Father's glory and not his own (cf. Jn 8:50); and finally, because he was completely obedient, becoming "obedient unto death, even death on a cross" (Phil 2:8): cf. *Commentary on Heb,* ad loc. Christ's faithfulness, moreover, extended over all nations and not just the people of Israel, which was the case with Moses.

Christ takes precedence over the Prophet not only because he is God's Son but also because he has much more authority. The comparison of the builder of a house and the house itself (connecting with the image of the people of God as God's house) gives the writer a further opportunity to exalt the figure of Christ. Moses and the Law come under Christ by virtue of a sovereign divine disposition establishing Christ as true high priest and new lawgiver. "Christ built the house, that is, the Church. For Christ himself, the author of grace and truth, built the Church: he gave it its laws whereas Moses only built it in the sense of transmitting the Law" (St Thomas, *Commentary on Heb*, 3, 1).

But it goes further than that: the Father who built all things (cf. v. 4) created all things through the Son, and therefore Christ is greater than Moses because he is also the Creator of the universe.

3:6b. "This house is the faithful", St Thomas writes; "they are Christ's house because they believe in Christ, and also because Christ dwells in them. So, this house is us, the Christian faithful" (*Commentary on Heb*, 3, 1). "The material, the physical structure, of a church should always remind you", John Paul II told the faithful in a suburb of Madrid, "that you are 'living stones' (1 Pet 2:5), that you should always be building yourselves into Christ, to the measure and example of Christ, in all your personal, family and social activities" (*Homily at Orcasitas*, 3 November 1982).

This is the ground on which the author invites his readers to hope and trust in God—a very appropriate exhortation, given the difficult circumstances in which his original readers found themselves. Hope is always an essential virtue, particularly when one is in a difficult situation, for it enables a person to focus

---

f. Greek *his*   **g.** Other ancient authorities insert *firm to the end*

Hebrews 3:7

The need for faith. The bad example given by the Chosen People

Ps 95:7–11

⁷Therefore, as the Holy Spirit says,
"Today, when you hear his voice,
⁸do not harden your hearts as in the rebellion,

---

on things eternal and thereby helps him stay true to his course. "One needs not only to be able to hold out but to have a stable, solid confidence, which is firmly grounded on faith, so as never to be overwhelmed by difficulties" (Chrysostom, *Hom. on Heb*, 5).

The writer boldly speaks of the joyful pride which comes from an awareness of divine filiation. "You are discouraged, why? Is it your sins and miseries? Is it your defeats, at times coming one after the other? A really big fall, which you didn't expect? [...] Take refuge in your divine sonship: God is your most loving father. In this lies your security, a haven where you can drop anchor no matter what is happening on the surface of the sea of life. And you will find joy, strength, optimism: victory!" (St Josemaría Escrivá, *The Way of the Cross*, VII, 2).

3:7–11. A long quotation from Psalm 95 introduces the theme of that "rest" which the people of the promise will attain at the end of their wayfaring.

In the book of Genesis we are told that when God finished his work of creation, he "rested". The "rest" prescribed in the Mosaic Law was a kind of imitation of what God did, sharing God's happiness, receiving the reward merited by a life of fidelity and hard work. The Jews had gradually come to a more spiritual understanding of "rest" or, as they termed it, "the place of rest". This idea reaches its highest form of expression in the apocryphal book of Esdras (4 Esdras), where the prayer is raised to God to grant the faithful departed "eternal rest", *Requiem aeternam dona eis, Domine*. The chosen people were helped to arrive at this notion of rest by reflecting on the spiritual meaning of the Exodus and the pilgrimage to the promised land. The Exodus was also seen as a new creation, with God "creating" his people. Like the first creation, this second creation would be followed by "rest"—entry into the promised land. The Letter to the Hebrews shares this interpretation of the Exodus but it gives it a Christian perspective by seeing the Exodus as the Redemption whereby Christ, a new Moses, leads us to eternal rest.

3:7. The author of the letter reaffirms that Sacred Scripture—in this case Psalm 95—is the work of the Holy Spirit. As such it always carries a contemporary message; it is a form God uses to speak to all men in all periods of history. Readiness to listen to God and do his will *today* and *now* is an important part of Christian living (cf. 3:13). A Christian should be docile to God speaking in his heart; he should be quick to respond to all the little invitations God gives him to deny himself and advance in holiness. No excuse is ever valid for delaying to give a positive response to grace. "Do your duty 'now', without looking back on 'yesterday', which has already passed, or worrying over 'tomorrow', which may never come for you" (St Josemaría Escrivà, *The Way*, 253). "Now! Return to your noble life now. Don't let yourself be fooled: 'now' is not too soon ... nor too late" (ibid., 254).

3:8. Man is free; he can resist grace, and unfortunately often does. "It is not God's goodness that is to blame for faith not

on the day of testing in the wilderness,
⁹where your fathers put me to the test
and saw my works for forty years.
¹⁰ Therefore I was provoked with that generation,
and said, 'They always go astray in their hearts;
they have not known my ways.'

---

coming to birth in men, but the inadequate dispositions of those who hear the preaching of the word" (St Gregory Nazianzen, *Oratio catechetica magna*, 31). Scripture calls this resistance to grace "hardness of heart" (cf., e.g., Ex 4:21; Rom 9:18; Deut 15:7; Jer 7:26; Acts 19:6).

When withholding belief or resisting conversion, people sometimes claim to have intellectual difficulties, but, very often, the real problem has to do with their dispositions, with not *wanting* to respond to grace. The disobedience and "hardness of heart" or stubbornness of the chosen people is a recurring subject in the Old Testament (cf., e.g., Ex 32:9; Deut 9:13; 2 Kings 17:14; Is 46:12; Jer 5:3; Ezek 2:4; etc.). Their rebellion against God's commands was due to pride, which turned them into a people whose forehead was as hard as brass, whose neck was "an iron sinew" (Is 48:4; cf. Acts 7:51), a people uncircumcised in heart, with uncircumcised ears (cf. Jer 9:26; 6:10). Conversion cannot operate if someone has that attitude. For this reason our Lord, and later his apostles, referred to the Jews' rejection of him, in order to make Christians steadfast in faith (cf. Is 6:9; Mt 13:13; Jn 12:40; Acts 28:26).

3:9. Psalm 95 contains a reference to the Israelites' rebellion when God put them to the test in the wilderness. The episode took place in Rephidim, on the border of the wilderness of Zin, in the south-east of the Sinai peninsula. Having made their way out of Egypt, the people grew impatient; they complained about how Yahweh was treating them, and put him to the test by asking him to work a miracle (Ex 17:1–7). God did work a miracle: at Horeb he ordered Moses to strike the rock with his rod, and out of it flowed water to relieve the people's thirst. The place was therefore given the name of Massah (meaning temptation) and Meribah (meaning fault-finding or exasperation). This episode in Jewish history came to symbolize the disgruntlement which typified the Jews in the desert, an attitude which even affected Moses in Kadesh (cf. Num 20:1–13). The leader of the chosen people, in circumstances similar to those of the earlier incident, struck the rock twice, not expecting anything to happen. On account of this he did not merit to enter the promised land: he was only allowed to see it from Mount Nebo, where he died (Deut 34:1–8).

"Putting God to the test", "tempting" him, is a sin of presumption. It involves exposing oneself imprudently and needlessly to physical or spiritual risk from which God's ordinary providence does not provide protection (cf. Mt 4:5–7).

In this passage, "putting God to the test" means demanding more proof than necessary that God is steadfast in his will and continues to protect his chosen people. "God should not be asked to account for his activities", St John Chrysostom comments; "if one asks him to prove his power, his providence, his solicitude, it is the same as not yet being fully convinced of his power and goodness and mercy" (*Hom. on Heb*, 6).

Hebrews 3:11

Num 14:21-23
2 Thess 2:3
1 Thess 5:11

¹¹ As I swore in my wrath,
'They shall never enter my rest.'"*
¹²Take care, brethren, lest there be in any of you an evil, unbelieving heart, leading you to fall away from the living God. ¹³But exhort one another every day, as long as it is called "today," that none of you may be hardened by the deceitfulness of sin.

3:11. There are three kinds of rest. The first is the "sabbath", when God rested after creating the world; then there is the rest provided by the promised land of Canaan after countless afflictions and difficulties; and "finally there is the true rest which belongs to the Kingdom of heaven, where the elect rest from their labours and afflictions: the sabbath is a reflection and symbol of that rest" (*Hom. on Heb*, 6).

St Thomas Aquinas applies the term "rest" to peace of body and soul and says that there are different kinds of peace—physical ease (cf. Lk 12:19); the peace of conscience a person has who does right in the sight of God; and the peace of eternal happiness in heaven (cf. *Commentary on Heb*, ad loc.).

3:12. "Falling away from the living God" seems to be something more serious than reverting to Judaism; it implies the sad possibility of total loss of belief in God. Thus, in the case of those to whom the epistle was written, a reversion from the Gospel to Judaism would not be simply a matter of returning to a previous religious position but rather a deliberate act involving voluntary resistance to grace and a complete break with God. For people who had not received the Revelation of Jesus Christ, the Jewish religion certainly did provide access to God; but for those who by embracing Christianity had thereby received the fullness of Revelation, renunciation of Christ would mean a virtually irreparable sin (cf. Heb 6:4–6). There is never a valid excuse for giving up the faith.

The Church teaches and prescribes to its children the need to be true to the faith even at the cost of life itself. From the very beginning this was the kind of fidelity practised by the martyrs and confessors of the faith."They cut our hands off, they nail us to crosses, they throw us to wild beasts, imprison us and burn us, and we submit to every kind of torture; yet everyone knows that we do not betray our faith. Rather, the worse our sufferings, the more there are who embrace faith and devotion in the name of Jesus" (St Justin, *Dialogue with Trypho*, 110, 4).

Some Christians today are called to stay true in the face of violent persecution; they and others also have to overcome fear of ridicule, and the temptation to hide their convictions from unbelievers. The words of the letter remind us that there is a danger that whereas in earlier times force failed to achieve its objective, nowadays fear of ridicule could cause us to be ashamed of Christ or to deny him. "'And in a paganized or pagan environment when my life clashes with its surroundings, won't my naturalness seem artificial?' you ask me. And I reply: 'Undoubtedly your life will clash with theirs; and that contrast—faith confirmed by works!—is exactly the naturalnesss I ask of you'" (St Josemaría Escrivá, *The Way*, 380).

3:13. The more Christians practise charity, the easier it is for them to be steadfast in the faith. Fraternity, mutual brotherly support, helps provide protection from the devil's efforts to make us sin: "'*Frater*

¹⁴For we share in Christ, if only we hold our first confidence firm to the end, ¹⁵while it is said,
"Today, when you hear his voice,
do not harden your hearts as in the rebellion."

_{Heb 6:11; 11:1}
_{Mk 4:19}
_{Rom 7:11}
_{2 Cor 9:4}
_{Ps 95:7f}

---

qui adiuvatur a fratre quasi civitas firma. Brother helped by brother is a fortress.' Think for a moment and make up your mind to live the fraternal spirit that I have always asked of you" (St Josemaría Escrivá, *The Way*, 460).

Aware of his personal weakness and of the need to help others and to let himself be helped, the Christian keeps striving to practise this fraternity. He loves the good he sees in others, and he tries to uproot in himself and others anything that implies a defect. Fraternity, therefore, leads to "fraternal correction", a word of advice which is always full of understanding, being the outcome of a desire to live in harmony with others and to remove divisions and barriers. Christian fraternity binds the Church together.

"Not in vain is there in the depths of man's being a strong longing for peace, for union with his fellow man, for mutual respect for personal rights, so strong that it seeks to transform human relations into fraternity. This longing reflects something which is most deeply imprinted upon our human condition: since we are all children of God, our fraternity is not a cliché or an empty dream; it beckons as a goal which, though difficult, is really ours to achieve" (St Josemaría Escrivá, *Friends of God*, 233).

3:14. This is a repetition of the exhortation in v. 6 to remain true to the end.

"Firm confidence" is the very opposite of the "falling away" mentioned in v. 12. From the very beginning of his calling, a Christian is already sharing in Christ's life and in his glory, but he will not share in it fully until after death, when he will be able actually to see the Lord.

This sharing in Christ's grace is a treasure which we carry in "earthen vessels" (2 Cor 4:7) and can lose at any time through sin. We need to nurture this grace and protect our faith by being watchful and active right through our life: "We have shared in Chirst's death through holy Baptism and we have been buried with him; we have shared in his resurrection provided we keep our faith intact" (Theodoret of Cyrrhus, *Interpretatio Ep. ad Haebreos*, 3).

The Christian life is a matter of constantly returning to God, beginning anew, and humbly and decisively correcting our course when we go astray through weakness or indifference.

"What does it matter that we stumble on the way, if we find in the pain of our fall the energy to pick ourselves up and go on with renewed vigour? Don't forget that the saint is not the person who never falls, but rather the one who never fails to get up again, humbly and with a holy stubbornness. If the book of Proverbs says that the just man falls seven times a day (cf. Prov 24:16), who are we poor creatures, you and I, to be surprised or discouraged by our own weaknesses and falls! We will be able to keep going ahead, if only we seek our fortitude in him who says: 'Come to me, all you who labour and are heavy laden and I will give you rest' (Mt 11:28). Thank you, Lord, *quia tu es, Deus, fortitudo mea* (Ps 42:2), because you, and you alone, my God, have always been my strength, my refuge and my support" (St Josemaría Escrivá, *Friends of God*, 131).

Hebrews 3:16

Ex 17:1ff
1 Cor 10:5, 10
Num 14:29
Num 14:22

¹⁶Who were they that heard and yet were rebellious? Was it not all those who left Egypt under the leadership of Moses? ¹⁷And with whom was he provoked forty years? Was it not with those who sinned, whose bodies fell in the wilderness? ¹⁸And to whom did he swear that they should never enter his rest, but to those who were disobedient? ¹⁹So we see that they were unable to enter because of unbelief.

Through faith we can attain God's "rest"

Gal 5:2
1 Cor 10:1–13

4 ¹Therefore, while the promise of entering his rest remains, let us fear lest any of you be judged to have failed to reach it. ²For good

---

3:16–19. The book of Exodus tells how the Israelites left Egypt under the leadership of Moses (cf. Ex 12:35–39), but their unbelief and infidelity prevented them, that particular generation, from taking possession of the promised land (cf. Num 14:20–23, 27–30, 36–37; 20:12). Their lack of faith in God and in Moses, their fault-finding and disobedience, which caused God to punish them in this way, are mentioned by the sacred writer because Christans also, through unfaithfullness, can fail to attain eternal life.

Unbelief leads to the temptation to disobey, and disobedience is a sign of unbelief. If a Christian makes a habit of not listening to God's calls, he is in danger of resisting grace more and more and can end up losing his faith. Unbelief is normally not something which happens all of a sudden; it is usually the outcome of a process of interior disobedience.

4:1–11. This chapter is a further exhortation to fidelity and develops the theme of that "rest" which the people of Israel failed to attain. The comparison between Moses and Jesus (cf. 3:1ff) is now extended to Jews and Christians. Moses tried to get the people of Israel to stay true to God and so enter their place of rest (cf. Deut 12:9–10). He laid down the precept of sabbath rest (Deut 5:12–15; Ex 20:8–11; 35:1–3; Num 15:32–36) in memory of God's resting after the Creation, and as a sign of the Covenant and a symbol of eternal rest. In the Gospel Christ promises a new kind of rest, an eternal one, in the house of the Father (cf. Jn 14:1–3, 27).

The history of the chosen people is not, then, a mere chronicle of past events. It is something meaningful to us today and full of lessons for Christian living. To Christians also, as members of the new Israel, God offers a "rest", one which is richer than the temporal rest the Jews obtained when they took possession of the promised land, for the rest promised to Christians is rest in heaven.

However, the Jews disobeyed God's commandments; they soiled themselves by worshipping idols and failed to grasp the significance of their own history. And they confused God's rest, their true destiny, with the sabbath rest—a physical rest which they practised in an almost exclusively external way (cf. Mk 3:1–6; Lk 13:10–17). Christians also can run a similar risk if they fail to hold on to everything which Jesus Christ, the mediator of the New Covenant, has won for them.

4:1. God's promise of rest remains valid, but to attain it one needs to be faithful —to have a vigilance that comes from holy fear of God, a fear of being excluded

news came to us just as to them; but the message which they heard did not benefit them, because it did not meet with faith in the hearers.ʰ ³For we who have believed enter that rest, as he has said,   Heb 3:11; 12:15   Ps 95:11

from eternal blessedness. The text can also be interpreted as meaning "Let us fear, lest any one of you despair because he thinks he has been excluded permanently"; that is, "let us fear despair".

In this context "rest" refers to all the supernatural graces we obtain through grace, particularly that of seeing and enjoying God in the future life. This rest, which will reach its perfection in heaven and which begins in this life with faith and grace, is man's true end or destiny. "God works with creative power by sustaining in existence the world that he called into being from nothing, and he works with salvific power in the hearts of those whom from the beginning he has destined for 'rest'" (John Paul II, *Laborem exercens*, 25).

The saints have often liked to describe the joy which heaven gives, that eternal rest which God deigns to grant souls who depart this world. "Who can measure the happiness of heaven, where no evil at all can touch us, no good will be out of reach; where life is to be one long laud extolling God, who will be all in all [...]. This, indeed, will be that ultimate sabbath that has no evening and which the Lord foreshadowed in the account of his creation [...]. Only when we are remade by God and perfected by a greater grace shall we have the eternal stillness of that rest in which we shall see that he is God. Then only shall we be filled with him when he will be all in all" (St Augustine, *The City of God*, 22, 30).

Losing this "rest" is the only thing one should really fear.

4:2. The good news was proclaimed to the Jews in the sense that they also heard the preaching of Moses which aimed at preparing the chosen people to be generous in their fidelity to the Lord's promises. The Israelites, however, rebelled against those who were the first to hear the message—Abraham, Isaac, Jacob, Moses himself, Joshua and the prophets.

The preaching of the Word can actually harden a person's heart if he does not listen to it with the right dispositions. "To obtain salvation it is not enough to hear the words. One needs to take them in with faith and keep a firm hold on them. What good was God's promise to those who received it if they did not receive it faithfully or failed to put their trust in his power—if they did not, so to speak, fuse with, become one with, the divine words?" (Theodoret of Cyrus, *Interpretatio Ep. ad Haebreos*, 4). What proves a person's true obedience to God's word is his solidarity with those to whom God has given the authority to proclaim it.

4:3–8. The believer can be said to "enter God's rest" because in this life he already begins to be intimate with the three divine Persons. In biblical terms the "rest" is connected with the Covenant which God establishes with men. "Rest" is the reward for faithfullness to the Covenant; it begins in this life in the form of serenity and interior peace and the enjoyment of material things (such as the promised land), but will reach its perfection only in heaven. In this sense, as Psalm 95 reminds us, God promised his people rest repeatedly: the psalm speaks of a "today" when they will enter his "rest": everyone can begin to enjoy "today" the rest of divine friendship, provided he

h. Other manuscripts read *they were not united in faith with the hearers*

"As I swore in my wrath,
'They shall never enter my rest,'"
although his works were finished from the foundation of the world. ⁴For he has somewhere spoken of the seventh day in this way, "And God rested on the seventh day from all his works." ⁵And again in this place he said,
"They shall never enter my rest."
⁶Since therefore it remains for some to enter it, and those who formerly received the good news failed to enter because of disobedience, ⁷again he sets a certain day, "Today," saying through David so long afterward, in the words already quoted,
"Today, when you hear his voice,
do not harden your hearts."
⁸For if Joshua had given them rest, God[i] would not speak later of another day. ⁹So then, there remains a sabbath rest for the people of God; ¹⁰for whoever enters God's rest also ceases from his labours as God did from his.

Gen 2:2, LXX
Ps 95:11
Heb 3:7f
Ps 95:7f
Deut 31:7
Josh 22:4
Rev 14:13

---

does not harden his heart, provided he repents and becomes faithful again.

Christians have received a further invitation from God to enter his rest: because many Jews proved to be unfaithful, a new people of God was established. This marks a new "today", a new point when one can opt for fidelity and enter the promised land. This "today" has two characteristics: it requires our free response to God's decision to call us; and it does not happen immediately: for the new people of God, also, there is a future "sabbath", that is, heaven.

To appreciate the subtle play on words, one should remember that the same term is used in Hebrew for the word "rest" and for the sabbath as a day of the week.

4:9–10. The peace and serenity of a Christian who has dominion over sin is described as "sabbath rest", a pledge and symbol of the "heavenly sabbath" of the blessed. "The spiritual sabbath consists in a holy and mystical rest, wherein the 'old man', being buried with Christ, is renewed to life and carefully applies himself to act in accordance with the spirit of Christian piety" (*St Pius V Catechism*, 3, 4, 15). This has been the experience of many holy people who have enjoyed peace of soul: St John of the Cross expresses it poetically in these words: "On a dark night, / afire with yearnings full of love / —O moment of delight!— / I slipped out unnoticed / while all my household slept" (*Poems*, I).

In this life a person's interior peace is dependent on his effort to control his passions.

"Let us remember that our life is a form of combat; let us never seek repose; let us never see affliction as something exceptional. We must be like the athlete who is always ready for the test. The time for rest has not yet come: we still need to be made perfect by suffering" (Chrysostom, *Hom. on Heb*, 5).

---

i. Greek *he*

¹¹Let us therefore strive to enter that rest, that no one fall by the same sort of disobedience.

The power of God's word

¹²For the word of God is living and active, sharper than any two-edged sword, piercing to the division of soul and spirit, of joints and

Is 49:2
Wis 7:22–30
Eph 6:17
1 Pet 1:23
Rev 1:16

4:11. The sacred writer ends his commentary on Psalm 95 with a short, concise exhortation summing up what he has been saying and inviting his readers to enter God's rest without delay.

"There are a number of reasons why the text speaks of striving to enter (God's) rest," St Thomas comments. "First, because, there is a long road ahead. Then because time is short—and we do not know how much time we have. Third, because ours is a pressing interior call which urges us on with the stimulus of love. Finally, because of the danger of delaying, as happened in the case of the foolish virgins (Mt 25:1–13), who arrived late and failed to gain entry" (*Commentary on Heb*, 4, 2).

The central idea is not only urgency and eagerness but also dogged perseverance with the help of grace.

4:12–13. The "word of God", which the text speaks about, probably refers to Revelation taken as a whole, particularly Holy Scripture; but it may also refer to the *Logos* or Word, the second person of the Holy Trinity. The "word" of God is presented as an expression of God's power: it is that active word (Gen 1:3ff; Ps 33:9) which creates everything out of nothing. In the Wisdom books we find this word personified (Sir 42:15; 43:26; Wis 9:1; 18:15; Ps 148:1–5). But this living and active word of God is also to be seen in the New Testament (Gal 3:8, 22) and in its full and perfect form in Christ himself (Jn 1:1; Rev 9:13).

God's word is also very much at work in Revelation: "In the sacred books the Father who is in heaven comes lovingly to meet his children, and talks to them. And such is the force and power of the Word of God that it serves the Church as her support and vigour, and the children of the Church as strength for their faith, food for the soul, and a pure and lasting fount of spiritual life" (Vatican II, *Dei Verbum*, 21).

God's word is consoling and life-giving, but it also inspires fear in those who try to ignore it. "The word of his truth is hotter and brighter than the sun, and pierces the very depths of hearts and minds" (St Justin, *Dialogue with Trypho*, 121, 2). The depths of a person's heart, his deepest thoughts, attitudes and intentions, lie open to God's all-seeing eye. "What a person does or thinks is expressed in his actions, but one can never be sure of what motivates his actions. That, however, is never hidden from God" (St Thomas, *Commentary on Heb*, 4, 2).

The last judgment, which is a hidden backdrop to these words of the sacred text, calls us to present conversion. "The Apostle of God wrote this not only for his [immediate] readers but also for us. It behoves us therefore always to keep that divine judgment before our minds, and to be full of fear and trembling and to keep God's commandments faithfully and be ever hopeful of that rest promised us which we shall attain in Christ" (Theodoret of Cyrus, *Interpretatio Ep. ad Haebreos*, ad loc.).

marrow, and discerning the thoughts and intentions of the heart. ¹³And before him no creature is hidden, but all are open and laid bare to the eyes of him with whom we have to do.

3. CHRIST, OUR HIGH PRIEST, IS GREATER THAN THE PRIESTS OF THE MOSAIC LAW

Heb 5:5–10; 7:26; 9:11, 24; 10:21; Eph 4:10
Heb 2:17f
Rom 8:3

Our confidence is based on Christ's priesthood

¹⁴Since then we have a great high priest who has passed through the heavens, Jesus, the Son of God, let us hold fast our confession. ¹⁵For we have not a high priest who is unable to sympathize with

---

4:14–16. The text now reverts to its main theme (cf. 2:17), that is, the priesthood of Christ. It highlights the dignity of the new high priest, who has passed through the heavens; and his mercy, too, for he sympathizes with our weaknesses. We have, therefore, every reason to approach him with confidence. "The believers were at that time in a storm of temptation; that is why the Apostle is consoling them, saying that our high priest not only knows, as God, the weakness of our nature: as man, he has also experienced the sufferings that affect us, although he was free from sin. Since he knows our weakness so well, he can give us the help we need, and when he comes to judge us, he will take that weakness into account in his sentence" (*Interpretatio Ep. ad Haebreos*, ad loc.).

We should respond to the Lord's goodness by staying true to our profession of faith. The confession or profession of faith referred to here is not simply an external declaration: external confession is necessary but there must also be commitment and a spirit of fidelity. A Christian needs to live up to all the demands of his calling; he should be single-minded and free from doubts.

4:15. "If we should some time find ourselves sorely tempted by our enemies, it will greatly help us to remember that we have on our side a high priest who is most compassionate, for he chose to experience all kinds of temptation" (*St Pius V Catechism*, 4, 15, 14). In order to understand and help a sinner to get over his falls and cope with temptation, one does not oneself need to have experience of being tempted; in fact, only one who does not sin knows the full force of temptation, because the sinner gives in prior to resisting to the end. Christ never yielded to temptation. He therefore experienced much more than we do (because we are often defeated by temptation) the full rigour and violence of those temptations which he chose to undergo as man at particular points in his life. Our Lord, then, allowed himself to be tempted, in order to set us an example and prevent us from ever losing confidence in our ability to resist temptation with the help of grace (cf. notes on Mt 4:1–11 and par.).

"There is no man", St Jerome comments, "who can resist all tests except he who, made in our likeness, has experienced everything but sin" (*Comm. in Ionam*, 2, 46). Christ's sinlessness, often affirmed in Holy Scripture (Rom 8:3; 2 Cor 5:21; Jn 8:46; 1 Pet 1:19; 2:21–24), follows logically from his being God and from his human integrity and holiness. At

our weaknesses, but one who in every respect has been tempted as we are, yet without sin. ¹⁶Let us then with confidence draw near to the throne of grace, that we may receive mercy and find grace to help in time of need.

Rom 3:25
2 Cor 5:21
1 Jn 3:21

Christ has been made high priest by God the Father

5 ¹For every high priest chosen from among men is appointed to act on behalf of men in relation to God, to offer gifts and

Heb 2:17; 7:28

---

the same time Christ's weakness, which he chose to experience out of love for us, is a kind of invitation from God to pray for strength to resist sin. "Let us adore Christ who emptied himself to assume the condition of a slave. He was tempted in every way that we are, but did not sin. Let us turn in prayer to him, saying, 'You took on our human weakness. Be the eyes of the blind, the strength of the weak, the friend of the lonely'" (*Divine Office*, Christmas Day, evening prayer I).

4:16. The "throne" is the symbol of Christ's authority; he is King of the living and the dead. But here it speaks of a "throne of grace": through the salvation worked by Christ, the compassionate Priest and intercessor, God's throne has become a judgment seat from which mercy flows. Christ has initiated for mankind a time of forgiveness and sanctification in which he does not yet manifest his position as sovereign Judge. Christ's priesthood did not cease to operate with his death; it continues in heaven, where he forever pleads on our behalf, and therefore we should have confident recourse to him.

"What security should be ours in considering the mercy of the Lord! 'He has but to cry for redress, and I, the ever merciful, will listen to him' (Ex 22:27). It is an invitation, a promise that he will not fail to fulfill. 'Let us then with confidence draw near to the throne of grace, and we may receive mercy and find grace to help in time of need.' The enemies of our sanctification will be rendered powerless if the mercy of God goes before us. And if through our own fault and human weakness we should fall, the Lord comes to our aid and raises us up" (St Josemaría Escrivá, *Christ Is Passing By*, 7).

5:1–10. The central theme of the epistle, broached in 2:17 and taken up again in 4:14–15, is discussed from here up to the start of chapter 10—the theme of Christ as high priest, the high priest who really can free us from all sin. In fact, Christ is the only perfect Priest: other priests—in both natural religions and the Jewish religion—are only prefigurements of Christ. The first thing to be emphasized, because the writer is addressing people of Jewish background, is that Christ's priesthood is on a higher plane than that of the priests of the Old Law. However, the argument applies not only to the priesthood of Aaron, to whose family all Israelite priests belonged, but also, indirectly, to all forms of priesthood before Christ. But there is a basic difference, in that whereas other priests were chosen by men, Aaron was chosen by God. Scripture introduces him as Moses' brother (cf. Ex 6:20), acting as his interpreter to Pharaoh (because Moses was "slow of speech": Ex 4:10; cf. 7:1–2) and joining him to lead the people out of Egypt (cf. Ex 4:27–30). After the Israelites left Egypt, God himself instituted the priesthood of Aaron to minister and carry out divine worship at the tabernacle and later at the temple in Jerusalem (cf. Ex 28:1–5).

Hebrews 5:1

Divine intervention, therefore, brought to a close the period when sacrifice was offered by the head of the family or the chief of the tribe and when no specific calling or external ordination rite was connected with priesthood. Thus, for example, in the book of Genesis we read that Cain, and Abel, themselves offered sacrifices (cf. Gen 4:35), as did Noah after coming safely through the flood (cf. Gen 8:20); and the patriarchs often offered sacrifices to God in adoration or thanksgiving or to renew their Covenant —for example, Abraham (cf. Gen 12:8; 15:8–17; 22:1–13) and Jacob (cf. Gen 26:25; 33:20), etc.

Although for a considerable time after the institution of the Aaron priesthood, sacrifices continued to be offered also by private individuals—for example, in the period of the Judges, the sacrifice of Gideon (Judg 6:18, 25–26) or that of Samson's parents (Judg 13:15–20)— gradually the convictions grew that to be a priest a person had to have a specific vocation, one which was not given to anyone outside males of the line of Aaron (cf. Judg 17:7–13), whom God had chosen from out of all the people of Israel, identifying him by the sign of his rod sprouting buds (Num 17:16–24). God himself meted out severe punishment to Korah and his sons when they tried to set themselves up as rivals of Aaron: they were devoured by fire from heaven (cf. Num 16); and it was specified in Mosaic legislation time and time again that only the sons of Aaron could act as priests (cf. Num 3:10; 17:5; 18:7). This priesthood offered the sacrifices of Mosaic worship— the burnt offerings, cereal offerings, sin offerings and peace offerings (cf. Lev 6). To the descendants of Aaron, assisted by the Levites, was entrusted also the care of the tabernacle and the protection of the ark of the Covenant. They received their ministry and had it confirmed by the offering of sacrifice and by anointing of the man's head and hands with oil (Ex 29; Lev 8–9; Num 3:3). For all these reasons Hebrew priests were honoured and revered by the people and regarded (not without reason, because God had ordained them) as on a much higher plane than other priests, particularly those of the peoples of Canaan, the priests of Baal, for example. In Christ's time the high priest was the highest religious authority in Israel; his words were regarded as oracular statements, and his decisions could have important political repercussions.

However, Christ came with the very purpose of taking this ancient institution and transforming it into a new, eternal priesthood. Every Christian priest is, as it were, Christ's instrument or an extension of his sacred humanity. Christian priests do not act in their own name, nor are they mere representatives of the people: they act in the name of God. "Here we have the priest's identity: he is direct and daily instrument of the saving grace which Christ has won for us" (St Josemaría Escrivá, *In Love with the Church*, 39). It is really Christ who is acting through them by means of their words, gestures etc. All of this means that Christian priesthood cannot be separated from the eternal priesthood of Christ. This extension of God's providence (in the form of the Old Testament priesthood and the priesthood instituted by Christ in the New Testament and the mission entrusted to New Testament priests) should lead us to love and honour the priesthood irrespective of the human defects and shortcomings of these ministers of God: "To love God and not venerate his Priests ... is not possible" (St Josemaría Escrivá, *The Way*, 74).

5:1a. These words provide a very good short definition of what every priest is.

"The office proper to a priest", St Thomas Aquinas points out, "is to be a mediator between God and the people, inasmuch as he bestows divine things on the people (he is called *sacerdos* (priest), which means 'a giver of sacred things', *sacra dans* [...]), and again inasmuch as he offers the people's prayer to God and in some way makes satisfaction to God for their sins" (*Summa theologiae*, 3, 22, 1).

In this passage of the letter we can detect an echo of the description of Aaron in the book of Sirach: "He chose him out of all the living to offer sacrifice to the Lord, incense and a pleasing odour as a memorial portion, to make atonement for the people" (Sir 45:16). Four elements characterize the office of the high priest (the text speaks of the "high" priest in the strict sense, but it is applicable to all priests)—1) his special dignity, because although he is a man he has been specially chosen by God; 2) the purpose of his mission, which is the good of mankind ("to act on behalf of men"); 3) the "material" side of his office, that is, public divine worship; 4) the specific acts he must perform, the offering of sacrifice at appropriate times.

In the specific case of priesthood instituted by God—such as that of Aaron or the new priesthood instituted by Christ—the calling ("taken" or "chosen" from among men) is not simply an influence the person feels interiorly, or a desire to be a priest: its divine origin is confirmed by nomination by the proper authority, and by official consecration.

5:1b. A priest is "chosen from among men", that is, he should possess a human nature. This is a further sign of God's mercy: to bring about our salvation he uses someone accessible to us, one who shares our human condition, "so that man might have someone like himself to have recourse to" (St Thomas, *Commentary on Heb*, ad loc.). These words also indicate the extent of God's kindness because they remind us that the divine Redeemer not only offered himself and made satisfaction for the sins of all, but desired that "the priestly life which the divine Redeemer had begun in his mortal body by his prayers and sacrifice (should not cease). He willed it to continue unceasingly through the ages in his mystical body, which is the Church; and therefore he instituted a visible priesthood to offer everywhere a clean oblation (Mal 1:11), so that all men all over the world, being diverted from sin, might serve God conscientiously, and of their own free will" (Pius XII, *Mediator Dei*, 1).

He is "chosen from among men" also in the sense that he is given special consecration which in some way marks him off from the rest of the people of God. St John Chrysostom comments, recalling Jesus triple question to Peter after the Resurrection (cf. Jn 21:15–17): "When he asked Peter if he loved him, he did not do so because he needed to know whether his disciple loved him, but because he wanted to show how great his own love was; thus, when he says, 'Who then is the faithful and prudent servant', he does not say this because he does not know the answer, but in order to show us how unique and wonderful an honour it is, as can be deduced from the rewards: 'he will place him over all his goods.' And he concludes that the priest ought to be outstanding in holiness" (*De sacerdotio*, 2, 1–2).

"The priests of the New Testament", Vatican II reminds us, "are, by their vocation to ordination, set apart in some way in the midst of the people of God,

sacrifices for sins. ²He can deal gently with the ignorant and wayward, since he himself is beset with weakness. ³Because of this

Lev 9:7; 16:6

but this is not in order that they should be separated from that people or from anyone, but that they should be completely consecrated to the task for which God chose them" (*Presbyterorum ordinis*, 3). This calling, then, constitutes a distinction but not a separation because it is indissolubly linked to a specific mission: a priest is "chosen from among men" but for the purpose of acting "on behalf of men in relation to God". In this delicate balance between divine call and spiritual mission to men lies the essence of priesthood. Christians, therefore, should never view a priest as "just another person". "They want to find in the priest the virtues appropriate to any Christian and even any upright man —understanding, justice, commitment to work (priestly work, in this case), charity, good manners, social refinement. But the faithful also want to be able to recognize clearly the priestly character: they expect the priest to pray, not to refuse to administer the sacraments; they expect him to be open to everyone and not set himself up to take charge of people or become an aggressive leader of human factions, of whatever shade (cf. *Presbyterorum ordinis*, 6). They expect him to bring love and devotion to the celebration of Mass, to sit in the confessional, to console the sick and the troubled; to teach sound doctrine to children and adults, to preach the Word of God and no mere human science which— no matter how well he may know it—is not the knowledge that saves and brings eternal life; they expect him to give counsel and be charitable to those in need" (St Josemaría Escrivá, *In Love with the Church*, 42).

Priests "could not be the servants of Christ unless they were witnesses and dispensers of a life other than that of this earth. On the other hand, they would be powerless to serve men if they remained aloof from their life and circumstances" (*Presbyterorum ordinis*, 3). In this connexion, Pope John Paul II has made the following appeal: "Yes, you are chosen from among men, given to Christ by the Father, to be in the world, *in the heart of society*. You are appointed to act on behalf of men (Heb 5:1). The priesthood is the sacrament whereby the Church is to be seen as the society of the people of God; it is the 'social' sacrament. Priests should 'convoke' each of the communities of the people of God, around them but not for themselves—*for Christ!*" (*Homily at an ordination of priests*, 15 June 1980).

The specific function of the priest has, then, been clearly identified: he is concerned about his brethren but he is not here to solve temporal problems; his role is only "in relation to God". "Christian ministerial priesthood is different from any other priesthood in that it is not an office to which someone is appointed by others to intercede with God on their behalf; it is a mission to which a man is called by God (Heb 5:1–10; 7:24; 9:11–28) to be towards others a living sign of the presence of Christ, the only Mediator (1 Tim 2:5), Head and Shepherd of his people [...]. In other words, Christian priesthood is essentially (this is the only possible way it can be understood) an eminently sacred mission, both in its origin (Christ) and in its content (the divine mystery) and by the very manner in which it is conferred (a sacrament)" (A. del Portillo, *On Priesthood*, pp. 59f).

5:2–3. From the moral qualities a priest needs, these verses single out mercy and compassion, which lead him, on the one hand, to be gentle to sinners and, at the same time, to desire to make personal reparation for their sins. The Latin translation of v. 2a puts the emphasis on the fact that the priest shares in suffering for sin: he can "suffer along with" (*aeque condolere*) but in just measure on seeing those who go astray, and, imitating Christ, he can himself perform some of the penance those sinners should be doing. The original word translated here as "deal gently" recalls the profound, but serene, sorrow which Abraham felt when Sarah died (cf. Gen 23:2) and at the same time it alludes to the need for forbearance, generosity and understanding: a priest must be a person who, while rejecting sin, is understanding to the sinner and conscious that it may take him time to mend his ways. He is also inclined to put the sinner's intentions in the best light (cf. Gal 6:1): people do not always sin deliberately; they can sin out of ignorance (that is, not realizing the gravity of their actions) and, more often than not, out of weakness.

The Old Testament makes a clear distinction between sin committed unwittingly (cf. Lev 4:2–27; Num 14:24, 27–29) and sins of rebelliousness (cf. Num 15:22–31; Deut 17:12). Further on (cf. Heb 6:4–6; 10:26–27; 12:17), the letter will again refer to the gravity of sins committed out of malice. Here, however, it is referring to sin, whether grave or not, committed out of weakness. "Ignorant" and "wayward" are almost synonymous, for a person who sins out of ignorance is described in Hebrews by a word which means "he who goes astray, he who does not know the way". The basic reason why a priest should be understanding and compassionate is his awareness of his own weakness. Thus, the Church puts these words on his lips in Eucharistic Prayer I: "*nobis quoque peccatoribus*—for ourselves, too, sinners" (cf. Wis 9:5–6). A priest is compassionate and understanding because "he himself is beset with weakness". The word translated as "beset" contains the idea of surrounded or covered by or wrapped as if in a cloak. Pope Pius XI wrote: "When we see a man exercising this faculty (of forgiving sins), we cannot but repeat (not out of pharisaical scandal, but with reverent amazement) those words, 'Who is this, who even forgives sins?' (Lk 7:49). It is the Man-God, who had and has 'authority on earth to forgive sins' (Lk 5:24), and has chosen to communicate it to his priests, and thereby with the generosity of divine mercy to meet the human conscience's need of purification. Hence the great consolation the guilty man receives who experiences remorse and contritely hears the priest tell him in God's name, 'I absolve you from your sins.' The fact that he hears this said by someone who himself will need to ask another priest to speak the same words to him, does not debase God's merciful gift: it enhances it, for the hand of God who works this wonder is seen (as operating) by means of a frail creature" (Pius XI, *Ad catholici sacerdotii*).

5:3. Everyone, including the priest, is a sinner. In the Old Testament rites for the Day of Atonement (*Yom Kippur*), the high priest, before entering the Holy of Holies, offered a sin-offering for his own sins (cf. Lev 16:3, 6, 11; Heb 9:6–14); so too the priests of the New Testament have a duty to be holy, to reject sin, to ask for forgiveness of their own sins, and to intercede for sinners. The model the priest should always have before him is Jesus Christ, the eternal high priest. "The main motive force actuating a priest should be the determination to attain the closest union with the divine Redeemer

> ^{Ex 28:1; Jn 3:27}
> ^{Ps 2:7, LXX}
> ^{Heb 4:14}
> he is bound to offer sacrifice for his own sins as well as for those of the people. ⁴And one does not take the honour upon himself, but he is called by God, just as Aaron was. ⁵So also Christ did not exalt

[...]. He should continually keep Christ before his eyes. Christ's commands, actions and example he should follow most assiduously, in the conviction that it is not enough for him to submit to the duties by which the faithful are bound, but that he must at a daily increasing pace pursue the perfection of life which the high dignity of a priest demands" (Pius XII, *Menti nostrae*, 7). But, one might object, Christ never had any defect, never sinned, because his human nature was perfect and totally holy: is he not therefore too perfect a model for men who when it comes down to it are sinners? The answer is, No, not at all, for he himself said, "I have given you an example, that you also should do as I have done to you" (Jn 13:15). Besides, when the text (v. 2) refers to "weakness" this may refer to two things—the weakness of human nature (of man as creature), and the imperfection resulting from his faults and his passions. The former kind of defect is one Christ shares with us; the second is one he does not. For this very reason, in the case of the priest, consciousness of his sins, plus his conviction that he has been called by Christ, moves him to be very committed to his apostolic ministry of reconciliation and penance; and in the first instance priests perform this ministry for one another. "Priests, who are consecrated by the anointing of the Holy Spirit and sent by Christ, mortify the works of the flesh in themselves and dedicate themselves completely to the service of people" (Vatican II, *Presbyterorum ordinis*, 12). As Pope John Paul II has stressed, "the priest's celebration of the Eucharist and administration of the other sacraments, his pastoral zeal, his relationship with the faithful, his communion with his brother priests, his collaboration with his bishop, his life of prayer—in a word, the whole of his priestly existence—suffers an inexorable decline if by negligence or for some other reason he fails to receive the sacrament of Penance at regular intervals and in a spirit of genuine faith and devotion. If a priest were no longer to go to confession or properly confess his sins, his *priestly being* and his *priestly action* would feel the effect of this very soon, and it would also be noticed by the community of which he was the pastor.

"But I also add that even in order to be a good and effective minister of Penance the priest needs to have recourse to the source of grace and holiness present in this sacrament. We priests, on the basis of our personal experience, can certainly say that, the more careful we are to receive the sacrament of Penance and to approach it frequently and with good dispositions, the better we fulfil our own ministry as confessors and ensure that our penitents benefit from it. And on the other hand this ministry would lose much of its effectiveness if in some way we were to stop being good penitents. Such is the *internal logic* of this great sacrament. It invites all of us priests of Christ to pay renewed attention to our personal confession" (*Reconciliatio et paenitentia*, 31).

What John Paul II says here ultimately stems from the fact that "as ministers of the sacred mysteries, especially in the sacrifice of the Mass, priests act in a special way in the person of Christ who gave himself as a victim to sanctify men" (*Presbyterorum ordinis*, 13).

In this way, "Christ the shepherd is present in the priest so as continually to actualize the universal call to conversion and repentance which prepares for the coming of the Kingdom of heaven (cf. Mt 4:17). He is present in order to make men understand that forgiveness of sins, the reconciliation of the soul and God, cannot be the outcome of a monologue, no matter how keen a person's capacity for reflection and self-criticism. He reminds us that no one, alone, can calm his own conscience; that the contrite heart must submit its sins to the Church-institution, to the man-priest, who in the sacrament of Penance is a permanent objective witness to the radical need which fallen humanity has of the man-God, the only Just One, the only Justifier" (A. del Portillo, *On Priesthood*, p. 62).

5:7–9. This brief summary of Christ's life stresses his perfect obedience to the Father's will, his intense prayer and his sufferings and redemptive death. As in the hymn to Christ in Philippians 2:6–11, the point is made that Christ set his power aside and, despite his being the only-begotten Son of God, out of obedience chose to die on the cross. His death was a true self-offering expressed in that "loud voice" when he cried out to the Father just before he died, "into thy hands I commit my spirit" (Lk 23:46). But although Jesus' obedience was most obvious on Calvary, it was a constant feature of "the days of his flesh": he obeyed Mary and Joseph, seeing in them the authority of the heavenly Father; he was obedient to political and religious authorities; and he always obeyed the Father, identifying himself with him to such a degree that he could say, "I have glorified thee on earth, having accomplished the work which thou gavest me to do [...]. All mine are thine, and thine are mine" (Jn 17:4, 10).

The passage also points to Jesus' prayer, the high point of which occurred in Gethsemane on the eve of his passion. The reference to "loud cries and supplications" recalls the Gospel account of his suffering: "And being in an agony he prayed more earnestly; and his sweat became like great drops of blood falling down upon the ground" (Lk 22:44).

Hebrews 5:7–9 is probably referring not so much to his prayer in the Garden, still less to any prayer of Christ asking to be delivered from death, but to our Lord's constant prayer for the salvation of mankind. "When the Apostle speaks of these supplications and cries of Jesus," St John Chrysostom comments, "he does not mean prayers which he made on his own behalf but prayers for those who would later believe in him. And, due to the fact that the Jews did not yet have the elevated concept of Christ that they ought to have had, St Paul says that 'he was heard', just as the Lord himself told his disciples, to console them, 'If you loved me, you would have rejoiced, because I go to the Father; for the Father is greater than I' [...]. Such was the respect and reverence shown by the Son, that God the Father could not but take note and heed his Son and his prayers" (*Hom. on Heb*, 11).

5:7. "In the days of his flesh", a reference to the Incarnation. "Flesh" is synonymous with mortal life; this is a reference to Christ's human nature—as in the prologue to St John's Gospel (cf. Jn 1:14) and many other places (Heb 2:14; Gal 2:20; Phil 1:22–24; 1 Pet 4:1–2) including where mention is made of Jesus being a servant and capable of suffering (cf. Phil 2:8; Mt 20:27–28). Jesus' human nature "in the days of his flesh" is quite different from his divine nature and also from his human nature after its glorification (cf. 1 Cor

Hebrews 5:6

himself to be made a high priest, but was appointed by him who said to him,
"Thou art my Son,
today I have begotten thee";*

⁶as he says also in another place,
"Thou art a priest for ever,
after the order of Melchizedek."

⁷In the days of his flesh, Jesusʲ offered up prayers and supplications, with loud cries and tears, to him who was able to

Ps 110:4
Heb 7:1–28

Mt 26:39f
Ps 22:25
Lk 22:41–44;
23:46

15:50). "It must be said that the word 'flesh' is occasionally used to refer to the weakness of the flesh, as it says in 1 Corinthians 15:50: 'flesh and blood cannot inherit the kingdom of God'. Christ had a weak and mortal flesh. Therefore it says in the text, 'In the days of his flesh', referring to when he was living in a flesh which seemed to be like sinful flesh, but which was sinless" (St Thomas Aquinas, *Commentary on Heb*, 5, 1). So, this text underlines our Lord's being both Victim and Priest.

"Prayers and supplications": very fitting in a priest. The two words mean much the same; together they are a form of words which used to be employed in petitions to the king or some important official. The plural tells us that there were lots of these petitions. The writer seems to have in mind the picture of the Redeemer who "going a little farther fell on his face and prayed, 'My Father, if it be possible, let this cup pass from me; nevertheless, not as I will, but as thou wilt'" (Mt 26:39). St Thomas comments on this description of Christ's prayer as follows: "His action was indeed one of offering prayers and supplications, that is, a spiritual sacrifice: that was what Christ offered. It speaks of prayers in the sense of petitions because 'The prayer of a righteous man has great power' (Jas 5:16); and it speaks of supplications to emphasize the humility of the one who is praying, who falls on his knees, as we see happening in the case of him who 'fell on his face and prayed' (Mt 26:39)" (*Commentary on Heb*, 5, 1).

To emphasize the force of Christ's prayer, the writer adds, "with loud cries and tears". According to rabbinical teaching, there were three degrees of prayer, each stronger than the last—supplications, cries and tears. Christian tradition has always been touched by the humanity of the Redeemer as revealed in the way he prays. "Everything that is being said here may be summed up in one word—humility: that stops the mouths of those who blaspheme against Christ's divinity saying that it is completely inappropriate for a God to act like this. For, on the contrary, the Godhead laid it down that [Christ's] human nature should suffer all this, in order to show us the extreme to which he truly became incarnate and assumed a human nature, and to show us that the mystery of salvation was accomplished in a real and not an apparent or fictitious manner" (Theodoret of Cyrus, *Interpretatio Ep. ad Haebreos,* ad loc.). Christ's prayer, moreover, teaches us that prayer must 1) be fervent and 2) involve interior pain. "Christ had both [fervour and pain], for the Apostle by mentioning 'tears' intends to show the interior groaning of him who weeps in this way

---

j. Greek *he*

save him from death, and he was heard for his godly fear. ⁸Although he was a Son, he learned obedience through what he

Phil 2:8

[...]. But he did not weep on his own account: he wept for us, who receive the fruit of his passion" (St Thomas, *Commentary on Heb*, ad loc.).

"He was heard for his godly fear." Chrysostom's commentary is very apposite: "'He gave himself up for our sins', he says in Galatians 1:4; and elsewhere (cf. 1 Tim 2:6) he adds, 'He gave himself as a ransom for all'. What does he mean by this? Do you not see that he is speaking with humility of himself, because of his mortal flesh? And, nevertheless, because he is the Son, it says that he was heard for his godly fear" (*Hom. on Heb*, 8). It is like a loving contention between Father and Son. The Son wins the Father's admiration, so generous is his self-surrender.

And yet Christ's prayer did not seem to be heeded, for his Father God did not save him from ignominious death—the cup he had to drink—nor were all the Jews, for whom he prayed, converted. But it was only apparently so: in fact Christ's prayer *was* heard. It is true that, like every one, the idea of dying was repugnant to him, because he had a natural instinct to live; but, on the other hand, he wished to die through a deliberate and rational act of his will; hence in the course of the prayer, he said, "not my will, but thine, be done" (Lk 22:42). Similarly Christ wanted to save all mankind—but he wanted them to accept salvation freely (cf. *Commentary on Heb*, ad loc.).

5:8. In Christ there are two perfect and complete natures and therefore two different levels of knowledge—divine knowledge and human knowledge. Christ's human knowledge includes 1) the knowledge that the blessed in heaven have, that is, the knowledge that comes from direct vision of the divine essence; 2) the knowledge with which God endowed man before original sin (infused knowledge); and 3) the knowledge which man acquires through experience. This last-mentioned knowledge could and in fact did increase (cf. Lk 2:52) in Christ's case. Christ's painful experience of the passion, for example, increased this last type of knowledge, which is why the verse says that Christ learned obedience through suffering. There was a Greek proverb which said, "Sufferings are lessons." Christ's teaching and example raise this positive view of suffering onto the supernatural level. "In *suffering there is concealed* a particular *power that draws a person interiorly close to Christ*, a special grace [...]. A result of such a conversion is not only that the individual discovers the salvific meaning of suffering but above all that he becomes a completely new person. He discovers a new dimension, as it were, of *his entire life and vocation*" (John Paul II, *Salvifici doloris*, 26).

In our Lord's case, his experience of suffering was connected with his generosity in obedience. He freely chose to obey even unto death (cf. Heb 10:5–9; Rom 5:19; Phil 2:8), consciously atoning for the first sin, a sin of disobedience. "In his suffering, sins are cancelled out precisely because he alone as the only-begotten Son could take them upon himself, accept them *with that love for the Father which overcomes* the evil of every sin; in a certain sense he annihilates this evil in the spiritual space of the relationship between God and humanity, and fills this space with good" (*Salvifici doloris*, 17). Christ "learned obedience" not in the

Jn 17:19 — suffered; ⁹and being made perfect he became the source of
Is 45:17; Heb 9:12 — eternal salvation to all who obey him, ¹⁰being designated by God
Ps 110:4 — a high priest after the order of Melchizedek.

sense that this virtue developed in him, for his human nature was perfect in its holiness, but in the sense that he put into operation the infused virtue his human soul already possessed. "Christ knew what obedience was from all eternity, but he learned obedience in practice through the severities he underwent particularly in his passion and death" (St Thomas Aquinas, *Commentary on Heb*, ad loc.).

Christ's example of obedience is something we should copy. A Christian writer of the fifth century, Diadochus of Photike, wrote: "The Lord loved (obedience) because it was the way to bring about man's salvation and he obeyed his Father unto the cross and unto death; however, his obedience did not in any sense diminish his majesty. And so, having—by his obedience—dissolved man's disobedience, he chose to lead to blessed and immortal life those who followed the way of obedience" (*Chapters on Spiritual Perfection*, 41).

5:9. Obviously Christ as God could not increase in perfection. Nor could his sacred humanity become any holier, for from the moment of his Incarnation he received the fullness of grace, that is, he had the maximum degree of holiness a man could have. In this connexion Thomas Aquinas points out that Christ had grace to an infinite degree. In Christ there is a dual grace: one is the grace of union (that is, the personal union to the Son of God gratuitously bestowed on human nature): clearly this grace is infinite as the person of the Word is infinite. The other grace is habitual grace which, although it is received in a limited human nature, is yet infinite in its perfection because grace was conferred on Christ as the universal source of the justification of human nature (cf. *Summa theologiae*, 3, 7, 11). In what sense, then, could Christ be "made perfect"? St Thomas provides the answer: Christ, through his passion, achieved a special glory—the impassibility and glorification of his body. Moreover, he attained the same perfections as we shall participate in when we are raised from the dead in glory, those of us who believe in him (cf. *Commentary on Heb*, ad loc.). For this reason our Redeemer could exclaim before his death, "It is finished" (Jn 19:30)— referring not only to his own sacrifice but also to the fact that he had completely accomplished the redeeming atonement. Christ triumphed on the cross and attained perfection for himself and for others. In Hebrews the same verb is used for what is translated into English as "to be made perfect" and "to finish". Christ, moreover, by obeying and becoming a perfect victim, truly pleasing to the Father, is more perfectly positioned to perfect others. "Obedience" is essentially docility to what God asks of us and readiness to listen to him (cf. Rom 1:5; 16:26; 2 Cor 10:5; Heb 4:3). Christ's obedience is a source of salvation for us; if we imitate him we will truly form one body with him and he will be able to pass on to us the fullness of his grace.

"Now, when you find it hard to obey, remember your Lord: *'factus obediens usque ad mortem, mortem autem crucis:* obedient even to accepting death, death on a cross!'" (St Josemaría Escrivá, *The Way*, 628).

5:10. As the epistle repeatedly teaches, Christ is a high priest "after the order of

The need for religious instruction

¹¹About this we have much to say which is hard to explain, since you have become dull of hearing. ¹²For though by this time you

1 Cor 3:1–3
Heb 6:1
1 Pet 2:2

Melchizedek". Two essential characteristics come together here: he is the eternal Son of God, as announced in the messianic Psalm 2:7: "You are my Son, today I have begotten you"; and he is at the same time high priest not according to the order which God instituted with Aaron but according to the order of Melchizedek, also established by God. Further on the letter explains in what sense this "order of Melchizedek" is superior to that of Levi and Aaron. What it stresses at this point is the connexion between Christ's priesthood and his divine sonship. Christ, the Son of God, was sent by the Father as Redeemer and mediator, and the mediation of Christ, who is God and true man, is exercised by way of priesthood. So, in the last analysis Christ is Priest both by virtue of being the Son of God and by virtue of his Incarnation as man. "The abyss of malice which sin opens up has been bridged by his infinite charity. God did not abandon men. His plans foresaw that the sacrifices of the Old Law would be insufficient to repair our faults and re-establish the unity which had been lost. A man who was God would have to offer himself up. To help us grasp in some measure this unfathomable mystery, we might imagine the Blessed Trinity taking counsel together in their uninterrupted intimate relationship of intimate love. As a result of their eternal decision, the only-begotten Son of God the Father takes on our human condition and bears the burden of our wretchedness and sorrow, to end up sewn with nails to a piece of wood" (St J. Escrivá, *Christ Is Passing By*, 95).

It was appropriate that the divine person who became incarnate should be the Son or Word, for "the Word has a kind of essential kinship not only with rational nature but also universally with the whole of creation, since the Word contains the essences of all things created by God, just as man the artist in the conception of his intellect comprehends the essences of all the products of art [...]. Wherefore all things are said to be made by the Word. Therefore, it was appropriate for Word to be joined to creature, that is, to human nature" (St Thomas, *Summa contra gentiles*, 4, 42). Finally, it was fitting that Redemption from sin should be brought about by way of a sacrifice offered by the same divine person.

So it is that Christ, the only-begotten Son, to whom God said, "You are my son, today I have begotten you", is also the priest to whom God swears, "Thou art a priest for ever, after the order of Melchizedek".

5:11–14. The writer explains in what sense Christ is called a "priest for ever, after the order of Melchizedek", because he is afraid his readers will not understand, despite their being Jews and therefore familiar with Melchizedek. This is a very important subject, calling for an extensive and complex explanation, and therefore it needs to be followed carefully. The people to whom the letter is addressed would have been very familiar with Holy Scripture and would have received catechesis prior to and subsequent to Baptism. By rights, at this stage they should be teachers of other Christians, well able to give them a clear exposition of the truths of faith. And yet they need to be told again about the rudiments of Christianity in the same sort of way as children need to be taught the

Hebrews 5:13

<small>Eph 4:13f</small>
<small>Phil 1:10</small>
<small>Gen 2:17</small>
<small>Rom 16:19</small>

ought to be teachers, you need some one to teach you again the first principles of God's word. You need milk, not solid food; [13]for every one who lives on milk is unskilled in the word of righteousness, for he is a child. [14]But solid food is for the mature, for those who have their faculties trained by practise to distinguish good from evil.

<small>Heb 9:14</small>
<small>Acts 20:21</small>
<small>Acts 6:6</small>
<small>1 Tim 4:14</small>

6 [1]Therefore let us leave the elementary doctrine of Christ and go on to maturity, not laying again a foundation of repentance from dead works and of faith toward God, [2]with instruction[k] about ablutions, the laying on of hands, the resurrection of the dead, and eternal judgment. [3]And this we will do if God permits.[l]

---

basics of language—the alphabet and pronunciation. The Jewish Christians to whom the letter is addressed, have become, because of their doubts and wavering, rather like those first Christians in Corinth, recent converts and already divided into separate parties, whom the Apostle calls "babes" and "men of the flesh" (cf. 1 Cor 3:1–3). Like small children they need to be given light food; they cannot yet take solid food. Although these words contain a reproach, because they are addressed to grown-up people, they are said in a tone of tenderness and affection. The rabbis in fact used to affectionately call their disciples "children of the breast", and described themselves as "teachers of children" (cf. Rom 2:20). St Paul often used the image of a child at the breast to describe the situation of those who did not yet know the truth and were therefore blamelessly ignorant (cf. 1 Cor 13:11; Gal 4:1,3; Eph 4:14). Sometimes he compared his preaching with the loving vigilance of a mother nursing her child (cf. 1 Thess 2:7; Gal 4:20). St Peter also calls recently baptized people "newborn babes" (1 Pet 2:2). So, in spite of being reproachful, the author of the letter sees himself as a teacher and spiritual father. Like little children, his readers need to go back and study the basics of the faith; they are not yet ready to understand the "word of righteousness", that is, the mystery of justification (Rom 6:16; 9:30), nor can they yet distinguish good from evil (cf. Rom 2:18; Phil 1:10; Gen 3:5). He is extending an implicit invitation to become spiritually mature, for a Christian should attain the wisdom and maturity of the perfect man, according to the measure of Christ's perfection (cf. Eph 4:10; 1 Cor 14:20; Col 1:28).

In this connexion St Thomas reminds us that Christian perfection calls for a continuous effort to purify the intentions behind one's actions, to have one's mind and other faculties properly trained, to keep repeating acts of virtue so as to develop good habits, and to distinguish between good and better, bad and worse (cf. *Commentary on Heb*, ad loc.). This is what is involved in having one's "faculties trained by practice".

6:1–3. The sacred writer wishes to strengthen Christians' faith and confidence, and therefore he reminds his readers that it is not a matter of going over elementary teaching, which is based on repentance for sin and a desire to begin a new life, but of developing this teaching so as to understand it better and draw practical

---

k. Other ancient manuscripts read *of instruction* **l.** Other ancient manuscripts read *let us do this if God permits*

conclusions: "Let us go on to maturity." Basic catechesis or instruction of the faithful was usually imparted before and after Baptism and consisted of various elements, as we can see from the text. It explained who Jesus Christ is and what his mission is (cf. Acts 8:35, 37), and, in particular, that he is the Son of God; it went into the need for penance and for seeking forgiveness of sin (cf. Mk 4:17; Mk 1:15); it dealt with faith in God, the sacraments and the last things—resurrection of the body and the Judgment.

Here we have an admirably clear and simple summary of the basic elements of Christian catechesis. Given its antiquity and the fact that it is inspired, this text bears important witness to the fact that even in the apostolic era there existed a summary of those truths which had to be expounded and accepted before a person could be baptized—a summary which was an early outline of what later became the Creed or Symbol of Faith. The very order in which these articles of faith are given reflects the pedagogical wisdom of the Church, guided by the Holy Spirit—first, faith, then the sacraments, then the last things.

The purpose of catechesis, as St Thomas tells us, is to acquire that teaching "whereby Christ begins to dwell in us through our knowledge of the faith". It involves establishing a vital, active solidarity with our Lord and Redeemer. The Christian can then go on to deepen in this knowledge. "The primary and essential object of catechesis is [...] 'the mystery of Christ'. Catechizing is in a way to lead a person to study this Mystery in all its dimensions [...]. It is therefore to reveal in the Person of Christ the whole of God's eternal design reaching fulfilment in that Person. It is to seek to understand the meaning of Christ's actions and words and of the signs worked by him, for they simultaneously hide and reveal his mystery. Accordingly, the definitive aim of catechesis is to put people not only in touch but in communion, in intimacy, with Jesus Christ: only he can lead us to the love of the Father in the Spirit and make us share in the life of the Holy Trinity" (John Paul II, *Catechesi tradendae*, 5).

6:2. Christian salvation goes hand in hand with using certain material things which confer grace: these are the sacraments. The text alludes to this in very few words. Firstly, there is instruction about "ablutions" or, as the original text suggests, "baptisms". The use of the plural has puzzled scholars because clearly there is only one Baptism—"one hope, one faith, one baptism" (cf. Eph 4:5). But it can be explained fairly easily if one bears in mind that Baptism used to be administered by triple immersion; that there are different forms of Baptism (of water, of blood or of desire); and that people used to be baptized in groups. However, it is more likely that the verse refers to the difference between the sacrament of Baptism and the "baptisms" or ritual washings the Jews frequently practised (cf. Mk 7:3–4); the phrase would, in that case, mean "instruction about the difference between Judaic ablutions and Christian Baptism".

The laying on of hands may refer to the rite of Confirmation, which included anointing with chrism (cf. Acts 8:17; 19:6), or to the rite of other sacraments, for example, that of Order (cf. 1 Tim 4:14; 5:22; 2 Tim 1:6; Acts 6:6; 13:3; etc.), Penance or Anointing of the Sick (cf. Jas 5:14). It may perhaps be a reference to the sacraments in general.

It should be remembered that in the New Testament, as St Thomas points out, the laying on of hands refers to a number

The danger of apostasy and the need for perseverance

Heb 10:26f; 12:17; Mt 12:31; 1 Jn 5:10; 1 Pet 2:3

⁴For it is impossible* to restore again to repentance those who have once been enlightened, who have tasted the heavenly gift,

---

of different things. For example, when Christ used to lay his hands on sick people to heal them (cf. Lk 4:40), that action did not have a sacramental character: it conferred a gift externally and visibly. In other cases, the laying on of hands was sacramental and referred mainly to the sacraments of Order and Confirmation, which produced an interior change and renewal (cf. *Commentary on Heb,* ad loc.).

6:4–6. In the context of an exhortation to fidelity and growth in maturity, the letter gives a severe warning about the danger of apostasy. It is true that it is very difficult for an apostate to return to the true faith, very difficult for him to change his attitudes, difficult also for someone to find the right words to get him to change, for he previously had knowledge of the truth and then voluntarily rejected it. However, it is not impossible for him to return, for God is infinitely merciful, as is shown in the episode of Simon Peter's denials and repentance. "In the case of physical illnesses", St Thomas comments, "there is no more dangerous situation than that of those who suffer a relapse; so too in the spiritual sphere if someone falls into sin after receiving grace it is more difficult for him to recover and do good" (*Commentary on Heb,* ad loc.).

To appreciate these strong words, it should be remembered that the early Christians had a high sense of the dignity of their calling. It is not possible to be really a Christian and at the same time be in league with sin—particularly if it is a sin of apostasy, which involves denial of the faith and therefore of the very source of salvation. On the other hand, the first recipients of the letter seem to have been living in a hostile environment: rejected by the society in which they had been brought up, they had to shed certain Jewish religious practices; they felt isolated and rejected, and therefore the temptation to revert to Judaism was strong. That is why the writer reminds them, firstly, of the gifts their calling to Christianity has brought them: they have been "enlightened", that is, they have received Baptism, "which is the principle of spiritual rebirth whereby the mind is enlightened by faith" (*Commentary on Heb,* ad loc.); God has also given them the light of the Gospel; they have been filled with the "heavenly gift", that is, the Holy Spirit who fills the soul with sweetness (cf. 1 Pet 2:3; Ps 34:9); they have been nourished with the Eucharist, and they have experienced the reassurance of the Good News and the power of the Kingdom of God and all the gifts in its train—divine filiation, joy, gratitude, faith, hope and charity, all of which are the beginnings of eternal life.

The situation referred to in v. 6 suggests a calamitous fall, rather like that of Adam (cf. Rom 5:15–20). It may be similar to that sin against the Holy Spirit which our Lord himself said would not be forgiven either in this world or in the next (cf. Mt 12:31–32; Mk 3:28–29; Lk 12:10). It echoes what St Peter says about an apostate being like a dog going back to its vomit or a sow that is washed but then wallows in the mire: they are worse off than when they started (cf. 2 Pet 2:30–22). Like a skilled preacher the sacred writer wants to show his readers the full horror which rejection of faith involves.

and have become partakers of the Holy Spirit, ⁵and have tasted the goodness of the word of God and the powers of the age to come, ⁶if they then commit apostasy, since they crucify the Son of God

Gen 1:11f
Deut 11:11
Heb 10:29

Many heretics have used this text to argue that there are sins which the Church cannot forgive—specifically, the sins of murder, adultery and apostasy. However, if one denies the Church that power it is equivalent to denying the sacrament of Penance. That is why all the Fathers have met this rigourism head on, because it almost always leads to outright laxism. Here is how St John Chrysostom put the case: "'There is no such thing as penance', they say. But penance does exist; what does not exist is second Baptism. Penance exists; it is very powerful and it can free from the burden of sins even a person who is deeply submerged in sins, provided he wants to be freed; it can make someone who is in danger completely safe, even though he may have plumbed the depths of evil [...]. If we so desire, Christ can be formed in us anew. Listen to what Paul says: 'My little children, with whom I am again in travail until Christ be formed in you!' (Gal 4:9). All that we need do is lay hold of Penance. See how kind God is to us! [...] 'We have fallen once again!' Yet not even then did he punish us: instead, he gave us the medicine of Penance, which is powerful enough to destroy and eliminate all our sins, provided we know what type of medicine it is and how to use it" (*Hom. on Heb*, 6). God in his mercy always receives the repentant sinner who has recourse to the sacrament of Penance, no matter how much he has sinned, no matter what sins he has committed. "What depths of mercy there are in God's justice! For, in the judgments of men, he who confesses his fault is punished; and in the judgment of God, he is pardoned. Blessed be the holy Sacrament of Penance!" (St Josemaría Escrivá, *The Way*, 309).

"To restore again to repentance": this points to the fact that the purpose and outcome of interior renewal is repentance and changed behaviour. It is describing the situation of a person who, having been influenced by interior grace and external preaching, takes his first steps on the road of repentance.

It is even more difficult to grasp all the implications of the second part of this verse: "since they crucify the Son of God on their own account and hold him up to contempt". Many Fathers and theologians see here a reference to the impossibility of being baptized a second time, because in baptism we share in the effects of the passion and death of Christ (cf. Rom 6:3–6; 1 Cor 1:13). If apostates were to try to be baptized again to obtain forgiveness, it would be like asking, in a way, for Christ to be crucified again. But Christ is no longer mortal and therefore it is not possible for Baptism to be repeated. Thus, for example, St Thomas comments: "When he says, 'they crucify again (the Son of God)', he is giving the reason why Baptism is not repeated, that is, because Baptism is a kind of conforming to the death of Christ, as we see in Romans 6:3—'all of us who have been baptized into Christ'—and this does not happen more than once because 'Christ being raised from the dead will never die again' (Rom 6:9). So those who would want to be baptized again would want to crucify Christ again" (*Commentary on Heb*, ad loc.).

Without excluding this meaning, a more obvious explanation, proposed by other Fathers, is that sinners are despising Penance even more than they are Baptism, for Penance also cleanses us by virtue of the merits of the passion and death of

2 Pet 2:21 — on their own account and hold him up to contempt. ⁷For land which has drunk the rain that often falls upon it, and brings forth vegetation useful to those for whose sake it is cultivated, receives a blessing from God. ⁸But if it bears thorns and thistles, it is worthless and near to being cursed; its end is to be burned. ⁹Though we speak thus, yet in your case, beloved, we feel sure of better things that belong to salvation. ¹⁰For God is not so unjust

Gen 3:17f
Mt 7:16

Heb 10:32–34;
3:14; Rom 15:25,
31; 2 Cor 8:4

Christ, and, as long as they remain obstinate in their sins, they crucify him on their own account and hold him up to contempt in the sense that they fail to appreciate the fruits of our Lord's passion: that is the reason they cannot repent or obtain forgiveness. St Thomas comments: "Those who sin after Baptism crucify Christ again, insofar as they can, for Christ died for our sins once and for all. You, who are baptized and commit sin, are crucifying Christ again insofar as you can; you are thus holding him up to contempt, for you are soiling yourself again after being cleansed by his blood" (*Commentary on Heb*, ad loc.).

6:7–8. To support its exhortations to fidelity the sacred text uses a parable which has a very evangelical ring to it: good ground receives the blessings of God; barren ground is only good for burning. This is a clear evocation of Christ's teaching: the ground is man's heart, his disposition towards God; God, for his part, sows seed generously through those whom he has sent, as in the parable of the sower (cf. Lk 8:5–15 and par.); and he also sends rain as needs be—preaching or instruction or grace itself which works in the interior of the soul (cf. Mt 5:45). The passage is also reminiscent of things that God often said to the chosen people through his prophets. The land is also the vineyard tended by the Almighty with loving care (cf. Is 5:1–6).

This parable dwells further on the sad consequences of unfaithfulness. The heart of the irreligious person or of the apostate is like barren land, which produces only thorns and thistles, as happened after the fall of Adam (cf. Gen 3:18). All it produces is sins, which merit condemnation to eternal fire (cf. Mt 25:41).

God's desire is to encourage everyone to be faithful. "We should tremble, dearly beloved," St John Chrysostom says, "for this warning does not come from Paul; these are not man's words: they are spoken by the Holy Spirit, it is Christ who is speaking through Paul [...]. Let us be filled with fear, therefore, let us be filled with fear. 'The wrath of God is revealed from heaven' (Rom 1:18). For it is manifested not only in regard to irreligion but in regard to every sin, great or small. But the mercy of God is also highlighted here too for it says, 'it is worthless and near to being cursed'. What consolation this word brings! For it says, 'near to being cursed'—not 'cursed'. And one is comforted not only by this phrase but also by the one that follows: for it does not say 'it will be burned' but 'its end is to be burned'. What does this mean? That if it remains in this state until the end, it will be subjected to fire. Therefore, if we cut and burn the thistles, we will be able to enjoy innumerable benefits, we will be appreciated and will receive the blessing" (*Hom. on Heb*, ad loc.).

6:9–12. The letter now changes to a tone of encouragement. "After speaking harshly about the position of the faithful, to

as to overlook your work and the love which you showed for his sake in serving the saints, as you still do. ¹¹And we desire each one of you to show the same earnestness in realizing the full assurance

---

prevent their falling into despair he now reveals why he has written what he has: he wants to lead them well away from danger. And so, in the first place, he tells them what confidence he has in them, and then gives the reason why they should feel confident themselves—because God is not unjust" (St Thomas Aquinas, *Commentary on Heb*, 4, 3).

The readers are called "beloved"; this was how St Paul normally addressed those who embraced the faith through his preaching (cf. 1 Thess 2:8; 1 Cor 10:14; 15:58; 2 Cor 7:1; 12:19; Rom 1:7; Phil 2:12; 4:1; etc.). The writer wants to see the situation improve, perhaps to see the trials pass or become easier; certainly he wants his readers to use their tribulation to help them to achieve salvation. He is moved when he recalls the charity they have shown one another: theirs has been an active fraternity, shown in deeds of service to the "saints", which was the way St Paul often referred to the brethren (cf. Rom 1:7; 1 Cor 1:2; 2 Cor 1:1; Eph 1:1; Phil 1:1; Col 1:2; etc.); their charity is practised "for his sake", for God. In their present circumstances, in the persecution they are experiencing, God will not abandon them (cf. Heb 10:33–34), for they have been generous in the almsgiving and hospitality that is so proper to Christians (cf. Rom 15:25, 31; 1 Cor 16:15; Eph 1:15; 2 Cor 8:4; 9:1, 12). "Now that we hear this—I beg you—let us serve the saints!, for every member of the faithful is a saint by the mere fact of belonging to the faithful [...]. Let us not be charitable only towards monks who live in the mountains. It is true that their faith and their lives make them saints, but many of those who live here are also saints: all are saints by virtue of their faith, and many are saints by virtue of their lives too. So, if you see someone suffering, do not doubt it for one moment: his very suffering gives him the right to be helped" (St John Chrysostom, *Hom. on Heb*, 10). It is not enough, however, to have a history of doing good: it is necessary to persevere in doing good, as if to say: By seeing through to the end what you have started you shall obtain everything you hope for. They must do good right "to the end", for he who endures to the end will be saved (cf. Mt 10:22; 24:13; *Commentary on Heb*, 4, 3). "Eternal life should be set before those who persevere in good works 'to the end' (cf. Mt 10:22) and who hope in God; it should be set before them as being the grace that God, through Jesus Christ, has mercifully promised his sons and 'as the reward' which, according to God's personal undertaking, most assuredly will be given them for their good works and merits (cf. St Augustine, *De natura et gratia*, 8, 20)" (Council of Trent, *De iustificatione*, chap. 16).

However, there is always the danger of slowing down: lazy people often excuse their inaction by pointing to the suffering and difficulties that doing good involves. The strength of one's resolutions is shown by the way one copes with difficulties: "You will convince me that you sincerely want to achieve your goals when I see you go forward unwaveringly. Do good [...]; practise the virtue of justice, right where you are, in your normal surroundings, even if you end up exhausted. Foster happiness among those around you by cheerfully serving the people you work with and by striving to

Hebrews 6:12

_{1 Cor 11:1}
_{Phil 3:17; 4:9}
_{Gal 3:14, 19}

of hope until the end, ¹²so that you may not be sluggish, but imitators of those who through faith and patience inherit the promises.

The promises made to Abraham were confirmed by oath and cannot be broken

_{Rom 4:20}
_{Gen 22:16f}

_{Ex 22:10}

¹³For when God made a promise to Abraham, since he had no one greater by whom to swear, he swore by himself, ¹⁴saying, "Surely I will bless you and multiply you." ¹⁵And thus Abraham,ᵐ having patiently endured, obtained the promise. ¹⁶Men indeed swear by a greater than themselves, and in all their disputes an oath is final for

---

carry out your job as perfectly as you can, showing understanding, smiling, having a Christian approach to life. And do everything for God, thinking of his glory, with your sights set high and longing for the definitive homeland, because there is no other goal worthwhile" (St Josemaría Escrivá, *Friends of God*, 211).

6:13–15. Abraham is an example, for every generation, of faith that is full of hope and patience; he is a man with great strength of character (cf. Rom 5:3–5). Already in the Letter to the Romans Abraham is cited as an example of faith and hope (cf. Rom 4:18–22). There St Paul highlights Abraham's faith in the Lord's promise that he would have innumerable descendants in spite of the fact that he was already an old man and unlikely to father children (cf. Gen 15:5; 17:1, 17). The Apostle may also have been alluding to the episode (cf. Gen 22), when God asked the patriarch to sacrifice Isaac, the son he had so yearned for: at that point Abraham did indeed "believe against hope" (cf. Rom 4:18; Gen 22:15–17). Here, on the other hand, of all the various promises made to Abraham of blessings and numerous offspring (cf. Gen 12:2–3, 7; 13:14–17; 15:5–7; 13:16; 17:4–8, 19), what is explicitly mentioned is the promise made after God prevented him from sacrificing his son. That was the first occasion the Lord "swore by himself" to a man. This divine promise, supported by an oath and seen as the most solemn "word of Yahweh", was the foundation of Israel's hope for thousands of years. Abraham himself recalled it when he was dying (cf. Gen 24:7); it was the support of Moses in all his great endeavours (cf. Ex 13:5, 11; 32:13); David, too, gave thanks to God for it (1 Chron 16:16; Ps 105:9); and at the dawn of the Redemption Zechariah rejoiced over it (Lk 1:73): it was "the oath which God swore to our Father Abraham" and it was fulfilled in Christ and in the Church (cf. Gal 4:21–31).

Abraham "obtained the promise" in the sense that he was enabled to see with his own eyes his promised son, Isaac, who was born to Sarah despite her old age. Not alone that: the New Testament tells us (cf. Jn 8:56; Gal 3:8) that he was given some sort of prophetic vision which allowed him to see the day of Christ and rejoice at it.

6:16. Secular writers of antiquity used to define an oath as something attached to a statement which cannot be proved, to provide a divine guarantee (cf. Pseudo-Aristotle, *Speech to Alexander*). This meant that they regarded an oath as a proof at law, to be put alongside the text of the law, the evidence of witnesses, agree-

---

m. Greek *he*

confirmation. ¹⁷So when God desired to show more convincingly to the heirs of the promise the unchangeable character of his purpose, he interposed with an oath, ¹⁸so that through two unchangeable things, in which it is impossible that God should prove false, we who have fled for refuge might have strong encouragement to seize the

Num 23:19
1 Sam 15:29

---

ment between the parties, and a confession of guilt. The Jews regarded an oath as something so awesome, so solemn, that they never dared swear an oath by God directly; instead they would swear by angels or by the life of men, such as the Messiah, Moses, Solomon, or by the gates of the temple, etc. (cf. Mt 5:34–36; 23:16–22). Philo of Alexandria, an heir to Jewish tradition and Greco-Roman thought, says that "by means of oaths, matters subject to doubt before the courts are resolved; what was not clear is made clear; and what was regarded as unreliable is rendered reliable" (*De sacrificio Abel*, 91).

St Thomas Aquinas developed and combined these ideas by saying that "an oath is an act of the virtue of religion which gives reliability to something previously in doubt. For in the sphere of knowledge nothing becomes certain unless it be demonstrated from something which is more certainly known. When oaths are taken, this certainty is obtained because the oath is sworn on God, who is the greatest and surest there is, since for men nothing is truer than God" (*Commentary on Heb*, ad loc.). The Thomist definition has become widely accepted because it also fits in with the commonly held view that swearing an oath is a way of honouring the sacred name of God. When an oath is properly made—meeting the necessary traditional requirements of truth, justice and judgment—that is, when it is made sincerely, for good reasons and not lightly, it is a morally good and meritorious act because it does honour to God's infinite truthfullness.

On Christ's teachings concerning oath-taking see the notes on Mt 5:33–37 and 23:16–22.

6:17–18. "Through two unchangeable things": in promises made by God his veracity is doubly committed—as the taker of the oath and as its guarantor.

God's covenant with Abraham and his oath to give him descendants took place at separate times (cf. Gen 15:7–18; 22:16–18). However, both episodes stem from a single act of God's will, in that he wanted to reward Abraham's obedience and at the same time commit himself by the use of external formalities proper to Hebrew legal practice. Among the Hebrews, when people made a pact, they sacrificed animals; the victims were then quartered and the contracting parties walked between the carcasses to symbolize that they would die the same death if they failed to keep the pact. God passed between the pieces of the animals Abraham sacrificed, in the form of a flaming torch, thereby giving him to understand that he (God) was under a most solemn obligation to do what he promised. In the second episode this rite was not repeated, but he "interposed with an oath", renewing as it were the "passing between" rite that accompanied the covenant.

God chose to express his promise by following this human form of contract in order to make his words more intelligible and to give us greater confidence.

Lev 16:2, 12
Heb 9:3; 10:20
Mt 27:51
Phil 110:4
Heb 5:6, 10

hope set before us. ¹⁹We have this as a sure and steadfast anchor of the soul, a hope that enters into the inner shrine behind the curtain, ²⁰where Jesus has gone as a forerunner on our behalf, having become a high priest for ever after the order of Melchizedek.

6:19–20. God's promise and oath are the gateway to our salvation, an anchor which makes us feel safe no matter what hazards threaten us. The Christian, who is, through faith, the true descendant of Abraham (cf. Rom 4:12) and the heir of the promise (cf. Gal 3:14, 16, 29), is therefore certain that God will keep his word. That is why the text says that we should "have strong encouragement to seize the hope set before us" (v.18). Hope is a kind of hold on what is promised, a kind of anchor that is "sure and steadfast". "For just as the anchor thrown overboard prevents the ship from moving, even if it is being battered by countless winds, but instead keeps it in one place, hope has the same effect" (Chrysostom, *Hom. on Heb*, 11). Greek and Roman authors often used the simile of an anchor in connexion with being steadfast in virtue and hopeful of happier times. The anchor has always been a motif in Christian art expressive of much more than a human sense of safety: it symbolizes the Christian's faith, his certainty in the resurrection of the Lord and in his own resurrection; it is a symbol of a confidence which stems from his intimate union with Christ. The sacred text brings together all those ideas: in a certain sense the anchor is Christ himself who through his redemptive sacrifice gives us the conviction that we can with him enter "into the inner shrine", that is, the heavenly sanctuary. "I have asked you to keep on lifting your eyes up to heaven as you go about your work, because hope encourages us to grasp the strong hand which God never ceases to reach out to us, to keep us from losing our supernatural point of view. Let us persevere even when our passions rear up and attack us, attempting to imprison us within the narrow confines of our selfishness; or when puerile vanity makes us think we are the centre of the universe. I am convinced that unless I look upward, unless I have Jesus, I will never accomplish anything. And I know that the strength to conquer myself and to win comes from repeating that cry, 'I can do all things in him who strengthens me' (Phil 4:13), words which reflect God's firm promise not to abandon his children if they do not abandon him" (St Josemaría Escrivá, *Friends of God*, 213). "A man should be tied to hope in the same way as the anchor is tied to the ship. But there is a difference between the anchor and hope: the anchor reaches down to get its hold, whereas hope reaches upwards, laying hold of God" (*Commentary on Heb, ad loc.*).

6:20. The sacrifice, resurrection and glorification of Christ are the grounds of our hope. In the Old Testament, the high priest entered the Holy of Holies once a year, on the Day of Atonement; this he did after offering one sacrifice in expiation of his own sins and another for the sins of the entire people. By his sacrifice on the cross, Christ entered into the true sanctuary of heaven and gave all men access to it. The reason for our firm hope is the fact that Christ has entered heaven. "It was not into the Holy of Holies (where Moses entered) but behind the curtain, into heaven, that he, Christ Jesus, went as our forerunner and was made a priest forever. He went not like

Jesus Christ is a priest after the order of Melchizedek

7 ¹For this Melchizedek, king of Salem, priest of the Most High God, met Abraham returning from the slaughter of the kings   Gen 14:17-20

Aaron, to offer the sacrificial victims, but to offer prayer for all the nations, like Melchizedek" (St Ephraem, *Comm. in Epist. ad Haebreos*, 6).

The description here of Christ as a "forerunner" has great depth and beauty. This is the only time this word is used in the New Testament, although Christian tradition soon came to use it, on the basis of the prophecy of Malachi (Mal 3:1), to describe St John the Baptist, the envoy sent in advance of Jesus to prepare his way (cf. Mk 1:2; Lk 1:76). Here the perspective is slightly different: it has to do not with preparing for the proclamation of the Gospel but with attaining final beatitude. Christ has gone before us into heaven to prepare a place for us (cf. Jn 14:2): he is our hope (cf. Col 1:27; 1 Tim 1:1), our life (cf. Col 3:4), our way (cf. Jn 14:6), whereby we have access to the Father (cf. Eph 2:18; 2:7). Christ is a "forerunner" in the literal sense of the word—one who "runs ahead", who went on ahead of the party to announce its arrival; or it can be understood in the sense of the first one to reach the finish, the first to finish the race. For our Lord is the first-born among the dead, the first in everything (cf. Col 1:18), the first fruits of those who will arise (cf. 1 Cor 15:20). By his merits he has already obtained the prize that we hope to win. Christian hope cannot falter, for it is based on the perennial value of the sacrifice and priesthood of Christ. Thus, the last words of this chapter remind us of the main theme of the letter.

Chap. 7. In keeping with biblical interpretation as practised by Jews of the time, the sacred writer now puts forward certain arguments in support of the superiority of Christ's priesthood over the Levitical priesthood. He wants to show the reader that the priesthood of Aaron and his descendants, that is, the Levitical priesthood, which was responsible for divine service in the temple of Jerusalem, was something good and very fitting. However, it was destined to disappear, and part of its mission was to prepare the way for Christ's priesthood, which is eternal and immutable. Earlier, in chapters 5 and 6, the relationships between Judaism and Christianity were examined from the point of view of the Covenant. In this chapter, they are looked at from the point of view of priesthood.

To do this, the writer brings in an Old Testament figure shrouded in mystery and much revered by the Jews—the priest Melchizedek. He appears first in Genesis 14:18-20 as king of Salem, when he comes out to meet Abraham to bless him after his victory over the invading kings. The passage also says that he was a priest of "God Most High" and that he offered Abraham bread and wine and received from the latter a tenth of his booty. In Psalm 110, which deals with the priesthood of the Messiah, Melchizedek is referred to again as being a "priest for ever", invested with an eternal priesthood which the Messiah King will also enjoy.

The Letter to the Hebrews uses and comments on these two Old Testament texts, taking them as well-known; it does not stop to explore their mysterious aspects. Chapter 7 consists of two parts. The first (7:1-10) may be summarized as saying that Melchizedek's priesthood is superior to the Levitical priesthood; and, because Christ's priesthood belongs to

and blessed him; ²and to him Abraham apportioned a tenth part of everything. He is first, by translation of his name, king of

the order of Melchizedek, it also is superior to the Levitical.

The second part (7:11-25) hinges on direct comparison of Christ's priesthood with that of the Old Law. The superiority of Christ's priesthood is clear to see, for it is perfect, permanent and sealed by God with an oath. In fact, because it is a permanent, eternal priesthood, it is unique: Christ is the only true high priest, whereas prior to his coming "the former priests were many in number, because they were prevented by death from continuing in office."

Christ's priesthood (which was heralded by that of Melchizedek), is prolonged in the Christian ministerial priesthood. However, Christ continues to be the only true priest, interceding for us with the Father: Christian priests are only vicars or ministers of Christ, not his successors.

At the end of the chapter (vv. 26-28) Christ's priesthood is extolled as being holy, blameless, unstained, perfect, and exalted above the heavens.

7:1-3. Melchizedek has special characteristics which make him a "figure" or "type" of Christ. The connexions between Christ and Melchizedek are expounded in accordance with the rules of rabbinical bible commentary; this is particularly obvious in the use of the phrase "without father or mother or genealogy" to refer to the eternity of Melchizedek. It is not surprising that the writer brings in the figure of Melchizedek, for the mysterious mention of this personage in Genesis 14:18-20 and in Psalm 110:4 had for some time intrigued Jewish commentators. For example, Philo of Alexandria sees Melchizedek as a symbol for human reason enlightened by divine wisdom (cf. *De legum allegoria*, 3, 79-82). Also, apocryphal literature identified Melchizedek with other biblical figures—for example, with Shem, Noah's first-born son, or with the son of Nir, Noah's brother. Certainly the epistle is in line with Jewish tradition on one important point: Melchizedek belongs to a priesthood established by God in pre-Mosaic times.

The Jewish historian Flavius Josephus (AD 37-100) refers to Melchizedek as a "prince of Canaan", who founded and was high priest of Jerusalem. The name Melchizedek, meaning "my king is righteous" or "King of Righteousness", was a Canaanite name (cf. Josh 10:13). "Salem" is probably an abbreviation of Jerusalem (cf. Ps 76:2); and *Elioh*, that is, God Most High, may also have been the name of one of the divinities worshipped by the inhabitants of Palestine before the Jewish conquest. Genesis tells us that, in spite of living in a Canaanite and polytheistic environment, Melchizedek was a priest of the true God. Despite not being a member of the chosen people, he had knowledge of the Supreme God. Psalm 110 adds a further revelation to that contained in Genesis: the promised Messiah, a descendant of David, will not only be a king (which they already knew) but also a priest; and he will not be a priest of Aaron: by a new disposition of God he will be a priest according to the order, or as the Hebrew text says, "after the manner of Melchizedek".

The Letter to the Hebrews views the Genesis episode through the prism of Psalm 110: Melchizedek is above all a representative of a new priesthood instituted by God independently of the Mosaic Law. That is why it gives so much importance to

righteousness, and then he is also king of Salem, that is, king of peace. ³He is without father or mother or genealogy, and has neither beginning of days nor end of life,* but resembling the Son of God he continues a priest for ever.

Jn 7:27
Ps 110:4

the words of Genesis: Melchizedek is "king of righteousness", according to one popular etymology, and he is also "king of Salem", that is, "king of peace" according to another which changes the second vowel of the Hebrew word *shalom*, which means "peace". Thus, in Melchizedek the two foremost characteristics of the messianic kingdom meet—righteousness and peace (cf. Ps 85:10; 89:14; 97:2; Is 9:5–7; 2:4; 45:8; Lk 2:14). Moreover, since Genesis says nothing about Melchizedek's background (he did not belong to the chosen people), the sacred writer, following a common rabbinical rule of interpretation (what is not in Scripture—in the Torah—has no existence in the "real world"), sees Scripture's silence on this point as symbolic: Melchizedek, since his genealogy is unknown, is a figure or "type" of Christ, who is eternal.

"Resembling the Son of God": it is not Christ who resembles Melchizedek but Melchizedek who is like Christ—indeed, who has been made to resemble Christ. Christ is the perfection of priesthood. Melchizedek was created and made like Christ so that we by reflecting on him might learn something about the Son of God.

Theodoret of Cyrus develops on this idea: "Christ the Lord possesses all these qualifications really and by nature. He is 'without mother', for God as Father alone begot him. He is 'without father', for he was conceived by mother alone, that is, the Virgin. He is 'without genealogy', as God, for he who was begotten by the unbegotten Father has no need of genealogy. 'He has not beginning of days', for his is an eternal generation. 'He has no end of life', for he possesses an immortal nature. For all those reasons Christ himself is not compared to Melchizedek but Melchizedek to Christ" (*Interpretatio Ep. ad Haebreos*, ad loc.). St Ephraem put this very nicely: "Thus, Melchizedek's priesthood continues for ever—not in Melchizedek himself but in the Lord of Melchizedek" (*Comm. in Epist. ad Haebreos*, ad loc.).

7:3. A priest of the true God, of the Most High God, yet not a member of the chosen people, Melchizedek is an example of how God sows the seeds of saving truth beyond limitations of geography, epoch or nation. "The priesthood of Christ, of which priests have been really made sharers, is necessarily directed to all people and all times, and is not confined by any bounds of blood, race, or age, as was already typified in a mysterious way by the figure of Melchizedek. Priests, therefore, should recall that the solicitude of all the churches ought to be their intimate concern" (Vatican II, *Presbyterorum ordinis*, 10).

At the same time the sacred text, by saying that Melchizedek was "without father or mother", gives grounds for thinking that also in the case of the consecration of Christ's priests they, in order to fulfil their mission, should be ready to leave their family behind—which is what often in fact happens. "The character and life of the man called to be a minister in the worship of the one true God bear the marks of a halo and a destiny to be 'set apart'. This puts him in some way outside and above the common history of other men—*sine patre, sine*

Melchizedek's priesthood is greater than that of Abraham's line

Gen 14:20
Num 18:21, 25
Deut 14:22

⁴See how great he is! Abraham the patriarch gave him a tithe of the spoils. ⁵And those descendants of Levi who receive the priestly office

---

matre, sine genealogia, as St Paul says of the mysterious prophetic Melchizedek" (A. del Portillo, *On Priesthood*, p. 44).

Addressing Christians, particularly those consecrated to the service of God, St John of Avila writes: "*Forget your people* (Ps 45:10) and be like another Melchizedek, whom we are told had no father or mother or genealogy. In this way [...] example is given to the servants of God who must be so forgetful of their family and relations that they are like Melchizedek in this world, as far as their heart is concerned—having nothing that ties their heart and slows them up on their way to God" (*Audi, filia*, 98).

7:4–10. The superiority of Melchizedek's priesthood over the Levitical priesthood is argued on two points—tithing and blessing. The same principle applies in each case, as is explicitly stated in v. 7 in regard to blessing: the inferior pays tithes to the superior, and it is the superior who blesses the inferior. Therefore, all the evidence indicates that Melchizedek was superior to Abraham because he was the one who received the tithe and gave the blessing. But Levi, the founder of the priestly line, was "in the loins" of his father Abraham when Abraham made his act of submission to Melchizedek; therefore, Levi is inferior to Melchizedek. Moreover, whereas the Levites or priests of the Mosaic Law are mortal men, Melchizedek is said to "live", because he has "no end of life".

Be that as it may, the passage does underline the exalted nature of priesthood. This applies to the Levitical priesthood, which has a prominent place among the Jewish people, for only priests of the family of Aaron were entitled to receive tithes and not have to pay them (cf. Num 18:26–32). Other Levites, not priests, received tithes of agricultural produce (cf. Deut 12:17–19; 14:22–27; 26:12–13) and livestock (cf. Lev 27:30–32), but they, in their turn, had to pay the tithe of the tithe—the "offering of Yahweh"—to their brothers who were priests. Tithing was a sign of God's absolute power over all things, and, in this sense, by their dedication to the service of God, the Levites also evidenced God's dominion: they were dedicated to Yahweh, standing in for all the first-born of Israel (cf. Num 3:12–13), because every first-born belonged to the Lord. The Levites, therefore, did not have territory assigned to them to cultivate and support themselves on: their "portion" and "lot" was God himself (cf. Ps 16:5–6). That was why they had a right to live on the tithes which every Israelite had a duty to pay to God.

However, despite the dignity of the Levitical priesthood, that of Melchizedek was worthier still. To him no less a personage than Abraham, the first father (the "Patriarch") of all Israel pays the tithe—despite the fact that the king of Salem was not of his tribe. And he pays him tithe of the best part of his booty (according to the Greek text), almost anticipating the Mosaic precept which prescribed that God be given the best portion of the Levitical tithe (cf. Num 18:30). In other words, although the priesthood of the sons of Aaron is on a very high level, Melchizedek's priesthood is more elevated still.

7:5. In the Law of Moses, that is, the Pentateuch or Torah, the regulations about

have a commandment in the law to take tithes from the people, that is, from their brethren, though these also are descended from Abraham. ⁶But this man who has not their genealogy received tithes from Abraham and blessed him who had the promises. ⁷It is beyond dispute that the inferior is blessed by the superior. ⁸Here tithes are received by mortal men; there, by one of whom it is testified that he lives. ⁹One might even say that Levi himself, who receives tithes, paid tithes through Abraham, ¹⁰for he was still in the loins of his ancestor when Melchizedek met him.

Gen 14:17

¹¹Now if perfection had been attainable through the Levitical priesthood (for under it the people received the law), what further

Ps 110:4

---

tithing changed somewhat over the course of the history of Israel (cf. Deut 12:6–17; 14:22–27; 26:12–15; Lev 27:30–33; 2 Chron 31:6); they developed gradually and, after the Exile (around the end of the sixth century), they became quite complex (cf. Neh 13:5, 10–12; Mal 3:8; Sir 35:8–10). A whole series of oral precepts grew up, which were later codified in rabbinical writings and, in some cases, led Jesus to reproach the Pharisees for their hypocrisy and over-emphasis on detail (cf. Mt 23:23; Lk 11:42; 18:12 and notes on same). It is quite likely that this verse, in speaking of "a commandment in the law", is referring to precepts of the oral as well as the written law.

Although it belongs to the Law of Moses and has therefore been replaced by the Law of Christ, the precept about paying tithes is a precept of natural justice and therefore "it was in the Law and is also in the New Testament, where it says, 'the labourer deserves his food' (Mt 10:10) or 'the labourer deserves his wages' (Lk 10:7). But now it is up to the Church to specify these tithes, just as previously, in the Old Testament, the Law specified them" (St Thomas Aquinas, *Commentary on Heb*, ad loc.).

7:7. A priest's blessing always does the recipient good because it draws down on him the holiness of the Church. Some people, for example, members of heretical groups, wrongly treated blessings with contempt. It should be remembered that the beneficial effect of rites and sacred signs established by the Church (sacramentals) derives not from the virtue of the minister but from the prayer of the Church and the dispositions of the recipient.

7:11–14. On the basis of the superiority of Melchizedek's priesthood over that of Levi, the writer now begins his "demonstration" of the superiority of Christ's priesthood over that of Aaron. If the Levitical priesthood had been able to achieve "perfection", that is, to fulfil God's design perfectly and bring about the salvation of mankind, why should there have been any need to replace it? If it has been replaced it is because that priesthood was unable to do what God designed it for—to bring the Mosaic Law to perfection; the priesthood of Aaron could only proclaim or promise.

It is clear that Christ is not only called (Ps 110:4) a priest "after the order", that is, in line with the role of and in succession to Melchizedek and not after the order of Aaron; but also, as the prophecies repeatedly say (cf., e.g., Num 24:17; Gen 48:10; 2 Sam 7:1; etc.), he belongs to the tribe of Judah—which had no priestly assignment under the Mosaic

need would there have been for another priest to arise after the order of Melchizedek, rather than one named after the order of Aaron? ¹²For when there is a change in the priesthood, there is necessarily

Law. No Israelite outside the tribe of Levi might perform priestly duties—under pain of death (cf. Num 1:51; 3:10, 38).

7:11. Broadly, the "perfection" referred to here has to do with true union with God, and therefore must include sanctifying grace and forgiveness of sin.

The Levitical priesthood was at the service of the Law, and the Law was salvific only through faith in the coming of Christ. Thus the Levitical priesthood was intrinsically orientated to Christ: "for, as it would be written (Heb 7:19), 'the law made nothing perfect' [...]; it did not provide the ultimate fullness of the heavenly fatherland because it did not enable people to enter Life" (St Thomas, *Commentary on Heb*, 7, 2).

In Romans 3:20 and Galatians 2:16–19 the same idea, so typical of St Paul, is to be found. It is summed up by the Council of Trent in these words: "As the Apostle St Paul testifies, there was no perfection under the former Testament because of the insufficiency of the Levitical priesthood. It was therefore necessary (according to the merciful ordination of God the Father) that another priest arise according to the order of Melchizedek, our Lord Jesus Christ, who could perfect all who were to be sanctified (cf. Heb 10:14)" (*De SS. Missae sacrificio*, chap. 1).

7:12. On the necessary connexion between priesthood and covenant, St Thomas writes: "The Law was subject to the ministry of its priests; so, when the priesthood changed, the Law too had to change. This is why that change had to take place: when the end is changed, the means for attaining the end must also change [...]. Just as human law regulates how men should live together and how society be arranged, so spiritual and divine law has to do with the order established by God. This divine disposition of things is essentially bound up with priesthood" (*Commentary on Heb,* ad loc.). This teaching, supported by Hebrews, was used by the Council of Trent to explain the connexion between the sacrifice of the New Testament and Christian priesthood: "By divine decree sacrifice and priesthood are so closely connected that both are present in every law. Since the catholic Church received by divine institution the holy and visible sacrifice of the Eucharist, there must be located in her also an external, visible priesthood, which derives from the transfer of the old priesthood [to the New Law]" (*De Sacram. ordinis*, chap. 1). The connexion between priesthood, sacrifice and law is also explained in the *St Pius V Catechism* (2, 7, 8): "The period previous to the written law must have had its priesthood and its spiritual power since it is certain that it had its law; for these two, as the Apostle testifies, are so closely connected that if the priesthood is transferred, the law must necessarily be transferred also. Guided, therefore, by a natural instinct, men recognized that God is to be worshipped; and hence it follows that in every nation some, whose power might in a certain sense be called spiritual, were given the care of sacred things and of divine worship. This power was also possessed by the Jews; but though it was superior in dignity to that with which priests were invested under the law of nature, yet it must be regarded as far

a change in the law as well. ¹³For the one of whom these things are spoken belonged to another tribe, from which no one has ever served at the altar. ¹⁴For it is evident that our Lord was descended from Judah, and in connection with that tribe Moses said nothing about priests.

¹⁵This becomes even more evident when another priest arises in the likeness of Melchizedek, ¹⁶who has become a priest, not according to a legal requirement concerning bodily descent but by the power of an indestructible life. ¹⁷For it is witnessed of him,
   "Thou art a priest for ever,
   after the order of Melchizedek."

Gen 49:10
Is 11:1
Lk 1:78
Rom 1:3
Rev 5:5

Ps 110:4
Heb 5:6

---

inferior to the spiritual power that is found in the New Law. For the latter is heavenly, and surpasses all the power of angels; it is derived not from the Mosaic priesthood, but from Christ our Lord who was a priest, not according to the order of Aaron, but according to the order of Melchizedek. For he it is who, himself endowed with the supreme power of granting grace and remitting sins, left to his Church this power, although he limited it in extent and attached it to the sacraments."

7:13. "The one of whom these things are spoken": the true priest, then, is not Melchizedek, who had only a symbolic role, but Christ, who is truly eternal, higher, perfect, unchangeable, and who brings Redemption.

7:15–19. The superiority of Christ's priesthood is now demonstrated by reference to the inferiority of the Old Law, in line with the inferiority of its priesthood. The Law is defined as "a legal requirement concerning bodily descent" as opposed to something spiritual (cf. 1 Cor 2:13–15; Gal 6:1; Eph 1:3; Col 1:8; 2 Cor 3:6–8); it is "weak" as opposed to effective; "useless" as opposed to being able to do what it is designed for. From this two things follow: the Law made nothing perfect (cf. note on 7:11); and its function was that of "introducing" us to a better law—that of Christ, a law that is full of hope, and hope enables us to draw near to God (cf. Rom 3:21; Gal 3:24; 1 Tim 1:8).

The epistle's verdict on the Law of Moses may seem somewhat harsh, but it fits in exactly with the gratuitous nature of glorification: "The Law", Theodoret comments, "has come to an end, as the Apostle says, and its place is taken by hope of better things. The Law has ended, however, not because it was bad, as some heretics foolishly say, but because it was weak and was not perfectly useful. But we must understand that it is the [now] superfluous parts of the Law that are described as weak or useless—circumcision, the sabbath precept, and similar things. For, the New Testament insistently commands observance of the 'Thou shalt not kill, Thou shalt not commit adultery' and the other commandments. In place of the old precepts we have now received hope of future good things, a hope that makes us God's own household" (*Interpretatio Ep. ad Haebreos,* ad loc.). St Thomas Aquinas points out that the commandments were and are useful. The Old Testament was not in itself bad, but it is unsuited to the new times; there is no reason why the new priesthood should

Hebrews 7:18

Heb 9:9
Rom 7:7; 8:3

[18] On the one hand, a former commandment is set aside because of its weakness and uselessness [19] (for the law made nothing perfect); on the other hand, a better hope is introduced, through which we draw near to God.

Christ is perfect high priest and his priesthood endures forever

Ps 110:4

[20] And it was not without an oath. [21] Those who formerly became priests took their office without an oath, but this one was addressed with an oath,
 "The Lord has sworn
 and will not change his mind,
 'Thou art a priest for ever.'"

Heb 8:6–10

[22] This makes Jesus the surety of a better covenant.

---

continue the ways of the old (cf. Ps 40:6f). That was why the Old Law was abrogated—because it was weak and served no purpose: "We say something is weak when it fails to produce its [designed] effect; and the effect proper to the Law and the priesthood is justification [...]. This the Law was unable to do, because it did not bring man to beatitude, which is his end. However, in its time it was useful, in that it prepared men for faith" (*Commentary on Heb*, 7, 3).

7:20–22. The third reason why Christ's priesthood is superior is that it has been sealed with an oath (cf. Heb 9:15–18). There is an implicit repetition here of what was said apropos of the promise made to Abraham (6:13–18): God's oath provides absolute certainty because the oath is made by Truth itself and supreme Truth bears witness to it. Psalm 110:4 is again quoted but with attention focused on the oath itself: "The Lord has sworn and will not change his mind." In developing his argument the author of Hebrews is using different aspects of the Psalm. First he bases his argument on "Thou art a priest [...] after the order of Melchizedek" to show that Christ's priesthood is different from and superior to the Levitical priesthood. Then he comments on the words "Thou art a priest forever" to contrast the eternal nature of Christ's priesthood with the contingent and temporary nature of the Levitical priesthood. And finally he focuses on the words "The Lord has sworn and will not change his mind", to show the force and permanence of the divine decision.

7:22. "The surety [mediator] of a better covenant": Christ is mediator (cf. 8:6; 9:15; 12:24) because he is priest, for every priest is established as a mediator between God and men (cf. 1 Tim 2:5; Heb 5:1). Christ's priesthood is superior to the Levitical priesthood because it has been established with an oath, whereas the Levitical has not. Given that covenant or law is bound up with priesthood, the New Covenant is therefore "better" than the old. "The function of a mediator is to get two extremes to agree. Christ brought us the divine gifts, for through him we have become partakers of the divine nature (cf 2 Pet 1:4) [...]. In the Old Covenant certain temporal benefits were promised; whereas now it is eternal ones" (*Commentary on Heb*, 7, 2).

²³The former priests were many in number, because they were prevented by death from continuing in office; ²⁴but he holds his priesthood permanently, because he continues for ever. ²⁵Consequently he is able for all time to save those who draw near to God through him, since he always lives to make intercession for them.

Rom 8:34
Rev 1:18
1 Jn 2:1
Heb 9:24

7:23–25. Christ's priesthood is everlasting. Just as Melchizedek had no "end of life", so too the Son of God holds his priesthood permanently. The Levites are mere mortal men; Christ, however, has not been instituted as priest by "bodily descent but by the power of an indestructible life" (v. 16); that is why he can truly be said to be a priest "for ever". This makes sense, for death is a consequence of sin, and Christ has conquered sin and death. Moreover, death makes it necessary for there to be a succession of human priests in order to provide continuity; whereas the everlasting character of Christ's priesthood renders any further priesthood unnecessary.

St Thomas comments that this shows Christ to be the true and perfect Priest in the strict sense of the word, for it was impossible for the Jewish priests to be permanent mediators because death naturally deprived them of their priesthood. The case of Christian priests is quite different, because they are not mediators strictly speaking. There is only one Mediator, Jesus Christ; they are simply representatives of his, who act in his name. Christ is to the Levites as the perfect (which is necessarily one) is to the imperfect (which is always multiple): "Incorruptible things have no need to reproduce themselves […]. Christ is immortal. As the eternal Word of the Father, he abides forever: his divine eternity is passed on to his body, for 'being raised from the dead (he) will never die again' (Rom 6:9). And so 'because he continues for ever, he holds his priesthood permanently.' Christ alone is the true Priest; the others (priests) are his ministers" (*Commentary on Heb*, ad loc.).

The eternal character of Christ's priesthood, St John Chrysostom points out, gives us reason for great confidence: "It is as if the Apostle were saying, 'Do not be afraid or think that (although) he loves us and has the Father's full confidence he cannot live forever: on the contrary, he does live forever!'" (*Hom. on Heb*, 13). We can put our trust in Christ the Priest because his priesthood is an enduring expression of his heartfelt love for all mankind: "The living Christ continues to love us still; he loves us today, now, and he offers us his heart as the fountain of our redemption: 'he always lives to make intercession for (us)' (Heb 7:25). We are always—ourselves and the entire world—embraced by the love of this heart 'which has loved men so much and receives such poor response from them'" (John Paul II, *Homily in Sacré Cœur*, Montmartre, Paris, 1 June 1980).

Christ's priesthood is an expression of his Love, from which it cannot be separated; since his Love is everlasting, so too is his priesthood. In the first place, his priesthood is everlasting because it is linked to the Incarnation, which is something permanent; secondly, because Christ's mission is that of saving all men in all periods of history and not simply one of helping them by his teaching and his example; thirdly, because Christ continues to be present—St Ephraem says—not in the victims of the sacrifices of Mosaic worship, but in the prayer of the Church (cf. *Comm. in Epist. ad*

Hebrews 7:26

Heb 4:14f
Lev 16:6, 11, 15

²⁶For it was fitting that we should have such a high priest, holy, blameless, unstained, separated from sinners, exalted above the heavens. ²⁷He has no need, like those high priests, to offer sacrifices daily, first for his own sins and then for those of the people; he did this once for all when he offered up himself.

Haebreos, ad loc.), particularly in the permanent efficacy of the sacrifice of the Cross constantly renewed in the Mass, and in the praying of the Divine Office. Finally, it is everlasting because Christ's sacrifice is perpetuated until the end of time in the Christian ministerial priesthood, for bishops and priests "in virtue of the sacrament of Order, are consecrated as true priests of the New Testament to preach the Gospel and shepherd the faithful and celebrate divine worship" (Vatican II, *Lumen gentium*, 28).

Christ not only interceded for us when he was on earth: he continues to make intercession for us from heaven: "This 'always' points to a great mystery," St John Chrysostom observes; "he lives not only here but also there, in heaven; not only here and for a while, but also there, in life eternal" (*Hom. on Heb*, 13). In saying that Christ "makes intercession" for us, the inspired text is saying that Christ "takes the initiative, addresses the Father, presents him with a request or a demand", as if Christ were an advocate before the Father, a help, a defender (a "paraclete": cf. 1 Jn 2:1). But in what sense does he continue to make intercession for us, given that he cannot merit any more than he did when he was on this earth? He intercedes, St Thomas replies, first by again presenting his human nature to the Father, marked with the glorious signs of his passion, and then by expressing the great love and desire of his soul to bring about our salvation (cf. *Commentary on Heb*, 7, 4). Christ, so to speak, continues to offer the Father the sacrifice of his longsuffering, humility, obedience and love. That is why we can always approach him to find salvation. "Through Christ and in the Holy Spirit, a Christian has access to the intimacy of God the Father, and he spends his life looking for the Kingdom which is not of this world, but which is initiated and prepared in this world. We must seek Christ in the Word and in the Bread, in the Eucharist and in prayer. And we must treat him as a friend, as the real, living person he is—for he is risen. Christ, we read in the Epistle to the Hebrews [Heb 7:24–25 follows]" (St Josemaría Escrivá, *Christ Is Passing By*, 116).

7:26–28. These last verses form a paean in praise of Christ, summing up and rounding off what has gone before. Christ is proclaimed to be "holy, blameless, unstained," that is, sinless, totally devoted to God the Father, just and faithful. Holy Scripture uses similar language to describe people of outstanding holiness, such as Zechariah and Elizabeth (cf. Lk 1:6), Simeon, who was "righteous and devout", Joseph of Arimathea (cf. Lk 23:50), the centurion Cornelius (cf. Acts 10:22), etc. The praise given Christ here, however, hints at a perfection which is more than human. Christ is, at the same time, "separated from sinners", not in the sense that he refuses to have any dealings with them or despises them, for, on the contrary, we know that the Pharisees abused him, saying, "Behold, a glutton and a drunkard, a friend of tax collectors and sinners" (Mt 11:19) and "This man

Hebrews 7:28

²⁸Indeed, the law appoints men in their weakness as high priests, but the word of the oath, which came later than the law, appoints a Son who has been made perfect for ever.

Heb 5:9

receives sinners and eats with them" (Lk 15:2; cf. Mt 9–11:13 and par.; Lk 7:34); he is "separated from sinners" because he can have no sin in him, since the presence of sin in his human nature is absolutely incompatible with the holiness of the unique person that Christ is—the divine Word. He is the perfect embodiment of all the ancient prerequisites for a priest of the true God (cf. Lev 21:4, 6, 8, 15). Christ, finally, from the point of view of his human nature also, has been "exalted above the heavens" not only ethically speaking, by virtue of his sublime holiness, but also in his very body, through his glorious ascension (cf. Acts 2:33–26; 10:42); he is therefore the "Son who has been made perfect forever".

"Who was Jesus Christ?" St Alphonsus asks himself. "He was, St Paul replies, holy, blameless, unstained or, even better, he was holiness itself, innocence itself, purity itself" (*Christmas Novena*, 4). And St Fulgentius of Ruspe extols Christ in these beautiful terms: "He is the one who possessed in himself all that was needed to bring about our redemption, that is, he himself was the priest and the victim; he himself was God and the temple—the priest by whose actions we are reconciled; the sacrifice which brings about our reconciliation; the temple wherein we are reconciled; the God with whom we have been reconciled. Therefore, be absolutely certain of this and do not doubt it for a moment: the only-begotten God himself, the Word made flesh, offered himself to God on our behalf in an odour of sweetness as sacrifice and victim—the very one in whose honour as well as that of the Father and the Holy Spirit, the patriarchs, prophets and priests used to offer sacrifices of animals in Old Testament times; and to whom now, that is, in the time of the New Testament, in the unity of the Father and the Holy Spirit, with whom he shares the same unique divinity, the holy catholic Church never ceases to offer on behalf of the entire universe the sacrifice of the bread and wine, with faith and charity" (*De fide ad Petrum*, 22).

The sublimity of Christ's priesthood is a source of encouragement, hope and holy pride for the priests of the New Testament, given that "every priest in his own way puts on the person of Christ and is endowed with a special grace. By this grace, the priest, through his service of the people committed to his care and all the people of God, is able the better to pursue the perfection of Christ, whose place he takes. The human weakness of his flesh is remedied by the holiness of him who became for us a high priest, 'holy, blameless, unstained, separated from sinners' (Heb 7:26)" (Vatican II, *Presbyterorum ordinis*, 12). For all these reasons St Pius X, addressing priests, wrote: "We ought, therefore, to represent the person of Christ and fulfil the mission he has entrusted to us; and thereby attain the end which he has set out to reach [...]. We are under an obligation, as his friends, to have the same sentiments as Jesus Christ, who is 'holy, blameless, unstained' (Heb 7:26). As his ambassadors we have a duty to win over men's minds to accept his law and his teaching, beginning by observing them ourselves; insofar as we have a share in his power, we are obliged to set souls free from the bonds of sin, and we must ourselves be very careful to avoid falling into sin" (*Haerent animo*, 5).

4. CHRIST'S SACRIFICE IS MORE EXCELLENT THAN ALL THE SACRIFICES OF THE OLD LAW

Ps 110:1
Heb 4:14
Acts 2:36

Christ is high priest of a New Covenant, which replaces the Old

8 ¹Now the point in what we are saying is this: we have such a high priest, one who is seated at the right hand of the throne of

---

8:1–2. The key point of the epistle is now proclaimed with great formality—the superiority of Christ's priesthood. This links up what was already said in 1:3 (about Christ being enthroned at the right hand of the Majesty) with what will be developed in chapters 9 and 10 (about the new temple and new form of worship). In Christ the Old Covenant, which offered worship by means of sacrifice and offerings, finds its total perfection; from Christ onwards the New Covenant begins, with a new sacrifice and a new temple. Little by little, consideration of the priesthood of the Mosaic form of worship gives way to examination of Christ's new form of divine service.

It is not just a matter of one temple or stone being replaced by another or by many such temples. The old temple has given way to a heavenly sanctuary, heaven itself. This is why Christ's ascension and enthronement at the right hand of the Father is so important: it marks the definitive entry of Jesus Christ's sacred humanity into his true temple, one not made by human hands. This makes it easier to understand the sense in which the temple of Jerusalem and the worship connected with it were a foreshadowing of future events.

Christ, then, possesses the true, definitive priesthood, for he exercises his ministry in the sanctuary of heaven, where he is seated at the right hand of the Father. This heavenly ministry of Christ is a further confirmation of the superiority of his priesthood. Firstly, because he is seated at the right hand of the Majesty in heaven (cf. Ps 110:1)—"Majesty" meaning the Godhead itself, for it is a way of referring to God (cf. the "throne of grace" in 4:16). Moreover, the "throne of the Majesty" is the equivalent of supreme authority to rule and judge. This can be seen from descriptions of the Last Judgment: "When the Son of man comes in his glory, and all the angels with him, then he will sit on his glorious throne" (Mt 25:31; cf. Rev 3:21; 20:11; Mt 19:28; etc.). Secondly, Christ carries out his ministry in a new sanctuary and a new tabernacle ("tent"), which are "true" in the sense that the sanctuary and tabernacle of Moses were only an "image" of them. The earthly liturgy is a reflection of the true, heavenly liturgy, which is the eternal continuation of Christ's priesthood in the presence of the Father, for "in the earthly liturgy we take part in a foretaste of that heavenly liturgy which is celebrated in the Holy City of Jerusalem toward which we journey as pilgrims, where Christ is sitting at the right hand of God, Minister of the holies and of the true tabernacle" (Vatican II, *Sacrosanctum Concilium*, 8).

Some Fathers see the true sanctuary and tabernacle as representing the Church, in its total sense of Church militant plus Church triumphant. And St Cyril of Alexandria, for example, points out in one of his works that "the old tabernacle was set up in the desert by Moses and it was highly suitable for performing all the sacred ceremonies of the Law. But the mansion which is appropriate to Christ is the city on high, that is, heaven, the

the Majesty in heaven, ²a minister in the sanctuary and the true tent[n] which is set up not by man but by the Lord. ³For every high priest is appointed to offer gifts and sacrifices; hence it is necessary for this priest also to have something to offer. ⁴Now if he were on earth, he would not be a priest at all, since there are priests who offer gifts according to the law. ⁵They serve a copy and shadow of the heavenly sanctuary; for when Moses was about to erect the tent,[n] he was instructed by God, saying, "See that you make everything according to the pattern which was shown you on the mountain." ⁶But as it is, Christ[o] has obtained a ministry which is as much more excellent than the old as the covenant he mediates is better, since it is enacted on better promises. ⁷For if that first covenant had been faultless, there would have been no occasion for a second.

Num 24:6, LXX
Heb 5:1

Ex 25:40
Col 2:17
Acts 7:44

Heb 7:22; 9:15; 12:24
1 Tim 2:5

---

divine tent which is not the product of human handiwork but rather something holy and begotten by God. Christ, established therein, offers to God the Father those who believe in him, those sanctified by the Spirit" (St Cyril, *Explanation of Heb*).

8:3–6. To compare the earthly and heavenly tabernacles, the author resorts to analogy and metaphor, which is all that he can do. Bearing this in mind, one should not interpret the words of this passage as meaning that Jesus Christ consummated his sacrifice only in heaven, for the sacrifice of Calvary happened only once and was complete in itself. What this passage is saying is that, in heaven, Christ, the eternal Priest, continuously presents to the Father the fruits of the cross. In the New Covenant there is only one sacrifice—that of Jesus Christ on Calvary; this single sacrifice is renewed in an unbloody manner every day in the sacrifice of the Mass; there Jesus Christ—the only Priest of the New Law—immolates and offers, by means of priests who are his ministers, the same victim (body and blood) which was immolated in a bloody manner once and for all on the cross.

8:7–12. The comparison between the two covenants, the Old made with Moses and written on stone, and the New, engraved on the minds and hearts of the faithful (cf. 2 Cor 3:3; Heb 10:16, 17) is developed with the help of a quotation from Jeremiah (Jer 31:31–34), where the prophet announces the spiritual alliance of Yahweh with his people. Jeremiah's words, quoted from the Greek translation (very close to the original Hebrew), refer directly to the restoration of the Jews after the Exile. Now that the chosen people have been purified by suffering they are fit to be truly the people of God: "I will be their God, and they shall be my people"; this promise of intimate friendship is the core of the prophecy. That is what it means when it says the Law will be written on the minds and hearts of all, and all—even the least—shall know God. It may be that Jeremiah sensed the messianic restoration that lay beyond the restoration of the chosen people on its return from exile; certainly we can see that this oracle finds its complete

n. Or *tabernacle* **o.** Greek *he*

Hebrews 8:8

Jer 31:31–34

⁸For he finds fault with them when he says:
"The days will come, says the Lord,
when I will establish a new covenant with the house of Israel
and with the house of Judah;

Ex 19:5f

⁹ not like the covenant that I made with their fathers
on the day when I took them by the hand
to lead them out of the land of Egypt;
for they did not continue in my covenant,
and so I paid no heed to them, says the Lord.

Heb 10:16f
2 Cor 3:3;
6:16–18

¹⁰ This is the covenant that I will make with the house of Israel
after those days, says the Lord:
I will put my laws into their minds,
and write them on their hearts,
and I will be their God,
and they shall be my people.

¹¹ And they shall not teach every one his fellow
or every one his brother, saying, 'Know the Lord,'
for all shall know me,
from the least of them to the greatest.*

¹² For I will be merciful toward their iniquities,
and I will remember their sins no more."

Rom 10:4
2 Cor 5:17
Rev 21:4f
Heb 9:18

¹³In speaking of a new covenant he treats the first as obsolete. And what is becoming obsolete and growing old is ready to vanish away.

The rites of the Old Covenant prefigure those of the New

Ex 25:23, 30f
2 Chron 13:11
LXX

9 ¹Now even the first covenant had regulations for worship and an earthly sanctuary. ²For a tent^p was prepared, the outer one, in

---

fulfilment only with the New Covenant: the return from Babylon was merely an additional signal/symbol of the perfect Covenant which Christ would establish. For it is in that New Covenant that God truly forgives sins and remembers them no more.

The Old Covenant is said not to have been faultless, or sinless. This does not mean it was bad; rather; as St Thomas explains, it was powerless to atone for sins, it did not provide people with the grace to avoid committing sins, it simply showed people how to recognize sins; those who lived under the Old Law continued to be subject to sin (cf. *Commentary on Heb*, 7, 2).

9:1–10. In the preceding chapters the superiority of Christ's priesthood is discussed. Now the letter examines the excellence of his sacrifice. To do so, it

p. Or *tabernacle*

which were the lampstand and the table and the bread of the Presence;^q it is called the Holy Place. ³Behind the second curtain stood a tent^p called the Holy of Holies, ⁴having the golden altar of incense and the ark of the covenant covered on all sides with gold, which contained a golden urn holding the manna, and Aaron's rod that budded, and the tables of the covenant; ⁵above it were the cherubim of glory overshadowing the mercy seat. Of these things we cannot now speak in detail.

⁶These preparations having thus been made, the priests go continually into the outer tent,^p performing their ritual duties; ⁷but into the second only the high priest goes, and he but once a year,

Ex 26:31–33
Ex 16:33; Ex 25:1 20; 16:21
Num 17:25
Ex 25:18, 22

Num 18:3f
Ex 30:10; Lev 16:2, 14f, 18f
Heb 7:27

---

describes the sanctuary of the Old Covenant, the tent or tabernacle, where Yahweh dwelt during the period when the people of Israel were making their way through the wilderness and in the early years in the promised land. It also refers to the sacrifice on the great Day of Atonement or Yom Kippur (cf. Lev 16:1–34; 23:26–32; Num 29:7–11), whereby Israel was reconciled with its God by purification and the forgiveness of all those sins committed during the year for which no atonement had been made. Both the sanctuary and the rites celebrated in it on this solemn day are a prefigurement of the new sanctuary and new form of worship inaugurated by Christ. This leads on to a discussion of the most essential and specific function of priesthood—sacrifice.

It should be noted that in describing the sanctuary of the Old Covenant the epistle does so in terms not of the temple of Jerusalem but of the tent in the desert. In addition to having certain more traditional connotations and allowing the ark of the Covenant to be included in the description (the ark was destroyed in 587 BC when Nebuchadnezzar sacked the temple), reference to the tabernacle is closely connected with an idea which underlies the entire letter: the Christian is making his way in a new exodus towards his homeland in heaven, entry into which has been opened by Christ's sacrifice (cf. 3:7–11).

9:3. "The second curtain": separating the Holy Place from the Holy of Holies. It is called the "second curtain" to distinguish it from the curtain at the entrance to the Holy Place, which would have been the first curtain. It was not, then, that there were two tents: there was only one, which was divided into two sections by this "second curtain".

9:6–7. This is a reference to the most solemn sacrifice of the Old Testament Day of Atonement—a penitential service on the tenth day of the month of Tishri (September–October), five days before the feast of Tabernacles. It was the only day in the year when the high priest was permitted to enter the Holy of Holies, whereas priests entered the Holy Place every day to do things connected with divine service (renew the incense, change the loaves of proposition, etc.). The ceremonies of the Day of Atonement are described in more detail in the Introduction to this volume.

This celebration purified the people of Israel, priests and leaders included,

---

q. Greek *the presentation of the loaves* **p.** Or *tabernacle*

Hebrews 9:8

<small>Heb 10:19f</small>

and not without taking blood which he offers for himself and for the errors of the people. ⁸By this the Holy Spirit indicates that the way into the sanctuary is not yet opened as long as the outer tent is still standing ⁹(which is symbolic for the present age). According to this arrangement, gifts and sacrifices are offered which cannot perfect the conscience of the worshipper, ¹⁰but deal only with food and drink and various ablutions, regulations for the body imposed until the time of reformation.

<small>Lev 11:2; 15:18
Num 19:13
Col 2:16f</small>

Christ sealed the New Covenant with his blood once and for all

<small>Heb 4:14;
10:1, 20
2 Cor 5:1</small>

¹¹But when Christ appeared as a high priest of the good things that have come,ʳ then through the greater and more perfect tentᵖ (not from their sins and atoned for the faults and uncleanness which the ordinary sacrifices could not erase; the sanctuary itself was also rendered clean of any contamination.

Yom Kippur is one of the most important feasts in the Jewish calendar, the others being the Passover, Pentecost, Tabernacles, and the celebration of the New Year.

"The errors of the people" probably refers to every kind of sin, both sins which Leviticus terms "sin" and what it calls "guilt" (cf. Lev 7:37). However, by referring to them as "errors", sins of ignorance, the point is being made that voluntary sins cannot be pardoned by the ceremony of Yom Kippur. There were certain rabbis in fact who taught that animal sacrifices were insufficient to erase the graver types of sin. For that it was necessary for God himself to replace the sacrifices offered by men with a divine sacrifice of infinite atoning value.

9:8–10. Old Testament liturgy was a symbol of the new liturgy, whose centre is the sacrifice of Christ, which alone is capable of sanctifying man, of "perfecting the conscience of the worshipper". The existence of an outer tent blocking the way to the inner tent symbolizes this inability of the liturgy to effect justification. Once the curtain is removed the way is open to man to attain union with God—holiness symbolized by entry into the Holy of Holies. By his death Christ tore the curtain (cf. Mt 27:51). He is our Way (cf. Jn 14:6), the Door (cf. Jn 10:7), allowing entry into the heavenly sanctuary. Therefore, as long as there exists the first tabernacle, that is, the Holy Place, separated from the Holy of Holies by the curtain, sacrifices and gifts offered cannot bring about man's interior perfection, because Christ's sacrifice has not yet taken place, the sacrifice which will make satisfaction for the sins of all mankind.

Also, the existence of the tabernacle is a symbol of the ineffectiveness of Jewish rites in the present era, when the redemptive sacrifice has already been offered. It should be remembered that when the Letter to the Hebrews was being written, the old liturgy was still being enacted in the temple. But the rites of the Old Law were valid only up to the Redemption wrought by Christ, that is, up to his death and resurrection.

9:11–14. The sacrifices of the Old Law could only promise ephemeral benefits,

---

r. Other manuscripts read *good things to come*   **p.** Or *tabernacle* made with hands, that is, not of this creation) ¹²he[s] entered once for all into the Holy Place, taking not the blood of goats and calves but his own blood, thus securing an eternal redemption.

Heb 7:27
Lk 24:21
Dan 9:24

---

whereas Christ's redemptive sacrifice obtained for man, once and for all, "the good things to come", that is, the heavenly and eternal benefits proper to the messianic age—sanctifying grace and entry to heaven. Like the high priest on the Day of Atonement, Christ entered once for all into the Holy of Holies, through the curtain. This sanctuary which he entered is the heavenly one; that is why it is "greater and more perfect" and not made by men (cf. 8:2). Christ passed through the heavens into the very presence of the Father (cf. 7:26) and is seated in heaven at his right hand (cf. 8:1).

Many Fathers, Doctors of the Church and modern scholars see the expression "through the greater and more perfect tent" as referring to the sacred humanity of our Lord, virginally conceived in the womb of Mary, that is, "not made with hands". The tent or tabernacle would be our Lord's body, in which the Godhead dwells. The text then says that it is "not of this creation", because Jesus as man was conceived without the action of a man and without original sin: he did not follow "the law of nature which holds sway in the created world" (Theodoret, *Interpretatio Ep. ad Hebraeos*, ad loc.). In this case the inspired text would be saying that Christ redeemed us by means of his human nature (cf. v. 12). However, the words "through the greater and more perfect tent" can also be understood as referring to heaven, in the sense of a greater and more perfect sanctuary. In any event, whether by passing through the heavens or through his most sacred body, Christ achieved Redemption by offering his own blood. This does not have a temporary value—like the blood of animals shed each year when the priest entered the Holy of Holies: Jesus secured eternal Redemption. In the Old Law the Jews were cleansed by the blood of sacrificed animals from legal impurities which prevented them from taking part in the liturgy; but Christ's blood does so much more, for it cleanses man of his sins. "Do you want to know how effective the blood of Christ is? Let us go back to the symbols which foretold it and remind ourselves of the ancient accounts of (the Jews in) Egypt. Moses told them to kill a year-old lamb and put its blood on the two doorposts and the lintel of each house [...]. Would you like an additional way to appreciate the power of Christ's blood? See where it flowed from, what its source is. It began to flow from the very cross and its source was the Lord's side. For, as the Gospel says, when our Lord was already dead, one of the soldiers went up to him with a lance and pierced his side and at once there came out water and blood—water, the symbol of Baptism; blood, the symbol of the Eucharist. The soldier pierced his side, he opened a breach in the wall of the holy temple, and there I discover the hidden treasure and I rejoice at the treasure I have found" (Chrysostom, *Baptismal catechesis*, 3, 13–19).

And so the Church includes in the prayers it recommends to be said after Mass, one which reads: "I beseech thee, most sweet Lord Jesus, may your passion be the virtue which strengthens, protects and defends me; your wounds, food and drink to nourish, inebriate and delight me; your death, everlasting life for me;

---

s. Greek *through*

Hebrews 9:13

Num 19:9, 17–20
1 Pet 1:18f
1 Jn 1:7
1 Cor 15:45
2 Cor 13:13

¹³For if the sprinkling of defiled persons with the blood of goats and bulls and with the ashes of a heifer sanctifies for the purification of the flesh, ¹⁴how much more shall the blood of Christ, who through the eternal Spirit offered himself without blemish to God, purify your[t] conscience from dead works to serve the living God.

---

your cross, my eternal glory" (*Roman Missal of St Pius V*, recommended prayer of thanksgiving after Mass).

9:12. "Thus securing an eternal redemption": the Greek text uses "having found", here translated as "securing". St John Chrysostom points out that the verb "to find" in this context has a shade of meaning that implies finding something unexpected: the reference is to finding, "as it were, something very unknown and very unexpected" (*Hom. on Heb*, ad loc.). However, taking into account the whole context and the possible Hebraic background of the expression, the verb "to find" is synonymous with "to search keenly, to reach, to attain": in other words, Christ eagerly sought to redeem man and he did so by his sacrifice. The verse refers to an "eternal" redemption, in contrast to the provisional nature of Mosaic sacrifices.

9:13. These words refer to a ceremony of purification described in the Old Testament (cf. Num 19). To cleanse a person from certain transgressions of the Law, the Israelites could avail of certain expiatory ablutions. These were done with water mixed with the ashes of a heifer, which the high priest had sacrificed in front of the tabernacle and then burned in its entirety. Into the fire cedarwood, hyssop and scarlet wool (9:19) had also to be thrown. Thus lustral water was only useful for legal purification or "purification of the flesh", as distinct from purification of the spirit.

9:14. The Messiah acts "through the eternal Spirit", which may be taken as a reference to the Spirit, as St Thomas, for example, interprets it: "Christ shed his blood, because the Holy Spirit did so; that is to say, it was by the Spirit's influence and prompting, that is, out of love of God and love of neighbour, that he did what he did. For it is the Spirit who purifies" (*Commentary on Heb*, ad loc.).

Pope John Paul II referred to this text to show the presence of the Holy Spirit in the redemptive sacrifice of the Incarnate Word: "In the sacrifice of the Son of Man the Holy Spirit is present and active just as he acted in Jesus's conception, in his coming into the world, in his hidden life and in his public ministry. According to the Letter to the Hebrews, on the way to his 'departure' through Gethsemani and Golgotha, the same *Jesus Christ* in his own humanity *opened himself totally* to this *action of the Spirit-Paraclete*, who from suffering enables eternal salvific love to spring forth" (*Dominum et Vivificantem*, 40).

The Son of God desired that the Holy Spirit should turn his death into a perfect sacrifice. Only Christ "in his humanity was worthy to become this sacrifice, for *he alone* was 'without blemish' (Heb 9:14). But he offered it 'through the eternal Spirit', which means that the Holy Spirit acted in a special way in this absolute self-giving of the Son of Man, in order to transform this suffering into redemptive love" (ibid.).

t. Other manuscripts read *our*

¹⁵Therefore he is the mediator of a new covenant, so that those who are called may receive the promised eternal inheritance, since a death has occurred which redeems them from the transgressions under the first covenant.ᵘ ¹⁶For where a will is involved, the death

1 Tim 2:5
Heb 8:6; 12:24
Gal 3:19; 4:1–7

It is also possible that "the eternal Spirit" is a more general reference to the Godhead present in Christ; in which case it would be the same as saying that Christ, being God and man, offered himself as an unblemished victim and therefore this offering was infinitely efficacious. Thus, as Pius XII says, Christ "laboured unceasingly by prayer and self-sacrifice for the salvation of souls until, hanging on the cross, he offered himself as a victim unblemished in God's sight, that he might purify our consciences and set them free from lifeless observances to serve the living God. All men were thus rescued from the path of ruin and perdition and set once more on the way to God, to whom they were now to give due glory by co-operating personally in their sanctification, making their own the holiness that springs from the blood of the unspotted Lamb" (*Mediator Dei*, 1).

Christ's sacrifice purifies us completely, thereby rendering us fit to worship the living God. As St Alphonsus puts it, "Jesus Christ offered himself to God pure and without the trace of a fault; otherwise he would not have been a worthy mediator, would not have been capable of reconciling God and sinful man, nor would his blood have had the power to purify and cleanse our conscience from 'dead works', that is, from sins which are given that name because (our) works are in no way meritorious or else are worthy of eternal punishment. 'So that you might serve the living God'" (*Reflections on the Passion*, 9, 2).

9:15–22. The covenant is shown to be new because it has been ratified by the death and by the shedding of the blood of the testator or mediator. "Man, having fallen into sin, was in debt to divine justice and was the enemy of God. The Son of God came into the world and clothed himself in human flesh; being both God and man he became the mediator between man and God, the representative of both sides, so as to restore peace between them and obtain divine grace for man, giving himself as an offering to pay man's debt with his blood and his death. This reconciliation was prefigured in the Old Testament in all the sacrifices that were offered in that period and in all the symbols which God ordained—the tabernacle, the altar, the veil, the lampstand, the thurible and the ark where the rod of Aaron and the tables of the Law were kept. All these were a sign and type of the promised redemption; and it was because that redemption would come about through the blood of Christ that God specified the blood of animals—a symbol of the blood of the divine Lamb —and laid it down that all the symbolic objects mentioned above should be sprinkled with blood: 'Hence even the first Covenant was not ratified without blood'" (ibid., 9, 2).

For a third time Christ is stated to be the mediator of a New Covenant. Hebrews 7:22 and 8:6 say that he is the mediator of a better covenant because it can give eternal life. Here, as in 12:24, it is explained that Christ is the mediator of a New Covenant, ratified by blood which

---

u. The Greek word here used means both *covenant* and *will*

of the one who made it must be established. ¹⁷For a will[u] takes effect only at death, since it is not in force as long as the one who made it is alive. ¹⁸Hence even the first covenant was not ratified

---

gives an eternal inheritance. The emphasis is on the sacrificial aspect: Christ is the mediator insofar as he is the atoning victim and at the same time the offerer of the sacrifice: in his sacrifice he is both priest and victim. "Christ is priest indeed; but he is priest for us, not for himself. It is in the name of the whole human race that he offers prayer and acts of human religious homage to his Eternal Father. He is likewise victim; but victim for us, since he substitutes himself for guilty mankind. Now the Apostle's exhortation, 'Yours is to be the same mind as Christ Jesus showed' (Phil 2:5), requires all Christians, so far as human power allows, to reproduce in themselves the sentiments that Christ had when he was offering himself in sacrifice—sentiments of humility, of adoration, praise, and thanksgiving to the divine Majesty. It requires them also to become victims, as it were; cultivating a spirit of self-denial according to the precepts of the Gospel, willingly doing works of penance, detesting and expiating their sins" (*Mediator Dei*, 22).

Christ's sacrifice is not only effective to forgive our sins; it is a manifestation of our Redeemer's love for us and it sets an example which we should follow. "And if God forgives us our sins it is so that we might use the time that remains to us in his service and love. And the Apostle concludes, saying, 'Therefore he is the mediator of a new covenant.' Our Redeemer, captivated by his boundless love for us, chose to rescue us, at the cost of his blood, from eternal death; and he succeeded in doing so, for if we serve him faithfully until we die we shall obtain from the Lord forgiveness and eternal life. Such were the terms of the testament, mediation or compact between Jesus Christ and God" (*Reflections on the Passion*, 9, 2).

9:15–17. As the RSV note points out the Greek word can be translated as either "covenant" or "will". The context and the parallel with the covenant of Sinai suggest the idea of covenant or pact, since the covenant with the chosen people was an unilateral pact, that is, a concession granted by God; however, it too can also be taken in a broad sense as a "will". Both the word "mediator" and the word "testator" (the one who makes the will) applied here to Christ serve to emphasize that his death needed to involve the shedding of blood. His is a death whereby we are called to "receive the promised eternal inheritance": "The work of our Redemption has been accomplished. We are now children of God, because Jesus has died for us and his death has ransomed us. *Empti enim estis pretio magno!* (1 Cor 6:20), you and I have been bought at a great price.

"We must bring into our life, to make them our own, the life and death of Christ. We must die through mortification and penance, so that Christ may live in us through Love. And then follow in the footsteps of Christ, with a zeal to coredeem all mankind" (St Josemaría Escrivá, *The Way of the Cross*, XIV).

9:18–22. The shedding of Christ's blood was necessary for the ratification of the New Covenant, just as the shedding of blood was needed for that of the Sinai covenant. Moses' action following on his

---

u. The Greek word here used means both *covenant* and *will*

solemn dialogue with God is described here in more detail than in the Exodus 24 account, probably following a Jewish oral tradition. Verse 22 gives the reason why Moses sprinkled the book of the Law, the people, the tabernacle and the ritual vessels: he did so to purify them; it is formulating a very important principle, which rounds off the whole point being made in this chapter—that the shedding of blood is needed for purification and for forgiveness of sins.

Although the Old Testament had "purifications" carried out with water, fire or cereal offerings—for example, cleansing from leprosy and from legal uncleanness (cf. Lev 22:6; 14:1ff), or the purification of booty captured from idolators (cf. Num 31:22–23)—in keeping with the Law (cf. Lev 17:11) almost everything was purified with blood in the sense that the sprinkling or anointing which the high priest carried out implied involvement in the essential act of sacrifice—the shedding of blood.

The Jews thought that the principle of life resided in blood, because no one could live without blood. Life and blood were taken as almost identical, and therefore God, the Lord of Life, was also the only owner of the blood. Hence the prohibition, in the Law of Moses, on eating food with blood in it: when a sacrifice was offered, the blood of the victim was reserved to Yahweh. Since many types of purification were done by blood offerings, the text says that "almost everything is purified by blood".

In the case of the simpler types of purification, sprinkling with blood was the most perfect but not the only method; but when it was a matter of obtaining "forgiveness" of sins and not just legal purification, the only recourse was a blood offering. That is why the rabbis used to say, "There is no atonement without blood". It is true that the Old Testament does speak of sins being forgiven through almsgiving (cf. Tob 4:8–11; 12:9; Dan 4:27), fasting, prayers and other penitential practices, but it is referring to attitudes which express repentance. These attitudes or dispositions would have been ineffective were they not accompanied by worship of the true God by means of sacrifice. In fact both blood sacrifices and interior sacrifices (fasting and penance) were all orientated towards the ultimate sacrifice—the shedding of Christ's blood. Therefore, the principle enunciated by the rabbis, which is the background to v. 22, finds its perfect fulfilment only in Christ's sacrifice: without the shedding of his blood, there is no forgiveness of sin.

"In our case it was Christ, not Moses, who sprinkled us with blood, through the words he spoke: 'This is the blood of the new covenant for the forgiveness of sins.' By these words, not by hyssop smeared by blood, did he sprinkle all. Previously, people's bodies were cleansed externally, because it was a matter of physical purification; whereas now, since the cleansing is spiritual, it penetrates the soul and purifies it, not by mere sprinkling but, as it were, by a fount which wells up in our souls" (St John Chrysostom, *Hom. on Heb*, 16).

The shedding of Christ's blood is in some way renewed when any sacrament is being administered, particularly so at the eucharistic consecration when the priest repeats the words of consecration, "this is the cup of my blood, the blood of the new and everlasting covenant. It will be shed for you and for all so that sins may be forgiven". Therefore, the Church, in awe at the efficacy of Christ's sacrifice, commemorates his passion in these words: "But when thirty years were over, / time had made that fame mature; / now, his long-predestined passion / Christ will

Hebrews 9:19

^{Ex 24:3-8}
^{Lev 14:4}
^{Num 19:6}

^{Ex 24:8}
^{Mt 26:28}
^{Heb 7:22}

^{Lev 8:15, 19}
^{Ex 40:9; Lev 17:11; Eph 1:7}

^{Heb 8:5}

without blood. ¹⁹For when every commandment of the law had been declared by Moses to all the people, he took the blood of calves and goats, with water and scarlet wool and hyssop, and sprinkled both the book itself and all the people, ²⁰saying, "This is the blood of the covenant which God commanded you." ²¹And in the same way he sprinkled with the blood both the tent^p and all the vessels used in worship. ²²Indeed, under the law almost everything is purified with blood, and without the shedding of blood there is no forgiveness of sins.

²³Thus it was necessary for the copies of the heavenly things to be purified with these rites, but the heavenly things themselves

---

willingly endure: / on the cross the Lamb is lifted— / Lo! the Victim they secure. / Of the gall he drinks, out-wearied, / thorns and nails and spear have vied, / till the blood and water issue / from his gentle riven side: / earth, sea, stars, yea all creation / lave them in that cleansing tide" (*Divine office*, Hymn at lauds in Passiontide, trs. Fitzpatrick).

9:23–28. In these verses the sacred writer adds some additional considerations to the main line of his argument. His thought centres on linking the sanctuary, the sacrifices which were offered in the Old Testament sanctuary, and the sacrifice of the New Covenant. It was "necessary" for Christ to shed his blood so that men might "receive the promised eternal inheritance" (9:15), that is, forgiveness of their sins (cf. 9:14). This shedding of blood is also necessary for the "purification" of the heavenly things (9:23). The sacrifices of the Mosaic liturgy purified the things of the old sanctuary and, in some way, pointed to forgiveness of sins (9:9, 10). The sacrifice of Christ, on the other hand, really does blot out sin and opens for us the way to heaven itself, giving us entry into that new sanctuary (7:25; 9:12). But the parallel is not a perfect one, for the old sacrifices were multiple and were constantly repeated in petition of forgiveness (9:25). The sacrifice of Christ, on the contrary, is a unique sacrifice, because it is eternally effective (7:27; 9:12). Moreover, whereas the high priest offered a sacrifice not with his own blood but with the blood of animals, Christ offered his own blood in sacrifice. Therefore, Christ has offered himself "once" (7:28; 9:12, 26, 28) in the same sort of way as every man has to die only once and then undergoes judgment. Furthermore, through his sacrifice Christ has passed through the heavens once and for all and will not return to earth to renew his sacrifice. He will not return until the end of time, when he will come in glory.

Two truths interweave here a number of times. The first is that Christ entered forever not into a temple made by man but into heaven itself (9:24; 7:26; 8:1). The second is that Christ also enables us to enter into glory; that is, his sacrifice and his entry into heaven enable man to attain his last end.

9:23. The text might seem to be saying that the heavenly sanctuary, like the Mosaic sanctuary, also needs purification. However, it is impossible for heavenly things to need purification from any stain or imperfection. This has led to many different interpretations being offered to

p. Or *tabernacle*

with better sacrifices than these. ²⁴For Christ has entered, not into a sanctuary made with hands, a copy of the true one, but into heaven itself, now to appear in the presence of God on our behalf. ²⁵Nor was it to offer himself repeatedly, as the high priest enters the Holy Place yearly with blood not his own; ²⁶for then he would have had to suffer repeatedly since the foundation of the world.

1 Cor 10:6, 11
Gal 4:4
1 Pet 1:20
Heb 12
1 Jn 3:5

---

explain what the purification mentioned here means. Some have seen the "heavenly things" as referring to the Church on earth, an as yet imperfect image of the Church in heaven and still in need of purification. Others see them as referring to the Church in heaven, the Church triumphant, in the sense that it has to purify sinners so as to be able to receive them into its bosom and destroy the roots of evil. St Thomas interprets the text as referring to the abolition of impediments to entry to the sanctuary. Men need to be purified of sin in order to enter heaven.

The words "heavenly things" seem to refer to the dedication or inauguration of heaven—conceived as a sanctuary, where God has his dwelling-place—with the blood of Christ. The old sanctuary was inaugurated and dedicated by a large number of blood sacrifices (cf. 1 Kings 8:62–64; 1 Mac 4:52–56). The new worship in the heavenly sanctuary cannot begin without the shedding of Christ's blood. Although the Christian has access to the sanctuary which Christ has inaugurated, he needs to remember that because it is so great and so perfect he cannot enter it if he has any stain or imperfection. Therefore, God has established that the souls of those who die in his friendship but who are not completely free from venial sin, are to be cleansed in purgatory. "To that [the beatific] vision no rational creature can be elevated unless it be thoroughly and entirely purified [...]. But it does at times happen that such purification is not entirely perfected in this life; one remains a debtor for the punishment [...]. Nevertheless, he is not entirely cut off from the reward, because such things can happen without mortal sin, which alone takes away the charity to which the reward of eternal life is due [...]. They must, then, be purged after this life before they achieve the final reward" (St Thomas Aquinas, *Summa contra gentiles*, 4, 91, 6).

9:24. By his glorious ascension into heaven Jesus Christ crowns his redemptive sacrifice and thenceforth intercedes for us as our advocate in the presence of God the Father (cf. Heb 4:14; 7:25; 8:1; 9:11–12). "What is this the Apostle is saying here about its being fitting that Christ, after suffering on our behalf, should go up into heaven and sit at the right hand of the Father, appearing before the face of God? What is this, Lord? He had to do this for us so that he could stand before the Father's house and show him his wounds and his sufferings, and say to him, 'Eternal Father, if you truly love me, so also truly love those whom I gave birth to and for whom I have laboured'" (St John of Avila, *Sermon 31 on Whit Monday*).

9:25–26. Between the sacrifices of the Old Covenant and the sacrifice of Christ there are numerous points of contact and a degree of continuity, for the former are a foreshadowing of the latter. However, there are also substantial differences: the sacrifices of the Mosaic Law were mul-

> Gen 3:19
> Is 53:12
> Heb 10:12, 14
> 1 Tim 6:14
>
> But as it is, he has appeared once for all at the end of the age to put away sin by the sacrifice of himself. ²⁷And just as it is appointed for men to die once, and after that comes judgment, ²⁸so

tiple, Christ's sacrifice was unique; the Mosaic sacrifices did not really have the power to forgive sins, Christ's sacrifice does; the Mosaic ones were done with the blood of animals, Christ shed his own blood; the Mosaic ones belong to the time of waiting and preparation, Christ's sacrifice marks the beginning of "the fullness of time" (cf. Mt 13:40–49; 24:3; 28:20; 1 Cor 10:11; Gal 4:4; Eph 1:10).

On the excellence of Christ's sacrifice over those of the Old Law, a further short proof is added, similar to that used in 8:3–5: if Christ's sacrifice consists essentially in his passion, and if the passion did not have the power to forgive all past, present and future sins, it would have had to be repeated, but that would be absurd, for Christ could die only once; therefore, Christ's sacrifice, offered once for all, is infinitely efficacious.

The celebration of the sacrifice of the Mass is not at odds therefore with the efficacy and unicity of the sacrifice of Christ, because the Mass is not a new sacrifice involving the shedding of blood, a numerical repetition of the sacrifice of the cross: it is an unbloody renewal of that sacrifice, to apply its infinite efficacy. "It is one and the same victim—he who now makes the offering through the ministry of priests and he who then offered himself on the cross; the only difference is in the manner of the offering" (Council of Trent, *De SS. Missae sacrificio*, chap. 2), since the sacrifice of Calvary was a blood sacrifice whereas the Mass is an unbloody sacrifice; "a commemorative showing forth of the death which took place in reality on Calvary is repeated in each Mass, because by distinct representations Christ Jesus is signified and shown forth in the state of victim" (Pius XII, *Mediator Dei*, 20).

The Mass, then, receives all its efficacy from Christ's death on the cross, and applies that sacrifice in time and space.

"Among the instruments for distributing to believers the merits that flow from the cross of the divine Redeemer, the august sacrifice of the altar is pre-eminent: 'As often as the commemoration of this victim is celebrated, the work of our Redemption is performed' (*Roman Missal*, 9th Sunday after Pentecost). This in no way derogates from the dignity of the sacrifice of the Cross; on the contrary, it is a clear proof—as the Council of Trent asserts—of its greatness and necessity. The daily immolation is a reminder to us that there is no salvation but in the cross of our Lord Jesus Christ (cf. Gal 6:14) and that the reason why God wills the continuation of this sacrifice 'from the rising of the sun to its setting' (Mal 1:11) is in order that there may be no pause in that hymn of praise and thanksgiving. This is a debt which men owe and to their Creator precisely because they stand in constant need of his help, and in constant need of the divine Redeemer's blood to destroy the sins that call for just retribution" (*Mediator Dei*, 21).

9:27–28. These verses look at three basic truths of Christian belief about the last things—1) the immutable decree of death; 2) the fact that there is a judgment immediately after death; 3) the second coming of Christ, in glory.

"Not to deal with sin": this phrase means that the second coming of Christ, or Parousia, will not be for the purpose of redeeming men from sin but rather to

Hebrews 9:28

Christ, having been offered once to bear the sins of many, will appear a second time, not to deal with sin but to save those who are eagerly waiting for him.

Phil 3:20
1 Pet 2:24

---

bring salvation, that is, glory, to those who placed their hope in him. Christ will come into the world for a second time, but not as Redeemer, for his sacrifice has already eliminated sin once for all; rather, he will come as Judge of all. His coming "is appointed": it is as necessary as death and judgment. These three truths are closely interconnected.

Although man is mortal, "a spiritual element survives and subsists after death, an element endowed with consciousness and will, so that the 'human self' subsists. To designate this element, the Church uses the word 'soul', the accepted term in the usage of Scripture and Tradition" (SCDF, *Letter on Certain Questions concerning Eschatology*, 17 May 1979).

Man, then, is made up of a spiritual and immortal soul and a corruptible body. However, when God originally endowed man with supernatural grace, he gave him additional gifts, the so-called "preternatural" gifts, which included bodily immortality. Adam's disobedience resulted in the loss of his friendship with God and the loss of this preternatural gift. From that point onwards death is "the wages of sin" (Rom 6:23), and it is to this divine decision that the text refers when it says that it "is appointed for men to die" (cf. Gen 3:19, 23; Rom 5:12). The Church has repeatedly stressed that death is a punishment; cf., for example, Pius VI, *Auctorem fidei*, prop. 1, 7: "in our present state (death) is inflicted as a just punishment for sin"; immortality was an "unmerited gift and not a natural condition". Verses 27–28 are an implicit exhortation to watchfullness (cf. also 1 Cor 7:29; Sir 14:12; and *Lumen gentium*, 48).

Immediately after death everyone will be judged on the conduct of his life. All "are to give an account of their lives; those who have done good deeds will go into eternal life; those who have done evil will go into everlasting fire" (*Athanasian Creed*). This is something which reason with the help of God's Word can discover, because people with a correct moral sense realize that good deserves to be rewarded and evil punished, and that it is impossible for this to occur completely in this life. It is difficult to say whether Hebrews 9:27 is referring to the "particular judgment", which happens immediately after death, or to the general judgment, which will take place on the last day. Both interpretations can be supported, for the judgment the verse refers to is connected, on the one hand, with death, and on the other with the second coming of Christ. In any event, it is clear that what is meant is a "personal" judgment, a trial at which each individual will be judged by Christ (cf. 2 Cor 5:10; Rom 14:10). The existence of a general judgment does not conflict with the certainty that there is a particular judgment, for the Church, in line with Holy Scripture, although it awaits the glorious revealing of our Lord Jesus Christ on the last day, sees that event as distinct from and separate in time from the judgment which every individual will undergo immediately after death (cf. *Letter on Eschatology*, op. cit.).

The idea of death and judgment, however, should not only inspire fear; it should also lead us to hope in Christ, for our Lord will come a second time to show himself a merciful judge to "those who are eagerly waiting for him".

Christians, therefore, combine their joyful hope in the establishment of the Kingdom of God, which they whole-

Hebrews 10:1

The sacrifices of the Old Covenant could not take away sins

Col 2:17
Heb 7:19; 8:5

10 ¹For since the law has but a shadow of the good things to come instead of the true form of these realities, it can never, by the same sacrifices which are continually offered year after year, make perfect those who draw near.* ²Otherwise, would they

---

heartedly desire, with a desire to make the best possible use of the time allotted to them in this life. "This urgent solicitude of the Church, the Spouse of Christ, for the needs of men—for their joys and hopes, their griefs and labours—is nothing other than her intense desire to share them in full, in order to illuminate men with the light of Christ and to gather together and unite all in him who alone is the Saviour of each one of them. This solicitude must never be taken to mean that the Church conforms herself to the things of this world, or that her longing for the coming of her Lord and his eternal reign grows cold" (Paul VI, *Creed of the People of God*).

10:1. The sacred writer once more compares the Old Testament sacrifices with the sacrifice of Christ (cf. 7:27; 9:9–10, 12–13), examining them now from the point of view of their efficacy.

The Law is "a shadow", that is, something without substance. The term used to be employed by artists to describe the first sketch on a canvas, a bare outline before the application of colour. Thus, the Old Law in relation to the New Testament is like a first sketch as compared with the finished painting. However, because it speaks of the New Testament as "the true form of these realities", it allows us to see the New Covenant as not yet giving possession of these "good things to come", but as being a kind of anticipation of them, a reflection of them. Yet it is a true, a faithful, reflection, insofar as the New Law already has the power to forgive sins and to link men with God through charity. "The New Law", St Thomas says, "represents the good things to come more clearly than does the Old. Firstly, because in the words of the New Testament express mention is made of the good things to come and the promise, whereas in the Old reference is made only to material good things. Secondly, because the New Testament draws its strength from charity, which is the fullness of the Law. And this charity, even if it be imperfect, is similar to Christ's charity by virtue of the faith to which it is joined. That is why the new law is called the 'law of love'. And that is also why it is called the 'true form', because it has imprinted on it the image of the good things to come" (*Commentary on Heb*, ad loc.).

Moreover, an image, to some degree at least, coincides with the reality it reflects: Christ himself, for example, is the image of God. Therefore, "in Christ one already possesses, in a permanent way, these good things of heaven—both the present ones and the future ones" (Chrysostom, *Hom. on Heb*, ad loc.).

10:2–4. These verses repeat and complete what is said in v. 1 and in 9:12–13. "Tell me, then, what is the point of having more victims and more sacrifices when a single victim would suffice for atonement for sins [...]. Multiple sacrifices in effect show that the Jews needed to atone for their sins because they had failed to find forgiveness: it points to the inefficacy of the victims offered, rather than to their power" (Chrysostom, *Hom. on Heb*, 17). The ultimate reason for this inefficacy is

not have ceased to be offered? If the worshippers had once been cleansed, they would no longer have any consciousness of sin. ³But in these sacrifices there is a reminder of sin year after year. ⁴For it is impossible that the blood of bulls and goats should take away sins.

Num 5:15, LXX
Is 1:11

Christ's offering of himself has infinite value
⁵Consequently, when Christ^v came into the world, he said,
  "Sacrifices and offerings thou hast not desired,
   but a body hast thou prepared for me;
  ⁶ in burnt offerings and sin offerings thou hast taken no
    pleasure.

Ps 40:7–9

---

explained by a striking statement: "It is impossible that the blood of bulls and goats should take away sins" (v. 4). There is here an echo of those proclamations of the prophets which reminded the people that true purification comes not from external actions but from conversion of heart (cf. Jer 2:22; 4:14; 11:15; Mic 6:7–8; Ps 51:18–19; etc.).

And yet, is it not the case that the priests of the New Testament renew Jesus' sacrifice in the Mass every day? St John Chrysostom answers: "Yes, that is true, but not because we regard the original sacrifice, Christ's sacrifice, as ineffective or impotent. We priests repeat it to commemorate his death. We have but one victim, Christ—not many victims [...]. There is but one and the same sacrifice [...], one Christ whole and entire, here as elsewhere, the same everywhere—the same Christ on all the altars. Just as Jesus Christ, although offered in different places, has only one body, so everywhere there is but one sacrifice [...]. What we do is a commemoration of Christ's offering, for at the Supper he said, 'Do this in memory of me.' Therefore, we do not offer, as the high priest of the Law did, a new, additional, victim: it is not one sacrifice more, but always the same one" (*Hom. on Heb*, 17).

v. Greek *he*

The Mass "is the sacrifice of Christ, offered to the Father with the cooperation of the Holy Spirit—an offering of infinite value, which perpetuates the work of the Redemption in us and surpasses the sacrifices of the Old Law. The holy Mass brings us face to face with one of the central mysteries of our faith, because it is the gift of the Blessed Trinity to the Church. It is because of this that we can consider the Mass as the centre and the source of a Christian's spiritual life. It is the final end of all the sacraments" (St Josemaría Escrivá, *Christ Is Passing By*, 86–87).

10:5–10. This passage carries a quotation from Psalm 40:7–8, but one taken from the Greek translation, the Septuagint, not from the Hebrew. Where the Hebrew says, "thou hast opened my ears", the Greek reads, "a body thou hast prepared for me". The difference is not substantial, because the Hebrew expression points to the docility and obedience of the speaker, who is the Messiah himself. The Greek translation gives the sentence a more general meaning: God has not only opened the ears of the Messiah; he has given him life as a man (cf. Phil 2:7). The words of this psalm "allow us as it were to sound the unfathomable depths of this

Hebrews 10:7

⁷ Then I said, 'Lo, I have come to do thy will, O God,' as it is written of me in the roll of the book."

⁸When he said above, "Thou hast neither desired nor taken pleasure in sacrifices and offerings and burnt offerings and sin offerings" (these are offered according to the law), ⁹then he added, "Lo, I have come to do thy will." He abolishes the first in order to establish the second. ¹⁰And by that will we have been sanctified through the offering of the body of Jesus Christ once for all.

¹¹And every priest stands daily at his service, offering repeatedly the same sacrifices, which can never take away sins. ¹²But

1 Sam 15:22
Jn 6:38
Heb 9:14, 28
Eph 5:2

Heb 10:1–4
Deut 10:8

---

self-abasement of the Word, his humiliation of himself for love of men even to death on the cross [...]. Why this obedience, this self-abasement, this suffering? The Creed gives us the answer: 'for us men and for our salvation' Jesus came down from heaven so as to give man full entitlement to ascend (to heaven) and by becoming a son in the Son to regain the dignity he lost through sin [...]. Let us welcome Him. Let us say to him, 'Here I am; I have come to do your will'" (John Paul II, *General Audience*, 25 March 1981).

The author of the letter, elaborating on the text of the psalm, asserts that the Messiah's sacrifice is greater than the sacrifices of the Old Law, unbloody as well as bloody, sin-offerings as well as burnt offerings as they were called in the liturgy (cf. Lev 5:6; 7:27). The sacrifice of Christ, who has "come into the world", has replaced both kinds of ancient sacrifice. It consisted in perfectly doing the will of his Father (cf. Jn 4:34; 6:38; 8:29; 14:31), even though he was required to give his life to the point of dying on Calvary (Mt 26:42; Jn 10:18; Heb 5:7–9). Christ "came into the world" to offer himself up to suffering and death for the redemption of the world. "He knew that all the sacrifices of goats and bulls offered to God in ancient times were incapable of making satisfaction for the sins of men; he knew that a divine person was needed to do that [...]. My Father (Jesus Christ said), all the victims offered you up to this are not enough and never will be enough to satisfy your justice; you gave me a body capable of experiencing suffering, so that you might be placated by the shedding of my blood, and men thereby saved; '*ecce venio*, here I am, ready'; I accept everything and in all things do I submit to your will. The lower part of his human nature naturally felt repugnance and reacted against living and dying in so much pain and opprobrium, but its rational part, which was fully subject to the Father's will, had the upper hand; it accepted everything, and therefore Jesus Christ began to suffer, from that point onwards, all the anguish and pain which he would undergo in the course of his life. That is how our divine Redeemer acted from the very first moments of his coming into the world. So, how should we behave towards Jesus when, come to the use of reason, we begin to know the sacred mysteries of Redemption through the light of faith?" (St Alphonsus, *Meditations for Advent*, 2, 5).

The psalm speaks of "the roll of the book": this may refer to a specific book or else to the Old Testament in general (cf. Lk 24:27; Jn 5:39, 46, 47).

10:11–14. Teaching given elsewhere in the letter (8:5; 9:9–10, 12–13, 25; 10:1–4)

when Christ[w] had offered for all time a single sacrifice for sins, he sat down at the right hand of God, ¹³then to wait until his enemies should be made a stool for his feet. ¹⁴For by a single offering he has perfected for all time those who are sanctified. ¹⁵And the Holy Spirit also bears witness to us; for after saying,

¹⁶ "This is the covenant that I will make with them
after those days, says the Lord:
I will put my laws on their hearts,
and write them on their minds,"
¹⁷ then he adds,
"I will remember their sins and their misdeeds no more."
¹⁸ Where there is forgiveness of these, there is no longer any offering for sin.

Ps 110:1
Acts 2:33
Mt 22:44

Jn 17:19

Heb 8:10
Jer 31:33

Heb 8:12
Jer 31:34

---

is now reiterated in order to show the universal efficacy of Christ's sacrifice. However, here it is expounded by comparing the posture of the Old Testament priests with that of Christ. They did in fact have to *stand* in the presence of Yahweh, offering victims repeatedly. Standing was the correct posture for servants and employees. The reference is to Old Testament priests who repeatedly, every day, went through the same motions and offered the same sacrifices. By contrast, Christ, as is stated in Psalm 110:1, after his Ascension is *seated* at the right hand of God the Father (see notes on Mt 16:19 and Heb 1:3). In addition to conveying the idea of repose and rest, being seated would be equivalent to receiving royal investiture or to exercising authority (cf. Heb 7:26; 8:1); also, a king's chief minister or heir used to sit on the right of the king, as in a place of special honour (cf. Mt 26:24; Mk 14:62; Lk 26:69); and it might be pointed out that David pitched his tent to the right of the tabernacle: cf. 2 Sam 7:18). What has happened is that by virtue of the efficacy of his single sacrifice, Christ has taken possession of heaven for ever more and has merited royal dignity; all that remains to happen, and it shall happen, is for all his enemies to submit to him (cf. 1 Cor 15:25–28). So fruitful is his sacrifice that those who take part in it, "those who have been sanctified", are thereby perfected: they obtain forgiveness of sins, purity of conscience, access to and union with God. In other words, the source of holiness in men is the sacrifice of Calvary.

10:15–18. The last proof of the superiority of Christ's sacrifice for the forgiveness of sins is based on this passage of Jeremiah 31:33–34, already quoted in 8:10–12. The letter is insisting on the spiritual character of the New Covenant —ratified with the blood of Christ—which is impressed on the hearts and minds of men. And it is also emphasizing the effects of this Covenant—forgiveness of sins by God.

---

w. Greek *this one*

PART TWO

Faith and perseverance in faith

5. A CALL FOR LOYALTY

Motives for staying loyal to Christ

Jn 14:6
Heb 6:19ff; 9:8, 11f

¹⁹Therefore, brethren, since we have confidence to enter the sanctuary by the blood of Jesus, ²⁰by the new and living way

10:19–21. Throughout the letter there is a constant interweaving of dogmatic and moral considerations, with the former points often giving rise to exhortations to the faithful to be unwavering in faith and hope. The letter now moves on from its theological reflections on Christ's priesthood to its practical application in the Christian life: the Christian should put his trust in the efficacy of Christ's sacrifice, and through faith, hope and charity associate himself with Christ's priesthood. He should do this for three reasons —the redemptive value of the blood of Jesus, the access to glory signified by his entry into the sanctuary of heaven, and Christ's enthronement at the right hand of the Father. The sprinkling of the blood of Christ gives the believer full assurance that he too will enter heaven, because the paschal mystery of Christ—his passion, death and resurrection—has made this possible.

"The new and living way": a translation of the original Greek expression, which literally reads "the recently sacrificed and living way"; this is a metaphorical expression indicating that Christ is a way, and that this way has been recently opened up, has been sacrificed and is alive. There is, then, a personification of "way" which recalls what Jesus said about his being "the way, and the truth, and the life" (Jn 14:6); and there is also a reference to Christ's sacrifice, to the fact that his body did not experience corruption and that he lives for ever (cf. Heb 7:25).

The *Pius V Catechism*, referring to the benefits brought us by Christ's passion, specifies how he opened to us the gates of heaven, closed due to mankind's sin: "Nor are we without a type and figure of this mystery in the Old Law. For those who were prohibited to return into their native country before the death of the high priest (cf. Num 35:25) typified that no one, however just and holy may have been his life, could gain admission into the celestial country until the eternal High Priest, Jesus Christ, had died, and by his death immediately opened heaven to those who, purified by the sacraments and gifted with faith, hope and charity, become partakers of his passion" (1, 5, 14).

The reference to Christ's flesh as a "curtain" not only recalls the curtain in the temple separating the Holy of Holies from the rest of the sanctuary, but also points to the fact that the deepest dimension of Christ is his Godhead, in which the Christian must believe, but without separating it from his humanity. Christ's human nature is at the same time a "way" because it reveals his divinity, and a "curtain" because it masks it. "Just as the priest (of the Old Law) entered the Holy of Holies, so too if we want to enter holy

which he opened for us through the curtain, that is, through his flesh, ²¹and since we have a great priest over the house of God, ²²let us draw near with a true heart in full assurance of faith, with our hearts sprinkled clean from an evil conscience and our bodies washed with pure water. ²³Let us hold fast the confession of our hope without wavering, for he who promised is faithful; ²⁴and let us consider how to stir up one another to love and good works, ²⁵not neglecting to meet together, as is the habit of some, but encouraging one another, and all the more as you see the Day drawing near.

Zech 6:11ff
Eph 5:26; Ezek 36:25; Heb 3:6; 4:16; Rom 6:4
Heb 4:14
Heb 3:13
2 Thess 2:1
Jas 2:2

---

glory, we must enter by way of Christ's flesh, the curtain (concealing) his divinity [...]. For, faith in the one God is insufficient if one does not have faith in the Incarnation" (St Thomas Aquinas, *Commentary on Heb*, ad loc.).

10:22–25. The letter now exhorts its readers to purity of heart, steadfastness in faith and mutual charity.

It speaks of a clean heart, recalling the purity which the water of Baptism brings. The Christian should stay true to the faith he received and professed at Baptism, and maintain the purity which it brings. To live in this way the baptized should count on the help provided by the Church and on the grace God continually gives. As Vatican I teaches, referring to those who have received the light of faith, "God does not abandon them, unless he is abandoned [...]. Therefore, the position of those who have embraced Catholic truth by the heavenly gift of faith, and of those who have been misled by human opinions and follow a false religion is by no means the same, for the former, who have accepted the faith under the teaching authority of the Church, can never have just reason for changing that faith or calling it into question" (*Dei Filius*, chap. 3).

Along with its exhortation to practise the three theological virtues, the passage includes a call not to neglect to attend Christian assemblies. We know that the first Christians were expected to come together daily or weekly (cf. Acts 2:46; 20:7) and, as we can see here, some gave up going to those meetings through carelessness, or because they preferred private to public prayer, or because they did not want others to know they were Christians. In Judaism much emphasis was placed on the duty to attend synagogue meetings. The meetings referred to in this passage, whether for the celebration of the Christian liturgy or for instruction in apostolic teaching, had a clearly eschatological focus in the sense that they built up people's hope in the coming of our Lord (cf. 1 Thess 5:4; 1 Cor 3:13; Rom 13:12; Phil 4:5; Jas 5:8; 1 Pet 4:7). The author's insistence on the need to meet together recalls another exhortation which goes back to the early Church: "Now that you are members of Christ, do not choose to cut yourselves off from the Church by failing to attend the assembly; having Christ your head present and in touch with you, as he promised, do not underestimate yourselves or choose to separate the Saviour from his members, or divide or scatter his body, or give your everyday needs more importance than the Word of God; rather, on the Lord's Day leave everything aside and come to the Church" (*Didache*). On the basis of the apostolic tradition, the Church has established a grave obligation to attend Mass

Hebrews 10:26

Heb 6:4–8; 12:17
2 Tim 3:7; 2 Pet
2:21; Is 26:11,
LXX
Num 35:30
Deut 17:6

²⁶For if we sin deliberately after receiving the knowledge of the truth, there no longer remains a sacrifice for sins, ²⁷but a fearful prospect of judgment, and a fury of fire which will consume the adversaries. ²⁸A man who has violated the law of Moses dies without mercy at the testimony of two or three witnesses. ²⁹How

on Sundays (cf. *Code of Canon Law*, can. 1247). "On this day Christ's faithful are bound to come together into one place. They should listen to the word of God and take part in the Eucharist, thus calling to mind the passion, resurrection and glory of the Lord Jesus and giving thanks to God, 'who has begotten them anew to a living hope through the resurrection of Jesus Christ from the dead' (1 Pet 1:3)" (Vatican II, *Sacrosanctum Concilium*, 106).

In the same way—by listening to and meditating on the Word of God—Christians fulfil their equally serious obligation to improve their understanding of Christian doctrine.

10:26–31. This passage is not saying that there are some sins that are unforgivable (cf. Heb 6:4–6), as early rigorists taught. The Church has received from her divine Redeemer the power to forgive all sins, no matter how grave (cf. Mt 18:18; Jn 20:18–20). Pope St Gelasius I explained this as follows: "So, there is no sin for whose forgiveness the Church does not pray; no sin which, by virtue of the God-given power it has, that cannot be forgiven; for it was (the Church) that was told, 'If you forgive the sins of any ...' (cf. Jn 20:23); 'whatever you loose on earth shall be loosed in heaven' (Mt 18:18). The word 'whatever' covers everything, no matter how grave the sins be, or what kind they be. That view is correct which argues that there is to be no forgiveness for him who persists in committing sins; but that does not apply to one who later repents of them" (*Ne forte*, 4). The letter speaks of "deliberate" sins, sins a person commits knowing that they are sins and consenting in them *and* acting maliciously; that is, fully deliberate sins—what the Old Testament calls "acting presumptuously" (cf. Deut 17:12; 18:22). Because the sinner is pertinacious, in practice there is no hope of his repenting. It is similar to what is called in the Gospel "speaking against [or blaspheming] the Holy Spirit" (cf. Mt 12:32 and note): "'blasphemy' does not properly consist in offending against the Holy Spirit in words; it consists rather *in the refusal to accept the salvation which God offers to man through the Holy Spirit*, working through the power of the Cross. If man rejects the 'convincing concerning sin' which comes from the Holy Spirit and which has the power to save, he also rejects the 'coming' of the Counsellor—that 'coming' which was accomplished in the Paschal Mystery, in union with the redemptive power of Christ's blood—the blood which 'purifies the conscience from dead works'" (John Paul II, *Dominum et Vivificantem*, 46).

Specifically, the writer seems to be referring to Christian apostates who had already received "the knowledge of the truth", which may mean instruction prior to Baptism and reception of the Eucharist; no part of Christ's redeeming sacrifice can help people in that position, because they have deliberately and explicitly rejected Redemption. All they can look forward to is condemnation when God comes to judge them, and punishment by fire (cf. the fate of Korah, Dathan and Abiram: Num 16:16–35). Punishment by

much worse punishment do you think will be deserved by the man who has spurned the Son of God, and profaned the blood of the covenant by which he was sanctified, and outraged the Spirit of grace? ³⁰For we know him who said, "Vengeance is mine, I will repay." And again, "The Lord will judge his people." ³¹It is a fearful thing to fall into the hands of the living God.

Heb 2:3; 6:6;
9:20; Ex 24:8
Deut 32:35f
Ps 135:14
Rom 12:19
Mt 10:28

---

fire is also something often proclaimed by the prophets as a part of divine justice on the day of Yahweh (cf. Is 66:24). The fire referred to here has to do not only with God's fury but with eternal torment (cf. Mk 9:47–49; Rev 11:5).

To emphasize the gravity of the sin of apostasy, which outrages the Holy Spirit, profanes the redeeming sacrifice of Christ and shows contempt for the very Son of God, the letter recalls that under the Law of Moses, there were certain sins which on the evidence of two or three witnesses (cf. Deut 19:15–21), merited capital punishment. This was the case, for example, with fully conscious deliberate and scandalous sins (cf. Num 15:30–31), blasphemy (Lev 24:13–16), adultery, incest, sodomy, bestiality, murder, idolatry and prophecy in the name of other gods. If sinners who committed such sins did not deserve "remission", obstinate apostates deserve it less.

Some commentators see this passage as also saying that there cannot be second baptism, contrary to the position taken by certain heretics.

10:31. This verse rounds off an entire passage designed to inspire horror of deliberate grave sin and to encourage Christians to have a holy fear of God. This fear includes, firstly, fear of eternal punishment and a sense of shame at the moral ugliness of sin, which are characteristics of attrition. But it can also include other dispositions which are proper to contrition, to the extent that one's fear is motivated by a sense of the outrage done to Christ, who suffered out of love for us; in which case love and fear are linked; in fact, the right kind of fear is filial fear, that of someone who is afraid of offending his father. Sorrow for having offended our heavenly Father is one of the key features of the Law of Christ.

"There are two motives which lead a person to do good and avoid evil. The first is fear. The motive that first leads a person to avoid sin is the thought of the pains of hell and the Last Judgment [...]. It is true that a person who refrains from sinning simply out of fear is not just; but that is where his justification begins. That is how the Law of Moses works to draw people away from sin and lead them to do good [...]. But this method, the method of fear, is inadequate; the Law promulgated by Moses was inadequate: it relied on that kind of fear to frustrate sin; although it did discourage a person from actually committing sin, it failed to purify his intentions. There is, however, another way to draw people away from sin and encourage them to act rightly—the way of love. That is the way followed by the Law of Christ, that is, the law of the Gospel, which is the law of love" (St Thomas Aquinas, *On the two commandments*, 1).

"'*Timor Domini sanctus*. The fear of God is holy.' Fear which is the veneration of a son for his Father; never a servile fear, for your Father-God is not a tyrant" (St Josemaría Escrivá, *The Way*, 435).

Hebrews 10:32

Heb 6:4
Eph 5:14
1 Cor 4:9
Phil 4:14
Heb 13:3
Mt 5:40; 6:20

Heb 11:6
Is 26:20, LXX

³²But recall the former days when, after you were enlightened, you endured a hard struggle with sufferings, ³³sometimes being publicly exposed to abuse and affliction, and sometimes being partners with those so treated. ³⁴For you had compassion on the prisoners, and you joyfully accepted the plundering of your property, since you knew that you yourselves had a better possession and an abiding one. ³⁵Therefore do not throw away your confidence, which has a great reward. ³⁶For you have need of

---

10:32–34. A Christian is called to share the persecution which Christ suffered. "A disciple is not above his teacher", our Lord said (cf. Mt 10:22–25; Lk 12:11–12; Jn 15:18); anyone who wanted to follow him would have to carry his cross (cf. Mt 10:38; 16:24; Mk 8:34; Lk 9:23; 14:27). These words of our Lord have always been borne out in practice. In the Acts of the Apostles we are told of how the Sanhedrin persecuted the apostles, and of how certain Jews acted against Stephen, and Herod against James and Peter, etc. The early Christians bore these afflictions bravely and even availed of them to spread the faith—first to Samaria, then to Antioch, and later throughout the whole Roman empire. The text here speaks of their courage. It may be thinking of the severe persecution instituted by Nero after the burning of Rome. Given these circumstances, the addressees, and Christians in general, need to keep their baptismal faith, their "enlightenment", intact: they should be mindful of "the former days" and copy those who compete and fight in public not minding that they are making a "public exhibition" of themselves (cf. 1 Cor 4:9).

Undoubtedly the persecution suffered by Christians who were converted from Judaism was severe. They were subject to "abuse" and "affliction", words which point to affronts, insults, ridicule, and treatment typical of religious persecution —confiscation of property, imprisonment and even flogging and other forms of punishment. Our early brethren in the faith not only bore these afflictions but also showed their solidarity and charity by generously sharing the suffering of those who were thrown in gaol.

And yet even these persecutions had very good effects (cf. 1 Pet 1:6–9; Jas 1:3–4), in that they helped the people concerned to be detached from material things and place their hope in divine rewards. In the same type of way, every Christian needs to face up to the difficulties and contradictions he experiences in life.

"Are things going against you? Are you going through a rough time? Say very slowly, as if relishing it, this powerful and manly prayer: 'May the most just and lovable will of God be done, be fulfilled, be praised and eternally exalted above all things. Amen. Amen.' I assure you that you will find peace" (St Josemaría Escrivá, *The Way*, 691).

10:35–39. The "confidence" mentioned in v. 35 is a translation of a Greek word which refers to the ease and trusting frankness with which a person addresses a good friend or God.

The sacred writer renews his call to endurance in the face of persecution. St John Chrysostom compares the situation of the Christians addressed in this letter with that of an athlete who has won a

endurance, so that you may do the will of God and receive what is promised. ³⁷ "For yet a little while, and the coming one shall come and shall not tarry; ³⁸ but my righteous one shall live by faith, and if he shrinks back, my soul has no pleasure in him." ³⁹ But we are not of those who shrink back and are destroyed, but of those who have faith and keep their souls.

Jn 14:19
Hab 2:3
Jas 5:8
Hab 2:4
Rom 1:17

1 Pet 1:9
1 Tim 6:9
1 Thess 5:9

The good example of the patriarchs

11 ¹Now faith is the assurance of things hoped for, the conviction of things not seen. ²For by it the men of old

Heb 3:14
Rom 1:16; 8:24

competition and is now simply waiting for the president of the games to award him the laurels. "From now on there is no further combat; all you must do is hold on to the merit you have won, and you will not lose your reward [...]. No further combat is called for: all that is necessary is perseverance. Just hold out and you will gain your laurels; you have already suffered all you need to obtain them—contentions, chains, pain, loss of property. What more could you have done? All that remains for you to do is wait patiently for the prize to be given you. If there is a delay, it will only be for a short while" (*Hom. on Heb*, ad loc.).

Here, as St Thomas comments, endurance refers to two things—the strength that enables one to stay loyal despite persecution, and the assurance of one who is confident of obtaining certain things he does not yet possess. The letter's exhortation to endurance is supported by two quotations from Sacred Scripture. The first, from Isaiah 26:20, is a reminder that God will soon judge the impious; the second from Habakkuk 2:3–4 (also quoted by St Paul in Rom 1:17; Gal 3:11), announces the coming liberation of the people of Israel. The sacred text accurately prophesied that those Jews who remained faithful to God would be released from captivity in Babylon and survive the experience. Moved by the Holy Spirit, the present writer states that the ancient prophecy has been fulfilled in Christ; he is "the coming one", that is, he will come a second time. Therefore, the Christian should await the outcome of persecution loyally and cheerfully. "Stand your ground like an anvil under the hammer. The mark of a true champion is to stand up to punishment and still come out victorious. It is our duty, particularly when the cause is God's, to accept trials of all kinds, if we ourselves are to be accepted by him" (St Ignatius of Antioch, *Letter to Polycarp*, 3, 1).

11:1. Although the text does not aim to provide a precise definition of faith, it does in fact very clearly describe the essence of that virtue, linking it to hope in future things and to certainty concerning supernatural truths. By means of faith, the believer acquires certainty concerning God's promises to man, and a firm conviction that he will obtain access to heaven. The Latin translates as "*substantia*" the word the RSV translates as "assurance"; *substantia*, which literally means "that which underlies", here refers to the solid basis provided by hope.

This verse indicates that faith, which is a type of knowledge, is different from other types of human knowledge. Thus, man can know things by direct evidence, by reasoned proof or by someone else's testimony. As regards knowledge based on information provided by someone else, that is, knowledge based on faith, we can distinguish two types—human faith, when it is another human being whose word one relies on (as in the case of pupil/teacher, child/parent), and supernatural faith (when the testimony comes from God himself, who is Supreme Truth). In this latter case the knowledge provided is most certain.

However, the object of supernatural faith, that is, *what* one believes in (God and the unchanging decrees of his will), is not something that is self-evident to man, nor is it something that can be attained by the use of unaided reason. That is why it is necessary for God himself to bear witness to what he reveals. Faith, then, is certain knowledge, but it is knowledge of things which are not self-evident, things which one does not see but which one can hope for.

The verse also says that faith is "conviction" concerning things not seen. It is therefore different from opinion, suspicion or doubt (none of which implies certainty). By saying that it has to do with things unseen, it is distinguishing faith from knowledge and intuitive cognition (cf. *Summa theologiae*, 2-2, 4, 1).

Summing up, we can say that "when God makes a revelation, we are obliged to render by faith a full submission of intellect and will. The faith, however, which is the beginning of human salvation, the catholic Church asserts to be a supernatural virtue whereby, with the inspiration and help of God's grace, we believe that what he has revealed is true —not because its intrinsic truth is seen by the natural light of reason, but because of the authority of God who reveals it, of God who can neither deceive nor be deceived" (Vatican I, *Dei Filius*, chap. 3).

It is, therefore, a feature of faith that it makes us *certain* about things which are not self-evident. That is why in order to believe one must want to believe, why the act of believing is always free and meritorious. However, faith can, with God's help, reach a certainty greater than any proof can provide. "This faith", St John of Avila comments, "is not based on reasons [...]; for when a person believes on the basis of reasons, he is not believing in such a way that he is totally convinced, without any doubt or scruple whatever. But the faith which God infuses is grounded on divine Truth, and it causes one to believe more firmly than if one saw it with one's own eyes, and touched it with one's own hands—and to believe more certainly than he who believes that four is greater than three, the sort of thing that is so obvious that the mind never hesitates a moment, nor can it even if it wants to" (*Audi, filia*, chap. 43).

The faith which God gives a person —supernatural faith—is necessarily the point of departure for hope and charity: it is what is usually called "living faith".

When one lives with this kind of faith it is easy to see that the three "theological" virtues (faith, hope and charity) are bound up with one another. Faith and hope lead a person to unite himself to God as the source from which all good things flow; charity unites us to God directly, by loving affection, because God is the supreme Good. Faith is as it were the first step: it means accepting what God says as true. We then unite ourselves to him through hope, insofar as we rely on God's help to attain beatitude. The goal of this process is charity, the fullness

received divine approval. ³By faith we understand that the world was created by the word of God, so that what is seen was made out of things which do not appear.

⁴By faith Abel offered to God a more acceptable sacrifice than Cain, through which he received approval as righteous, God bearing witness by accepting his gifts; he died, but through his

Gen 1
Rom 1:20

Gen 4:4, 10
Mt 23:35

---

of which is eternal possession of God, the Supreme Good. "Let us grow in hope, thereby strengthening our faith which is truly 'the assurance of things hoped for, the conviction of things not seen' (Heb 11:1). Let us grow in this virtue, let us beg our Lord to increase his charity in us; after all, one can only really trust what one loves with all one's might. And it is certainly worthwhile to love our Lord" (St Josemaría Escrivá, *Friends of God*, 220).

If hope in general is the conviction of being able to obtain something worthwhile in the future, something difficult to obtain, theological hope is the conviction of being able, with the help of God, to attain heaven. And faith is precisely what provides certain knowledge of those two truths—that heaven is our goal and that God wants to help us to get there (cf. *Summa theologiae*, 2-2, 17, 5 and 7). Therefore, nothing should dishearten us on this road to our ultimate goal because we put our trust in "three truths: God is all-powerful, God has a boundless love for me, God is faithful to his promises. And it is he, the God of mercies, who enkindles this trust within me, so that I never feel lonely or useless or abandoned but, rather, involved in a plan of salvation which will one day reach its goal in Paradise" (John Paul I, *Address*, 20 September 1978).

11:3. The creation of the world from nothing is one of the first articles of faith. The text is reminiscent in a way of v. 1, in that faith gives conviction about things we cannot see; that is how we know the origin of all created things and discover God from things we can see.

Essentially the text is emphasizing the importance of belief in God as Creator and in Creation as coming from nothing. This is a truth found in all the creeds and it has been often defined by the Church Magisterium (cf., for example, Lateran IV and Vatican I). "We believe in one God, the Father, the Son and the Holy Spirit, Creator of what is visible—such as this world where we live out our lives—and of the invisible—such as the pure spirits which are also called angels" (Paul VI, *Creed of the People of God*).

11:4. The book of Genesis (4:3–5) tells of the offerings made to Yahweh by Cain and Abel, the sons of Adam and Eve. God was pleased with Abel's offering but not with Cain's. God said to Cain, "Why are you angry, and why has your countenance fallen? If you do well, will you not be accepted? And if you do not do well, sin is couching at the door ready to waylay you" (Gen 4:6–7). Many Jewish commentators saw this as meaning that Cain's sin may have been one of meanness because he did not offer the best of his crop. Additionally there would have been a sin of envy towards Abel (Wisdom 10:3 speaks of Cain's evil and his fratricidal hatred). In contrast to Cain, the prototype of the envious, selfish, violent and fratricidal man, Jewish literature extolled Abel as an example of generosity, uprightness and piety.

Hebrews 11:5

Gen 5:24
Sir 44:16
Wis 4:10

faith he is still speaking. ⁵By faith Enoch was taken up so that he should not see death; and he was not found, because God had taken him. Now before he was taken he was attested as having

---

Against this background of Jewish religious thought come the words of Jesus (Mt 23:25) and St John (1 Jn 3:12) who describe Abel as "righteous", that is holy and devout. The Hebrews text stresses that what made Abel's offering the better one was his faith, commitment to God and generosity. That was why God bore witness to his righteousness by accepting the victims he offered and perhaps—according to an ancient oral Jewish tradition—sending fire down upon them to burn them. For God "looked more to the offerer than to what he offered, because the acceptability of an oblation is determined by the righteousness of the offerer, in cases other than of a sacrament," as St Thomas Aquinas says (*Commentary on Heb*, ad loc.). The text says literally that "God himself bore witness to his offerings", as if to imply that he "came down" or that he "sent down fire" to consume them (cf. the famous oblation of Elijah in 1 Kings 18:38; that of Moses and Aaron in Leviticus 9:24; and that of Gideon in Judges 6:21).

"He died, but through his faith he is still speaking": this is reminiscent of the passage in Genesis where God tells Cain that "the voice of your brother's blood is crying to me from the ground" (Gen 4:10). Abel is God's witness, his "martyr", because he confesses God's greatness by his faith, sacrifice and generosity. "By leading others towards virtue, Abel proves to be an eloquent speaker. Any words must be less effective than (the example of) this martyrdom. So, just as heaven speaks to us by simply revealing itself to us, this great saint exhorts us simply by impinging on our memory" (St John Chrysostom, *Hom. on Heb*, 22).

It is comforting to know that the first example of faith in God was given by the son of Adam and Eve, and that it took the form of a sacrifice. It is understandable therefore that Fathers have, in fact, seen Abel as a figure of Christ: he was a shepherd, he offered an oblation pleasing to God, he shed his blood, and was therefore a "martyr for the faith".

When renewing Christ's sacrifice, the Liturgy asks God to look with favour on the offerings and accept them as once he accepted the gifts of his "servant Abel" (cf. *Roman Missal*, Eucharistic Prayer I).

11:5. There was also quite an amount of Jewish tradition about Enoch, one of the patriarchs from the pre-Flood period; this stemmed from the fact that the book of Genesis, instead of rounding off mention of him with the usual words "and he died" (as is the case with the other patriarchs), says that he "walked with Elohim, and he was not, for God took him" (cf. Gen 5:21–24). This led people to think that Enoch did not die and that therefore he was in the presence of God preparing the way for the Messiah who would set man free: that is, he must be one of the Messiah's precursors, like Elijah, of whose death also there is no mention. The Greek translation of the Old Testament (the Septuagint) elaborates a little on the Hebrew text of Genesis 5:23: it says, "Enoch walked with God; and he was not, for the Lord took him", and the RSV Genesis passage reflects this. It might also be pointed out that the book of Sirach mentions Enoch with great respect, proposing him as an example to all generations; it says that "Enoch pleased the Lord, and was taken up" (Sir 44:16),

pleased God. ⁶And without faith it is impossible to please him. For whoever would draw near to God must believe that he exists and

Heb 7:25; 10:35
Ex 3:14

and elsewhere it adds that "no one like Enoch has been created on earth" (Sir 49:14). In apocryphal Jewish writing Enoch came to assume great importance: he was attributed great power as an astrologer and described as engaging in a series of fantastic exploits to prepare the way for the Messiah. It therefore became widely believed that Enoch would return to the world prior to the coming of the Anointed.

The Letter to the Hebrews uses the Sirach texts and the Greek version of Genesis as its ground for stating that Enoch "was attested as having pleased God", and therefore it proposes Enoch as an example of faith.

The sentence "Enoch was taken up so that he should not see death" is not just referring to his being an upright man: it connects him with the coming of the Messiah and with the end of the world. The text is not saying or denying that Enoch died, but simply that he was "taken up". In view of the fact that it is decreed that all men should die (cf. Heb 9:27), for death is a consequence of original sin (cf. Rom 5:12), most probably the words "was taken up" should be seen as a reference to death, and the following words, "so that he should not see death," should be taken either in a moral sense—that is, "not experience the spiritual death of sin"—or else as meaning that he arose immediately after our Lord's death, as happened in the case of some saints (cf. Mt 27:52–53).

11:6. Faith is a virtue which is necessary for salvation, but faith alone is insufficient; it must be "faith working through love" (Gal 5:6). However, faith is of decisive importance because it is "the beginning of man's salvation" (St Fulgentius, *De fide ad Petrum*, 1) and because it is "the foundation and source of all justification" (Council of Trent, *De iustificatione*, chap. 8); we are referring not only to faith in the sense of a personal act—the act of faith—but also to faith in the sense of a body of truths which one holds as certain. Thus, theology says that two things are necessary—the faith by which one believes (the attitude of the believer) and the truths of faith which have to be believed (articles of faith). The verse speaks of both, but it dwells mainly on the second—the content or "object" of faith—whereas earlier (11:1) it looked more at the importance of the act as such. No one can please God unless he draws near him; but it is not possible to do that without faith; therefore no one can please God unless he has faith. God himself moves us and helps us to approach him, but man needs to respond freely to God's action; it is by the act of faith that he does so: faith is that disposition of soul "by which we yield our unhesitating assent to whatever the authority of our Holy Mother the Church teaches us has been revealed by God; for the faithful cannot doubt those things of which God, who is truth itself, is the author" (*St Pius V Catechism*, 1, 1, 1).

That is why, among truths of faith, we distinguish those which are accessible to human reason and those which man could never come to know on his own; the latter are called "mysteries". The former can be reduced to three—the existence of God, the immortality of the soul, and the existence of a moral order established by God.

It is clear that if one does not believe in the existence of God and in the moral

Hebrews 11:6

order established by him there is no possibility of salvation. What does the passage mean when it says that "whoever would draw near to God must believe that he exists and that he rewards those who seek him"? We might reply, with St Thomas, that, after original sin, no one can be saved unless he have faith in the promised Mediator (Gen 3:15). For pagans, who have received no revelation, it was and is sufficient to believe that God rewards good and punishes evil (cf. *Commentary on Heb*, ad loc.).

The words of the sacred writer also pose another problem: how can those be saved who do not know Christ? The first thing to bear in mind is the absolute necessity of true and upright faith. Man has an obligation to seek truth, particularly religious truth, and he must not content himself with just any religion, as if all religions were more or less equal (cf. Pius IX, *Syllabus of Errors*, 15 and 16). That is why adult pagans who request Baptism when they are in danger of death or in a situation of dire need must be given before Baptism a short instruction (adapted to the situation and to their intellectual capacity) on the main mysteries of faith—the Trinity and the Incarnation (cf. *Reply of the Holy Office*, 26 January 1703).

All this, however, does not mean that people who are not Christians cannot be saved. What it means, Vatican II teaches, is that "they could not be saved who, knowing that the Catholic Church was founded as necessary by God through Christ, would refuse either to enter it, or to remain in it" (*Lumen gentium*, 14). "Those who, through no fault of their own, do not know the Gospel of Christ or his Church, but who nevertheless seek God with a sincere heart, and, moved by grace, try in their actions to do his will as they know it through the dictates of their conscience—those too may achieve eternal salvation. Nor shall divine providence deny the assistance necessary for salvation to those who, without any fault of theirs, have not yet arrived at an explicit knowlege of God, and who, not without grace, strive to lead a good life" (*Lumen gentium*, 16).

Therefore, when in its apostolic and missionary work, the catholic Church encounters other religions, it "rejects nothing of what is true and holy in these religions. It has a high regard for the manner of life and conduct, the precepts and doctrines which, although differing in many ways from its own teaching, nevertheless often reflect a ray of that truth which enlightens all men. Yet it proclaims, and is in duty bound to proclaim without fail, Christ who is the way, the truth and the life (Jn 14:6). In him, in whom God reconciled all things to himself (cf. 2 Cor 5:18–19), men find the fullness of their religious life" (Vatican II, *Nostra aetate*, 2). In the last analysis, "although in many ways known to himself God can lead those who, through no fault of their own, are ignorant of the Gospel to that faith without which it is impossible to please him (Heb 11:6), the Church, nevertheless, still has the obligation (cf. 1 Cor 9:16) and also the sacred right to evangelize. And so, today as always, missionary activity retains its full force and necessity" (Vatican II, *Ad gentes*, 7).

Similarly every Christian should always desire to seek God and have others seek him also. "If there is someone who is going to reward us, let us do everything possible not to lose the reward that is given to virtue [...]. But, how can one find the Lord? Think of how gold is found—by much effort and trouble [...].

that he rewards those who seek him.* ⁷By faith Noah, being warned by God concerning events as yet unseen, took heed and constructed an ark for the saving of his household; by this he condemned the world and became an heir of the righteousness which comes by faith.

Gen 6:8ff
Heb 7:1
Rom 3:22
2 Pet 2:5
1 Pet 3:20

⁸By faith Abraham obeyed when he was called to go out to a place which he was to receive as an inheritance; and he went out, not

Gen 12:1, 4

So, we must seek God in the same way as we look for something we have lost. Is it not true that we rack our brains? Don't we look everywhere? Don't we look in out of the way places? Don't we spend money searching? If, for example, we have lost a child, what will we not do? What regions, what seas, will we not cross? How much more in the case of God, given that those who seek him have such need of him!" (St John Chrysostom, *Hom. on Heb*, 22).

11:7. When Noah received God's order to build the ark (cf. Gen 6–9; Mt 24:37–39; 1 Pet 3:20; 2 Pet 2:5), there was as yet no sign of a flood; in other words, he had to rely totally on God's word. He took heed, he acted "*reveritus*", with religious fear, that is, with a deeply religious attachment to God, an attitude which led him to obey very exactly what God told him to do.

Noah's faith "condemned the world" because the worldly and unbelieving men of his time jeered at him when he was making the ark. "What do these words mean—'by this he condemned the world'? They mean that he showed up the world as deserving of punishment, because even though they saw him building (the ark) they did not mend their ways or repent" (*Hom. on Heb*, 23, 1). By acting in line with his faith Noah condemns, unknown to himself, the incredulity of his contemporaries. Today also the life of a person of faith can be a reproach to those around him, but that should not lead him to act any differently.

11:8. Abraham, "our father in faith", is the greatest example, in the Old Testament, of faith in God (cf. Gen 12:1–4; Rom 4:1ff; Gal 3:6–9; Heb 6:13ff). It is not surprising that the author pauses to dwell on the faithful life of the father of the chosen people. Putting all his trust in the divine word, Abraham gave up all the security and comfort of his native land in Ur of the Chaldees, to set out for a distant and unknown place, the land of Canaan, which God had promised to give his descendants. "Neither the love for his homeland nor the pleasure of his neighbours' company nor the comforts of his father's home were able to weaken his resolve. He set out courageously and ardently to where God willed to lead him. What self-abasement and abandonment! One cannot love God perfectly unless one renounces all attachment to perishable things" (St Francis de Sales, *Treatise on the Love of God*, book 10). Abraham symbolizes the need for detachment if one is to obtain redemption and to be a good servant of God and of others.

"Never forget that Christ cannot be reached without sacrifice. You have to get rid of everything that gets in the way [...]. You have to do the same in this battle for the glory of God, in this struggle of love and peace by which we are trying to spread Christ's kingdom. In order to serve the Church, the Pope and all souls, you must be ready to give up everything superfluous" (St Josemaría Escrivá, *Friends of God*, 196).

Hebrews 11:9

^{Gen 23:4; 26:3; 35:12}
^{Rev 21:10-22}
^{Gen 17:19; 21:2}
^{Rom 4:19-21}
^{Gen 22:17; 32:13; Dan 3:36, LXX; Ex 32:13}

knowing where he was to go. ⁹By faith he sojourned in the land of promise, as in a foreign land, living in tents with Isaac and Jacob, heirs with him of the same promise. ¹⁰For he looked forward to the city which has foundations, whose builder and maker is God. ¹¹By faith Sarah herself received power to conceive, even when she was past the age, since she considered him faithful who had promised. ¹²Therefore from one man, and him as good as dead, were born descendants as many as the stars of heaven and as the innumerable grains of sand by the seashore.

11:9–10. Abraham, and his son Isaac and grandson Jacob like him, far from settling down comfortably in a permanent place, lived a nomadic existence, strangers in a foreign land (cf. Gen 23:4). By faith the patriarch "looked forward to the city which has foundations", the city God would build. Instead of the provisionality of tents and the weak foundations of cities built by men, a heavenly city was being established, eternal and permanent, built by God on solid foundations, which Abraham hoped one day to possess. The promised land was a symbol of the definitive fatherland to which God called the father of Israel. There was even a late Jewish tradition which spoke of Abraham being given a vision of the heavenly Jerusalem after he ratified his covenant with God.

Christians live in the world by the will of God, and they love the world, but at the same time they realize they should not settle down in it as if it were the final goal of their lives. "They are residents at home in their own country but their behaviour is more like that of people who are passing through [...]. For them any foreign country is a homeland, and any homeland a foreign country" (*Letter to Diognetus*, 5, 5).

11:11–12. Sarah, like Abraham, was very elderly when God announced that she was going to have a child. At first she was puzzled and even sarcastically sceptical (cf. Gen 18:9f), but soon her attitude changed into a faith which God rewarded by her conceiving Isaac. The faith of Sarah and her husband can be said to exceed that of the earlier patriarchs because what God promised could come true only by means of a miracle, since Abraham, like his wife, was old and incapable of begetting children. That is why it says that from one man "and him as good as dead" innumerable descendants were born. God is generous in rewarding man's faith. "'*Si habueritis fidem, sicut granum sinapis!*—If your faith were the size of a mustard seed! ...' What promises are contained in this exclamation of the Master!" (St Josemaría Escrivá, *The Way*, 585).

The conception of Isaac is also a "type" of that of Christ. "All the miraculous conceptions which occurred in the Old Testament were prefigurements of the greatest of all miracles, the Incarnation of the Word. It was fitting that his birth from a Virgin should be prefigured by other births so as to prepare people's minds for faith. But there is this difference: God miraculously enabled Sarah to conceive by means of human seed, whereas the blessed Virgin conceived without it" (St Thomas Aquinas, *Commentary on Heb*, 11, 3).

¹³**These all died in faith, not having received what was promised, but having seen it and greeted it from afar, and having acknowledged that they were strangers and exiles on the earth.**

_{Jn 8:56; Gen 23:4; 1 Chron 29:15; Ps 39:13 1 Pet 1:1; 2:11}

11:13–16. After speaking about the faith of Abel, Noah and Abraham, the sacred writer goes on to give a brief panoramic account of the entire history of the patriarchs and the Exodus. It does not deal with events in chronological order. By recalling that the patriarchs left their own country to journey abroad "seeking a homeland", he brings in the exodus from Egypt. Between Abraham, who left Ur to travel to the land of Canaan, and the people of Israel, who left Egypt for the promised land, there is an obvious parallel, which is even more marked if one bears in mind that neither Abraham nor the Israelites led by Moses were destined to take possession of the land: that was reserved to their descendants. The only thing Abraham managed to do was to purchase the cave of Machpelah, near Hebron, and the land immmediately around it, for which he had to pay a very high price in silver. The cave became the burial ground of Sarah, Abraham himself, Isaac, Rebecca, Jacob and Leah. But Abraham publicly admitted he was "a stranger and a sojourner" in Canaan when he bought the cave from the Hittites (Gen 23:4). Nor did the Hebrews of Moses' generation manage to enter Canaan. The nearest they got to it was descriptions brought by their spies; and Moses himself was only able to view it from a distance, from Mount Nebo, just prior to his death (cf. Deut 32:49–52; 33:1–4). Abraham, and later Isaac and Jacob (who led a nomadic existence in Canaan), like the Israelites in the wilderness, prefigure Christians, who are also in search of a land of their own, a better homeland, that is, heaven (cf. Heb 13:14). It certainly is moving to recall the patriarchs and the Exodus, and very helpful to the faith and hope of Christians amid the difficulties they encounter in this world. Those men of faith are said to have "seen" what was promised: this may be a reference to some special grace God gave them, as was the case with Abraham (cf. Jn 8:56), or else to the intuitive vision of supernatural things which faith provides (cf. Aquinas, *Commentary on Heb*, ad loc.). "They greeted it from afar," happy to do so. "They greeted the promises and rejoiced," St John Chrysostom says, "for they already had such faith in those promises that they could make signs of greeting. This comparison is taken from seafaring: when from afar sailors espy the city they are making for, even before entering the port they cheer in greeting" (*Hom. on Heb*, 23).

The patriarchs' attitude was a true indication of their faith in a future life, for, as St Thomas points out, by describing themselves as strangers and sojourners (Gen 23:4; 47:9; cf. Deut 26:5) they showed they were heading towards their homeland, the heavenly Jerusalem. They did not set their hearts on an earthly homeland, or on their parental homestead, for if so they could in fact have chosen to return to it (cf. *Commentary on Heb*, ad loc.). Thus the promises made to them found their fulfilment not in something earthly but in the eternity of heaven: "Therefore God is not ashamed" to be called the God of Abraham and Isaac and Jacob: seeing their faith and fidelity, he overlooked their sins and faults. And he is disposed to act in the same way towards Christians.

In vv. 14 and 16, in the Greek text and the New Vulgate—and in the RSV—

Hebrews 11:14

Ex 3:6
Rev 21:2
Mt 23:32

Gen 22; Jas 2:21; Sir 44:20
Gen 21:12, LXX; Rom 9:7

¹⁴For people who speak thus make it clear that they are seeking a homeland. ¹⁵If they had been thinking of that land from which they had gone out, they would have had opportunity to return. ¹⁶But as it is, they desire a better country, that is, a heavenly one. Therefore God is not ashamed to be called their God, for he has prepared for them a city.

¹⁷By faith Abraham, when he was tested, offered up Isaac, and he who had received the promises was ready to offer up his only son, ¹⁸of whom it was said, "Through Isaac shall your descendants be named."

---

the verbs are in the present tense, as distinct from the past (aorist) used generally in this passage. This is because the whole paragraph is recalling the life of the patriarchs, but with the intention of stressing that their faith is an example to all generations. What we have here is a mixture of history and sapiential writing, using verbs which indicate that the action—or at least some of its effects—is still going on.

11:17–19. It is very difficult for us to imagine what Abraham thought when God asked him to sacrifice Isaac, the son of the promise, his only son, in the mountains of Moriah (cf. Gen 22:2). The Old Testament shows how resolute Abraham was, his absolute docility, his serenity even in the midst of suffering, his trust in God (cf. Gen 22:1–18). This is revealed in the touching conversation between the patriarch and his son, when Isaac asks him where is the lamb for the offering and Abraham replies, "God will provide himself with the lamb for a burnt offering, my son." In St Paul's letters generally Abraham's faith is proposed as an example (cf. Gal 3:7; Rom 4:3, 11–12; 4:17–22); but that was in the context of his faith in God's promise that he would have a multitude of descendants. Here, however, the patriarch's faith is to be seen in the way he approaches a commandment which seems to negate that promise: how could God possibly ask him to sacrifice his only son? The answer lies in the fact that God knew that Abraham had faith in his ability to bring the dead back to life.

Abraham's obedience to God in this episode is the most striking proof of his faith. Here most of all the patriarch "believed against hope [...]; he grew strong in his faith as he gave glory to God" (Rom 4:18, 21). "The patriarch hears words which deny the promise; he hears the very author of the promise contradict himself, but he is not dismayed; he is going to obey as if everything were completely consistent. And in fact the two things were compatible: the two things God said were contradictory as far as human logic was concerned; but faith brought them into agreement [...].

"God tested Abraham's faith. Did he not know the strength and integrity of that great man? Undoubtedly he did, very well. Why, then, did he put them to the test? He did not do it to prove to himself the patriarch's virtue; he did it to show the world how excellent Abraham was. The Apostle, moreover, shows the Hebrews one of the causes of our temptations, so that anyone who is afflicted should not think that God has abandoned him" (Chrysostom, *Hom. on Heb*, 25). We know, moreover, that precisely on account of Abraham's generosity and faith, God renewed his promise to him, now ratifying it with an oath (cf. Gen 22:16; Heb 6:13–18).

¹⁹He considered that God was able to raise men even from the dead; hence, he did receive him back, and this was a symbol. ²⁰By faith Isaac invoked future blessings on Jacob and Esau. ²¹By faith Jacob,

Rom 4:17
Gen 27:27-29, 39f; Gen 47:31, LXX; 48:15f

11:19. "Hence he did receive him back, and this was a symbol": after offering Isaac, Abraham was given him back, because God stepped in before Isaac was sacrificed (Gen 22:11–12). And he received him as "a symbol" (literally, as "a parable"). Tradition has seen the sacrifice of Isaac, the only Son, as a symbol of the redemptive sacrifice of Christ; and, particularly, it has seen God's intervention on Mount Moriah as a symbol of the Resurrection. "He saw it as a symbol," Theodoret comments, "that is, as a prefigurement of the Resurrection. (Isaac) was brought to death by his father's will, and then brought back to life by the voice which prevented his death. All this amounts to a prefiguring of the passion of the Saviour, and that is why the Lord told the Jews, 'Your father Abraham rejoiced that he was to see my day; he saw it and was glad' (Jn 8:56)" (*Interpretatio Ep. ad Haebreos*, ad loc.).

Origen, a writer of Christian antiquity, reflects this tradition very beautifully when he says that the sacrifice of Isaac helps us to understand the mystery of Redemption. "Isaac carrying the wood for the burnt offering is a symbol of Christ, who carried his (own) cross. But it is also the function of the priest to carry the wood for the burnt offering […]. Christ is the Word of God, but the Word made flesh. Therefore, there is in Christ an element which comes from above and another which comes from human nature, which he took on in the womb of the Virgin. This is why Christ experiences suffering: he suffers in the flesh, and he dies, but what suffers death is the flesh, and the ram is a figure of this, as St John said, 'Behold the Lamb of God, who takes away the sin of the world' (Jn 1:29) […]. Christ is at one and the same time victim and high priest. Thus, according to the spirit he offers the victim to his father; according to his flesh, he himself is offered on the altar of the cross" (*Homilies on Genesis*, 8, 6 and 9).

For all these reasons, Eucharistic Prayer I links Christ's sacrifice with those of Abel, Isaac and Melchizedek.

11:20. Prompted by his mother Rebecca, Jacob disguised himself as Esau and managed to obtain from Isaac the blessing that belonged to Esau as first-born; as a result the promises made to Abraham passed to Jacob (cf. Gen 27:27–29). When Isaac discovered that he had been tricked, he saw in this trick a design of Providence and he confirmed what he had done (cf. Gen 27:33): "I ate it before you came, and I have blessed him—yes, and he shall be blessed." The only blessing that could then be bestowed on Esau was a general blessing to the effect that he was free to go his own way and would possess a land which was far from fertile. Isaac is an example of faith, because it was his faith which allowed him to recognize and accept God's plans.

Isaac bestowed "future blessings"—not material goods but hope in the future fulfilment of God's promises.

11:21. "Bowing in worship over the head of his staff": two gestures of Jacob are combined here. One was when he had finished blessing his sons, the ancestors of the twelve tribes: "he drew up his feet into the bed, and breathed his last, and was gathered to his people" (Gen 49:32); the other, slightly earlier, had to do with

Hebrews 11:22

<small>Gen 50:24</small>

when dying, blessed each of the sons of Joseph, bowing in worship over the head of his staff. ²²By faith Joseph, at the end of his life, made mention of the exodus of the Israelites and gave directions concerning his burial.ˣ

The faith of Moses, the judges and the prophets

<small>Ex 2:2f
Acts 7:20</small>

²³By faith Moses, when he was born, was hid for three months by his parents, because they saw that the child was beautiful; and they were

---

the patriarch's final illness (cf. Gen 47:31). He had Joseph swear that he would bury him in the promised land; then he took ill and "bowed himself upon the head of his bed". The Greek translation of the Old Testament (the Septuagint), by a slight change of vowels in one Hebrew word, said that "Jacob bowed reverentially over the head of his staff". What the sacred writer is stressing here is Jacob's reverence towards God: he ended his life with an act of adoration of God.

11:22. When Joseph was on the point of dying he remembered the ancient promise made by God to Abraham (cf. Gen 15:13f), according to which, after a period of slavery and oppression in a foreign country, the children of Israel would return to the promised land. Although Joseph enjoyed a privileged position in Egyptian society, he still firmly believed in God's promise to his forefathers to give them the land of Canaan, and he wanted his body to lie there: "I am about to die; but God will visit you, and bring you up out of this land to the land which he swore to Abraham to Isaac, and to Jacob [...]. God will visit you, and you shall carry up my bones from here" (Gen 50:24-25; cf. Ex 13:19; Josh 24:32).

11:23-29. After the patriarchs, Moses was the figure most revered by the Jewish people; he was for them the founder and lawgiver of their nation (cf. Heb 3:1-5

and notes). This passage sketches key episodes in his life when he gave great example of faith, and it begins with the faith of his parents, who dared to disobey Pharaoh's edict (cf. Ex 1:16, 22). The book of Exodus (cf. Ex 2:2) tells us of his mother's tender care, but Hebrew tradition speaks also of his father's decision to disobey the edict. The reason they disobeyed Pharaoh would initially have been parental love and the fact that the child was so beautiful. However, St Stephen (cf. Acts 7:20) says that Moses was "beautiful before God", that is, pleasing to God: his beauty was a sign of God's favour; so, his parents must have in some way realized that the child was specially favoured by God (cf. Aquinas, *Commentary on Heb*, ad loc.).

Another example of Moses' faith was the fact that he left Pharaoh's court (and the career that was opening up before him, and for which his entire education equipped him: cf. Acts 7:22) over an incident to do with repression of the Israelites; he killed an Egyptian overseer and had to flee for his life (cf. Ex 2:11-15). When Yahweh charged him with the mission of liberating his people, Moses was not afraid to confront Pharaoh. He unleashed the plagues; exposed the magicians of Egypt; and strove relentlessly until he achieved his goal. To do all this he drew his strength from the vision he had seen on Mount Sinai, when the invisible God revealed himself to him in

x. Greek *bones*

not afraid of the king's edict. ²⁴By faith Moses, when he was grown up, refused to be called the son of Pharaoh's daughter, ²⁵choosing rather to share ill-treatment with the people of God than to enjoy the fleeting pleasures of sin. ²⁶He considered abuse suffered for the Christ greater wealth than the treasures of Egypt, for he looked to the reward. ²⁷By faith he left Egypt, not being afraid of the anger of the king; for he endured as seeing him who is invisible. ²⁸By faith he kept the Passover and sprinkled the blood, so that the Destroyer of the first-born might not touch them.

²⁹By faith the people crossed the Red Sea as if on dry land; but the Egyptians, when they attempted to do the same, were drowned. ³⁰By faith the walls of Jericho fell down after they had

Ex 2:11
Ps 69:10, LXX;
89:51f, LXX
Heb 10:35
Ex 2:15
1 Tim 1:17
Ex 12:11, 21–23
Ex 14:22, 27
1 Cor 10:10
Wis 18:25
Josh 6:20

---

the mysterious burning bush. Finally the text recalls the faith of all those Israelites who followed Moses in the epic journey of the Exodus. God enabled them to cross the Red Sea without wetting their feet, whereas the army of the Egyptians there met its doom (cf. Ex 14:26–31).

The central point of the teaching in this passage is the choice which faith obliges—the pleasures of sin v. ill-treatment shared with the people of God; "the treasures of Egypt" v. "abuse suffered for the Christ". This last expression indicates that the sufferings of the Israelites in Egypt prefigured the sufferings of the Messiah.

Jewish teachers in the time of St Paul usually saw the future Messiah as being a new and greater Moses: the Anointed would embody, again and definitively, all the functions of Moses—liberator, convoker of the people, lawgiver, mediator of the Covenant, wonder-worker etc. Hence the inevitable Moses–Christ parallel.

"Abuse suffered for the Christ" also refers to suffering and contempt experienced by Christ's followers. There is no earthly prize comparable to attaining the Lord through grace. For the true disciple of Christ no suffering is too great provided he can follow the Messiah and be like him.

"The true servants of Jesus Christ, when they find themselves despised and ill-treated because of their love for him, regard it as a great honour [...]. Moses could have escaped Pharaoh's wrath simply by letting himself be taken for the son of the king's daughter, but he rejected such kinship and preferred (to share) the affliction of his Hebrew brethren" (St Alphonsus, *Shorter Sermons*, 40, 2, 1).

Our faith should be like that of Moses: we should despise the "fleeting pleasures of sin" in order to suffer with Christ. This commitment to stay with Christ, to stand by his cross, is what gives serenity and joy. "Is it not true that as soon as you cease to be afraid of the Cross, of what people call the cross, when you set your will to accept the Will of God, then you find happiness, and all your worries, all your sufferings, physical or moral, pass away?

"Truly the Cross of Jesus is gentle and lovable. There, sorrows cease to count; there is only the joy of knowing that we are co-redeemers with him" (St Josemaría Escrivá, *The Way of the Cross*, II).

11:30. By putting their faith in the word of God, who had given Joshua detailed instructions about how to take Jericho (cf. Josh 6:2–5), the Israelites obtained

been encircled for seven days. ³¹By faith Rahab the harlot did not perish with those who were disobedient, because she had given friendly welcome to the spies.

³²And what more shall I say? For time would fail me to tell of Gideon, Barak, Samson, Jephthah, of David and Samuel and the prophets—³³who through faith conquered kingdoms, enforced justice, received promises, stopped the mouths of lions, ³⁴quenched raging fire, escaped the edge of the sword, won strength out of weakness, became mighty in war, put foreign armies to flight. ³⁵Women received their dead by resurrection. Some were tortured,

---

victory: the walls protecting the city crumbled before their eyes. "Even if it lasted for ten centuries", St John Chrysostom comments, "the sound of trumpets could not knock walls down, whereas for faith nothing is impossible" (*Hom. on Heb*, 27).

11:31. Before embarking on the conquest of the promised land Joshua sent two spies to bring back detailed information about Jericho. When they reached the city they lodged in the house of Rahab, a prostitute, who hid them and helped them to escape when the king's men came searching. Rahab believed in the true God and she also believed that the Hebrews were his chosen people: that was why she risked her life for them. She asked them to swear to leave herself and her family untouched (cf. Josh 2:1–21). Joshua kept the promise the spies made her, but the rest of the inhabitants of Jericho, who were unbelieving, perished (cf. Josh 6:22–25).

Because of her action and despite the fact that she was a prostitute and a foreigner, Rahab has ever since been the object of praise. The Fathers often saw her as a symbol of "the Church of the Gentiles", that is, of pagans who find their way into the Church.

11:32–38. Up to now, the passage has been recalling outstanding examples of faith from the time of the Patriarchs down to that of Joshua (18th to 13th century BC). The epistle now goes on to their exploits and sufferings, wherein their faith brought them victory; the sacred writer then mentions the testimony of faith of heroes, judges, kings, prophets and martyrs from the time of the conquest of Palestine to that of the Maccabees (13th to 2nd centuries BC). Not in any strict chronological order, he mentions only the most important Judges (Gideon, Barak, Samson and Jephthah), the greatest of the kings (David) and the most famous of the early prophets (Samuel). Finally he refers to exploits and other deeds inspired by faith and fidelity, without giving names.

We know from Holy Scripture that many of these people had shortcomings and, in some cases, committed grave sins. However, those weaknesses did not prevent their filling key roles in God's plans: they let themselves be used by God to apply his policy and are therefore worthy of being proposed as examples of faith.

11:33–35a. "Through faith (they) conquered kingdoms": a reference to the men who conquer the promised land: Barak, who overcame the Canaanites (cf. Judg 11), Gideon, who conquered the Midianites (cf. Judg 7), Jephthah, who conquered the Amonnites (cf. Judg 11), Samson, who defeated the Philistines (cf. Judg 14), and David, who succeeded in

refusing to accept release, that they might rise again to a better life. ³⁶Others suffered mocking and scourging, and even chains

Jer 20:37f
2 Chron 24:21
Mt 23:37

---

subduing all the enemies of Israel (cf. 2 Sam 5:17–25; 8:1f; 10).

"Enforced justice": a reference to the authority exercised by the Judges on a tribal basis, and by Samuel and the kings over the whole of Israel (cf. 1 Sam 12:3; 2 Sam 8:15); it can also be understood as meaning those who practised righteousness in God's name and made it effective, the prophets being the oustanding examples.

"Received promises": the righteous of the Old Testament received an earnest of the messianic promises in the form of the fulfilment of certain prophecies made by God. Barak defeated Sisera as God had promised (cf. Judg 4:14f); Gideon overcame the Midianites (cf. Judg 6:14; 7:7); David brought peace to the whole land, as Nathan had predicted (cf. 2 Sam 7:11); etc.

"Stopped the mouths of lions": a reference to feats performed by Samson (cf. Jud 14:6), David (cf. 1 Sam 17:34–35), and Benaiah (cf. 2 Sam 23:20); it especially recalls the episode of Daniel in the lion's den: when thrown there by the king on account of his faith, he told him, "My God sent his angel and shut the lions' mouths, and they have not hurt me" (Dan 6:22).

Sacred history also includes people who "quenched raging fire" (like the three young men in the fiery furnace in Babylon: cf. Dan 3:21–94); or who "escaped the edge of the sword" (as Moses did, in his flight from Pharaoh's wrath: cf. Ex 18:4); or like David, who "won strength out of weakness" in his victories over Goliath and Saul (cf. 1 Sam 17:34ff; 18:11; 19:11). Thanks to his faith Elijah found protection from Jezebel's persecution (cf. 1 Kings 19:1f);

and the Jewish people were able to escape extermination during King Ahasuerus' reign thanks to the prayer and intercession of Esther and Mordecai (cf. Esther 3:6ff).

Through faith King Hezekiah was miraculously cured of mortal illness (cf. Is 38) and Samson received his strength after becoming weak and blind (cf. Judg 15:19; 16:28–30). Faith enabled the Hebrews, under the judges, to take on and defeat the pagan peoples of Palestine; it led Judith to behead Holofernes and bring about the destruction of his army; and it enabled the Maccabees to repel the foreign armies of Antiochus (cf. 1 Mac 1:38).

Then there is the example of the widow of Zarephath, who sheltered Elijah and had her son restored when the prophet cured him (cf. 1 Kings 17:17f). And Elisha brought back to life the son of the Shunammite widow (cf. 2 Kings 4:33f).

All these examples show the effectiveness of faith, when it involves a person's whole life and lifestyle, influencing both everyday events and great exploits.

11:35b–36. Faith not only enables people to perform exploits and miracles: it also enables them to persevere in doing good and to bear all kinds of moral and physical pain, even torture and the most cruel forms of death. And so the text refers to various sorts of suffering inflicted on the prophets and many other just members of the people of Israel.

The writer may have in mind, for example, the death of Eleazar (cf. 2 Mac 6:19ff) and of the seven brothers (cf. 2 Mac 7), who underwent most cruel torture during the persecution mounted by Antiochus IV Epiphanes. The king had promised them their lives if they

and imprisonment. ³⁷They were stoned, they were sawn in two,ʸ they were killed with the sword; they went about in skins of sheep and goats, destitute, afflicted, ill-treated—³⁸of whom the world was not worthy—wandering over deserts and mountains, and in dens and caves of the earth.

³⁹And all these, though well attested by their faith, did not receive what was promised, ⁴⁰since God had foreseen something better for us, that apart from us they should not be made perfect.

1 Pet 1:10–12; 3:19

---

gave up their faith and laws by eating forbidden meat; but they stayed true to God and were mercilessly martyred. However, they had unshakeable faith in the rightness of God's judgment and in future resurrection (2 Mac 7:19, 14, 23, 29). They desired to "rise again to a better life": they put their faith in an incomparably more valuable, more real, life than that of a few more years on earth, which would have been the reward of apostasy. "They did not escape death," St Thomas writes, "not because God was not looking after them but so that they might obtain eternal life, which is a more excellent thing than being set free from any present affliction or being raised up again to this life" (*Commentary on Heb*, 11, 35).

The example of these men and women whom faith strengthened to endure suffering, should encourage Christians to face persecution courageously and defend their faith at all costs. "Let us pray to God that we do not suffer persecution, but if that does happen, let us bear it bravely. It befits a prudent man not to fling himself lightly into danger, but it befits a brave man to rise to the occasion when danger falls on him" (*Hom. on Heb*, 5).

11:37–38. Some righteous men were stoned for their faith—Zechariah, for example, who was killed by order of King Joash (cf. 2 Chron 24:20–21); Naboth, condemned to death through the lies spread by Jezebel (cf. 1 Kings 21:13);

and the prophet Jeremiah also, according to an ancient tradition. Others were sawn in two—Isaiah, for example, whom another Jewish tradition says was martyred by King Manasseh.

Elijah, in flight from persecution, went around dressed in skins (cf. 1 Kings 19:3ff); similarly Mattathias and his sons during the war against the Seleucid kings, were forced to hide in the mountains and had only goatskins to wear (cf. 1 Mac 2:28).

In our own time there are also people who profess their faith in God by undergoing comparable persecution; but usually hatred of Christ and his followers takes more subtle forms.

11:40. This verse is the conclusion following from all the examples provided. The righteous of the Old Law were outstanding for their faith and endurance, but for all that they did not have the strength that the grace of Christ bestows; Jesus remarked, when John the Baptist was praised to him, "Truly, I say to you, among those born of women there has arisen no one greater than John the Baptist; yet he who is least in the kingdom of heaven is greater than he" (Mt 11:11); and he reminded his disciples of their privileged position: "Blessed are the eyes which see what you see! For I tell you that many prophets and kings desired to see what you see, and did not see it, and to hear what you hear, and did not hear it" (Lk 10:23–24; cf. Mt 13:16–17).

---

y. Other manuscripts add *they were tempted*

6. THE EXAMPLE OF CHRIST AND THE DUTIES OF CHRISTIANS

The example of Christ

12 ¹Therefore, since we are surrounded by so great a cloud of witnesses, let us also lay aside every weight, and sin which

1 Tim 6:12
2 Tim 4:7

God did not deny their reward to the righteous of the Old Testament, but he postponed it until heaven's gates were opened by the death and resurrection of our Lord. They too now enjoy eternal life and they will attain their final perfecting when their bodies rise in glory on the last day. God is like a good father, St John Chrysostom comments, who says to his beloved children when they finish their work, that he will not give them their supper until their other brothers come back also. "And you, are you annoyed because you have not received your reward? What should Abel do, then. He was the first to gain the victory, but remained uncrowned. And Noah? And all those of those times who are waiting for you and for those who will come after you? Do you not see how much better off we are? That is why he says: God in his providence had arranged something better for us. And, in order that it should not be thought that those people were superior to us because they received their crown earlier, God disposed that all should be crowned at the very same time; and he who won his many years earlier will be crowned along with you [...]. For if we are all the one body, this body will the more rejoice if all are crowned at the same time and not one by one" (*Hom. on Heb*, 28).

12:1–3. After recalling the exemplary faith and fidelity of the righteous of the Old Testament, a moral lesson is now drawn: Christians should be no less faithful—particularly since they have as a model not only patriarchs, kings and prophets but also Christ Jesus himself, "the pioneer and perfecter of our faith", in other words, he is the perfect example of obedience, of faithfulness to his mission, of union with the Father, and of endurance in suffering.

Christ is depicted as the strong, generous athlete who runs a good race (cf. 1 Cor 9:24; 1 Tim 6:12; 2 Tim 2:6), who starts and finishes well, who does not flag and who wins the race. A Christian should live in the same way (cf. Gal 2:2; Phil 2:16; 5:7). It is as if we were listening again to what St Paul says in Philippians 2:5–9: "Have this mind among yourselves, which was in Christ Jesus." Christ's example helps us to overcome contempt and it reminds us that we should not be surprised to meet up with humiliation and hostility rather than success and rejoicing (cf. Mt 10:24; Lk 6:40). "Cross, toil, anguish: such will be your lot as long as you live. That was the way Christ went, and the disciple is not above his Master" (St Josemaría Escrivá, *The Way*, 699).

12:1. This verse contains three remarkable expressions which stress the need to be faithful in spite of difficulties. The first is the "cloud of witnesses", a reference to the multitude of holy people in the course of the history of Israel who stayed faithful to God (cf. 11:2, 4, 5, 39); they are a cloud, a huge number filling the sky. In classical literature one often finds an army advancing in battle array being compared with a storm forming in the

Hebrews 12:2

Mt 25:21
Ps 110:1
Heb 2:10

clings so closely, and let us run with perseverance the race that is set before us,* ²looking to Jesus the pioneer and perfecter of our

sky. Also, the image of the cloud suggests that these witnesses are high up, near the sun, a sign of their spiritual stature.

They are "witnesses", that is, active spectators of the combat in which Christians are involved. This evokes the idea of spectators at the Games who follow the events from the stands, applauding, shouting and gesticulating.

"Sin which clings so closely": one interpretation of the original is "sin which watches us closely, like an enemy, to see where he can attack us". It is the same kind of idea as occurs in 1 Peter 5:8, where it says that the devil prowls around like a roaring lion seeking whom he may devour, and as in Genesis 4:7 where God describes sin as couching at the door (like a hungry wild animal ready to pounce). The verb used to describe sin indicates it is something which surrounds one on all sides (cf. RSV) and can easily get a foothold and is persistent. "We may have here an allusion to occasions of sin, to the fact that sin is present all around us, that is, in the world, in the flesh, in our neighbour and in the devil" (St Thomas, *Commentary on Heb*, ad loc.). Sin is also a "weight" which hinders our movements and reduces our agility; there may also be a reference here to being overweight. The athlete needs to shed any surplus weight and keep to a strict training schedule involving many small renunciations (cf. 1 Cor 9:25). His only hope of success in the Games depends on this.

Finally, Christians are invited to "run with perseverance". Theirs is not a short race but a long test which calls for endurance and an ability to cope with pain and fatigue. "Just as in a race and in combat we need to shed everything that cramps our movements, the same happens in the struggle of tribulation. 'I have fought the good fight, I have finished the race,' St Paul says (2 Tim 4:7). So, he who wants to run well towards God in the midst of tribulation should shed all useless weight. The Apostle describes this encumbrance as 'weight, and sin which clings so closely'. This weight is the sins we have committed, which pull the soul downwards and incline it to sin again" (*Commentary on Heb*, ad loc.).

Essentially, the verse emphasizes the need for detachment if one is to win in the struggle of life: "Anything that does not lead to God is a hindrance. Root it out and throw it far from you" (St Josemaría Escrivá, *The Way*, 189).

12:2. The Christian should fix his gaze on Jesus, in the same way as a runner, once the race has begun, lets nothing distract him from his determination to reach his goal.

"If you want to be saved," St Thomas writes, "look at the face of your Christ. He is the pioneer of our faith, in two senses. He teaches it through his preaching and he also impresses it on our heart. In two senses also is he the perfecter of our faith: he confirms faith by his miracles and it is he who gives faith its reward" (*Commentary on Heb*, ad loc.).

Christ is the "pioneer" of our faith in the sense that he has marked out the path Christians should take. He is the captain and guide of all the faithful, the champion who takes the lead and opens the way, setting the pace. The reference evokes what Hebrews 6:20 says about Jesus being our "forerunner".

Christ is the "pioneer" of our faith, the cause of our faith; it is he that we first believe in and, as author of grace, it is he

faith, who for the joy that was set before him endured the cross, despising the shame, and is seated at the right hand of the throne of God. ^{Phil 2:8}

³Consider him who endured from sinners such hostility against himself, so that you may not grow weary or fainthearted. ^{Lk 2:34 Gal 6:9}

---

who infuses this virtue into our souls. The title of "pioneer", initiator, may also indicate that Christ is for the Christian—and for the universe—beginning and end, alpha and omega (cf. Rev 1:17; 2:8; 22:13). In the same line, Jesus is also the "perfecter" of our faith, for it is he who will lead us to perfection in faith and will transform it into the perfection of glory. He will crown his work in us (cf. St Augustine, *Letter,* 194, 5), for if we believe it is because he has moved us to faith, and if we are glorified it will be because he has helped us to stay true to the end.

Everything Christ did in his life is a perfect example for us to follow, particularly the way he underwent his passion. "In the passion of Christ there are three things to consider: in the first place what he gave up, then what he suffered, and thirdly what he merited. As far as the first is concerned, (Hebrews) speaks of his leaving 'the joy that was set before him', that is, joy or happiness here on earth, as when the crowd sought him out to make him king and he fled to the mountain despising that honour [...]. Then describing the happiness of eternal life as his reward, he 'endured the cross': that is the second thing, namely, that he suffered the cross. 'He humbled himself and became obedient unto death, even death on a cross' (Phil 2:8). In this the terrible severity of his suffering is manifested, for he was nailed to the cross by his hands and feet, and the opprobrium of this death, for it was an ignominous death [...]. The third thing, that is, what he merited, is being seated at the right hand of the Father. Thus, the exaltation of Christ's human nature was the reward for his passion" (*Commentary on Heb*, ad loc.).

Christ is the pioneer of our faith by his death on the cross, and its perfecter by his glorification. Only those who share in Christ's sufferings will be raised up like him in glory (cf. Rom 6:8). The Christian life begins in Christ and finds its climax in him.

To bring about our redemption any form of suffering would have sufficed; but such was our Lord's love for us that he accepted the ignominy of death on a cross.

"By now they have fastened Jesus to the wooden cross. The executioners have ruthlessly carried out the sentence. Our Lord, with infinite meekness, has let them have their way.

"It was not necessary for him to undergo so much torment. He could have avoided those trials, those humiliations, that ill-usage, that iniquitous judgment, and the shame of the gallows, and the nails and the lance.... But he wanted to suffer all this for you and for me. And we, are we not going to respond?

"Very likely there will be times, when alone in front of a crucifix, you find tears coming to your eyes. Don't try to hold them back.... But try to ensure that those tears give rise to a resolution" (St J. Escrivá, *The Way of the Cross*, XI, 1).

12:3. "What does Christ teach you from the height of the cross, from which he chose not to come down, but that you should arm yourself with valour against those who revile you, and be strong with

Hebrews 12:4

Perseverance in the midst of trials

Heb 10:32-36
Prov 3:11f,
LXX

⁴In your struggle against sin you have not yet resisted to the point of shedding your blood. ⁵And have you forgotten the exhortation which addresses you as sons?—

---

the strength of God?" (St Augustine, *Enarrationes in Psalmos*, 70, 1). The difficulties Jesus had to contend with were quite exceptional: Jews and Gentiles opposed him; he suffered every kind of humiliation, to the extreme of his passion and death; but what pained him most was the hardheartedness, spiritual blindness and impenitence of those whom he had come to save. The "sinners" who proved "hostile" to Jesus are not only Caiaphas, Herod, Pilate etc. but also those who continue to sin despite his redemptive sacrifice. Yet our Lord bore all this patiently and exhibited to a supreme degree the virtues and qualities he asks of his disciples.

In Christ, and in Christians, weakness becomes strength, humiliation and glory. "(Jesus) dies nailed to the Cross. But if at the same time in this *weakness* there is accomplished his *lifting up*, confirmed by the power of the Resurrection, then this means that the weaknesses of all human sufferings are capable of being infused with the same power of God manifested in Christ's Cross" (John Paul II, *Salvifici doloris*, 23).

The sacred text seeks to inspire the faithful with hope and strength by suggesting that they contemplate Christ's sufferings. That in fact has led many Christians to turn over a new leaf. St Teresa of Avila describes how it changed her: "By this time my soul was growing weary, and, though it desired to rest, the miserable habits which now enslaved it would not allow it to do so. It happened that, entering the oratory one day, I saw an image which had been procured for a certain festival that was observed in the house and had been taken there to be kept for that purpose. It represented Christ sorely wounded; and so conducive was it to devotion that when I looked at it I was deeply moved to see him thus, so well did it picture what he suffered for us. So great was my distress when I thought how ill I had repaid him for those wounds that I felt as if my heart were breaking, and I threw myself down beside him, shedding floods of tears and begging him to give me strength once for all so that I might not offend him" (*Life*, 9, 1).

12:4-13. Following Christ's example, Christians should struggle to avoid sin; they should put up with tribulation and persecution because if such adversity arises it means that the Lord permits it for our good. The letter's tone of encouragement seems to change here to one of reproach. It is as if the writer were saying, "Christ gave his life for your sins, contending even to the point of dying for you; how is it that you do not put up with suffering, out of love for him? It is true that you are being persecuted: God is disciplining you as a Father disciplines his children. But you are children of God and therefore your attitude should be one of abandonment to his will even when it seems hard. That is the way a Father brings up his children."

The main point is that the only important thing is fidelity to God, and that the sin of apostasy is the greatest of all misfortunes. "Don't forget, my son, that for you on earth there is but one evil, which you must fear and avoid with the grace of God: sin" (St Josemaría Escrivá, *The Way*, 386).

"My son, do not regard lightly the discipline of the Lord,
nor lose courage when you are punished by him.
⁶ For the Lord disciplines him whom he loves,   Rev 3:19
and chastises every son whom he receives."
⁷It is for discipline that you have to endure. God is treating you as sons; for what son is there whom his father does not discipline? ⁸If you are left without discipline, in which all have participated, then

---

12:5–11. Suffering, the sacred writer teaches, is a sign of God's paternal love for us; it proves that we really are his children.

This teaching is supported by the quotation from Proverbs 3:11–12, taken from a long discourse in which a father exhorts his son to acquire true wisdom. In the present passage the father is identified with God and we with the sons whom he is addressing.

By being incorporated into Christ through Baptism a person becomes a child of God: this is the very basis of the Christian life and it should be a source of serenity and peace in every difficulty we meet in the course of life. The term "discipline" which appears so much in this passage does not convey the full richness of the original Greek word, *paideia*, which has to do with the educational upbringing of child by parent, of pupil by teacher, and also the punishment meted out in this context. Here the focus is largely on the second aspect. However, it should be remembered that in ancient times education and instruction always involved the idea of punishment. God, therefore, should not be seen as a cruel or pitiless father, but as a good father who brings up his children in an affectionate yet firm way. Adversity and suffering are a sign that this divine teaching method is at work: God uses them to educate us and discipline us. "You suffer in this present life, which is a dream, a short dream. Rejoice, because your Father-God loves you so much, and if you put no obstacles in his way, after this bad dream he will give you a good awakening" (St Josemaría Escrivá, *The Way*, 692). If we were illegitimate children he would not bother to educate us; but because we are true sons he disciplines us, to make us worthy of bearing his name. "Everything that comes to us from God," an ancient ecclesiastical writer reminds us, "and that we initially see as beneficial or disadvantageous, is sent to us by a father who is full of tenderness and by the wisest of physicians, with our good in mind" (Cassian, *Collationes*, 7, 28).

When the soul has this kind of attitude, that is, when the trials the Lord sends are willingly accepted, "with peaceful fruit of righteousness", it yields fruit of holiness which fills it with peace: "Jesus prays in the garden: *Pater mi* (Mt 26:39), *Abba, Pater!* (Mk 14:36). God is my Father, even though he may send me suffering. He loves me tenderly, even while wounding me. Jesus suffers, to fulfil the Will of the Father.... And I, who also wish to fulfil the most holy Will of God, following in the footsteps of the Master, can I complain if I too meet suffering as my travelling companion?

"It will be a sure sign of my sonship, because God is treating me as he treated his own divine Son. Then I, as he did, will be able to groan and weep alone in my Gethsemane; but, as I lie prostrate on the ground, acknowledging my nothingness, there will rise up to the Lord a cry from the depths of my soul: *Pater mi, Abba, Pater, ... fiat!*" (St Josemaría Escrivá, *The Way of the Cross*, I, 1).

Num 16:22	you are illegitimate children and not sons. ⁹Besides this, we have had earthly fathers to discipline us and we respected them. Shall we not much more be subject to the Father of spirits and live? ¹⁰For they disciplined us for a short time at their pleasure, but he disciplines us for our good, that we may share his holiness. ¹¹For the moment all discipline seems painful rather than pleasant; later it yields the peaceful fruit of righteousness to those who have been trained by it.
2 Cor 4:17
Jas 3:18	
Is 35:3
Prov 4:26, LXX
Ps 34:15
Rom 12:18
Mt 5:8f
1 Jn 3:2
2 Tim 2:22 | ¹²Therefore lift your drooping hands and strengthen your weak knees, ¹³and make straight paths for your feet, so that what is lame may not be put out of joint but rather be healed.

Striving for peace. Purity. Reverent worship |
| Deut 29:17, LXX; Acts 8:23 | ¹⁴Strive for peace with all men, and for the holiness without which no one will see the Lord. ¹⁵See to it that no one fail to obtain the |

12:12–13. This exhortation follows logically from the previous one. It seems to evoke the world of athletic competition referred to at the beginning of the chapter. Verse 12 is like a shout of encouragement to a runner who is beginning to flag in the middle of a race.

The author uses a quotation from Isaiah (Is 35:3) in which drooping hands and weak knees indicate moral decline (cf. 2 Sam 2:7; 4:1; Jer 47:3). He then goes on to use words from Proverbs 4:26 to encourage right living: "make straight steps with your feet": if the Christian perseveres in his efforts even if he is somewhat "lame", that is, even if he is someone whose faith is weak and is in danger of apostasy, he will be able to return to fitness in spite of everything.

However, this exhortation can be taken as addressed not only to those who need to mend their ways but also to Christians in general, who should be exemplary and never in any way be a stumbling-block to their weaker brethren.

12:14. These words echo what our Lord says in the Sermon on the Mount: "Blessed are the peacemakers, for they shall be called sons of God". Jesus promises those who promote peace that they will be sons of God and therefore share in God's inner life, which makes man holy. The apostles and disciples of the Lord often repeat this teaching (cf. Jas 3:18; Rom 12:18; 1 Pet 3:11). Being at peace with God, which comes from docility to his plans (v. 11), necessarily leads one to foster and maintain peace with others. Peace with God and with one's neighbour is inseparable from the search for holiness. Christ brings about the fulfilment of the ancient promises which foretold a flowering of peace and righteousness in the messianic times (cf. Ps 72:3; 85:11–12; Is 9:7; etc.).

"Holiness": it is not just a matter of avoiding sin. One needs to cultivate virtue and to desire to attain holiness with the help of grace. Holiness or Christian perfection is the common goal of all Christ's disciples. Salvation and holiness are really one and the same thing, for only saints can obtain entry into the presence of God: only those who are holy can see the Holy One.

"You must be perfect, as your heavenly Father is perfect" (Mt 5:48). These

grace of God; that no "root of bitterness" spring up and cause trouble, and by it the many become defiled; ¹⁶that no one be immoral or irreligious like Esau, who sold his birthright for a single meal. ¹⁷For you know that afterward, when he desired to inherit the blessing, he was rejected, for he found no chance to repent, though he sought it with tears.

Gen 25:33f
Gen 27:30–40
Heb 6:4–6

words of our Lord are always echoing through the Church; today more than ever. "Today, once again, I set myself this goal and I also remind you and all mankind: this is God's will for us, that we be saints.

"In order to bring peace, genuine peace, to souls; in order to transform the earth and to seek God our Lord in the world and through the things of the world, personal sanctity is indispensable" (St Josemaría Escrivá, *Friends of God*, 294).

12:15. Theodoret comments on this passage as follows: "Do not be concerned only about yourselves; rather let each of you look after the other; strengthen the waverer and assist him who needs your helping hand" (*Interpretatio Ep. ad Haebreos,* ad loc.). A Christian needs to be concerned not only about his own soul, his own salvation; on his conscience should also lie the salvation of his brothers and sisters in the faith. He should be like a gardener who cares for his plants and makes sure no weeds or diseases spread through his garden. In the Old Testament, the man who denies his faith is described as a root bearing poisonous and bitter fruit (cf. Deut 29:18). Anyone who is indifferent to a brother's infidelity endangers those around him, for bad example can spread like an epidemic. This passage is reminiscent of St Paul's reproach to the Corinthians: "Do you not know that a little leaven leavens the whole lump?" (1 Cor 5:6).

Hence the need to be ever vigilant to ensure that no one through his own fault loses the gifts God has given him; "the true apostle is on the lookout for occasions of announcing Christ by word, either to unbelievers to draw them towards the faith, or to the faithful to instruct them, strengthen them, incite them to a more fervent life; 'for Christ's love urges us on' (2 Cor 5:14), and in the hearts of all should the Apostle's words find echo: 'Woe to me if I do not preach the Gospel' (1 Cor 9:16)" (Vatican II, *Apostolicam actuositatem*, 6).

12:16–17. Esau is an example of the way excessive interest in temporal things can lead to irresponsible behaviour. In rabbinical literature the first-born son of Isaac gained notoriety as a man inclined to vice through his marriages to Hittite women (cf. Gen 26:34–35; 27:46). The letter describes him as a "fornicator" (translated by RSV as "immoral", the word can be interpreted in a strict sense as meaning "unchaste"); but it can also be taken metaphorically as indicating apostasy, which is often its sense in the Old Testament. Esau is also described as "irreligious", that is, "impious", lacking in the piety due to his parents, because he sold his birthright (cf. Gen 25:29–34). He later tried to obtain from his father, Isaac, the blessing proper to the first-born, which Jacob had inherited through deceit (Gen 27). But he did not succeed in getting his father to change his mind and bless him, even though he pleaded with him with tears in his eyes, according to ancient Jewish tradition.

Esau "did not repent of having sold his birthright; he repented of having lost

Hebrews 12:18

¹⁸For you have not come to what may be touched, a blazing fire, and darkness, and gloom, and a tempest, ¹⁹and the sound of a trumpet, and a voice whose words made the hearers entreat that no further messages be spoken to them. ²⁰For they could not endure the order that was given, "If even a beast touches the mountain, it shall be stoned." ²¹Indeed, so terrifying was the sight that Moses said, "I tremble with fear." ²²But you have come to Mount Zion and to the city of the living God, the heavenly Jerusalem, and to innumerable angels in festal gathering, ²³and to the assembly^z of

Ex 19:12, 16, 18; Deut 4:11; Ex 19:16. 19; 20:18f; Ex 19:12f; Deut 9:19; Rev 14:1; Ps 74:4; Gen 4:26; Rev 21:2; Lk 10:20; 2 Tim 4:8

---

it; what pained him was not the sin of selling (it) but the disadvantage of losing (it). That is why his repentance was not accepted—because it was not sincere" (*Commentary on Heb*, 12, 3).

The moral teaching contained in these verses has to do with fidelity. Christians are first-born, but they are capable of falling into an infidelity from which there is no return, losing the gift of faith.

12:18–21. The text recalls in detail all the physical signs which accompanied the manifestation of God on the heights of Sinai (cf. Ex 19:12–16; 20:18), and to these it adds other things taken from Jewish oral tradition.

All this helps to inspire feelings of religious reverence and fear, which explains why the people begged God not to speak further, for they were afraid they would die. To assert his transcendence God forbade anyone to put foot on the mountain (Ex 19:12, 21); this was a way of showing this as yet uncivilized people the difference between the true God and idols.

There is no mention in the Pentateuch of Moses being frightened of the vision he saw when God manifested himself on Sinai; when his fear is mentioned (Deut 9:19) it is in the context of the second time he went up the mountain to be given replacements for the tables he had broken in a fit of rage (Deut 9:15–18; Ex 32:19–20). His fear was that God would punish with death those who had adored the golden calf. When telling (cf. Acts 7:32) the story of God's first revelation to Moses in the burning bush, St Stephen says that "Moses trembled and did not dare to look": thus, the presence of divinity provokes in him the deepest feelings of reverence and fear (cf. the attitude of Abraham: Gen 15:12; of Zechariah: Lk 1:12; of Isaiah: Is 6:4–5; of Jeremiah: Jer 1:6; of Gideon: Judg 6:22–23; etc.).

12:22–24. The sacred text dramatically contrasts two scenes—that of the establishment of the Covenant on Sinai, and the vision of the heavenly city, the dwelling-place of the angels and saints. The comparison implies a rhetorical question: if the setting of the Old Covenant was so solemn and awesome, and if the Covenant itself was so supernatural and divine, what must not be said of the New Covenant?

We have therefore overwhelming reasons for staying faithful: what awaits us is not an austere and vengeful God but, rather, the joy and splendour of the heavenly city. For the Hebrew people Mount Sinai was the most important symbol of their special connexion with God, reminding them that the Almighty was also the Supreme Judge who claimed their exclusive devotion and who abominated idolatry. Similarly, another mountain, Mount Zion, on which the temple was built, represented God's

---

z. *Or angels, and to the festal gathering and assembly*

protective presence in the midst of his people. Both mountains, Sinai and Zion, prefigured the mountain from which the Messiah-King would reign and towards which all peoples would flock to worship the true God (cf. Ps 2:6; Is 2:2).

The vision which Judaism, on the basis of Scripture, had elaborated of heaven as the "new Jerusalem" is now extended: not only is it the holy mountain, the source of the light and glory of Yahweh (cf. Is 8:18; 28:16; 60:1–11; Ps 50:2; 74:2; Joel 3:17), the city of peace (cf. Is 33:20); it is the city where the angels and saints dwell and rejoice, the domain of the living God and of Jesus—the heavenly and everlasting Jerusalem, which is also illustrated in the book of Revelation (cf. Rev 21:15–17; 22:1–5).

The text once more recalls the Exodus (cf. Heb 3:1618; 4:1–2; 9:18–20; 10:19–22). Christians are making their way to heaven, their lasting homeland, their true place of rest, just as the ancient Israelites made their way out of Egypt and crossed the desert to reach the land promised to their forefathers.

However, despite this parallel there are differences: the Old Covenant, although it did include expressions and promises of joy and jubilation, was set in an atmosphere of religious fear and trembling; whereas the New Covenant is full of joy and exultation, although in the midst of suffering.

"It is a question [...] of the glorious and supernatural joy, prophesied for the new Jerusalem redeemed from the exile and loved with a mystical love by God himself [...]. Through the course of many centuries and in the midst of most terrible trials, these promises wonderfully sustained the mystical hope of ancient Israel. And it is ancient Israel that transmitted them to the Church of Jesus Christ, in such a way that we are indebted to ancient Israel for some of the purest expressions of our hymn of joy. And yet, according to faith and the Christian experience of the Holy Spirit, this peace which is given by God and which spreads out like an overflowing torrent when the time of 'consolation' comes, is linked to the coming and presence of Christ" (Paul VI, *Gaudete in Domino*, 2–3).

12:22. The mention of Zion recalls the other mountain on which the Covenant was made (Sinai), as also the many prophetical texts which proclaimed that the Messiah's reign would begin on Zion, his holy mountain (cf. Ps 2:6; Is 2:2–4; 25:6; Zech 14:4). Thus, Mount Zion, the city of the living God, and the heavenly Jerusalem all mean the Church in triumph in heaven.

St Thomas emphasizes that part of eternal happiness in heaven consists in the vision of the heavenly assembly: "for in the glory of heaven there are two things which most cause the blessed to rejoice—enjoyment of the Godhead and the fellowship of the saints" (*Commentary on Heb*, ad loc.).

"Proceeding from the love of the eternal Father (cf. Tit 3:4), the Church was founded by Christ in time and gathered into one by the Holy Spirit (cf. Eph 1:3, 5, 6, 13–14, 23). It has a saving and eschatological purpose which can be fully attained only in the next life. But it is now present here on earth and is composed of men; they, the members of the earthly city, are called to form the family of the children of God in this present history of mankind and to increase it continually until the Lord comes" (Vatican II, *Gaudium et spes*, 40).

12:23. "The assembly of the first-born who are enrolled in heaven": the blessed,

Hebrews 12:24

Heb 11:40
1 Pet 1:2

the first-born who are enrolled in heaven, and to a judge who is God of all, and to the spirits of just men made perfect, ²⁴and to Jesus, the mediator of a new covenant, and to the sprinkled blood that speaks more graciously than the blood of Abel.

Heb 2:3

²⁵See that you do not refuse him who is speaking. For if they did not escape when they refused him who warned them on earth, much less shall we escape if we reject him who warns from

---

including the righteous of the Old Testament, the apostles and all Christians who have attained the beatific vision. They are called first-born because, as in the case of the patriarchs, they were the first to have faith; because, as in the case of the apostles, it was they who received Christ's call initially, to pass it on to others; and, finally, because, as in the case of faithful Christians, they were chosen by God from among the pagans (cf. Rom 8:29; Phil 3:20; Col 1:18; Rev 1:5; 14:4). Their names are written in heaven (cf. Lk 10:20; Rev 2:17; 3:5; 13:8; 17:8).

12:24. As Incarnate Word and High Priest, Jesus is the mediator of the New Covenant (cf. Heb 8:6; 9:15; 1 Tim 2:5; cf. Heb 2:17; 13:1; 7:25). The letter focuses for a moment on the most significant point in the alliance—the shedding of our Lord's blood, which ratifies the Covenant and cleanses mankind (cf. Ex 24:8; Heb 9:12–14, 20; 10:19, 28–29; 13:20; 1 Pet 1:2). This blood "speaks more graciously than the blood of Abel", "for the shedding of Christ's blood was represented figuratively by the shedding of the blood of all the just there has been since the beginning of the world [...]. Therefore, the spilling of Abel's blood was a sign of this new spilling of blood. But the blood of Christ is more eloquent than that of Abel, because Abel's called for vengeance whereas the blood of Christ claims forgiveness" (St Thomas Aquinas, *Commentary on Heb*, ad loc.). The confidence the blood of Christ gives us makes us feel happy to be sinners who, repentant, take refuge in his wounds.

"Sinners, says the Letter, you are fortunate indeed, for after you sin you have recourse to the crucified Jesus, who shed all his blood so that he might stand as mediator to make peace between God and sinners, and win you forgiveness from him. If your evildoing shouts against you, the Redeemer's blood cries aloud in your favour, and divine justice cannot but listen to what this blood says" (St Alphonsus, *The Love of Jesus Christ*, 3).

12:25. The Old Covenant was ratified in a solemn manner in order to inspire respect and veneration. The much greater importance and dignity of the New Covenant, sealed with the blood of Christ, carries with it an increased obligation of fidelity. If those were condemned who opposed Moses, who "received living oracles to give us" (Acts 7:38), there is much more reason for us to be punished if we cut ourselves off from "him who warns from heaven".

"There is never reason to look back (cf. Lk 9:62). The Lord is at our side. We have to be faithful and loyal; we have to face up to our obligations and we will find in Jesus the love and the stimulus we need to understand other people's faults and overcome our own. In this way even depression—yours, mine, anyone's—can also be a pillar for the kingdom of Christ" (St Josemaría Escrivá, *Christ Is Passing By*, 160).

heaven. ²⁶His voice then shook the earth; but now he has promised, "Yet once more I will shake not only the earth but also the heaven." ²⁷This phrase, "Yet once more," indicates the removal of what is shaken, as of what has been made, in order that what cannot be shaken may remain. ²⁸Therefore let us be grateful for receiving a kingdom that cannot be shaken, and thus let us offer to God acceptable worship, with reverence and awe; ²⁹for our God is a consuming fire.

Hag 2:6, 21
Mt 24:29

Is 33:1
Deut 4:24; 9:3
Rom 1:9

12:26–27. Quoting from the prophet Haggai (Hag 2:6), the sacred writer shows that just as the earth trembled at Sinai when God sealed the Covenant with Moses, so too did earth, and heaven also, tremble when the New Covenant was made (cf. Mt 27:51–52). He is stressing that the New Covenant will last forever, whereas the Old was provisional. The Law of Moses disappeared insofar as it was temporary and earthly; everything of permanent value in it remains.

Although it is more likely that the text is referring to the establishment by Christ of the New Law in place of that of Moses, this passage can be interpreted in an eschatological sense, as some Fathers of the Church have done: "Scripture teaches us that heaven and earth will be destroyed 'once more', as if this event had already happened. I think that it refers to the irresistible establishment of a new state of creation. We must believe Paul when he says that the final upheaval of the world will be nothing other than the second coming of Christ and that the existing universe will be transformed and will give way to another, definitive and unchangeable universe" (St Gregory Nazianzen, *Oratio*, 21).

Whichever interpretation applies, the practical consequences of this teaching are the same. Earthly things are impermanent; therefore, we should desire things which last—heavenly things. "Why do you grieve when you suffer in this world which cannot last, in this world which soon will pass away? [...]. No one does any building in a city which is going to be destroyed. Tell me, please: if someone told you that in a year's time a particular city was going to be completely demolished, and also that some other one was going to endure: would you build in the one which was going to be pulled down? That is why I am telling you now: let us not build in this world; in a little time it will all collapse and disappear" (Chrysostom, *Hom. on Heb*, ad loc.).

12:28–29. The high point of the epistle is v. 28, which proclaims the establishment of a "kingdom that cannot be shaken", that will last forever. This Kingdom is the heavenly Jerusalem, of which the Church is an anticipation. Christians who are true to their calling are preparing the way for the coming of the Kingdom and in some way they make it present on earth. "A kingdom that is ruled by truth, by the dignity of man, by responsibility, by the conviction of being (made in) the likeness of God. A kingdom where there takes effect the divine plan for man, a plan based on love, true freedom, mutual service and reconciliation of men with God and with one another" (John Paul II, *Audience for young people*, 3 November 1982).

Christians are full citizens of this Kingdom, with a perfect right to share in the benefits which flow from it. However,

Hebrews 13:1

<small>Rom 12:13; 1 Thess 4:9; Gen 18:2f; 19:1–3; Judg 6:11–24; 13:3–20; Tob 5:4f Jas 6:11–24; Mt 25:36; Heb 10:34; Eph 5:5</small>

Duties towards others—charity, hospitality, fidelity in marriage

13 ¹*Let brotherly love continue. ²Do not neglect to show hospitality to strangers, for thereby some have entertained angels unawares. ³Remember those who are in prison, as though in prison with them; and those who are ill-treated, since you also are in the body. ⁴Let marriage be held in honour among all, and let the

---

these rights at the same time create certain obligations—to keep the grace of God and offer him acceptable worship. Some translations, including the RSV, take the original Greek to mean "let us be grateful to God": however, it seems more likely, given the context, that it means that it is grace which enables us to offer God acceptable worship. In other words, let us jealously hold onto this supernatural gift—sanctifying grace and the other supernatural graces—which makes us subjects of the Kingdom established by Christ's covenant.

The description of God as a "consuming fire" is evocative of various Old Testament passages (cf., e.g., Deut 4:24; 9:3; Ex 24:17; Is 33:14). God's justice will deal severely with those who do not accept the grace Christ offers them: it will follow its course inexorably.

13:1–3. The teaching on moral questions which takes up this chapter follows on logically from the trend of the whole letter, particularly the previous chapter: faithfulness to Christ means being faithful to him as a person and to his teaching. As he himself said, "If you love me, you will keep my commandments" (Jn 14:15). Among the essential teachings of our faith is the supreme importance of charity: "A new commandment I give to you, that you love one another; even as I have loved you, that you also love one another. By this all men will know that you are my disciples, if you have love for one another" (Jn 13:34–35). As Tertullian attests, pagans bore witness to how well the early Christians practised this virtue, when they would say, "See how they love one another: they are ready to die for one another" (*Apologeticum*, 39).

Brotherly love expresses itself in all kinds of ways. One of them is hospitality, which is one of the traditional corporal works of mercy. The virtue of hospitality is given high praise in this passage which contains implicit references to episodes in the life of Abraham and Sarah (Gen 18), Lot (cf. Gen 19), Manoah (cf. Judg 13:3–22) or Tobit (cf. Tob 12:1–20), who gave hospitality to wayfarers who turned out to be angels. Similarly, Christians who practise this virtue are in fact welcoming Christ himself (cf. Mt 25:40). They should also see Christ in everyone who is experiencing any kind of suffering. "He himself is the one who in each individual experiences love; he himself is the one who receives help, when this is given to every suffering person without exception. He himself is present in this suffering person, since his salvific suffering has been opened once and for all to every human suffering" (John Paul II, *Salvifici doloris*, 30).

13:4. For anyone to practise charity towards God and towards others, the virtue of chastity is essential. It expands one's capacity for love. The text earnestly exhorts Christians to show their appreciation of marriage by practising marital chastity. Marriage is a personal calling by God to seek holiness in that state in life. "In God's plan, all husbands and wives are called in marriage to holiness, and

marriage bed be undefiled; for God will judge the immoral and adulterous. ⁵Keep your life free from love of money, and be content with what you have; for he has said, "I will never fail you nor forsake you." ⁶Hence we can confidently say,
> "The Lord is my helper,
> I will not be afraid;
> what can man do to me?"

Deut 31:6, 8
Gen 28:15
Josh 1:5
1 Tim 6:8
Ps 118:6

Religious duties—obeying lawful pastors; religious worship
⁷Remember your leaders, those who spoke to you the word of God; consider the outcome of their life, and imitate their faith.

Lk 22:26
1 Tim 5:17

---

this lofty vocation is fulfilled to the extent that the human person is able to respond to God's command with serene confidence in God's grace and in his or her own will" (John Paul II, *Familiaris consortio*, 34).

However, this also calls for marital chastity, which is a manifestation and proof of true love. "Human love—pure, sincere and joyful—cannot subsist in marriage without the virtue of chastity, which leads a couple to respect the mystery of sex and ordain it to faithfullness and personal dedication [...].

"When there is chastity in the love of married persons, their marital life is authentic; husband and wife are true to themselves, they understand each other and develop the union between them. When the divine gift of sex is perverted, their intimacy is destroyed, and they can no longer look openly at one another" (St J. Escrivá, *Christ Is Passing By*, 25).

13:5–6. In teaching against love of money and exaggerated desire for material things, the text may be echoing what our Lord said: "Do not lay up for yourselves treasures on earth, where moth and rust consume and where thieves break in and steal, but lay up treasures in heaven [...]" (Mt 6:19–20). The letter is encouraging us to trust God at all times and to be detached from earthly things. "Detach yourself from the goods of the world. Love and practise poverty of spirit: be content with what enables you to live a simple and sober life [...]" (St Josemaría Escrivá, *The Way*, 631).

It uses some words spoken by Moses on God's behalf to remind the reader that it is God himself who has told man that he will never abandon him (cf. Deut 31:6). These words should fill us with consolation, allowing us to say with the psalmist (cf. Ps 118:6) that we can do anything provided God helps us, and there is nothing for us to fear provided we abandon ourselves to divine providence (cf. Mt 6:25–32).

"If Christ is yours, then wealth is yours; he satisfies all your wants. He will look after you, manage all your affairs for you most dutifully; you will need no human support to rely on [...]. Put all your trust in God; centre in him all your fear and all your love; he will make himself responsible for you, and all will go well as he sees best" (*The Imitation of Christ*, 1, 2–3).

13:7–19. In this passage this more practical section of the letter examines specifically ecclesial duties, placing special emphasis on the Christian's duty to maintain unity with and to obey and

Hebrews 13:7

respect those who have the mission to govern the community. This exhortation is made twice (vv. 7 and 17) to show the importance of obedience to lawful pastors (cf. 1 Thess 5:12–13; 1 Cor 16:16). We should see in the pastors of the Church a model of how we should practise the faith (v. 7; cf. Phil 3:17), and in particular we should see them as Christ's representatives (cf. Gal 4:12–14). Obedience to the hierarchy of the Church naturally involves accepting its teaching and eschewing heretical opinions (v. 9; cf. 1 Tim 6:3; Gal 1:6–9). Unity of faith, moreover, has to be expressed in unity of worship (v. 10; cf. Phil 3:3; Eph 4:4–5): no one may take part in Christian worship while continuing to take part in Jewish worship (cf. 1 Cor 10:16–21), nor is it lawful to regard rabbinical rules about food as still applying (v. 9; Col 2:16–18; 1 Tim 4:3–5). One needs to undergo a real conversion (vv. 11–13; Rom 3:23–26) and to put aside outdated rites and practices if one is to share in Christ's cross (1 Cor 2:21–25; Gal 6:14–15). We must not put our trust in earthly things, but instead bear in mind that our end and goal is heaven (cf. Phil 3:20). Finally, unity of faith, discipline and sacraments must express itself in a consistent, coherent lifestyle whereby we are always in the presence of God, use everything as an opportunity for prayer and sacrifice, and practise a continuous charity towards others (vv. 15–16; cf. Gal 6:9–10; Rom 12:9–13; Eph 5:1–2; etc.). This short passage gives a very attractive outline of what Christian life involves. As Vatican II put it, "A life like this calls for a continuous exercise of faith, hope and charity. Only the light of faith and meditation on the Word of God can enable us to find everywhere and always the God 'in whom we live and move and have our being' (Acts 17:28); only thus can we seek his will in everything, see Christ in all men, acquaintance or stranger, and make sound judgments on the true meaning and value of temporal realities both in themselves and in relation to man's end" (*Apostolicam actuositatem*, 2).

13:7–14. The text emphasizes the need to be at one with those in charge, the pastors and teachers of the Christian communities. Reference, in the past tense, to their faith suggests it is referring to those who have already obtained the crown of martyrdom—people like Stephen and St James the Greater (cf. Acts 7:59–60; 12:2), and other members of the community who were victims of Jewish persecution (cf. Acts 8:1; Heb 6:10; 10:32–34). They were admirable people; however, unity with one's leaders was not and is not conditional on the personal quality of these leaders: "What a pity that whoever is in charge doesn't give you good example! But, is it for his personal qualities that you obey him? Or do you conveniently interpret Saint Paul's '*obedite praepositis vestris*: obey your leaders' with a qualification of your own ... , 'always provided they have virtues to my taste'?" (St J. Escrivá, *The Way*, 621).

Faithfulness to and solidarity with one's lawful pastors is faithfulness towards Christ himself, for the "bishops, as vicars and legates of Christ, govern the particular churches assigned to them by their counsels, exhortations and example, but over and above that also by the authority and sacred power which indeed they exercise exclusively for the spiritual development of their flock in truth and holiness, keeping in mind that he who is greater should become as the lesser, and he who is the leader as the servant (cf. Lk

Hebrews 13:9

⁸Jesus Christ is the same yesterday and today and for ever. ⁹Do not be led away by diverse and strange teachings; for it is well that the

Eph 4:14; Col 2:7; Rom 14:17 1 Cor 8:8

22:26–27)" (Vatican II, *Lumen gentium*, 27). Thus, it is rightly said that he who hears them hears Christ (cf. Lk 10:16). For their part, pastors should have the same love and solicitude for those in their charge as our Redeemer had; in this wonderful unity of charity the mystery of Christ will shine forth; it is Christ's right "to be the sole ruler of the Church; and for this reason also he is likened to the Head. The head (to use the words of St Ambrose) is 'the royal citadel' of the body (*Hexameron*, 6, 9, 55), and because it was endowed with more perfect gifts it naturally rules all the members, being purposely placed above them to have them under its care. In like manner the divine Redeemer wields the supreme power and government over the whole commonwealth of Christians" (Pius XII, *Mystici Corporis*, 16).

The mystery of the Incarnation is indissolubly linked to the mystery of the Church, in such a way that the unity of the Church is a sign of the unity of the Lord's Body, which is one body with many different members (cf. 1 Cor 12:1–12; *Lumen gentium*, 7). Therefore, fidelity to the Church derives not from human reasons but from a desire to be faithful to Christ himself.

Fidelity to Christ, his preaching, to his commandments and the sacraments he instituted leads to loving fulfilment of everything the Church lays down with regard to worship—particularly to interior practice of the faith, repentance for sin and fervent reception of the sacraments (cf. Council of Trent, *De iustificatione*, chaps. 6 and 8; Rom 3:22–24; 11:16; Eph 2:8; 1 Cor 4:7; 15:10; 2 Cor 3:5). There are no clean or unclean foods (cf. Col 2:16; Rom 14:2–4), whether they are offered to idols or not (cf. 1 Cor 8; 10: 14–33), whether they are eaten or abstained from on certain days (cf. Rom 14:5; Col 2:16; Gal 4:10); there is no food which renders a person unclean or leads him to salvation (cf. Mk 7:15, 18; Rom 14:17, 20): for one whose heart is pure all things are pure (cf. Tit 1:15). The important thing is the grace of God, which is given us in the sacraments and which enables us to practise all the commandments out of love for God. The letter moves from these remarks about legal purity and impurity to point out that there is now an entirely new situation and what really matters is sharing in the paschal mystery of Christ, that is, in his passion, death and resurrection.

13:8. This verse expresses the foundation of the life of every Christian. It is a wonderful expression of faith constituting an act of adoration and reverence similar to the praise of the one God in Deuteronomy 6:4 ("The Lord our God is one Lord") or of the eternal God in Psalm 102:12 ("Thou, O Lord, art enthroned for ever; thy name endures to all generations"), only here it is Jesus Christ who is being extolled. Though their first teachers and guides may have died to bear witness to their faith, Christians will always have a teacher and guide who will never die, who lives for ever crowned with glory. Men come and go but Jesus remains for ever. He exists from all eternity, he is the Alpha and the Omega, the Beginning and the End (cf. Rev 1:8; 22:13); he lived "yesterday" among men in a specific period of history; he lives "today" in heaven, at the right hand of the Father, and he is "today" at our side providing us

Hebrews 13:10

Heb 8:4f

heart be strengthened by grace, not by foods, which have not benefited their adherents.* ¹⁰We have an altar from which those

with grace and forever interceding for us (cf. Mt 28:20; Heb 4:14); he will remain "for ever" as High Priest and Redeemer (cf. Heb 6:20; 7:17) until he establishes his Kingdom and hands it to his Father (cf. 1 Cor 15:24–28).

It is moving to think that Christ did not take on human nature for a limited period only. The Incarnation was decreed from all eternity, and the Son of God, born of the Virgin Mary, in time and space, in the reign of Caesar Augustus, remains a man for ever, with a glorious body bearing the resplendent marks of his passion. In Christ's human nature, now indissolubly joined to the divine person of the Son, all Creation is in some way glorified (cf. Col 1:15–20; Eph 1:9–10). Therefore, we can be absolutely sure that Christ's teaching cannot change: it is as immutable as he is and it will eventually transform the world. We know that all dimensions of human life—work, family life, life in society, affections, suffering—acquire in Christ a new and lasting purpose. "The Church believes that Christ, who died and was raised for the sake of all, can show man the way and strengthen him through the Spirit in order to be worthy of his destiny: nor is there any other name under heaven given among men by which they can be saved. The Church likewise believes that the key, the centre and the purpose of the whole of man's history is to be found in its Lord and Master. She also maintains that beneath all that changes there is much that is unchanging, much that has its ultimate foundation in Christ, who is the same yesterday, and today, and forever" (Vatican II, *Gaudium et spes*, 10). This is the source of the Christian's confidence. "Jesus is the way. Behind him on this earth of ours he has left the clear outlines of his footprints. They are indelible signs which neither the erosion of time nor the treachery of the evil one have been able to erase. *Iesus Christus heri, et hodie; ipse et in saecula.* How I love to recall these words! Jesus Christ, the very Jesus who was alive yesterday for his Apostles and the people who sought him out—this same Jesus lives today for us, and will live forever" (St Josemaría Escrivá, *Friends of God*, 127).

13:9. This verse contains two commandments. The first is to hold on to sound teaching and not be led astray by those who argue that the precepts of the Old Law still apply (cf. Acts 20:29–30; Gal 1:6, 7; 3:2–4; 5:12). Christians should not yield to the attraction of new teachings which are "diverse" (that is, contradictory and changeable, whereas there is only one truth and it does not change) and "strange", that is, alien to the teaching of Christ.

The second commandment, stated implicitly, was probably very clear to the first readers of the letter, who were familiar with the strange practices of religious sects of the time. It states a basic principle: what strengthens one's resolve and leads to upright conduct is not special regulations about food but Christ's grace. Grace and food are counterposed, but the latter is not said to be something bad. Special dietary laws or food-related religious practices are of no use to anyone; but grace is always useful. This is very reminiscent of John 6:63: "It is the spirit that gives life, the flesh is of no avail."

13:10. Very probably the term "altar" refers to the "eucharistic table" and possibly also to Christ in the Eucharist. It

who serve the tent[a] have no right to eat. ¹¹For the bodies of those animals whose blood is brought into the sanctuary by the high priest as a sacrifice for sin are burned outside the camp. ¹²So Jesus also suffered outside the gate in order to sanctify the people through his own blood. ¹³Therefore let us go forth to him outside the camp and bear the abuse he endured.* ¹⁴For here we have no

Lev 16:27
Mt 21:39
Jn 19:20
Acts 7:58
Heb 11:26
Heb 11:10
Phil 3:20

is not possible to take part in Christian worship if one has another religious allegiance, and vice versa (cf. 1 Cor 10:21).

The text is saying that the Old Testament form of worship has been replaced by Christian worship: Christian worship is the real thing; Old Testament worship was only its shadow or prefigurement.

13:11–13. This passage should be read against the background of the Old Testament rites of the Day of Atonement (cf. Heb 9:7–9; 4:14; 9:24; 10:20; Lev 16:27). Jesus Christ, crucified outside the walls of Jerusalem (for the mound of Calvary was outside the gate of Ephraim, to the northeast of the city) has acted out what was prefigured by the sacrificed victims which were burned outside the camp. By sacrificing the heifer and the male goat to atone for the sins of the people, the high priest was enabled to enter the sanctuary; so too the shedding of Christ's blood has opened the way to the sanctuary of heaven. The skin, bones and flesh of the victims were burned outside the camp; so too Christ went out of the city; but his exit is symbolic in another sense also: it means leaving Jewish worship behind and declaring it obsolete. The people to whom the epistle was initially written—obviously Christians of Jewish background—are being invited to leave behind the comfortable position they enjoyed as Jews (Judaism being recognized by the Roman empire as a "lawful religion") and not to be afraid of the risks—the "abuse"—involved in following Christ (the enmity of Jews and persecution by Gentiles).

"Abuse" may be a reference to the fact that contact with the remains of animals sacrificed on the Day of Atonement meant legal impurity (cf. Lev 16:24, 26, 28); but it clearly refers to the Cross (or "stumbling block" to Jews: cf. 1 Cor 1:23) and to the contempt suffered by our Lord. This exhortation also has a wider application—to Christians of all times, who need to leave behind anything which prevents them from being good disciples of Christ. "We too have to imitate him who chose to undergo the cross for the sake of our salvation; we have to leave this world, or, better, leave the empty affairs of this world" (Chrysostom, *Hom. on Heb*, 33).

13:14. Using the cyclic method found elsewhere in the letter (cf. 9:18–22, 25), the sacred writer links the notion of atoning sacrifice to the Exodus. In fact, three points in salvation history are linked together. Firstly, the Exodus, with the celebration of the Passover and the establishment of the Covenant on Sinai. This first episode is set in the framework of the sacrifice of expiation on Sinai, when Moses sprinkled the blood over the people and the book of the Law. A second episode, or, better, a second reference point, is the ceremonial of the Day of Atonement which was celebrated in the encampment during the pilgrimage in the wilderness and later on in the

a. Or *tabernacle*

Hebrews 13:15

Lev 7:12
2 Chron 29:31
Ps 50:14, 23

lasting city, but we seek the city which is to come. [15]Through him then let us continually offer up a sacrifice of praise to God, that is,

---

temple of Jerusalem. Both the Exodus and the Day of Atonement had a spiritual meaning: the people were petitioning God for forgiveness of their sins and were asking to be set free of them; and God's mercy was being celebrated, as was the Israelites' entry into the promised land. The third episode is, clearly, the passion, death and resurrection of Christ, the fulfilment and perfecting of everything symbolized by those earlier "types".

The life of Christians is an exodus (cf. Heb 4:1–11) because it involves leaving sin behind and living in union with God, sharing in our Lord's cross. It is an exodus because we shall have to leave this earth in order to enter heaven. Death, which is a punishment for sin (cf. Rom 6:23), is something we must undergo if we are to become fully identified with Christ (cf. Rom 6:10–11): "For whoever would save his life will lose it; and whoever loses his life for my sake, he will save it" (Lk 9:24; cf. Mt 10:39; 16:25; Mk 8:35; Jn 12:25).

The verse also points to the need for Christian detachment (cf. 2 Cor 5:1–2; Phil 3:20; Col 1:5; 1 Pet 1:4): " God did not create us to build a lasting city here on earth, 'this world is the way to that other, a dwelling place free from care' (Jorge Manrique). Nevertheless, we children of God ought not to remain aloof from earthly endeavours, for God has placed us here to sanctify them and make them fruitful with our blessed faith" (St Josemaría Escrivá, *Friends of God*, 210).

The Second Vatican Council also points to this tension which Christian life involves: "the expectation of a new earth must not weaken but rather stimulate our concern for cultivating this one. For here grows the body of a new human family, a body which even now is able to give some kind of foreshadowing of the new age. Hence, while earthly progress must be carefully distinguished from the growth of Christ's Kingdom, to the extent that the former can contribute to the better ordering of human society, it is of vital concern to the Kingdom of God" (*Gaudium et spes*, 39).

13:15–16. The text presupposes the Old Testament distinction between the "sin offering" and other offerings. The sin offering was made publicly on the great Day of Atonement. The other offerings, particularly those not involving the shedding of blood—first fruits, fruit and loaves, which the faithful presented to God in thanksgiving and praise—were called "peace offerings", among which the most prominent was the "sacrifice of thanksgiving" (cf. Lev 7:12; Ps 50:14; 116:17).

In the New Testament the faithful, exercising their spiritual priesthood (cf. Rom 12:1; Heb 12:28), offer sacrifices acceptable to God—prayer (made by lips which confess God), good works, alms, etc.

Already, through the prophets, God had made it plain that he abhorred sacrifices which were merely external (cf. 1 Sam 15;22; Is 1:11–17; Jer 6:20; Amos 5:21–22): what he wanted was a pure and humble heart (cf. Is 58:6–8). Jesus said the same (cf. Mt 5:23–24; Mk 11:25; Lk 18:9–14). So too, in the New Covenant, Christ wants all followers to exercise that priesthood which consists in doing good and offering to God all the little sacrifices each day involves: "Since he wishes to continue his witness and his serving

the fruit of lips that acknowledge his name. ¹⁶Do not neglect to do good and to share what you have, for such sacrifices are pleasing to God.

Is 57:19; Hos 14:3; Mal 1:11
Phil 4:18; 2 Cor 8:4

¹⁷Obey your leaders and submit to them; for they are keeping watch over your souls, as men who will have to give account. Let them do this joyfully, and not sadly, for that would be of no advantage to you.

1 Thess 5:12
Ezek 3:18

¹⁸Pray for us, for we are sure that we have a clear conscience, desiring to act honourably in all things. ¹⁹I urge you the more earnestly to do this in order that I may be restored to you the sooner.

Rom 15:30
Eph 6:19
Col 4:3
Philem 22

Words of farewell

²⁰Now may the God of peace who brought again from the dead our Lord Jesus, the great shepherd of the sheep, by the blood of the eternal covenant, ²¹equip you with everything good that you may do his will, working in you[b] that which is pleasing in his sight, through Jesus Christ; to whom be glory for ever and ever. Amen.

Is 63:11
Zech 9:11
Is 55:3
Jer 32:40
Ezek 37:26
Jn 10:11
1 Pet 2:25
Rom 16:27

---

through the laity also, the supreme and eternal priest, Christ Jesus, vivifies them with his spirit and ceaselessly impels them to accomplish every good and perfect work" (Vatican II, *Lumen gentium*, 34).

13:17–19. Emphasis is put here on the duty all Christians have to pray especially for those who are placed in authority over them.

"We owe two things to those who govern us in the spiritual sphere. First, obedience, to do what they tell us; and then reverence, to honour them like parents and accept the discipline they propose" (Chrysostom, *Hom. on Heb*, 13, 3).

"You are under an obligation to pray and sacrifice yourself for the person and intentions of whoever is 'in charge' of your apostolic undertaking. If you are careless in fulfilling this duty, you make me think that you lack enthusiasm for your way" (St Josemaría Escrivá, *The Way*, 953).

13:20–21. The epistle ends in the same kind of way as the Pauline epistles do— with a doxology and some words of farewell. In these verses "the God of peace" is invoked; he is the only one who can give true peace, decreeing that men should be reconciled to him through the action of Christ; and Jesus is described as "the great shepherd": once more there is this paralleling the Exodus/Old Covenant with entry into heaven. Just as Moses brought the people of Israel into the promised land the way a shepherd leads his sheep (cf. Is 63:11), so Jesus Christ, the shepherd *par excellence* (cf. Jn 10:10–16; 1 Pet 2:25; 5:4), has led his sheep into the glory of heaven.

Verse 21 links Christian teaching on grace with man's response to that grace. Commenting on this passage St Thomas Aquinas explains that the words "equip you with everything good that you may do his will" is the same as saying "may God make you desire everything good",

---

b. Other ancient authorities read *us*

Hebrews 13:22

2 Tim 4:3
1 Pet 5:12
Acts 16:1

²²I appeal to you, brethren, bear with my word of exhortation, for I have written to you briefly. ²³You should understand that our brother Timothy has been released, with whom I shall see you if he comes soon. ²⁴Greet all your leaders and all the saints. Those who come from Italy send you greetings. ²⁵Grace be with all of you. Amen.

---

because it is God's will that we act of our own free will. If we did not act freely, our will would not be good; if we do God's will we will always be doing what is good for us (cf. Aquinas, *Commentary on Heb*, ad loc.). God has disposed man's will to choose to do what is right. It is up to man to respond to God's design. In this sense God "equips us with everything good that you may do his will".

13:22–24. The "word of exhortation" conveys the idea of a speech or text that seeks to give consolation and encouragement. It may even be an allusion to the type of addresses given in synagogues (cf. Acts 13:15)—as if the author were conveying in written form something he was unable to do orally.

"Our brother Timothy": a reference to that well-known figure in the early Church, a disciple and travelling-companion of St Paul, to whom the Apostle wrote two letters that bear his name.

The greeting to the "leaders" shows the respect and reverence people had for those in charge of the community (cf. Heb 13:7, 17). On the phrase "all the saints", see the notes on Rom 1:7; 1 Cor 1:2; Eph 1:1.

"Those who come from Italy": as many Fathers and early commentators thought, this letter was almost certainly written in Rome.

13:25. The ending is similar to that of letters of St Paul, especially Ephesians, Colossians, 1 Timothy, 2 Timothy and Titus. "Grace" is the whole ensemble of supernatural gifts which God gives man through Jesus Christ. It is what all apostolic endeavour is seeking—that all men should obtain grace and that none should lose it. Theodoret, commenting on this passage, points out that "he adds the customary ending, praying that they all be partakers of grace. Let us praise the lawgiver of both old and new [laws] and, in order to obtain his help, let us pray that by fulfilling his divine commands we shall attain the promised good things to come, in Jesus Christ our Lord, to whom belongs glory together with the Father and the Holy Spirit now and for ever and for ever more. Amen" (*Interpretatio Ep. ad Haebreos*, ad loc.).

THE CATHOLIC LETTERS

The Revised Standard Version, with notes

General Introduction to the Catholic Letters

The canon of the books of the New Testament includes, along with the Pauline corpus (thirteen letters plus Hebrews), a group of seven letters described as the "Catholic Letters"—James; 1 and 2 Peter; 2 and 3 John; and Jude.

Apparently the reason why they are grouped like this is not because of similarities of style or doctrine, but simply to distinguish them from the Pauline corpus. The grouping is found as early as the fourth century AD[1] but they were not always put in the same place in the canon: the great early codexes—the Codex Vaticanus and the Codex Sinaiticus—put them after the Acts of the Apostles; from St Jerome onwards, they always appear in bibles just after the writings of St Paul, before the book of Revelation. Nor do they always occur in the same order within the group; often the two letters of St Peter come first,[2] although from St Jerome onwards they are usually positioned in manuscripts in the order familiar to us.

The name "catholic" was given by Origen to 1 Peter, 1 John, and Jude.[3] Later Eusebius and St Jerome extended the title to all seven. It would seem that they were described in this way because they were letters addressed to the whole Church and not just to specific churches or individuals, as in the case of St Paul's letters. The Second and Third Letters of St John do have particular addressees but they are put into the "catholic" category for the sake of convenience.[4]

CANONICITY

Some early commentators explained the title "catholic" as meaning "canonical", indicating that everyone regarded these as inspired books.[5] However, this explanation is not very convincing. Five of seven were slow to receive unanimous acceptance as canonical (this is dealt with in the introductions to the particular letters); these five are the so-called "deuterocanonical" letters—James, 2 Peter, 2 and 3 John and Jude. In his famous canon Eusebius locates all five among the disputed books (*antilegómena*) but acknowledges that most people accepted them as inspired.[6]

---

1. Cf. Eusebius of Caesarea, *Ecclesiastical History*, 3, 25, 2–3. **2.** This is the case in the list of canonical books issued by the Council of Trent. **3.** Cf. Eusebius, *Ecclesiastical History*, 6, 25,8. **4.** Cf. ibid., 2, 23, 25; St Jerome, *On Famous Men*, 2, 4. **5.** Cf. St Isidore of Seville, *Eytmology*, 6, 24. **6.** Cf. *Ecclesiastical History*, 3, 25, 3.

General Introduction to the Catholic Letters

In the West they were unanimously accepted as canonical from the fourth century onwards (this is confirmed by the provincial council of Hippo, 393, and the third and fourth councils of Carthage, 397 and 419). The Syrian Church gradually came round to accepting them and by the end of the seventh century, it is fair to say, the entire Church accepted them.

In the sixteenth century, the Protestants began to resurrect the old doubts about the canonicity of some of these letters—but for new reasons, as shall be explained in the particular introductions. This led the Council of Trent solemnly to define the witness of Tradition—that all these books have to be received "as sacred and canonical in their entirety, with all their parts, according to the text usually read in the Catholic Church".[7]

COMMON FEATURES

Each letter has a specific purpose and content of its own, and they have very few features in common. St Augustine says that they all have to do with refuting errors which were beginning to appear.[8] And all of them evidence the teaching and catechesis given to the early Christians communities. For the most part the tone is pastoral and the letters contain religious instruction and moral teaching encouraging people to lead deeply Christian lives.

---

7. Council of Trent, *De libris sacris*. 8. Cf. *De fide et operibus*, 14, 21.

Introduction to the Letter of St James

The Letter of St James heads up the list of "Catholic Letters". Over the course of the centuries it has not been commented on to any great extent, probably because it has to do with moral as distinct from doctrinal matters; from the sixteenth century onwards commentators focused mostly on the subject of faith and works (cf. 2:14–26). Because of the paucity of commentaries and the complexity of the letter's language (it is written in very sophisticated Greek, and the background of the language is clearly Semitic), scholars even nowadays raise questions about its authorship, date of composition, etc. However, in recent decades this letter has attracted a lot of attention due to the fact that it is a very faithful reflection of the very vital, spontaneous exposition given to the Christian message in the first communities, and because it very clearly points up the unity between the Old and New Testaments.

THE AUTHOR

At the beginning of the letter the writer introduces himself simply as "James, a servant of God and of the Lord Jesus Christ" (1:1). In the Old Testament the expression "servant of God" is applied to people like Abraham (Ps 105:42), Moses (Josh 14:7), David (Ps 89:3) or the prophets (Amos 3:7) who had a prominent mission; in the New Testament St Paul describes himself as "a servant of Jesus Christ" (cf., e.g., Rom 1:1; Phil 1:1). The rest of the letter hardly gives us any further information about the writer except that he includes himself among the teachers (3:1); that, as such, he teaches with authority (1:13ff; 3:13ff), he reproaches his readers (1:21ff; 4:13ff) and takes them to task (4:1ff) and even threatens them (5:1ff). The author of the letter then, is someone called James who is well-known to the early Christians, someone held in high regard.

The name James—*Iaaqob* in Hebrew—was very common, so it is not surprising that up to five men called James appear in the New Testament— James, the son of Zebedee, called the Greater (Mt 10:2; Lk 8:51; Acts 1:13; 12:2); James, the son of Alphaeus, also an Apostle, called the Less (Mt 10:3; Mk 3:18; Lk 6:15; Acts 1:13); James, "the Lord's brother" (Gal 1:19; cf. Mt 13:55; Mk 6:3); James, bishop of Jerusalem (Acts 12:17; 15:13; 21:18; Gal 1:19); and James, to whom the risen Jesus appeared (1 Cor 15:17). Scholars are generally agreed that the "brother of the Lord" (that is, his cousin or

Introduction to the Letter of St James

relative: cf. note on Mt 6:1–3) is the bishop of Jerusalem, to whom the risen Lord appeared; this reduces the number of possible Jameses to three—James the Greater, James the Less, and James, the Lord's brother and bishop of Jerusalem. The first-mentioned was martyred by Herod Agrippa around AD 44 (Acts 12:12) and it is unlikely that he could have been the author of the letter. As regards the two remaining Jameses, we cannot be sure that they were one and the same person but the likelihood is that they were: in fact, St Luke and St Paul, after the death of James the Greater, make reference only to one James, the bishop of Jerusalem and brother of the Lord (Acts 12:17; Gal 2:9, 12).

This James was a relative of Jesus, the son of one of the Marys who kept our Lady company at the foot of the cross (Mt 25:56; Jn 19:25). After St Peter went to Rome, this James stayed behind as head of the Jerusalem community (cf. Acts 12:17; 21:18ff) and as such was visited by St Paul after his conversion (cf. Gal 1:19). He was martyred around the year 62 at the instigation of the high priest Annas II.[1]

Summing up, it is fairly clear that the letter was written by James, "the Lord's brother" and bishop of Jerusalem, who was probably the same person as the James, son of Alphaeus, listed in the Gospel as an apostle (cf. Mt 10:3; Mk 3:18).

The text of the letter confirms this attribution; on the one hand, the background to the language is Semitic, the Old Testament is frequently quoted, and the Aramaic turns of phrase indicate an author of Jewish background; on the other hand, a Christian spirit clearly imbues the entire letter. Its eminently pastoral character suggests that it was written by someone who was responsible for a Christian community (as the bishop of Jerusalem was). The objection often raised that the letter is written in very good Greek (such as one would not expect someone from Palestine to use) can be explained by James' employing a secretary or amanuensis (common at the time) who had a good knowledge of Greek.

Some non-Catholic commentators assign the letter to an anonymous pre-Christian Jew of the first century BC, arguing that it was later touched up to "christianize" it; but this theory does not hold up in the light of the arguments outlined above. Nor is there any basis for the "pseudo-epigraphic theory", which argues that the letter was written around the end of the first century or beginning of the second century AD by an unknown author who credited it to James in order to reinforce its authority.

CANONICITY

Explicit references in the Fathers to the Letter of St James are to be found from the third century. However, there are earlier allusions to it, even in letters

---

1. Cf. Flavius Josephus, *Jewish Antiquites*, 20, 9, 1; Eusebius of Caesarea, *Ecclesiastical History*, 2, 23, 19–23.

of St Paul and in St Jude.² There are also references in writers as early as St Clement of Rome (end of first century), St Justin (mid second century) and St Irenaeus (second half of the second century).

The first explicit acknowledgment comes from Origen (185–255),³ who echoes a second-century Egyptian tradition that the letter was inspired. From the time of Origen onwards the church of Alexandria was in no doubt about the letter's canonicity. Eusebius of Caesarea lists it among the "disputed" books, even though he admits that most people accepted it,⁴ and he himself, bearing witness to the Palestinian tradition, considers it canonical.

From the time of the provincial Council of Laodicea (c.360) the letter appears in all lists of inspired books. No doubts were raised about its canonicity from then until the sixteenth century, when Luther rejected it for the simple reason that he found its teaching at odds with his doctrine of justification. The Council of Trent, basing itself on the centuries-old tradition of the Church, solemnly defined it to be canonical.

DATE OF COMPOSITION

There are two possible dates, depending on the relationship between St James and St Paul in their treatment of the topic of faith and good works and who depends on whom. Given that, in treating of this subject, the same biblical texts are used here and in Romans and Galatians, some scholars have argued that St James was the first to speak about it, and did so prior to the problems solved by the Council of Jerusalem (49/50) raised their head. According to this view, the Letter of St James is the earliest New Testament text.

However, we cannot rule out the possibility that St James was acquainted with St Paul's Letters to the Galatians and Romans (written in 54 and 58 respectively) and that, without making mention of them, he wrote his letter to counter mistaken conclusions some people were trying to draw from what St Paul had said. In this case the date of composition would be around AD 60, shortly before the author died a martyr's death.

As we have indicated, there is no sound basis for the theory that the letter was written by a pre-Christian author, nor for the suggestion that it was written in the second century AD, by which time all the apostles were dead.

IMMEDIATE READERSHIP

The letter is addressed to "the twelve tribes in the Dispersion" (1:1), that is, the Jews who lived outside Palestine, among the Gentiles. Those who say that

---

2. Cf., e.g., Jas 1:1 with 1 Pet 1:1 and Jude 1; Jas 1:18 with 1 Pet 1:23; Jas 1:2–3 with 1 Pet 1:6; Jas 4:6–20 with Pet 5:5–9. **3.** Cf. *In Iesu Nave*, 7; *In Ioann. Comm.*, 19, 6. **4.** *Ecclesiastical History*, 3, 25, 3.

the letter is pre-Christian Jewish base their argument mainly on these few words; yet there are many pointers to its Christian origin, for example, the explicit references to Jesus Christ (1:1; 2:1), the allusion to the "honourable name" (2:7) and to the second coming of the Lord (5:7–8). Moreover, the letter's moral exhortations are very akin to the sayings of Jesus, particularly the Sermon on the Mount as reported by Matthew (Mt 5–7)—for example, joy in suffering (cf. 1:2, 12 and Mt 5:11ff); the poor will inherit the Kingdom (cf. 2:5 with Mt 5:3); the merciful will obtain mercy (cf. 2:13 with Mt 5:7); prohibition of oaths (cf. 5:12 with Mt 5:37); etc.

Besides, Christians also can be described as "the tribes in the Dispersion", for they are the heirs of the promises made to the Patriarchs and are pilgrims in alien lands in this life (cf. 1 Pet 1:1; 2:11; Heb 11:13); and there was even more justification for describing in this way Christians of Jewish background living outside Jerusalem.

Given that the letter was addressed originally to Jewish converts, it is easy to see why James uses expressions familiar to people of Hebrew origin—for example, "hearers of the word" (cf. 1:22–25); "assembly" (synagogue, in the Greek text: 2:2); the mention of Old Testament characters (Abraham, Rahab, Job, Elijah); the use of the title "Lord of hosts" (5:4); etc. On the other hand sins more frequent among pagans, such as idolatry, dissolute lifestyles, drunkenness, etc., are not mentioned, whereas these sins are referred to by St Paul when he addresses Christians of Gentile background (cf. 1 Cor 6:9–11; Gal 5:19–21; etc.). But, as we have already pointed out, the entire letter is imbued with Christian thinking.

As regards the circumstances which led James to write the letter, we know little other than what it tells us itself, that is, that various defects were threatening the progress of these Christian communities. Almost all the disorders denounced in the letter have to do with behaviour towards one's neighbour—grumbling (5:9), jealousy and covetousness (3:13–16; 4:1–3); evil speech (4:11f), etc., and particularly discord between rich and poor: he has some very harsh things to say on this score (cf. 2:1–13; 5:1–6), making it very clear that people must not selfishly turn their back on the disadvantaged.

CONTENT

Running right through the letter is an emphasis on the need for consistency between a Christian's faith and actions: everything a Christian does should reflect the faith he or she professes.

Naturally enough, the letter is not structured like a systematic treatise. As in the case of Jewish wisdom writing (Proverbs, Ecclesiastes and Wisdom are good examples), the letter is structured in what we might call a psychological and pedagogical manner: one thought leads off to another, using similar-

Introduction to the Letter of St James

sounding words, repeating the same idea more than once (as in a series of concentric circles), pressing short maxims into service, etc. This type of writing makes it easier for the listener or reader to commit its message to memory. All this undermines the theory that the letter is a composite of homilies delivered on different occasions and copied down much later. Clearly there is an underlying unity to the various counsels contained in the letter.

Accepting that the letter does not have any rigid structure, we can divide it into three sections, the second of which deals specifically with the basic teaching about consistency between the faith one professes and the works one does. The first section contains preparatory instructions and the third a series of applications of the basic principle.

1. The *first section* (1:1—2:13), which begins after the short heading and greeting (1:1), consists of a series of instructions so interlinked that it is difficult to say where one ends and the next begins: it teaches the value of suffering (1:2–12); it emphasizes that only good can come from God and therefore God never tempts man or seeks to harm him (1:13–18); accepting what comes from God means doing what he says (1:19–27) and not being a respecter of persons (2:1–13). All these teachings point to the need for there to be no discrepancy between what one receives from God and the way one puts it into practice.

2. The *second section* (2:14–26) develops the central idea: a faith which does not translate into good works is a dead faith (2:14–19). This point is made again and again, like a refrain running right through the passage; the argumentation is based mainly on the example of well-known biblical personalities (2:20–26).

3. In the *third section* (3:1—5:6) practical applications of this teaching are piled one on another and woven together. Christians are exhorted to control the tongue (3:1–12), to seek true wisdom and reject false wisdom (3:13–18), to recognize the source of disagreement (4:1–12), and to put all their trust in divine providence and not be preoccupied by their private affairs (4:13–17) or riches, for that only leads to flagrant injustice (5:1–6). In this part of the letter the sacred writer speaks with greater severity, not mincing his words, in order to make people see that actions of the kind he condemns are incompatible with the profession of the Christian faith.

4. The letter concludes with a series of pithy counsels (5:7–20): it insists on the need to keep true to the faith with patience and constancy (5:7–11); it teaches the value of prayer (5:13–18), encouraging prayer at all times; it speaks about the sacrament of the Anointing of the Sick (5:14–15); and finally it encourages Christians to have concern for one another (5:19–20).

Introduction to the Letter of St James

DOCTRINAL AND MORAL QUESTIONS

The main purpose of the epistle is a moral and ascetical one, hence the predominance of exhortations and warnings about how to cope with difficulties and temptations, about the need to be objective in one's judgment of others and to avoid backbiting etc.; about detachment from material things, and the need to be concerned about the poor and needy; the practice of prayer; the correction of those who go astray. These are the main themes of the letter.

Although it does not overtly deal with doctrinal matters, these underlie the whole letter. There are many references to God's attributes and actions: he is the Creator (1:17; 5:4; 3:9), Father (1:27; 3:10), Rewarder and Judge (4:12), merciful Saviour (2:13). Except for 1:1 and 2:1 there is no explicit mention of Jesus Christ but he is portrayed as Lord and Saviour; his second coming is alluded to (5:8) and the fact that he is Judge (5:9), and his teachings echo throughout the epistle. The Church is spoken of as a community of believers (2:2), in which teachers (3:1) and elders (5:14) have specific functions of government and of administration of the sacraments (1:18; 2:7; 5:14).

1. *The sacrament of the Anointing of the Sick*

Apart from the allusion to this sacrament in Mark 6:13, this letter is the only place in the New Testament where there is explicit mention of the Anointing of the Sick: "Is any among you sick? Let him call the elders of the church, and let them pray over him, anointing him with oil in the name of the Lord; and the prayer of faith will save the sick man, and the Lord will raise him up; and if he has committed sins, he will be forgiven" (5:14–15). As explained in the notes on this passage, these words of St James identify the elements of this sacrament: it is a sensible sign with remote matter (oil), proximate matter (anointing), form (liturgical prayer), minister (elders, that is, priests), subject (the sick Christian) and effects (curing and salvation). The Church has solemnly defined that this sacrament was instituted by Christ; and this passage of St James is referred to in Vatican II's recommendation of the sacrament: "By the sacred anointing of the sick and the prayer of the priests the whole Church commends those who are ill to the suffering and glorified Lord that he may raise them up and save them (cf. Jas 5:14–16). And indeed she exhorts them to contribute to the good of the people of God by freely uniting themselves to the passion and death of Christ (cf. Rom 8:17; Col 1:24; 2 Tim 2:11–12; 1 Pet 4:13)."[5]

2. *Faith and works*

The central teaching of the letter has to do with consistency between faith and works. In a simple and lively way, the sacred author outlines this teaching particularly in 2:14–26, a passage whose tone is reminiscent of the wisdom

---

5. Vatican II, *Lumen gentium*, 11.

books of the Old Testament, and which may well be an example of the formal religious instruction imparted to those first Christian communities. The passage begins by pointing to the absurdity of the behaviour of a person who, finding someone in need, instead of coming to his aid is content simply with giving him good advice (vv. 14–16); these lives are followed by the enunciation of a key moral principle: "So faith by itself, if it has no works, is dead" (v. 17). This teaching is supported by well chosen examples: the demons have faith but it does them no good (v. 19), whereas Abraham and Rahab, whose faith expressed itself in actions, were thereby justified (vv. 20–26).

This Catholic teaching was accepted unquestionably up to the time of the Reformation, when this text was seen as an unsurmountable obstacle for the theory of justification by faith alone; Luther was the most outspoken enemy of this letter, which he described as "an epistle of straw".

From that point onwards, in Protestant circles, the claim is made that this text was written as a correction to what St Paul says in Romans 3:20–31 and Galatians 2:16; 3:2, 5, 11. There is undoubtedly a parallel between James and those two passages: the argumentation is along the same lines, as is even the wording: both make reference to Abraham as a model of how a man is justified (Jas 2:21–25 and Rom 4:1–3), and both speak of faith, works, and justification. The following two verses show the similarly in language and apparent contradiction.

> Jas 2:24 "You see that a man is justified by works and not by faith alone."
>
> Rom 3:28 "We hold that a man is justified by faith apart from works of the law" (cf. Gal 2:16).

However, although the terms used are identical, the perspective is different and there is no contradiction: St Paul says that faith works through love (Gal 5:6); but in his argument with the Judaizers he denies that the works of the Old Law are necessary: it is faith that is important. St James is emphasizing above all that faith must be reflected in one's behaviour. Arguably St James is interpreting St Paul and correcting erroneous conclusions which might be drawn from a misreading of Paul.

For St James, "works" are morally correct behaviour, which must be in line with the religious faith one professes. For St Paul "works" are the legal rules of the Old Law, which no longer have validity, now that Christ has promulgated the New Law.

In this letter "justification" means moral perfection, which is attained, once grace has been conferred, by the practice of virtue, by upright conduct; it is for St Paul what is usually termed "first justification", that is, the union with God that comes with initial grace.

Introduction to the Letter of St James

Clearly the two inspired authors are not contradicting one another: in both instances one needs to adhere to God ("faith" in St Paul), which includes assenting to revealed truths ("faith" in St James), which has to find expression in a coherent Christian life ("works" in St James). This consistency between faith and works is something St Paul calls for when he says that faith "works through love" (Gal 5:6; cf. 1 Thess 1:3; 2 Thess 1:11), or "he who loves his neighbour has fulfilled the law" (Rom 13:8) or when he says in connexion with the just judgment of God that "he will render to every man according to his works" (Rom 2:6).

THE LETTER OF JAMES

The Revised Standard Version, with notes

Greeting

1 ¹James, a servant of God and of the Lord Jesus Christ, To the twelve tribes* in the Dispersion: Greeting.

1 Pet 1:1
Acts 12:17
Jn 7:35

1. OPENING INSTRUCTIONS

The value of suffering

²Count it all joy, my brethren, when you meet various trials, ³for you know that the testing of your faith produces steadfastness.

1 Pet 1:6
1 Pet 1:7

1:1. The author of the letter is St James, who was in charge of the Christian community of Jerusalem for a number of years (cf. Acts 12:17; 15:13; 21:19), a close relative of our Lord. As to the author being the apostle St James the Less, the son of Alphaeus, cf. the Introduction to this letter, pp. 13–14.

James introduces himself as "a servant of God and of the Lord Jesus Christ". The title of "servant of God" was given to people in the Old Testament who were outstandingly faithful to the Lord (cf. Ps 34:22), such as Moses, David, the prophets; the title applies in a special way to the Messiah, the "Servant of Yahweh" (cf. Is 42–53). In the New Testament it is applied to all Christians, particularly the apostles (cf. Acts 4:29; 16:17; Rev 1:1). At the start of their letters, St Peter, St Paul and St Jude sometimes describe themselves in this way to make the point that they are mere messengers of divine truth.

The term "Lord"—*Kyrios* in Greek—which is applied to Jesus Christ is used in the second-century BC Septuagint Greek version of the Old Testament to translate the name of Yahweh. St Paul also uses it frequently. It is an explicit profession of faith in the divinity of Jesus Christ, part of the Christian creed from the very beginning.

The letter is addressed "to the twelve tribes in the Dispersion" or Diaspora. The term *diaspora* originally meant Jews domiciled outside Palestine. Here it refers to Christians—the twelve tribes of the new, true Israel—who were to be found all over the Greco-Roman world. It is very likely that it refers particularly to Jewish converts to Christianity.

The salutation used by James—which the New Vulgate translates as "health" and the RSV gives as "greeting"—literally means "rejoice". It was the customary form of greeting in the Greek of the time. The same word is used in v. 2, perhaps to make it quite clear what kind of joy he means.

1:2–12. In these opening verses, St James points out how Christians should behave in the face of trials: they should accept them with joy (vv. 2–4); if they find it difficult to see why they are experiencing difficulties, they should ask God to give them the necessary wisdom (vv. 5–8); the poor and well-to-do should have the same attitude to things (vv. 9–11); finally, he reminds them that the reward God promises to those who endure trials is blessedness (v. 12). The whole passage clearly reflects the Beatitudes of the Sermon on the Mount (cf. Mt 5:1–12).

The problem of the suffering experienced by the righteous in contrast with the prosperity of the impious in this life is one often dealt with in the Old

James 1:4

^{Mt 5:48}
^{Rom 5:3}
⁴And let steadfastness have its full effect, that you may be perfect and complete, lacking in nothing.

^{Prov 2:3–6}
^{Mt 7:7}
⁵If any of you lacks wisdom, let him ask God, who gives to all men generously and without reproaching, and it will be given him.

^{Mt 21:21}
⁶But let him ask in faith, with no doubting, for he who doubts is like

---

Testament, particularly in the Psalms and in the book of Job. But it was not fully and finally solved until the coming of Jesus Christ, who by his teaching and his life revealed the redemptive value of suffering, and the great reward which heaven holds. "It is through Christ and in Christ that light is thrown on the riddle of suffering and death which, apart from his Gospel, overwhelms us" (Vatican II, *Gaudium et spes*, 22).

Human suffering has a redemptive value when borne in union with Christ: "The Gospel of suffering", Pope John Paul II says, "is being written unceasingly, and it speaks unceasingly with the words of this strange paradox: the springs of divine power gush forth precisely in the midst of human weakness. Those who share in the sufferings of Christ preserve in their own sufferings a very special *particle of the infinite treasure* of the world's Redemption, and can share this treasure with others" (*Salvifici doloris*, 27).

1:2–4. The "trials" referred to here do not seem to be persecutions, but rather everyday adversity—perhaps poverty especially (cf. 1:9; 2:5–7)—which tests the Christian's faith: for this reason the word is sometimes translated as "temptations". These trials act as a test of perseverance in the pursuit of good, and help the soul to grow in patience, a much needed virtue: "There is nothing more pleasing to God", St Alphonsus comments, "than to see a soul who patiently and serenely bears whatever crosses it is sent; this is how love is made, by putting lover and loved one on the same level [...]. A soul who loves Jesus Christ desires to be treated the way Christ was treated—desires to be poor, despised and humiliated" (*The Love of Jesus Christ*, chap. 5).

Patience, steadfastness, is quite different from mere passive endurance of suffering; it comes from the virtue of fortitude and leads one to accept suffering as something sent by God. It is grounded on hope (cf. 1 Thess 1:3) and on faith put to the test (Jas 1:3); it is very fruitful (cf. Lk 8:15), particularly in terms of Christian joy (cf. Acts 5:41), and implies sustained effort to the point of perfection.

1:5–8. The wisdom that St James refers to views everything in the light of Christ crucified—the wisdom of the cross in the phrase of St Paul (cf. 1 Cor 1:18ff), which is the only type of insight that enables one to be joyful in the midst of adversity and suffering, because it allows one to see these things as an opportunity to share in our Lord's suffering. When we find it difficult to view things in this light, we need to ask God to give us wisdom.

Our prayer for wisdom should be a prayer full of faith: "Whatever you ask for in prayer, you will receive, if you have faith" (Mt 21:22). The *St Pius V Catechism* (4, 7, 3) reminds us that "believe, we must, both in order to pray, and that we be not wanting in that faith which renders prayer fruitful. For it is faith that leads to prayer, and it is prayer that, by removing all doubts, gives strength and firmness to faith. This is the

a wave of the sea that is driven and tossed by the wind. ⁷,⁸For that person must not suppose that a double-minded man, unstable in all his ways, will receive anything from the Lord.

⁹Let the lowly brother boast in his exaltation, ¹⁰and the rich in his humiliation, because like the flower of the grass he will pass away. ¹¹For the sun rises with its scorching heat and withers the grass; its flower falls, and its beauty perishes. So will the rich man fade away in the midst of his pursuits.

Jas 2:5
Is 40:6
1 Tim 6:17
Is 40:7

---

meaning of the exhortation of St Ignatius to those who approach God in prayer: 'Be not of doubtful mind in prayer; blessed is he who hath not doubted' (*Ep. X ad Heronem*). Therefore, to obtain from God what we ask, faith and an assured confidence are of first importance, according to the admonition of St James: 'Let him ask in faith, with no doubting' (Jas 1:6)."

1:5. "Who gives to all men generously and without reproaching": God always listens to our requests, and he answers them without humiliating us, without reminding us of our unworthiness. This should help us address the Lord with complete confidence, not being inhibited by our shortcomings and sins. "You are so conscious of your misery", St Josemaría Escrivá says, "that you acknowledge yourself unworthy to be heard by God. But, what about the merits of Mary? And the wounds of your Lord? And ... are you not a son of God? Besides, he listens to you '*quoniam bonus ..., quoniam in saeculum misericordia ejus*: because he is good, because his mercy endures for ever'" (*The Way*, 93).

1:7–8. "A double-minded man": an indecisive soul who is unsure whether to trust in the efficacy of prayer or not. St Bede comments: "A double-minded person is one who kneels down to ask God for things and beseeches him to grant them, and yet feels so accused by his conscience that he distrusts his ability to pray. A double-minded person is also one who, when he does good deeds, looks for external approval rather than interior reward. The wise man is right when he says, 'Woe to the sinner who walks along two ways!' (Sir 2:12) [...] People of this type are inconstant in all their ways, for they are very easily overpowered by adverse circumstances and entrapped by favourable ones, with the result that they stray from the true path" (*Super Iac. expositio*, ad loc.).

1:9–11. Apparently poverty was one of the hardest trials these Christians were experiencing. The Semitic mind was fond of expressing itself in terms of contrasts, and this may make it difficult for us to grasp the full thrust of St James' maxims; to do so we need to draw on our general knowledge of Christian doctrine. God and the Church have a predilection for the poor, and Christ describes the poor as blessed (cf. Mt 5:3 and par.): this teaching applies in the first instance to those who experience material need, but material need is a symbol of the truly poor, that is, those who, independently of whether they have many or few material possessions, realize that they are in dire need of God (cf. note on Lk 6:24). In principle, it may be easier for a materially poor person to feel in need of God, whereas someone who is well off needs to be detached from possessions in order to trust fully in God.

James 1:12

Dan 12:2
1 Cor 9:25
1 Pet 5:4

¹²Blessed is the man who endures trial, for when he has stood the test he will receive the crown of life which God has promised to those who love him.

The source of temptation

Sir 15:11-20

¹³Let no one say when he is tempted, "I am tempted by God"; for God cannot be tempted with evil and he himself tempts no one; ¹⁴but

---

The sacred writer does not require people who have possessions to give them up: what they have to do is to realize that material possessions are transitory, impermanent things to be used in the service of others and of society, and not just for oneself.

The impermanence of earthly possessions—indicated here by the simile of the flower of the grass (cf. Is 40:6-8)—is an idea which occurs frequently in Holy Scripture (cf., e.g., Job 27:13-23; Ps 49:17-20; Mt 6:19f; Lk 12:16-21).

1:12. These words, which expand on the idea contained in vv. 2-4, echo our Lord's own words: "Blessed are you when men revile you and persecute you and utter all kinds of evil against you falsely on my account. Rejoice and be glad, for your reward is great in heaven" (Mt 5:11-12). The simile of the crown—a mark of victory and kingship—is used to convey the idea of definitive triumph with Christ: the Lord will appear crowned in glory (Rev 14:14); the Woman of the Apocalypse, symbolizing the Church and the Blessed Virgin, is also described as crowned (cf. Rev 12:1); and this reward is promised to those who stay true to God in this life (cf. Rev 2:10; 3:11). It is also to be found in other New Testament passages to convey the idea of the ultimate reward of heaven (cf. 1 Cor 9:25; 2 Tim 4:8; 1 Pet 5:4).

This means that Christians should not be depressed or cowed by the difficulties which God permits them to experience; on the contrary, they should see them as a series of tests which with God's help they should surmount in order to receive the reward of heaven. "The Lord does not allow his followers to experience these trials and temptations unless it be for their greater good," St John of Avila comments. "[...] He disposed things in this way: endurance in adversity and struggle against temptation prove who his friends are. For the mark of a true friend is not that he keeps you company when times are good, but that he stands by you in times of trial [...]. Companions in adversity and later in the Kingdom, you should strive to fight manfully when you meet opposition that would separate you from God, for He is your help here on earth and your reward in heaven" (*Audi, filia*, 29).

1:13-18. These verses identify the source of the temptations man experiences: they cannot come from God but are, rather, the effect of human concupiscence (vv. 16-18).

Sometimes temptation means putting a person's faithfulness to the test; in this sense it can be said that God "tempts" certain people, as happened in the case of Abraham (cf. Gen 22:1ff). However, here the reference is to temptation in the strict sense of incitement to sin: God never tempts anyone in this way, he never encourages a person to do evil (cf. Sir 15:11-20). Therefore, we cannot attribute to God our inclination to sin, nor can it be argued that by endowing us with

each person is tempted when he is lured and enticed by his own desire. ¹⁵Then desire when it has conceived gives birth to sin; and sin when it is full-grown brings forth death.

¹⁶Do not be deceived, my beloved brethren. ¹⁷Every good endowment and every perfect gift is from above, coming down from the Father of lights with whom there is no variation or shadow due to change.ᵃ ¹⁸Of his own will he brought us forth by the word of truth that we should be a kind of first fruits of his creatures.

Rom 7:7–8
Rom 7:10
Mt 7:11
Jn 3:3
Jas 3:15–17
1 Jn 1:5
Jn 1:13
1 Pet 1:23
Rev 14:4

---

freedom he is the cause of our sin. On the contrary, the natural and supernatural gifts we have received are resources which help us act in a morally good way.

1:14–15. St James' teaching is that the source of temptation is to be found in our own passions. Elsewhere he says that the world (cf. 1:27; 4:4) and the devil (4:7) are causes of temptation; but to actually commit sin the complicity of one's own evil inclinations is always necessary.

Concupiscence ("desire"), here as elsewhere in the New Testament (cf., e.g., Rom 1:24; 7:7ff; 1 Jn 2:16), means all the disordered passions and appetites which, as a result of original sin, have a place in men's hearts. Concupiscence as such is not a sin; but rather, according to the Council of Trent, "since it is left to provide a trial, it has no power to injure those who do not consent and who, by the grace of Jesus Christ, manfully resist"; and if it is sometimes called sin (cf. Rom 6:12ff) it is "only because it is from sin and inclines to sin" (*De peccato originali*, 5).

Using the simile of generation St James describes the course of sin from the stage of temptation to that of the death of the soul. When one gives in to the seduction of concupiscence sin is committed; this in turn leads to spiritual death, to the soul's losing the life of grace. This is the opposite process to the one described earlier (cf. vv. 2–12), which begins with trials (temptations in the broad sense: cf. note on 1:2–4) and ends up in heaven; whereas in this passage, the process also begins with temptation but because of sin ends up with the death of the soul. John Paul II describes the process as follows: "Man also knows, through painful experience, that by a conscious and free act of his will he can change course and go in a direction opposed to God's will, separating himself from God (*aversio a Deo*), rejecting loving communion with him, detaching himself from the life-principle which God is, and consequently choosing death" (*Reconciliatio et paenitentia*, 17).

1:16–18. "The Father of lights": a reference to God as Creator of the heavenly bodies (cf. Gen 1:14ff; Ps 136:7–9) and, in the symbolism of light, as the source of all good things, material and, especially, spiritual. Unlike heavenly bodies, which change position and cast shadows, there is no variation or shadow in God: no evil can be attributed to him (cf. v. 13), but only good things.

"First fruits of his creatures": Christians, who have been recreated by God by "the word of truth" (the Gospel) already constitute the beginning of the new heaven and the new earth (cf. Rev 21:1) and are a sign of hope for all mankind and for the whole of Creation (cf. Rom 9:19–23).

---

a. Other ancient authorities read *variation due to a shadow of turning*

James 1:19

Doers of the word, not hearers only

Eccles 7:9
Sir 5:11

¹⁹Know this, my beloved brethren. Let every man be quick to hear, slow to speak, slow to anger, ²⁰for the anger of man does not work the righteousness of God. ²¹Therefore put away all filthiness and rank growth of wickedness and receive with meekness the implanted word, which is able to save your souls.

Rom 2:13
1 Jn 3:18

²²But be doers of the word, and not hearers only, deceiving yourselves.* ²³For if any one is a hearer of the word and not a

---

1:19–27. In the previous verse the sacred writer referred to the effectiveness of "the word of truth". Now he makes the point that although the Gospel has this effectiveness, it is not enough just to hear it: we need to listen to it with docility (vv. 19–21) and put it into practice (vv. 22–27). Further on he will emphasize this connexion between faith and works (cf. 2:14–26).

1:19–20. These counsels occur often in the wisdom books of the Old Testament (cf., e.g., Prov 1:5; 10:19; Sir 5:12–13; 20:5–8). To put doctrine into practice one needs to listen to it with a good disposition (v. 21). The letter will have more to say about prudence in speech (cf. 1:26; and especially 3:1ff).

"The anger of man does not work the righteousness of God": a Hebrew expression meaning that someone who gives way to anger is not acting justly in God's eyes.

Anger is one of the "capital" sins (one of the "seven deadly sins"), capital because they lead to many other sins; anger leads particularly to the evil desire for vengeance. Speaking of the effects of anger St Gregory the Great explains that it clouds one's judgment when making decisions, makes it difficult to get on with others, causes discord and makes it difficult to see where the truth lies. Moreover, "it deprives one of righteousness, as it is written, 'The anger of man does not work the righteousness of God' (Jas 1:20) because when one's mind is not at peace, one's critical faculty is impaired and one judges to be right whatever one's anger suggests" (*Moralia*, 5, 45). This sin is avoided by the practice of the virtue of patience, of which St James spoke a few verses earlier (cf. 1:2–4, 12; also 5:7–11).

1:21. "First he calls", St Bede comments, "for the cleansing of mind and body from vice, so that those who receive the word of salvation can live in a worthy manner. A person who does not first turn his back on evil cannot do good" (*Super Iac. expositio,* ad loc.).

To listen docilely to the word of God one needs to try to keep evil inclinations at bay. Otherwise, pride—deceiving itself with all sorts of false reasons—rebels against the word of God (which it sees as a continuous reproach for a habit of sin it is unwilling to give up).

1:22–25. Holy Scripture frequently exhorts us to put the word of God into practice: "Everyone who hears these words of mine and does not do them will be like a man who built his house upon the sand" (Mt 7:26; cf., e.g., Ezek 33:10–11; Mt 12:50; Rom 2:13; Jas 2:14–26).

The comparison of the man looking in the mirror is a very good one: the word of God is frustrated unless it leads to examination of conscience and a firm resolution to mend one's ways. Those who are doers of the word will be "blessed";

doer, he is like a man who observes his natural face in a mirror; ²⁴for he observes himself and goes away and at once forgets what he was like. ²⁵But he who looks into the perfect law, the law of liberty, and perseveres, being no hearer that forgets but a doer that acts, he shall be blessed in his doing.

²⁶If any one thinks he is religious, and does not bridle his tongue but deceives his heart, this man's religion is vain.

Ps 19:8
Jn 13:17
Rom 8:2

Ps 34:14
Jas 3:2

our Lord says the same thing when he describes as blessed those who "hear the word of God and keep it" (Lk 11:28).

St James' counsels in this passage are a clear call for the consistency a Christian must seek at all times. Pope John Paul II comments: "These are very serious, very severe, statements; a Christian should always be genuine, should never be content with words alone. The mission he has received is a delicate one: he should be leaven in society, light of the world, salt of the earth. As time goes by, the Christian becomes more and more aware of his commitment, and the difficulties it entails: he discovers he has to swim against the tide, he has to bear witness to truths which are absolute, yet invisible; he has to lose his earthly life in order to gain eternity; he needs to feel responsible not just for himself but also for his neighbour—for whom he should light the way, and edify and save. However, he realizes that he is not alone in all this [...]. The Christian knows that not only did Jesus Christ, the Word of God, become man to reveal saving truth and redeem mankind; he has also chosen to stay with us on earth, mysteriously renewing the sacrifice of the Cross by means of the Eucharist and becoming spiritual food for the soul and accompanying it on its journey through life" (*Homily*, 1 September 1979).

1:25. "The perfect law, the law of liberty": that is, the good news brought by Christ, who has made us children of God (cf. Jn 1:12; 1 Jn 3:1ff) and set us free from every kind of servitude, both that of the Old Law (cf., e.g., Gal 2:4 and 4:21ff and notes on same) and subjection to the devil, to sin and to death.

It can also be regarded as a law of freedom because when man obeys it he is expressing his freedom to the fullest degree (cf. Jn 8:31ff), and he is happy in this life and will be blessed in the next (cf., e.g., Ps 1:1ff; 119:1ff). Thus, when a person sins and turns his back on this law, he becomes not a free man but a slave: "Such a person may show that he has acted according to his preferences," St Josemaría Escrivá explains, "but he does not speak with the voice of true freedom, because he has become the slave of his decision and he has decided for the worst, for the absence of God, where there is no freedom to be found.

"I tell you once again: I accept no slavery other than that of God's love. This is because, as I have told you on other occasions, religion is the greatest rebellion of men, who refuse to live like animals, who are dissatisfied and restless until they know their Creator and are on intimate terms with him. I want you to be rebels, free and unfettered, because I want you—it is Christ who wants us!—to be children of God. Slavery or divine sonship, this is the dilemma we face. Children of God or slaves to pride, to sensuality, to the fretful selfishness which seems to afflict so many souls" (*Friends of God*, 37–38).

1:26–27. St James now gives some examples of what doing "the word of truth"

James 1:27

²⁷Religion that is pure and undefiled before God and the Father is this: to visit orphans and widows in their affliction, and to keep oneself unstained from the world.

Impartiality

1 Cor 2:8

2 ¹My brethren, show no partiality as you hold the faith of our Lord Jesus Christ, the Lord of glory. ²For if a man with gold

---

(v. 18), that is, the Gospel, means—controlling one's tongue, being charitable and not letting oneself be stained by the world.

The Old Testament often refers to widows and orphans as deserving of special attention (cf. Ps 68:5; 146:9; Deut 27:19), and the first Christians made arrangements for the care of widows in the early communities (cf. Acts 6:1ff; 9:39; 1 Tim 5:3ff). Concern for widows and orphans is included in the works of mercy ("by which the temporal or spiritual wants of our neighbour are relieved": *St Pius X Catechism*, 943), which our Lord will take into account at the Last Judgment (cf. Mt 25:31–46).

"World" here has the pejorative meaning of "enemy of God and of Christians" (cf. also 4:4; and other passages of Scripture, e.g., Jn 1:10; 7:7; 16:8–11; Eph 2:2; 2 Pet 2:20); one needs to be constantly on the alert to avoid contamination. On other meanings of "world" in the Bible, see the note on John 17:14–16.

"God and the Father": this is the literal meaning of the Greek. In New Testament Greek the term "God" when preceded by the definite article normally means not the divine nature but the person of the Father. In this case by adding the words "and the Father" St James does not mean another, distinct, divine person; he is simply making explicit the meaning of the term "the God". It could also be translated by the paraphrase "before him who is God and Father".

2:1–13. Apparently some of the Christians to whom this letter was addressed were guilty of discriminating against people on the grounds of social standing—a clear instance of inconsistency between faith and actions, a key theme James has already touched on (cf. 1:19–27) and will develop later (cf. 2:14–26). He may well be taking an example from something that actually happened (vv. 1–4) to make the very vigorous point that discrimination is opposed to the Gospel (vv. 5–7) as indeed to the Law (vv. 8–11); and he makes it plain that this type of behaviour will be severely punished by God when he comes to judge (vv. 12–13).

2:1–4. God "is not partial and takes no bribe" (Deut 10:17). Discrimination among people is often condemned in the Old Testament—in the Law as well as in the Prophets and the Wisdom books (cf., e.g., Lev 19:15; Is 5:23; Mic 3:9–11; Ps 82:2–4). In the Gospel even our Lord's enemies admit that he is impartial and does not make unfair distinctions (cf. Mt 22:16).

In line with this teaching, the Church takes issue with every form of discrimination. "All men are endowed with a rational soul and are created in God's image; they have the same nature and origin and, being redeemed by Christ, they enjoy the same divine calling and destiny; there is here a basic equality between men and it must be given ever greater recognition. Undoubtedly not all men are alike as regards physical capacity

rings and in fine clothing comes into your assembly, and a poor man in shabby clothing also comes in, ³and you pay attention to the one who wears the fine clothing and say, "Have a seat here, please," while you say to the poor man, "Stand there," or, "Sit at my feet," ⁴have you not made distinctions among yourselves, and become judges with evil thoughts? ⁵Listen, my beloved brethren. Has not God chosen those who are poor in the world to be rich in faith and heirs of the kingdom which he has promised to those who love him? ⁶But you have dishonoured the poor man. Is it not the rich who

1 Cor 1:26
Rev 2:9

---

and intellectual and moral powers. But forms of social or cultural discrimination in basic personal rights on the grounds of sex, race, colour, social conditions, language or religion, must be curbed and eradicated as incompatible with God's design" (*Gaudium et spes*, 29).

2:1. "The faith of our Lord Jesus Christ, the Lord of glory": literally "the faith of our Lord Jesus Christ of glory." This phrase can be interpreted in slightly different ways depending on how one understands "of glory". The most likely interpretation is that this is an instance of a Semitic genitive used in place of the adjective "glorious" or "glorified"; in which case St James is referring to Jesus Christ who, after his ascension and resurrection, enjoys, also in his capacity as man, the highest honour and glory.

The RSV takes up the idea found in 1 Corinthians 2:8 where St Paul calls Christ "the Lord of glory": since in the Old Testament "glory" was the splendour of the majesty of Yahweh (cf. Ex 24:16), by applying this divine attribute to Christ his divinity is being explicitly asserted. If this is the correct translation, it may be a form of words taken from early Christian liturgy.

Some translate it in another way which puts even greater stress on Christ's divinity: "The faith of the glory [that is, the divinity] of our Lord Jesus Christ."

All these translations are compatible with one another and complementary to one another.

2:5–7. Many of the people to whom the letter was written must have been quite poor (cf. note on 1:2–4; 1 Cor 1:26–29). St James reminds them that God wants to make them rich in faith and heirs of the Kingdom of heaven. Jesus in fact had given as a sign of his messiahship the fact that the Gospel is proclaimed to the poor (cf. Mt 11:5; Lk 7:22) and he also taught that "Blessed are the poor in spirit, for theirs is the kingdom of heaven" (Mt 5:3). "Christ was sent by the Father 'to preach good news to the poor ... to heal the contrite of heart' (Lk 4:18), 'to seek and to save the lost' (Lk 19:10). Similarly, the Church encompasses with her love all those who are afflicted by human misery and she recognizes in those who are poor and who suffer, the image of her poor and suffering founder. She does all in her power to relieve their need and in them she strives to serve Christ" (Vatican II, *Lumen gentium*, 8).

Of the rich, on the other hand, the apostle speaks with unusual harshness. As elsewhere in Scripture, those who deserve such severe condemnation are people who are bent on building up their possessions as if ownership were the only purpose in life, not minding what means they used, and oppressing and ill-treating the poor (cf. note on Lk 6:24).

oppress you, is it not they who drag you into court? ⁷Is it not they who blaspheme that honourable name which was invoked over you?*

⁸If you really fulfil the royal law, according to the scripture, "You shall love your neighbour as yourself," you do well. ⁹But if you show partiality, you commit sin, and are convicted by the law as transgressors. ¹⁰For whoever keeps the whole law but fails in one point has become guilty of all of it.* ¹¹For he who said, "Do

Lev 19:18
Mt 22:39
Mk 12:31
Mt 5:19
Gal 3:10

Behaviour of this type is so serious that it amounts to "blaspheming that honourable name by which you are called" (v. 7)—blasphemy by scandalous action rather than by words. This "name" can mean both the name "Jesus"—called down on them at Baptism—and that of "Christian", a name already being given to those first followers of the Master (cf. Acts 11:26).

What St James says here can in no sense be used to justify the "class struggle" which some materialistic doctrines propose. The Magisterium of the Church has often pointed out that the application of Christian principles should make for harmony and concord between the various groups in society (cf. Leo XIII, *Rerum novarum*, 14). James' words certainly do urge everyone to make a real effort to promote the human dignity of all: "The evil inequities and oppression of every kind which afflict millions of men and women today openly contradict Christ's Gospel and cannot leave the conscience of any Christian indifferent" (SCDF, *Libertatis conscientia*, 57).

2:8–11. The Apostle extends his argument against discrimination, recalling what is said in the Old Testament (with which his original readers would have been familiar, since many of them were Jewish converts to Christianity). As we have pointed out previously (cf. note on 2:1–4) all unjust discrimination is condemned in the Old Testament.

2:8. "The royal law" is spelled out in the book of Leviticus (19:18). St James calls it this perhaps because, in addition to commanding love of God above all things, it is the basis and root of all the other commandments (cf. Mt 22:34–40).

Jesus corrected narrow interpretations of that law of charity (cf. Mt 5:43–48; Lk 10:25–37) and formulated the "new commandment" at the Last Supper: "that you love one another, even as I have loved you, that you also love one another" (Jn 13:34). In proposing this new standard ("as I have loved you") our Lord gives new content and meaning to the precept of brotherly love. This commandment is the law of the new people of God, the Church (cf. *Lumen gentium*, 9).

2:10–11. Each and every commandment of the Law of God is an expression of his will. Therefore, any sin—even if it is against only one precept—is always an offence against God. And if the sin is a grave sin, it destroys the virtue of charity and the supernatural life of grace.

When explaining this point, St Augustine reminds us that charity is the fullness of the law (cf. Rom 13:9f); the Law and the Prophets are grounded on charity in its two dimensions of love of God and love of neighbour (cf. Mt 22:34–40).

"And no one loves his neighbour," he goes on, "unless he loves God and tries his best to get that neighbour (whom he loves as himself) to love God too. If he

not commit adultery," said also, "Do not kill." If you do not commit adultery but do kill, you have become a transgressor of the law. ¹²So speak and so act as those who are to be judged under the law of liberty. ¹³For judgment is without mercy to one who has shown no mercy; yet mercy triumphs over judgment.

Deut 5:17–18
Ex 20:13–14

Jas 1:25

Mt 5:7; 18:29,
34; 25:45f

2. FAITH AND GOOD WORKS

Faith without good works is dead

¹⁴What does it profit, my brethren, if a man says he has faith but has not works? Can his faith save him?* ¹⁵If a brother or sister is

Mt 7:21; 21:29

---

does not love God, then he does not love himself, nor does he love his neighbour. That is why whoever would keep the whole law but fails in one point has become guilty of all of it, for he has acted against charity, on which the whole law depends. One becomes guilty of all the commandments when one sins against that (virtue) from which they all derive" (*Letter*, 167, 5, 16).

2:12. He again refers to the "law of liberty". Earlier (cf. 1:25 and note) he meant the new law brought by Jesus Christ; now the expression is used to mean the law of charity, on which we will be judged at the Last Day (cf. Mt 25:31–46 and notes).

2:13. Neglect and disdain for the poor implies acting without mercy, and anyone who acts like that will be judged without mercy. These words are a direct echo of what our Lord says: "Blessed are the merciful, for they shall obtain mercy" (Mt 5:7), and "With the judgment you pronounce you will be judged, and the measure you give will be the measure you get" (Mt 7:2).

Mercy "triumphs over [condemnatory] judgment": anyone who practises mercy will be confident and even happy to face God's judgment because he knows that God will show him mercy.

Commenting on this verse, St Augustine says: "When the just King sits in judgment, who will claim to be pure in heart? Who will boast of being free from sin? What hope could there be if mercy did not prevail over judgment? But that mercy will be applied to those who are themselves merciful" (*Letter*, 167, 6, 20).

2:14–26. This passage forms the core of the letter. The sapiential method (often used in the Old Testament) and pedagogical style of the passage help to engrave the message on the readers' minds: unless faith is accompanied by works, it is barren, dead. This basic message, with different variances, is stated up to five times (vv. 14, 17, 18, 20, 26), in a cyclical, repetitive way.

The initial rhetorical question (v. 14) and the simple, vivid example of a person who is content with giving good advice to someone in urgent need of the bare essentials (vv. 15–16), catch the disciples' attention and predispose them to accept the core message, which is couched in the form of a sapiential maxim (v. 17).

The narrative retains its conversational tone, with a series of questions; we are given three examples of faith: firstly

ill-clad and in lack of daily food, ¹⁶and one of you says to them, "Go in peace, be warmed and filled," without giving them the things needed for the body, what does it profit? ¹⁷So faith by itself, if it has no works, is dead.

1 Jn 3:17

(a negative example), the faith of demons, which is of no avail (vv. 18–19); contrasting with this, the faith of Abraham, the model and father of believers (vv. 20–23); and finally, the faith of a sinner whose actions won her salvation, Rahab the prostitute (vv. 24–25). The last sentence once again repeats the essential idea: "faith apart from works is dead" (v. 26).

2:14. This teaching is perfectly in line with that of the Master: "Not every one who says to me, 'Lord, Lord', shall enter the kingdom of heaven, but he who does the will of my Father who is in heaven" (Mt 7:21).

A faith without deeds cannot obtain salvation: "Even though incorporated into the Church, one who does not however persevere in charity is not saved. He remains indeed in the bosom of the Church, but 'in body' not 'in heart'. All children of the Church should nevertheless remember that their exalted condition results not from their own merits but from the grace of Christ. If they fail to respond in thought, word, and deed to that grace, not only shall they not be saved, but they shall be the more severely judged" (Vatican II, *Lumen gentium*, 14).

In the Christian life, therefore, there needs to be complete consistency between the faith we profess and the deeds we do. "Unity of life", one of the key features of the spirituality of Opus Dei, tries to counter the danger of people leading a double life, "on the one hand, an inner life, a life related to God; and on the other, as something separate and distinct, their professional, social and family lives, made up of small earthly realities [...]".

There is only one life, made of flesh and spirit. And it is that life which has to become, in both body and soul, holy and filled with God: we discover the invisible God in the most visible and material things" (St Josemaría Escrivá, *In Love with the Church*, 52).

2:15–16. This very graphic example is similar to that in the First Letter of St John: "If any one has the world's goods and sees his brother in need, yet closes his heart against him, how does God's love abide in him?" (1 Jn 3:17); and the conclusion is also along the same lines: "Little children, let us not love in word or speech but in deed and in truth" (1 Jn 3:18). St Paul gives the same teaching: "the kingdom of God does not consist in talk but in power" (1 Cor 4:20). Actions, works, measure the genuineness of the Christian life; they show whether our faith and charity are real.

Almsgiving, for example, so often praised and recommended in Scripture (cf., e.g., Deut 15:11; Tob 4:7–11; Lk 12:33; Acts 9:36; 2 Cor 8:9), is very often a duty. Christ "will count a kindness done or refused to the poor as done or refused to himself [...]. Whoever has received from the divine bounty a large share of temporal blessings whether they be external or material, or gifts of the mind, has received them for the purpose of using them for the perfecting of his own nature, and, at the same time, that he may employ them, as the steward of God's providence, for the benefit of others" (Leo XIII, *Rerum novarum*, 24).

2:17. As well as involving firm adherence to revealed truth, faith must influence a

¹⁸But some one will say, "You have faith and I have works." Show me your faith apart from your works, and I by my works will show you my faith. ¹⁹You believe that God is one; you do well. Even the demons believe—and shudder.

Gal 5:6

Examples from the Bible

²⁰Do you want to be shown, you shallow man, that faith apart from works is barren? ²¹Was not Abraham our father justified by works,

Gen 22:9
Heb 11:17

Christian's ordinary life and be a standard against which he measures his conduct When one's works are not in accordance with one's beliefs, then one's faith is dead.

Christian teaching also describes as "dead faith" the faith of a person in mortal sin: because he is not in the grace of God he does not have charity, which is as it were the soul of all the other virtues. "Faith without hope and charity neither perfectly unites a man with Christ nor makes him a living member of his body. Therefore it is said most truly that 'faith apart from works is dead' (Jas 2:17ff) and useless" (Council of Trent, *De iustificatione*, 7).

2:18. The apostle makes it crystal clear that faith without works makes no sense at all. "The truth of faith includes not only inner belief, but also outward profession, which is expressed not only by declaration of one's belief, but also by the actions by which a person shows that he has faith" (St Thomas, *Summa theologiae*, 2–2, 124, 5).

2:19. St James goes as far as to compare a faith without works with the kind of faith devils have, for they do believe: they are forced to believe by the evidence of the signs (miracles and prophecies, for example) which support Christian teaching (cf. *Summa theologiae*, 2–2, 5, 2). However, that faith is not saving faith; on the contrary, it causes them to cringe by reminding them of divine justice and eternal punishment.

Commenting on this verse, St Bede says that it is one thing to believe God, another thing to believe in God, and another to believe "towards" God (*credere in illum*). "Believing him is believing that what he says is true. Believing in him is believing that he is God. Believing 'towards' him is loving him. Many people, even bad people, believe that God tells the truth; they believe it is the truth and they do not want to, are too lazy to, follow the way truth points. Believing that he is God is something the devils are able to do. But believing and tending towards him is true only of those who love God, who are Christians not in name only but whose actions and lives prove them to be so. For without love faith is of no avail. With love, it is the faith of a Christian; without love, it is the faith of the devil" (*Super Iac. expositio*, ad loc.).

2:20–26. The original addressees of the letter (Christians of Jewish background steeped in Scripture) would have been very familiar with the two examples from the Old Testament (Abraham and Rahab).

The patriarch Abraham is a model of faith (cf. especially Heb 11:8ff). St James highlights the fact that his faith was manifested in deeds (v. 22), so much so that he was ready to sacrifice his own son when God, to test him, asked him to do so (cf. Gen 22:1ff). The text of Genesis 15:6 quoted here (v. 23) is also used by

James 2:22

Gen 15:6
Rom 4:3
Is 41:8
2 Chron 20:7
Jn 8:39

when he offered his son Isaac upon the altar? ²²You see that faith was active along with his works, and faith was completed by works, ²³and the scripture was fulfilled which says, "Abraham believed God, and it was reckoned to him as righteousness"; and he was called the friend of God. ²⁴You see that a man is justified by works and not by faith alone. ²⁵And in the same way was not also

St Paul in his polemic against the Judaizers, to show that "first justification" comes from faith and not from works of the Mosaic Law (cf. Rom 4:1–25; Gal 3:6–9); that is, Abraham was justified from the very moment he believed in God; his works would not have had any value without that direct reference to God. In Abraham, as in every Christian who acts consistently, faith and works totally imbue each another: works show forth faith, and faith inspires and performs works (vv. 22, 24).

The story of Rahab (v. 25) is told in the book of Joshua (2:1–21; 6:17–25): this woman, who was living among the Canaanites, saved the lives of two Israelite spies whom Joshua had sent into Jericho, and for this reason she and her family were saved when the Israelites took the city. Her actions showed her faith (cf. Josh 2:9–14; Heb 11:31), and led not only to her coming out unscathed and becoming a member of the people of Israel; it also won her the honour of being one of the four foreign women mentioned in the Gospel in our Lord's ancestral tree (cf. Mt 1:5).

These two examples clearly show that God calls all men to believe and that all can and should manifest their faith by exemplary living.

2:22–24. The Magisterium of the Church quotes these verses when it teaches that justification, righteousness, received as a free gift in the sacrament of Baptism, grows in strength as the Christian responds to grace by keeping the commandments of God and of the Church; the righteous, the just, "increase in the very justice which they have received through the grace of Christ, their faith is completed by works (cf. Jas 2:22), and they are justified the more, as it is written: 'Let the righteous still do right' (Rev 22:11), [...] and again: 'You see that a man is justified by works and not by faith alone (Jas 2:24)" (Council of Trent, *De iustificatione*, 10).

2:23. "It was reckoned to him as righteousness": St Paul (cf. Gal 3:6 and note) uses these words of Genesis 15:6 to explain that righteousness is attained not just by Abraham's descendants but by all who believe the word of God, whether they be Jews or not; St James, from another perspective, quotes this text to show that Abraham's faith made him righteous, that is, holy. Both teachings are complementary. Abraham believed in the divine promise that he would be the father of a great people despite his age and his wife's sterility; but that faith was reinforced and manifested when it met the test God set—that of sacrificing his only son, while still believing in the earlier promise. The same thing happens in the case of the Christian: his initial faith is strengthened by obedience to the commandments, and he thereby attains holiness.

"The friend of God": Scripture also gives this touching title to Abraham (cf. Is 41:8; Dan 3:35, New Vulgate) and our Lord uses it to describe his apostles: "I have called you friends" (Jn 15:15).

Rahab the harlot justified by works when she received the messengers and sent them out another way? ²⁶For as the body apart from the spirit is dead, so faith apart from works is dead.

_{Josh 2:4f; 6:17}
_{Heb 11:31}

_{Jas 2:17}

3. PRACTICAL APPLICATIONS

Controlling one's tongue

3 ¹Let not many of you become teachers, my brethren, for you know that we who teach shall be judged with greater strictness. ²For we all make many mistakes, and if any one makes no

_{Jas 1:26}
_{Sir 14:1}

These are not just isolated examples, for God calls all to be his friends; he wishes to be as intimate with everyone as he was with Abraham and the apostles: "We do not exist in order to pursue just any happiness. We have been called to penetrate the intimacy of God's own life, to know and love God the Father, God the Son, and God the Holy Spirit, and to love also—in that same love of the one God in three divine Persons—the angels and all men" (St Josemaría Escrivá, *Christ Is Passing By*, 133).

2:26. In speaking of "the spirit" St James is referring to the "breath of life", "breathing". The comparison (like all those in the letter) is very graphic: we recognise a body to be alive by its breathing; if it is not breathing it is a corpse; similarly, a faith that is alive expresses itself in actions, especially in acts of charity.

"Just as when a body moves we know it is alive," St Bernard explains, "so too good works show that faith is alive. The soul gives life to the body, causing it to move and feel; charity gives life to faith, causing it to act, as the Apostle says, 'faith working through love' (Gal 5:6). Just as the body dies when its soul leaves it, so faith dies when charity grows cold. Therefore, when you see someone who is active in good works and happy and eager in his conduct, you can be sure that faith is alive in him: his life clearly proves it to be so" (*Second Sermon on the Holy Day of Easter*, 1).

3:1–18. There is now an apparently sudden change of subject; but in fact the themes dealt with in the letter from this point onwards are practical applications of the principle outlined in the second section (consistency between faith and works). Firstly, it deals with control of the tongue, prudent speech; after warning of occupational hazards of teachers (vv. 1–2), it denounces the sins the tongue can cause (vv. 2–12), and goes on to describe the characteristics of true and false wisdom (vv. 13–18).

3:1–2. St James draws attention to the responsibility that goes with holding a position of authority: all those who are teachers, in addition to answering to God for their own actions, are responsible to some degree for the actions of their disciples. That is why the Church has always encouraged prayer for those whose job it is to guide their brethren: "Nor should (lay people) fail to commend to God in their prayers those who have been placed over them, who indeed keep watch as having to render an account

James 3:3

mistakes in what he says he is a perfect man, able to bridle the whole body also. ³If we put bits into the mouths of horses that they may obey us, we guide their whole bodies. ⁴Look at the ships also; though they are so great and are driven by strong winds, they

---

of our souls, that they may do this with joy and not with grief (cf. Heb 13:17)" (Vatican II, *Lumen gentium*, 37).

"We all make many mistakes": Holy Scripture repeatedly draws attention to the sinful condition of man and the frequency with which he offends God (cf., e.g., Ps 19:13; 51:3ff; Prov 20:9; 1 Jn 1:8). The Council of Trent recalls these words of St James when it teaches that no one can go through life without committing some venial sin, "except by a special privilege granted by God, as the Church teaches happened in the case of the Blessed Virgin" (*De iustificatione*, can. 23; cf. chap. 16).

The great saints, from whom we can learn much, have attained holiness because they recognized that they were sinners: "I shall love you, Lord, and shall give thanks to you and confess your name," St Augustine exclaims, because "you have forgiven me such great sins and evil deeds [...]: for what might I have not done, seeing that I loved evil solely because it was evil? I confess that you have forgiven all alike—the sins I committed on my own motion, the sins I would have committed but for your grace [...]. If any man has heard your voice and followed it and done none of the things he finds me here recording and confessing, still he must not scorn me: for I am healed by the same doctor who preserved him from falling into sickness, or at least into such grievous sickness. But let him love you even more—seeing me rescued out of such sickness of sin, and himself saved from falling into such sickness of sin, by the one same Saviour" (*Confessions*, 2, 7).

3:2–12. The sacred writer focuses on sins of the tongue, possibly because of their frequency. In the wisdom books of the Old Testament these sins are referred to particularly often (cf., e.g., Prov 10:11–21; Sir 5:9–15; 28:13–26).

He basically makes three points—first, a positive point, by way of summing up what follows: "If any one makes no mistakes in what he says he is a perfect man" (v. 2). Then with three graphic comparisons (typical of this letter) he shows how difficult it is to control the tongue (vv. 3–6), but controlled it must be, otherwise great harm will be done (vv. 7–12).

"A perfect man" (v. 2): this does not mean that he cannot commit other sins; it implies that if one succeeds in restraining one's tongue one has self-control, which means that one is putting up good resistance to temptation.

3:3–6. Three simple, easy-to-understand examples (used also by other ancient writers in Greco-Latin and Jewish literature) show how something small—a horse's bit, a boat's rudder, a small fire—can have very big effects; the tongue has a similar influence in social life.

The *St Pius V Catechism*, recalling this teaching, says: "From these words we learn two truths. The fact is that sins of the tongue are very prevalent [...]. The other truth is that the tongue is the source of innumerable evils. Through the fault of the evil-speaker are often lost the property, the reputation, the life, and the salvation of the injured person, or of him who inflicts the injury. The injured person, unable to bear patiently the contumely, avenges it without restraint. The offender,

are guided by a very small rudder wherever the will of the pilot directs. ⁵So the tongue is a little member and boasts of great things. How great a forest is set ablaze by a small fire! ⁶And the tongue is a fire. The tongue is an unrighteous world among our members, staining the whole body, setting on fire the cycle of nature,ᵇ and set on fire by hell.ᶜ ⁷For every kind of beast and bird, of reptile and sea creature, can be tamed and has been tamed by humankind, ⁸but no human being can tame the tongue— a restless evil, full of deadly poison. ⁹With it we bless the Lord and Father, and with it we curse men, who are made in the likeness of God. ¹⁰From the same mouth come blessing and cursing. My brethren, this ought not to be so. ¹¹Does a spring pour forth from the same opening fresh water and brackish? ¹²Can a fig tree, my brethren, yield olives, or a grapevine figs? No more can salt water yield fresh.

Mt 15:11; 12:36f
Prov 16:27

Gen 9:2

Ps 140:4
Gen 1:27
Eph 4:29

Mt 7:16

---

on the other hand, deterred by a perverse shame and a false idea of what is called honour, cannot be induced to make reparation to him whom he has offended" (3, 9, 1). It should be remembered that if one unfairly damages another's reputation one has an obligation to make reparation by doing what one can to restore his or her good name.

"Do you know what damage you may cause by throwing stones with your eyes blindfolded? Neither do you know the harm you may cause—and at times it is very great—by letting drop uncharitable remarks that to you seem trifling, because your eyes are blinded by thoughtlessness or passion" (St Josemaría Escrivá, *The Way*, 455).

3:6. St James uses this graphic language to emphasize that if one does not control one's tongue it can cause much evil, affecting one's entire life. In itself very useful, the tongue can wreak havoc, so it is not surprising that the enemies of our sanctification seek to get control of it:

"though their voices sound like cracked bells, that have not been cast from good metal and have a very different tone from the shepherd's whistle call, they so distort speech, which is one of the most precious talents ever bestowed on men by God, a most beautiful gift for the expression of deep thoughts of love and friendship towards the Lord and his creatures, that one comes to understand why St James says that the tongue is 'an unrighteous world' (Jas 3:6). So great is the harm it can do—lies, slander, dishonour, trickery, insults, tortuous insinuations" (St J. Escrivá, *Friends of God*, 298).

3:9–12. The sacred writer uses further examples, equally simple and familiar to his readers, to stress the need for control of the tongue. Experience shows that it is as easy to put it to a good purpose as to an evil one. Besides, misuse of the tongue is a sign that one's heart is not in the right place: as our Lord already warned us, "out of the abundance of the heart the mouth speaks" (Mt 12:34).

---

b. Or *wheel of birth* **c.** Greek *Gehenna*

James 3:13

True and false wisdom

Margin references: Gal 5:23; Jas 2:18; 1 Pet 2:12; Rom 2:8; Eph 4:31; Col 3:3; Jas 1:5, 17

¹³Who is wise and understanding among you? By his good life let him show his works in the meekness of wisdom. ¹⁴But if you have bitter jealousy and selfish ambition in your hearts, do not boast and be false to the truth. ¹⁵This wisdom is not such as comes down from above, but is earthly, unspiritual, devilish. ¹⁶For where jealousy and selfish ambition exist, there will be disorder and every vile practise. ¹⁷But the wisdom from above is first pure, then peaceable, gentle, open to reason, full of mercy and good fruits, without uncertainty or insincerity. ¹⁸And the harvest of righteousness is sown in peace by those who make peace.

Margin references: Is 32:17; Mt 5:9; Phil 1:11

3:13–18. These verses point out the qualities of Christian wisdom (cf. 1:5). After exhorting his readers to manifest their wisdom by their actions (v. 13), he attacks the signs of false wisdom (vv. 14–16) and explains the qualities of the true (vv. 17–18).

St Paul also makes a distinction between worldly wisdom—the wisdom of man when he veers away from his correct goal—and the wisdom of God, which reaches its highest expression on the cross (cf. 1 Cor 1:18 3:3). St James pays particular attention to the practical effects of godly wisdom—meekness, mercy and peace.

False wisdom, on the contrary, leads to bitter zeal, rivalry and resentment: it is "earthly" because it rejects things transcendental and supernatural; "unspiritual" (merely natural, "psychic" in the original Greek), as befits people who follow their nature as wounded by original sin, deprived of the help of the Spirit (cf. notes on 1 Cor 2:14–16; Jude 19–20); "devilish", in the sense that such people are inspired by the devil, who is envious (cf. Wis 2:24), "a liar and the father of lies" (Jn 8:44).

3:18. What this verse means is that the "peacemakers" of the Beatitudes (cf. Mt 5:6 and note) create around themselves an environment making for righteousness (holiness), and they themselves benefit from the peace they sow. "There can be no peace," John XXIII says, "between men unless there is peace within each of them: unless, that is, each one builds up within himself the order wished by God" (*Pacem in terris*, 165).

The "harvest of righteousness" is the equivalent of righteousness itself: it is keeping the law of the Gospel, doing good works, which show true wisdom. The passage is reminiscent of Isaiah 32:17–18: "and the effects of righteousness will be peace, and the result of righteousness, quietness and trust for ever. My people will abide in a peaceful habitation, in secure dwellings and in quiet resting places."

Every Christian who strives to live in accordance with his vocation is a sower of holiness and justice-with-peace: "Through your work, through the whole network of human relations," St J. Escrivá says, "you ought to show the charity of Christ and its concrete expression in friendship, understanding, human affection and peace. Just as Christ 'went about doing good' (Acts 10:38) throughout Palestine, so must you also spread peace in your family circle, in civil society, at work, and in your cultural and leisure activities" (*Christ Is Passing By*, 166).

James 4:4

The source of discord

4 ¹What causes wars, and what causes fightings among you? Is it not your passions that are at war in your members? ²You desire and do not have; so you kill. And you covet^d and cannot obtain; so you fight and wage war. You do not have, because you do not ask. ³You ask and do not receive, because you ask wrongly, to spend it on your passions. ⁴Unfaithful creatures! Do not

Rom 7:23
1 Pet 2:11

Rom 8:7
1 Jn 2:15

4:1—5:6. Contrasting with the peace possessed and spread by those who practise true wisdom (cf. 3:17–18), one often finds discord and contention among Christians which makes it difficult for them to live together in harmony. St James severely reproaches this sort of behaviour, pointing out that it originates in greed in all its various forms.

These verses are a further collection of teachings—warnings addressed to various groups in the Christian community, censuring the graver kinds of moral deviation, which all show that people are not practising the faith they profess. First comes discord (vv. 1–12); then, empty-headed boasting about one's own abilities (vv. 13–17); and, lastly, the injustice of the rich who oppress the weak (5:1–6).

In reproaching the faithful for dissension and division (vv. 1–12), the main causes are identified as greed and envy (vv. 1–3), disordered love of things of the world, and pride (vv. 4–10), and, stemming from that, complaints and evil speech (vv. 11–12).

4:1. "Wars" and "fighting" are an exaggerated reference to the contention and discord found among those Christians. "Passions", as elsewhere in the New Testament, means concupiscence, hedonism, pleasure-seeking (cf. v. 3; Lk 8:14; Tit 3:3; 2 Pet 2:13).

St James points out that if one fails to fight as one should against one's evil inclinations, one's inner disharmony overflows in the form of quarrelling and fighting. The New Testament often refers to the good kind of fight, which confers inner freedom and is a prerequisite for salvation (cf., e.g., Mt 11:12; Rom 7:14–25; 1 Pet 2:11).

"How can you be at peace if you allow passions you do not even attempt to control to drag you away from the 'pull' of grace? Heaven pulls you upwards; you drag yourself downwards. And don't seek excuses—that is what you are doing. If you go on like that, you will tear yourself apart" (St Josemaría Escrivá, *Furrow*, 851).

4:2–3. St James is describing the sad state to which free-wheeling hedonism (specifically, greed for earthly things) leads.

"You do not receive, because you ask wrongly": "He asks wrongly who shows no regard for the Lord's commandments and yet seeks heavenly gifts. He also asks wrongly who, having lost his taste for heavenly things, seeks only earthly things —not for sustaining his human weakness but to enable him to indulge himself" (St Bede, *Super Iac. expositio*, ad loc.).

4:4–6. The sacred writer warns that inordinate love of the world, which stems from ambition, is incompatible with the

---

d. Or *you kill and you covet*

know that friendship with the world is enmity with God? Therefore whoever wishes to be a friend of the world makes himself an enemy of God. ⁵Or do you suppose it is in vain that the scripture says, "He yearns jealously over the spirit which he has made to dwell in us"? ⁶But he gives more grace; therefore it says,

Gen 2:7
Prov 3:34
Job 22:29

---

love of God. "World" here has the meaning of "enemy of God", opposed to Christ and his followers (cf. note on 1:26–27). The teaching contained in these verses echoes that of our Lord: "No one can serve two masters; for either he will hate the one and love the other, or he will be devoted to the one and despise the other. You cannot serve God and mammon" (Mt 6:24).

The saints have frequently reminded us—by their lives as well as their teachings—that inordinate love of the world is incompatible with the love of God: "Worldly society has flowered from a selfish love which dared to despise even God, whereas the communion of saints is rooted in a love of God that is ready to trample on self" (St Augustine, *The City of God*, 14, 28).

"Unfaithful creatures!": the original Greek simply says "Adulterers" (fem.) and the New Vulgate, "Adulterers" (masc.). This echoes the symbol the prophets often use (cf., e.g., Hos 1:2ff; Jer 3:7–10; Ezek 16:1ff) of the marriage of God and his people sealed by the Covenant. St James, therefore, is not referring to the sin of adultery; he is berating those whose excessive love for the things of this world makes them unfaithful to God.

4:5. The original Greek is open to various interpretations and the quotation as given here is not to be found in the Bible. Translated word for word it means: "Jealously he loves the spirit which dwells in us." It is not clear who "loves"—God or the spirit; and "the spirit" may mean the soul or the Holy Spirit; moreover, the jealousy can be either something good or something bad (like envy). It might perhaps be translated as "The Spirit who dwells in us jealously loves us" (which is how the New Vulgate translates it).

Although this sentence does not appear literally in the Bible, St James may be referring not so much to a specific passage as to an idea which often occurs in the Bible when it depicts God as a jealous lover (cf., e.g., Ex 20:5; 34:14; Zech 1:14; 8:2), who expects his love to be returned wholeheartedly; this very human kind of language is a most moving evocation of God's immense love for man. St Alphonsus teaches: "Since he loves us with infinite love, he desires all our love; that is why he is jealous when he sees others having a share in hearts which he wants entirely for his own. 'Jesus is jealous', St Jerome said (*Epistle*, 22), in the sense that he does not want us to love anything that is outside himself. And if he sees that some creature has a part of your heart, he is in a sense envious of it, as the apostle James writes, because he tolerates no rival for our love; he wants to have all our love" (*The Love of Jesus Christ*, chap. 11).

4:6. The sacred writer foresees the possibility that some may draw back from this "jealous" love God expects to be reciprocated: but God never expects the impossible; he gives us all the grace we need to do what he asks: "All my hope is naught," St Augustine exclaims, "save in your great mercy. Grant what you command, and command what you will" (*Confessions*, 10, 29).

"God opposes the proud, but gives grace to the humble." ⁷Submit yourselves therefore to God. Resist the devil and he will flee from you. ⁸Draw near to God and he will draw near to you. Cleanse your hands, you sinners, and purify your hearts, you men of double mind. ⁹Be wretched and mourn and weep. Let your

1 Pet 5:5
Eph 6:12
1 Pet 5:8f
Zech 1:3
Jas 1:8

However, only people who are humble are given this grace, and have it bear fruit. The proud, who are full of self-love, even fail to realize that they need grace, and so they do not ask for it, or do not ask for it properly. The second part of the verse is a literal quotation from Proverbs 3:34 (according to the Septuagint Greek): it is an example of the "poetic" form, with the characteristic antithetical parallelism of Hebrew verse. St Augustine, in his explanation of the fact that the Bible refers in places to the sins of prominent men, urges his readers to be humble, commenting that "there is scarcely a page in the sacred books which does not echo the fact that 'God resists the proud and gives grace to the humble'" (*De doctrina christiana*, 3, 23).

4:7-10. Some ways of countering pride are identified here: basically what is required is a sincere and deep conversion, which must begin with the humility of recognizing that we are sinners and in need of purification. The tone of these verses is reminiscent of the way the Old Testament prophets upbraid the people of Israel for their unfaithfulness to Yahweh.

To draw near to God the sinner needs purification. "Cleaning your hands" should not be understood as referring to the physical ablutions of the Jews (cf. Ex 30:19-21; Mk 7:1-5); but should be taken in a moral sense—purification from sins, and upright actions (e.g., Is 1:15-17; 1 Tim 2:8). Of all the possible ways of being purified and converted (for example, the penitential rite at Mass, a visit to a shrine, or fasting), "none is more significant," John Paul II reminds us, "more divinely efficacious or more lofty and at the same time easily accessible as a rite than the sacrament of Penance. [...]. For a Christian, *the sacrament of Penance is the ordinary way* of obtaining forgiveness and the remission of serious sins committed after Baptism" (*Reconciliatio et paenitentia*, 28 and 31).

4:7. When someone resists the devil's temptations, the devil leaves him alone: he cannot force a man to commit sin. *The Shepherd of Hermas* (a work by an anonymous Christian writer, around the middle of the second century) elaborates on the same idea: "Be converted, you who walk in the commandments of the devil, commandments that are hard, bitter, cruel and foul. And do not fear the devil either, because he has no power against you [...]. The devil cannot lord it over those who are servants of God with their whole heart and who place their hope in him. The devil can wrestle with, but not overcome them. So, if you resist him, he will flee from you in defeat and confusion" (11th commandment, 4, 6 and 5, 2).

4:9. "Be wretched": "To acknowledge one's sin—penetrating still more deeply into the consideration of one's own personhood—*to recognize oneself as a sinner*, capable of sin and inclined to commit sin, is the essential first step in returning to God" (*Reconciliatio et paenitentia*, 13).

Mourning and weeping are the external expression of sincere repentance (cf. Mt 5:4 and note; Tob 2:6; Amos 8:10):

James 4:10

_{Mt 23:12}
_{1 Pet 5:6}

laughter be turned to mourning and your joy to dejection. ¹⁰Humble yourselves before the Lord and he will exalt you.

¹¹Do not speak evil against one another, brethren. He that speaks evil against a brother or judges his brother, speaks evil against the law and judges the law. But if you judge the law, you are not a doer of the law but a judge. ¹²There is one lawgiver and judge, he who is able to save and to destroy. But who are you that you judge your neighbour?

_{Rom 14:4}
_{Mt 10:28}

Trust in divine providence

_{Prov 27:1}
_{Lk 12:19f}
_{Job 14:1f}
_{Acts 18:21}

¹³Come now, you who say, "Today or tomorrow we will go into such and such a town and spend a year there and trade and get gain"; ¹⁴whereas you do not know about tomorrow. What is your life? For you are a mist that appears for a little time and then vanishes. ¹⁵Instead you ought to say, "If the Lord wills, we shall live and we shall do this or that." ¹⁶As it is, you boast in your

---

"You are crying? Don't be ashamed of it. Yes, cry: men also cry like you, when they are alone and before God. Each night, says King David, I soak my bed with tears. With those tears, those burning manly tears, you can purify your past and supernaturalize your present life" (St Josemaría Escrivá, *The Way*, 216).

4:11–12. Thinking evil of one's neighbour (judging him) and speaking evil of him (defaming him) goes against the commandment of charity, which sums up the Law and the Prophets (cf. Mt 22:3440). Therefore, anyone who acts like that breaks the whole Law: it means taking the law into one's own hands, usurping the place of God, the supreme Lawgiver and Judge. In other words it is for God to make laws and, in line with them, "to save and to destroy", that is, to reward and to punish.

4:13–17. Overweening self-confidence is a type of pride because it means one is forgetful of God who, in his providence, rules over the lives of men. St James reminds those who are totally caught up in their business affairs that human life is something very impermanent (v. 14). He made the same point earlier with the simile of the flower of the grass (cf. 1:9–11); now he puts it in terms of the fleetingness of mist (a familiar Old Testament image: cf., e.g., Job 7:7–16; Ps 102:4; Wis 2:4). "Earthly life is a wearisome thing," St Gregory the Great reminds us, "more unreal than fables, faster than a runner, with many ups and downs caused by unreliability and weakness; we shelter in houses made of clay (in fact, life itself is mere clay); our fortitude, our resolution, has no substance; such rest and repose as we get in the midst of our activities and difficulties is of no help" (*Exposition on the seven penitential psalms*, Ps 109, prologue).

A Christian should trustingly abandon himself into the hands of God, but that does not in any sense mean that he may irresponsibly opt out of his duties or avoid exercising his rights.

4:15. "If the Lord wills": this expression is to be found elsewhere in the New Testament; St Paul uses the same words

arrogance. All such boasting is evil. ¹⁷Whoever knows what is right to do and fails to do it, for him it is sin.

Lk 12:47
Rom 14:23

A warning to the rich

5 ¹Come now, you rich, weep and howl for the miseries that are coming upon you. ²Your riches have rotted and your garments are moth-eaten. ³Your gold and silver have rusted, and their rust will be evidence against you and will eat your flesh like fire. You

Lk 6:24
Mt 6:19
Sir 29:10
Prov 16:27

(cf. 1 Cor 4:19) or ones like them, when speaking about his personal plans (cf. Acts 18:21; Rom 1:10; 1 Cor 16:7). It is a saying which has passed into popular Christian speech and it shows a readiness to leave one's future in God's hands, trusting in divine providence.

4:17. As elsewhere in the letter, St James ends this passage with a general maxim (cf. 1:12; 2:13; 3:18). In this instance, to emphasize the need to prove one's faith and one's grasp of the faith by action (cf. 2:14–16), he gives a warning about sins of omission. Once again, the Master's teachings are reflected in what the sacred writer says: "the servant who knew his master's will, and did not make ready or act according to his will, shall receive a severe beating" (Lk 12:47).

5:1–6. With exceptional severity and energy the sacred writer again (cf. 2:5–7) criticizes the sins of the well-to-do. In tones reminiscent of the Prophets (cf., e.g., Is 3:13–26; Amos 6:1ff; Mic 2:1ff), he reproves their pride, vanity and greed (vv. 2–3) and their pleasure-seeking (v. 5), warning them that the judgment of God is near at hand (vv. 3, 5). The opening exhortation—"weep and howl" —is a very forceful call to repentance.

The Church has constantly taught that we have a duty to do away with unjust inequalities among men, which are frequently denounced in Scripture. The Second Vatican Council made an urgent call for a more just, fraternal society, a call for solidarity: "To fulfil the requirements of justice and equity, every effort must be made to put an end as soon as possible to the immense economic inequalities which exist in the world and increase from day to day, linked with individual and social discrimination, provided, of course, that the rights of individuals and the character of each people are not disturbed" (*Gaudium et spes*, 66).

People who are well-to-do should use their resources in the service of others. In this connexion, the Church teaches that "they have a moral obligation not to keep capital unproductive and in making investments to think first of the common good. [...] The right to private property is inconceivable without responsibilities to the common good. It is subordinated to the higher principle which states that goods are meant for all" (SCDF, *Libertatis conscientia*, 87).

5:2–3. Greed, an inordinate desire for material things, is one of the seven deadly sins. An avaricious person offends against justice and charity and becomes insensitive to his neighbour's needs, so keen is he on his self-aggrandisement. "If you are inclined to avarice," says St Francis de Sales, "think of its folly: it makes us slaves to that which was intended to serve us. Remember how we must leave everything when we die; perhaps those who get our wealth then will only

James 5:4

Lev 19:23
Deut 24:14, 15
Is 5:9
Jer 12:3
Lk 16:19–25

have laid up treasure[e]* for the last days. ⁴Behold, the wages of the labourers who mowed your fields, which you kept back by fraud, cry out; and the cries of the harvesters have reached the ears of the Lord of hosts. ⁵You have lived on the earth in luxury and in

---

squander it, and even to their ruin" (*Introduction to the Devout Life*, 4, 10).

Our Lord also speaks about the moth and the rust which consume earthly treasures, and tells us that the true treasure is good works and upright actions, which will earn us an everlasting reward from God in heaven (cf. Mt 6:19–21).

"You have laid up treasure for the last days": a reference to the Day of Judgment, as in v. 5: "you have fattened your hearts in a day of slaughter" (cf. e.g., Is 34:6; Jer 12:3; 25:34). It can also be translated as "you have laid up treasure in the last days", which would be a reference to the present time, which (ever since the coming of the Messiah) is seen as in fact the last days, the beginning of the eschatological era. The two renderings are compatible because they both have reference to the Judgment.

5:4. Cheating workers of their earnings was already condemned in the Old Testament (cf., e.g., Lev 19:13; Deut 24:14–15; Mal 3:5). It is one of the sins which "cries out to heaven" for immediate, exemplary punishment; the same applies to murder (cf. Gen 4:10), sodomy (Gen 18:20–21) and oppression of widows and orphans (Ex 22:22–24).

The Church has often reminded the faithful about the duty to pay fair wages: "remuneration for work should guarantee man the opportunity to provide a dignified livelihood for himself and his family on the material, social, cultural and spiritual level to correspond to the role and the productivity of each, the relevant economic factors in his employment, and the common good" (Vatican II, *Gaudium et spes*, 67).

"The Lord of hosts": a common Old Testament description of God, manifesting his omnipotence, as Creator and Lord of the whole universe; it is used to acclaim God in the *Sanctus* of the Mass: "Lord God of power and might" ("Dominus Deus Sabaoth").

5:5. This description of the lifestyle of these rich people (vv. 2, 3, 5) recalls the parable of the rich man and Lazarus (cf. Lk 16:19ff). Those who live in this way do well to listen to the Master's warning: "Take heed to yourselves lest your hearts be weighed down with dissipation and drunkenness and cares of this life, and that day come upon you suddenly like a snare" (Lk 21:34).

Against the hedonism condemned by the sacred writer, Christians should be conscious of the duty to promote a just society: "Christians engaged actively in modern economic and social progress and in the struggle for justice and charity must be convinced that they have much to contribute to the prosperity of mankind and to world peace. Let them, as individuals and as group members, give a shining example to others. Endowed with the skill and experience so absolutely necessary for them, let them preserve a proper sense of values in their earthly activity in loyalty to Christ and his Gospel, in order that their lives, individual as well as social, may be inspired by the spirit of the Beatitudes, and in particular by the spirit of poverty.

---

e. Or *will eat your flesh, since you have stored up fire*

pleasure; you have fattened your hearts in a day of slaughter. ⁶You have condemned, you have killed the righteous man; he does not resist you.

Hos 1:6

4. FINAL COUNSELS

A call for constancy

⁷Be patient, therefore, brethren, until the coming of the Lord. Behold, the farmer waits for the precious fruit of the earth, being

Deut 11:14
Jer 5:24

"Anyone who in obedience to Christ seeks first the kingdom of God will derive from it a stronger and purer love for helping all his brethren and for accomplishing the task of justice under the inspiration of charity" (*Gaudium et spes*, 72).

5:6. "The righteous man": according to St Bede (cf. *Super Iac. expositio,* ad loc.), this refers to our Lord, who is just *par excellence* and is described as such in other passages of Scripture (cf., e.g., Acts 3:14; 7:52). This interpretation is quite appropriate, given the fact that in the needy we should see Jesus Christ himself (cf. Mt 25:31–45); they often suffer at the hands of those who refuse to recognize even their most elementary rights: "The bread of the needy is the life of the poor; whoever deprives them of it is a man of blood. To take away a neighbour's living is to murder him; to deprive an employee of his wages is to shed blood" (Sir 34:21–22).

"Every man has the right to possess a sufficient amount of the earth's goods for himself and his family. This has been the opinion of the Fathers and Doctors of the Church, who taught that men are bound to come to the aid of the poor and to do so not merely out of their superfluous goods.[...] Faced with a world today where so many people are suffering from want, the Council asks individuals and governments to remember the saying of the Fathers: 'Feed the man dying of hunger, because if you do not feed him you are killing him!' and it urges them according to their ability to share and dispose of their goods to help others, above all by giving them aid which will enable them to help and develop themselves" (*Gaudium et spes*, 69).

5:7–11. Just before he ends his letter, St James again (cf. 1:2–4, 12) exhorts his readers to be patient, perhaps in case some are tempted to avenge themselves on the rich. He uses the simile of the farmer, who patiently waits for the earth to yield the fruits of his work: in the same kind of way the oppressed will be rewarded for all their afflictions when the Lord comes. St James encourages them also by reminding them of the patience and long-suffering of the prophets and of Job.

Christian hope, and the patience it induces, enables people to put up with injustice in this present life; but it is not an easy way out of one's responsibilities nor an invitation to be passive. A Christian should strive to make this world a place of justice and peace, but should realize it is a transient place, and not make these temporal ideals an absolute goal. "God did not create us to build a lasting city here on earth. [...] Nevertheless, we

James 5:8

_{1 Thess 3:13}
_{Mt 24:33}
_{Mt 5:12}

patient over it until it receives the early and the late rain. ⁸You also be patient. Establish your hearts, for the coming of the Lord is at hand. ⁹Do not grumble, brethren, against one another, that you may not be judged; behold, the Judge is standing at the doors. ¹⁰As an example of suffering and patience, brethren, take the prophets who spoke in the name of the Lord. ¹¹Behold, we call those happy

---

children of God ought not to remain aloof from earthly endeavours, for God has placed us here to sanctify them and make them fruitful with our blessed faith, which alone is capable of bringing true peace and joy to all men wherever they may be [...]. We urgently need to christianize society. We must imbue all levels of mankind with a supernatural outlook, and each of us must strive to raise his daily duties, his job or profession, to the order of supernatural grace. In this way all human occupations will be lit up by a new hope that transcends time and the inherent transience of earthly realities" (St Josemaría Escrivá, *Friends of God*, 210).

5:7–9. St James' words show how vividly the early Christians realized that the Christian life should be a time for watchfulness and for looking forward to the Parousia of the Lord, when our redemption will be finally sealed (cf. Lk 21:28). Jesus did not choose to reveal the precise moment of his coming (cf. Mt 24:36); he stressed, rather, the need to be watchful, to make sure it found us ready (cf. Mt 24:42, 44; 25:13). Therefore, every Christian should live in the expectation of that event which surely will come, though he knows not when. This is also what the Apostle means when he says "the coming of the Lord is at hand" and "the Judge is standing at the doors", for he may come at any moment.

5:10–11. The lives of the prophets are a very good model of patience and endurance in adversity. Some of them in particular (Elijah, Isaiah, Jeremiah) underwent great suffering on account of their obedience to God.

"You have seen the purpose of the Lord": this is the interpretation of St Bede and St Augustine, referring to the example of patience set by Jesus in his passion and death on the cross. Most commentators prefer the other possible translation, "You have seen the outcome the Lord gave him", referring to Job, who bore patiently the trials God sent to him (cf. Job 42:10ff), because, for one thing, it avoids having to give the term "Lord", which appears twice in the same verse (v. 11), two different meanings—Jesus Christ and God one and three.

5:11. "The Lord is compassionate and merciful": Holy Scripture often describes the Lord as a God of mercy, attributing to him human sentiments like "abounding in steadfast love", "bowels of mercy", meaning that he has tender, even maternal, feelings towards us (cf., e.g., Ex 34:6; Joel 2:13; Lk 1:78).

St Thomas Aquinas, who often says that divine omnipotence is displayed particularly in the form of mercy (cf. *Summa theologiae*, 1, 21, 4; 2–2, 30, 4) explains very simply and graphically that God's mercy is abundant and infinite: "To say that a person is merciful is like saying that he is sorrowful at heart (*miserum cor*), that is, he is afflicted with sorrow by the misery of another as though it were his own. Hence it follows that he endeavours to dispel the misery of

who were steadfast. You have heard of the steadfastness of Job, and you have seen the purpose of the Lord, how the Lord is compassionate and merciful. ^{Ps 103:8; 111:4} ^{Job 1:21f;} ^{Jas 1:12}

On oath-taking

¹²But above all, my brethren, do not swear, either by heaven or by earth or with any other oath, but let your yes be yes and your no be no, that you may not fall under condemnation. ^{Mt 5:34–37}

The value of prayer. The sacrament of the Anointing of the Sick

¹³Is any one among you suffering? Let him pray. Is any cheerful? Let him sing praise. ¹⁴Is any among you sick? Let him call for the ^{Mk 6:13}

---

the other person as if it were his own; and this is the effect of mercy. God cannot feel sorrow over the misery of others, but it does most properly belong to him to dispel that misery, whatever form that shortcoming or deprivation takes" (*Summa theologiae*, 1, 21, 3).

In Christ, Pope John Paul II taught, the mercy of God is very clear to see: "*he himself makes it incarnate* and personifies it. *He himself, in a certain sense, is mercy.* To the person who sees it in him—and finds it in him—God becomes 'visible' in a particular way as the Father 'who is rich in mercy' (Eph 2:4)" (*Dives in misericordia*, 2).

5:12. This exhortation is almost an exact echo of the words of the Lord: "Let what you say be simply 'Yes' or 'No'; anything more than this comes from evil" (Mt 5:37). The Jews of the time tended to take oaths far too readily and had developed an elaborate casuistry about them (cf. note on Mt 5:33–37); our Lord criticized these abuses, and St James repeats his teaching. However, that does not mean that oath-taking is always wrong: in fact Holy Scripture itself praises it when it is done in the right way for good reasons (cf. Jer 4:2), and St Paul sometimes resorts to it (cf., e.g., Rom 1:9; 2 Cor 1:23). Hence the Church teaches that it is lawful and even does honour to God to take an oath when it is strictly necessary and provided one acts in accordance with truth and justice.

St James' "let your yes be yes and your no be no" is in fact a summing up of the virtue of sincerity, a virtue which is very pleasing to God (cf. Jn 1:47) and essential in human relationships.

5:13–18. In these final counsels, St James has most to say on the subject of prayer. He teaches that it is a necessary and effective counter to sadness ("suffering": v. 13); the prayer of priests, while anointing the sick with oil, is the sacrament of Anointing (vv. 14–15); prayer for others helps bring forgiveness of sins (v. 16). All this is supported by the example of Elijah (vv. 17–18).

5:13. "Suffering": the Greek word, which can be translated as "experiencing sadness", includes the idea of suffering under some evil, so the "sadness" can be taken as some type of affliction, or sickness of the soul.

St Bede describes the attitude a Christian should adopt when he or she feels overwhelmed by the "pest" of sadness, regardless of its cause: "Have recourse to the Church; kneel in prayer before the Lord, asking him to send the grace of his consolation, and do not imbibe the world's sadness, which only leads to death" (*Super Iac. expositio*, ad loc.). Sadness, gloominess, is a powerful ally of the devil and one of the subtlest weapons he uses to lead a person to commit sin; one needs to react against it immediately.

"Being children of God, how can we be sad? Sadness is the end product of selfishness. If we truly want to live for God, we will never lack joy, even when we discover our errors and wretchedness. Cheerfulness finds its way out into our life of prayer, so much so that we cannot help singing for joy. For we are in love, and singing is a thing that lovers do" (St Josemaría Escrivá, *Friends of God*, 92).

14–15. The Church's Magisterium teaches that this text promulgates the sacrament of the Anointing of the Sick: cf. the Council of Trent: "This holy anointing of the sick was initiated as a true and proper sacrament of the New Testament by Christ our Lord; it is implied in St Mark (cf. Mk 6:13) and it is commended to the faithful and promulgated by the Apostle, St James, the brother of the Lord [...] (Jas 5:14f). In these words, as the Church has learned from the apostolic Tradition transmitted to her, he teaches the matter, the form, the proper minister and the effects of this life-giving sacrament" (*De Sacramento extremae unctionis*, chap. 1; cf. can. 1).

The matter of the sacrament is "oil blessed by a bishop, because anointing very fittingly symbolizes the grace of the Holy Spirit, who anoints the soul of the sick person in an invisible manner" (ibid.). It is true that among ancient peoples (including the Jews: cf. Is 1:6; Jer 8:21–22; Lk 10:34) oil was much appreciated for its curative powers; hence the symbolism of this sacramental sign. But St James is looking at medicinal effects on the soul rather than on the body, for he says that the sick man will be saved and his sins will be forgiven. The Church expressly teaches that the anointing stands for the grace of the Holy Spirit. The oil of the sick is solemnly blessed by the bishop in the Chrism Mass; in case of necessity it can also be blessed by the priest at the time he administers the Anointing (cf. *The Rite of Anointing of the Sick*, 21).

The form of the sacrament is the prayer which the priest recites as he anoints the sick person on the forehead and hands. The Greek words of St James —"let them pray over him, anointing him"—are so couched that they lead one to conclude that from the very beginning the praying and the anointing took place simultaneously and therefore the formula "pray over" refers to a liturgical gesture.

As far as the minister of the sacrament is concerned, the Council of Trent, referring to these verses, says: "They indicate that the proper ministers of this sacrament are the presbyters of the Church. This does not refer to the older men nor to the more influential men in the community but to the bishops or the priests duly ordained by the bishops through the laying on of hands of the presbyterate (cf. 1 Tim 4:14)" (*De Sacramento extremae unctionis*, chap. 3; cf. can. 4). The term "elder" which St James uses also means someone older in age; but here as in other New Testament passages (cf., e.g., Acts 11:10; 14:23; 15:2; 20:17; 1 Tim 5:17–19) it clearly refers to the bishops and priests of the Church.

elders of the church, and let them pray over him, anointing him with oil in the name of the Lord; ¹⁵and the prayer of faith will save   Mk 16:18

As regards the effects of the sacrament, "Furthermore the complete effect of this sacrament is explained in the words: 'and the prayer of faith will save the sick man, and the Lord will raise him up, and if he be in sins, they shall be forgiven him' (Jas 5:15). For this effect is the grace of the Holy Spirit, whose anointing takes away sins, if there are any still to be expiated, and removes the traces of sin: and it comforts and strengthens the soul of the sick person. It gives him great confidence in the divine mercy. Encouraged by this, the sick man more easily bears the inconvenience and trials of the illness and more easily resists the temptations of the devil who lies in wait for his heel. This anointing occasionally restores health to the body if health would be of advantage to the salvation of the soul" (ibid., chap. 2).

Finally, as regards the recipient of the sacrament and when it should be administered, the words of the letter point to an illness of some seriousness, because the priests are asked to go to the sick person's house. The Second Vatican Council says that this sacrament is not only for those who are at the point of death and that "as soon as anyone of the faithful begins to be in danger of death from sickness or old age, the fitting time for him to receive this sacrament has certainly already arrived" (*Sacrosanctum Concilium*, 73). The Code of Canon Law lays down that "pastors of souls and those who are close to the sick are to ensure that the sick are helped by this sacrament in good time" (can. 1001).

It is important, therefore, to avoid delaying it unduly through fear of causing anxiety or upset. "In public and private catechesis, the faithful should be encouraged to ask for the anointing and, as soon as the time for the anointing comes, to receive it with complete faith and devotion" (*The Rite of Anointing the Sick*, 13).

This sacrament is a wonderful expression of divine mercy and of God's tender loving care for every single soul: "our merciful Redeemer willed that his servants should always be provided with salutary safeguards against all weapons of all enemies. Accordingly he prepared great helps in the other sacraments to enable Christians to keep themselves throughout their lives untouched by any serious spiritual harm, and likewise he protected them at the end of life with the invincible strength of the sacrament of extreme unction. For even if our adversary seeks occasions throughout the whole of life and goes about that he may devour our souls in any way he can (cf. 1 Pet 5:8), there is no time at which he is more vehemently intent on using all the forces of his cunning to destroy us completely and, if possible, to disturb our trust in the divine mercy, than when he sees the end of life approaching us" (Council of Trent, *De Sacramento extremae unctionis*, prologue).

5:15. "Will save the sick man": from the way St James uses the same verb elsewhere (cf. 2:21; 2:14; 4:12; 5:20) we can see that he is referring to the salvation of the soul. Secondarily, and to the degree that it makes for spiritual health, this sacrament can also heal the body; it seems clear that the sacred writer does not mean to say that physical health will always be restored, as if the Anointing of the Sick were a guarantee that one would not die. And it is quite clear that, by

the sick man, and the Lord will raise him up; and if he has committed sins, he will be forgiven.* ¹⁶Therefore confess your sins to one another, and pray for one another, that you may be healed. The prayer of a righteous man has great power in its

virtue of the grace of the sacrament, the sick person is strengthened to face the trauma of illness and death with supernatural outlook and joy. "Nothing conduces more to a tranquil death than to banish sadness, await with a joyous mind the coming of our Lord, and be ready willingly to surrender the deposit entrusted whenever it shall be his will to demand it back. To free the minds of the faithful from this solicitude, and fill the soul with pious and holy joy is, then, an effect of the sacrament of Extreme Unction" (*St Pius V Catechism*, 2, 6, 14).

"If he has committed sins, he will be forgiven": although the sacrament of Anointing of the Sick is a sacrament "of the living", that is, it should be received in the state of grace, Catholic teaching, based on these words, says that Anointing can forgive the mortal sins of a sick person who is repentant but has not been able to go to Confession (cf., e.g., *Summa theologiae*, Supplement, 30, 1). Hence the importance of conferring this sacrament "upon sick people who have lost consciousness or lost the use of reason, if as Christian believers they would have asked for it were they in control of their faculties" (*Rite of Anointing of the Sick*, 14).

5:16. "Therefore confess your sins to one another": it is impossible to say exactly what type of confession is being referred to. Some—St Augustine, for example (cf. *In Ioann. Evang.*, 58, 5)—interpret these words as referring to a pious custom of confessing sins to others in a public act of contrition at which people prayed for one another; in which case it could be the origin of the penitential rite at the beginning of Mass. Others, including St Thomas (cf. *Summa theologiae*, Supplement, 6, 6), apply these words to sacramental confession; in which case one would have to understand it as meaning confession to priests. St Bede in his commentary links these two possible interpretations while distinguishing between venial and mortal sin: "In this sentence a distinction should be made: we should confess to each other our lesser, daily sins, and believe that we are saved by the daily prayer of others. But, as the law lays down, we should show to the priest the uncleanness of graver leprosy and be sure to purify ourselves in the manner and for the period that his decision specifies" (*Super Iac. expositio*, ad loc.).

Without intending to define the meaning of this text, the Council of Trent refers to it when it teaches that it is a matter of divine law that all mortal sins be confessed in the sacrament of Penance. "From the time of the institution of the sacrament of Penance, already explained, the universal Church has always understood that integral confession of sins (cf. Jas 5:16; 1 Jn 1:9; Lk 17:14) was also instituted by the Lord, and that it is by divine law necessary (for the forgiveness) of all falls committed after Baptism, for our Lord Jesus Christ, when he was about to ascend from earth to heaven, left priests to take his place (Mt 16:19; 18:18; Jn 20:23), as presidents and judges, before whom Christ's faithful should confess all the mortal sins they might commit, so that by the power of the keys they (priests) might pass sentence of absolution or retention of sins" (*De Sacramento paenitentiae*, chap. 5).

effects. ¹⁷Elijah was a man of like nature with ourselves and he prayed fervently that it might not rain, and for three years and six months it did not rain on the earth. ¹⁸Then he prayed again and the heaven gave rain, and the earth brought forth its fruit.

<small>1 Kings 17:1</small>

<small>1 Kings 18:42</small>

Concern for one another

¹⁹My brethren, if any one among you wanders from the truth and some one brings him back, ²⁰let him know that whoever brings back a sinner from the error of his way will save his soul from death and will cover a multitude of sins.

<small>Gal 6:1</small>
<small>Prov 10:12</small>
<small>1 Pet 4:8</small>

5:17–18. As a palpable example of the power of prayer, St James mentions Elijah, whose prayer obtained that no rain should fall in Israel for a period, and then that it should come in abundance (cf. 1 Kings 17–18; Sir 48:3).

He thereby demonstrates the immense power of prayer, even for obtaining God's help in our material needs. We must remember that good prayer identifies our will with that of God, who is almighty. This has always been the way the saints have understood it: "God has never and will never refuse anything to those who ask him for his graces in the right way," the Curé of Ars says. "Prayer is the great recourse we have for escaping from sin, for persevering in grace, for moving God's heart and drawing down upon ourselves all manner of heavenly blessings, whether for our soul or to meet our temporal needs" (*Selected Sermons*, Fourth Sunday after Easter).

5:19–20. St James' letter ends with an encouraging exhortation to apostolic concern for those who stray from the right path. This is something extremely important, causing St Teresa of Avila to exclaim: "Whenever I read in the lives of saints of how they converted souls, I seem to feel much more devout, tender and envious of them than when I read of all the martyrdoms that they suffered. This is an inclination given me by our Lord; and I think he prizes one soul which by his mercy, and through our diligence and prayer, we may have gained for him, more than all the other services we can render him" (*Book of Foundations*, 1, 7). The Second Vatican Council teaches that apostolic concern stems from the Christian vocation itself and therefore is something all Christians should have; referring to the apostolate of lay people, it says specifically that it is "a sharing in the salvific mission of the Church. Through Baptism and Confirmation all are appointed to this apostolate by the Lord himself" (*Lumen gentium*, 33).

Introduction to the First Letter of St Peter

ST PETER THE APOSTLE

The Gospels and the Acts of the Apostles give us the main features of St Peter's character, but do not provide enough information for a biography of the Apostle.

He was originally called Simeon, in Hebrew (cf. Acts 15:14; 2 Pet 1:1), or Simon, the Greek form of the same name;[1] but Jesus surnamed him Cephas (cf. Jn 1:42). From this word, which in Aramaic (the language mostly spoken by the Jews of the time) means stone or rock, comes the name Peter, the Greek for rock.

Like most of our Lord's first disciples, Simon Peter was a native of Bethsaida (cf. Jn 1:44), a city of Galilee on the north-east shore of Lake Tiberius or Gennesaret. Like his father John[2] and his brother Andrew, he was a fisherman (cf. Mt 4:18). We also know that he was married, because Jesus cured his mother-in-law, who was living in Capernaum (cf. Mt 8:14).

Before meeting Jesus, he had very probably been a disciple of the Baptist, along with his brother Andrew (cf. Jn 1:35, 40). It was Andrew who brought him to Jesus (cf. Jn 1:40–42), thereby beginning a relationship which was to give a new direction to his life.

We can take it that he was present at the first miracle Jesus worked, at the wedding in Cana (cf. Jn 2:1–11), after which he went down with him to Capernaum (cf. Jn 2:12). He continued to work as a fisherman, listening to our Lord's teaching and witnessing his miracles (cf. Lk 4:31–5:7) up to the time when he was called to be one of the Twelve. Peter answered the call immediately, along with Andrew and the two sons of Zebedee, James and John: they left everything to follow Christ (cf. Lk 5:11; Mt 4:22; Mk 1:18).

He now was part of the Lord's circle of disciples. Prior to the Sermon on the Mount, after spending the night in prayer (cf. Lk 6:12), Jesus "called his disciples, and chose from them twelve, whom he named apostles" (Lk 6:13), which means "sent out". The apostles are listed four times in the New Testament and Simon Peter heads each list.[3] Within the apostolic college he, with James and John, constituted an inner group, the only ones to witness the resurrection of the daughter of Jairus (cf. Mk 5:37), the transfiguration of our Lord (cf. Mk 9:2), and his agony in the garden of Olives (cf. Mk 14:33).

---

1. Cf. Mt 16:17; Lk 22:31; Jn 1:42; 21:15–17. **2.** Cf. Jn 1:42; 21:15–17. In Mt 16:17 he is called Jona, which was a shortened form of the Hebrew *Johanan* (John). **3.** Cf. Mt 10:2–4; Mk 3:16–19; Lk 6:14–16; Acts 1:13.

Introduction to the First Letter of St Peter

Peter often acts as the spokesman for the apostles: he asks Jesus to explain the parable about purity of heart (cf. Mt 15:15); he asks about what reward they will get for having left everything (cf. Mt 19:27); after the eucharistic discourse in the synagogue of Capernaum, which led many disciples to abandon the Master, it is Peter again who speaks on behalf of the apostles: "Lord, to whom shall we go? You have the words of eternal life; and we have believed, and have come to know, that you are the Holy One of God" (Jn 6:68–69).

One episode at Caesarea Philippi is particularly important—when our Lord asked the Twelve, "But who do you say that I am?" and Simon Peter replied, "You are the Christ, the Son of the living God" (Mt 16:15–16). Christ went on to make a solemn promise to Peter that he would have charge of his Church: "And I tell you, you are Peter, and on this rock I will build my church, and the powers of death shall not prevail against it. I will give you the keys of the kingdom of heaven, and whatever you bind on earth shall be bound in heaven, and whatever you loose on earth shall be loosed in heaven."[4]

Although Jesus had foreknowledge of Peter's weakness and denials, he made this revelation to him in the Upper Room: "Simon, Simon, behold Satan demanded to have you, that he might sift you like wheat, but I have prayed for you that your faith may not fail; and when you have turned again, strengthen your brethren."[5] Finally, after his resurrection, Christ confers on Peter those powers of nourishing and governing the whole Church in his name.[6]

After our Lord's ascension, Peter, without any debate, is the leading apostle; it is he who proposes and presides over the election of Matthias to take the place of the traitorous Judas, specifying the requirements for candidacy (cf. Acts 1:15–22); he delivers the first address to evangelize the people on the day of Pentecost (cf. Acts 2:14–40); he speaks out before the Sanhedrin to justify the apostles' preaching (cf. Acts 3:6–7; 5:15; 9:36–41); he condemns Ananias and Sapphira (cf. Acts 5:1–11) as he does Simon the magician (cf. Acts 8:18–24); instructed by the Lord in a vision, he receives the first pagan family into the Church, that of Cornelius (cf. Acts 10:9–48; 11:1–18). And St Paul, after his conversion and despite receiving the Gospel in a revelation from Jesus Christ (cf. Gal 1:11–12), went up to Jerusalem around the year 39, to see Cephas (as he usually called him), and stayed with him for two weeks (cf. Gal 1:18–19)—a clear sign of the veneration St Paul had for the man chosen by the Lord to be the visible head of the Church.

The Jewish authorities, too, were aware of the leading place St Peter had in the early Church, as can be seen from the fact that, around the year 43, Herod Agrippa I had him imprisoned with the intention of putting him to death (cf. Acts 12:3–4). On that occasion the Church "made earnest prayer" to God for him (Acts 12:5); after he was miraculously released from prison "he departed

---

4. Mt 16:18–19; cf. note on Mt 16:13–20. **5.** Lk 22:31–32; cf. note on Lk 22:31–34. **6.** Cf. Jn 21:15–17 and note on same.

Introduction to the First Letter of St Peter

and went to another place" (Acts 12:17)—probably Antioch or Rome. We do know that he spent some time in Antioch (cf. Gal 2:11–14), but it is not clear whether it was at this juncture (tradition tells us that he occupied the see of Antioch for a while). We do know for certain that he was present at the apostolic Council of Jerusalem in the year 49 (cf. Acts 15:7–11), at which, once again, he played a key role in promoting the unity of the Church.

There is evidence to support an ancient tradition of St Peter spending a period in Rome, as its bishop, and suffering a martyr's death there under the emperor Nero. What is not clear is when exactly he arrived in Rome or how long he stayed there; nor is the precise date of his martyrdom known. Some commentators think that he went to Rome twice—once, when he left Jerusalem, around the year 49, the date of the Council. Prior to the year 60 he would have returned to Rome, although he was probably away from the city for periods, on missionary journeys. This theory would explain why he is not mentioned in the greetings in St Paul's Letter to the Romans (in 57–58), nor in connexion with Paul's first imprisonment in Rome (in 61–63). Other scholars, however, think that St Peter went to Rome only once, during the reign of Nero (54–68).

As far as his death is concerned, it is certain that he suffered martyrdom in Rome under Nero (the tradition is that he was crucified, head down). On the basis of information supplied by Eusebius,[7] and by St Jerome, some put the likely date at the year 67, which was when St Paul also died; however, others suggest the year 64, when, after the burning of Rome, Nero was responsible for the persecution and death of very many Christians.

A very ancient tradition, supported by archaeological excavations, says that the tomb of the prince of the Apostles lies under the altar of St Peter's basilica.

THE AUTHOR

The greeting at the start of the letter gives the author as the apostle St Peter (cf. 1 Pet 1:1), a witness of the sufferings of Christ (cf. 1 Pet 5:1). This is consistent both with the external testimony of Tradition and with examination of the text itself.

Throughout Christian antiquity, no doubts were raised about the Petrine authorship of the letter or about its being a canonical, inspired, text. As far back as the end of the second century, St Irenaeus of Lyons quotes from it several times, attributing it expressly to St Peter.[9] The same is true of Clement of Alexandria (d. 214),[10] the author of the first commentary on the letter.[11]

In addition to the explicit testimonies, there are implicit ones of an even earlier time—the first half of the second century. Although they do not

---

7. Cf. *Chronicon*, book 2.   **8.** *On Famous Men*, 1, 5.   **9.** Cf. *Against Heresies*, 4, 9, 2; 16, 5; 5, 7, 2.
10. Cf. *Stromata*, 4, 7, 47.   **11.** Cf. *Hypotyposeis*.

mention the author, they do show that this letter was regarded even then as having the authority of an inspired document. Thus, St Polycarp cites it a number of times in his *Letter to the Philippians*, as does Papias of Hierapolis, according to fragments of his writing contained in the work of Eusebius of Caesarea.[12] Eusebius (d. 339 or 340) summarizes Christian tradition prior to his time when he says that this epistle belongs to those New Testament writings accepted by all and rejected by none.[13]

All the ancient canons (lists of inspired books) which have come down to us mention this letter (all, that is, except the Muratorian Canon; but this exception may be due to the fact that part of that document is missing). Thus, the epistle appears in the canons of the provincial councils of Laodicea (*c*.360), Hippo (393), and the third and fourth councils of Carthage (397 and 419), as also in Pope St Innocent I's letter to Exuperius, bishop of Toulouse (405).

Examination of the content of the letter supports its Petrine origin: there are very obvious similarities between the teaching contained in it and the discourses of St Peter recorded in the Acts of the Apostles; for example: the portrayal of Jesus as the Servant of Yahweh (cf., e.g., 1 Pet 2:22–25; Acts 3:13) and the cornerstone rejected by the builders (cf. 1 Pet 2:4–8; Acts 4:11); and the resurrection of our Lord as the kernel of the Christian faith and of the proclamation of the Gospel.

Silvanus' part in the letter. "By Silvanus," St Peter says at the end of his letter, "a faithful brother as I regard him, I have written briefly to you" (1 Pet 5:20). This seems to be the Silvanus who worked with St Paul in the evangelization of Asia Minor (cf. 2 Cor 1:9; 1 Thess 1:1; 2 Thess 1:1), who is called Silas in the Acts of the Apostles (cf., e.g., Acts 15:22ff; 16:19, 25). He would therefore have known very well the people the letter was addressed to.

St Peter's very brief mention of Silvanus does not make it quite clear what role he played in connexion with the letter; he may simply have been the bearer and commentator of the letter; he may have been an amanuensis who took down the apostle's dictation (which was Tertius' role in the Letter to the Romans: cf. Rom 16:22); or he may have acted as editor or redactor, who faithfully put into writing ideas given him by St Peter.

St Jerome uses the last-mentioned possibility to explain the differences in style between the First and Second Letters of St Peter: "As the need arose, he [Peter] used different interpreters."[14] Some modern scholars also favour this theory because it may best explain the letter's flowing Greek, the ease with which the author quotes and draws inspiration from the Greek version of the Old Testament (the Septuagint), and the coincidences noticeable between this letter and certain letters of St Paul (particularly Romans and Ephesians). This theory does seem to be the best one.

---

12. Cf. *Ecclesiastical History*, 3, 39, 17.   **13.** Cf. ibid., 3, 1; 3, 25, 2.   **14.** *Epist. ad Hedibiam*, 120, 11.

Introduction to the First Letter of St Peter

In any event, if Silvanus was in fact the redactor of the epistle, that does not take anything away from its authenticity as a Petrine text, for St Peter clearly makes it his own (cf. 1 Pet 1:1; 5:12).

IMMEDIATE READERSHIP AND DATE OF COMPOSITION

The letter is addressed to a number of Christian communities in different parts of Asia Minor (cf. 1:1). No indications are given as to whether St Peter knew these Christians personally (the region in question had been evangelized by St Paul, accompanied in fact by Silvanus: cf. Acts 15:40ff). These young communities were located in a hostile environment, which could have made it difficult for them to persevere in the faith. It is possible that when the Apostle learned of the trials they were experiencing he decided it would be good to write them some words of encouragement.

From the letter itself it is clear that quite a number of these Christians were converts from paganism. For example, there are references to their "former ignorance" (1:14) about God, who "called (them) out of darkness into his marvellous light" (2:9), so that those who were formerly no people are now become "God's people" (cf. 2:10). These and other features of the letter (cf. 1:18; 2:25; 4:2–4) suggest that these were first-generation Christians, who had only recently embraced the faith—which also explains why St Peter frequently reminds them of their Baptism (cf. 1:3, 23; 2:2; 3:21).

As regards the date, certain things point to the letter's having been written around the year 64. For example, the opening greeting (cf. 1:1) implies that Christianity has already spread through Asia Minor, and therefore the letter should be dated after St Paul's last journey in the region (50–57). Also, there is no mention of St Paul, which seems to indicate that he had already left Rome, after being set free from captivity in the spring of 63. On the other hand, the letter was probably written prior to the persecution under Nero (July 64), because that is not mentioned. As indicated at the end of the letter, it was written in "Babylon" (5:13), undoubtedly a reference to Rome, the capital of the Empire, often given the symbolic name of "Babylon" (cf. Rev 14:8; 16:19; 17:5; 18:2, 10, 21).

CONTENT

The main purpose of the letter seemingly was to console and exhort Christians to stand firm in the midst of difficulties. It does not have any very clear structure. Very often doctrinal points are developed in the course of the exhortation. However, the fact that it follows no particular plan does not mean that it is not a single, coherent whole.

Introduction to the First Letter of St Peter

The *prologue* (1:1–12) consists of the usual greeting (1:1–2) and an introductory hymn of thanksgiving (1:3–12), which mentions the difficulties of those Christians who are being exhorted to perseverance.

The body of the letter (1:13–5:11) can be divided into three sections, followed by final exhortations.

1. *The first part* (1:13—2:10) is a stirring invitation to seek holiness. This is based on two main points—the holiness of God who called them (1:13–16) and the blood of Christ which rescued them from sin (1:17–21). Holiness should express itself in charity (1:22–25) and in their effort to grow in the Christian life (2:1–3), conscious of the fact that, like living stones, they form the edifice of the Church (2:4–10).

2. *The second part* (2:11—3:12) identifies the kinds of obligations Christians have in society—exemplary lives to be led by all in a pagan environment (2:11–12); citizens' duties to legitimate authority (2:13–17); servants' duties to their masters (2:18–25); the duties of husband and wife in family life (3:1–7); and the duty of all to practise the greatest fraternity (3:8–12).

3. *The third part* (3:13—4:19) expands on the way Christians should cope with persecution and trials: the baptized have a part to play in the redemptive mystery of Christ. When they suffer unjustly they can count themselves blessed (3:13–17), for Christ suffered unto death before he was glorified (3:18–22). The Christian, who is a member of Christ's body, has broken with sin (4:1–6) and has to practise charity (4:7–11). This section ends by speaking about the spiritual value of suffering unjust persecution (4:12–19).

4. At the end of the letter St Peter addresses a series of *exhortations* to priests (5:1–4) and to all the faithful (5:5–11), encouraging all to put their trust in the Lord.

As in other New Testament letters, the *epilogue* (5:12–14), sends greetings from the church of the sender and concludes with some words of blessing.

TRIALS

St Peter may have been spurred to write this letter by the various trials (cf. 1:6–7) these Christians were experiencing, including unjust accusation (cf. 2:12–15), revilement (cf. 3:9–17) and abuse (cf. 4:4); he goes so far as to describe these trials as a "fiery ordeal" (cf. 4:12–16) which he fears may cause them to waver.

It is unlikely that he is referring to official persecution: the persecution instigated by Nero did not extend to the provinces of Asia Minor; empire-wide

Introduction to the First Letter of St Peter

persecution did not occur until much later in the time of Domitian (d. 96) and Trajan (d.117). These latter persecutions were so severe that he would have written in more dramatic terms if he had been referring to them. He must therefore mean opposition in different forms from the pagan world around them, a world which felt affronted by the lifestyle of these recent converts (cf. 4:4) and which therefore discriminated against them in various ways.

These Christian communities felt alienated by their fellow-citizens (cf. 2:11–12); but the clash of lifestyles also occurred within the family circle, where slaves had to bear injustice from their masters (cf. 2:18–25) and wives intolerance from their husbands (cf. 3:1–3).

The letter is clearly written in a tone of consolation and exhortation. The trials they have to bear have a positive side: they should avail of them to draw closer to God; he, not men, is their true Judge (cf. 4:19). They should realize that their imitation of Jesus will bring good results and will even attract their persecutors to the faith (cf. 2:12). The sacred writer does not confine himself to giving occasional advice on humility (cf. 5:5–7) but tells them, in line with our Lord's teaching (cf. Mt 5:10–12), that they are blessed, and encourages them to bear their sufferings joyfully (cf. 4:13). He develops a particularly profound and consoling idea: the Christian is built into Christ and shares in his paschal mystery; just as Jesus, in order to redeem man, underwent his passion and death and afterwards was raised to everlasting life, so too Christians will attain their own salvation, and that of many others, by bearing trials well. Jesus Christ is their model and it is also he who gives full meaning to trials as Christian experiences (cf. 4:12–19).

BAPTISM

Although he explicitly mentions Baptism only once (cf. 3:21), St Peter frequently alludes to this sacrament which makes us members of Jesus Christ and marks the start of a new life: by God's "great mercy we have been born anew to a living hope" (1:3). These references help to identify elements of baptismal liturgy and pre-baptismal catechetical instruction. From his teaching we can notice three things: Baptism means a rebirth; it sets one free from sin (it is prefigured in the liberation of the Israelites from Egypt); the salvation of Noah is a "type" of the salvation effected by this sacrament.

In the New Testament Baptism is often depicted as a *new birth* (cf., e.g., Jn 3:3ff; Tit 3:5; 1 Jn 2:29). St Peter sees Christians as "born anew" of imperishable seed (cf. 1:23; 1:3) and he encourages them, as "newborn babes" (2:2), to live in goodness and simplicity, desirous of the spiritual nourishment that they receive from the Word of God and from the sacraments.

Baptism is also *liberation from the slavery of sin*. Christians have broken with sin (cf. 4:1–6) and have passed from slavery to the freedom of the children of God, because they have been ransomed "with the precious blood of Christ, like that of a lamb without blemish or spot" (1:19; cf. note on 1:1–2).

Without formally citing them, the letter contains many references which recall the exodus of the Israelites from the land of Egypt, as if that ancient liberation worked by God prefigured what happens in Baptism. Thus, St Peter teaches the Christians that previously they were not a people but now they are "God's own people" (2:10); previously they lived in ignorance, but now they are called to holiness (cf. 1:14–15). The mention of the "lamb without blemish or spot" (1:19) recalls the paschal lamb (cf. Ex 12:5) whose blood the Israelites smeared on the lintels of their doors; and the advice to "gird up" their minds (cf. 1:13) seems to be an allusion to the passages in which the Israelites are told to eat the paschal lamb girded as for a journey (cf. Ex 12:11).

Moreover, Christians are "a chosen race, a royal priesthood, a holy nation, God's own people" (2:9): the text is interwoven with a quotation from the book of Exodus (cf. Ex 19:5–6), which explains the consequences of God's Covenant with his people, and another from Isaiah (cf. Is 43:20–21) which recalls the epic journey of the Israelites in the wilderness. The new people of God (cf. 2:10), born through Baptism, have a duty—a stricter one than that imposed on the Israelites—to imitate God's holiness (cf. 1:15–16; Lev 19:2; 20:7–8) and to give up their former concupiscence (cf. 1:14).

Reference to the events of the exodus to show what happens at Baptism is something very common in the Tradition of the Church: "Reflect with me", St Cyril of Jerusalem taught neophytes in the fourth century, "on the passage from the old things to the new, the passage from figure to reality. There Moses was sent by God to Egypt; here Christ is sent to the world from the bosom of his Father. There it was a question of bringing the chosen people out of Egypt; here Christ must set free those who in the world were enslaved by sin; there the blood of the lamb deflected the exterminator; here the blood of the immaculate Lamb, Jesus Christ, acts as a refuge against the demons."[15] And the liturgy includes the reading of the account of the passage of the Red Sea (cf. Ex 14:15—15:1) in the Easter Vigil, in which Baptism is solemnly administered.

Finally, the letter mentions *the salvation of Noah as a type of Baptism.* The only time the letter explicitly uses the word "Baptism" (cf. 3:21) is when it compares the salvation of Noah and his family from the flood with that of the Christian faithful, who are saved by the water of Baptism (cf. 3:18–22). St Peter is not saying that there is an exact parallel between both events, but he is clearly teaching about the efficacy of the sacrament of Baptism.

Water on its own only serves to remove dirt (cf. 3:21); the sacrament of Baptism cleanses the soul of original sin and of every other sin, purifying the heart from all stain by bathing the body with pure water (cf. Heb 10:22). By receiving Baptism one is asking God "for a clear conscience, through the

---

15. *Mystagogical Catechesis*, 1, 3.

Introduction to the First Letter of St Peter

resurrection of Jesus Christ" (3:21): these words imply, above all, a moral cleansing in the Christian; but they may also contain a reference to the commitment to keep the faith which the neophyte professed; they may even refer to what later came to be known as the baptismal "character".[16]

OTHER DOCTRINAL ASPECTS

Possibly following the style of a baptismal catechism, the letter includes doctrinal points important for helping Christians to stay true to their faith (cf. 5:9).

For example, it recalls (though not systematically) the dogma of the Blessed Trinity (cf. 1:2–12; 4:14); the divinity of Jesus Christ with his title of *Kyrios*, Lord (cf. 1:3; 2:3; 3:15), and his redemptive work: by his passion, death and resurrection he has obtained salvation for all mankind (cf. 1:17–21; 3:18–22); in Baptism the faithful become members of him in such a way as to have a share in his sufferings and glory (cf. 2:18–25; 3:13ff).

Although the Church is not named as such, it is present throughout the letter: Christians, who are brothers to one another, are living stones in the spiritual building which has Christ as its cornerstone (cf. 2:4–10); they are the new priestly people established by God (cf. 2:9); Christ is their Shepherd (cf. 2:25) and in his name pastors must tend souls disinterestedly and lovingly (cf. 5:1–4).

Hope of eternal life should encourage Christians on their earthly pilgrimage (cf. 1:1, 17; 2:11); they have been reborn so as to obtain an imperishable inheritance (cf. 1:4); the difficulties and trials they experience will not last for long, for the hour will come when the faithful will receive their definitive, glorious reward, and when the guilty will be punished (cf. 4:17–19). This hope of theirs is a distinctive mark of believers and they should always be ready to explain it to others (cf. 3:15).

These truths of our faith form the basis of the apostle's exhortations, which are sometimes addressed to Christians in general and sometimes to particular groups—servants (cf. 2:18–25), women (cf. 3:1–6), husbands (cf. 3:7), priests (cf. 5:1–4), young people (cf. 5:5). Particular stress is laid on humility (cf. 2:18–25; 3:8–9; 5:5ff) and on the joy which should govern the Christian life, no matter how difficult times are (cf. 1:2–12; 4:12–19).

---

16. Cf. note on 1 Pet 3:21.

THE FIRST LETTER OF PETER

The Revised Standard Version, with notes

Greeting

1 ¹Peter, an apostle of Jesus Christ, To the exiles of the Dispersion in Pontus, Galatia, Cappadocia, Asia, and Bithynia,* ²chosen and destined by God the Father and sanctified by the Spirit for obedience to Jesus Christ and for sprinkling with his blood:

May grace and peace be multiplied to you.

Jas 1:1
Rom 8:29
Heb 12:24
2 Thess 2:13

Praise and thanksgiving to God

³Blessed be the God and Father of our Lord Jesus Christ! By his great mercy we have been born anew to a living hope through the

Eph 2:4

1:1–2. In his greeting the sacred writer uses the name conferred on him by Jesus: Peter is the Greek translation of the Aramaic word *cephas*, which means rock (cf. 1 Jn 1:42 and note). He introduces himself as "an apostle of Jesus Christ", a trustworthy witness to our Lord's life.

The "Dispersion" (Diaspora) originally referred to Jews who were resident outside Palestine, but here the term is given a deeper meaning: St Peter addresses those who are "exiles of the Dispersion", that is, Christians, who are living on this earth like wayfarers journeying towards their lasting homeland, heaven. On this idea, often found in Scripture (cf., e.g., Gen 47:9; the entire book of Exodus; Ps 39:13; 119:19; Heb 11:13), he will insist further (cf. 1:17; 2:11).

The regions mentioned in v. 1 were in Asia Minor (present-day Turkey). Perhaps the first news they received of Christianity came from Jews who had been converted on the day of Pentecost and were domiciled in these places (cf. Acts 2:9). Later, St Paul evangelized part of this region.

Verse 2 explains the sublime choice that has been made of Christians: by an eternal design of God they have been chosen from all eternity (cf. Rom 8:28–30; Eph 1:4–6) and sanctified by the Holy Spirit. Their election has a double purpose—to obey Jesus Christ by faith and good works, and to enable them to be "sprinkled with his blood", that is, take a full share of the fruits of Redemption. The words are evocative of the events on Sinai: when Moses read the book of the Covenant to the people, they pledged obedience to Yahweh and then Moses sprinkled them with the blood of the sacrifices to seal the Covenant (cf. Ex 24:7–8). By referring to obedience and to sprinkling with blood, the apostle is reminding them that Christ brought about the new and enduring Covenant, sealed by the blood he shed on the cross. This whole verse, therefore, is really a short, profound profession of faith in the Blessed Trinity: to the Father is attributed the choice made from all eternity; to the Son, redemption; to the Holy Spirit, sanctification.

The grace and peace he wishes his readers is a type of Christian greeting, often used by St Paul (cf. note on Rom 1:7; also 2 Pet 1:2): it expresses a wish for God's blessing (which comes in the form of sanctifying grace and the gifts of the Holy Spirit) and inner peace, the effect of the reconciliation with God which Jesus has brought about.

1:3–12. This passage, a hymn of praise and gratitude to God, developing what is proclaimed in v. 2, is more explicit about the action of each person of the Blessed Trinity: by making his choice of Christians, God the Father has destined us to a marvellous heritage in heaven (vv.

1 Peter 1:4

Col 1:5, 12
Rom 5:2
2 Cor 4:17
Heb 12:11

resurrection of Jesus Christ from the dead, [4]and to an inheritance which is imperishable, undefiled, and unfading, kept in heaven for you, [5]who by God's power are guarded through faith for a salvation ready to be revealed in the last time. [6]In this you rejoice,[a] though now for a little while you may have to suffer various trials,

---

3–5); to attain this we need to love and believe in Jesus Christ our Lord (vv. 6–9); the Holy Spirit, who earlier proclaimed salvation by the mouth of the Old Testament prophets, is now, through those who preach the Gospel, announcing that salvation has arrived (vv. 10–12).

1:3–5. When the fruits of the Redemption are applied to us, a kind of rebirth takes place. St Peter is the only New Testament writer to use the Greek term translated here "we have been born anew" (cf. also 1:23); but the same idea occurs elsewhere: St John speaks of the action of the Holy Spirit at Baptism as causing one to be born again (cf. Jn 3:1ff; also, e.g., 1:12–13; 1 Jn 2:29; 3:9); St Paul refers to "a new creation" to describe the effects of Redemption (cf., e.g., Gal 6:15; 2 Cor 5:17); and St James calls Christians the "first fruits of his creatures" (Jas 1:16–18).

Through this being born again, God destines us "to a living hope", which centres on the inheritance of heaven, here described as "imperishable" (it is eternal), "undefiled" (it contains no evil) and "unfading" (it will never grow old). The sacred writer uses these adjectives of negation to show that heavenly things are not subject to any of the imperfections and defects of earthly things.

For those Christians who stay true to their calling, this inheritance is "kept in heaven". This key theme will be addressed in various parts of the letter (cf. 2:18–25; 3:13–17; 4:12–19; 5:5–11); the letter is very much aimed at encouraging the faithful to bear sufferings with joy, knowing that they are a means to and a guarantee of heaven.

1:3. God brought about the work of Redemption "by his great mercy". For "God, who is rich in mercy, out of the great love with which he loved us, even when we were dead through our trespasses, made us alive together with Christ" (Eph 2:4–5). And just as the work of Creation is a manifestation of God's omnipotence, so his new Creation is an expression of his mercy (cf. *Summa theologiae*, 2–2, 30, 4; cf. the note on 2 Cor 5:17).

"Through the resurrection of Jesus Christ from the dead": the resurrection of our Lord marks the climax of his salvific work, for it assures men of their redemption and their own resurrection. In its Easter liturgy the Church joyfully reminds us of this: "He is the true Lamb who took away the sins of the world. By dying he destroyed our death; by rising he restored our life" (*Easter Preface*, I).

1:6–9. Hope of obtaining the inheritance of heaven gives Christians joy in the midst of trials which test their faith. At the centre of that faith is Jesus, whom they strive to love above all, thereby attaining "unutterable and exalted joy", a foretaste of the joy of heaven itself.

Exhortations to be joyful in the midst of affliction occur often in the New Testament (cf., e.g., Mt 5:11–12; 2 Cor 1:3–7; Jas 1:2) and reflect a deep Christian conviction, which St Bede refers to in his commentary: "St Peter says that it is

---

a. Or *Rejoice in this*

⁷so that the genuineness of your faith, more precious than gold which though perishable is tested by fire, may redound to praise and glory and honour at the revelation of Jesus Christ. ⁸Without having seen[b] him you[c] love him; though you do not now see him you[c] believe in him and rejoice with unutterable and exalted joy. ⁹As the outcome of your faith you obtain the salvation of your souls.

¹⁰The prophets who prophesied of the grace that was to be yours searched and inquired about this salvation; ¹¹they inquired

Prov 17:3
Rom 2:7, 10
Jas 1:3; Mal 3:3

Jn 17:20; 20:29
2 Cor 5:7
Rom 6:22

---

good to suffer trials because eternal joys cannot be obtained except through the afflictions and sorrows of this passing world. 'For a little while', he says, however, because when one receives an eternal reward, the afflictions of this world—which appeared so heavy and bitter—seem then to have been very short-lived and slight" (*Super 1 Pet. expositio*, ad loc.).

Christian joy is the fruit of faith, hope and love. "You should realize that God wants us to be happy and that, if you do all you can, you will be happy, very, very happy, although you will never be a moment without the Cross. But that Cross is no longer a gallows. It is the throne from which Christ reigns" (St Josemaría Escrivá, *Friends of God*, 141).

1:7. The refining of gold by fire is often referred to in Scripture (cf., e.g., Ps 66:10; Prov 17:3; 1 Cor 3:12–13; Rev 3:18) to explain that the sufferings of this life help to improve the quality of one's faith. "If I experience pain," St Augustine teaches, "relief will come in due course. If I am offered tribulation, it will serve for my purification. Does gold shine in the craftsman's furnace? It will shine later, when it forms part of the collar, when it is part of the jewellery. But, for the time being, it puts up with being in the fire because when it sheds its impurities it will acquire its brilliant shine" (*Enarrationes in Psalmos*, 61, 11).

The thought of Christ coming in glory (cf. 1:5–13; 4:13) should greatly encourage the Christian to bear trials cheerfully.

1:10–12. These verses of thanksgiving (vv. 3–12) end with a reference to the role of the Holy Spirit in salvation: he acted in the Old Testament through the prophets by announcing salvation, and now, through preachers of the Gospel, he reveals that it has come about.

The passage is a clear acknowledgment of the unity and continuity of the Old and New Testaments: in the Old the sufferings and subsequent glorification of Christ are proclaimed, in such a way that "what the prophets predicted as future events," says St Thomas, "the apostles preached as something which had come true" (*Commentary on Eph* 2:4). "The economy of the Old Testament was deliberately orientated to prepare for and declare in prophecy the coming of Christ, Redeemer of all men, and of the messianic Kingdom (cf. Lk 24:44; Jn 5:39; 1 Pet 1:10) [...]. God, the inspirer and author of the books of both Testaments, in his wisdom has so brought it about that the New should be hidden in the Old and that the Old should be made manifest in the New. For although Christ founded the New Covenant in his blood (cf. Lk 22:20; 1 Cor 11:25), still the books of the Old Testament, all of them caught up into the

---

b. Other ancient authorities read *known*   **c.** Or omit *you*

1 Peter 1:12

<small>Is 53; Mt 13:17
Lk 24:27

Eph 3:10</small>

what person or time was indicated by the Spirit of Christ* within them when predicting the sufferings of Christ and the subsequent glory. ¹²It was revealed to them that they were serving not themselves but you, in the things which have now been announced to you by those who preached the good news to you through the Holy Spirit sent from heaven, things into which angels long to look.

1. A CALL TO HOLINESS

Christians are called to be saints

<small>Lk 12:35</small> ¹³Therefore gird up your minds, be sober, set your hope fully upon the grace that is coming to you at the revelation of Jesus Christ.

Gospel message, attain and show forth their full meaning in the New Testament (cf. Mt 5:17; Lk 24:27; Rom 16:25-26; 2 Cor 3:14-16) and in their turn, shed light on it and explain it" (Vatican II, *Dei Verbum*, 15-16).

These verses show the Holy Spirit's role as cause and guide of the evangelizing activity of the Church. In the early days of the spread of Christianity, as described in Acts, the action of the third Person of the Blessed Trinity was palpable.

1:12. The Greek word translated at the end of this verse as "look" contains the idea of bending over carefully in order to get a better look. This metaphor, then, depicts the angels in heaven contemplating with joy the mystery of salvation. St Francis de Sales, referring to this passage, exclaims: "Now in this complacency we satiate our soul with delights in such a manner that we do not yet cease to desire to be satiated [...]. The fruition of a thing which always contents never lessens, but is renewed and flourishes incessantly; it is ever agreeable, ever desirable. The perpetual contentment of heavenly lovers produces a desire perpetually content" (*Treatise on the Love of God*, 5, 3).

1:13—2:10. Having focused their attention on the sublimity of the Christian calling, St Peter exhorts the faithful to a holiness in keeping with it. He provides some reasons why they should strive for holiness—the holiness of God (vv. 13–16) and the price paid for their salvation, the blood of Christ (vv. 17–21). He then goes on directly to refer to the importance of love (vv. 22–25); and he encourages them to grow up in their new life (2:1–3) so that as "living stones" they can form part of the spiritual building of the Church, which has Christ as its cornerstone (vv. 4–10).

1:13–16. Israel was chosen by God from all the peoples of the earth to implement his plan of salvation: he set the people of Israel free from the slavery of Egypt, established a covenant with them and gave them commandments about how to live. These commandments in their highest form tell them to be holy as God is holy (cf. Lev 19:2). However, those events in the life of Israel were only an imperfect foreshadowing of what would happen when Jesus Christ came: Christians constitute the new chosen people; by Baptism they have been set free from sin and have been called to live in a fully holy way, with God himself as their model.

1 Peter 1:17

¹⁴As obedient children, do not be conformed to the passions of your former ignorance, ¹⁵but as he who called you is holy, be holy yourselves in all your conduct; ¹⁶since it is written, "You shall be holy, for I am holy."

Rom 12:2
Eph 4:17; 2:3
Lev 11:44; 19:2; 20:7

The blood of Christ has ransomed us
¹⁷And if you invoke as Father him who judges each one impartially according to his deeds, conduct yourselves with fear

Jer 3:19; Mt 6:9
Rom 2:11
2 Cor 5:11

The Second Vatican Council solemnly declared that all are called to holiness (cf., e.g., *Lumen gentium*, 11, 40, 42). St Josemaría Escrivá, who anticipated the Council's teaching on this and other points, had constantly preached about this universal call to holiness: "Christ bids all without exception to be perfect as his heavenly Father is perfect. For the vast majority of people, holiness means sanctifying their work, sanctifying themselves in it, and sanctifying others through it—thereby finding God as they go about their daily lives [...]. Since the foundation of the Work in 1928, my teaching has been that sanctity is not the reserve of a privileged few; all the ways of the earth, every state in life, every job, every honest occupation, can be divine" (quoted in Bernal, 3, 3).

1:13. "Gird up your minds": a metaphor based on the custom of the Jews, and Middle Easterners in general, of gathering up their rather full garments prior to setting out on a journey, to let them walk with greater ease. In the account of the Exodus we are told that God laid it down that when the Israelites celebrated the Passover they should do so with their loins girt, their sandals on and a staff in their hand (cf. Ex 12:11), because they were about to start on the journey to the promised land. St Peter evokes this image (which our Lord also used: cf. Lk 12:35ff), because Baptism, the new Exodus, marks the start of the Christian pilgrimage to heaven, our lasting home (cf. 1:17; 2:11); and he applies it to sobriety: we need to control our feelings and inclinations if we are to walk with joy along the route which will take us to the glorious coming of the Lord.

"The revelation of Jesus Christ": this is a reference, above all, to his eschatological coming at the end of time. The revelation of Jesus began with his incarnation and will reach its climax at the end of this world. Therefore, the "grace" mentioned should be understood not only as sanctifying grace but also the whole ensemble of benefits the Christian receives at Baptism, which will find their full expression in heaven.

1:14. "Your former ignorance": the writer contrasts his hearers' present position with their former one. He does not mean that prior to Baptism they were perverse and ignorant, but that the Christian vocation brings such clear knowledge of God and so many aids to practise virtue that their previous position can be viewed as one of concupiscence and ignorance. "The followers of Christ, called by God, not in virtue of their works but by his design and grace, and justified in the Lord Jesus, have been made sons of God in the baptism of faith and partakers of the divine nature, and so are truly sanctified" (Vatican II, *Lumen gentium*, 40).

1:17–21. The Christian has attained the honour of being a son or daughter of

1 Peter 1:18

Is 52:3
1 Cor 6:20; 7:23
Heb 9:14
Jn 1:29
Rom 16:25f
Rom 4:24
Col 1:27

throughout the time of your exile. ¹⁸You know that you were ransomed from the futile ways inherited from your fathers, not with perishable things such as silver or gold, ¹⁹but with the precious blood of Christ, like that of a lamb without blemish or spot. ²⁰He was destined before the foundation of the world but was made manifest at the end of the times for your sake. ²¹Through him you have

---

God. The sacred writer summarizes God's plan for man's salvation, which comes about in Christ: from all eternity, it was God's design to save men through Christ; this design was made manifest "at the end of the times", when our Lord offered himself as an expiation for the sins of men, and then rose from the dead and was glorified. This is a further reason why Christians should grow in their desire for holiness.

"You were ransomed" (v. 18): the image of ransoming used here to explain Redemption is probably taken from sacred manumission (common at the time in Asia Minor and Greece) whereby slaves were set free through a sum of money being deposited in the temple. When exhorting Christians not to return to their former sins, St Paul also stresses the great size of the ransom (cf. 1 Cor 6:20 and note). The amount of the ransom, St Ambrose points out, "was not reckoned in terms of money but in terms of blood, for Christ died for us; he has set us free with his precious blood, as St Peter also reminds us in his letter [...]; precious because it is the blood of a spotless Lamb, the blood of the Son of God, who has ransomed us not only from the curse of the Law, but also from that never-ending death which impiety implies" (*Expositio Evangelii sec. Lucam*, 7, 117).

"The blood of Christ, like that of a lamb without blemish or spot" (v. 19): in the sacrifice of Jesus was fulfilled the prophecy of Isaiah about the Messiah's expiatory suffering; and it also finally completed the liberation of the Israelite first-born in Egypt through the blood of the paschal lamb (Ex 12; cf. Introduction to this letter). So, when in the New Testament the figure of the Lamb is applied to Christ, this is a way of referring to the atoning sacrifice of the cross and, also, the spotless innocence of the Redeemer (cf. note on Jn 1:29).

1:17. "If you invoke as Father": this may be a reference to the saying of the Our Father, which Christians may have recited at the Baptism ceremony from the very beginning. We do know (cf. the *Didaché*, or *Teaching of the Twelve Apostles*, an anonymous text of the apostolic era) that Christians used to pray the Our Father three times a day (cf. 8, 3). Frequent reflection on the fact that God is our Father fills us with peace and joy and stirs us to act as befits children of such a Father, knowing that God sees us and judges our actions. Therefore, divine filiation can never be taken as a kind of safe-conduct which allows us to be casual about our duties: "Worldly souls are very fond of thinking of God's mercy. And so they are encouraged to persist in their follies.

"It is true that God our Lord is infinitely merciful, but he is also infinitely just: and there is a judgment, and he is the Judge" (St Josemaría Escrivá, *The Way*, 747).

1:21. The resurrection of Jesus is the basis of Christian faith and hope and is the main proof of Jesus' divinity and his divine mission (cf., e.g., 1 Cor 15 and

confidence in God, who raised him from the dead and gave him glory, so that your faith and hope are in God.ᵈ

Brotherly love

²²Having purified your souls by your obedience to the truth for a sincere love of the brethren, love one another earnestly from the heart. ²³You have been born anew, not of perishable seed but of imperishable, through the living and abiding word of God; ²⁴for

"All flesh is like grass
and all its glory like the flower of grass.
The grass withers, and the flower falls,
²⁵ but the word of the Lord abides for ever."

That word is the good news which was preached to you.

1 Jn 3:9
Jas 1:18

Is 40:6, 7
Jas 1:10f

Is 40:8

Like newborn babies

2 ¹So put away all malice and all guile and insincerity and envy and all slander. ²Like newborn babes, long for the pure spiritual milk, that by it you may grow up to salvation; ³for you have tasted the kindness of the Lord.

Eph 4:22
Jas 1:21
Mt 18:3
1 Cor 3:2
Heb 5:12f
Ps 34:9

---

notes on same). The apostles were, first and foremost, witnesses of our Lord's resurrection (cf. Acts 1:22; 2:32; etc.), and the proclamation of the Resurrection was the core of apostolic catechesis (cf. the discourses of St Peter and St Paul in the Acts of the Apostles).

Jesus Christ rose from the dead by his own power, the power of his divine person (cf. *Creed of the People of God*, 12); the *St Pius V Catechism* points out that "we sometimes, it is true, read in Scripture that he was raised by the Father; but this refers to him as man, just as those passages, on the other hand, which say that he rose by his own power relate to him as God" (1, 6, 8).

1:22–25. Fraternal love is one of the main signs of holiness. Jesus said that this love would be the distinguishing mark of Christians, and the apostles often repeat this teaching in the instruction they impart (cf., e.g., 1 Cor 13; Jas 2:8; 1 Jn).

The new people of God, Vatican II says, "are reborn, not from a corruptible seed, but from an incorruptible one through the word of the living God (cf. 1 Pet 1:23); the law of this people is the new commandment to love as Christ loved us (cf. Jn 13:34)" (*Lumen gentium*, 9).

2:1–3. The liturgy applies this text to the newly baptized (cf. Second Sunday of Easter, entrance antiphon): they are like babies recently born to the new life of grace (cf. 1:23). These verses are an exhortation to have the sincerity and simplicity of children.

Just as little children clamour for their food, Christians should long for the spiritual nourishment that lies in the Word of God and the sacraments. St Bede comments: "Just as children have a natural desire for their mother's milk [...], so should you desire to know the rudiments of the faith [...], so that by learning well you may come to receive the living Bread

---

d. Or *so that your faith is hope in God*

1 Peter 2:4

The priesthood that all believers share

Acts 4:11
Eph 2:21f
Rom 12:1

⁴Come to him, to that living stone, rejected by men but in God's sight chosen and precious; ⁵and like living stones be yourselves

---

that has come down from heaven, through the sacraments of the Lord's incarnation; these sacraments cause you to be born again and give you nourishment that enables you to contemplate the majesty of God" (*Super 1 Pet. expositio*, ad loc.).

Psalm 34, to which St Peter refers in v. 3 says, "Taste and see that the Lord is good" (v. 8); by applying these words to Christ, his divinity is being asserted (cf. note on 1:10–12). Among the early Christians it was quite usual for Holy Communion to be given during the baptismal ceremony (in which this psalm was sung in honour of the Eucharist). "This hymn", St Cyril of Jerusalem teaches, "is a divine melody inviting us to partake of the divine mysteries: 'O taste and see the Lord is good.' It is not your tongue but your sound faith that forms your judgment. For it is not bread and wine that you are tasting, but the body and blood which they contain" (*Mystagogical Catechesis*, 5, 20).

2:2. "Like new-born babies": although this simile applies here to people who have only recently received Baptism, all Christians should throughout their lives have the simplicity and trust of children. "Unless you turn and become like children, you will never enter the kingdom of heaven" (Mt 18:3). Spiritual childhood, whereby we always see ourselves as small children in God's eyes, is one way of growing in intimacy with him. "In our interior life", St Josemaría Escrivá recommends, "it does all of us good to be *quasi infantes*, like those tiny tots who seem to be made of rubber and who even enjoy falling over because they get up right away and are running around again, and also because they know their parents will always be there to console them whenever they are needed.

"If we try to act like them, our stumbling and failures in the interior life (which, moreover, are inevitable) will never result in bitterness. Our reaction will be one of sorrow but not discouragement, and we'll smile with a smile that gushes up like fresh water out of the joyous awareness that we are children of that Love, that grandeur, that infinite wisdom, that mercy, that is our Father. During the years I have been serving our Lord, I have learned to become a little child of God. I would ask you to do likewise, to be *quasi modo geniti infantes*, children who long for God's word, his bread, his food, his strength, to enable us to behave henceforth as Christian men and women" (*Friends of God*, 146)

"Spiritual milk": this may be an allusion to the promises God made to the chosen people to bring them into "a land flowing with milk and honey" (Ex 3:8), and it could be that from those words the custom grew in the early baptismal liturgy of giving the recently baptized milk mixed with honey (a custom suppressed towards the end of the fourth century). The expression refers to all the graces our Lord gives in Baptism to enable a person attain salvation.

2:4–10. Baptism makes us members of the Church. The sacred writer uses the idea of constructing a building (vv. 4–8) to explain that Christians together go to make up the one, true people of God (vv. 9–19). The whole passage is built on quotations from the Old Testament, possibly ones used in early apostolic catechesis.

built into a spiritual house, to be a holy priesthood, to offer spiritual sacrifices acceptable to God through Jesus Christ. ⁶For it stands in scripture:
> "Behold, I am laying in Zion a stone, a cornerstone chosen and precious,
> and he who believes in him will not be put to shame."

⁷To you therefore who believe, he is precious, but for those who do not believe,
> "The very stone which the builders rejected
> has become the head of the corner,"

⁸and
> "A stone that will make men stumble,
> a rock that will make them fall";

for they stumble because they disobey the word, as they were destined to do. ⁹But you are a chosen race, a royal priesthood, a holy nation, God's own people,ᵉ that you may declare the wonderful deeds of him

Is 28:16
Rom 9:33

Ps 118:22
Mt 21:42

Is 8:14f

Ex 19:6
Deut 7:6
Eph 5:8
Phil 2:15
Acts 26:18

The Church is like a spiritual building of which Christ is the cornerstone, that is, the stone which supports the entire structure (cf. *Lumen gentium*, 6). Christians have to be living stones united to Christ by faith and grace, thereby forming a solid temple in which "spiritual sacrifices" are offered which are "acceptable to God" (v. 5). The closer their union with Christ, the stronger the building: "All of us who believe in Christ Jesus", Origen explains, "are called 'living stones' [...]. For if you, who are listening to me, want to prepare yourself better for the construction of this building, and be one of the stones closest to the foundation, you need to realize that Christ himself is the foundation of the building we are describing. As the Apostle Paul tells us, 'no other foundation can any one lay than that which is laid, which is Jesus Christ' (1 Cor 3:11)" (*In Iesu nave*, 9, 1).

2:8. Applying to Christ what the prophet Isaiah says of Yahweh (cf. Is 8:14; note on 1 Pet 2:13), St Peter shows how, for those who do not believe in Christ, the cornerstone becomes a "stone that will make men stumble, a rock that will make them fall"; Simeon prophesied as much to the Blessed Virgin in the temple (cf. Lk 2:34).

"As they were destined to do": this does not mean that God predestined some to damnation. God wants all men to be saved (cf. 1 Tim 2:4), and that was why Jesus Christ became man; but for someone to be saved, his free response is necessary, and man can oppose God's salvific plan and reject grace. It should be remembered that in the language of the Bible, particularly the Old Testament, sometimes no distinction is made between what God orders or wills and what he simply allows to happen (cf. Rom 9:14–33 and notes on same).

2:9–10. In contrast with those who reject faith (vv. 7–8), believers form the true Israel, the true people of God; in it the titles applied to Israel in the Old Testament find their full meaning: they

e. Greek *a people for his possession*

1 Peter 2:10

Hos 1:6; 9; 2:3, 25
Rom 9:25

who called you out of darkness into his marvellous light. ¹⁰Once you were no people but now you are God's people; once you had not received mercy but now you have received mercy.

---

are "a chosen race" (cf. Ex 19:5–6), a people convoked by God to sing his praises (cf. Is 43:20–21). Their election is not only something Christians should glory in; it makes demands on them: Christians are set apart for God, they belong to him (cf. 1 Cor 6:19), for the blood of Christ has been paid as their ransom (cf. 1 Pet 1:18–21). So, they must not remain passive; they have to preach the greatness of God and draw many other souls to him: "the Good News of the Kingdom which is coming and which has begun is meant", says Pope Paul VI, "for all people of all times. Those who have received the Good News and who have been gathered by it into the community of salvation can and must communicate and spread it" (*Evangelii nuntiandi*, 13).

In this people there is only one priest, Jesus Christ, and one sacrifice, that which he offered on the cross and which is renewed in the Mass. But all Christians, through the sacraments of Baptism and Confirmation, obtain a share in the priesthood of Christ and are thereby equipped to mediate in a priestly way between God and man and to take an active part in divine worship; by so doing they can turn all their actions into "spiritual sacrifices acceptable to God" (1 Pet 2:5). Theirs is a true priesthood, although it is essentially different from the ministerial priesthood of those who receive the sacrament of Order: "Though they differ essentially and not only in degree, the common priesthood of the faithful and the ministerial or hierarchical priesthood are none the less ordered one to another; each in its own proper way shares in the one priesthood of Christ. The ministerial priest, by the sacred power that he has, forms and rules the priestly people; in the person of Christ he effects the eucharistic sacrifice and offers it to God in the name of all the people. The faithful indeed, by virtue of their royal priesthood, participate in the offering of the Eucharist. They exercise that priesthood, too, by the reception of the sacraments, prayer and thanksgiving, the witness of a holy life, abnegation and active charity" (Vatican II, *Lumen gentium*, 10; cf. *Presbyterorum ordinis*, 2).

And the same Council says, apropos of those "spiritual sacrifices" (v. 5) by which Christians sanctify the world from within, that "all their works, prayers and apostolic undertakings, family and married life, daily work, relaxation of mind and body, if they are accomplished in the Spirit—indeed even the hardships of life if patiently borne—all these become spiritual sacrifices acceptable to God through Jesus Christ (cf. 1 Pet 2:5). In the celebration of the Eucharist these may most fittingly be offered to the Father along with the body of the Lord. And so, worshipping everywhere by their holy actions, the laity consecrate the world itself to God" (*Lumen gentium*, 34).

2:10. A passage from the book of Hosea is applied to the faithful: Yahweh tells the prophet to name two of his children "Not pitied" and "Not my people" (Hos 1:6, 8), to symbolize the unfaithfulness of the people of Israel, for which they deserved to be rejected by God. However, a little further on (Hos 2:22f), when he speaks of the new covenant he is thinking of making, Yahweh says, "I will have pity on Not pitied, and I will say to Not my people, 'You are my people'; and he shall say,

2. THE OBLIGATIONS OF CHRISTIANS

Setting an example for pagans

¹¹Beloved, I beseech you as aliens and exiles to abstain from the passions of the flesh that wage war against your soul. ¹²Maintain

Ps 39:13
Gal 5:17, 24

'Thou art my God'". St Peter indicates that this prophecy has found its fulfilment in the Church, the new people of God.

"Christ instituted this new covenant, namely the new covenant in his blood (cf. 1 Cor 11:25); he called a race made up of Jews and Gentiles which would be one, not according to the flesh, but in the Spirit, and this race would be the new people of God. For those who believe in Christ, who are reborn, not from a corruptible seed, but from an incorruptible one through the word of the living God (cf. 1 Pet 1:23), not from flesh, but from water and the Holy Spirit (cf. Jn 3:5–6), are finally established as a 'chosen race, a royal priesthood, a holy nation ... who in times past were not a people, but now are the people of God' (1 Pet 2:9–10)" (*Lumen gentium*, 9).

2:11—3:12. After outlining the fact that their vocation requires Christians to be holy, the apostle goes on to describe how their conduct will attract Gentiles to the faith (2:11–12)—exemplary behaviour in social and civic life, obeying lawful authority (vv. 13–17); obedience of servants to masters (vv. 18–25); and mutual respect between husband and wife (3:1–7). Finally, he encourages all to practise fraternal charity (3:8–12).

2:11–12. The letter contains many appeals to Christians to stay true to the faith even when pagans criticize them (2:12), cause them to suffer (3:13–15), or insult them for following Christ (4:14). Some authors, reading these remarks as referring to state persecution unleashed by Roman emperors—especially Domitian (d. 96) and Trajan (d. 117)—give the letter a much later date, even a second-century date; but all the information available to us favours a much earlier date, around the year 64 (cf. Introduction). St Peter seems to be referring rather to the trials the faithful met at the hands of their fellow-citizens. At that time Christians often encountered misunderstanding, rejection and discrimination, and even the loss of property (cf., e.g., Acts 19:23–31; 2 Thess 2:14).

This context explains why the apostle encourages these recent converts (he once again reminds them they are wayfarers: cf. 1:1, 17) to lead exemplary lives, so that those among whom they live, although they may initially misinterpret their conduct, will end up glorifying God: "Let your light so shine before men, that they see your good works and give glory to your Father who is in heaven" (Mt 5:16). Good example is enormously effective in drawing souls closer to God. St John Chrysostom exhorted his flock in this way: "There would be no need for preaching if our life were a beacon of virtues—no call for words if we had deeds to show. There would be no pagans if we were truly Christians—if we kept Jesus Christ's commandments, if we put up with unjust treatment and deception, if we blessed those who cursed us, if we returned good for evil. No one would be such a monster not to embrace the true religion immediately if we really lived like that" (*Hom. on 1 Tim*, 10).

In addition to being mindful of exterior difficulties, St Peter does not

1 Peter 2:13

Jas 3:13
Mt 5:16
Is 10:3

good conduct among the Gentiles, so that in case they speak against you as wrongdoers, they may see your good deeds and glorify God on the day of visitation.

Obedience to civil authority

Rom 13:1, 7
Tit 3:1

¹³Be subject for the Lord's sake to every human institution,ᶠ whether it be to the emperor as supreme, ¹⁴or to governors as sent by him to punish those who do wrong and to praise those who do right. ¹⁵For it is God's will that by doing right you should put to

---

forget that the greatest danger lies in personal evil inclinations which "wage war against your soul" (v. 11). Constant effort is called for if one is to control one's passions and overcome temptation (cf., e.g., Mt 10:38–39; 1 Cor 9:24–27; 1 Tim 6:12): "There are people who want to be humble," St Gregory the Great teaches, "but without being despised; who want to be content with their lot, provided they have all they need; to be chaste, but without mortifying their body; to be patient, provided no one offends them. When they try to acquire virtues but avoid the effort which virtues involve, it is as if, with no experience of combat on the battlefield, they want to win the war without moving from the city" (*Moralia*, 7, 28).

"The day of visitation": this may refer to the time when the Lord will come in glory at the end of the world; but from the context it seems, rather, to refer to his coming to the hearts of the Gentiles through the grace of conversion (cf. Lk 19:44).

2:13–17. Christians should be exemplary in all their dealings with others, obeying the emperor and other people in authority "for the Lord's sake". Jesus taught the obligation of conscientious fulfilment of civic duties (cf. Mt 22:21–22; 17:24–27);

and St Paul, echoing the Master's teaching, reminds us that all authority comes from God (Rom 13:1–7; cf. Jn 19:11). The first Christians, in the midst of trials and persecutions, were heroically faithful to their civic duties; not only did they not react violently against unjust persecution, but they prayed for their persecutors (cf. note on Rom 13:1–7).

As regards relations between citizen and State, the Magisterium of the Church teaches that, on the side of the State, authority "must be exercised within the limits of the moral order and directed toward the common good (understood in the dynamic sense of the term) according to the juridical order legitimately established or due to be established. Citizens, then, are bound in conscience to obey (cf. Rom 13:5). Accordingly, the responsibility, the dignity, and the importance of civic rulers is clear.

"When citizens are under the oppression of a public authority which oversteps its competence, they should still not refuse to give or to do whatever is objectively demanded of them by the common good; but it is legitimate for them to defend their own rights and those of their fellow citizens against abuses of this authority within the limits of the natural law and the law of the Gospel" (Vatican II, *Gaudium et spes*, 74).

---

f. Or *every institution ordained for men*

silence the ignorance of foolish men. ¹⁶Live as free men, yet without using your freedom as a pretext for evil; but live as servants of God. ¹⁷Honour all men. Love the brotherhood. Fear God. Honour the emperor.

Gal 5:13
Prov 24:21
Mt 22:21
Rom 12:10

Duties towards masters. Christ's example
¹⁸Servants, be submissive to your masters with all respect, not only to the kind and gentle but also to the overbearing. ¹⁹For one is approved if, mindful of God, he endures pain while suffering unjustly. ²⁰For what credit is it, if when you do wrong and are beaten for it you take it patiently? But if when you do right and suffer for it you take it patiently, you have God's approval. ²¹For

Eph 6:5

Mt 5:10
1 Pet 3:14, 17;
4:13f
Mt 16:24
Rom 4:12

2:16. By obeying political authority, the faithful are not surrendering their freedom; on the contrary, they are correctly using, in generous service of God and of others, the freedom which Christ has won for them. St Peter encourages them to "live as free men", conscious that they are "servants of God".

The Second Vatican Council teaches that Christians "should be a shining example by their sense of responsibility and their dedication to the common good; they should show in practice how authority can be reconciled with freedom, personal initiative with the solidarity and the needs of the whole social framework, and the advantages of unity with profitable diversity" (*Gaudium et spes*, 75).

2:17. The Christian's social and political duties are summed up here in four points. "Honour all men": that is, treat them as befits their human dignity (cf. *Gaudium et spes*, 12–22). "Love the brotherhood," that is, everyone in the Church, thereby keeping our Lord's new commandment (cf. 1 Pet 1:22; Jn 13:34). "Fear God," the source of all wisdom, avoiding all selfishness (cf. Prov 1:7; 1 Jn 4:17–18 and note). "Honour the emperor": give to Caesar the things that are Caesar's (cf. Mt 22:21 and note).

2:18–25. The writer now addresses all domestic servants (the Greek word means all who work in household tasks). He exhorts them to obey their masters, even if they are harsh (v. 18), because God is pleased if they put up with unfairness for his sake (vv. 19–20); in doing so they are imitating the example of Jesus (vv. 21–25). St Paul, when addressing slaves in his letters (cf. Eph 5:5–9; Col 3:22–24), never encourages them to rebel. Christian teaching on social issues is not based on class struggle but on fraternal love: love eventually does away with all discrimination, for all men have been created in the image of God and are equal in his sight. This peaceable policy gradually made for the suppression of slavery, and it will also lead to the solution of all social problems (cf. *Gaudium et spes*, 29).

The fact that St Peter addresses only servants and does not go on to say anything to masters (as St Paul usually does: cf. Eph 6:5–9; Col 3:23ff) has led some commentators to suggest that most of the Christians addressed in this letter must have been people of humble condition.

2:21–25. This passage is a beautiful hymn to Christ on the cross. Christ's sufferings, which fulfil the prophecies about the Servant of Yahweh contained in the book

1 Peter 2:22

<small>Is 53:9
Jn 8:46
Is 53:12
Mt 5:39
Is 53:4, 5, 12
2 Cor 5:21
Heb 9:28
Rom 3:24f; 6:11
Is 53:6
Ezek 34:5
Jn 10:12
1 Pet 5:4</small>

to this you have been called, because Christ also suffered for you, leaving you an example, that you should follow in his steps. ²²He committed no sin; no guile was found on his lips. ²³When he was reviled, he did not revile in return; when he suffered, he did not threaten; but he trusted to him who judges justly. ²⁴He himself bore our sins in body on the tree,^g that we might die to sin and live to righteousness. By his wounds you have been healed. ²⁵For you were straying like sheep, but have now returned to the Shepherd and Guardian of your souls.

---

of Isaiah (52:13 53:12), have not been in vain, for they have a redemptive value. He has taken our sins upon himself and brought them with him onto the cross, offering himself as an atoning sacrifice. This means that we are free of our sins ("dead to sin") and can live "to righteousness", that is, can live for holiness with the help of grace.

The example of the suffering Christ is always a necessary reference point for Christians: however great the trials they experience, they will never be as great or as unjust as those of our Lord. Reflecting on Christ's suffering led St Bernard to comment: "I have come to see that true wisdom lies in meditating on these things [...]. Some have provided me with wholesome, if bitter, drink, and I have used others as gentle and soothing unction. This gives me strength in adversity and helps me to be humble in prosperity; it allows me to walk with a sure step on the royal road of salvation, through the good things and the evil things of this present life, free from the dangers which threaten to right and left" (*Sermons on the Song of Songs*, 43, 4).

2:25. The messianic prophecy about the Servant of Yahweh includes the image of the scattered flock (cf. Is 53:6), to which Jesus alludes in his allegory of the Good Shepherd (cf. Jn 10:11–16). St Peter, to whom our Lord had given charge of his flock (cf. Jn 21:15–19), would have had a special liking for imagery connected with shepherding.

Jesus Christ is "the Shepherd and Guardian of your souls" and "the chief Shepherd" (1 Pet 5:4). The etymology of the Greek word—*epíscopos* (guardian)—means "overseer"; the word was used in civic life to designate those who were responsible for seeing that the law was kept. In the Dead Sea manuscripts the Hebrew equivalent (*mebaqqer*) is used to designate the religious leaders of the schismatic community of Qumran. Whatever might be the origin of the term, in the New Testament the word *epíscopos* is often used to mean the pastor of the Church (cf., e.g., Acts 20:28; see the note on 1 Pet 5:1–4). Here St Peter applies to Christ the words the prophet Ezekiel places on the lips of God: "I will seek out my sheep, and I will rescue them from all places where they have been scattered" (Ezek 34:12). Our Lord founded the Church as a sheepfold "whose sheep, although watched over by human shepherds, are nevertheless at all times led and brought to pasture by Christ himself, the Good Shepherd and prince of shepherds (cf. Jn 10:11; 1 Pet 5:4), who gave his life for his sheep (cf. Jn 10:11–16)" (Vatican II, *Lumen gentium*, 6).

g. Or *carried up ... to the tree*

1 Peter 3:9

Exemplary family life

3 ¹Likewise you wives,* be submissive to your husbands, so that some, though they do not obey the word, may be won without a word by the behaviour of their wives, ²when they see your reverent and chaste behaviour. ³Let not yours be the outward adorning with braiding of hair, decoration of gold, and wearing of fine clothing, ⁴but let it be the hidden person of the heart with the imperishable jewel of a gentle and quiet spirit, which in God's sight is very precious. ⁵So once the holy women who hoped in God used to adorn themselves and were submissive to their husbands, ⁶as Sarah obeyed Abraham, calling him lord. And you are now her children if you do right and let nothing terrify you.

⁷Likewise you husbands, live considerately with your wives, bestowing honour on the woman as the weaker sex, since you are joint heirs of the grace of life, in order that your prayers may not be hindered.

Eph 5:22
1 Cor 7:16

1 Pet 2:12
Is 3:18, 24
1 Tim 2:9
Rev 17:4

Gen 18:12
Prov 3:25

Love of the brethren

⁸Finally, all of you, have unity of spirit, sympathy, love of the brethren, a tender heart and a humble mind. ⁹Do not return evil for

Rom 12:16

3:1–7. The counsels and appeals in this passage are not meant to cover all aspects of the sacrament of Marriage; in contrast with the morality of the time, St Peter simply exhorts married people, both men and women, to live in a Christian way, and offers them practical advice.

"Joint heirs of the grace of life" (v. 7): St Peter identifies the source of the dignity of women, who up to then (especially in the East) were regarded as inferior to men: according to Christian teaching man and woman are equal in dignity, because both are children of God and have the same supernatural destiny. The essential equality of men and women does not gainsay their different roles in marriage.

3:1–2. Again he reminds them of the importance of good example (cf. 2:11–12). Throughout the history of the Church, many women have converted husbands who were pagans or separated from God.

St Augustine movingly describes the example of his mother, St Monica: "she served (her husband) as her lord. She made every effort to win him to you, speaking of you to him by her behaviour, by which you made her beautiful to her husband, respected and loved by him and admirable in his sight. For she bore his acts of unfaithfulness quietly, and never had any jealous scene with her husband about them. She hoped that your mercy would come upon him and that he believing in you might become chaste [...]. The upshot was that towards the very end of his life she won her husband to you; and once he was a Christian she no longer had to complain of the things she had had to bear with before he was a Christian" (*Confessions*, 9, 9).

3:8–12. St Peter now addresses the faithful in general, emphasizing their membership of the Church. The exhortation ends with a quotation from Psalm 34

1 Peter 3:10

<small>Mt 5:39, 44
1 Thess 5:15

Ps 34:13–17
Jas 1:26</small>

evil or reviling for reviling; but on the contrary bless, for to this you have been called, that you may obtain a blessing. ¹⁰For
"He that would love life
and see good days,
let him keep his tongue from evil
and his lips from speaking guile;
¹¹ let him turn away from evil and do right;
let him seek peace and pursue it.
¹² For the eyes of the Lord are upon the righteous,
and his ears are open to their prayer.
But the face of the Lord is against those that do evil."

3. THE CHRISTIAN'S ATTITUDE TO SUFFERING

Undeserved suffering is a blessing

<small>Rom 8:34

Mt 5:10</small>

¹³Now who is there to harm you if you are zealous for what is right? ¹⁴But even if you do suffer for righteousness' sake, you will

---

(vv. 12–16), a psalm he quoted earlier (cf. 2:3).

Love is the virtue that must govern the Christian life (vv. 8–9; cf. 1:22–25). This theological virtue influences all the moral virtues (St Peter here makes mention of unity, fraternity, compassion and humility, all of which replace the law of vengeance). He also stresses that their Christian calling dictates the way they should act: they have been chosen to inherit the blessings of God and therefore they in their turn should bless, not curse, others.

3:13—4:19. The sacred writer now makes a series of appeals designed to give hope to Christians suffering unjustly on account of Jesus' name: he reminds them that every baptized person is called to share in the paschal mystery of Christ, that is, in his sufferings and in his glorification; just as he, after suffering unjustly, was glorified (3:18–22), so too those who now suffer for Christ will have a part in his glorious triumph (4:13–14).

The section begins and ends speaking about the Christian meaning of tribulation (3:13–17 and 4:12–19): trials should not make them feel cowed or ashamed, nor should they come as a surprise; on the contrary, they should fill them with joy and lead them to glorify God for letting them partake in our Lord's suffering.

The apostle also points to one of the reasons for the misunderstandings they experience: after Baptism they have broken with their previous sinful life and that is something pagans cannot understand (4:1–6). Also, Christians should remember that life is something very transient, and therefore they should practise prayer and charity (4:7–11).

3:13–17. These verses act as an introduction to the central theme of this section

1 Peter 3:17

be blessed. Have no fear of them, nor be troubled, ⁱ⁵but in your hearts reverence Christ as Lord. Always be prepared to make a defence to any one who calls you to account for the hope that is in you, yet do it with gentleness and reverence; ¹⁶and keep your conscience clear, so that, when you are abused, those who revile your good behaviour in Christ may be put to shame. ¹⁷For it is better to suffer for doing right, if that should be God's will, than for doing wrong.

Is 8:13
1 Pet 1:3

1 Pet 2:12

(3:13—4:19). They seem to be directed to people who are surprised to encounter persecution despite doing good (v. 13). Opposition should not dismay them; their calumniators will come to realize their mistake (v. 16).

St Peter's words of advice have a very positive ring about them; they are really an application of the beatitude in which our Lord says, "Blessed are you when men revile you and persecute you and utter all kinds of evil against you falsely on my account. Rejoice and be glad, for your reward is great in heaven" (Mt 5:11–12).

St Peter's teachings have a perennial value for disciples of Christ, for (as history clearly shows) fidelity to the Master brings with it persecution (cf. Jn 15:18–22; 2 Tim 3:12), sometimes open and violent persecution, sometimes persecution of a more subtle type, in the form of calumny, humiliation and other hazards.

3:15. "Reverence Christ as Lord": literally, "Hallow", as in the Our Father. The words imply recognition of the divinity of Jesus Christ: he is called Lord (*Kyrios*), a name proper to God; and they are told to "glorify" or "reverence" him, that is, render him the worship that is due to God alone. Even in the midst of difficulties the entire Christian life should be a hymn of praise to God; by acting in this way, Christians are living out their holy, royal priesthood (1 Pet 2:4–10; cf. Vatican II, *Presbyterorum ordinis*, 1).

"To account for the hope that is in you": he is not referring to defending oneself before the courts, for official persecution had not yet become widespread in Asia Minor (cf. note on 2:11–12). He seems, rather, to be referring to the obligation to bear witness to their faith and hope, for all baptized persons should always, by word and example, make their faith known to others.

3:18–22. This passage may include parts of a Creed used in early Christian baptismal instruction. It very clearly expresses the essence of faith in Jesus Christ, as preached from the beginning by the apostles (cf. Acts 2:14–36; 1 Cor 15:1ff) and as articulated in the Apostles' Creed: "He was crucified, died and was buried. He descended into hell; the third day he rose again from the dead. He ascended into heaven and sits at the right hand of God the Father Almighty."

Jesus Christ, who suffers for the sins of mankind—"the righteous for the unrighteous"—and then is glorified, gives meaning to the sufferings of Christians. "Oh, how great thanks am I bound to return to you for having shown me and all the faithful the right and good way to your everlasting kingdom! For your life is our life; and by holy patience we walk on to you, who are our crown. If you had not gone before and taught us, who

1 Peter 3:18

Christ's suffering and glorification

1 Pet 2:21, 24
Rom 6:10
Heb 9:28
1 Pet 4:6
2 Pet 3:9
Gen 7:7, 17

[18] For Christ also died[h] for sins once for all, the righteous for the unrighteous, that he might bring us to God, being put to death in the flesh but made alive in the spirit; [19] in which he went and preached to the spirits in prison, [20] who formerly did not obey, when God's patience waited in the days of Noah, during the

---

would care to follow? Alas, how many would have stayed afar off and a great way behind if they had not had before their eyes your wonderful example!" (*The Imitation of Christ*, 3, 18).

3:18. "Christ has died for sins once for all": our Lord's sacrifice is unrepeatable (cf. Heb 9:12–28; 10:10) and superabundantly sufficient to obtain the remission of all sins. The fruits of the cross are applied to man, in a special way, by means of the sacraments, particularly by taking part in the Mass, the unbloody renewal of the sacrifice of Calvary.

"Being put to death in the flesh but made alive in the spirit": there is disagreement among commentators as to what "flesh" and "spirit" mean here. Some identify them with our concepts of body and soul—"dead as regards the body, alive as regards the soul". Others see them as equivalent to the humanity-divinity of our Lord: "dead as far as his human nature is concerned, alive (continues to live) as far as his divinity is concerned". Finally, having regard to the meaning these terms have in the Old Testament, the phrase may refer to the earthly condition of our Lord compared with the glorious condition he had after his resurrection; in which case it would be an early form of words used to convey the idea that Jesus Christ, on dying, left his mortal condition behind for ever in order to move into his glorious, immortal state through his resurrection (cf. 1 Cor 15:35–49).

3:19–20. "In which", that is, in the spirit. The ambiguity of the original text (referred to in the previous note) continues, so it is possible to understand the "in which" in the three ways outlined. Some take it as meaning that Christ went to preach to the spirits in prison "with his soul", separated from his body; for some he went "in his glorious condition", which is not incompatible with the resurrection in the strict sense happening afterwards.

In any event, these verses are one of the clear references in the New Testament to our Lord descending into hell (cf. also Mt 12:38–41; Acts 2:24–36; Rom 10:6–7; Eph 4:8–9; Rev 1:18). After dying on the cross, Jesus Christ went to bring his message of salvation "to the spirits in prison": many Fathers and commentators are inclined to the view that this is a reference to the just of the Old Testament who, not being able to enter heaven until the Redemption took place, were kept in the bosom of Abraham, which is also called the "limbo" of the just (cf. *St Pius V Catechism*, 1, 6, 1–6).

The reference to the contemporaries of Noah is probably explained by the fact that, for the Jews of the time, those people (along with the people of Sodom and Gomorrah: cf. Mt 24:36–39; Lk 17:26–30) were the classic inveterate sinners. By bringing in this reference St Peter is teaching that the Redemption embraces all men: even the contemporaries of Noah, if they repented, could have attained salvation through the merits of Christ.

---

h. Other ancient authorities read *suffered*

building of the ark, in which a few, that is, eight persons, were saved through water. ²¹Baptism, which corresponds to this, now saves you, not as a removal of dirt from the body but as an appeal to God for a clear conscience, through the resurrection of Jesus Christ, ²²who has gone into heaven and is at the right hand of God, with angels, authorities, and powers subject to him.

Heb 10:22

Eph 1:21
Ps 110:1

The Christian has broken with sin

4 ¹Since therefore Christ suffered in the flesh,ⁱ arm yourselves with the same thought, for whoever has suffered in the flesh ⁱ

Rom 6:2, 7

3:21–22. The waters of the Flood are a figure of Baptism: in the same way as Noah and his family were saved by being in the Ark, now men are saved through Baptism, which makes them members of Christ's Church.

"As an appeal to God for a clear conscience, through the resurrection of Jesus Christ": the obvious meaning of this is that the Christian asks for perseverance in the good way of life he entered into at Baptism. However, the Greek word translated as "appeal", a rarely used one, contains the idea of "commitment". It is possible that this may be a reference to a part of the baptismal rite—for example, the profession of faith the neophyte made, and his promise to stay true to it. Or it may refer to a permanent effect of Baptism whereby the Christian is given a share in "the resurrection of Christ": it would not be surprising if St Peter were referring to what later came to be known as the baptismal "character". In fact, the context suggests something permanent and indelible: just as Noah's salvation was a lasting one and there was never again a flood, so too the condition of the Christian is something permanent; now that he has risen Jesus can never die again (cf. Rom 6:3) and neither can the baptized return to their former sinful condition.

Verse 22, possibly taken from a baptismal hymn, is a very concise account of the glorification of Christ. After descending into hell, he arose and ascended into heaven, where he is seated "at the right hand of God": this phrase, already common in early Christian catechesis (cf., e.g., Mt 22:41–46; Mk 16:19; Acts 2:33) means that our Lord, who is equal to the Father in his divinity, also, as man, occupies at his side the place of honour over all other created beings. This universal lordship of Christ is further emphasized by the statement that all heavenly beings are subject to him (cf. Phil 2:10; Eph 1:21); three degrees of angels are mentioned, that is, all the angels, because the number three symbolizes totality.

4:1–6. The apostle continues his exposition, possibly following the pattern of baptismal instruction. Christians have to identify with Christ, dead and risen: they have died with him, to rise with him (cf. Rom 6:3); their lives can no longer be the way they were before Baptism, even if the change of lifestyle results in their being misunderstood and reviled. They should remember that they will in due course appear before the Judge of the living and the dead, Jesus Christ.

"Whoever has suffered in the flesh has ceased from sin" (v. 1): this looks like a legal adage, meaning that one who has suffered the pain of death has paid for all his crimes (cf. Rom 6:7). St Peter

---

i. Other ancient authorities add *for us*; some *for you*

1 Peter 4:2

^{1 Jn 2:16f}
^{Tit 3:3}
^{Rom 1:28}

has ceased from sin,* ²so as to live for the rest of the time in the flesh no longer by human passions but by the will of God. ³Let the time that is past suffice for doing what the Gentiles like to do, living in licentiousness, passions, drunkenness, revels, carousing, and lawless idolatry. ⁴They are surprised that you do not now join them in the same wild profligacy, and they abuse you; ⁵but they will give account to him who is ready to judge the living and the dead. ⁶For this is why the gospel was preached even to the dead, that though judged in the flesh like men, they might live in the spirit like God.

^{Acts 10:42}
^{1 Pet 3:19}
^{Rom 8:10}
^{1 Cor 5:5}

A call for charity

^{1 Cor 10:11}
^{Prov 10:12}
^{1 Cor 13:7}

⁷The end of all things is at hand; therefore keep sane and sober for your prayers. ⁸Above all hold unfailing your love for one another,

---

would have adapted it to give it a theological meaning: Christians, by dying mystically with Christ in Baptism, have had all their sins forgiven and therefore it does not make sense to continue to live in them (cf. Rom 6:1ff; 1 Jn 3:9; 5:18).

This new mode of behaviour has led to opposition from pagans, who cannot understand why they have given up the vices they previously indulged in. Some of the sins mentioned (sins not common among Jews), and the reference to abuse by Gentiles, suggest that the letter was originally written to Christian converts from paganism. The reaction of the pagans to their behaviour, constituting as it does a moral reproach for their sinful lives, is nothing new: Why did Cain kill Abel, St John asks himself, and he replies, "Because his deeds were evil and his brother's righteous" (1 Jn 3:12). This type of reaction is always liable to occur.

In this connexion the apostle reminds them that Judgment is nigh (cf. note on 4:7), and that judgment will show everything up in its true light. He who "is ready to judge the living and the dead" (v. 5) is Jesus Christ; in many other passages of the New Testament it reads "who will come to judge" (cf. 5:4; Acts 10:42; 2 Tim 4:1): this must have been a standard formula in early Christian catechesis, which passed into the Apostles' Creed.

4:6. "The gospel was preached even to the dead": it is not easy to work out what this means; it may be an allusion to our Lord descending into the bosom of Abraham (cf. 3:19–20). However, St Peter is possibly referring to Christians who have already died without seeing, in this life, the final victory of Christ: the preaching they heard, and their lives according to the Gospel (which brought them insults from their contemporaries), have not been in vain.

In either case, St Peter would be referring to those who remained faithful to God, whose life seemed folly to people without supernatural outlook. This passage is evocative of the following text from the book of Wisdom: "The souls of the righteous are in the hand of God, and no torment will ever touch them. In the eyes of the foolish they seemed to have died, and their departure was thought to be an affliction, and their going from us to be their destruction; but they are at peace. For though in the sight of men they were punished, their hope is full of immortality" (Wis 3:1–4).

4:7–11. "The end of all things is at hand": the incarnation of Jesus Christ marked

since love covers a multitude of sins. ⁹Practise hospitality ungrudgingly to one another. ¹⁰As each has received a gift, employ

Jas 5:20
1 Pet 1:22
Lk 12:42

the beginning of the last days, a period which extends to the end of the world and the Last Judgment (cf. note on 1 Jn 2:18). That is why the last stage of the world "is at hand", or, as some translate it, "has arrived".

Because the End is imminent (cf. 4:5), St Peter urges them to practise prayer and charity, Christ's "new commandment" (cf. Jn 13:34–35), and also hospitality, which was highly valued among the Semites and encouraged among Christians (cf., e.g., Rom 12:13; 1 Tim 3:2; 5:10).

This readiness to make available to others the gifts one has received from God, will cause God to be glorified in everything through Jesus Christ (v. 11). The passage ends with a doxology or hymn in praise of Christ (possibly as a formula used in early liturgy and familiar to the first Christians). As elsewhere in the New Testament, the doxology does not appear at the end of the letter (cf. Rom 1:25; 9:5; Gal 1:5; Eph 3:21); in fact only three epistles end with a doxology (Romans, Jude and 2 Peter). Therefore, the fact that the doxology comes at this point does not mean that it originally marked the end of the letter; it may indicate that St Peter has been following up to this point the structure of an early form of baptismal catechesis. The themes dealt with in the rest of the letter, the style, and even the vocabulary, all support the view that the same author is writing throughout.

4:8. "Love covers a multitude of sins": this quotation from the Old Testament (Prov 10:12; cf. Jas 5:20) can be taken to refer both to other people's sins (which charity understands and forgives) and to one's own. After teaching us to pray in the Our Father, "Forgive us our trespasses as we forgive those who trespass against us", our Lord added: "if you forgive men their trespasses, your heavenly Father also will forgive you" (Mt 6:12, 14). And, when he pardoned the sinful woman, he said, "her sins, which are many, are forgiven, for she loved much" (Lk 7:47).

The Church teaches that perfect love for God wins pardon for sins, but it stresses that that love includes a desire to receive the sacrament of Penance, for one cannot love God without wanting to do what he has laid down: "The Sacred Council also teaches that even if it sometimes happens that a person has this contrition made perfect by charity and becomes reconciled to God prior to receiving this sacrament, his reconciliation should not be attributed to his contrition but rather to his desire for the sacrament which is included in his contrition" (Council of Trent, *De sacramento paenitentiae*, chap. 4).

4:10–11. The Christian receives various gifts from God, that is, charisms or graces given mainly for the benefit of others: they should not be kept for oneself but used for the purpose for which they were intended.

Speaking of the apostolic action of the faithful, the Second Vatican Council recalls that "the Holy Spirit sanctifies the people of God through the ministry and the sacraments. However, for the exercise of the apostolate he gives the faithful special gifts besides (cf. 1 Cor 12:7), 'apportioning them to each one as he wills' (1 Cor 12:11), so that each and all, putting at the service of others the grace received, may be 'as good stewards of God's varied grace' (1 Pet 4:10), for the

1 Peter 4:11

<small>Rom 3:2; 12:7
1 Cor 10:31
Rom 16:27</small>

it for one another, as good stewards of God's varied grace: ¹¹whoever speaks, as one who utters oracles of God; whoever renders service, as one who renders it by the strength which God supplies; in order that in everything God may be glorified through Jesus Christ. To him belong glory and dominion for ever and ever. Amen.

<small>1 Pet 1:6f
Acts 5:41
Rom 8:17

2 Tim 2:12
Jas 1:2

Is 11:2
Ps 89:51f</small>

The Christian meaning of suffering

¹²Beloved, do not be surprised at the fiery ordeal which comes upon you to prove you, as though something strange were happening to you. ¹³But rejoice in so far as you share Christ's sufferings, that you may also rejoice and be glad when his glory is revealed. ¹⁴If you are reproached for the name of Christ, you are blessed,

---

building up of the whole body in charity (cf. Eph 4:16). From the reception of these charisms, even the most ordinary ones, there arises for each of the faithful the right and duty of exercising them in the Church and in the world for the good of men and the development of the Church" (*Apostolicam actuositatem*, 3).

4:12–19. St Peter now returns to the main theme of this part of the letter (3:13 4:19)—the trials Christians unjustly suffer on account of being followers of Christ (cf. 1:6–7; 2:18–25; 3:13–17). They should not be surprised or ashamed by this; rather, it should make them happy and lead them to glorify God, for if they share in Christ's suffering it means they will also share in his exaltation. St John of Avila wrote: "God wants to open our eyes and have us realize what favours are being done us in things the world regards as disadvantages, and how honoured we are to be scoffed at for seeking the honour of God, and what great reward awaits us for our present depression, and how God's gentle, sweet and loving arms are opened wide to receive those wounded in doing battle on his behalf" (*Letter*, 58).

Moreover, the "spirit of God" will rest on them (v. 14): our Lord promised the special assistance of the Holy Spirit to persecuted Christians hauled before courts on account of their faith (cf. Mt 10:19–20); St Peter here calls him "the spirit of glory", because his indwelling in the Christian is a guarantee and an anticipation of eternal glory (cf. 2 Cor 1:22).

Before the divine judgment which lies ahead (it is one of the frequent themes of the letter) no one can be complacent (vv. 17–18). The Apostle's severe warnings are reminiscent of those Jesus gave the women of Jerusalem on his way to Calvary: "if they do this when the wood is green, what will happen when it is dry?" (Lk 23:31). However, if one has suffered on Christ's account in this life it is clear that one can approach the judgment with greater confidence (cf. Mt 5:11–12; 10:32).

4:13. "To the prospect of the Kingdom of God," Pope John Paul II teaches, "is linked hope in that glory which has its beginning in the Cross of Christ. The Resurrection revealed this glory—eschatological glory—which in the Cross of Christ was completely obscured by the immensity of suffering. Those who share in the suffering of Christ are also called, through their own sufferings, to share *in glory*" (*Salvifici doloris*, 22).

because the spirit of glory[j] and of God rests upon you. ¹⁵But let none of you suffer as a murderer, or a thief, or a wrongdoer, or a mischief-maker; ¹⁶yet if one suffers as a Christian, let him not be ashamed, but under that name let him glorify God. ¹⁷For the time has come for judgment to begin with the household of God; and if it begins with us, what will be the end of those who do not obey the gospel of God? ¹⁸And

    "If the righteous man is scarcely saved,
    where will the impious and sinner appear?"

¹⁹Therefore let those who suffer according to God's will do right and entrust their souls to a faithful Creator.

Lk 10:6; Acts 5:41; 1 Pet 2:20
Acts 11:26; 26:28; Phil 1:20
Ezek 9:6; Jer 25:29; Lk 23:31; 1 Cor 11:32
2 Thess 1:8
Prov 11:31
Lk 23:46

4. FINAL EXHORTATIONS

To priests

5 ¹So I exhort the elders among you, as a fellow elder and a witness of the sufferings of Christ as well as a partaker in the glory that is to be revealed. ²Tend the flock of God that is your

Mt 17:5
Rom 8:17
2 Jn 1
Jn 21:16
Acts 20:28
Philem 14
Tit 1:7

4:16. This is one of the three places in the New Testament in which Christ's disciples are described as "Christians" (cf. Acts 11:26; 26:28). As St Luke explains in Acts, they were first given this name in Antioch, the capital of the Roman province of Syria (cf. Acts 11:26).

Being a Christian should never cause one to be cowed or ashamed; it should be a motive for gratitude to God and for holy pride: "Christians who become cowed or inhibited or envious in the face of the licentious behaviour of those who have not accepted the Word of God, show that they have a very poor idea of the faith. If we truly keep the law of Christ—that is, if we make the effort to do so, because we will not always fully succeed—we will find ourselves endowed with a wonderful gallantry of spirit that does not need to look elsewhere to discover the full meaning of human dignity" (St Josemaría Escrivá, *Friends of God*, 38).

5:1–4. In many New Testament texts, the Greek terms *presbýteros* and *epískopos* mean the same, being used indiscriminately to designate pastors of local communities (cf., e.g., Acts 11:30; 20:28; and notes on same). From the second century on, the terminology became fixed: *epískopoi* (bishops) have the fullness of the sacrament of Order and are responsible for local churches; *presbýteroi* (elders, later designated priests) carry out the priestly ministry as co-workers of the bishops. The Acts of the Apostles tell us that Paul and Barnabas ordained priests in the various churches of Asia Minor (cf. Acts 14:23), to which St Peter is now writing (1 Pet 1:1).

The leader of the apostles here addresses them formally. Although he refers to himself as one of them—a "fellow elder [priest]"—he is distinguishing himself as a witness of the sufferings of Christ and "a partaker in the glory that

---

j. Other ancient authorities insert *and of power*

1 Peter 5:3

2 Cor 1:24
Tit 2:7
Phil 3:17
1 Cor 9:25
Heb 13:20
1 Pet 2:25

charge,ᵏ not by constraint but willingly,ˡ not for shameful gain but eagerly, ³not as domineering over those in your charge but being examples to the flock. ⁴And when the chief Shepherd is manifested you will obtain the unfading crown of glory.

Prov 3:34; Jn 13:4, 14; Eph 5:21; Jas 4:6

To all the faithful

⁵Likewise you that are younger be subject to the elders. Clothe

---

is to be revealed" (this is possibly an allusion to the Transfiguration, at which he was given a foretaste of that glory: cf. Mt 17:1ff; 2 Pet 1:16–18).

St Peter's exhortations (vv. 2–3) recall those of our Lord when he spoke about the Good Shepherd (Jn 10:1ff) and when he told Peter after the Resurrection, "Feed my lambs.... Feed my sheep" (Jn 21:15–17). The Magisterium of the Church has often drawn inspiration from these words when reminding pastors of their duties: "As to the faithful, they (the priests) should bestow their paternal attention and solicitude on them, whom they have begotten spiritually through baptism and instruction (cf. 1 Cor 4:15; 1 Pet 1:23). Gladly constituting themselves models of the flock (cf. 1 Pet 5:3), they should preside over and serve their local community in such a way that it may deserve to be called by the name which is given to the unique People of God in its entirety, that is to say, the Church of God (cf. Cor 1:2; 2 Cor 1:21; and passim). They should be mindful that by their daily conduct and solicitude they display the reality of a truly priestly and pastoral ministry both to believers and unbelievers alike, to Catholics and non-Catholics; that they are bound to bear witness before all men of the truth and of the life, and as good shepherds seek after those too (cf. Lk 15:4–7) who, whilst having been baptized in the catholic Church, have given up the practice of the sacraments,

or even fallen away from the faith" (*Lumen gentium*, 28; cf. No. 41).

If they approach their responsibilities in this way, they will have no reason to fear the Judgment (v. 4); the Lord will make himself present to them as "the chief Shepherd", whom they have tried to imitate in their care of the flock, and they will receive "the unfading crown of glory" (cf. note on Jas 1:12). "When the moment comes for them to enter God's presence, Jesus will go out to meet them. He will glorify forever those who have acted on earth in his Person and in his name. He will shower them with that grace of which they have been ministers" (St Josemaría Escrivá, *In Love with the Church*, 50).

5:3. St Gregory the Great teaches that the pastor of souls "should always give the lead, to show by his example the way to life, so that his flock (who follow the voice and the actions of the pastor) are guided more by example than by words; his position obliges him to speak of elevated things, and also to manifest them personally; the word more easily gains access to the hearts of hearers when it carries with it the endorsement of the life of him who when giving instructions assists in their fulfilment by his own example" (*Regulae pastoralis*, 2, 3).

5:5–11. The apostle concludes his exhortation with a call to humility, which should express itself in complete docility

---

k. Other ancient authorities add *exercising the oversight* **l.** Other ancient authorities add *as God would have you*

yourselves, all of you, with humility toward one another, for "God opposes the proud, but gives grace to the humble."

⁶Humble yourselves therefore under the mighty hand of God, that in due time he may exalt you. ⁷Cast all your anxieties on him, for he cares about you. ⁸Be sober, be watchful. Your adversary the

Job 22:29
Ps 55:23
Mt 6:25

---

in the face of the trials God permits (vv. 6–7). This last piece of advice is often found in Scripture: "Cast your burden on the Lord, and he will sustain you" (Ps 55:22); Jesus also teaches that we should trust in God's fatherly providence (cf. Mt 6:19–34). "You have such care for each one of us", St Augustine exclaims, "as if you had no others to care for" (*Confessions*, 3, 11).

However, abandonment in God does not mean irresponsibility, so St Peter reminds them there is always need to be watchful against the assaults of the devil, who will pounce on us if we lower our guard (v. 8).

The description of the devil (etymologically the word means liar, detractor: cf. Rev 12:9–10) as a roaring lion seeking someone to devour has often been taken up by the saints. "He moves round each one of us", St Cyprian says, "like an enemy who has us surrounded and is checking the walls to see if there is some weak, unsecured part, where he can get in" (*De zelo et livore*).

Christians "firm in the faith" will resist the attacks of the devil. The trials they suffer (cf. 1:6–7; 4:13; 5:1–4) serve to purify them and are a pledge of the glory God will give them: "For this momentary affliction is preparing for us an eternal weight of glory beyond all comparisons" (2 Cor 4:17). "So great is the good that I hope for, that any pain is for me a pleasure" (St Francis of Assisi, *Reflections on Christ's Wounds*, 1).

5:5. "You who are younger": it is not clear whether he is addressing people who are young in age, or Christians who are not "elders" (priests), that is, lay people.

"God opposes the proud, but gives grace to the humble": a quotation from Proverbs (cf. Jas 4:6 and note on same), containing an idea which runs right through the Old Testament (cf., e.g., Job 12:19; Ps 18:88; 31:34) and the teachings of Christ (cf., e.g., Lk 14:11). The Blessed Virgin proclaims this truth in the *Magnificat*: "he has put down the mighty from their thrones, and exalted those of low degree" (Lk 1:52).

"Humility is the source and foundation of every kind of virtue," the Curé of Ars teaches; "it is the door by which all God-given graces enter; it is what seasons all our actions, making them so valuable and so pleasing to God. Finally, it makes us masters of God's heart, to the point, so to speak, of making him our servant; for God has never been able to resist a humble heart" (*Selected Sermons*, 10th Sunday after Pentecost).

5:8. For the third time, St Peter exhorts the faithful to be sober; earlier he referred to the importance of sobriety so as to put one's hope in heavenly things (1:13) and to help one to pray (4:7). Now he stresses that it puts us on guard against the devil.

Man should use the goods of this world in a balanced, temperate way, so as to avoid being ensnared by them, thereby forgetting his eternal destiny: "Detach yourself from the goods of the world. Love and practise poverty of spirit: be content with what enables you to live a simple and sober life. Otherwise, you will never be an apostle" (St Josemaría Escrivá, *The Way*, 631).

1 Peter 5:9

<small>1 Thess 5:6
Jas 4:7
Rev 5:5
Eph 6:11, 13

1 Thess 2:12</small>

devil prowls around like a roaring lion, seeking some one to devour. ⁹Resist him, firm in your faith, knowing that the same experience of suffering is required of your brotherhood throughout the world. ¹⁰And after you have suffered a little while, the God of all grace, who has called you to his eternal glory in Christ, will himself restore, establish, and strengthen*ᵐ* you. ¹¹To him be the dominion for ever and ever. Amen.

Words of farewell

<small>Acts 15:22–27
Heb 13:22

Acts 12:12
2 Jn 13</small>

¹²By Silvanus, a faithful brother as I regard him, I have written briefly to you, exhorting and declaring that this is the true grace of God; stand fast in it. ¹³She who is at Babylon,* who is likewise chosen, sends you greetings; and so does my son Mark. ¹⁴Greet one another with the kiss of love.
Peace to all of you that are in Christ.

5:12. Silvanus, called Silas in the Acts of the Apostles (Acts 15:22) accompanied St Paul on his second apostolic journey through Asia Minor and Greece (cf. Acts 15:36—18:22); he was therefore well known to the Christians addressed in this letter.

From the reference St Peter makes to him here, it is not possible to say for sure whether Silvanus was simply the bearer of the letter, or acted as an amanuensis who took down the apostle's dictation, or was an editor or redactor of ideas the apostle gave him (on this subject, see the Introduction to this letter).

5:13. "Babylon": this is a symbolic way of referring to Rome, the prototype of the idolatrous and worldly city of the era. Some centuries earlier Babylon had been the subject of severe reproaches and threats by the prophets (cf., e.g., Is 13:47; Jer 50–51). In the book of Revelation Rome is also referred to by this name (cf. e.g., Rev 17–18).

The Mark referred to is the author of the Second Gospel. Tradition says that he acted as St Peter's interpreter in Rome. The apostle calls him "son", meaning that he was spiritually his son, and implying that they had been close to each other for a long time.

5:14. "The kiss of love": St Paul also, at the end of some of his letters, refers to the "holy kiss" (cf. Rom 16:16; 1 Cor 16:20; 2 Cor 13:12; 1 Thess 5:26), a mark of supernatural charity and shared faith. With this meaning the gesture passed into primitive eucharistic liturgy (cf. note on 1 Cor 16:20).

The final words, "Peace to all of you that are in Christ", are similar to the way St Paul ends many of his letters; since the first age of the Church it has been used in liturgical celebrations. St Cyril of Jerusalem, for example, ends his baptismal catechism with these words: "May the God of peace hallow you entirely, and your body and your soul remain unsullied until the coming of our Lord Jesus Christ, to whom be glory for ever and ever. Amen" (*Mystagogical Catechesis*, 5, 23).

---

m. Other ancient authorities read *restore, establish, strengthen and settle*

Introduction to the Second Letter of St Peter

THE AUTHOR

At the start of the letter the writer introduces himself by his two names—Simon (in the original, Simeon, the Semitic form: cf. Acts 15:14) and Peter—adding reference to his vocation, "apostle of Jesus Christ". In the course of the letter he makes some allusions to himself: he was an eyewitness of the transfiguration of Jesus (cf. 1:16–18); this is the second time he is writing to his readers (cf. 3:1), a reference no doubt to 1 Peter; he calls St Paul "our beloved brother" (3:15); and he speaks about his death, possibly referring to Jesus' prophecy of his martyrdom (cf. Jn 21:18–19).

Despite this information, this is the New Testament text whose authenticity has been most debated. In the first two centuries Tradition provides no clear reference to St Peter being its author; from the third and fourth century onwards there are numerous testimonies to Petrine authorship, among them those of Clement of Alexandria (d. 214), according to Eusebius.[1] Towards the middle of the third century, Origen, who was aware of the doubts about the letter's authenticity, quotes 2 Peter 1:4 as words of St Peter;[2] and elsewhere he remarks that "Peter proclaims with the trumpets of his two epistles."[3] Dating from the same period is the testimony of Firmilian, bishop of Caesarea in Cappadocia, in his *Letter to Cyprian*.[4]

In his *Ecclesiastical History* Eusebius of Caesarea includes this letter among the "disputed" New Testament writings, that is, those not accepted by all, although accepted by most;[5] he himself did not regard it as canonical.[6] On the other hand, several fourth-century writers—including St Athanasius, St Basil, St Gregory Nazianzen, and Didymus of Alexandria—made use of it in their works.

What St Jerome has to say is particularly interesting. On the one hand, he mentions doubts about its Petrine authorship and the reasons for those doubts: Peter "wrote two epistles which are called 'catholic', the second of which many say is not his, because of the difference in style from the first."[7] At another point he offers a solution to this difficulty: "The two epistles which bear Peter's name differ from one another in both style and character. From which we conclude that, in accordance with his needs, he used different secretaries."[8]

---

1. Cf. *Ecclesiastical History*, 6, 14, 1.   **2.** Cf. *In Lev. hom.*, 6, 4.   **3.** *In Iesu nave*, 7, 1.   **4.** Cf. 75, 6.
5. Cf. *Ecclesiastical History*, 3, 25, 3.   **6.** Cf. ibid., 3, 3, 1.   **7.** *On Famous Men*, 1.   **8.** *Epist. ad Hedibiam*, 120, 11.

Introduction to the Second Letter of St Peter

The main difficulties about attributing the letter to St Peter come from study of the text itself. The vocabulary and style are noticeably different from those in the First Letter of St Peter, with expressions that seem better suited to a later period; there is the mention of the apostles and "fathers";[9] the letter's view of the second coming of Christ seems to be different;[10] St Paul's letters are, in 2 Peter, already regarded as Scripture (cf. 3:15–16); finally, the letter seems to have been written after the Letter of St Jude, from which it seems to quote.

These difficulties do not rule out St Peter as the author. In fact, there are also notable similarities between the letter and 1 Peter[11] and also between it and the discourses of Peter recorded in Acts.[12] For this reason some Catholic authors suggest that 2 Peter was written in Rome, around the year 64 or 67, shortly before the apostle was martyred.

It is also possible that an anonymous disciple of St Peter, under the inspiration of the Holy Spirit, chose to pass on certain teachings which were in line with those of the apostle. By using Peter's name and authority, he would be resorting to a device common at the time (pseudonymous writing), well aware that the ideas he was giving were not his own but those of the apostle Peter. In this case, the redactor would not be trying to usurp St Peter's name but rather to acknowledge the paternity of ideas contained in the letter.

If the letter was in fact written pseudonymously, it could date from around the years 80–90. However, there are insufficient grounds for dating the letter well into the second century, as some have tried to do.

As far as its being an inspired and therefore canonical letter is concerned, it is of secondary importance whether it was written by St Peter or by an anonymous disciple of his. The letter appears in the earliest lists of canonical books, such as those of the Council of Laodicea (360), Hippo (393), the third and fourth Councils of Carthage (397 and 419) and the letter of Pope Innocent I (405). The Council of Trent issued a declaration to the effect that this letter and the other texts of the Bible are inspired.[13]

IMMEDIATE READERSHIP

As it says in its opening words, this letter is addressed "to those who have obtained a faith of equal standing with ours" (2 Pet 1:1), that is, Christians in general. Some expressions suggest that the immediate addressees may have been the Christian community of Greece or Asia Minor. For example, we know for a fact that St Paul also wrote to those Christians (cf. 3:15–16);

---

9. Cf. 2 Pet 3:2–4 and notes on same. **10.** Cf. 2 Pet 3:1–10 and notes on same. **11.** Cf., e.g., 1 Pet 1:7–9 and 2 Pet 3:1–10; 1 Pet 1:10–12 and 2 Pet 1:19–21; 1 Pet 22 and 2 Pet 1:12; 1 Pet 3:20 and 2 Pet 2:5. **12.** Cf. Acts 2:14ff; 3:11ff; 5:29ff; 10:34ff. **13.** Cf. *De libris sacris*.

besides, one gets the impression that the writer knows them personally (cf. 1:12–16) and that they were the same persons as those to whom he wrote the First Letter (cf. 3:1). Although originally addressed to particular groups of the faithful, the general tone of the letter shows that the sacred writer had in mind Christians in general.

It is not easy to say where the letter was written. If it was written by St Peter, he must have written it from Rome, where he was living. If it was by a disciple, it could have been written from Rome or else from somewhere in Asia Minor or Egypt. We do not have enough information to be sure.

LINKS BETWEEN 2 PETER AND THE LETTER OF ST JUDE

When 2 Peter and Jude are compared, one immediately notices similarities in the way the ideas are developed: even the wording is the same at times. Specifically, between 2 Peter 2:1–3:3 and Jude 4–18 the parallels are such that the only explanation seems to be that the two texts are linked in some way.

The most likely answer is that 2 Peter is dependent on Jude. Thus, it tends to explain and paraphrase ideas which appear in a much more concise form in Jude; it omits allusions or quotations from Jewish apocryphal writings (especially the *Book of Enoch*) which appear in Jude, and logically the letter which omits these would be the later one; the text of 2 Peter is more elaborate: for example, when it refers to the punishment inflicted by God (cf. 2:4–8) it keeps to a chronological order (angels, the Flood, Sodom), whereas in the parallel passage in Jude (cf. Jud 5–7) that is not the case (his order is: Israelites in the wilderness, angels, Sodom).

These and other little things suggest that the author of this letter was familiar with that of Jude.

CONTENT

The epistle has a fairly clear structure. It begins with a greeting similar to that in other New Testament writings (1:1–2) and ends with an exhortation to perseverance (3:17–18). The body of the letter has three distinct parts: the *first part* (1:3–21) is an appeal for fidelity to teaching received; the *second part* (2:1–22) is a long denunciation of false teachers, immoral people who try to corrupt others; the *third part* (3:1–16) deals with the second coming of Christ; it refutes false views and expounds the true teaching.

From the doctrinal point of view, we might point particularly to what it has to say about the Parousia, its refutation of erroneous theories on that subject, and consequent exhortation.

Introduction to the Second Letter of St Peter

THE FINAL COMING OF THE LORD

The main doctrinal point controverted by the false teachers was the Parousia of the Lord (cf. 3:3–4). This is a subject which comes up often in the New Testament, particularly in the First Letter of St Peter, where the apostle bases his appeal for fidelity in the midst of trials on hope of the next life. The author of 2 Peter faces right into this subject, first, making it quite clear that the Lord will come; and he takes issue with the arguments put forward by the false teachers.

His unequivocal teaching about the coming of Christ at the end of time is based firstly on the episode of the Transfiguration, which was an anticipation of Christ's glorious manifestation (cf. 1:16–18); also, the word of the prophets and of the Old Testament in general confirms this truth (cf. 1:19), because their constant teaching is that God will reward the good and punish the wicked.

One of the false teachers' arguments was that the Parousia was too long in coming. Without going into the ins and outs of this subject, the sacred writer clearly teaches that time is something very relative from the point of view of the eternity of God, for whom "one day is as a thousand years" (3:8), and if God puts off the final moment he does so in his mercy, "not wishing that any should perish" (3:9). One thing is clear: they must remain watchful, for the Day of the Lord will come without warning (cf. 3:10).

Another of their objections was that so much time had gone by and there was as yet no sign of the natural phenomena which were meant to herald the total change the end would bring (cf. 3:3–4). The sacred writer reproaches them for their lack of faith: God created the world by his word alone and in the same way brought about the punishment of the Flood, which involved vast ecological changes (cf. 3:5–6). Therefore, we must believe that it will be his word too that will cause all creation to undergo the profound change which will bring about "new heavens and a new earth" (cf. 3:7, 10, 12, 13).

As regards the specific form the glorious coming of Christ will take and the details of same, the letter contains expressions which are difficult to interpret. It is possible that the sacred writer is using obscure language (as our Lord himself did: cf. Mt 24:36ff and par.) to encourage the faithful to be vigilant, and also to underline the sublimity of this mysterious design of God's.

That Jesus Christ will come in glory to judge the living and the dead has formed part of the Church's creed from the very beginning and was solemnly defined as a dogma of faith by Benedict XII in the constitution *Benedictus Deus* (AD 1336).

THE FALSE TEACHERS

In chapter 2 the sacred writer describes false teachers as men who are greedy (cf. 2:3, 14), dissipated (cf. 2:13), blinded by passion (cf. 2:10, 14, 18), and

Introduction to the Second Letter of St Peter

seducers (cf. 2:14, 18, 19). In chapter 3 he emphasizes, rather, their doctrinal errors: they are scoffers who do not believe in the second coming of Jesus Christ (cf. 3:3–4). By their evil conduct and their false theories they deny the Lord (cf. 2:1) and lead many to perdition (cf. 2:14, 18, 19).

There is no reason to think that the author is taking issue with organized heresy (as some have suggested, to support the theory that this is a text written much later on). Scarcely any details are given about these heresies, whereas St John, for example, does give details in his letters.[14]

The author is mainly concerned to forewarn Christians and thereby draw them away from the moral depravity of the false teachers.

MORAL CONDUCT

In view of the loose morality being promoted by the false teachers, the sacred writer stresses fidelity to the teaching they have received (cf. 1:2, 3, 8; 2:20, 21; 3:18) and perseverance in virtue (cf. 1:5–7; 2:21; 3:11, 14).

At the beginning of the letter (cf. 1:5–7) he gives a list of virtues.[15] This is not meant to cover all Christian morality; it is simply a short, practical survey. Faith, the beginning of the Christian life, is listed first; charity, its climax, comes at the end; and six other inter-connected virtues are listed, like links in the one chain.

Throughout the letter there is much emphasis on motives: on the one hand, the Christian calling (cf. 1:3, 10) and the initiative of God, who gives us promises and a share in his divine nature (cf. 1:4), require us to respond by growing in virtue and avoiding the sins of the past (1:9); on the other hand, the goal that lies ahead (access to the eternal Kingdom of the Lord: cf. 1:11) should encourage us to persevere in good living. If we remember the prophecy of the coming of Christ we will remain vigilant at all times (cf. 1:12–21) and persevere in godliness (cf. 3:11), for we do not know when that time will come (cf. 3:10).

---

14. Cf. "Introduction to the First Letter of St John", below. **15.** Similar lists appear elsewhere in the New Testament (cf., e.g., Rom 5:3; Gal 5:22–23; Rev 2:19).

THE SECOND LETTER OF PETER

The Revised Standard Version, with notes

2 Peter 1:3

1 ¹Simon Peter, a servant and apostle of Jesus Christ,   Acts 15:14
To those who have obtained a faith of equal standing with ours in the righteousness of our God and Saviour Jesus Christ:[a]

²May grace and peace be multiplied to you in the knowledge of   Jude 2
God and of Jesus our Lord.

1. A CALL TO FIDELITY

Divine largesse

³His divine power has granted to us all things that pertain to life   1 Pet 2:9
and godliness, through the knowledge of him who called us to[b] his   2 Cor 4:4, 6

1:1–2. As in other New Testament writings and in ordinary letters of the time, the opening greeting gives the name of the sender, that of the addressees and the greeting as such.

"Simon": the original Greek text says "Simeon", using the Hebrew form of the same name (cf. Acts 15:14). To this he adds that of "Peter", the name the Lord gave him when he promised to make him the head of the apostles (cf. Jn 1:42).

The original addressees of the letter may have been the faithful of the communities of Greece or Asia Minor (cf. the Introduction).

The greeting contains two words frequently used in this setting—"grace and peace" (cf. 1 Pet 1:2 and note)—which sum up the benefits the Christian has received. The true "knowledge of God and of Jesus" is a frequent point of reference in the letter (cf. 1:1, 8; 2:20; 3:18). It is not just intellectual knowledge, but rather the knowledge that comes from familiarity with the Lord and conduct consistent with the faith (cf. 1:5–7). The author emphasizes this point from the very start, because he wants to forestall the influence of false teachings which undermine the faith.

"The righteousness of our God and Saviour Jesus Christ": this may be a reference to God the Father *and* Jesus; but, given that the Greek text uses only one definite article, it is probably a title of Jesus Christ, whom he calls "God and Saviour", in the same way as elsewhere he describes him as "Lord and Saviour" (1:11; 2:20; 3:2, 18). Thus, the divinity of Jesus Christ, which is often proclaimed in the New Testament, is openly acknowledged at the very start of the letter.

1:3–21. The first part of the letter is an appeal for steadfastness and for growth in Christian life. Firstly, Peter encourages his readers to pursue virtue; the reasoning he uses is both simple and profound (vv. 3–11): by his power, God has chosen the apostles and conferred on them wonderful graces in which all the faithful share (vv. 3–4); they must respond to this divine initiative by practising virtue so as to reach the goal and fullness to which the Christian is called (vv. 5–11).

He goes on (vv. 12–21) to remind them that hope in our Lord's second coming is something well founded, something that belongs to the deposit of faith: the transfiguration of our Lord was a foretaste of

---

a. Or *of our God and the Saviour Jesus Christ*   **b.** Or *by*

own glory and excellence, ⁴by which he has granted to us his precious and very great promises, that through these you may escape from the corruption that is in the world because of passion, and become partakers of the divine nature.*

Christian virtues

Gal 5:6
1 Thess 4:9

⁵For this very reason make every effort to supplement your faith with virtue, and virtue with knowledge, ⁶and knowledge with self-

---

his final coming (vv. 16–18); it was something foretold in many prophecies and no one has the right to argue against it (vv. 19–21). Therefore, the final coming of the Lord is something quite certain and helps to keep our hope alive.

1:3–4. In these verses the same pronoun is repeated three times: "granted to *us*", "called *us*", "granted to *us*"; although he may mean all Christians, it is more likely that he is referring only to the apostles.

The basis of Christian morality and of the practice of virtue (vv. 5–9) is God's initiative in calling the apostles (v. 3) and endowing them with graces (promises) sufficient to make all Christians "partakers of the divine nature".

"His divine power": usually in the Bible calling is attributed to God the Father (cf., e.g., 1 Pet 1:15; 2:9; 5:10); by emphasizing here that it is Jesus Christ who calls "by his own glory and excellence", the author is clearly acknowledging Jesus as God.

"His precious and very great promises": the promises made in the Old Testament, especially those to do with the coming of the Messiah and Saviour. Jesus Christ brought about the Redemption, whereby all men have access to the supernatural good things of which the prophets spoke.

"Partakers of the divine nature": this succinct phrase sums up the fruits that the good things (especially grace) produce in Christians. This sharing in God's own life is both the beginning and the final goal of Christian life. It is the beginning insofar as it is incorporation in Christ through Baptism, and brings with it (through grace and adoptive divine filiation) a sharing in God's own life. It is the final goal of the Christian life since this participation attains its fullness and enduring perfection in heaven, with the contemplation of God "as he is" (1 Jn 3:2 and note on same).

Of course, already in this life the Blessed Trinity dwells in the soul in grace (cf., e.g., Jn 14:17–23; 1 Cor 3:16; 6:19; and notes on same). "Our faith teaches us that man, in the state of grace, is divinized —filled with God" (St Josemaría Escrivá, *Christ Is Passing By*, 103).

Partaking of the divine nature is a basic feature of the Christian vocation. Pope Pius XII reminds us of this marvellous fact, which is closely linked to the mystery of the Incarnation: "If the Word 'emptied himself, taking the form of a servant' (Phil 2:7), he did so in order that his brethren according to the flesh might be made partakers of the divine nature (cf. 2 Pet 1:4), both during this earthly exile by sanctifying grace and in the heavenly home by the possession of eternal beatitude. For this reason the Only-begotten of the Father chose to become a son of man, that we might be made conformable to the image of the Son of God (cf. Rom 8:29) and be renewed according to the likeness of him who created us (cf. Col 3:10)" (*Mystici Corporis*, 20).

control, and self-control with steadfastness, and steadfastness with godliness, ⁷and godliness with brotherly affection, and brotherly affection with love. ⁸For if these things are yours and abound, they keep you from being ineffective or unfruitful in the knowledge of our Lord Jesus Christ. ⁹For whoever lacks these things is blind and shortsighted and has forgotten that he was cleansed from his old sins. ¹⁰Therefore, brethren, be the more zealous to confirm your call and election, for if you do this you will never fall; ¹¹so there will be richly provided for you an entrance into the eternal kingdom of our Lord and Saviour Jesus Christ.

Gal 6:10

1 Jn 2:9, 11

1 Thess 1:4

Jn 3:5f

On this subject, see also the notes on Rom 8:14–15 and Gal 4:6.

1:5–9. Lists of Christian virtues are also to be found in other parts of the New Testament (cf., e.g., Gal 5:22–23; 1 Tim 6:11; Rev 2:19). This passage provides a list which is well conceived from a pedagogical point of view—simple to remember, because each virtue is linked with the one before it; and the emphasis is on faith and charity, which mark the beginning and end of the list. St Ignatius of Antioch commented on the value of these two theological virtues: "Given an unswerving faith and love for Jesus Christ, there is nothing in all this that will not be obvious to you; for life begins and ends with those two qualities. Faith is the beginning, and love is the end; and the two together lead to God. All that makes for a soul's perfection follows in their train, for nobody who professes faith will commit sin, and nobody who possesses love can feel hatred" (*Letter to the Ephesians*, 14, 1–2).

For Christians, virtues are not an end in themselves but a means necessary for attaining knowledge of Christ (cf. note on 1:1); but union with the Lord calls for works, and if we failed to practise virtues we could not see Christ (v. 9). St Teresa of Avila constantly stresses the need to combine contemplation and action: "I repeat that if you have this in view you must not build upon foundations of prayer and contemplation alone, for, unless you strive after the virtues and practise them, you will never grow to be more than dwarfs. God grant that nothing worse than this may happen—for, as you know, anyone who fails to go forward begins to go back" (*Interior Castle*, 8, 4,9).

1:10–11. Practice of the virtues not only assures one's vocation and election; it is essential for attaining entry to the eternal kingdom. Holy Scripture teaches that the ultimate prize is a gift from God; it conveys this idea by saying "there will be richly provided for you an entrance", which shows that it is God who bestows the prize—but he counts on man's free response. The Council of Trent solemnly taught that "eternal life should be set before those who persevere in good works to the end (cf. Mt 10:22) and who hope in God. It should be set before them as being the grace that God, through Jesus Christ, has mercifully promised his children, and 'as the reward' which, as God himself promised, must assuredly be given them for their good works and merits" (*De iustificatione*, 16).

"Lord and Saviour Jesus Christ": this expression, which occurs only in this letter (cf. 2:20; 3:2, 18), has become part of Christian tradition, because it is a

2 Peter 1:12

Spiritual testimony

Jude 5
2 Cor 5:1

Jn 21:18, 19

¹²Therefore I intend always to remind you of these things, though you know them and are established in the truth that you have. ¹³I think it right, as long as I am in this body,[c] to arouse you by way of reminder, ¹⁴since I know that the putting off of my body[c] will be soon, as our Lord Jesus Christ showed me. ¹⁵And I will see to it that after my departure you may be able at any time to recall these things.

Mt 17:1–8
Mk 9:2–8
Lk 9:28–35
Jn 1:14

The Transfiguration, an earnest of the Second Coming

¹⁶For we did not follow cleverly devised myths when we made known to you the power and coming of our Lord Jesus Christ, but we were eyewitnesses of his majesty.* ¹⁷For when he received honour and glory from God the Father and the voice was borne to him by the Majestic Glory, "This is my beloved Son,[d] with whom

---

perfect summary of faith in Jesus as God and Redeemer. It acknowledges who Jesus Christ is and what he has achieved.

1:12–15. This passage summarizes the purpose of the letter—to remind people about Christian truths and to encourage them to practise virtue.

The sacred author is moved to write by his apostolic zeal and the fact that he is soon to die. Both reasons accurately reflect the personality and spirit of St Peter the apostle.

As far as his foreknowledge of his death is concerned, we do not have much to go on: what he says may be a reference to what our Lord told him (cf. Jn 21:18ff); or it may refer to a later revelation, which certain traditions about the apostle's martyrdom report (for example, that of *Quo vadis?* given in an apocryphal book, *Acts of St Peter*, chap. 35).

The image of the tent ("body": v. 13; cf. Is 38:12) is very expressive of the ephemeral character of man's life on earth. St Paul also uses it (cf. 2 Cor 5:1 and note).

The letter is a kind of spiritual testimony (v. 15); hence its warning about staying true to the faith is a particularly solemn one.

1:16–18. The transfiguration of Jesus Christ, at which the voice of God the Father was heard (vv. 16–18), and the testimony of the Old Testament prophets (vv. 19–21) are a guarantee of the doctrine of Christ's second coming.

"The power and coming of our Lord Jesus Christ": this phrase sums up the purpose of apostolic preaching: "power" indicates that Jesus Christ is God and is almighty like the Father; the "coming" (literally "Parousia") means the same as his manifestation in glory at the end of time. This is not a matter of "myth"; it will be as real as his sojourn on this earth, of which the apostles are "eyewitnesses". When speaking of the Transfiguration, the sacred writer refers to the "majesty" of Jesus Christ (an attribute which he always possesses, because he is God) and the "voice" of the Father confirming Christ's divine nature (cf. Mt 17:5). The

---

c. Greek *tent* **d.** Or *my son, my* (or *the*) *Beloved*

I am well pleased," ¹⁸we heard this voice borne from heaven, for we were with him on the holy mountain.

Prophecy and the Second Coming
¹⁹And we have the prophetic word made more sure. You will do well to pay attention to this as to a lamp shining in a dark place, until the day dawns and the morning star rises in your hearts. ²⁰First of all you must understand this, that no prophecy of

Rev 2:28
Lk 1:78

simple line of argument is that if Jesus Christ allowed his divinity to be glimpsed just for a moment, he will also be able to manifest it in its fullness and forever at the end of time.

"On the holy mountain": this wording indicates that he is referring to the transfiguration and not to the baptism of our Lord (Mt 3:16–17). The mountain is described as "holy" because a theophany occurred there; similarly, in the Old Testament Zion is called a "holy mountain" because God revealed himself there (cf. Ps 2:6; Is 11:9).

1:19–21. "The prophetic word" finds its complete fulfilment in Jesus Christ (cf. Heb 1:1). This does not refer to a particular prophecy; at that time "the prophetic word" meant the messianic prophecies or (more usually) all the Old Testament insofar as it proclaims the enduring salvation to come.

These verses encapsulate the whole notion of biblical prophecy—its value, interpretation and divine origin. They also show the close connexion between the Old and the New Testaments. "The books of the Old Testament, all of them caught up into the Gospel message, attain and show forth their full meaning in the New Testament (cf. Mt 5:17; Lk 24:27; Rom 16:25–26; 2 Cor 3:14–16) and, in their turn, shed light on it and explain it" (Vatican II, *Dei Verbum*, 16).

By reaching their fulfilment in Jesus Christ, the Old Testament prophecies confirm the truthfulness of what Jesus said and did. Together with the Transfiguration they constitute a guarantee of the second coming of the Lord.

The comparison of prophecy to the morning star is a very good one, for that star is designed to bring light and announce the coming of day. Similarly, the fullness of Revelation which begins with the earthly life of Christ will reach its climax when he comes in glory.

1:20. Prophecy and Holy Scripture in general are not man-made; they are the word of God: there is nothing in the Bible that is not inspired by the Holy Spirit (v. 21). Therefore, against the false teachers of his time and of all eras, the sacred writer rejects any interpretation of Scripture based exclusively on human ingenuity; as the Second Vatican Council reminds us, it is "the Church which exercises the divinely conferred commission and ministry of watching over and interpreting the Word of God" (*Dei Verbum*, 12).

These words repeat the teaching of the Council of Trent: "No one should dare to rely on his own judgment in matters of faith and morals […] to distort Holy Scripture to fit meanings of his own that are contrary to the meaning that holy Mother Church has held and now holds; for it is her office to decide on the true sense and interpretation of Holy Scripture" (*De libris sacris*; cf. Vatican I, *Dei Filius*, chap. 2).

2 Peter 1:21

2 Tim 3:16
Acts 3:21

scripture is a matter of one's own interpretation, ²¹because no prophecy ever came by the impulse of man, but men moved by the Holy Spirit spoke from God.ᵉ

2. FALSE TEACHERS DENOUNCED

Deut 13:2–6
Mt 24:24
1 Thess 4:1
Jude 4

The harm done by false teachers

2 ¹But false prophets also arose among the people, just as there will be false teachers among you, who will secretly bring in destructive heresies, even denying the Master who bought them,

---

1:21. This verse makes it clear that there is such a thing as biblical interpretation (cf. 2 Tim 3:13ff), and it specifies what it is. Scripture has been written under the inspiration of the Holy Spirit; God and the human author are involved in the writing of the sacred books in such a way that the end-product is, at one and the same time, entirely of God's making and entirely of man's.

"Holy Mother Church, relying on the faith of the apostolic age, accepts as sacred and canonical the books of the Old and the New Testaments, whole and entire, with all their parts, on the grounds that, written under the inspiration of the Holy Spirit (cf. Jn 20:31; 2 Tim 3:16; 2 Pet 1:19–21; 3:15–16), they have God as their author, and have been handed on as such to the Church herself. To compose the sacred books, God chose certain men who, all the while he employed them in this task, made full use of their powers and faculties so that, although he acted in them and by them, it was as true authors that they consigned to writing whatever he wanted written, and no more" (*Dei Verbum*, 11).

2:1–22. The sacred writer wants to expose the false teachers who are doing such damage among the Christians to whom he is writing. Before refuting their basic error (denying the Parousia), he denounces their immoral conduct, particularly their greed (vv. 3, 14) and impurity.

The section begins by pointing out how evil the actions of these imposters are (vv. 1–3). He warns that eternal punishment awaits them (vv. 4–10); goes on to describe their corrupt conduct (vv. 10–19); and points out how seriously wrong it is for people who have become Christians to revert to their former life of sin (vv. 20–22).

The outspoken description of the false teachers, and the references to the punishment they will receive, must have made an impression on the original recipients of the letter and led them to distance themselves from the false teachers.

The parallel passage in the Letter of St Jude (vv. 4–16), from which the author of this letter seems to have drawn inspiration (cf. Introduction) fills out and illustrates the teaching contained in this chapter.

2:1–3. The Old Testament contains a good deal of warning and criticism of the false teachers who were sowing confusion among the people of Israel (cf., e.g., Deut 13:2–6; Jer 14:13–16; Ezek 13:1ff). Here similar warnings are given about people at work in the Christian communities;

e. Other authorities read *moved by the Holy Spirit holy men of God spoke*

bringing upon themselves swift destruction. ²And many will follow their licentiousness, and because of them the way of truth will be reviled. ³And in their greed they will exploit you with false words; from of old their condemnation has not been idle, and their destruction has not been asleep.*

Is 52:5
Acts 9:2

Rom 16:18
1 Thess 2:5

The punishment that awaits them
⁴For if God did not spare the angels when they sinned, but cast them into hell[f] and committed them to pits of nether gloom to be

Gen 6:1–4
Mt 8:29
Jude 6

---

although the warning concerns events in the future (it is somewhat reminiscent of our Lord's prophecies about his coming again: cf. Mt 24:11), it is quite clear from things in the rest of the letter (cf. 2:12ff) that the false teachers were already at work. From the tone of these verses, it seems that they were Christians who had gone astray but still formed part of the community of the faithful.

The sacred writer bemoans the terrible damage they are doing: their bad example is leading many astray (St Jude says in the parallel passage that "they pervert the grace of our God into licentiousness": v. 4) and doing great harm to the Church by giving it a bad name: the "way of truth will be reviled" (literally: "blasphemed").

"The way of truth" (v. 2): as in Acts this word "way" is used to refer to the Christian way of life or the Gospel itself (cf. note on Acts 9:3).

2:4–10. To depict the eternal punishment awaiting the false teachers, he uses three well known biblical examples—the rebellious angels, the Flood, and the destruction of Sodom and Gomorrah. In the parallel passage in St Jude (vv. 5–10), instead of the Flood the example given is the punishment of the rebellious Israelites in the desert. Given that the examples here are more detailed and are in a chronological order, commentators think that this letter is the later one (cf. Introduction).

Another feature of this passage is the stress it puts on the salvation of the godly (along with the punishment that awaits the wicked)—Noah in the midst of a perverse generation, and Lot, all alone in a wicked world. The Lord will judge each according to his merits.

2:4. Holy Scripture does not explain what kind of sin was committed by the angels who were cast into hell. Many saints (including St Augustine and St Thomas Aquinas) think it was a sin of pride. Christian religious instruction usually explains it in this way: "the angels were not all faithful to God; many of them through pride claimed to be equal to him and independent of him, and for this sin they were forever shut out from heaven and condemned to hell" (*St Pius X Catechism*, 39).

"Hell": the original has *tartarus*, the name given in Greek mythology to the place of torment kept for the enemies of the gods. "Pits of nether gloom": the Gospel also speaks of darkness when referring to the horrors of hell (cf. Mt 22:13; 25:30).

The fact that the angels were condemned should serve as a severe warning: even though they were privileged creatures they did not escape punishment. The nature of the punishment helps to show how evil sin is.

---

f. Greek *Tartarus*

2 Peter 2:5

Gen 8:18
1 Pet 3:6
Gen 19:24f
Jude 7
Gen 19:6f
Ezek 9:4
1 Cor 10:13
Jude 6
Rev 3:10
Jude 7, 8, 16

kept until the judgment; ⁵if he did not spare the ancient world, but preserved Noah, a herald of righteousness, with seven other persons, when he brought a flood upon the world of the ungodly; ⁶if by turning the cities of Sodom and Gomorrah to ashes he condemned them to extinction and made them an example to those who were to be ungodly; ⁷and if he rescued righteous Lot, greatly distressed by the licentiousness of the wicked ⁸(for by what that righteous man saw and heard as he lived among them, he was vexed in his righteous soul day after day with their lawless deeds), ⁹then the Lord knows how to rescue the godly from trial, and to keep the unrighteous under punishment until the day of judgment, ¹⁰and especially those who indulge in the lust of defiling passion and despise authority.

2:5. "A herald of righteousness": the Old Testament describes Noah as "righteous" (Gen 6:9); perhaps that is how the sacred writer deduces that he preached righteousness by his word and example. He may be evoking certain Jewish traditions (mentioned by Flavius Josephus) to the effect that, prior to the Flood, the patriarch preached to his contemporaries to try to convert them.

2:6–10. The destruction of Sodom and Gomorrah, cities proverbial for vice, is *the* biblical example of divine punishment of sinners; our Lord often reminded people about it (cf., e.g., Mt 10:15; 11:23–24; Lk 17:26–29). Despite harrassment, Lot stayed true to God in the midst of the corruption all round him (cf. Gen 18–19); that was why God saved him and his family when the two cities were wiped out. Similarly, when the Day of Judgment comes, God will save the godly and punish the ungodly. By mentioning Lot, the sacred writer seems to be saying that the ancient punishment is not just a warning to the wicked; it also helps the godly to persevere doing good, even in a hostile environment.

Apparently the main sin of the false teachers and the one to which the faithful were being drawn was that of lust (v. 10), as was the case in Sodom and Gomorrah. This vice so clouds the mind that a person who becomes steeped in it ends up despising the "authority" of the Lord (literally, "lordship": cf. notes on Jude 8–10).

"Do not forget," St Josemaría Escrivá writes, "that when someone is corrupted by the concupiscence of the flesh he cannot make any spiritual progress. He cannot do good works. He is a cripple, cast aside like an old rag. Have you ever seen patients suffering from progressive paralysis and unable to help themselves or get up? Sometimes they cannot even move their heads. Well, in the supernatural order, the same thing happens to people who are not humble and have made a cowardly surrender to lust. They don't see, or hear, or understand anything. They are paralysed. They are like people gone mad. Each of us here ought to invoke our Lord, and his Blessed Mother, and pray that he will grant us humility and a determination to avail devoutly of the divine remedy of confession" (*Friends of God*, 181).

2:10–19. Without mincing his words, the sacred writer describes the perverse behaviour of the false prophets: they are arrogant and blasphemous (vv. 10–13); their lives are more suited to animals, for they let themselves be led by their passions, particularly lust and greed (vv. 13–16); despite their claims, they have no teaching

Their arrogance and immorality
Bold and wilful, they are not afraid to revile the glorious ones, [11]whereas angels, though greater in might and power, do not pronounce a reviling judgment upon them before the Lord. [12]But these, like irrational animals, creatures of instinct, born to be caught and killed, reviling in matters of which they are ignorant, will be destroyed in the same destruction with them, [13]suffering wrong for their wrongdoing. They count it pleasure to revel in the daytime. They are blots and blemishes, revelling in their dissipation,[g] carousing with you. [14]They have eyes full of adultery,

Jude 9

Ps 49:13
Jude 10

Jude 12

---

to offer (v. 17); with false promises of liberation they are leading the recent converts astray (vv. 18–19).

The parallel passage in St Jude (vv. 8–16) clarifies the meaning of some expressions here.

2:10–13. In their arrogance, these ungodly people "are not afraid to revile the glorious ones" (literally, "the glories", that is, the angels). It is not easy to say whether this is a reference to the angelic world in general or (as most commentators in fact think) to the fallen angels. In any event, it is clear that, blinded as they are by their pride, they are blaspheming creatures who are on a higher plane than they; the arrogance is all the greater when not even the angels themselves dare to revile the demons.

Nor can we say what form this blasphemy took: they may have been underestimating the power of the demons, judging them incapable of harming them —which would mean they felt they could continue their depraved lifestyle. Or they may have been invoking the fallen angels as patrons of their vices (cf. note on parallel passage in Jude: vv. 8–10).

2:13–16. Because these men were motivated exclusively by greed and a desire for sensual pleasure, they were really living like animals; their degraded conduct, which is denounced here very vigorously, should serve as a warning, because the same thing can happen to people who let their passions get the better of them.

God inspired Balaam to bless the people of Israel on a number of occasions (cf. Num 22–24) but Balaam later led the Israelites into idolatry and fornication (cf. Num 31:16; Rev 2:14). In Jewish tradition he is the epitome of an evil and avaricious person; which is why the sacred writer refers to him when describing the greed and seductiveness of the false teachers. In the corresponding passage of St Jude (v. 11) Cain and Korah are also referred to (cf. note on Jude 11).

2:13–14. "Revelling in their dissipation [love feasts], carousing with you" (v. 13): from the letter of St Jude (v. 12) we can deduce that the false preachers used these occasions to indulge their greed and spread their errors. Intemperance (greed and lust, mainly) had made them slaves to their passions, unable to seek anything but sensual pleasure.

Christians should never let temporal things cloud their wisdom if they want to have a supernatural approach to life. Speaking of the value of the virtue of purity, the Church stresses "that everyone should have a high esteem for the virtue of chastity, its beauty and its power of attraction. This virtue increases the human person's dignity and enables him to love truly, disinterestedly, unselfishly and with

---

g. Other ancient authorities read *love feasts*

2 Peter 2:15

Num 22:5
Jude 11
Rev 2:14

Num 22:28f

Jude 12, 13
Jude 16

insatiable for sin. They entice unsteady souls. They have hearts trained in greed. Accursed children! ¹⁵Forsaking the right way they have gone astray; they have followed the way of Balaam, the son of Beor, who loved gain from wrongdoing, ¹⁶but was rebuked for his own transgression; a dumb ass spoke with human voice and restrained the prophet's madness.

¹⁷These are waterless springs and mists driven by a storm; for them the nether gloom of darkness has been reserved. ¹⁸For, uttering

---

respect for others" (SCDF, *Declaration on Sexual Ethics*, 1). And, referring to the means to achieve this, it goes on to say: "the faithful of the present time, and indeed today more than ever, must use the means which have always been recommended by the Church for living a chaste life. These means are: discipline of the senses and the mind, watchfulness and prudence in avoiding occasions of sin, the observance of modesty, moderation in recreation, wholesome pursuits, assiduous prayer and frequent reception of the sacraments of Penance and the Eucharist. Young people especially should earnestly foster devotion to the Immaculate Mother of God" (ibid.).

2:17. The deceitfulness, emptiness and barrenness of these people's conduct is illustrated by two images ("waterless springs", "mists driven by a storm") which as it were summarizes those used by St Jude (vv. 12–13). "He calls them dry springs", St Augustine comments, "that is, springs insofar as they have been given knowledge of the Lord Christ; dry, on the other hand, because they do not live in keeping with that knowledge" (*De fide et operibus*, 1, 25). Vanity and hypocrisy are usually features of people who try to justify their doctrinal and moral deviations (cf. Mt 7:15–20).

2:18–19. These false teachers, sadly, have led some recent converts astray: those converts had only turned their back on sin and now they are being led astray

again, with promises of liberation, as if liberation could be found by following one's passions and instincts. What they are doing is becoming slaves to sin: "Every one who commits sin is a slave to sin" (Jn 8:34).

Christian freedom ("the glorious liberty of the children of God": Rom 8:21) has been gained for mankind by Christ through his death on the cross. From the beginning, some misinterpreted this freedom, and the apostles had to correct those who took it as "a pretext for evil" (1 Pet 2:16) or "as an opportunity for the flesh" (Gal 5:13), perverting "the grace of God into licentiousness" (Jude 4). Living in freedom does not mean ignoring the Law of God; in fact, the Law of Christ is "the perfect law, the law of liberty" (Jas 1:25; cf. note on same). "If you continue in my word, you are truly my disciples," the Master teaches, "and you will know the truth, and the truth will make you free" (Jn 8:31–32).

"Christ, our Liberator, has freed us from sin and from slavery to the Law and to the flesh, which is the mark of the condition of sinful mankind. Thus it is the new life of grace, fruit of justification, which makes us free. This means that the most radical form of slavery is slavery to sin. Other forms of slavery find their deepest root in slavery to sin. That is why freedom in the full Christian sense, characterized by the life of the Spirit, cannot be confused with a licence to give in to the desires of the flesh. Freedom is a new life in love" (SCDF, *Libertatis nuntius*, 4, 2).

loud boasts of folly, they entice with licentious passions of the flesh men who have barely escaped from those who live in error. ⁱ⁹They promise them freedom, but they themselves are slaves of corruption; for whatever overcomes a man, to that he is enslaved.

Jn 8:34
Rom 6:16

Apostasy, a grave sin
²⁰For if, after they have escaped the defilements of the world through the knowledge of our Lord and Saviour Jesus Christ, they are again entangled in them and overpowered, the last state has become worse for them than the first. ²¹For it would have been better for them never to have known the way of righteousness than after knowing it to turn back from the holy commandment delivered to them. ²²It has happened to them according to the true proverb, The dog turns back to his own vomit, and the sow is washed only to wallow in the mire.

Mt 12–45
Lk 11:24

Lk 12:47, 48

Prov 26:11
Mt 7:6

3. THE SECOND COMING OF CHRIST

The teaching of Tradition

3 ¹This is now the second letter that I have written to you, beloved, and in both of them I have aroused your sincere mind

2 Pet 1:13

2:20–22. The sacred writer uses two popular proverbs (v. 22) to show the serious situation of those who return to a life of sin after knowing the saving teaching of Christ. These verses can apply to the false teachers themselves as well as to those they lead astray. "The last state has become worse for them than the first": our Lord said the same thing about someone who after having had a devil cast out of him fell under his sway once more: "the last state of that man becomes worse than the first" (Mt 12:45).

St Gregory the Great applies this passage to those who bewail their sins but do not give them up: "When the dog vomits, it is clearly throwing up food it cannot take; but when it returns to its vomit it once again burdens itself with a burden it had shed. So too, those who weep over the sins they have committed are undoubtedly casting away the iniquity with which they wrongly stuffed themselves and which oppressed their soul; an iniquity which they ingest once again when, after confession, they repeat it. A sow, for example, when she rolls in the mire to clean herself, comes out filthier than ever. So too, a person who weeps for his sin and yet does not give it up becomes guilty of a greater fault; because he scorns the forgiveness which he could obtain by weeping, and then wallows in the mire. When, despite his tears, he prevents his life being cleansed, then in the sight of God he causes those very tears to be stained" (*Regulae pastoralis liber*, 3, 30).

3:1–16. The truth most explicitly rejected by the false teachers was that of the second coming of the Lord (cf. v. 4); by rejecting it they were able to tone down

2 Peter 3:2

Jude 17

by way of reminder; ²that you should remember the predictions of the holy prophets and the commandment of the Lord and Saviour through your apostles.

1 Tim 4:1
Jude 18
Is 5:19

Mistaken notions

³First of all you must understand this, that scoffers will come in the last days with scoffing, following their own passions ⁴and

---

the moral demands of Christianity. The sacred writer now sets about refuting their arguments and outlining correct teaching on eschatology. Because we do not know exactly what kind of heresy is being refuted, some parts of the text are difficult to understand.

The whole passage is very well structured: a brief reference to the teaching of the prophets and apostles (vv. 1–2); fallacious ideas of the opponents (vv. 3–4); correct teaching about the second coming of our Lord (vv. 5–10); and an appeal for hope and vigilance, because we do not know the hour of the Lord's coming (vv. 11–16).

3:1–2. The letter referred to is probably 1 Peter, which also dealt with the subject of the Parousia (cf. 1 Pet 1:10–12; 5:12). Even if the author of the "second letter" was not St Peter but a disciple of his (cf. Introduction), the reference could still be to 1 Peter, which at that time would have already been well known to Christians generally.

"I have aroused your sincere mind by way of reminder", that is, I have given you a correct understanding of the true doctrine so that you can see where the false teachers have gone wrong. Having a sincere mind is not only a matter of holding on to the true doctrine, but also of detecting doctrinal or moral error.

The reference to the apostles alongside that of the prophets shows that from the beginning the apostles, as authorized messengers of Revelation, had a role similar to that of the prophets in the Old Testament.

"The commandment of the Lord and Saviour" may mean the commandment of love (cf. Jn 13:34), insofar as it covers the whole Christian life, but here (cf. also 2:21) it seems to refer more to all the truths taught by Jesus, elsewhere these are described as the "gospel" (Gal 1:9; cf. Mk 1:14), "the word of the Lord" (Acts 8:25); "the mystery of God" (1 Cor 2:1) and "the faith" (Gal 1:23). As the Second Vatican Council teaches: "What was handed on by the apostles comprises everything that serves to make the People of God live their lives in holiness and increase their faith. In this way the Church, in her doctrine, life and worship, perpetuates and transmits to every generation all that she herself is, all that she believes" (*Dei Verbum*, 8).

3:3–4. Jesus had predicted that false teachers would appear and try to lead Christians astray (cf. Mt 24:24; Mk 13:22). The warnings which are often found in the New Testament about false ideas of one kind or another show how easy it is for us to wander away from the truth (cf., e.g., Acts 20:29–31; 1 Tim 4:1; 2 Tim 3:1–5; 1 Jn 2:19). St Jude uses almost the same words to unmask the scoffers of Christ, who let their passions gain the upper hand (cf. Jude 18 and note).

The false prophets referred to in the letter deny the second coming of Christ on the grounds that things are still the same, none of the catastrophes they

saying, "Where is the promise of his coming? For ever since the fathers fell asleep, all things have continued as they were from the beginning of creation."

Ezek 12:22
Mt 24:48

True teaching about the End

⁵They deliberately ignore this fact, that by the word of God heavens existed long ago, and an earth formed out of water and by means of water, ⁶through which the world that then existed was deluged with water and perished. ⁷But by the same word the heavens and

Gen 1:2, 6, 9

Gen 7:21
2 Pet 2:5

---

expected have occurred (they may have misinterpreted what our Lord said about the signs of the second coming and of the end of the world: cf. Mk 13:21ff).

"The fathers": some take this as meaning the first generation of Christians, most of whom had already died; the false teachers would have argued that the second coming should have happened during the lifetime of that generation. It could also be a reference to Old Testament forebears, especially, the ancestors of the entire human race; in which case the scoffers referred to may have been influenced by a current of Greek culture and philosophy which held that the world was eternal and unchanging; they would argue that no substantial change had occurred from the beginning up to now—which was a good indication that nothing was going to happen in the future, either.

3:5–7. These errors are replied to with information familiar to all: the world is not unchangeable, for creation and the Flood shows that its being and continued existence depend on the word of God. Besides, the delay in the second coming is understandable if one remembers that time does not count in the eternity of God (v. 8), and, moreover, by leaving this interval, divine mercy is giving men an opportunity to mend their ways (vv. 9–10).

Creation and the Flood, therefore, show that changes in the cosmos are a function of the will of God: with a mere word he caused a mass of earth and water to appear, later to be separated out into dry land and sea (cf. Gen 1:6–10); in the Flood, God's word caused the waters once again to drown the earth in punishment of men's sins, returning things to the original state of chaos in some way, until dry land appeared again (cf. Gen 8:3–14).

The sacred writer does not mean to provide any kind of scientific explanation of the origin of the world. He limits himself to recalling what the first chapters of the Bible say in a simple, figurative language suited to a more primitive mind (cf. Gen 1–11)—ideas his readers accepted unquestioningly, as we know from the rabbinical writings of the time. However, the conclusions he draws are perfectly valid: if the word of God caused Creation and the Flood, that same word can bring about a final day of conflagration.

It is interesting how much the sacred writer stresses the cosmic role of "fire" in the final upheaval (cf. 3:7, 10, 12). It may be that he is picking up a biblical tradition which uses fire as an image for the presence of God (cf., e.g., Ex 3:1–4; 13:21–22; Deut 4:24; Mic 1:3–4, 6), for the punishment he inflicts (e.g., Deut 32:22; Is 5:24–25; 66:15–16; Zeph 1:15–18) and for when he intervenes to purify man (e.g., Is 6:7; 30:27–28; 66:18–22; Mal 4:1–3). Therefore, it is likely that the writer wants in this way to stress that the end of

earth that now exist have been stored up for fire, being kept until the day of judgment and destruction of ungodly men. ⁸But do not ignore this one fact, beloved, that with the Lord one day is as a thousand years, and a thousand years as one day. ⁹The Lord is not slow about his promise as some count slowness, but is forbearing toward you,ʰ not wishing that any should perish, but that all should reach repentance. ¹⁰But the day of the Lord will come like a thief, and then the heavens will pass away with a loud

---

the world will involve a special kind of divine intervention, similar to that which took place at Creation and at the Flood; that one of its effects will be the punishment of the ungodly; and that it will also involve a special kind of purification through a profound transfiguration: "new heavens and a new earth" (v. 13). It is possible (in what way we cannot say) that fire may be used by God to bring these events about.

There is therefore no basis here for the theory which sees this cosmic fire as a reflection of Persian or Stoic philosophical notions. In Persian philosophy the end of the world is seen in terms of a last battle between good and evil; the Stoics had a theory that the cosmos evolved in a cyclical way; every time it is destroyed a new cycle starts, just like the previous one.

3:8. This passage from v. 4 of Psalm 90 was often cited by Jewish rabbis in their calculations about how long the messianic times would last and when the end of the world would be; later on, milleniarists would use it as a basis for their far-fetched theories about Christ and his saints bearing temporal rule for a thousand years over an earthly kingdom prior to the End. The author of the letter cites the psalm as an authority for the view that time is a function of Creation and has no connexion with the eternity of God: the fact that the Parousia has not happened is no reason to deny that it will happen.

3:9–10. In this passage we are reminded that God, in his great mercy, does not seek our condemnation but, rather, wants all men to be saved (cf. 1 Tim 2:4; Rom 11:22) and shows wonderful patience towards them. The fact that the Parousia has not yet come about is quite compatible with the certainty that it will happen, and happen all of a sudden; therefore, far from being an excuse for making Christian life less demanding, the Parousia is a spur to stay vigilant (the Master himself used the simile of the thief: cf. Mt 24:43–44; Lk 12:39). "Since we know neither the day nor the hour, we should follow the advice of the Lord and watch constantly so that, when the single course of our earthly life is completed (cf. Heb 9:27), we may merit to enter with him into the marriage feast and be numbered among the blessed (cf. Mt 25:31–46) and not, like the wicked and slothful servants (cf. Mt 25:26), be ordered to depart into the eternal fire (cf. Mt 25:41)" (Vatican II, *Lumen gentium*, 48).

"The earth and the works that are upon it": there are so many variants in the Greek manuscripts that it is almost impossible to reconstruct the original text: but they all convey the idea that the earth will be affected by this universal cataclysm.

---

h. Other ancient authorities read *on your account*

noise, and the elements will be dissolved with fire, and the earth and the works that are upon it will be burned up.

Moral lessons to be drawn
¹¹Since all these things are thus to be dissolved, what sort of persons ought you to be in lives of holiness and godliness, ¹²waiting for and hastening^i the coming of the day of God, because of which

Is 34:4

3:11–16. The writer now follows up these considerations with a moral exhortation, based on the conviction that the old world will disappear (v. 12), producing new heavens and a new earth (v. 13), and that men living in the period prior to this cataclysm will not know when it is going to happen (v. 15).

All this should not make Christians afraid; in fact, it should bolster their hope (vv. 12–14). God will keep his promise to grant heaven to those who persevere in good; but this hope of future reward should not lead one to neglect temporal affairs: "Far from diminishing our concern to develop this earth, the expectancy of a new earth should spur us on, for it is here that the body of a new human family grows, foreshadowing in some way the age which is to come" (Vatican II, *Gaudium et spes*, 39).

Hope opens the way to upright conduct (v. 11) of an even higher standard (v. 14). Christians should realize that they have a pressing duty to grow in virtue as long as they live in this world (v. 15): "God may have given us just one more year in which to serve him. Don't think of five, or even two. Just concentrate on this one year, that has just started. Give it to God, don't bury it! This is the resolution we ought to make" (St Josemaría Escrivá, *Friends of God*, 47).

The practice of virtue leads to holiness and enduring union with God (v. 14; cf. 1 Thess 3:13). "'While we are at home in the body we are away from the Lord' (2 Cor 5:6) and, although we have the first fruits of the Spirit, we groan inwardly (cf. Rom 8:23) in our anxiety to be with Christ (cf. Phil 1:23). The same love urges us to live more for Him who died for us and who rose again (cf. 2 Cor 5:15). We make it our aim, then, to please the Lord in all things (cf. 2 Cor 5:9) and we put on the armour of God that we may be able to stand against the wiles of the devil and resist the evil day (cf. Eph 6:11–13)" (*Lumen gentium*, 48).

3:12. "Waiting for and hastening": these two verbs convey the idea that Christian hope is something dynamic; it is in no way passive. Contrary to a view quite widespread among the Jews of the time, it does not mean that the Parousia will come sooner, the more meritorious men are; what it means is that the more closely united to Christ they are, the nearer they are to his glory. Therefore, it is urgent that all should embrace faith in Christ. We who have this faith pray in the Our Father, "Thy kingdom come." The first Christians made the same petition in their ejaculatory prayer, "Marana tha", "Come, Lord" (1 Cor 16:22; Rev 22:20), referring to the second coming of the Lord.

"The day of God": the usual expression in the New Testament is "the day of the Lord" (1 Cor 1:8; 5:5; 1 Thess 5:2; 2 Thess 2:2; 2 Pet 3:10); both expressions refer to the point at which Christ will come to judge the living and the dead.

---

i. Or *earnestly desiring*

the heavens will be kindled and dissolved, and the elements will melt with fire! ¹³But according to his promise we wait for new heavens and a new earth in which righteousness dwells.

¹⁴Therefore, beloved, since you wait for these, be zealous to be found by him without spot or blemish, and at peace. ¹⁵And count the forbearance of our Lord as salvation. So also our beloved brother Paul wrote to you according to the wisdom given him, ¹⁶speaking of this* as he does in all his letters. There are some things in them hard to understand, which the ignorant and unstable twist to their own destruction, as they do the other scriptures.

Is 65:17; 66:22
Rev 21:1, 27

Jude 24

Rom 2:4
1 Tim 1:15, 16

3:13. "New heavens and a new earth": one of things promised for the End is that creation will be renewed, re-fashioned: the prophets proclaimed this (cf. Is 65:17), and the New Testament speaks of drinking new wine at the heavenly banquet (cf. Mt 14:25), being given a new name (cf. Rev 2:17), singing a new song (cf. Rev 5:9), living in a new Jerusalem (Rev 21:3). All this imagery conveys the idea that the whole universe will be transformed, man included (cf. Rom 8:19–22). "We know neither the moment of the consummation of the earth and of man (cf. Acts 1:7) nor the way the universe will be transformed. The form of this world, distorted by sin, is passing away (cf. 1 Cor 7:31), and we are taught that God is preparing a new dwelling and a new earth in which righteousness dwells (cf. 2 Cor 5:2; 2 Pet 3:13), whose happiness will fill and surpass all the desires of peace arising in the hearts of men" (*Gaudium et spes*, 39).

3:15–16. The reference to the writing of St Paul is clear evidence of the fact that from the very beginning of Christianity unity in faith was considered essential. It is difficult to say whether the sacred writer is thinking of some specific passage, for themes and even wording found in this letter are to be found in many Pauline letters—for example, on the subject of God's forbearance in waiting for men to mend their ways (cf. Rom 2:4–11; 1 Tim 1:16); or that of holiness as the Christian goal (cf. 1 Cor 1:7–8; Col 1:21–22; Eph 1:5–14).

The "wisdom" of St Paul may be a reference to the special endowments the Apostle had for the spread of the Gospel; or it may refer to the charism of divine inspiration, thereby acknowledging that the Letters of St Paul are sacred scripture, because it would mean putting them on the level of the other sacred books (v. 16).

"Some things ... difficult to understand": he does not mention any specific subject; the point he is making is that the false teachers can do damage if they base their errors on arbitrary misinterpretations of Pauline texts. In his time St Augustine warned about the fact that "the heresies and perverse dogmas which entrap souls and hurl them into the abyss originate simply in a bad understanding of good scriptures, and the rashness and audacity with which people put forward their misinterpretations" (*In Ioann. Evang.*, 18, 1).

That is why the Church, while at the same time giving people every encouragement to read Scripture, has established precise rules to avoid erroneous interpretations and to obtain the maximum possible fruit from assiduous reading. "It is for the bishops, 'with whom the apostolic doctrine resides' [St Irenaeus]

Final exhortation and doxology

¹⁷You therefore, beloved, knowing this beforehand, beware lest you be carried away with the error of lawless men and lose your own stability. ¹⁸But grow in the grace and knowledge of our Lord and Saviour Jesus Christ. To him be the glory both now and to the day of eternity. Amen.

Mk 13:5
Rom 16:27
Jude 25

---

suitably to instruct the faithful entrusted to them in the correct use of the divine books, especially of the New Testament, and in particular of the Gospels. They do this by giving them translations of the sacred texts which are equipped with necessary and really adequate explanations. Thus the children of the Church can familiarize themselves safely and profitably with the Sacred Scriptures, and become steeped in their spirit" (Vatican II, *Dei Verbum*, 25).

3:17–18. The letter ends with a very succinct summary of some of its main points —pastoral concern, ways to defend oneself against false teachers, and faith in the divinity of Christ.

"Beloved": the faithful are referred to in this solicitous way elsewhere in the letter (3:1, 8, 14). The warnings and threats made by the sacred writer are born of his pastoral zeal to establish them in the truth (1:12) and remind them what the true teaching is (3:1).

When he encourages them not to lose their "own strength", he is reminding them that firmness in the faith is an essential weapon for protecting themselves against deceitful teachers who are causing their faith and morals to waver (cf. 2; 3:16). Understanding and love should be shown towards those who are in error, but this should not "make us indifferent to truth and goodness. Love, in fact, impels the followers of Christ to proclaim to all men the truth which saves" (*Gaudium et spes*, 28).

"To him be the glory": most of the doxologies which appear in the New Testament are in praise of God the Father (cf. Jude 25; Rom 16:27); this one is addressed to Christ, whose divinity, as in other passages of the letter, is openly confessed. He has the same glory as the Father: the doxology is not simply expressing a desire but stating a fact. The eternal love of Jesus Christ is the basis of the Christian's hope. "While she slowly grows to maturity, the Church longs for the completed Kingdom and, with all her strength, hopes and desires to be united in glory with her King" (*Lumen gentium*, 5).

Introduction to the First Letter of St John

According to a tradition which goes back to the second century, the apostle St John wrote his three letters in Ephesus, on his return from exile on Patmos around the years 95–96. The authenticity of the first letter is well documented from early on; its internal structure confirms that it was written by the same person as wrote the Fourth Gospel.

The first explicit testimony comes from St Irenaeus, bishop of Lyons. Born around the year 140 in Smyrna (Asia Minor), Irenaeus had there known St Polycarp, a direct disciple of St John.[1] In his book *Against Heresies*[2] Irenaeus makes use of New Testament texts dealing with the Incarnation of the Word of God, including a series of quotations from St John ("the disciple of the Lord"), deriving both from the Fourth Gospel and from 1 John.[3]

Clement of Alexandria (150–214), in addition to writing a commentary on this letter, only fragments of which have come down to us, frequently quotes it in his work, attributing it explicitly to the apostle John.[4] The same is true of Tertullian (d. 222),[5] and Origen (d. 253), who makes a point of underlining the relationship between the Fourth Gospel and 1 John.[6]

This epistle is included in all the early catalogues or canons of inspired books, with St John named by its author. For example, the famous Muratorian Fragment, containing a canon composed in Rome around the year 180, expressly mentions the prologue of the letter, attributing it to St John.

Detailed analysis of the text confirms that it was written by the same person as wrote the Fourth Gospel. There are very obvious similarities of style; structure; phrases; vocabulary; and ideas. Typical Johannine expressions occur in both texts—for example, being born of God, being of God, abiding in God, abiding in the truth, walking in the light, etc. In both, too, we find the frequent use of certain contrasts, much favoured by Semites—light/darkness, truth/lies, love/hate, death/life, God/the devil, righteousness/sin.

There is also evidence in the two texts of interest in certain doctrinal themes. Thus, Christ is described as the Word (Logos: 1 Jn 1:1 and Jn 1:1), the only Son (1 Jn 4:9 and Jn 1:18), and the Saviour of the world (1 Jn 4:14 and Jn 4:42). St John also puts stress on the reality of the Incarnation (cf. the

---

1. St Polycarp (d. probably 22 February 156) actually refers to 1 John 4:2–3 in his *Letter to the Philippians* (chap. 7). **2.** 3, 16, 5, 8. **3.** E.g., 1 Jn 2:18, 19, 21; 4:1–3; 5:1. **4.** Cf. *Stromata*, 2, 15, 66; 3, 4, 32; 5, 44; 6:45. **5.** Cf. *Adversus Praxeam*, 15; *Scorpiace*, 12; *Adversus Marcionem*, 5, 16. **6.** Cf. Eusebius of Caesarea, *Ecclesiastical History*, 6, 25, 8.

prologues of the letter and the Gospel) and points to its redemptive value "to take away sins" (1 Jn 3:5; cf. Jn 1:29).

The beginning of the Christian life is seen as passing "out of death into life" (e.g., 1 Jn 3:14 and Jn 5:24), or as being "born of God" (1 Jn 3:9; 4:7; 5:1, 4; and Jn 1:13; 3:3), so that the Christian becomes a "child of God" (1 Jn 3:1–2 and Jn 1:12) and comes "to have life" (cf. 1 Jn 5:12 and Jn 3:36). Similarly, the true disciple of Christ should be recognized by the fact that he keeps the commandments, God's "word" (1 Jn 2:5 and Jn 14:21, 23). And following Christ's example (1 Jn 2:6 and Jn 13:15), he should particularly practise brotherly love (1 Jn 3:11 and Jn 13:34), which is called the "new commandment" (1 Jn 2:7–8 and Jn 13:34).

There has never been any real doubt about the canonicity of the letter. As we here said, it has figured in all the early lists of inspired books; and from the second century onwards it is cited by many Greek and Latin Fathers. It appears on the lists of secred books compiled by all the earliest councils which dealt with this subject—Laodicea (*c*.360), Rome (382), Hippo (393), the third Council of Carthage (397), etc.

In his *Ecclesiastical History*[7] Eusebius of Caesarea echoes this constant tradition by classifying 1 John among these writings which everyone always accepted as sacred and canonical (*homologúmena*). And St Jerome states that it was accepted the world over as canonical "by all competent men of the Church".[8]

In its fourth session[9] the Council of Trent solemnly declared this letter, along with all the other books in the two Testaments, to be canonical.

IMMEDIATE READERSHIP

The First Letter of St John carries no heading, unlike the other New Testament epistles (with the exception of Hebrews) and ordinary secular correspondence of the time. In fact, it makes no mention of the writer's name or the addressees' names, and contains none of the usual opening greeting(s) and no special words of farewell.

The fact that the addressees are not named suggests that this is a kind of circular letter sent to all the Christian communities of some region.

According to a tradition passed down by St Irenaeus,[10] the apostle John, on his return from exile on the island of Patmos, spent the last years of his life in Ephesus, at that time the capital of the Roman province of Asia. From there he ruled over the various churches of Asia Minor whose names are given in the book of Revelation (Rev 2–3). It is quite likely therefore that the faithful of those communities were the people to whom this letter was originally sent.

7. Cf. 3, 24, 17.   **8.** *On Famous Men*, 9, 18.   **9.** *De librir sacris*.   **10.** *Against Heresies*, 3, 1, 1.

Introduction to the First Letter of St John

DATE OF COMPOSITION

The letter must have been written after the year 95/96 when, during Nerva's reign, St John returned from Patmos. Although the question is still open, most experts are inclined to the view that this letter is later than the Fourth Gospel, since it seems to presuppose the teachings contained therein. Finally, of the three New Testament letters which bear St John's name, this one is probably chronogically the latest, having been written towards the end of the first century of the Christian era.

THE REASON FOR THE LETTER

As is obvious from its content, some false teachers (antichrists, deceivers, children of the devil, as St John calls them: cf. 2:18, 26; 3:7, 10; 4:1) had appeared in these young churches and, although they probably no longer had any links with them (cf. 2:19), they still were a threat to purity of faith and Christian morality. The apostle is writing to denounce their errors and stress then the faith of believers.

We do not know exactly who these heretics were. From the tenor of the letter, it appears that they were spreading both doctrinal and moral errors to do with the person and salvific work of Christ, denying that Jesus was the Messiah, the Son of God (cf. 2:22; 4:3, 14f). Also, St John's insistence of the fact that Jesus Christ "has come in the flesh" (4:2) suggests that they denied the Incarnation;[11] the rather mysterious reference to Jesus Christ having come "by water and blood, ... not with the water only but with the water and the blood" (5:6) also seems to be directed against the same errors.

All this points to the Gnostic heresy of Cerinth, according to which Jesus was not born of a virgin but was the son of Joseph and Mary, and his birth had been like that of anyone else. Therefore, he was not the true Son of God; the divine Word merely dwelt in him for a period of time, from his baptism in the Jordan up to the time of his passion—which meant that the blood of Christ shed on the cross had no redemptive value. St John asserts, to the contrary, that Christ's blood "cleanses us from all sin" (1:7), that Christ "is the expiation for our sins" and "for the sins of the whole world" (2:2).

Along with these Christological errors, errors on questions of morals were being spread—an erroneous concept of the Christian life: they thought they were without sin (cf. 1:8); they claimed to have acquired a special knowledge of God which exempted them from keeping his commandments (cf. 2:4–6). Practical errors of this type confirm the influence of these heretics of Gnostic ideas, which had begun to spread towards the end of the first century.

---

11. Cf. also the prologue of the letter: 1:1–4.

Introduction to the First Letter of St John

CONTENT

In the structure of the letter it is fairly easy to identify a *prologue* (1:1–4) and a brief *epilogue* (5:13) followed by an appendix (5:14–21). The prologue, which is very like that of the Fourth Gospel, states the basic idea of the letter—the communion or union of the Christian with God, which manifests itself in faith in Jesus Christ, and in the practice of brotherly love. This communion results in the life which the Christian receives in and through Jesus Christ, the incarnate Son of God. This idea is summed up in the epilogue: "I write this to you who believe in the name of the Son of God, that you may know that you have eternal life" (5:13).

However, it is not easy to find any clear breaks in the central part of the letter, because its thought does not develop linearly but, rather, in a spiral way: again and again the same basic ideas occur, focused on from different angles. Therefore, the division we have chosen is not meant to indicate that the text has any rigid structure; it is merely designed to highlight the main themes so as to facilitate reading.

The first part (1:5—2:29), which begins with the message that "God is light", outlines the demands implied by the Christian life, which is depicted as walking in the light". The light/darkness (cf. 1:5, 7; 2:8–11) and truth/lies (cf. 1:6, 8; 2:4, 21–27) antithesis are repeatedly referred to.

This holy life of the Christian is made possible by the fact that the blood of Jesus "cleanses us from all sin" (1:7), for he is our "advocate with the Father" (2:1). To stay in communion with God one needs to recognize oneself as a sinner (3:2) and to strive not to sin (1:8—2:2), keep the commandments (especially that of brotherly love: 2:3–11), not love the world (2:12–17), and not listen to the "antichrists" (2:18–29).

The second part (3:1–24), which begins with a statement about the Christian's divine filiation, puts further stress on the same demands, viewed from the perspective of the fact that Christians are children of God. Divine filiation will attain its fullness when we shall be gloriously transfigured at the second coming of the Lord so as to "see him as he is" (3:2). It is this hope that sustain and encourages Christians on the road to holiness, and that brings them to struggle against sin (3:3–10) and practise brotherly love and the other commandments of the Lord (3:11–24).

The third part (4:1—5:12) develops still further in breadth and depth the main ideas of the letter, arranging them in a kind of literary triptych—faith in Jesus Christ (4:1–6), love (4:7–21) and, again, faith in our Lord (5:1–12). Believers, unlike the false prophets, are "of God" (4:2, 4, 6); and "God is love" (4:8, 16) and all genuine love comes from God (cf. 4:7); our union with God is founded on this love. At the same time, this divine love poured into our hearts equips us and obliges us to love others, who are our brothers (cf. 4:11–16). In sum, love of God and love of neighbour are inseparable (cf. 4:17–21).

Once again the decisive role of faith in Christ is underlined (cf. 5:1)—a living faith which expresses itself in deeds (cf. 5:1–5) and is grounded on the witness borne by God the Father and the Holy Spirit about the Son (cf. 5:6–12).

After a short conclusion (cf. 5:13) which summarizes the central theme of the letter, St John adds, as a kind of appendix, some final counsels (cf. 5:14–21).

TEACHING

1. *Communion with God.* St John gives a full outline of the doctrine of the communion or union of the Christian with God. He does so partly because the false teachers were claiming that they had a higher understanding of God, a *gnosis*, unconnected with traditional Christian teaching, and an enduring union with him, thanks to which they did not feel obliged to keep the commandments, particularly that of fraternal charity.

To counter these errors, St John stresses that only those who stay in communion with the apostles and accept their message can attain union with the Father and the Son (cf. 1:3). To describe this communion he uses clear, bold language: knowing God (cf. 2:3, 13, 14; 3:1, 6; 4:6–8; 5:20), being in God (cf. 2:5; 5:20) or in the light (cf. 2:9); having the Father (cf. 2:23) or the Son (cf. 5:12) and therefore eternal life (cf. 3:15; 5:12); and, above all, the expression "abiding" in God (cf. 2:6, 24, 26; 3:6, 24), articulated most strongly when he says that "all who keep his commandments abide in him, and he in them" (3:4; cf. 4:13–16).

The basic requirement for being in communion with God is confessing true faith in Christ as the Son of God (cf. 2:23; 4:15), since it is he who has brought us the revelation of the Father and he who gives us divine life (cf. 5:12). To guarantee this orthodox faith, Christians receive interior instruction from the Holy Spirit (through the "anointing" given at Baptism: cf. 2:20, 27) and external teaching from apostolic tradition (cf. 2:24).

As usual in the language of the Bible, knowledge of God is not something purely speculative, for a person only really knows God when he is united to him by charity, which is love of God and love of neighbour for God. In this way faith and love build each other up: knowing God better leads to brotherly love, and brotherly love enables one the bettter to love God: "he who loves ... knows God. He who does not love does not know God; for God is love" (4:7–8). A love-impregnated knowledge of God expresses itself in keeping his commandments (cf. 2:3–6), for "he who loves ... knows God. He who does not love does not know God; for God is love" (3:24); love of God is particularly visible when you keep the commandment of brotherly love (cf.

2:9–11; 3:14–17; 4:12). In a word, "he who abides in love abides in God, and God abides in him" (4:16); whereas, as St Augustine will later say, "acting against charity is acting against God".[12]

2. *Faith in Jesus Christ.* From start (cf. 1:1–3) to finish (cf. 5:13, 20) the letter keeps stressing faith in the person and redemptive work of the Son of God, Jesus Christ. Both to expose demons and to fortify Christians in the faith they have had from the beginning, the apostle places the emphasis on the divinity of Jesus Christ, on his redemptive Incarnation, and on his role as the only Mediator betweed God and man.

The very prologue summarizes important dogmatic truths about Christ:[13] he is the Word (1:1), that is, the second person of the Blessed Trinity, the Son of God (1:3); he exists eternally alongside the Father (cf. 1:1–2); he took on a true human nature (ibid.). He is that imperishable Life, which through him is communicated to believers.

These statements are developed in the course of the letter. Thus, the title of "Son" of God is mentioned repeatedly:[14] the Greek word *hyiós* is used; it is never used when speaking of the divine filiation of the Christian, but only for the "only Son" (4:9), who is "true God" (5:20). So, against the "antichrists" who denied that Jesus was the Christ (cf. 2:22), Christian faith professes that "Jesus is the Christ" (5:1), "Jesus is the Son of God" (5:5). God the Father has borne witness concerning his Son (cf. 5:9–11) and has commanded us to believe in the name of his Son Jesus Christ (3:25); only if we obey shall we be united to the Father (2:26; 4:15) and have eternal life (5:11–13). On the other hand, those who deny the Son are making God out to be a liar (5:10).

In addition to denying Christ's divinity, the heretics also denied his redemptive incarnation. St John answers them by categorically stating that Christ is true man, that the Incarnation did take place: "the life was made manifest" (1:2); Jesus Christ "has come in the flesh" (4:2). He stresses the redemptive value of Christ's life and death: he came to take away sins (3:5) and to destroy the works of the devil (3:8); "he is the expiation for our sins, and not for ours only but also for the sins of the whole world" (2:2). Christians have their sins forgiven "for his sake" (2:12) and in his blood are cleansed from all sin (1:7). In a word: God sent him as the Saviour of the world (4:14).

Finally, Jesus Christ is the Mediator between God and man: he reveals the Father to us, unites us to him and gives us divine life. Because he is the Word of God, the very fact that he has become man is revelation itself. He came to make the true God known to us (5:20); his redemptive incarnation is the supreme proof of the Father's love for men (cf. 3:16; 4:9–10).

By confessing belief in Jesus Christ, we become united to the Father (cf. 2:23; 4:15). This union is not just something external; it is fellowship with the

---

12. *In Epist. Ioann. ad Parthos*, 7, 5. **13.** 1:1–4. Cf. the prologue of St John's Gospel (Jn 1:1ff) with which it is so closely related. **14.** 1:3, 7; 2:22–23; 3:8, 23; 4:9, 14, 15; 5:5, 9–13.

Introduction to the First Letter of St John

Father (1:3), because through Jesus Christ and in him we are in the true God (5:20), really sharing in the eternal life of God (cf. 5:11–13). In other words, we are children of God in Christ and through Christ.

In order to abide in communion with God, the Christian should live as Christ lived (2:6), by keeping the commandments. Since Christ is pure (3:3) and without sin (3:5), the Christian who should strive to purify himself (3:3); since Christ is righteous, so too the Christian should be righteous (3:7), that is, live a holy life. Above all, Jesus is the model of love: by dying for us he has shown us what true love means (3:16).

3. *Charity*. This is the central theme of the letter. St John uses both the noun "love"[15] and the verb "to love".[16] Twice he develops the theme to the point where he says, "God is love" (4:8, 16). As St Augustine comments, in this letter the apostle "said many things, practically all of them about charity".[17]

God is love because in himself, in life within the Trinity, he is a living community of love. St John arrives at this understanding through deep meditation (under the inspiration of the Holy Spirit) on the way God works in the history of salvation and, particularly, in effecting the redemptive Incarnation: "In this the love of God was made manifest among us, that God sent his only Son into the world, so that we might live through him" (4:9).

To understand this wonderful proof of God's love for men, we need to reflect on the fact that the Father *sent his only Son*, the Beloved, with whom he is well pleased (cf. Mt 3:17 and par.); he sent him *to the world*, that is, sinful mankind, the enemy of God (cf. Jn 3:16), as *expiation for our sins*, dying on the cross (4:10) to communicate divine life to us, *making us his children* by means of grace (cf. 3:1). The fullness of love is found in God. We are made to partake of that fullness, through Christ: we become God's children. It is Christ who, by his incarnation and his redemptive death (3:16), reveals to us and bestows on us this love of the Father.

Divine love is bestowed on us by supernatural rebirth in Baptism. The Christian, as St John frequently puts it, "is born of God" (3:9; 4:7; 5:1, 2, 4); he receives as a gift the infused virtue of charity which equips him (and at the same time obliges him) to love both God and his neighbour.

In line with this double precept of charity, as Jesus taught it (cf. Mt 22:37–40 and par.), the Christian's response to the love which the Father has shown him in Christ should embrace both love of God and love of neighbour.

Love for God (cf. 4:19–21; 5:2) should manifest itself in keeping his commandments (5:3; cf. 3:3–5, 24), in not loving the world insofar as it is the enemy of God (cf. 2:15–16) and in striving to cleanse oneself of all sin (cf. 3:3, 4, 6; 2:8–9)—in a word, living in a holy way (cf. 3:7). Above all, God's

---

15. 18 times. In the original Greek the word used is always the same (*ágape*), but in translation it is sometimes given as "love" and sometimes as "charity". **16.** 28 times. **17.** *In Epist. Ioann. ad Parthos*, prologue.

commandment is that "we should believe in the name of his Son Jesus Christ and love one another" (3:23).

St John presents brotherly love as the new commandment, although it is also an old commandment (2:7; cf. Jn 13:34–35), a message which was passed on and heard from the beginning (3:11; cf. 3:23); and as a debt we have contracted, a required response to the love of the Father and of the Son. God the Father loved us so much that he sent his own Son; therefore, "we also *ought* to love one another" (4:11). Jesus Christ "laid down his life for us; and we ought to lay down our lives for the brethren" (3:16). Since this love of the Father and of the Son is a love expressed in deeds, the apostle exhorts us "not (to) love in word or speech but in deed and in truth" (3:18).

Love for our neighbour is also a logical consequence of divine filiation, for "every one who loves the parent [God] loves the child" (5:1), that is, his brothers. Therefore, brotherly love is one of the best criteria for identifying the children of God: "for he who does not love his brother whom he has seen, cannot love God whom he has not seen" (4:20); rather, he is a liar and belongs to the devil's faction (cf. 3:10). Finally, brotherly love is the way to God, the way to be in communion with him: "if we love one another, God abides in us and his love is perfected in us" (4:12; cf. 2:10; 3:14).

4. *Divine filiation*. Communion with God, and the life of grace received from Jesus Christ, make the Christian a child of God: "see what love the Father has given us, that we should be called children of God; and so we are" (3:1).

Although different from Christ's natural filiation to God,[18] the Christian's divine filiation is a marvellous supernatural fact. God, through Christ, gives men his Life, making them partakers of his own divine nature (cf. 2 Pet 1:4); and so St John often refers to Christians as "born of God" (cf. 2:29; 3:9; 4:7; 5:1, 4). It is not a matter, therefore, of just an extrinsic relationship (like a title of honour, or adoption human-style): we *are really* children of God (cf. 3:1). In this life, divine filiation brings with it a mysterious identification with Christ, but the seed of divine life will not attain its full growth until eternal life, when we shall see him "as he is" (3:2).

The third chapter further spells out the demands made on us as children of God—avoiding sin (cf. 3:3–10) and practising fraternal love (cf. 3:11–24). However, in other parts of the letter there are also many references to the way those born of God, those who belong to God, live: they do right (2:29); they overcome the evil one (4:4) and the world (5:4); and, especially, they believe in Jesus Christ and keep the commandments, practising brotherly love (cf. 5:1–2).

St John goes so far as to say that "no one born of God commits sin; … he cannot sin" (3:9; cf. 5:18 and note); he does not mean an impeccability based

---

18. St John even uses different words in Greek to refer to the Son of God (*hyiós*) and to Christians as children of God (*tekna*). When addressing his disciples, affectionately calling them "little children", he uses other terms—*teknia, paidía*.

Introduction to the First Letter of St John

on one's own efforts, or something natural to man, which was what the Gnostics thought, for in the same letter he speaks of the need to recognize that we are sinners (cf. 1:8–10). What the apostle is saying, rather, is that the Christian counts on the guarantee and strength he has been given to overcome sin—grace, divine filiation, Jesus Christ himself (cf. 3:9).

Finally, and by way of contrast, St John counterposes the children of God and "the children of the devil",[19] telling us how to distinguish between them: the children of the devil sin (cf. 3:8); they do not do right; nor do they practise charity (cf. 3:10).

---

19. 3:10. Not to be taken in a literal sense; in a typical Semitic circumlocution, St John uses the term to describe those whose actions indicate they are on the devil's side, that is, they are people who through sin have broken with God and gone over to the Enemy (cf. notes on 3:6–9; 3:10).

THE FIRST LETTER OF JOHN

The Revised Standard Version, with notes

Prologue

Jn 1:1–18; 20–20, 25, 27; 1 Jn 2:13; Lk 24:39; Jn 1:4, 14; 14:6; 15:27

1 ¹*That which was from the beginning, which we have heard, which we have seen with our eyes, which we have looked upon and touched with our hands, concerning the word of life—²the life

1:1–4. Since the time of the Fathers, these verses have been described as the "prologue", like the prologue of the Fourth Gospel (Jn 1:1–18). In fact, there are many similarities in doctrine, style and even language between the two.

Both passages sing the praises of the mystery of the Incarnation: the Word of God who existed from all eternity, "from the beginning", became man (has been seen, heard, looked upon and touched) so that men might partake of divine life—might have "fellowship", communion, with the Father and the Son. Like the Gospel prologue, this one is written in a rhythmical way—"That which was ..., which we have heard ..., which we have seen ...". And many of the ideas are the same—for example, the reference to "the beginning" (cf. Jn 1:1); the term "the Word" to refer to the second Person of the Blessed Trinity; the reference to "life" (cf. Jn 1:4).

As St Bede points out, "from the very start of the epistle we are being taught the divinity and, at the same time, the humanity of our God and Lord Jesus Christ" (*In I Epist. S. Ioannis*, ad loc.).

1:1. "That which was from the beginning": although the pronoun used is neuter—as if to indicate the ineffable character of the mystery of Christ—the whole phrase refers not to a thing or an abstract teaching, but to the divine Person of the Son, who in the fullness of time was made manifest (v. 2), assuming a human nature. In other words, St John, as in his Gospel, is teaching that Jesus, a historical person (the apostles have lived with him, have seen him, have heard him speak) is the eternal Word of God (cf. Jn 1:1 and note).

"That which we have heard, ... seen ..., touched ... ": all those references to perception by the senses show the apostle's desire to make it clear that God really did become man. This may be because heretics were denying the Incarnation, or it may simply be that he thought it necessary to spell out this fundamental truth of our faith. He did so in the Gospel (cf., e.g., Jn 20:30–31); and in this letter we frequently find phrases like "Jesus Christ has come in the flesh" (4:2); "Jesus is the Christ" (2:22; cf. 5:1); "Jesus is the Son of God" (4:15; cf. 5:1, 12, 20).

We have recently been reminded that "the Church reverently preserved the mystery of the Son of God, who was made man, and in the course of the ages and of the centuries has propounded it for belief in a more explicit way"; moreover, what the Church teaches "concerning the one and the same Christ the Son of God, begotten before the ages in his divine nature and in time in his human nature, and also concerning the eternal persons of the Most Holy Trinity, belongs to the immutable truth of the Catholic faith" (SCDF, *Mysterium Filii Dei*, 2 and 6).

1:2. St John introduces this verse by way of parenthesis to explain what he means by "the word of life". In the Gospel he had written, "In him [the Word] was life" (Jn 1:4) and elsewhere he records Jesus' statement, "I am the bread of life" (Jn 6:35, 48). These expressions declare that the Son of God has life in all its fullness, that is, divine life, the source of all life, natural and supernatural. Jesus in fact identified himself with Life (cf. Jn 11:25;

was made manifest, and we saw it, and testify to it, and proclaim to you the eternal life which was with the Father and was made manifest to us—³that which we have seen and heard we proclaim also to you, so that you may have fellowship* with us; and our fellowship is with the Father and with his Son Jesus Christ. ⁴And we are writing this that our joy[a] may be complete.

Mt 13:17
Acts 4:20
1 Cor 1:9
Jn 15:11
2 Jn 12

14:6). By the Incarnation, the Word of God *manifests* true life and at the same time makes it possible for that life to be communicated to men—imperfectly, by means of grace, while they are in this world, and perfectly in heaven, by means of the beatific vision (cf. 1 Jn 5:11–12).

"And we testify to it": the testimony of the apostles is something unique in the history of the Church, because (unlike those who succeed them) they know our Lord personally, they have been "witnesses" of his life, death and resurrection (cf. Lk 24:48; Acts 1:8).

"With the Father": the Greek implies closeness, difference, and the mutual relationship between Father and Son, so providing a glimpse of the mystery of the Blessed Trinity (cf. note on Jn 1:1).

1:3–4. This testimony about Christ is designed to lead to fellowship and complete joy.

Fellowship with the apostles (the Greek word is *koinonía*) means, firstly, having the same faith as those who lived with Jesus: "They saw our Lord in the body," St Augustine reminds us, "and they heard words from his lips and have proclaimed them to us; we also have heard them, but we have not seen him [...]. They saw him, we do not see him, and yet we have fellowship with them, because we have the same faith" (*In Epist. Ioann. ad Parthos*, 1, 3).

To have fellowship with the Father and the Son we need to have the same faith as the apostles: "St John openly teaches that those who desire to partake of union with God must first partake of union with the Church, learn the same faith and benefit from the same sacraments as the apostles received from the fullness of Truth made flesh" (St Bede, *In I Epist. S. Ioannis*, ad loc.). The Church, the Second Vatican Council teaches, is not simply a collection of people who think the same way; it is the people of God "whom Christ established as a communion of life, love and truth" (*Lumen gentium*, 9).

Fellowship, communion, with the apostles, with the Church, has as its purpose to bring about union with God ("with the Father and with his Son Jesus Christ"); this is a subject St John develops over the course of this letter, as he previously did in his Gospel (cf., e.g., Jn 17:20ff). Here he uses expressions such as "to have the Son", and, in respect of the Son, "to have the Father" (2:23; 5:11ff); "to be in God" (2:5; 5:20); "to abide in God" (2:6, 24; 3:24; 4:13, 15, 16). This deep, intimate communion means that, without losing his personality, man shares in a wonderful and real way in the life of God himself. If Holy Scripture uses many different expressions in this connexion, it is due to the fact that the human mind, because it is so limited, cannot fully grasp the marvellous truth of communion with God.

Complete joy is the outcome of this communion. Most manuscripts say "our joy"; others, including the Vulgate, say "your joy". The difference is not important, because "our" involves the apostles and the faithful, particularly in view of

a. Other ancient authorities read *your*

1. UNION WITH GOD

God is light

⁵This is the message we have heard from him and proclaim to you, that God is light and in him is no darkness* at all.

1 Tim 6:16
Jas 1:17

the mutual fellowship previously mentioned (cf. Jn 15:11; 17:13). This joy, which will reach its fullness in the next life, is already in this life in some sense complete, insofar as knowledge of Jesus is the only thing that can satisfy man's aspirations.

1:5—2:29. This section describes what communion with God is, and the demands it makes on us. We can say there are two parts in the section: the first (1:5—2:11) teaches that communion with God means walking in the light and, therefore, rejecting sin and keeping the commandments. The second (2:12–19) warns the readers to guard against worldly concupiscence and not trust false teachers.

St John is writing as a pastor of souls who has lived the life of the Lord and reflected deeply upon it. His teaching interweaves truths of faith with moral and ascetical demands because he wants Christians to live in a way consistent with their faith. Therefore, the text does not really divide into a doctrinal section and a moral section.

1:5. "God is light": the imagery of light/darkness was much employed in ancient times—sometimes to promote the notion that the world had two principles, one good and the other evil. In St John the image clearly has a different meaning, one connected with biblical teaching on light. When God reveals himself to men, in one way or another light usually plays a part: examples range from the burning bush (cf. Ex 3:1ff) to the coming of the Holy Spirit in the form of tongues of fire (cf. Acts 2:1ff). This imagery is used to show God's sublimity—as we find also in St Paul: "the Lord of Lords, ... who dwells in unapproachable light, whom no man has ever seen or can see" (1 Tim 6:15–16).

The image of light also helps to show what revelation involves: God has made himself known to us, enlightening our hearts (cf. 2 Cor 4:6). Thus, we can say that God is light, Jesus Christ has made him known to us, and Christian revelation is the splendour of that light. In St John's Gospel the idea of Christ as the light which enlightens the world occurs very often (cf., e.g., Jn 1:4, 9; 8:12; 9:5). St Thomas Aquinas explains, in this connexion, that philosophers prior to Christ had a certain light which allowed them to attain some knowledge of God through reason; the people of Israel had much more light, through divine revelation in the Old Testament; angels and saints, because they have greater knowledge of God by virtue of grace have divine light to a special degree; but only the Word of God is the true light, because he is by his very essence the light which enlightens (cf. *Commentary on St John*, 1, 9).

The expression "God is light" has also a moral dimension: in God there is no darkness because there is no sin; he is sovereign good and all perfection. The light/darkness imagery, therefore, helps to underline the gravity of sin: "the light has come into the world, and men loved darkness rather than light, because their deeds were evil" (Jn 3:19). Those who lead a holy life are called children of light (Jn 12:36; Lk 16:8; Eph 5:8; 1 Thess 5:5); whereas those who do evil

1 John 1:6

Jn 3:19
Lk 25:53
1 Thess 5:4
Mt 26:28
Heb 9:12, 14
Rev 1:5; Ps 51
Prov 20:9
Rom 3:10

Walking in the light. Rejecting sin

⁶If we say we have fellowship with him while we walk in darkness, we lie and do not live according to the truth; ⁷but if we walk in the light, as he is in the light, we have fellowship with one another, and the blood of Jesus his Son cleanses us from all sin. ⁸If we say we

---

live in darkness (1 Thess 5:4), which is the symbol of sin (Lk 22:53).

St John uses the statement that "God is light" to encourage Christians to live in an upright way; as does St Augustine, who comments that we must be united to God and "darkness should be cast away from us so as to allow light to enter, because darkness is incompatible with light" (*In Epist. Ioann. ad Parthos*, 1, 5).

1:6–10. The clause "if we say" introduces three suppositions—very probably claims made by some early heretics, especially Gnostics (who boasted of having attained fullness of knowledge and thought they were incapable of sinning).

St John is using the literary technique of parallelism, much employed by Semitic writers: the first sentence states an idea which is repeated and filled out in the later ones. Here, the first statement ("we lie") is later extended to "we deceive ourselves" (v. 8) ..., and then to "we make him [God] a liar" (v. 10). This literary device shows that the author of the letter was familiar with this style of writing, very common in the Old Testament.

1:6–7. Walking in darkness/walking in the light—a graphic description of sinful conduct and upright conduct. St John insists that one cannot justify a life of sin by claiming to have communion with God: "mere confession of faith is in no sense sufficient", St Bede declares, "if that faith is not confirmed by good works" (*In I Epist. S. Ioannis*, ad loc.).

"Fellowship with one another": If there were an exact parallelism between the parts of the passage, we would expect it to read "fellowship with him", which is how some Fathers read it. If the text reads differently, it is because mutual communion, the fellowship with the Church to which St John is referring, is a pledge and sign of fellowship with God: "the Church, in Christ, is in the nature of a sacrament—a sign and instrument, that is, of communion with God and of unity among all men" (Vatican II, *Lumen gentium*, 1).

"The blood of his Son Jesus cleanses us from all sin": this idea is often found in the book of Revelation when it says that the blood of Christ sets us free (cf. Rev 1:5), cleanses souls and makes them white (cf. Rev 7:14), ransoms them for God (cf. Rev 5:9) and defeats the enemies of salvation (cf. Rev 12:11). It is made quite clear that the blood of Christ purifies all types of sin, past and present, mortal and venial. (On the blood of Christ as atonement for all sins, see the notes on Heb 9:12, 14.)

1:8. "If we say we have no sin": the Old Testament often says that all men are sinners (cf. 7:70; Job 9:2; 14:4; 15:14; 25:4; Prov 20:9; Ps 14:1–4; 51; etc.) and this is also clear from the New Testament (cf. especially Rom 3:10–18). The Council of Trent condemns anyone who says "that a man once justified cannot sin again and cannot lose grace" (*De iustificatione*, can. 23).

Loss of the sense of sin is a danger that threatens man in all epochs. The apostle's warning (to his contemporaries in the first instance) has particular rele-

have no sin, we deceive ourselves, and the truth is not in us. ⁹If we confess our sins, he is faithful and just, and will forgive our sins and cleanse us from all unrighteousness. ¹⁰If we say we have not sinned, we make him a liar, and his word is not in us.

Prov 28:13
Jas 5:16

2 ¹My little children, I am writing this to you so that you may not sin; but if any one does sin, we have an advocate with the Father, Jesus Christ the righteous; ²and he is the expiation for our sins, and not for ours only but also for the sins of the whole world.

Jn 14:16; Rom 8:34; Heb 7:25
Acts 3:14
1 Jn 4:10
Jn 11:51f
Rom 3:25

---

vance in our own time. "Deceived by the loss of the sense of sin," John Paul II reminds us, "and at times by an illusion of sinlessness which is not at all Christian, the people of today also need to listen again to St John's admonition, as addressed to each one of them personally: 'If we say we have no sin, we deceive ourselves, and the truth is not in us', and indeed 'the whole world is in the power of the evil one' (1 Jn 5:19). Every individual therefore is invited by the voice of divine truth to examine realistically his or her conscience, and to confess that he or she has been brought forth in iniquity, as we say in the *Miserere* Psalm (cf. Ps 51:7)" (*Reconciliatio et paenitentia*, 22).

1:9–10. "If we confess our sins": the Council of Trent quotes this text (without intending to define its exact meaning) when it teaches that confession of sins is of divine institution: "The Catholic Church has always understood that integral confession of sins was also instituted by the Lord (Jas 5:16; 1 Jn 1:9; Lk 17:14) and is by divine law necessary for all falls after Baptism" (*De Sacramento paenitentia*, chap. 5).

The sacred writer puts emphasis on the interior disposition of the Christian: he should humbly admit that he is a sinner; and St Augustine explains: "If you confess yourself to be a sinner, the truth is in you: the truth is light. Your life does not yet shine as brightly as it might, because there are sins in you; but now you are beginning to be enlightened, because you confess your iniquities" (*In Epist. Ioann. ad Parthos*, 1, 6).

"Faithful and just": a translation of two Hebrew words which literally have to do with love and faithfulness. The Old Testament uses this expression to stress that God's faithful love is always ready to forgive.

2:1–2. To make sure that no one makes a wrong appeal to divine mercy so as to justify their continuing to sin, St John exhorts all to avoid sin. It is one thing to acknowledge that we are sinners and to be conscious of our frailty; it is a very different matter to become completely passive or pessimistic, as if it were not possible to avoid offending God. "Jesus understands our weakness and draws us to himself on an inclined plane," St Josemaría Escrivá explains. "He wants us to make an effort to climb a little each day. He seeks us out, just as he did the disciples of Emmaus, whom he went out to meet. He sought Thomas, showed himself to him and made him touch with his fingers the open wounds in his hands and side. Jesus Christ is always waiting for us to return to him; he knows our weakness" (*Christ Is Passing By*, 75).

"My little children": it is difficult to translate this and other similar expres-

1 John 2:3

Keeping the commandments

³And by this we may be sure that we know him, if we keep his commandments.* ⁴He who says "I know him" but disobeys his commandments is a liar, and the truth is not in him; ⁵but whoever keeps his word, in him truly love for God is perfected. By this we

1 Jn 4:20
1 Jn 5:3
Jn 14:21, 23

---

sions in St John, charged as they are with tenderness and a sense of pastoral responsibility. They express a deep, strong love, like that of Jesus at the Last Supper (cf. Jn 13:33). This same Greek term appears six more times in this letter (2:12, 28; 3:7, 18; 4:4; 5:21); at other times he uses words equivalent to our "my little ones" (cf. 2:14, 18) or "dearly beloved" (2:7; 3:2, 21; 4:1, 7, 11; 3 Jn 2, 5, 11). All these expressions reflect how very close St John was to the faithful.

"We have an advocate with the Father": Jesus Christ, who is the only Mediator (cf. 1 Tim 2:5), intercedes for us. He, who has died for our sins (he is "the expiation"), presents his infinite merits to God the Father, by virtue of which the Father pardons us always. The Holy Spirit is also called Paraclete or Advocate insofar as he accompanies, consoles and guides each Christian, and the whole Church, on its earthly pilgrimage (cf. note on Jn 14:16–17).

"St John the apostle exhorts us to avoid sin", St Alphonsus says, "but because he is afraid we will lose heart when we remember our past faults, he encourages us to hope for forgiveness provided we are firmly resolved not to fall again; he tells us that we have to put our affairs in order with Christ, who died not only to forgive us but also (after dying) to become our advocate with the heavenly father" (*Reflections on the Passion*, chap. 9, 2).

2:3–6. "By this we may be sure": a phrase that occurs often in this letter (cf., e.g., 2:5, 18; 3:19, 24), usually to preface clear criteria for distinguishing doctrinal and moral truth from error. In this instance, it has to do with keeping the commandments being a sign of true knowledge of God.

For St John, knowing God is not a merely intellectual exercise nor does he mean that the immensity of God can be grasped by man's limited understanding. It refers to something much simpler and more important: knowing God means being united to him by faith and love—by grace. If this letter puts so much emphasis on knowing God (cf., e.g., 2:14; 3:1; 4:6–8; 5:20) or knowing Jesus Christ (cf. 2:13–14; 3:6), it may be because the heretics (particularly the Gnostics) were boasting of having attained special knowledge of God, superior to that of ordinary faithful. And so the apostle describes what true knowledge of God consists in, using expressions which complement one another—knowing him (v. 4); in him who knows God "truly love for God is perfected" (v. 5); abiding in him (v. 6).

"Keeping his commandments" (vv. 3 and 4), "Keeping his word" (v. 5), "walking in the same way in which he walked" (v. 6): keeping the commandments is absolutely necessary, because there is no room for faith without works (cf. 1 Jn 3:17–18; Jas 2:14ff; Gal 5:6). Similarly, one must keep the word of God, that is, accept all revelation docilely (an idea found very often in John: cf., e.g., Jn 5:38; 8:31, 51; 1 Jn 2:14). But, above all, Christians must identify their life with Christ's; St Prosper comments: "Walk as he walked: does that not mean

may be sure that we are in him: ⁶he who says he abides in him ought to walk in the same way in which he walked.

⁷Beloved, I am writing you no new commandment, but an old commandment which you had from the beginning; the old commandment is the word which you have heard. ⁸Yet I am writing you a new commandment, which is true in him and in you, because[b] the darkness is passing away and the true light is already shining. ⁹He who says he is in the light and hates his brother is in the darkness still. ¹⁰He who loves his brother abides in the light, and in it[c] there is no cause for stumbling. ¹¹But he who hates his brother is in the darkness and walks in the darkness, and does not

Jn 13:15, 34

Deut 6:5
Mt 22:37–40

Jn 13:34
Rom 13:12
Jn 8:12
Jn 11:10
Jn 12:35–36

---

giving up the comforts he gave up, not being afraid of the kind of trials he bore, teaching what he taught [...], persevering in helping even those who show no appreciation, praying for one's enemies, being kind to evildoers, serenely tolerating the proud?" (*De vita contemplativa*, 2, 21).

2:7–8. In a play on words, St John draws his readers' attention to the commandment of brotherly love, which he goes on to describe in vv. 9–11. It is, he says, an old commandment (v. 7) and at the same time a new one (v. 8). Old, because Christianity and charity are inseparable and that is something the faithful have known "from the beginning", that is, since they first received instruction; in some way, it can be said that it is even pre-Christian, because it is impressed on the heart of man. Yet it is new, because it is not out of date and has become a reality in Christ and in Christians. The novelty lies not in the precept (which is to be found in the Old Testament: cf. Lev 19:18) but in the standard which Jesus sets ("even as I have loved you": Jn 13:34) and in the fact that it covers everyone: we must love everyone, friends and enemies, without distinction of race, or ideology, or social status (cf. note on Jn 13:34–35).

Moreover, Christian love is not limited to seeking the earthly happiness of others, but tries to lead all to faith and holiness: "What is perfection in love?" St Augustine asks. "Loving our enemies and loving them so that they may be converted into brothers. Our love should not be a material one. Wishing someone temporal well-being is good; but, even if he does not have that, his soul should be secured [...]. It is uncertain whether this life is useful or useless to someone; whereas life in God is always useful. Therefore, love your enemies in such a way that they become your brothers; love them in such a way that you attract them to fellowship with yourself in the Church" (*In Epist. Ioann. ad Parthos*, 1, 9).

2:9–11. In the special style of this letter, an application is made of the new commandment, possibly to counter false teachers, who despised the ordinary faithful and were sowing discord among the Christians. The rhythm of the language—hate, love, hate—in which the positive idea is placed between two opposed ideas, highlights the importance of brotherly love.

"The principal apostolate we Christians must carry out in the world," St Josemaría Escrivá writes, "and the best witness we can give of our faith, is to

b. Or *that* **c.** Or *him*

know where he is going, because the darkness has blinded his eyes.

The apostle's confidence in the faithful

¹²I am writing to you, little children, because your sins are forgiven for his sake. ¹³I am writing to you, fathers, because you know him who is from the beginning. I am writing to you, young men, because you have overcome the evil one. I write to you, children, because you know the Father. ¹⁴I write to you, fathers,

Margin references:
- 1 Jn 1:7; 2:2; 1 Cor 6:11
- 1 Jn 1:1; Jn 1:1
- Jn 5:38

---

help bring about a climate of genuine charity within the Church. For who indeed could feel attracted to the Gospel if those who say they preach the Good News do not really love one another, but spend their time attacking one another, spreading slander and quarrelling? It is all too easy, and very fashionable, to say that you love everyone, Christians and non-Christians alike. But if those who maintain this ill-treat their brothers in the faith, I don't see how their behaviour can be anything but 'pious hypocrisy'. By contrast, when in the Heart of Christ we love those 'who are children of the same Father, and with us share the same faith and are heirs to the same hope' (Minucius Felix, *Octavius*, 31), then our hearts expand and become fired with a longing to bring everyone closer to our Lord" (*Friends of God*, 226).

Light/darkness: the section which began at 1:5 ("God is light") ends with the repetition of this contrasting imagery.

2:12–14. These verses, which are a kind of aside, are not easy to translate. The main difficulty has to do with the meaning of the expression, "I am writing (or I insist) *because*". The Greek conjunction may have an explanatory meaning (as the New Vulgate translates it): "I am writing to you *that* your sins have been forgiven …"; in which case the apostle would be trying to build up the Christians' resistance to the arguments of the heretics; as if he were saying, "You can be sure that your sins have been forgiven …", that is, that it is you, not they, who are Christians.

However, it is also correct in the context to understand it as being the causal. In this way the apostle is invoking his authority over these Christians, confident that they will listen to him; it is as if he were saying, "I can tell you, and you have the duty and the right to pay heed to me, because your sins have been forgiven …".

The way he addresses his readers, calling them little children, children, fathers, young men, is also open to various interpretations. The first two (little children, children) are usually taken to mean all Christians, without distinction of age or the length of time they have been in the Church; whereas the other two (fathers, young men) would be addressed to those particular groups. However, it is possible that these are simply rhetorical devices, in which case what is said to young people is perfectly applicable to older people, and vice versa; this is the way St Augustine understood it: "Remember that you are fathers; if you forget Him who is from the beginning, you will have lost your paternity. Also see yourselves over and over again as young men: strive to win; win so as to be crowned; be humble in order not to succumb in the struggle" (*In Epist. Ioann. ad Parthos*, 2, 7).

because you know him who is from the beginning. I write to you, young men, because you are strong, and the word of God abides in you, and you have overcome the evil one.

Detachment from the world
¹⁵Do not love the world or the things in the world. If any one loves the world, love for the Father is not in him. ¹⁶For all that is in the world, the lust of the flesh and the lust of the eyes and the pride of life, is not of the Father but is of the world. ¹⁷And the world passes away, and the lust of it; but he who does the will of God abides for ever.

Jn 5:42; Jas 4:4
Prov 27:20
Tit 2:12
Jas 4:16
Mt 7:21
1 Pet 4:2

"Because you know him who is from the beginning": a reference to Jesus Christ, as distinct from the Father, who appears at the start of v. 14. St John puts emphasis on *knowing*, which covers not just theoretical knowledge but more particularly a knowledge that comes from faith and love (cf. note on 2:3–6).

2:13. "The evil one": the devil is explicitly mentioned several times in this letter; he is the enemy of the children of God (2:14; 5:18); a sinner from the beginning (3:8); and has the world in his power (5:18–19; cf. Jn 16:11).

"The apostle writes: '*You have overcome the evil one*'! And so it is. It is necessary to keep going back to *the origin of evil and of sin* in the history of mankind and the universe, just as Christ went back to these same roots in the Paschal Mystery of his Cross and Resurrection. There is no need to be afraid to call *the first agent of evil* by his name—*the Evil One*. The strategy which he used and continues to use is that of not revealing himself, so that the evil implanted by him from the beginning may receive its development from man himself, from systems and from relationships between individuals, from classes and nations—so as also to become ever more a '*structural' sin*, ever less identifiable as '*personal sin*'. In other words, so that man may feel in a certain sense 'freed' from sin but at the same time be ever more deeply immersed in it" (John Paul II, *Letter to Young People*, 31 March 1985, 15).

2:15–17. The term "world" has a number of meanings in Holy Scripture (cf. note on Jn 17:14–16). Here it has the pejorative sense of enemy of God and man (cf. also note on Jas 1:26–27), and includes everything that is opposed to God—the kingdom of sin. Following Christ involves a radical choice: "No one can serve two masters" (Mt 6:24); "friendship with the world is enmity with God" (Jas 4:4).

"The pride of life": this is the usual translation in Latin. The original Greek says more or less "the arrogance of earthly things"; the two translations are compatible because reliance on material things leads to pride.

The list St John gives here of the signs of a worldly life summarizes everything opposed to fidelity to the love of God. "Lust of the flesh is not limited to disordered sensuality. It also means softness, laziness bent on the easiest, most pleasurable, way, any apparent shortcut, even at the expense of fidelity to God [...]. We can and ought to fight always to overcome the lust of the flesh, because, if we are humble, we will always be granted the grace of our Lord.

"St John tells us that the other enemy is the lust of the eyes, a deep-seated

1 John 2:18

Not listening to heretics

1 Jn 2:22
2 Jn 7
1 Tim 4:1

¹⁸Children, it is the last hour;* and as you have heard that antichrist is coming, so now many antichrists have come;

---

avariciousness that leads us to appreciate only what we can touch. Such eyes are glued to earthly things and, consequently, they are blind to supernatural realities. We can, then, use this expression of Sacred Scripture to mean that disordered desire for material things, as well as that deformation which views everything around us—other people, the circumstances of our life and of our age—in a merely human way.

"Then the eyes of our soul grow dull. Reason proclaims itself capable of understanding everything, without the aid of God. This is a subtle temptation, which hides behind the power of our intellect, given by our Father God to man so that he might know and love him freely. Seduced by this temptation, the human mind appoints itself the centre of the universe, being thrilled with the prospect that 'you will be like God' (Gen 3:5). So filled with love for itself, it turns its back on the love of God.

"In this way does our existence fall prey unconditionally to the third enemy: pride of life. It's not merely a question of passing thoughts of vanity or self-love, it's a state of general conceit. Let's not deceive ourselves, for this is the worst of all evils, the root of every false step. The fight against pride has to be a constant battle, to such an extent that someone once said that pride only disappears twenty-four hours after each of us has died. It is the arrogance of the Pharisee whom God cannot transform because he finds in him the obstacle of self-sufficiency. It is the haughtiness which leads to despising others, to lording it over them, to mistreating them. For 'when pride comes, then comes disgrace' (Prov 11:2)" (St Josemaría Escrivá, *Christ Is Passing By*, 5–6).

2:18–27. This passage covers one of the main themes in St John's letters—the fidelity of Christians being tested by the heretics. The style, replete with contrasts and parallelisms, makes what he has to say very lively.

First he describes the circumstances these Christians find themselves in: the presence of heretics leads one to think that the antichrist predicted by our Lord (cf. Mt 24:5–24 and par.) has come already and the "last hour" (v. 18) has begun.

He goes on to unmask those who are cast in the role of antichrist, and contrasts them with true believers: 1) they are not of us (v. 19), whereas you know the truth (vv. 20–21); 2) the heretics are imposters who deny the basic truth that Jesus is the Christ (vv. 22–23), whereas you *abide* in the Father and in the Son (vv. 24–25); 3) they arrogantly present themselves as teachers, but the anointing *abides* in you and you have no need of spurious teachers (vv. 26–27).

The repetition of the word *abide* stresses the need to keep the teaching of the Church intact. The faithful have a right to practise their faith in peace, and it is part of the mission of pastors to strengthen them in the faith, as St John is doing here. When introducing his *Creed of the People of God*, Pope Paul VI said: "It is true that the Church always has a duty to try to obtain a deeper understanding of the unfathomable mysteries of God (which are so rich in their saving effects) and to present them in ways even more suited to the successive generations. However, in fulfilling this inescapable duty of study and research, it must do everything it can to ensure that Christian

therefore we know that it is the last hour. ¹⁹They went out from us, but they were not of us; for if they had been of us, they would have continued with us; but they went out, that it might be plain

Acts 20:30
1 Cor 11:18

teaching is not damaged. For if that happened, many devout souls would become confused and perplexed—which unfortunately is what is happening at present" (*Homily*, 30 June 1968).

2:18. "The last hour": this expression was probably familiar to the early Christians, who had a lively desire to see the second coming of Christ. As many passages in the New Testament indicate, the fullness of time already began with the Incarnation and the Redemption brought about by Christ (cf. Gal 4:4; Eph 1:10; Heb 9:26). From that point onwards, until the end of the world, we are in the last times, the last earthly stage of salvation history: hence the urgency Christians should feel about their own holiness and the spread of the Gospel. "To prevent anyone dragging his feet," St Augustine urges, "listen: 'children, it is the last hour', go on, run, grow; it is the last hour. It may be an extended one, but it is the last hour" (*In Epist. Ioann. ad Parthos*, 3, 3). This eschatological sense of the last times, which the prophets announced long before (cf. Is 2:2; Jer 23:20; 49:26), is also to be found in the Fourth Gospel (cf., e.g., Jn 2:4; 5:28; 17:1).

"The antichrist": a sign of "the last hour" foretold by our Lord and the apostles is the feverish activity of false prophets (cf. Mt 24:11–24; Acts 20:29–30; 2 Thess 2:2ff; 2 Tim 4:1ff; 2 Pet 3:3). Although this term is only to be found in the letters of St John (1 Jn 2:18, 22; 4:3; 2 Jn 7), the "antichrist's" features are similar to those of the "man of lawlessness", "the enemy" St Paul speaks about (cf. 2 Thess 2:1–12) and the "beasts" of the Apocalypse (cf., e.g., Rev 11:7; 13:1ff); the distinguishing mark they all share is their brutal opposition to Christ, his teaching and his followers. It is difficult to say whether the antichrist is an individual or a group. In St John's letters, the latter seems to be the case: it is a reference to all those who oppose Christ (the "many antichrists") who have been active since the start of Christianity and will continue to be so until the end of time.

2:19. "They were not of us": St John unmasks the antichrists; they could not have led the faithful astray had they not come from the community; but they were only pretending to be Christians—wolves in sheep's clothing (cf. Mt 7:15), "false brethren" (Gal 2:4)—and that is how they are able to sow confusion. Our Lord himself warned that both wheat and cockle would grow side by side in the Kingdom of God (cf. Mt 13:24–30); the sad fact that this is happening should not cause Christians to doubt the holiness of the Church. As St Augustine explains: "Many who are not of us receive, along with us, the sacraments; they receive Baptism with us, they receive with us what they know the faithful receive—the blessing, the Eucharist and the other holy sacraments; they receive communion from the same altar as we do, but they are not of us. Temptation reveals this to be so; when temptation overtakes them, they flee as if borne away by the wind, because they are not wheat. When winnowing begins on the threshing floor of the Lord on the day of judgment, they will all fly away; remember that" (*In Epist. Ioann. ad Parthos*, 3, 5).

1 John 2:20

1 Jn 2:27
2 Cor 1:21
2 Pet 1:12

1 Jn 4:3

that they all are not of us. ²⁰But you have been anointed by the Holy One, and you all know.ᵈ ²¹I write to you, not because you do not know the truth, but because you know it, and know that no lie is of the truth. ²²Who is the liar but he who denies that Jesus is the

---

2:20. "Anointed by the Holy One": it is difficult to say exactly what this means (cf. also v. 27); St John says that this anointing has the effect of countering the work of the antichrist. He may be referring to the sacrament of Baptism or that of Confirmation, or both, where anointing with chrism is part of the sacramental rite. In any case he is referring to the action of the Father and of the Son through the Holy Spirit on the soul of the Christian who has received these sacraments: this explains why the anointing "instructs" Christians "to know everything" (v. 27; RSV alternate reading).

"The Holy One": St John uses this expression to describe God the Father (cf., e.g., Rev 6:10; Jn 17:11), God the Son (cf. Jn 6:69; Rev 3:7), or simply God, without specifying which Person. The last-mentioned use was very common among Jews of the time, to refer to the one true God.

"You all know": not only about the anointing but about Christian teaching in general. Some important manuscripts, which the Sistine-Clementine Vulgate follows, read: "You know all" (cf. RSV alternate reading). Both readings are complementary, for the apostle is stressing that Christians do not need to listen to teachings other than those of the Church: they are being guided by the Holy Spirit, who gives them sureness of faith. The Second Vatican Council quotes this text when teaching about the "supernatural appreciation of the faith [*sensus fidei*] of all the faithful": "The whole body of the faithful, who have an anointing that comes from the Holy One (cf. 1 Jn 2:20 and 27), cannot err in matters of belief. This characteristic is shown in the supernatural appreciation of the faith of the whole people, when, 'from the bishops to the last of the faithful' they manifest a universal consent in matters of faith and morals" (*Lumen gentium*, 12).

2:22. "Jesus is the Christ": this is a basic truth of Christian faith. As in most of St John's writings, this wording means not only that Jesus is the Messiah but also that he is the Son of God (cf. Jn 20:31). From the earliest days of Christianity, faith in Jesus, which included both his messiahship and his divinity, could be expressed by applying to him the titles of "Messiah" and "Son of God", or simply one or other of those titles. Over the course of the centuries the Church has been developing and deepening its understanding of revealed truths about Christ—partly in reaction to heresies attacking that truth. In recent years also the Magisterium has taken issue with erroneous ideas: "The opinions according to which it has not been revealed and made known to us that the Son of God subsists from all eternity in the mystery of the Godhead, distinct from the Father and the Holy Spirit, are in open conflict with this belief; likewise the opinions according to which the notion is to be abandoned of the one person of Jesus Christ begotten in his divinity of the Father before all the ages and begotten in his humanity of the Virgin Mary in time; and lastly the assertion that the humanity of Christ existed not as being assumed into the eternal person of the Son of God but

---

d. Other ancient authorities read *you know everything*

Christ? This is the antichrist, he who denies the Father and the Son. ²³No one who denies the Son has the Father. He who confesses the Son has the Father also. ²⁴Let what you heard from the beginning abide in you. If what you heard from the beginning abides in you, then you will abide in the Son and in the Father. ²⁵And this is what he has promised us,ᵉ eternal life.

²⁶I write this to you about those who would deceive you; ²⁷but the anointing which you received from him abides in you, and you

1 Jn 4:15
Jn 5:23; 14:7, 9
1 Jn 1:3; 2:7
Jn 5:24
1 Jn 2:20; Jn 14:26; Jer 31:34

---

existed rather of itself as a person, and therefore that the mystery of Jesus Christ consists only in the fact that God, in revealing himself, was present in the highest degree in the human person Jesus.

"Those who think in this way are far removed from the true belief in Christ, even when they maintain that the special presence of God in Jesus results in his being the supreme and final expression of divine Revelation. Nor do they come back to the true belief in the divinity of Christ by adding that Jesus can be called God by reason of the fact that in what they call his human person God is supremely present" (SCDF, *Mysterium Filii Dei*, 3).

2:23. "Has the Father": a very graphic way of referring to union with God (cf. 2 Jn 9). St John, who has other ways of saying the same thing—for example, "knowing him" (1 Jn 2:3f; Jn 14:7); "seeing him" (Jn 14:7, 9)—may have had in mind the errors of the Gnostics, who held that union with God was attained through a special kind of knowledge (*gnosis*), available only to initiates of their sect. The apostle repeats the teaching given in his Gospel: only through Christ, through faith in him, can one attain union with and knowledge of the Father (cf. Jn 1:18; 14:9–10); Jesus and the Father are one, only God (Jn 14:11). So, faith in Christ is inseparable from faith in the Blessed Trinity; so, too, denial of the Son's divinity involves rejection of the Father. "Once the mystery of the divine and eternal person of Christ the Son of God is abandoned, the truth respecting the Most Holy Trinity is also undermined" (SCDF, *Mysterium Filii Dei*, 4).

2:27. The anointing (cf. note on 2:20) refers to the Holy Spirit, who acts on the faithful by instructing them "about everything". Our Lord had said this would be so: "the Counsellor, the Holy Spirit, whom the Father will send in my name, he will teach you all things" (Jn 14:26).

The apostle does not mean that the faithful have no need of the Magisterium of the Church (the very fact that he is writing to them shows otherwise); what he wants to make quite clear is that their true teacher is the Holy Spirit (he it is who guides the Magisterium in its teaching, and he also acts in the soul of the Christian, helping him or her to accept that teaching). "If his anointing teaches you everything, it seems that we [pastors] are toiling to no purpose; why so much shouting on our part [...]? This is the marvellous thing. The sound of our words is striking your ears, but the Master is within. Do not think that it is a question of somebody learning from a man; we can attract your attention by the power of our voice, but if he who does the teaching is not within, all our sermons will be in vain" (St Augustine, *In Epist. Ioann. ad Parthos*, 3, 13).

e. Other ancient authorities read *you*

have no need that any one should teach you; as his anointing teaches you about everything, and is true, and is no lie, just as it has taught you, abide in him.

²⁸And now, little children, abide in him, so that when he appears we may have confidence and not shrink from him in shame at his coming. ²⁹If you know that he is righteous, you may be sure that every one who does right is born of him.

1 Jn 4:17
2 Thess 1:9
1 Jn 3:7, 10

2. LIVING AS GOD'S CHILDREN

We are children of God

Rom 8:14-17
Eph 1:5
Jn 15:21; 17:25
Col 3:4

3 ¹See what love the Father has given us, that we should be called children of God; and so we are. The reason why the world does not know us is that it did not know him. ²Beloved, we

---

2:28-29. These two verses sum up what has gone before and also act as an introduction to a passage on divine filiation. The central idea which St John has been repeating—"abide in him"—now opens out on to the prospect of the Last Judgment: Jesus Christ, who will be our Judge, is the same person as gave us revelation and life. This is one of the foundations of Christian hope.

"We may have confidence": the sacred writer changes to the plural, to include himself: we all have to give an account of our actions and we should have confidence in Christ our Judge. The word translated as "confidence" is much richer in Greek than in English; it is the equivalent of freedom, frankness, confident audacity. "It will be a great thing at the hour of death", St Teresa of Avila writes, "to realize that we shall be judged by One whom we have loved above all things [...]. Once our debts have been paid we shall be able to walk in safety. We shall not be going into a foreign land, but into our own country, for it belongs to him whom we have loved so truly and who himself loves us" (*Way of Perfection*, 40, 8).

3:1-24. This entire chapter shows how moved the apostle is when he contemplates the marvellous gift of divine filiation. The Spirit, who is the author of all Holy Scripture, has desired John to pass on to us this unique revelation: we are children of God (v. 1).

It is not easy to divide the chapter into sections, because the style is very cyclic and colloquial and includes many repetitions and further thoughts which make for great vividness and freshness. However, we can distinguish an opening proclamation of the central message (vv. 1-2) and emphasis on two requirements of divine filiation—rejection of sin in any shape or form (vv. 3-10), and brotherly love lived to the full (vv. 11-24).

3:1. "We should be called children of God": the original Hebrew expression, which reads "we are called ...", is also used by our Lord in the Beatitudes (cf. Mt 5:9): "to be called" means the same as "to be called by God"; and in the language of the Bible, when God gives someone a name he is not simply conferring a title but is causing the thing that the name indicates (cf., e.g., Gen 17:5), for the

are God's children now; it does not yet appear what we shall be, but we know that when he appears we shall be like him, for we shall see him as he is.

Rom 8:29
Phil 3:21
1 Cor 13:12

---

word of God is efficacious, it does what it says it will do. Hence St John's adding: "and so we are".

Therefore, it is not just a matter of a metaphorical title, or a legal fiction, or adoption human-style: divine filiation is an essential feature of a Christian's life, a marvellous fact whereby God gratuitously gives men a strictly supernatural dignity, an intimacy with God whereby they are *domestici Dei*, "members of the household of God" (Eph 2:19). This explains the tone of amazement and joy with which St John passes on this revelation.

This sense of divine filiation is one of the central points in the spirituality of Opus Dei. Its founder wrote: "We do not exist in order to pursue just any happiness. We have been called to penetrate the intimacy of God's own life, to know and love God the Father, God the Son, and God the Holy Spirit, and to love also—in that same love of the one God in three divine Persons—the angels and all men.

"This is the great boldness of the Christian faith—to proclaim the value and dignity of human nature and to affirm that we have been created to obtain the dignity of children of God, through the grace that raises us up to a supernatural level. An incredible boldness it would be, were it not founded on the promise of salvation given us by God the Father, confirmed by the blood of Christ, and reaffirmed and made possible by the constant action of the Holy Spirit" (*Christ Is Passing By*, 133).

"The world does not know us, (because) it did not know him": these words are reminiscent of our Lord's at the Last Supper: "the hour is coming when whoever kills you will think he is offering service to God. And they will do this because they have not known the Father, nor me" (Jn 16:2–3). Divine filiation brings with it communion and a mysterious identification between Christ and the Christian.

3:2. The indescribable gift of divine filiation, which the world does not know (v. 1), is not fully experienced by Christians, because the seeds of divine life which it contains will only reach their full growth in eternal life, when we see him "as he is", "face to face" (1 Cor 13:12); "this is eternal life, that they know thee the only true God, and Jesus Christ whom thou hast sent" (Jn 17:3). In that direct sight of God as he is, and of all things in God, the life of grace and divine filiation achieve their full growth. Man is not naturally able to see God face to face; he needs to be enlightened by a special light, which is given the technical theological name of *lumen gloriae*, light of glory. This does not allow him to "take in" all of God (no created thing could do that), but it does allow him to look at God directly.

Commenting on this verse, the *St Pius V Catechism* explains that "beatitude consists of two things—that we shall behold God such as he is in his own nature and substance; and that we ourselves shall become, as it were, gods. For those who enjoy God while they retain their own nature, assume a certain admirable and almost divine form, so as to seem gods rather than men" (1, 13, 7).

"When he appears": two interpretations are possible, given that in Greek the verb has no subject: "when (what we shall be) is revealed we shall be as he is"; or, as the New Vulgate translates it,

1 John 3:3

A child of God does not sin

Mt 5:48
Lev 19:2

³And every one who thus hopes in him purifies himself as he is pure.

Jn 1:29
Is 53:5
1 Pet 2:24

⁴Every one who commits sin is guilty of lawlessness; sin is lawlessness. ⁵You know that he appeared to take away sins, and in

---

"when he (Christ) is revealed we will be like him (Christ)". The second interpretation is the more likely.

3:3. "Purifies himself": Christian hope, which is grounded on Christ, is something active and it moves the Christian to "purify himself". This verb is evocative of the ritual purifications required of priests in the Old Testament prior to engaging in divine service (cf. Ex 19:10; Num 8:21; Acts 21:24); here, and in other places in the New Testament, it means interior purification from sins, that is, righteousness, holiness (1 Pet 1:22; Jas 4:8). Our model is Jesus Christ, "as he is pure"; he is the One who has never had sin, the Righteous One (1 Jn 2:29; 3:7); a Christian has no other model of holiness, as Jesus himself said: "Learn from me" (Mt 11:29; cf. Jn 14:6). "We have to learn from him, from Jesus, who is our only model. If you want to go forward without stumbling or wandering off the path, then all you have to do is walk the road he walked, placing your feet in his footprints and entering into his humble and patient Heart, there to drink from the wellsprings of his commandments and of his love. In a word, you must identify yourself with Jesus Christ and try to become really and truly another Christ among your fellow men" (St Josemaría Escrivá, *Friends of God*, 128).

3:4–5. "Sin is lawlessness": although this is not strictly speaking a definition, it does convey a basic idea: every sin is more than a transgression of a precept of the moral law; it is above all, an offence against God, the author of that law, a despising and a rejection of his will.

To understand the scope of this assertion, one needs to start from the fact that man has been created by God and is ever-dependent on him. So, every sin involves a pretentious desire to be like God (cf. Gen 3:5), to build one's life without reference to, or even in opposition to, God. Everyone who sins severs his allegiance to God and takes the devil's side. In this the mystery and "lawlessness" of sin consists. "This expression," Pope John Paul II explains, "which echoes what St Paul writes concerning the *mystery of evil* (cf. 2 Thess 2:7), helps us to grasp the obscure and intangible element hidden in sin. Clearly, sin is a product of man's freedom. But deep within its human reality there are factors at work which place it beyond the merely human, in the border-area where man's conscience, will and sensitivity are in contact with the dark forces which, according to St Paul, are active in the world almost to the point of ruling it (cf. Rom 7:7–24; Eph 2:2; 6:12)" (*Reconciliatio et paenitentiae*, 14).

Moreover, now that Christ has brought about our Redemption, every sin implies an offence to our Redeemer; it means crucifying again the Son of God (cf. Heb 6:6). So, St John reminds us about the main purpose of the Incarnation: "he appeared to take away sins" (v. 5). There is an echo here of the words the apostle heard the Baptist say: "Behold the Lamb of God, who takes away the sins of the world!" (Jn 1:29).

Thus, as we profess in the Creed at Mass, "for us men and for our salvation

him there is no sin. ⁶No one who abides in him sins;* no one who sins has either seen him or known him. ⁷Little children, let no one deceive you. He who does right is righteous, as he is righteous. ⁸He who commits sin is of the devil; for the devil has sinned from the beginning. The reason the Son of God appeared was to destroy the works of the devil. ⁹No one born of God commits sin; for God's^f nature abides in him, and he cannot sin because he is^g born

Rom 6:14
1 Jn 2:29
Jn 8:44
Gen 3:15
1 Jn 3:6
5:18

---

he (the Word) came down from heaven". Being true God and therefore completely exempt from sin (v. 5), he took on our human nature, to burden himself with our sins and nail them to the cross. Therefore, the Christian, ransomed from the power of the devil by the precious blood of Christ, and intimately united to him by the life of grace, has broken with sin once for all.

3:6–9. This passage acts as a preface to v. 10, where the apostle spells out the criteria for distinguishing the children of God from the children of the devil—the practice of Christian virtues and the keeping of the commandments of God, especially that of brotherly love.

To understand correctly what St John is saying here, it is useful to remember his controversy with the false teachers (the Gnostics): these were trying to deceive the faithful (v. 7) and claimed to have a special knowledge of God (*gnosis*), which put them above good and evil, so that what the Church regarded as sin they saw as morally indifferent and as incapable of undermining the union with God they claimed they had.

To identify these heretics, the apostle has recourse to words of our Lord: "the tree is known by its fruit" (Mt 12:33). Thus, the genuine Christian is recognized by deeds of righteousness (v. 7), that is, by keeping the commandments of God and leading a holy life. And the qualities essential to the Christian life are incompatible with sin; these qualities are—divine filiation ("he is born of God": v. 9), intimate union with Christ ("who abides in him": v. 6), and sanctifying grace, together with the infused virtues and the gifts of the Holy Spirit (this seems to be what the expression "God's nature abides in him" means: v. 9). Thus it is understandable that "No one who abides in him (Christ) sins" (v. 6).

In fact, as long as "God's nature abides in him ... he cannot sin" (v. 9). Clearly St John does not mean that a Christian is incapable of sinning; at the start of the letter he said, "If we say we have no sin, we deceive ourselves" (1:8). What he wants to make quite clear is that no one can justify his own sin by the device of claiming to be a child of God: the righteousness of the children of God reflects itself in their actions, whereas "he who commits sin is of the devil" (v. 8), for sin cuts one off from God and means one has submitted to the slavery of the devil.

The ancient heresy has grown up again, in a way, in our own time: there are those who claim that union with God is not broken by transgression of his commandments, even in grave matter, provided one does not withdraw one's "fundamental option" for God. Against this error, the Magisterium of the Church reminds us that "care must be taken not to reduce mortal sin to an act of 'fundamental option'—as is commonly said today—against God, intending thereby an explicit and formal contempt for God

---

f. Greek *his*   **g.** Or *for the offspring of God abide in him, and they cannot sin because they are*

1 John 3:10

of God. ¹⁰By this it may be seen who are the children of God, and who are the children of the devil: whoever does not do right is not of God, nor he who does not love his brother.

---

or neighbour. For mortal sin exists also when a person knowingly and willingly, for whatever reason, chooses something gravely disordered. In fact, such a choice already includes contempt for the divine law, a rejection of God's love for humanity and the whole of creation: the person turns away from God and loses charity" (*Reconciliatio et paenitentia*, 17).

3:10. "Children of the devil": this is a common Semitic way of speaking, meaning "the devil's supporters". In St John's writings we find references to "children of the devil" (cf. Jn 8:44; Acts 13:10) and to people who are "of the devil" (v. 8), and Judas is even called a "devil" (Jn 6:70; but he never uses an expression like "born of the devil". Therefore, the expressions "children of the devil" and "children of God" cannot be put on the same plane.

Also, "children of God" refers here primarily to the moral dimension of Christian life, as a description (the opposite of "the children of the devil") of those whose actions show they are on God's side. However, being children of God has a radically different meaning from being children of the devil, because it derives from something transcendental —God's causing the Christian to partake of his own divine nature through the life of grace (cf. 1 Jn 3:1–2 and notes on same).

The criteria for distinguishing the two groups mentioned are: the practice of righteousness, that is, striving for holiness and fighting against sin, reviewed in the previous section (vv. 3–9), and the practice of brotherly love, as we shall see in the next section (vv. 11–24).

3:11–22. St John begins this important passage on the subject of brotherly love with the same elevated tone as in 1:5. As usual with his style, it is difficult to discern any rigid arrangement of concepts, but there is a clear connexion of ideas, expressed in paradoxes and contrasts. 1) Statement of the central theme —the commandment of love (v. 11). 2) Its counterpoint is the sin of Cain (v. 12); those who do not practise brotherly love are as much murderers as he was (vv. 13–15). 3) Our model (a new contrast) is Christ, who gave his life for us (v. 16); brotherly love, following our Lord's example, must go beyond mere talk; it must show itself in deed and in truth (vv. 17–18). 4) The consequence of brotherly love is total confidence in God, who knows everything (vv. 19–22).

This passage of St John has led to many beautiful, touching commentaries by the Fathers of the Church. "I believe this is the pearl the merchant in the Gospel was looking for, which when he found it led him to sell everything he had and buy it (Mt 13:46). This is the precious pearl—charity; unless you have it, everything else you have is of no use to you; and if you have it alone, you need nothing else. Now you see with faith; later on you will see with intuitive vision; if we love now, when we do not see, what degree of love shall we not attain when we do see! And, meanwhile, what should we be doing? We should be loving the brethren. You may be able to say, I have not seen God; but can you say, I have not seen man? Love your brother. If you love your brother whom you see, you will also see God, because you will see charity, and God dwells within it" (St Augustine, *In Epist. Ioann. ad Parthos*, 5, 7).

Loving one another

¹¹For this is the message which you have heard from the beginning, that we should love one another, ¹²and not be like Cain who was of the evil one and murdered his brother. And why did he murder him? Because his own deeds were evil and his brother's righteous. ¹³Do not wonder, brethren, that the world hates you. ¹⁴We know that we have passed out of death into life, because we love the brethren. He who does not love abides in death. ¹⁵Any one who hates his brother is a murderer, and you know that no

Margin references: 1 Jn 2:7; Jn 13:34; Gen 4:8; Jn 15:18; Jn 5:24; Mt 5:21f

---

3:11. The new commandment of brotherly love, which Jesus expressly taught at the Last Supper (cf. Jn 13:34–35 and note) is the "message" which Christians have learned from the beginning (cf. 1 Jn 2:7). There is no more sublime commandment, and all the commandments are summed up in it. As St Augustine explains, "Everyone can make the sign of the cross of Christ; everyone can answer, Amen; everyone can sing Alleluia; everyone can have himself baptized, can enter churches, can build the walls of basilicas. But charity is the only thing by which the children of God can be told from the children of the devil. Those who practise charity are born of God; those who do not practise it are not born of God. An important mark, an essential difference! You may have whatever you like, but if you lack this, just this, everything else is of no use whatsoever; and if you lack everything and have nothing but this, you have fulfilled the law!" (*In Epist. Ioann. ad Parthos*, 5, 7).

3:12. Cain is the prototype of those who belong to the devil; not only because he took his brother's life by violence, but because the hatred nestling in his heart prevented him from recognizing his brother's goodness. The same reaction can happen today: "Because you don't know, or don't want to know, how to imitate that man's upright manner of acting, your secret envy makes you seek to ridicule him" (St Josemaría Escrivá, *Furrow*, 911).

3:13. In this verse, an aside breaking the flow of the argument, St John seeks to encourage all Christians, particularly his immediate readers who were probably experiencing persecution (perhaps that ordered by the emperor Domitian). Jesus clearly predicted that his disciples would be persecuted as he was (cf. Jn 15:18–22).

For a Christian, difficulties should provide an opportunity to show firmness in the faith and not be sad or discouraged (cf. Jn 16:1–4): "If you are reproached for the name of Christ, you are blessed, because the spirit of glory and of God rests upon you" (1 Pet 4:14).

3:14–15. The Christian life involves passing from death to life, from sin to grace. Anyone who does not practise the commandment of love "remains in death [sin]".

"Anyone who hates his brother is a murderer." This unambiguous statement echoes the teaching of Jesus in the Sermon on the Mount: "every one who is angry with his brother shall be liable to judgment" (Mt 5:22). The internal sin of hatred has the same malicious root as the external act of murder.

By speaking in this way, St John makes it crystal clear that hatred of one's neighbour is incompatible with the Christian faith.

1 John 3:16

Jn 15:13
Jas 2:16
Deut 15:7
Mt 7:21
Jas 1:22; 2:15f

2 Jn 4
3 Jn 3–4
1 Jn 4:17
Heb 4:16
Mt 7:7

murderer has eternal life abiding in him. ¹⁶By this we know love, that he laid down his life for us; and we ought to lay down our lives for the brethren. ¹⁷But if any one has the world's goods and sees his brother in need, yet closes his heart against him, how does God's love abide in him? ¹⁸Little children, let us not love in word or speech but in deed and in truth.

¹⁹By this we shall know that we are of the truth, and reassure our hearts before him ²⁰whenever our hearts condemn us; for God is greater than our hearts, and he knows everything. ²¹Beloved, if our hearts do not condemn us, we have confidence before God;

3:16–18. From Jesus the Christian learns what love is and what demands it makes —not only through his teaching (like that about the Good Shepherd in John 10:1ff or his discourse at the Last Supper) but above all by his example: "he laid down his life for us", by dying on the cross. We "ought" to do the same; the Greek word St John uses implies a duty. That is, the precept of brotherly love imposes an obligation for two reasons—by the very nature of things, since all men are brothers and children of God; and because we are indebted to Christ and must respond to the infinite love he showed by giving his life for us.

Using an example very like that in the Letter of St James (cf. Jas 2:15–16), he shows that true love expresses itself in actions: anyone who "closes his heart" when he sees others in need does not truly love. The saints have constantly reminded us of St John's teaching: "what the Lord desires is works. If you see a sick woman to whom you can give some help, never be affected by the fear that your devotion will suffer, but take pity on her: if she is in pain, you should feel pain too; if necessary, fast so that she may have your food, not so much for her sake as because you know it to be your Lord's will. That is true union with his will. Again, if you hear someone being highly praised, be much more pleased than if they were praising you" (St Teresa of Avila, *Interior Castle*, 5, 3, 11).

3:19–22. The apostle reassures us: God knows everything; not only does he know our sins and our frailties, he also knows our repentance and our good desires, and he understands and forgives us (St Peter, on the Lake of Tiberias, made the same confession to Jesus: "Lord, you know everything, you know that I love you": Jn 21:17).

St John's teaching on divine mercy is very clear: if our conscience tells us we have done wrong, we can seek forgiveness and strengthen our hope in God; if our conscience does not accuse us, our confidence in God is ardent and bold, like that of a child who has loving experience of his Father's tenderness. The love of God is mightier than our sins, Pope John Paul II reminds us: "When we realize that God's love for us does not cease in the face of our sin or recoil before our offences, but becomes even more attentive and generous; when we realize that this love went so far as to cause the Passion and Death of the Word made flesh who consented to redeem us at the price of his own blood, then we exclaim in gratitude: 'Yes, the Lord is rich in mercy', and even: 'The Lord *is* mercy'" (*Reconciliatio et paenitentia*, 22).

This confidence in God makes for confidence in prayer: "If you abide in me,

²²and we receive from him whatever we ask, because we keep his commandments and do what pleases him. ²³And this is his commandment, that we should believe in the name of his Son Jesus Christ and love one another, just as he has commanded us. ²⁴All who keep his commandments abide in him, and he in them. And by this we know that he abides in us, by the Spirit which he has given us.

Jn 14:13–15
Jn 6:28; 13:34
Jn 15:10
1 Jn 4:13
Rom 8:9

3. FAITH IN CHRIST. BROTHERLY LOVE

Faith in Christ, not in false prophets

4 ¹Beloved, do not believe every spirit, but test the spirits* to see whether they are of God; for many false prophets have gone

1Jn 2:18
2 Jn 7
Mt 24:24
1 Tim 4:1

---

and my words abide in you, ask whatever you will, and it shall be done for you" (Jn 15:7; cf. 14:13f; 16:23, 26–27).

3:23–24. The commandments of God are summed up here in terms of love for Jesus and love for the brethren. "We cannot rightly love one another unless we believe in Christ; nor can we truly believe in the name of Jesus Christ without brotherly love" (St Bede, *In I Epist. S. Ioannis*, ad loc.). Faith and love cannot be separated (cf. Gal 5:6); our Lord himself told us what would mark his disciples out—their love for one another (Jn 13:34–35).

Keeping the commandments confirms to the Christian that he is abiding in God: "If you keep my commandments, you will abide in my love" (Jn 15:10). Moreover, it ensures that God abides in his soul, by the indwelling of the Holy Spirit: "If you love me you will keep my commandments. And I will pray the Father, and he will give you another Counsellor, to be with you for ever" (Jn 14:15–16).

"May God be your house and you God's; dwell in God that God may dwell in you. God dwells in you to support you; you dwell in God in order not to fall. Keep the commandments, have charity" (*In I Epist. S. Ioannis*, ad loc.).

4:1–6. In the third part of the letter (4:1–5:12), the sacred writer expands further on the two things which sum up God's commandments (3:23)—faith in Jesus (4:1–6; 5:1–12) and brotherly love (4:7–21).

He begins by giving criteria for recognizing the true spirit of God and for identifying false teachers (4:1–6), clearly echoing what he said in the second chapter (cf. 2:18–29). There the heretics were called "antichrists", here "false prophets". There he underlined the indwelling of the Blessed Trinity in believers ("you will abide in the Son and in the Father": 2:24), the anointing "abides in you" (2:27); here he emphasizes rather the fact of belonging to God or not. This idea is developed in three points: 1) he who confesses Jesus Christ "is of God"; 2) he who does not confess him "is not of God" (vv. 2–3); you "are of God", they "are of the world" (vv. 4–5); 3) we (he must surely mean the apostles) "are of God", and therefore apostolic teaching merits attention and must be listened to (v. 6).

1 John 4:2

1 Cor 12:3	out into the world. ²By this you know the Spirit of God: every spirit which confesses that Jesus Christ has come in the flesh is of
1 Jn 2:22	God, ³and every spirit which does not confess Jesus is not of God. This is the spirit of antichrist, of which you heard that it was
1 Jn 2:13–14	coming, and now it is in the world already. ⁴Little children, you are of God, and have overcome them; for he who is in you is
Jn 15:19	greater than he who is in the world. ⁵They are of the world, therefore what they say is of the world, and the world listens to
Jn 8:47; 14:17	them. ⁶We are of God. Whoever knows God listens to us, and he

---

"Being of God", in St John's language, does not refer to originating from God, because in fact everyone, good and bad, faithful or not, comes from God. It means, rather, belonging to a group ("to my sheep": Jn 10:26) and it also means a mode of existence: "he who is from the earth ... of the earth speaks" (Jn 3:31); "you are from below, I am from above" (Jn 8:23); "Everyone who is of the truth hears my voice" (Jn 18:37). Faith, therefore, is not a superficial thing, something that affects us on the outside only: it actually changes a person's inner life; belonging to the community of the children of God involves a new way of being, which can be seen from the fact that we live in accordance with the faith we profess.

4:2–3. "Every spirit which confesses that Jesus Christ has come in the flesh ...": according to this translation (which fits certain Greek manuscripts) the Apostle would be emphasizing the fact that the Incarnation really happened, as if the false prophets opposed to the faith were saying that Christ's human nature was not real but only apparent (that was the position of the Docetists).

In the context, the alternate reading—"every spirit which confesses Jesus Christ come in the flesh"—may fit in better, since St John often insists that the Christian's faith centres on the person of Jesus Christ, who, being God, became man (cf. 2:22; 4:15; 5:1–5). By emphasizing this he is taking issue with the Gnostics particularly, who were saying that Jesus was the Son of God only from his Baptism onwards (cf. note on 1 Jn 5:6).

On the antichrist, see the note on 2:18.

4:4. St John repeats his conviction that Christians are assured of victory in their battle against the evil one (cf. 2:13; 5:4, 18). But what makes them victorious is the power of Christ working in them; so, while bolstering their faith he is also calling on them to be humble: "Do not become proud; recognize who has conquered in you. Why did you win? 'Because he who is in you is more powerful than he who is in the world.' Be humble; carry your Lord; be a little donkey for your rider. It is in your best interest to have him guide and direct you; because if you do not have him as your rider, you will be inclined to toss your head and kick out; but woe to you if you have no guide! That freedom would mean your ending up as prey for wild beasts" (St Augustine, *In Epist. Ioann. ad Parthos*, 7, 2).

4:6. "Whoever knows God listens to us": as elsewhere in the letter, there is a change from "you" to "we" (cf. 2:18, 28; 3:13–14). One could argue that the apostle is simply including himself in the Christian community as a whole, as if to

who is not of God does not listen to us. By this we know the spirit of truth and the spirit of error.

God is love. Brotherly love, the mark of Christians

⁷Beloved, let us love one another; for love is of God, and he who loves is born of God and knows God. ⁸He who does not love does

1 Jn 4:16

---

say "Whoever knows God listens to the Christians." However, the obvious interpretation is that the "us" refers to those in authority in the Church, bringing it perfectly into line with what Jesus says: "He who hears you hears me" (Lk 10:16). Obedience to the living Magisterium of the Church is, therefore, the rule for distinguishing the spirit of truth from the spirit of error. It could not be otherwise, for it is the Holy Spirit himself who guides the Church in its teaching and leads the faithful to accept that teaching: "the assent of the Church can never be lacking to such definitions [of the Supreme Magisterium] on account of the same Holy Spirit's influence, through which Christ's whole flock is maintained in the unity of the faith and makes progress in it" (Vatican II, *Lumen gentium*, 25).

4:7–21. St John now expands on the second aspect of the divine commandment (cf. 1 Jn 3:23)—brotherly love. The argument is along these lines: God is love and it was he who loved us to begin with (vv. 7–10); brotherly love is the response which God's love calls for (vv. 11–16); when our love is perfect, we feel no fear (vv. 17–18); brotherly love is an expression of love of God (vv. 19–21).

This is not tiresome repetition of the ideas already discussed (2:7–11; 3:11–18): contrary to the false teaching which is beginning to be spread, charity is the sure mark, the way to recognize the genuine disciple.

St Jerome hands down a tradition concerning the last years of St John's life:

when he was already a very old man, he used always say the same thing to the faithful: "My children, love one another!" On one occasion, he was asked why he insisted on this: "to which he replied with these words worthy of John: 'Because it is the Lord's commandment, and if you keep just this commandment, it will suffice'" (*Commentary on Gal.*, 3, 6, 10).

4:7. The divine attributes, God's perfections, which he has to the highest degree, are the cause of our virtues: for example, because God is holy, we have been given a capacity to be holy. Similarly, because God is love, we can love. True love, true charity, comes from God.

4:8. "God is love": without being strictly speaking a definition (in 1:5 he says "God is light"), this statement reveals to us one of the most consoling attributes of God: "Even if nothing more were to be said in praise of love in all the pages of this epistle", St Augustine explains, "even if nothing more were to be said in all the pages of Holy Scripture, and all we heard from the mouth of the Holy Spirit were that 'God is love', there would be nothing else we would need to look for" (*In Epist. Ioann. ad Parthos*, 7, 5).

God's love for men was revealed in Creation and in the preternatural and supernatural gifts he gave man prior to sin; after man's sin, God's love is to be seen, above all, in forgiveness and redemption (as St John goes on to say: v. 9), for the work of salvation is the product of God's mercy: "It is precisely because sin

not know God; for God is love. ⁹In this the love of God was made manifest among us, that God sent his only Son into the world, so that we might live through him. ¹⁰In this is love, not that we loved God but that he loved us and sent his Son to be the expiation for

---

exists in the world, which 'God so loved ... that he gave his only Son' (Jn 3:16), that God, who 'is love' (1 Jn 4:8), *cannot reveal himself other than as mercy*. This corresponds not only to the most profound truth of that love which God is, but also to the whole interior truth of man and of the world which is man's temporary homeland" (John Paul II, *Dives in misericordia*, 13).

4:9. God has revealed his love to men by sending his own Son; that is, it is not only Christ's teachings which speak to us of God's love, but, above all, his presence among us: Christ himself is the fullness of revelation of God (cf. Jn 1:18; Heb 1:1) and of his love for men. "The source of all grace is God's love for us, and he has revealed this not just in words but also in deeds. It was divine love which led the second Person of the most holy Trinity, the Word, the Son of God the Father, to take on our flesh, our human condition, everything except sin. And the Word, the Word of God, is the Word from which Love proceeds (cf. *Summa theologiae*, 1, 43, 5, quoting St Augustine, *De Trinitate*, 9, 10).

"Love is revealed to us in the incarnation, the redemptive journey which Jesus Christ made on our earth, culminating in the supreme sacrifice of the cross. And on the cross it showed itself through a new sign: 'One of the soldiers pierced his side with a spear, and at once there came out blood and water' (Jn 19:34). This water and blood of Jesus speaks to us of a self-sacrifice brought to the last extreme: 'It is finished' (Jn 19:30) —everything is achieved, for the sake of love" (St Josemaría Escrivá, *Christ Is Passing By*, 162).

"Among us": it is difficult to convey in English everything the Greek contains. The Greek expression means that the love of God was shown *to* those who witnessed our Lord's life (the apostles) and to all other Christians, who participate in this apostolic witness (cf. note on 1 Jn 1:1–3; this idea is repeated in vv. 14 and 16). But it also means "*within* us", inside us, in our hearts, insofar as we partake of God's own life by means of sanctifying grace: every Christian is a witness to the fact that Christ has come so that men "may have life, and have it abundantly" (Jn 10:10).

4:10. Given that love is an attribute of God (v. 8), men have a capacity to love insofar as they share in God's qualities. So, the initiative always lies with God.

When explaining in what love consists, St John points to its highest form of expression: "he sent (his Son) to be the expiation of our sins" (cf. 2:2). Similar turns of phrase occur throughout the letter: the Son of God manifested himself "to destroy the works of the devil" (3:8); "he laid down his life for us" (3:16). All these statements show that: 1) Christ's death is a *sacrifice* in the strict sense of the word, the most sublime act of recognition of God's sovereignty; 2) it is an atoning sacrifice, because it obtains God's pardon for the sins of men; 3) it is the supreme act of God's love, so much so that St John actually says, "in this is love."

What is amazing, St Alphonsus teaches, "is that he could have saved us without suffering or dying and yet he

our sins. ⁱⁱBeloved, if God so loved us, we also ought to love one another. ¹²No man has ever seen God; if we love one another, God abides in us and his love is perfected in us.

¹³By this we know that we abide in him and he in us, because he has given us of his own Spirit. ¹⁴And we have seen and testify that the Father has sent his Son as the Saviour of the world. ¹⁵Whoever confesses that Jesus is the Son of God, God abides in

Mt 18:33
Jn 1:18
1 Jn 3:24
Rom 5:5
Jn 3:17; 4:42
1 Jn 5:5

---

chose a life of toil and humiliation, and a bitter and ignominious death, even death on a cross, something reserved for the very worst offenders. And why was it that, when he could have redeemed us without suffering, he chose to embrace death on the cross? To show us how much he loved us" (*The Love of Jesus Christ*, chap. 1).

4:11–12. The apostle underlines here the theological basis of brotherly love: the love which God has shown us by the incarnation and redemptive death of his Son, places us in his debt: we have to respond in kind; so we "ought" to love our neighbour with the kind of gratitude and disinterest that God showed by taking the initiative in loving us.

Moreover, by loving one another we are in communion with God. The deepest desire of the human heart, which is to see and to possess God, cannot be satisfied in this life, because "no man has ever seen God" (v. 12); our neighbour, on the other hand, we do see. So, in this life, the way to be in communion with God is by brotherly love. "Love of God is the first thing in the order of commands", St Augustine explains, "and love of neighbour is the first thing in the order of practice [...]. You, who do not yet see God, will, by loving your neighbour, merit to see him. Love of neighbour cleanses our eyes to see God, as John clearly says, If you do not love your neighbour, whom you see, how can you love God, whom you do not see? (cf. 1 Jn 4:20)" (*In Ioann. Evang.*, 17, 8).

4:13. Having the gift of the Holy Spirit is the sure sign of being in communion with God. Since the Holy Spirit is the love of the Father and of the Son, his presence in the soul in grace is necessarily something dynamic, that is, it moves the person to keep all the commandments (cf. 3:24), particularly that of brotherly love. This impulse shows that the third Person of the Blessed Trinity is at work within us; it is a sign of union with God.

The Spirit's action on the soul is a marvellous and deep mystery. "This breathing of the Holy Spirit in the soul," says St John of the Cross, "whereby God transforms it into himself, is so sublime and delicate and profound a delight to it that it cannot be described by mortal tongue, nor can human understanding, as such, attain to any conception of it" (*Spiritual Canticle*, stanza 39).

4:14–15. Once more (cf. v. 1:4) John vividly reminds his readers that he and the other apostles have seen with their own eyes the Son of God, made man out of love for us. They were eyewitnesses of his redemptive life and death. And in the Son, sent by the Father as Saviour of the world, the unfathomable mystery of God is revealed—that his very being is Love.

"It is 'God, who is rich in mercy' (Eph 2:4) whom Jesus Christ has revealed to us as Father: it is his very Son who, in himself, has manifested him and made him known to us (cf. Jn 1:18; Heb 1:1f)" (John Paul II, *Dives in misericordia*, 1).

him, and he in God. ¹⁶So we know and believe the love God has for us. God is love, and he who abides in love abides in God, and God abides in him. ¹⁷In this is love perfected with us, that we may have confidence for the day of judgment, because as he is so are we in this world. ¹⁸There is no fear in love, but perfect love casts out fear. For fear has to do with punishment, and he who fears is not perfected in love. ¹⁹We love, because he first loved us. ²⁰If any

Marginal references: 1 Jn 4:8; 1 Jn 2:28; Rom 8:15; 1 Jn 4:10; 1 Jn 2:4

4:16. "Knowing" and "believing" are not theoretical knowledge but intimate, experienced attachment (cf. notes on 2:3–6; 4:1–6; Jn 6:69; 17:8). Therefore, when St John says that they knew and believed "the love God has for us" he is not referring to an abstract truth but to the historical fact of the incarnation and death of Christ (v. 14), the supreme manifestation of the Father's love.

"He who abides in love abides in God, and God abides in him": St Thomas Aquinas explains "that in some way the loved one is to be found in the lover. And so, he who loves God in some way possesses him, as St John says (1 Jn 4:16) [...]. Also, it is a property of love that the lover becomes transformed into the loved one; so, if we love vile and perishable things, we become vile and perishable, like those who 'became detestable like the things they loved' (Hos 9:10). Whereas, if we love God, we are made divine, for the Apostle says, 'He who is united to the Lord becomes one spirit with him' (1 Cor 6:17)" (*On the Two Commandments of Love*, prol., 3).

4:17–18. The perfection of charity shows itself in serene confidence in God and consequent absence of fear. Love is perfected *"in* us", as a gratuitous gift from God, but it can also be said that it grows *with* us, thanks to our free response to grace.

Confidence for the day of judgment (cf. also the note on 2:28) is something we should have also in this life; a basis for it is to be found in the daring statement, "... because as he is so are we in this world". This is not just a reference to imitating Christ's virtues or qualities: it means the profound identification with Christ which the Christian should attain: "it is no longer I who live, but Christ who lives in me" (Gal 2:20).

The fear which is incompatible with charity is servile fear, which sees God only as one who punishes those who transgress his commandments. But filial fear, which *is* compatible with charity, is what gives a Christian a deep horror of sin because it is something which cuts him off from the love of God his Father. In the early stages of the Christian life, fear of God is very helpful (cf., e.g., Ps 111:10; Sir 1:27): the Council of Trent teaches that sinners "by turning from a salutary fear of divine justice to a consideration of God's mercy, are encouraged to hope, confident that God will be well-disposed to them for Christ's sake" (*De iustificatione*, 6).

4:18. "The solution is to love", St J. Escrivá says. "St John the Apostle wrote some words which really move me: 'qui autem timet, non est perfectus in caritate.' I like to translate them as follows, almost word for word: the fearful man doesn't know how to love. You, therefore, who do love and know how to show it, you mustn't be afraid of anything. So, on you go!" (*The Forge*, 260).

one says, "I love God," and hates his brother, he is a liar; for he who does not love his brother whom he has seen, cannot[h] love God whom he has not seen. ²¹And this commandment we have from him, that he who loves God should love his brother also.

Mt 22:37–40
Jn 15:17

Everyone who believes in Jesus overcomes the world

5 ¹Every one who believes that Jesus is the Christ is a child of God, and every one who loves the parent loves the child. ²By this we know that we love the children of God, when we love God

1 Jn 2:22
Mt 16:16

4:19. Commenting on this passage, St Augustine exclaims: "How could we have loved him if he had not first loved us? By loving him, we become his friends; but he loved us when we were his enemies, in order to make us his friends. He loved us first and gave us the boon of loving him. We did not yet love him, but on loving him we become beautiful. What is a misshapen and deformed man doing, loving a beautiful woman? [...] Can he, by loving, change and become beautiful? [...]. Our soul, my brethren, is ugly due to iniquity; loving God makes it beautiful. What kind of love is this which makes the lover beautiful? God is always beautiful, never deformed, never changeable. He, who is ever beautiful, first loved us" (*In Epist. Ioann. ad Parthos*, 9, 9).

"We love": this can also be translated as "we should love one another", repeating 4:11. But here it seems to have an emphatic meaning: we are capable of loving.

4:20–21. "He is a liar": this is a very harsh statement (cf. 1:6–10; 2:4): being a liar means being on the devil's side, for the devil is the father of lies (cf. Jn 8:44). Loving God means keeping all the commandments (cf. Jn 14:15; 15:10), and the principal commandment is that of charity; therefore, it is not possible to love God without loving one's neighbour. Clement of Alexandria records a beautiful phrase of Christian tradition on this point when he says, "Seeing your brother is seeing God" (*Stromata*, 1, 19; 2, 15).

St John concludes this exhortation to charity by giving a new format to Christ's commandment, which makes it quite clear that love of neighbour is inseparable from love of God: true charity is a current that runs from God to the Christian and from the Christian to his fellow men. "The true disciple of Christ is marked by love both of God and of his neighbour" (Vatican II, *Lumen gentium*, 42).

5:1–5. The fifth chapter is a summary of the entire letter, focusing on faith in Jesus Christ (vv. 6–12) and the confidence that faith gives (vv. 13–21).

In the opening verses (vv. 1–5) St John points to some consequences of faith: he who believes in Christ is a child of God (v. 1); he loves God and men, his brothers (v. 2); he keeps the commandments (v. 3) and shares in Christ's victory over the world (vv. 4–5).

5:1. "He who loves the parent ...": it is axiomatic that one who loves his father also loves his brothers and sisters, because they share the same parent. The New Vulgate clarifies the scope of this maxim in this letter by adding the word *Deum*: "He who loves God his father ..." loves him who is born of God; Christian fraternity is a consequence of divine filiation.

---

h. Other ancient authorities read *how can he*

1 John 5:3

Jn 14:25
Mt 11:30

1 Jn 2:13, 14
Jn 16:33

1 Jn 4:4

and obey his commandments. ³For this is the love of God, that we keep his commandments. And his commandments are not burdensome. ⁴For whatever is born of God overcomes the world; and this is the victory that overcomes the world, our faith. ⁵Who is it that overcomes the world but he who believes that Jesus is the Son of God?

Testimony borne to Christ

Jn 19:34

⁶This is he who came by water and blood, Jesus Christ, not with the water only but with the water and the blood. ⁷And the Spirit is

---

5:4. "This is the victory that overcomes the world, our faith": faith in Jesus Christ is of crucial importance because through it every baptized person is given a share in Christ's victory. Jesus has overcome the world (cf. Jn 16:33) by his death and resurrection, and the Christian (who through faith becomes a member of Christ) has access to all the graces necessary for coping with temptations and sharing in Christ's own glory. In this passage the word "world" has the pejorative meaning of everything opposed to the redemptive work of Christ and the salvation of man that flows from it.

5:6. The "water" and the "blood" have been interpreted in different ways, depending on whether they apply (following the more literal meaning) to events in the life of Christ, or are regarded as symbols of particular sacraments. The water, if referred to the life of Christ, would be an allusion to our Lord's baptism (cf. Mt 3:13–17 and par.), where the Father and the Holy Spirit bore witness to Christ's divinity; the blood would refer to the cross, where Christ, God and true man, shed his blood to bring Redemption. According to this interpretation, St John is answering the Gnostics, who said that Jesus of Nazareth became the Son of God through baptism and ceased to be the Son of God prior to his passion: therefore, only the man Jesus, devoid of divinity, died on the cross; which would be a denial of the redemptive value of Christ's death.

Understood as symbols of the sacraments, the water would refer to Baptism (cf. Jn 3:5), where we receive the Holy Spirit and the life of grace (cf. Jn 7:37–39); the blood would apply to the Eucharist, where we partake of the blood of Christ in order to have life in us (cf. Jn 6:53, 55, 56). Jesus came on earth to give his life for men (cf. Jn 10:10); we obtain that life in the first instance by means of the living water of Baptism (cf. Jn 4:14; 7:37ff); and also by the application of the blood of Christ, which cleanses us from all sin (cf. 1 Jn 1:7; 2:2; 4:10).

The two interpretations are compatible with one another, given that sacraments are sensible signs of the supernatural effects of Christ's redemptive death. Referring to Baptism, Tertullian wrote: "We have also a second laving, and it too is unique—the baptism with blood. The Lord spoke of this when he said, 'I have a baptism to be baptized with' (Lk 12:50), having had already been baptized once. So, he did come 'by water and blood' (1 Jn 5:6), as John writes, in order to be bathed by the water and glorified by the blood, in order to make us (who are called by water) chosen ones through blood. These two baptisms spring from the wound in his pierced side; so it is that those who believed in his blood would be washed by the water; those who were

the witness, because the Spirit is the truth. ⁸There are three witnesses,* the Spirit, the water, and the blood; and these three agree. ⁹If we receive the testimony of men, the testimony of God is greater; for this is the testimony of God that he has borne witness to his Son. ¹⁰He who believes in the Son of God has the testimony in himself. He who does not believe God has made him a liar, because he has not believed in the testimony that God has borne to his Son. ¹¹And this is the testimony, that God gave us eternal life, and this life is in his Son. ¹²He who has the Son has life; he who has not the Son of God has not life.

Jn 5:32, 37; 8:18

Jn 3:33
Rom 8:16

1 Jn 1;2; 5:20

Jn 3:36

---

washed in the water would also drink of the blood" (*De baptismo*, 6).

5:7–8. The Sistine-Clementine edition of the Vulgate included an addition which left the text reading as follows: "There are three who give witness *in heaven: the Father, the Word, and the Holy Spirit; and these three are one. And there are three who give witness on earth:* the Spirit, the water, and the blood; and these three agree." The words shown in italics (known as the Johannine "comma" or addition) were the subject of heated debate (around the end of the nineteenth century) as to their authenticity. The Holy Office (as it was then called) left theologians free to research the matter (cf. *Declaration*, 2 June 1927) and in fact it has been shown that the "comma" was introduced in Spain around the fourth century AD in a text attributed to Priscillian, and therefore does not belong to the original inspired text. The "comma" makes express mention of the Blessed Trinity; however, even without it the text proclaims that mystery of faith fairly clearly: it makes mention of Jesus Christ, the Son of God (vv. 5–6), and of the Holy Spirit (v. 7) and of the Father, both of whom bear witness to the Son (v. 9).

According to the legal prescriptions of the Old Testament, the testimony of one witness was insufficient at trials (Deut 17:6; cf. Jn 8:17). St John points to three witnesses (the Holy Spirit, water and blood), thereby refuting the Gnostic teaching; he is saying that the water and the blood, that is, Christ's baptism and his death on the cross, are a manifestation of his divinity. Clearly the word "witness" is used here in a broad sense: namely, in the sense that at those two important moments in his life, Christ makes known to us that he is true God.

The Fathers who interpreted these words as referring to the sacraments usually comment on the fact that in the sacraments the grace of God is communicated internally and is signalled externally. St Bede writes along those lines: "The Holy Spirit makes us adoptive sons of God; the water of the sacred fount cleanses us; the blood of the Lord redeems us: the spiritual sacrament gives us a dual witness, one visible, one invisible" (*In I Epist. S. Ioannis*, ad loc.).

5:9–12. In his characteristic style St John strings together a series of short phrases (and their opposites, as contrasts) which are full of meaning. In a very few words, he enunciates three important truths, which he expects Christians to be very familiar with: 1) God the Father has borne witness to his Son (v. 9); 2) this witness brings an obligation with it; if one does not believe one is making God out to be a liar (v. 10); 3) God has given us life in Christ (vv. 11–12).

1 John 5:13

4. CONCLUSION

Jn 1:12; 20:31

¹³I write this to you who believe in the name of the Son of God, that you may know that you have eternal life.

Prayer for sinners

1 Jn 3:21f
Mt 7:7
Jn 14:13

¹⁴And this is the confidence which we have in him, that if we ask anything according to his will he hears us. ¹⁵And if we know that

---

Earlier the apostle pointed out that faith in Jesus can be the object of reason because it is based on external proofs, and that its fruit is supernatural life (cf. 1 Jn 1:1–5). Now he adds that in addition to the aforementioned witnesses—the Spirit, the water and the blood (vv. 6–8) —God the Father bears witness. Although John does not expressly say so, it is clear that God bore witness to Jesus throughout his earthly life: Jesus' words, miracles, passion and death, and his resurrection are evidence God has supplied of Christ's divinity. The believer "has the testimony [of God] in him" (v. 10), within him, insofar as he accepts and makes the Christian message (Revelation) his own, convinced that it comes from God, who cannot deceive or be deceived. In his turn, he who believes in Jesus Christ manifests his faith to others, passing on to them the conviction that Jesus is true God.

Faith produces the fruit of supernatural life, which is the seed and firstfruit of eternal life (cf. 11–12); that life can be given us only by Jesus Christ, our Saviour. "To those of us who are still making our pilgrim way in this life has been given the hope of eternal life, which we shall only receive in its full form in heaven when we reach Him" (St Bede, *In I Epist. S. Ioannis*, ad loc.).

5:13–21. St John's words in v. 13 are evocative of the first epilogue to his Gospel, where he explains why he wrote that book: "that you may believe that Jesus is the Christ, the Son of God, and that believing you may have life in his name" (Jn 20:31). In this verse of the letter, the apostle stresses the efficacy of faith, which is already an anticipation of eternal life (cf. notes on 1 Jn 3:2; 5:9–12).

His final counsels are designed to strengthen our confidence in prayer and to urge the need for prayer on behalf of sinners (vv. 14–17); they also stress the conviction and confidence that faith in the Son of God gives the believer (vv. 18–21).

5:14–15. Earlier, the apostle referred to confidence in prayer and to how we can be sure of receiving what we pray for: that confidence comes from the fact that "we keep his commandments and do what pleases him" (1 Jn 3:22). Now he stresses that God always listens to us, if we ask "according to his will". This condition can be taken in two ways, as St Bede briefly explains: "insofar as we ask for the things he desires, and insofar as those of us who approach him are as he desires us to be" (*In I Epist. S. Ioannis*, ad loc.). The asker therefore needs to strive to live in accordance with God's will, and to identify himself in advance with God's plans. If one does not try to live in keeping with God's commandments, one cannot expect him to listen to one's prayers.

When prayer meets those requirements, "we know that we have obtained the requests made of him", as our Lord

he hears us in whatever we ask, we know that we have obtained the requests made of him. ¹⁶If any one sees his brother committing what is not a mortal sin, he will ask, and God[i] will give him life for those whose sin is not mortal. There is sin which is mortal; I do not say that one is to pray for that. ¹⁷All wrongdoing is sin, but there is sin which is not mortal.

Mt 12:31
Heb 6:4–6

---

himself assured us: "if you ask anything in my name, I will do it" (Jn 14:14). "It is not surprising, then," the Curé of Ars teaches, "that the devil should do everything possible to influence us to give up prayer or to pray badly, because he knows better than we do how much hell fears prayers and how impossible it is that God should refuse us what we ask him for in prayer. How many sinners would get out of sin if they managed to have recourse to prayer!" (*Selected Sermons*, 5th Sunday after Easter).

5:16–17. "Mortal sin": the meaning of the original text is "sin which leads to death". The gravity of this sin (St John does not specify its exact nature) recalls the gravity of blasphemy against the Holy Spirit (cf. Mt 12:31–32) and of the sin of apostasy which Hebrews speaks of (Heb 6:4–8).

The Fathers have interpreted this expression in various ways, referring to different grave sins. In the context of the letter (in the previous chapters St John often speaks about the antichrists and false prophets who "went out" from the community: 2:19) the best interpretation seems to be that of St Bede and St Augustine, who apply it to the sin of the apostate who, in addition, attacks the faith of other Christians. "My view is", St Augustine says, "that the sin unto death is the sin of the brother who, after knowing God by the grace of our Lord Jesus Christ, attacks brotherly union and in a passion of envy reacts against that very grace by which he was reconciled to God" (*De Sermo Dom. in monte*, 1, 22, 73).

If St John does not expressly command his readers to pray for these sinners, it does not mean that they are beyond recovery, or that it is useless to pray for them. Pope St Gelasius I teaches: "There is a sin of death for those who persist in that same sin; there is a sin not of death for those who desist from sin. There is, certainly, no sin for the pardon of which the Church does not pray or from which, by the power which was divinely granted to it, it cannot absolve those who desist from it" (*Ne forte*).

Referring to this passage of St John, Pope John Paul II says: "Obviously, the concept of *death* here is a spiritual death. It is a question of the loss of the true life or 'eternal life', which for John is knowledge of the Father and the Son (cf. Jn 17:3), and communion and intimacy with them. In that passage the sin *that leads to death* seems to be the denial of the Son (cf. 1 Jn 2:22), or the worship of false gods (cf. 1 Jn 5:21). At any rate, by this distinction of concepts John seems to wish to emphasize the incalculable seriousness of what constitutes the very essence of sin, namely the rejection of God. This is manifested above all in *apostasy* and *idolatry*: repudiating faith in revealed truth and making certain created realities equal to God, raising them to the status of idols and false gods (cf. 1 Jn 5:16–21)." And after referring to blasphemy against the Holy Spirit (cf. Mt 12:31–32) he adds: "Here of course it is a

---

i. Greek *he*

1 John 5:18

The Christian's confidence as a child of God

1 Jn 3:9
Jn 17:15

¹⁸We know that any one born of God does not sin, but He who was born of God keeps him, and the evil one does not touch him.

Gal 1:4

¹⁹We know that we are of God, and the whole world is in the power of the evil one.

---

question of extreme and radical manifestations—rejection of God, rejection of his grace, and therefore opposition to the very source of salvation (cf. St Thomas, *Summa theologiae* 2–2, 14, 1–3)—these are manifestations whereby a person seems to exclude himself voluntarily from the path of forgiveness. It is to be hoped that very few persist to the end in this attitude of rebellion or even defiance of God. Moreover, God in his merciful love is greater than our hearts, as St John further teaches us (cf. 1 Jn 3:20), and can overcome all our psychological and spiritual resistance. So that, as St Thomas writes, 'considering the omnipotence and mercy of God, no one should despair of the salvation of anyone in this life' (ibid., ad 1)" (*Reconciliatio et paenitentia*, 17).

5:18–20. "We know": each of these verses begins this way. He does not mean theoretical knowledge but that understanding that comes from living faith. St John is once again stressing the Christian's joyful confidence, which he has been expounding throughout the letter (cf. 2:3–6 and note). This confidence is grounded on three basic truths: 1) he who is born of God does not sin (cf. 1 Jn 3:6–9 and note); 2) "we are of God", and therefore we are particularly free of the world, which is still in the power of the evil one (cf. 4:4; 5:12); 3) the Son of God has become man (cf. 4:2; 5:1). The incarnation of the Word is the central truth which sheds light on the two previous ones, because our supernatural insight is the effect of the Incarnation (v. 20): Jesus Christ, true God and true man, is also eternal life, for only in him can we attain that life.

5:18. "In this Johannine affirmation", Pope John Paul II teaches, "there is an indication of hope, based on the divine promises: the Christian has received the guarantee and the necessary strength not to sin. It is not a question therefore of a sinlessness acquired through one's own virtue or even inherent in man, as the Gnostics thought. It is a result of God's action. In order not to sin the Christian has knowledge of God, as St John reminds us in this same passage. But a little earlier he had written: 'No one born of God commits sin; for God's seed [RSV: "nature"] abides in him' (1 Jn 3:9). If by 'God's seed' we understand, as some commentators suggest, Jesus the Son of God, then we can say that in order not to sin, or in order to gain freedom from sin, the Christian has within himself the presence of Christ and the mystery of Christ, which is the mystery of God's loving kindness" (*Reconciliatio et paenitentia*, 20).

5:19. "The whole world is in the power of the evil one": although the Greek term may be neuter and would allow a more abstract translation ("in the power of evil"), it is more consistent with the context to take it in a personal sense. St John is pointing up the contrast between Christ's followers and those of the evil one: whereas the world (in the pejorative sense) is like a slave in the power of the devil, true Christians are *in* Christ, as free people, with a share in Christ's own life.

²⁰And we know that the Son of God has come and has given us understanding, to know him who is true; and we are in him who is true, in his Son Jesus Christ. This is the true God and eternal life. ²¹Little children, keep yourselves from idols.

Jn 17:3
Rom 9:5

1 Cor 10:14

"We have been born of God through grace and have been reborn in Baptism through faith. On the other hand, those who love the world are in the power of the enemy, be it because they have not yet been liberated from him by the waters of regeneration or because, after their rebirth, they have once more submitted to his rule through sinning" (*In I Epist. S. Ioannis*, ad loc.).

5:20. "Him who is true": that is, the only true God as distinct from false gods; the Jews used to refer to God as "the True", without naming him. When St John goes on to say that "we are in him, who is true, in his Son Jesus Christ", he is confessing the divinity of Christ and the fact that he is the only mediator between the Father and mankind.

5:21. Although at first sight, this final exhortation may seem surprising, it was appropriate in its time, because these first Christians were living in the midst of a pagan world, and were exposed to the danger of idolatry.

However, St John may be speaking metaphorically: the true danger facing Christians, then and now, is that of following the idols of the heart—that is, sin; in which case he is giving this final counsel: Keep away from sin, be on your guard against those whose fallacious arguments could lead you to sin.

Introduction to the Second and Third Letters of St John

These two letters of St John, which on account of their brevity are also called the "lesser epistles", conform to the style of letters of the period in the Greco-Roman world: they begin in the usual formal way (with the sender's name, then that of the addressee, and the greeting) and end with a concluding salutation.

The author introduces himself in both as "the elder" (cf. 2 Jn 1; 3 Jn 1). The Second Letter is addressed "to the elect lady and her children" (2 Jn 1), a symbolic way of referring to a local church, very probably one in Asia Minor. The Third is addressed to a Christian called Gaius (3 Jn 1), and perhaps through him to a group of faithful.

THE AUTHOR

In neither letter does the sacred writer give his name. However, the wide circulation they received from the very beginning (despite their slightness) is an implicit testimony to the authority of the writer. To this must be added the many testimonies which, from earliest times, attribute these letters to St John the apostle.

Thus, St Polycarp (d. 156), a disciple of the apostle, in his *Letter to the Philippians*[1] seems to use the text of 2 John 7. St Irenaeus (d. 202), a disciple, in turn, of St Polycarp quotes 2 John 7 and 11, expressly attributing that letter to St John.[2] Also, Tertullian (d. c.222), a witness to tradition in north Africa, refers to 2 John 7.[3] An indirect testimony is to be found in Clement of Alexandria (d. 214), who, to introduce a quotation from 1 John, uses this form of words: "John in his longer epistle", implying that he knew of at least one other, shorter, letter by the same writer.[4] Explicit quotations from the two letters are to be found in many different writers of the third to fifth centuries—St Dionysius of Alexandria,[5] St Athanasius,[6] St Cyril of Jerusalem,[7] St Gregory Nazianzen,[8] St Augustine[9] etc.

Both letters, along with 1 John, figure as works of St John the apostle in the earliest lists or canons of inspired books. The Muratorian Canon, written

---

1. Cf. 7:1. **2.** Cf. *Against Heresies*, 1, 16, 3; 3, 16, 8. **3.** Cf. *De carne Christi*, 24. **4.** Cf. *Stromata*, 2, 16, 76. **5.** Cf. Eusebius of Caesarea, *Ecclesiastical History*, 7, 25, 11. **6.** *Epist.* 39. **7.** *Catechesis*, 4, 36. **8.** *Poems*, 1, 12, 37. **9.** *De doctrina christiana*, 2, chap. 8, 12.

around the year 180, which reflects the tradition of the Roman church, speaks of the letters (plural) of St John. The provincial Council of Laodicea (c.360), a witness to the tradition of Asia Minor, includes in its canon 60 a list of inspired books in which the three letters figure. The same is true of various African councils—Hippo (393) and the third and fourth councils of Carthage (397 and 419). Finally, we might mention a letter from Pope St Innocent I (20 February 405) to Exuperius, bishop of Toulouse, where in reply to a question from the bishop as to which books are inspired, he sends him the well-known list with St John's three letters among the New Testament writings.

Alongside this broad consensus, which reflects so many testimonies from different parts of the Church, there were, in the early centuries, some doubts as to whether St John was the author of these two letters.

Very early on, Origen (d. 253) mentions the doubts current at his time.[10] Eusebius places both letters among the "disputed writings" of the New Testament, that is, the books not accepted by all as canonical;[11] he himself did accept them.[12] The same has to be said of St Jerome, who regarded them as authentic Johannine texts but noted the doubts obtaining in his time.[13]

These doubts originate from the text by Papias of Hierapolis (written around the year 130) which rationalist criticism has also used to deny the authenticity of the Fourth Gospel.[14] In the passage from Papias, recorded by Eusebius it says: "If ever anyone came who had carefully followed the presbyters, I inquired as to the words of the presbyters or what Thomas or James or what John or Matthew or any other of the disciples of the Lord, and what Aristion and the presbyter [elder] John, the Lord's disciple, were saying."[15]

If some modern critics have chosen to attribute the Gospel to "John the elder", taking him to be a different person from the apostle, they are naturally ever more inclined to do this in regard to these two letters signed by "the elder". However, even in the case of these letters the arguments offered are not convincing because, as against this one ambiguous testimony from Tradition, which does not even mention the Johannine writings, there is almost complete unanimity from the second century onwards as regards their Johannine authenticity. Official church documents have always attributed both letters to St John the apostle.

In addition to the testimonies from Tradition, there are also similarities of language and content between these letters and the Fourth Gospel which speak in favour of St John as author.

There is certainly no doubt about both letters being by the same author: it is enough to compare the initial greetings and endings, which are almost identical in wording.[16] Also, both letters, especially the Second, contain a

---

10. Cf. *In Ionann. comm.*, 6, 3; see *Ecclesiastical History*, 6, 27, 7–10.   **11.** Cf. *Ecclesiastical History*, 3, 25, 3.   **12.** Cf. *Demonstration Evangelica*, 3, 5, 88.   **13.** Cf. *Epist. ad Paulinum*, 53, 8; *On Famous Men*, 9, 18.   **14.** Cf. *The Navarre Bible: St John* (2005), p. 13.   **15.** *Ecclesiastical History*, 3, 39, 4.   **16.** Compare 2 Jn 1 with 3 Jn 1; 2 Jn 4 with 3 Jn 3, 4; 2 Jn 12 with 3 Jn 13, 14.

Introduction to the Second and Third Letters of St John

series of expressions and ideas characteristic of St John. The typical turns of phrase are: "love in the truth" (1 Jn 3:18; 2 Jn 1: 3 Jn 1); "know the truth" (1 Jn 2:21; 2 Jn 1); "abiding in Christ" or "in the doctrine of Christ" (1 Jn 2:28; 2 Jn 9); "having the Father and the Son" (1 Jn 2:23; 2 Jn 9); reference to traditional Christian teaching by the phrase "as you have heard from the beginning" (1 Jn 2:24; 3:11; 2 Jn 6); insistence on brotherly love ("that we love one another": 1 Jn 3:11, 23; 4:7; 2 Jn 5), a commandment which is not new, but which we have had from the beginning (cf. 1 Jn 2:7; 2 Jn 5); love for God consists in keeping the commandments (cf. 1 Jn 5:3; 2 Jn 6); he who does right "is of God" (1 Jn 3:10; 3 Jn 11), whereas he who does evil "has not seen God" (1 Jn 3:6; 3 Jn 11).

The first two letters speak of "many antichrists", "false prophets" or "deceivers (who) have gone into the world" (1 Jn 2:18; 4:1; 2 Jn 7); they are people who do not confess "that Jesus Christ has come in the flesh" (1 Jn 4:2; 2 Jn 7). Also, in 1 and 2 John the apostle expresses the wish that "our joy may be complete" (1 Jn 1:4; 2 Jn 12).

As can be seen, there is scarcely a verse of 2 John that does not have its parallel in 1 John. In fact, the second is usually regarded as a first draft (or else a resume) of the first.

To conclude: both the testimony of Tradition and analysis of the texts agree in pointing to St John the apostle as the author.

As regards canonicity the doubts which arose in the second to fourth centuries had no great importance, and, as we have indicated, from the fourth century onwards these letters appear in all the lists of inspired books. In the Councils of Trent[17] and Vatican I,[18] the Church has solemnly declared them to be canonical.

---

17. Cf. *De libris sacris*. **18.** Cf. *Dei Filius*, chap. 2.

Special Introduction to the Second Letter of St John

This letter is addressed to "the elect lady and her children" (v. 1), probably not a noble Christian woman and her family, but a local church; at the end of the letter, in similar phrasing, the apostle describes as "your elect sister" (v. 13) the Christian community from which he is writing—probably Ephesus.

The counsels the writer gives have to do with the same subjects as are covered more extensively in 1 John—brotherly love and observance of the commandments (vv. 4–6), and the need to be on guard against deceivers (vv. 7–11). Since the latter do "not acknowledge the coming of Jesus Christ in the flesh" (v. 7), the apostle exhorts the faithful to abide in the doctrine of Christ (v. 9), who is the Son of the Father (v. 3), so as to live in communion with the Father and the Son (v. 9).

In the absence of other information in the Tradition of the Church, it is reasonable to suppose that this letter was written in the last years of the first century, as a warning at a time when danger from heretics was not yet as serious as that revealed in 1 John (1 John being a later letter).

THE SECOND LETTER OF JOHN

The Revised Standard Version, with notes

Greeting

¹The elder* to the elect lady* and her children, whom I love in the truth, and not only I but also all who know the truth, ²because of the truth which abides in us and will be with us for ever:

³Grace, mercy, and peace will be with us, from God the Father and from Jesus Christ the Father's Son, in truth and love.

<small>3 Jn 1
1 Pet 5:13
Jn 14:17

1 Tim 1:2
2 Tim 1:2</small>

1:1–3. The normal heading of a letter in the Greco-Roman world (cf. note on 1 Cor 1:1) included the name of the sender ("the elder"), that of the addressee ("the elect lady and her children"), and the greeting (v. 3).

Like St Paul, St John uses this format but gives it his personal, Christian seal, especially in the greeting. Thus, whereas normally the greeting sent good wishes, St Paul usually says "grace and peace" (cf. the note on Rom 1:7); St John adds "mercy" (cf. also 1 Tim 1:2; 2 Tim 1:2). This is a way of stressing his supernatural conviction that they are receivers of divine favours.

The letter is addressed to the elect lady and her children, a metaphor meaning a particular church of Asia Minor: this allows one to suppose that it may have been a circular letter, addressed in the first instance to one community, but meant to be read later in many other communities, at least in Asia Minor.

"The truth": this word is used four times in this short section. In New Testament language, especially in the writings of St John, "truth" means the revelation of God which reaches its climax in Jesus Christ ("I am the truth": Jn 14:6) and includes all the truths in which we have to believe (cf. Jn 17:17, 19); but it is above all an interior principle of supernatural life and activity (cf. 1 Jn 2:24). Therefore, "to love in the truth" is much more than "to love sincerely"; it means "loving in Christ", the formula which St Paul uses (cf., e.g., Rom 16:8) and which is equivalent to "loving with the same love as that with which Christ loves". Of course, this is presented as a goal which the Christian should aim at though he will never fully achieve it.

1:1. "The elder": this is the literal translation. Among the Jews, elders were the most prominent people in the communities and formed one of the "estates" in the Sanhedrin (cf. note on Mt 2:4). In the New Testament and in the first era of Christianity, the titles of "elder" and "bishop" were used indiscriminately to refer to pastors of local communities, pastors appointed by the apostles (cf. note on Acts 20:28; and also Acts 11:30; 14:23; 20:17; 1 Tim 4:14; 5:17–19; Tit 1:5, 7). Even St Peter describes himself as "a fellow elder" (1 Pet 5:1). Only much later did the terminology we now have become fixed, reserving the title of "bishop" to bishops, and that of "elder" to ordinary priests.

Here the definite article—*the* elder—indicates that the writer is a person well known to those he is addressing and one who has authority over them. That elder *par excellence* is none other than St John himself.

1:3. "From the Father and from Jesus Christ, the Father's Son": this phrase is one of many supportive of the dogma of the consubstantiality between the Father and the Son, that is, that the two have the same substance, are one, only God. St John attests here, St Bede teaches, "that the grace, mercy and peace that are given to the faithful also come from Christ, as

The law of love

⁴I rejoiced greatly to find some of your children following the truth, just as we have been commanded by the Father. ⁵And now I beg you, lady, not as though I were writing you a new commandment, but the one we have had from the beginning, that we love one another. ⁶And this is love, that we follow his commandments; this is the commandment, as you have heard from the beginning, that you follow love.

Marginal refs: 3 Jn 3; 1 Jn 2:7; 1 Jn 5:3

Precautions against heretics

⁷For many deceivers have gone out into the world, men who will not acknowledge the coming of Jesus Christ in the flesh; such a one is the deceiver and the antichrist. ⁸Look to yourselves, that

Marginal refs: 1 Jn 2:18; 4:1, 3; Gal 4:11

---

well as from God the Father; and in order to show that he is equal to the Father and coeternal with him he says that the gifts of the Son are the same as those of the Father" (*In II Epist. S. Ioannis*, ad loc.). Jesus, speaking about his consubstantiality with the Father, says, "whatever he [God the Father] does, that the Son does likewise" (Jn 5:19).

1:4–6. Among all similarities of language and content between the Second and Third Letters, this passage is a particularly significant one.

The apostle's joy (v. 4) is based on the fact that the Christians have learned that walking in the truth entails keeping the commandment of brotherly love, which they have had from the beginning. The verses sum up one of the main themes of the First Letter, where St John expounds these teachings at greater length (cf. 1 Jn 2:7–11; 3:11–24; 4:7–21 and notes on same).

"That you follow love": the Greek is ambiguous and literally says "that you follow it"; "it" could refer to the commandment (that is how the New Vulgate reads it) or to love. The sense is not very different, if one remembers that in St John's teaching the commandments reduce to love of God and love of neighbour: "Listen carefully to a brief precept", St Augustine exhorts, "love and do what you like" (*In Epist. Ioann ad Parthos*, 7, 8).

St John also emphasizes that this is a commandment they have had "from the beginning" (vv. 5 and 6); that is, Tradition is so definite on this point that anyone who teaches otherwise is a liar and a deceiver. This helps to explain the connexion between these verses and the ones which follow. In fact the false teachers were causing harm in two ways—by corrupting the faith and by destroying unity and mutual love.

1:7–11. These warnings are a summary of things said in the First Letter (cf. 2:18–29; 4:1–6; 5:1–5; and notes on same). St John shows how to recognize these heretics—by the fact that they do not acknowledge the divinity of Jesus Christ incarnate (cf. 1 Jn 4:2–3 and note); and he warns that anyone who turns his back on sound teaching is abandoning the Father and the Son (cf. 1 Jn 2:22–25 and notes). The passage ends with instructions on precautions to take in dealings with those people (vv. 10–11).

On the "antichrist" (v. 7), see the note on 1 Jn 2:18.

you may not lose what you[a] have worked for, but may win a full reward. ⁹Any one who goes ahead and does not abide in the doctrine of Christ does not have God; he who abides in the doctrine has both the Father and the Son. ¹⁰If any one comes to you and does not bring this doctrine, do not receive him into the house or give him any greeting; ¹¹for he who greets him shares his wicked work.

1 Jn 2:23

Conclusion and greetings

¹²Though I have much to write to you, I would rather not use paper and ink, but I hope to come to see you and talk with you

3 Jn 13f

1:8. "That you may not lose what you have worked for": many important codexes read "what we have worked for", referring to the efforts of the apostles. Both readings have equal support in the Greek codexes; both make sense and show that in order to persevere in the faith (and obtain the reward for doing so) care and effort are needed, on the part of both pastors and other faithful.

St Cyril of Jerusalem exhorted: "Keep careful watch, to ensure that the enemy does not make off with any who are off guard or remiss; and that no heretic may pervert part of what you have been given. Accepting the faith is like putting into the bank the money we have given you; God will ask you for an account of this deposit" (*Catechesis V, De fide et symbolo*).

1:10–11. John does not mince his words: faith, a most precious gift from God, needs to be protected from harm. The letter has to do with certain errors which were spreading at the time, but its teaching applies to all periods of history.

In the Middle East hospitality and greeting were not, as they are sometimes among us, mere marks of courtesy or good manners; they involved a real sense of solidarity and affinity. Hence the warning that reception of these people implied complicity in their evil deeds (v. 11), and the consequent danger of giving scandal to others.

Instructions of a similar kind are to be found in Mt 18:17; 1 Cor 5:9–13; Tit 3:10–11. The Church has a duty to safeguard the faith—and to try to get those who undermine it to mend their ways. In exceptional cases it may have recourse to disciplinary measures if "neither by fraternal correction or reproof, nor by any methods of pastoral care, can the scandal be sufficiently repaired, justice restored and the offender reformed" (*Code of Canon Law*, can. 1341).

St Vincent of Lerins warned: "If you were to tolerate, even just once, a doctrinal error, I shudder to describe the grave danger to religion that would result; once you give way in any area of catholic dogma you will give way in another and another, as something quite lawful and required by custom" (*Commonitorium*, 23).

1:12–13. The ending shows St John's great warmth and affection. Like St Paul (cf. Rom 1:11–12) he longs to visit those Christians as soon as possible to confirm

---

a. Other ancient authorities read *we*

2 John 1:13

face to face, so that our joy may be complete. ¹³The children* of your elect sister greet you.

them in the faith and for the sheer pleasure a meeting will give both him and them.

The greeting sent in v. 13 comes from the members of the church from which he is writing, probably that of Ephesus.

Special Introduction to the Third Letter of St John

Addressed to a Christian named Gaius (v. 1), this letter must have been written at a time of strife in some Christian community. All we know about Gaius is what can be gleaned from the letter; St John praises him for being a true Christian (vv. 3–4), as he showed by the welcome he gave the apostle's envoys (vv. 5–8). That welcome also revealed his respect for the person of St John. His attitude contrasts with that of Diotrephes, who must have been the man in charge of that community (v. 9); Diotrephes does not accept the apostle's authority, nor did he receive his envoys; he even dared to excommunicate those who did welcome them (vv. 9–10). That explains why a previous letter the apostle sent to the church (v. 9) has not had any effect.

A man called Demetrius is also mentioned, probably the bearer of the letter; "everyone" has good things to say about him (v. 12). It is usually supposed that Demetrius was commissioned either to replace Diotrephes at the head of the church or else to institute Gaius in that position. In fact, the ancient Christian text, the *Apostolic Constitutions* (7, 46) contains lists of bishops which include the names of Gaius and Demetrius as bishops of Pergamum and Philadelphia respectively; however, the historical accuracy of these data is in doubt.

Although it does not contain any new teachings, the letter is a valuable testimony to the way of life of the early communities, and a model of the letters of introduction and recommendation mentioned elsewhere in the New Testament (cf. Acts 18:27; 2 Cor 3:3).

THE THIRD LETTER OF JOHN

The Revised Standard Version, with notes

Greeting

¹The elder to the beloved Gaius, whom I love in the truth.

²Beloved, I pray that all may go well with you and that you may be in health; I know that it is well with your soul.

2 Jn 1

Praise of Gaius

³For I greatly rejoiced when some of the brethren arrived and testified to the truth of your life, as indeed you do follow the truth. ⁴No greater joy can I have than this, to hear that my children follow the truth.

2 Jn 4

1 Jn 3:19

1–2. Gaius was a common name in the classical world. In St Paul's life, for example, others of the same name appear (cf. Acts 19:29; 20:4; 1 Cor 1:14; Rom 16:23). We know nothing about this Gaius other than what the letter says. An ancient Christian text (*Apostolic Constitutions*, 7, 46) mentions a Gaius as bishop of Pergamum and a Demetrius (v. 12) as bishop of Philadelphia; but the historical accuracy of these data is in doubt. From what the apostle says here, Gaius does not—at least yet—seem to hold any hierarchical office; he seems to be simply a prominent Christian faithful to his responsibilities in the Church.

"Beloved Gaius": four times St John describes him as "beloved" (vv. 1, 2, 5, 11). This really shows the deep fellowship the first Christians practised—not for them cold formality—and not only were they intimately concerned for one another's spiritual welfare, they were also interested in their physical well-being. "How well the early Christians practised this ardent charity which went far beyond the limits of mere human solidarity or natural kindness. They loved one another, through the heart of Christ, with a love tender and strong. Tertullian, writing in the second century, tells us how impressed the pagans were by the behaviour of the faiithful at that time. So attractive was it both supernaturally and humanly that they often remarked: 'See how they love another' (*Apologeticum*, 39)" (St Josemaría Escrivá, *Friends of God*, 225).

3–8. With great simplicity St John says why his paternal heart feels so happy— because Gaius, as his charity shows (vv. 5–8), is such a good-living man (vv. 3–4).

He uses a typically Semitic turn of phrase to describe Gaius' upright life: "you follow the truth." In the Old Testament the patriarchs are praised for "walking with God" (cf., e.g., Gen 5:22, 24; 6:9). This image of the wayfarer took on great importance after the Exodus: the people of Israel by divine will made their way as pilgrims to the Promised Land and in the course of that journey the great event of the Covenant took place (cf. Ex 19:24). "Walking with God" means the same as "fulfilling what the Covenant requires", that is, the commandments (cf. 2 Jn 4). With the coming of Christ, who said of himself, "I am the way, and the truth, and the life" (Jn 14:6), it has become quite clear that walking in the truth means being totally attached to the person of Christ: "live in him" (Col 2:6), "walk in the light" (1 Jn 1:7), "follow the truth" (2 Jn 4), all means the same sort of thing —living in communion with Christ, being a genuine Christian in everything one thinks and does.

⁵Beloved, it is a loyal thing you do when you render any service to the brethren, especially to strangers, ⁶who have testified to your love before the church. You will do well to send them on their journey as befits God's service. ⁷For they have set out for his sake and have accepted nothing from the heathen. ⁸So we ought to support such men, that we may be fellow workers in the truth.

Tit 3:13

Mt 10:40
Heb 13:2

Diotrephes' misconduct
⁹I have written something to the church; but Diotrephes, who likes to put himself first, does not acknowledge my authority. ¹⁰So if I

Gaius' charity expressed itself in welcoming and helping the preachers sent by John (in the early times of the Church itinerant missionaries helped to keep alive the faith and promote solidarity among the scattered churches). They had set out "for his sake", that is, Christ's (v. 7; cf. Acts 5:41; Phil 2:9–10; Jas 2:7). By helping (even materially), Christians become "fellow workers in the truth" (v. 8) and merit the reward promised by our Lord: "He who receives you receives me, and he who receives me receives him who sent me" (Mt 10:40).

"Fellow workers in the truth": the Second Vatican Council applies these words to lay people when explaining how their apostolate and the ministry proper to pastors complement each other. And it goes on: "Lay people have countless opportunities for exercising the apostolate of evangelization and sanctification. The very witness of a Christian life, and good works done in a supernatural spirit, are effective in drawing people to the faith and to God; and that is what the Lord has said: 'Let your light shine so brightly before men, that they may see your good works and give glory to your Father who is in heaven' (Mt 5:16).

"This witness of life, however, is not the sole element in the apostolate; the true apostle is on the look-out for opportunities to announce Christ by word, either to unbelievers to draw them towards the faith, or to the faithful to instruct them, strengthen them and incite them to a more fervent life" (*Apostolicam actuositatem*, 6).

9–10. "I have written something to the the church": we do not know what he is referring to—possibly a letter which has not survived.

As regards Diotrephes, all we know about him is what the letter tells us. He seemed to have had a position of authority, similar to that of a bishop. His ambition led him astray: he does not recognize St John's authority and is spreading lies about him; he has refused to receive the brethren sent by the apostle (the itinerant missionaries) and even tries to prevent others doing so.

The defiant behaviour of Diotrephes reminds us, by contrast, that the attitude of someone in a position of authority in the Church should be the same as that of the Master, who "came not to be served but to serve, and to give his life as a ransom for many" (Mt 20:28). In this connexion, Vatican II reminds us that "in exercising his office of father and pastor, the bishop should be with his people as one who serves (cf. Lk 22:26–27), as a good shepherd who knows his sheep and whose sheep know him, as a true father who excels in his love and solicitude for

come, I will bring up what he is doing, prating against me with evil words. And not content with that, he refuses himself to welcome the brethren, and also stops those who want to welcome them and puts them out of the church.

Commendation of Demetrius

[11]Beloved, do not imitate evil but imitate good. He who does good is of God; he who does evil has not seen God. [12]Demetrius* has testimony from every one, and from the truth itself; I testify to him too, and you know my testimony is true.

1 Jn 3:6–7
Jn 19:25; 21:24

Conclusion and farewell

[13]I had much to write to you, but I would rather not write with pen and ink; [14]I hope to see you soon, and we will talk together face to face.

2 Jn 12

---

all, to whose divinely conferred authority all readily submit" (*Christus Dominus*, 16).

11. The apostle here provides a resume of the teaching contained in various passages of his First Letter (cf. 1 Jn 2:18–19; 3:3–10; 5;18–20): he who does right is showing that he is of God, a child of God, that he is united to Christ and abides in him; whereas he who commits sin breaks his link with God and goes over to the enemy.

"Do not imitate evil but imitate good": St John's warning is not an unnecessary one, for human nature is so weak that, despite being impressed by good example, we are more inclined to copy bad example. The Church is always putting the saints before us as models to imitate: "To look on the life of those who have faithfully followed Christ is to be inspired with a new reason for seeking the city which is to come (cf. Heb 13:14 and 11:10), while at the same time we are taught to know a most safe path by which, despite the vicissitudes of the world, and in keeping with the state of life and condition proper to each of us, we will be able to arrive at perfect union with Christ, that is, holiness. God shows to men, in a vivid way, his presence and his face in the lives of those companions of ours in the human condition who are more perfectly transformed into the image of Christ (cf. 2 Cor 3:18). He speaks to us in them and offers us a sign of his kingdom, to which we are powerfully attracted, so great a cloud of witnesses is there given (cf. Heb 12:1) and such a witness to the truth of the Gospel" (Vatican II, *Lumen gentium*, 50).

12. The only information we have about Demetrius is contained in this verse. He may have been one of the missionaries sent by St John, and perhaps the bearer of the letter.

In addition to being recommended by all who knew him. Demetrius is testified to by "the truth itself". This may be a reference to Christ (cf. Jn 14:6) or to the Holy Spirit (the Spirit of Truth: Jn 14:17; 15:26; 1 Jn 5:6); or it may refer to Demetrius' exemplary conduct (he is one of those who "follow the truth": vv. 3–4). As at other important moments (cf., e.g., Jn 19:35; 21:24; 1 Jn 1:1–4), St John offers his own testimony.

13–15. The ending is very reminiscent of that of 2 John. It is a further example of the apostle's warm affection for the faith-

¹⁵Peace be to you. The friends greet you. Greet the friends, every one of them.

---

ful in his charge: he asks Gaius to greet them "every one of them"—one by one.

"Peace be to you": this is the normal Hebrew salutation, which the apostles continued to use in their letters, giving it a Christian meaning (cf., e.g., Rom 1:7 and the note on same; 1 Pet 5:14), As he wrote these words the apostle (now an old man) would have heard the echo of our Lord's greeting on the evening of the day of the Resurrection: "Peace be with you" (Jn 20:19).

Introduction to the Letter of St Jude

THE AUTHOR

The author of this short letter introduces himself to his readers as "Jude, a servant of Jesus Christ and brother of James" (v. 1). The description "servant of Jesus Christ" is similar to that used in various New Testament epistles.[1] The term "servant" is appropriate to every Christian, but it particularly suits those who have a ministry in the Church, especially the apostles and their successors.[2]

The reference to "James" is to a prominent person highly respected by the original addressees of the letter. From information in the New Testament we know that this James was the "brother" (that is, cousin or close relative) of the Lord (cf. Gal 1:19; Mt 13:55), who along with St Peter and St John was one of the "pillars" of the Church (cf. Gal 2:9), and that he was bishop of Jerusalem (cf. Acts 12:17; 15:13; 21:18), where he was martyred in the year 62.

As in the case of the Letter of St James,[3] the question arises whether this Jude (the author of the letter, who figures among our Lord's "brethren": cf. Mt 13:55) is the apostle of the same name, or whether two different people are involved.

St Luke twice lists the apostles (cf. Lk 6:16; Acts 1:13) and both times he puts Jude second last and, to distinguish him from Judas the traitor (in Hebrew, Greek and Latin the two names are the same), he calls him, literally, "Judas of James", which can mean either son of James, or brother of James. Normally the reference would be to a person's father; however, there are exceptions: sometimes in the case of a specially important person the rest of the family is named with reference to him; since James the Less was the most famous member of his family, St Luke may have been referring to James' *brother* when he called him "Jude of James".[4]

In the other lists of apostles—in the Gospels of Matthew and Mark—he is mentioned by his surname, Thaddaeus (cf. Mt 10:4; Mk 3:18) to distinguish him from Judas Iscariot, and he comes after his brother, "James the son of Alphaeus".

Therefore, there are solid grounds for equating the author with the apostle Jude-Thaddeus but we cannot be absolutely sure about it.

1. Cf. Rom 1:1; Phil 1:1; Tit 1:1; 2 Pet 1:1; Jas 1:1. **2.** Thus, one of the Pope's titles is "Servant of the servant of God". **3.** Cf. "Introduction to the Letter of St James", above. **4.** St Mark calls one of the holy women "Mary the mother of James" (15:40) and also "Mary [the mother] of James" (16:1).

Introduction to the Letter of St Jude

AUTHENTICITY

Some authors are of the view that this letter was written by a later disciple of St Jude. In support of this they offer evidence to do with style and vocabulary, and some turns of phrase that would suggest a later date. However, from early times Church tradition has explicitly pointed to the letter as being by the apostle St Jude. This tradition is vouched for, for example, by Origen[5] and Tertullian[6] in the first half of the third century.

CANONICITY

As well as some more or less clear allusions to the letter in the *Didaché* (second century) and St Polycarp's *Letter to the Philippians* (*c*.AD 110), there is an explicit reference in the Muratorian Fragment (*c*.180) listing the Letter of St Jude among the canonical writings of the New Testament. To the testimony of Origen and Tertullian should be added that of Clement of Alexandria, who not only quoted from the letter in his writings[7] but wrote a commentary on it.[8]

In the fourth century St Athanasius[9] and St Cyril of Alexandria,[10] to mention just two, vouch for the letter's canonicity.

The ecclesiastical writer Eusebius of Caesarea (263–330) states that most people accepted it as canonical, although there were some who thought it was not; hence his putting it among the "disputed" writings.[11] St Jerome tells us the main reasons for these doubts: "Jude has left us a short epistle, which is one of the Catholic Letters; but since he quotes the apocryphal book of Enoch it is rejected by many; yet it deserves a place in Holy Scripture because of its antiquity and the use that is made of it."[12]

Jude does (in vv. 14–15) quote the *Book of Enoch*, a text held in high regard by the Jews. But that does not mean necessarily that the sacred writer approves everything contained in that book, much less that he regards it as inspired. Not even his statement "Enoch ... prophesied" (v. 14) leads to that conclusion, for it was common at the time to refer to a well known teacher as a "prophet" (cf., e.g., Jn 1:19–28). St Paul, for that matter, quotes on one occasion a verse from a pagan poet Epimenides of Knossos, referring to him as a "prophet" (Tit 1:12).

At any event, as St Jerome made clear in the text just quoted, the Letter of St Jude enjoyed great authority from very early on and was accepted by the Church as Holy Scripture: it figures in all the lists of inspired books from the

---

5. Cf. *In Rom. comm.*, 5, 1.   **6.** Cf. *De culta feminarum*, 1, 3.   **7.** Cf. *Paedagogus*, 3, 8; *Stromata*, 3, 2.   **8.** Cf. Eusebius of Caesarea, *Ecclesiastical History*, 6, 14.   **9.** Cf. *Epist.*, 39.   **10.** Cf. *Mystagogical Catechesis*, 4, 35.   **11.** Cf. *Ecclesiastical History*, 3, 25, 3; 6, 13, 6; 14, 1.   **12.** *Of Famous Men*, 4.

mid-fourth century onwards. Its canonicity, and that of the other books in both Testaments, was solemnly declared by the Council of Trent.

IMMEDIATE READERSHIP

We do not know exactly whom the letter was originally sent to, for the salutation uses a description applicable to Christians in general. It is fairly likely that the addressees were, for the most part, converts from Judaism. This would explain the allusions to extra-biblical Jewish traditions and apocryphal writings such as *The Assumption of Moses* (cf. v. 9) and the *Book of Enoch* (cf. vv. 14–15). Possibly the fact that no specific addressees are mentioned explains why the letter was included among the Catholic Letters from as early as the time of Origen.[13]

The fact that the letter actually mentions James (cf. v. 1) may indicate that it was sent to the same group of readers as the Letter of St James, among whom James would have been held in high regard. In the absence of any further information, this is also the only clue we have to help us date the letter. If in fact it was sent to the same readers as the Letter of James it would be reasonable to date it shortly after the death of St James, which occurred around the year 62; a similar conclusion is reached by some scholars who think it must have been written before the year 70 because it makes no reference to the destruction of Jerusalem (yet others say this silence proves nothing). However, we would not be far wrong in dating it around the year 70.

BACKGROUND AND PURPOSE

The author's purpose in writing is to exhort the faithful to protect the faith delivered to them "once and for all" (v. 3), reminding them of what the apostles already predicted about the appearance of evil men dominated by their passions (cf. 17–18).

His specific reason for writing may have been news to the effect that ungodly men of that type had already secretly wormed their way into those Christian communities (cf. v. 4).

According to the letter, their errors had more to do with morals than faith: they were people who "pervert the grace of our God into licentiousness" (v. 4) and were spreading a false interpretation of Christian freedom (an error which St Paul also exposed).[14] Sexual immorality (cf. vv. 4, 8, 11, 13, 23) and greed (cf. vv. 11, 16) are the main vices mentioned.

---

13. Cf. "General Introduction to the Catholic Letters", above. 14. Cf., e.g., Rom 6:1–15; 1 Cor 6:12ff; Gal 5:13ff.

Introduction to the Letter of St Jude

At all events, this heterodox movement seems to have been in its early stages: these people are creating divisions (cf. v. 19), but they still take part in the life of the community (cf. v. 12) and there seems to be some hope of winning many of them back (cf. vv. 22–23).

The problem of false teachers and their evil influence on the faithful is also dealt with in the Second Letter of St Peter; between that letter and Jude there is a great similarity of thought and even language, especially between Jude 4–18 and 2 Peter 2:1–3:3. A comparison of the two texts suggests that the Letter of St Jude influenced 2 Peter, where some of the things said are developed further and slightly modified.[15]

PLAN AND CONTENT

The structure of the letter is fairly clear. In addition to the opening greeting (vv. 1–2), followed by the reason for writing (vv. 3–4), and a solemn doxology at the end (vv. 24–25), the body of the letter has two main parts—one exposing the false teachers (vv. 5–16) and the other exhorting the faithful (vv. 17–23).

In the first section, after showing with some biblical examples the punishment awaiting these ungodly people (vv. 5–7), their blasphemous and evil behaviour is condemned (vv. 8–13) and divine retribution is further underlined (vv. 14–16).

In the exhortation St Jude reminds them that, even in the first instruction that they gave, the apostles warned that false teachers would arise (vv. 17–19); Jude encourages them to base their life on faith, prayer, charity and hope (vv. 20–21). Finally, he tells them how they should behave towards those who have been influenced by ungodly teaching (vv. 22–23).

---

15. Cf. "Introduction to the Second Letter of St Peter," above, which has more to say on this.

THE LETTER OF JUDE

The Revised Standard Version, with notes

Greeting and blessing

¹Jude, a servant of Jesus Christ and brother of James, To those who are called, beloved in God the Father and kept for Jesus Christ: ²May mercy, peace, and love be multiplied to you.

Mt 13:55

2 Pet 1:2

1–2. In line with the standard practice in the classical world (also followed in the other New Testament letters), the heading gives the name and title of the sender and the addressees (v. 1) as well as the greeting proper (v. 2).

The author of the letter is probably the apostle St Jude Thaddaeus (cf. Introduction). Although he was a relative of our Lord (cf. Mt 13:55), he does not refer to that, preferring what he regards as the better title of "servant of Jesus Christ". In the religious world of the Jews the expression "servant of God" was equivalent to "worshipper of God" (cf. note on Rom 1:1). Therefore, by introducing himself as "servant of Jesus Christ" (as some other apostles do: cf. Rom 1:1; Jas 1:1; 2 Pet 1:1) St Jude is implicitly acknowledging the divinity of Christ.

The letter is addressed to "those who are called, beloved in God the Father and kept for Jesus Christ"—three characteristics applicable to Christians in general; that was why the letter was included in the "Catholic Letters", that is, those addressed to Christians everywhere, although it would originally have been sent to a smaller group.

"Who are called": this is the literal translation: to the same Greek root belongs the word "church", which is the community of those whom God "called ... out of darkness into his marvellous light" (1 Pet 2:9), the new people of God, chosen freely by him without any merit on their part. By its regular practice of describing Christians as "called" (cf. Rom 1:7; 8:28; 1 Cor 1:24; Rev 17:4), the New Testament underlines the gratuitous nature of the gift of faith and the Christian vocation, which has its origin not in man's will but in a divine initiative.

"Beloved in God the Father": the Old Testament also was conscious of God's loving kindness towards all his creatures (cf. Wis 11:24), especially his chosen people. The prophets were always recalling God's predilection as evidenced by the history of Israel. The supreme manifestation of the Father's eternal love is the incarnation and redemptive death of his Son Jesus Christ "so that we might live through him" (1 Jn 4:9). And God's paternal love, which made us his children (cf. Jn 3:1), never ceases to work in our favour right through our lives (cf. Rom 8:32).

"Kept for Jesus Christ": this is the most likely translation; it could also be read as "kept through Jesus Christ". God's entire plan of salvation is orientated towards Jesus, Head of the Church (cf. Col 1:18) and of the whole cosmos (cf. Eph 1:3–10). "For those whom (God) foreknew he also predestined to be conformed to the image of his Son, in order that he might be the first-born among many brethren" (Rom 8:29).

The sacred writer uses these expressions to describe what being a Christian means: a Christian's life begins with a calling from God, develops thanks to the love of God and reaches its highpoint in Jesus Christ. Undoubtedly, a Christian's vocation and perseverance derives its full meaning from the ultimate good which lies ahead of him: "The Church, to which we are all called in Christ Jesus, and in

Jude 3

His reason for writing

2 Pet 1:5; 2:21 ³Beloved, being very eager to write to you of our common salvation, I found it necessary to write appealing to you to contend for the faith which was once for all delivered to the saints. ⁴For admission has

---

which by the grace of God we acquire holiness, will receive its perfection only in the glory of heaven" (Vatican II, *Lumen gentium*, 48).

2. The good wishes which letters usually include in the opening greeting have a rather original ring to them here. St Jude's style is to present his ideas in sets of threes; here he describes himself as Jude/a servant of Jesus Christ/brother of James; the addressees are called/beloved in God/kept for Jesus Christ; and the blessing includes mercy/peace/love (cf. also vv. 5–8, 11, 20–21).

The three benefits included in the blessing are closely interconnected and form a summary of the graces God gives.

By mercy God loves men despite their sins. Mercy has a long and rich history in the Old Testament, as Pope John Paul II reminds us: "It is significant that in their preaching the prophets link mercy, which they often refer to because of the people's sins, with the incisive image of love on God's part. The Lord loves Israel with the love of a special choosing, much like the love of a spouse, and for this reason he pardons its sins and even its infidelity and betrayals [...]. In the preaching of the prophets *mercy signifies a special power of love*, which *prevails over the sin* and infidelity of the chosen people" (*Dives in misericordia*, 4). The redemption can be said to be the work of divine mercy.

Peace is a consequence of God's mercy. In Jewish letters peace was usually mentioned in the heading. St Paul and St Peter usually say "grace and peace" (cf. note on Rom 1:7; 1 Pet 1:2).

Love is the highest gift, which has been revealed in all its fullness in the New Testament: the love of God stirs Christians to love God and man, and is the commandment which summarizes all the rest (cf. Mt 22:34–40).

Some Fathers gave an allegorical interpretation to this greeting and those in other letters, seeing in them an implicit reference to the Blessed Trinity: according to St Augustine, mercy is attributed to the Father, peace to the Son, and love to the Holy Spirit (cf. *Unfinished Exposition on the Epistle to the Romans*, 12).

3–4. These verses explain the reason and purpose of the letter. The author is writing to the faithful about "our common salvation" (v. 3) because he has received alarming reports about the damage being done by certain false teachers with their bad doctrine and loose morals. St Jude's zeal leads him to expose these evil men (vv. 5–16) and exhort Christians to protect the faith (vv. 17–23).

3. The faith one receives must be kept intact and handed on in all its fullness. Because the faith "delivered to the saints" implies an already formed deposit of truths, some have suggested that the presence of this term means the letter should be given a later date; however, many references to this unchanging deposit are also to be found in St Paul (cf., e.g., Gal 1:6–9; 1 Cor 11:23ff; 15:1ff).

This verse reminds us of the importance of Tradition. As we know, the deposit of Christian faith and morals was entrusted to the Church "to be preserved in a continuous line of succession until

been secretly gained by some who long ago were designated for this condemnation, ungodly persons who pervert the grace of our God into licentiousness and deny our only Master and Lord, Jesus Christ.[a]

Gal 2:4
2 Pet 2:16

1. FALSE TEACHERS DENOUNCED

The punishment that awaits them

[5]Now I desire to remind you, though you were once for all fully informed, that he[b] who saved a people out of the land of Egypt,

Num 14:35
1 Cor 10:5
2 Pet 1:12

---

the end of time. Hence the apostles, in handing on what they themselves had received, warn the faithful to maintain the traditions which they had learned either by word of mouth or by letter (cf. 2 Thess 2:15); and they warn them to fight hard for the faith that had been handed on to them once and for all (cf. Jude 3)" (Vatican II, *Dei Verbum*, 8).

Therefore, although the custody of the faith and its handing on is a basic responsibility of the Pope and the bishops of the Church, it is also an obligation which falls on all Christians, particularly those who have a teaching role—for example, parents, teachers, catechists. John Paul II says: "It is Christ alone who teaches; anyone else teaches to the extent that he is Christ's spokesman, enabling Christ to teach with his lips. Whatever the level of his responsibility in the Church, every catechist must constantly endeavour to transmit by his teaching and behaviour the teaching and life of Jesus" (*Catechesi tradendae*, 6).

4. "Admission has been secretly gained": the Greek verb meaning "to enter from outside" conveys very well the way these false teachers went about it; they were probably travelling preachers, who went from one community to the next. St Jude accuses them of two faults—one moral and practical, that of turning grace into licentiousness; the other doctrinal, that of denying Jesus Christ. On the latter point he has very little else to say (cf. v. 8), presumably because his letter is mainly pastoral in character.

"Pervert the grace of God into licentiousness": the deviations he goes on to condemn have their origin in this perversion of values. Christ with his grace has obtained our freedom; however, this truth was quite often taken as a pretext for toning down the need to fight against sin (cf. Rom 6:1, 15; Gal 5:13; 1 Pet 2:16; 2 Pet 2:19). To understand the true nature of freedom better, we need to look at Jesus Christ who, being God, emptied himself and became obedient unto death on a cross (cf. Phil 2:6–8 and notes on same). "Thus we come to appreciate that freedom is used properly when it is directed towards the good; and that it is misused when men are forgetful and turn away from the Love of loves […]. Freedom finds its true meaning when it is put to the service of the truth which redeems, when it is spent in seeking God's infinite Love which liberates us from all forms of slavery" (St Josemaría Escrivá, *Friends of God*, 26 and 27).

5–7. The writer makes use of three famous biblical examples as a warning to

---

a. Or *the only Master and our Lord Jesus Christ*   **b.** Ancient authorities read *Jesus* or *the Lord* or *God*

Jude 6

Gen 6:1–2
2 Pet 2:4–9

afterward destroyed those who did not believe. ⁶And the angels that did not keep their own position but left their proper dwelling have been kept by him in eternal chains in the nether gloom until

---

false teachers—the unbelieving and complaining Israelites in the wilderness (v. 5); the angels who in their pride rebelled against God and were cast into hell (v. 6); the people of Sodom and Gomorrah, whose cities were destroyed in punishment for their sins of lust (v. 7).

At the same time, he seems to be alluding to the three main sins of the heretics he is denouncing—unbelief, pride and lust (cf. also vv. 14–16).

In 2 Peter reference is also made to the punishment of the rebellious angels and of Sodom and Gomorrah (cf. 2 Pet 2:4–10 and notes on same).

5. "The Lord" [RSV alternate reading]. In other Greek manuscripts it says "Jesus", thereby expressly attributing to Christ the liberation of Israel from Egypt, and interpreting the Old Testament in the light of the New, which is its fullness (cf. 1 Cor 10:1–12). The reading "The Lord" allows one to take it as referring either to God the Father or to Christ.

In the book of Numbers (chap. 14) we are told how the people of Israel, once they had been set free from the slavery of Egypt, rebelled against God, complaining about the trials of the journey and mistrustful of God's help. To punish their unbelief God decreed that that entire generation (except for those who had remained faithful) would die during the forty-year sojourn in the desert and never enter the promised land (cf. Num 14:20ff).

St Jude applies the lessons of that event to the situation of Christians: through Baptism they have been set free from the slavery of sin; their sights are on the promised land of heaven. However, as long as they are making their way, they must persevere in the faith "delivered once for all" (v. 3) and lead lives in line with it.

"Though you were once for all fully informed": this translation follows the great majority of the papyri and early Greek manuscripts and so is different from that of the New Vulgate, which, by changing the order of the words, applies the "once for all" to the rescue from Egypt ("the Lord—after saving the people once for all").

6. God created angels as the most sublime of creatures to form his heavenly court and to help him in the government of the cosmos, especially as protectors of and messengers to man. From the beginning they were given the gift of grace, but because they were intelligent beings it was necessary that they should respond freely to God's gift. Scripture tells us that some of them rebelled against God (cf. Rev 12:7–9) and were thrown into hell.

Some apocryphal books (for example, the *Book of Enoch*) gathered together legendary accounts of the sin of the fallen angels (cf. note on v. 7). St Jude, however, simply says that angels did sin, and were immediately punished and that that, as in the case of all who are condemned, will become plain for all to see at the Last Judgment. The Church teaches that it was pride that caused the angels' rebellion against God; "although (the angels) were all endowed with celestial gifts, very many, having rebelled against God, their Father and Creator, were hurled from those high mansions of bliss, and shut up in the darkest dungeon of earth, there to suffer for eternity the

the judgment of the great day;* ⁷just as Sodom and Gomorrah and the surrounding cities, which likewise acted immorally and indulged in unnatural lust, serve as an example by undergoing a punishment of eternal fire.

Gen 19:4–25
Mt 10:15
2 Pet 2:6–10

Their immorality
⁸Yet in like manner these men in their dreamings defile the flesh, reject authority, and revile the glorious ones.ᶜ ⁹But when the

2 Pet 2:10

---

punishment of their pride" (*St Pius V Catechism*, 1, 2, 17).

7. The inhabitants of Sodom and Gomorrah were particularly depraved (cf. Gen 18:20ff): their sins—including unnatural vice (sodomy)—were proverbial (Jer 23:14; Ezek 16:48–50). The whole region was destroyed (cf. Gen 19:24–25) and its cities have always been cited as the classic example of the severity of God's punishment of evildoers (cf. Jer 49:18; 50:40; Amos 4:11).

These cities were located on the shore of the Dead Sea, where "evidence of their wickedness still remains: a continually smoking wasteland, plants bearing fruit that does not ripen" (Wis 10:7). Jesus also referred to Sodom and Gomorrah as symbols of divine punishment (cf. Mt 10:15; 11:13; Lk 10:12; 17:29).

"Which ... acted immorally": probably a reference to the angels, alluding to the mythical account in the *Book of Enoch* and other apocrypha, which thought that the sin of the angels had been one of impurity; this opinion was common among the Jews. The sacred writer is not saying that these accounts are true; he is simply using things in the popular imagination to show the gravity of sins and the severity of the punishment they attract.

"Undergoing a punishment of eternal fire": these words make it quite clear that God's decision as Judge is irrevocable; this passage is quoted in the *Creed of the People of God*, 12 to describe the suffering of the damned in hell: "Those who have responded to the love and compassion of God will go into eternal life. Those who have refused them to the end will be consigned to the fire that is never extinguished."

The existence of hell as a place of eternal punishment is constant in Christian teaching. God's purpose in revealing this truth was not to strike terror into us but to encourage us to be converted and to persevere in right living. It has led many people to return to the right path.

"There is a hell. Not a very original statement, you think. I will repeat it to you, then: there is a hell! Echo it for me, at the right moment, in the ear of one friend, and of another, and another" (St Josemaría Escrivá, *The Way*, 749).

8–10. The sacred writer wants to expose the arrogance of the false teachers, whose personal conduct is like that of the people just mentioned (vv. 5–7). They are led not by the truth but by dreams (cf. v. 8), like the false prophets of old (cf. e.g. Deut 13:1–5).

Their corrupt behaviour is summed up in three sins (v. 8), whose exact nature is difficult to identify: "defiling the flesh" with sins of impurity, making themselves like the people of Sodom and Gomorrah (cf. vv. 4 and 7); "rejecting authority" (literally, "rejecting lordship", probably

c. Greek *glories*

Jude 10

<small>Dan 10:13; 12:1
Zech 3:2
2 Pet 2:11
2 Pet 2:12

Gen 4:8
2 Pet 2:15
Num 16:22

Ezek 34:8
Prov 25:14</small>

archangel Michael, contending with the devil, disputed about the body of Moses, he did not presume to pronounce a reviling judgment upon him, but said, "The Lord rebuke you."* ¹⁰But these men revile whatever they do not understand, and by those things that they know by instinct as irrational animals do, they are destroyed. ¹¹Woe to them! For they walk in the way of Cain, and abandon themselves for the sake of gain to Balaam's error, and perish in Korah's rebellion. ¹²These are blemishes^d on your love

---

in the sense that their licentious behaviour amounted in practice to rejecting the lordship of Christ: v. 4); it may also refer to the Church, whose authority they despised.

"Reviling the glorious ones", that is, the angels. It is not clear, however, whether this refers only to the good angels or to angelic nature in general (including therefore demons). Nor do we know what kind of blaspheming is being referred to. Perhaps the depraved customs spoken about by St Irenaeus (cf. *Against Heresies*, 1, 31) and St Epiphanius (cf. *Adversus haereses Panarium*, 38) began around this time: towards the beginning of the second century some Gnostic heretics went as far as to invoke the angels as patrons of their licentious behaviour.

To illustrate the wickedness of these insults to the angels, St Jude points out that not even the Archangel St Michael dared to curse the devil; he simply exclaimed, "The Lord rebuke you." St Jude attributes these words to him when they were arguing over "the body of Moses" (he assumes his readers are familiar with the story, which was to be found in the apocryphal *Assumption of Moses* and in other Jewish writings, to the effect that St Michael and the devil disputed over the body of Moses). The sacred writer does not make these speculations his own (there is no mention of them in the Bible: cf. Deut 34:5–6); he simply uses them to make a moral point.

The archangel's prudence only serves to highlight these people's arrogance.

11. With three further biblical examples he shows how evil the deceivers are. Cain is depicted in the Bible as the model of unbelief and fratricide (cf. Gen 4:3ff; Heb 11:14; 1 Jn 3:12). Balaam, a famous soothsayer (Num 22–24), was the epitome of greed and seduction, having led the Israelites into idolatry and fornication (cf. Num 31:16; 2 Pet 2:15; Rev 2:4).

Korah and his followers rebelled against Moses and Aaron and were punished by Yahweh who made the earth open and swallow them (Num 16).

The evildoers denounced by St Jude were leading Christians astray in a similar way—encouraging apostasy and licentiousness and creating discord (v. 19).

12–13. Using similes from nature, Jude now provides a clear description of the false teachers which stresses their arrogance and hypocrisy; they are attractive superficially, but all emptiness within.

They take part in the Christians' fraternal meals or love feasts (*ágapes*: cf. note on 1 Cor 11:17–22), where they freely indulge their greed and spread their false ideas. They are "blemishes", stains in the proper sense or in a moral sense; that is how the New Vulgate translates the term used here. It can also mean "scandal", coming from the original Greek meaning a "reef", a rock lying

d. Or *reefs*

feasts, as they boldly carouse together, looking after themselves; waterless clouds, carried along by winds; fruitless trees in late autumn, twice dead, uprooted; ¹³wild waves of the sea, casting up the foam of their own shame; wandering stars for whom the nether gloom of darkness has been reserved for ever.

2 Pet 2:13, 17

Is 57:20

The judgment of God
¹⁴It was of these also that Enoch in the seventh generation from Adam prophesied, saying, "Behold, the Lord came with his holy

Gen 5:18–24

---

just under the water and therefore a danger to navigation. "Looking after themselves"; that is, insolent and ambitious; possibly also a reference to their not respecting Church authority (cf. vv. 8, 16).

Pointing to the sterility and falsehood of their lives, St Jude calls them "waterless clouds" (deceiving those who expect rain), and "fruitless trees of late autumn", trees which should have been laden with fruit and instead produce nothing. They are "twice dead": perhaps a reference to their abandonment of the faith, which leaves them worse off than they were before Baptism (cf. 2 Pet 2:20–22; "uprooted": "Every plant which my heavenly Father has not planted", our Lord had said, "will be rooted up" (Mt 15:13).

And so, just as the waves of the sea deposit filth and debris on the shore, these people are casting the bad example of their impure lives before the faithful. Appearing as stars which reflect light for a while, they turn out to be "wandering stars" which go nowhere.

"The nether gloom of darkness": a reference to the darkest of dark places, where punishment awaits the ungodly (cf. note on v. 7).

14–16. The letter contains various allusions to the *Book of Enoch*, and now it quotes directly from it. This apocryphal text, written many years before Jesus Christ, has come down to us mainly in Ethiopian and Coptic versions; it belongs to the category of "apocalyptic writing", which contains many legendary accounts linked to obscure Old Testament passages. Like almost all apocryphal books, the author is unknown and it is attributed (to give it authority) to a prominent Old Testament figure: Enoch appears in Genesis as the seventh in line from Adam, and is a man praised for his goodness (cf. Gen 5:22–24; Sir 44:16; 49:14; Heb 11:5). These apocryphal writings had considerable popularity as spiritual literature and undoubtedly did much good despite their inaccuracies; but they were never regarded by the people of Israel or by the Church as inspired.

"Behold, the Lord came with his holy myriads": without going into what these words mean in the *Book of Enoch*, it is clear that in this letter the Lord is Christ, who will come as Judge of all, accompanied by the angels (cf. Dan 7:10; Heb 12:22), as he himself foretold (cf. Mt 25:31). In the language of apocalyptic writing, which is also used by the prophets, future events are spoken of as if they had already occurred.

Although God's judgment will affect everyone, this passage speaks above all of the condemnation that awaits the wicked—specifically, the false teachers the letter is denouncing. That is why it actually repeats the main charges against them—rebellion against lawful church

Jude 15

myriads, [15] to execute judgment on all, and to convict all the ungodly of all their deeds of ungodliness which they have committed in such an ungodly way, and of all the harsh things which ungodly sinners have spoken against him." [16]These are grumblers, malcontents, following their own passions, loud-mouthed boasters, flattering people to gain advantage.

Mt 25:31
2 Pet 2:10, 18
Lev 19:15

2. EXHORTATION

False teachers were predicted

2 Pet 3:2

[17]But you must remember, beloved, the predictions of the apostles of our Lord Jesus Christ; [18]they said to you, "In the last time there

---

authority, unbelief, lust, pride and greed (vv. 4, 8, 10, 11).

Reflection on the eternal truths is a good antidote against sin: "For it often happens", Fray Luis of Granada teaches, "that when the sinner realizes the torment which lies ahead of him, even though he may not love God for his own sake, he begins to give up his evildoing and desires and tries to follow another way, and little by little with heaven's help he comes to love and serve the Lord wholeheartedly and willingly. For divine mercy is so great that it is extended to man in all kinds of ways and by many different routes" (*Compendium of Christian Doctrine*, 8).

17–23. Having denounced the false teachers (vv. 5–16), St Jude now turns to the faithful to remind them about apostolic teaching on future heresy (cf. vv. 17–19) and to exhort them to practise the Christian virtues (vv. 20–21). The letter ends with some practical pieces of advice about how to behave towards those who go astray (vv. 22–23).

17–19. In their initial oral teaching, the apostles who founded the various Christian communities warned of the danger of false teachers within the Church itself (cf. Acts 20:29f; 1 Tim 4:1–3; 2 Tim 3:1–5). These warnings can be traced back to what Christ himself said: "False Christs and false prophets will arise and show great signs and wonders, so as to lead astray, if possible, even the elect" (Mt 24:24).

The way the writer refers to "the apostles of our Lord Jesus Christ" does not mean that he was not one of them. He could be referring simply to the fact that some of them had already died. The other point about this verse is the importance it gives to Tradition (cf. note on v. 3).

"In the last time" (v. 18): in the prophets this expression refers to the messianic era (cf., e.g., Is 2:2; Mic 4:1), which brings to an end the long period of waiting for the promised Redeemer and marks the start of the Kingdom of God, which will last forever (cf. Dan 7:14, 27; Lk 1:33). The fullness of time (cf. Gal 4:4) began with the coming of Christ and will reach its zenith with his return in glory for the Last Judgment. In the New Testament perspective, therefore, "the last time" covers the entire period of the Christian era; it is the era of the Church. This earthly phase of the Kingdom of God is characterized, by, among other

will be scoffers, following their own ungodly passions." ¹⁹It is these who set up divisions, worldly people, devoid of the Spirit.

1 Tim 4:1
2 Pet 3:3
1 Cor 2:14

Faith, hope and charity
²⁰But you, beloved, build yourselves up on your most holy faith; pray in the Holy Spirit; ²¹keep yourselves in the love of God; wait for the mercy of our Lord Jesus Christ unto eternal life.

Col 2:7
1 Thess 5:11

Attitude towards waverers
²²And convince some, who doubt; ²³save some, by snatching them

Amos 4:11
Rev 3:4

---

things, the presence of the "good" and the "bad" side by side (cf. Mt 13:47–48), the cockle sown among the wheat (cf. Mt 13:24ff).

"Worldly people": *psychikoi*, literally, "animal" or "natural" men. As in some texts of St Paul (cf. 1 Cor 2:14; 15:44–46), these are the opposite of "spiritual" men, that is, Christians who have the Holy Spirit and are docile to him (cf. Rom 5:5; 8:14). On the other hand, those who are "devoid of the Spirit", who is the source of supernatural life, form judgments and make decisions under the sole guidance of human nature wounded by original sin. Theirs is a merely earthly wisdom (cf. Jas 3:15), a wisdom of the flesh (cf. 1 Cor 3:3).

20–21. The Christian life can be summed up as living the three theological virtues (faith, hope and charity, accompanied by prayer), through the action of each of the three divine Persons—the love of God the Father, the mercy of our Lord Jesus Christ, and fellowship with the Holy Spirit.

The spiritual building is founded on faith, that is, on the truths revealed by God for our salvation and delivered once for all to the Church (cf. v. 3). Therefore it is a "most holy" faith—of divine origin, worthy of the highest respect, and unchangeable. Prayer is essential for penetrating deeper and deeper into the unfathomable riches of the faith. The Christian prays "in the Holy Spirit" because, as St Paul teaches, "you have received the spirit of sonship. When we cry, 'Abba, Father!' ..." (Rom 8:15); and "the Spirit helps us in our weakness; for we do not know how to pray as we ought, but the Spirit himself intercedes for us with sighs too deep for words" (Rom 8:26). To the love of God (the source of divine filiation in the Holy Spirit) the Christian should respond by striving to abide in that love and constantly increase it. Trust in God's help and in his mercy build up our hope of ultimately seeing the Lord face to face.

The Second Vatican Council reminds us that the faithfulness of a Christian's life depends on active communion with Christ: "A life like this calls for a continuous exercise of faith, hope and charity. Only the light of faith and meditation on the Word of God can enable us to find God everywhere and always [...]. Those with such a faith live in the hope of the revelation of the sons of God, keeping in mind the cross and resurrection of the Lord [...]. With the love that comes from God's prompting, they do good to all, especially to their brothers in the faith (cf. Gal 6:10)" (*Apostolicam actuositatem*, 4).

22–23. The apostle now gives some practical advice on how to behave towards those who have been affected by false ideas.

Jude 24

out of the fire; on some have mercy with fear, hating even the garment spotted by the flesh.ᵉ

1 Thess 5:23
Phil 1:10
2 Pet 3:14

Rom 16:27

Final doxology

²⁴Now to him who is able to keep you from falling and to present you without blemish before the presence of his glory with rejoicing, ²⁵to the only God, our Saviour through Jesus Christ our Lord, be glory, majesty, dominion, and authority, before all time and now and for ever. Amen.

The Greek text can be read in various ways. According to some codexes and the Vulgate, it is referring to three categories of people—waverers; those who have already been harmed by error but can still be recovered; and those who persist in heresy. That is how the RSV translates it. Other codexes, followed by the New Vulgate, first give a counsel valid for dealings with everyone affected by error and then go on to distinguish two groups—those who can still be recovered and those who seem to be beyond help.

Christians should always show kindness to those who break with sound teaching. In this way they will attract many back to the faith; but there will be others with whom they will not succeed; in their case, particularly if their lifestyle is depraved, it will be necessary to be prudent (to hate "even the garment spotted by the flesh"), in order to avoid contagion; but one should still treat them affectionately and pray for them. "It is a characteristic of the perfect", St Augustine teaches, "not to hate anything in sinners other than their sins; and to love those people themselves" (*Contra Adimantum*, 17, 5).

24-25. The letter does not end with the usual greetings but with a solemn doxology or hymn of praise addressed to God the Father through Jesus Christ. It may have come from a liturgical hymn.

"Only God": this does not exclude the divinity of the Son and the Holy Spirit; it is simply confessing that there is only one God (cf. Jn 17:3).

God reveals his power particularly in the work of our salvation. We constantly need his grace if we are to avoid sin in this life and one day obtain the glory of heaven. Jesus Christ is the Mediator both of our salvation and of our praise of God. From the beginning the Church has had the custom of addressing liturgical prayer to the Father through Jesus Christ.

---

e. The Greek text in this sentence is uncertain at several points

New Vulgate Text

APOCALYPSIS IOANNIS

[1] ¹Apocalypsis Iesu Christi, quam dedit illi Deus palam facere servis suis, quae oportet fieri cito, et significavit mittens per angelum suum servo suo Ioanni, ²qui testificatus est verbum Dei et testimonium Iesu Christi, quaecumque vidit. ³Beatus, qui legit et qui audiunt verba prophetiae et servant ea, quae in ea scripta sunt; tempus enim prope est. ⁴Ioannes septem ecclesiis, quae sunt in Asia: Gratia vobis et pax ab eo, qui est et qui erat et qui venturus est, et a septem spiritibus, qui in conspectu throni eius sunt, ⁵et ab Iesu Christo, qui est testis fidelis, primogenitus mortuorum et princeps regum terrae. Ei, qui diligit nos et solvit nos a peccatis nostris in sanguine suo ⁶et fecit nos regnum, sacerdotes Deo et Patri suo, ipsi gloria et imperium in saecula saeculorum. Amen. ⁷*Ecce venit cum nubibus,* et *videbit* eum omnis oculus et qui eum *pupugerunt, et plangent se super eum omnes tribus terrae.* Etiam, amen. ⁸Ego sum Alpha et Omega, dicit Dominus Deus, qui est et qui erat et qui venturus est, Omnipotens. ⁹Ego Ioannes, frater vester et particeps in tribulatione et regno et patientia in Iesu, fui in insula, quae appellatur Patmos, propter verbum Dei et testimonium Iesu. ¹⁰Fui in spiritu in dominica die et audivi post me vocem magnam tamquam tubae ¹¹dicentis: «Quod vides, scribe in libro et mitte septem ecclesiis: Ephesum et Smyrnam et Pergamum et Thyatiram et Sardis et Philadelphiam et Laodiciam». ¹²Et conversus sum, ut viderem vocem, quae loquebatur mecum; et conversus vidi septem candelabra aurea ¹³et in medio candelabrorum *quasi Filium hominis, vestitum podere* et *praecinctum* ad mamillas zonam *auream*; ¹⁴*caput* autem *eius* et *capilli erant candidi tamquam lana alba, tamquam nix, et oculi eius velut* flamma *ignis,* ¹⁵*et pedes eius similes orichalco* sicut in camino ardenti, *et vox illius tamquam vox aquarum multarum,* ¹⁶et habebat in dextera manu sua stellas septem, et de ore eius gladius anceps acutus exibat, et facies eius sicut sol lucet in virtute sua. ¹⁷Et cum vidissem eum, cecidi ad pedes eius tamquam mortuus; et posuit dexteram suam super me dicens: «Noli timere! Ego sum primus et novissimus, ¹⁸et vivens et fui mortuus et ecce sum vivens in saecula saeculorum et habeo claves mortis et inferni». ¹⁹Scribe ergo, quae vidisti et quae sunt et quae oportet fieri post haec. ²⁰Mysterium septem stellarum, quas vidisti ad dexteram meam, et septem candelabra aurea: septem stellae angeli sunt septem ecclesiarum, et candelabra septem septem ecclesiae sunt. [2] ¹Angelo ecclesiae, quae est Ephesi, scribe: Haec dicit, qui tenet septem stellas in dextera sua, qui ambulat in medio septem candelabrorum aureorum: ²Scio opera tua et laborem et patientiam tuam, et quia non potes sustinere malos et tentasti eos, qui se dicunt apostolos et non sunt, et invenisti eos mendaces; ³et patientiam habes et sustinuisti propter nomen meum et non defecisti. ⁴Sed habeo adversus te quod caritatem tuam primam reliquisti. ⁵Memor esto itaque unde excideris, et age paenitentiam et prima opera fac; sin autem, venio tibi et movebo candelabrum tuum de loco suo, nisi paenitentiam egeris. ⁶Sed hoc habes, quia odisti facta Nicolaitarum, quae et ego odi. ⁷Qui habet aurem, audiat quid Spiritus dicat ecclesiis. Vincenti dabo ei edere de ligno vitae, quod est in paradiso Dei. ⁸Et angelo ecclesiae, quae est Smyrnae, scribe: Haec dicit Primus et Novissimus, qui fuit mortuus et vixit: ⁹Scio tribulationem tuam et paupertatem tuam —sed dives es— et blasphemiam ab his, qui se dicunt Iudaeos esse et non sunt, sed sunt synagoga Satanae. ¹⁰Nihil horum timeas, quae passurus es. Ecce missurus est Diabolus ex vobis in carcerem, ut tentemini, et habebitis tribulationem diebus decem. Esto fidelis usque ad mortem, et dabo tibi coronam vitae. ¹¹Qui habet aurem, audiat quid Spiritus dicat ecclesiis. Qui vicerit, non laedetur a morte secunda. ¹²Et angelo ecclesiae, quae est Pergami, scribe: Haec dicit, qui habet romphaeam ancipitem acutam: ¹³Scio, ubi habitas, ubi thronus est Satanae, et tenes nomen meum et non negasti fidem meam et in diebus Antipas, testis meus fidelis, qui occisus est apud vos, ubi Satanas habitat. ¹⁴Sed habeo adversus te pauca, quia habes illic tenentes doctrinam Balaam, qui docebat Balac mittere scandalum coram filiis Israel, edere idolothyta et fornicari; ¹⁵ita habes et tu tenentes doctrinam Nicolaitarum similiter. ¹⁶Ergo paenitentiam age; si quo minus, venio tibi cito et pugnabo cum illis in gladio oris mei. ¹⁷Qui habet aurem, audiat quid Spiritus dicat ecclesiis. Vincenti dabo ei de manna abscondito et dabo illi calculum candidum, et in calculo nomen novum scriptum, quod nemo scit, nisi qui accipit. ¹⁸Et angelo ecclesiae, quae est Thyatirae, scribe: Haec dicit Filius Dei, qui habet oculos ut flammam ignis, et pedes eius similes

orichalco: ¹⁹Novi opera tua et caritatem et fidem et ministerium et patientiam tuam et opera tua novissima plura prioribus. ²⁰Sed habeo adversus te, quia permittis mulierem Iezabel, quae se dicit prophetissam, et docet et seducit servos meos fornicari et manducare idolothyta. ²¹Et dedi illi tempus, ut paenitentiam ageret, et non vult paeniteri a fornicatione sua. ²²Ecce mitto eam in lectum et, qui moechantur cum ea, in tribulationem magnam, nisi paenitentiam egerint ab operibus eius. ²³Et filios eius interficiam in morte, et scient omnes ecclesiae quia ego sum scrutans renes et corda, et dabo unicuique vestrum secundum opera vestra. ²⁴Vobis autem dico ceteris, qui Thyatirae estis, quicumque non habent doctrinam hanc, qui non cognoverunt altitudines Satanae, quemadmodum dicunt, non mittam super vos aliud pondus; ²⁵tamen id quod habetis, tenete, donec veniam. ²⁶Et, qui vicerit et qui custodierit usque in finem opera mea, / *dabo illi* potestatem super *gentes,* / ²⁷et *reget illas in virga ferrea,* / *tamquam vasa fictilia confringentur,* / ²⁸sicut et ego accepi a Patre meo, et dabo illi stellam matutinam. ²⁹Qui habet aurem, audiat quid Spiritus dicat ecclesiis. [3] ¹Et angelo ecclesiae, quae est Sardis, scribe: Haec dicit, qui habet septem spiritus Dei et septem stellas: Scio opera tua, quia nomen habes quod vivas, et mortuus es. ²Esto vigilans et confirma cetera, quae moritura erant, non enim invenio opera tua plena coram Deo meo; ³in mente ergo habe qualiter acceperis et audieris, et serva et paenitentiam age. Si ergo non vigilaveris, veniam tamquam fur, et nescies qua hora veniam ad te. ⁴Sed habes pauca nomina in Sardis, qui non inquinaverunt vestimenta sua et ambulabunt mecum in albis, quia digni sunt. ⁵Qui vicerit, sic vestietur vestimentis albis, et non delebo nomen eius de libro vitae et confitebor nomen eius coram Patre meo et coram angelis eius. ⁶Qui habet aurem, audiat quid Spiritus dicat ecclesiis. ⁷Et angelo ecclesiae, quae est Philadelphiae, scribe: Haec dicit Sanctus, Verus, qui habet *clavem David, qui aperit, et nemo claudet; et claudit, et nemo aperit:* ⁸Scio opera tua —ecce dedi coram te ostium apertum, quod nemo potest claudere— quia modicam habes virtutem, et servasti verbum meum et non negasti nomen meum. ⁹Ecce dabo de synagoga Satanae, qui dicunt se Iudaeos esse et non sunt, sed mentiuntur; ecce faciam illos, ut veniant et adorent ante pedes tuos et scient quia ego dilexi te. ¹⁰Quoniam servasti verbum patientiae meae, et ego te servabo ab hora tentationis, quae ventura est super orbem universum tentare habitantes in terra. ¹¹Venio cito; tene quod habes, ut nemo accipiat coronam tuam. ¹²Qui vicerit, faciam illum columnam in templo Dei mei, et foras non egredietur amplius, et scribam super eum nomen Dei mei et nomen civitatis Dei mei, novae Ierusalem, quae descendit de caelo a Deo meo, et nomen meum novum. ¹³Qui habet aurem, audiat quid Spiritus dicat ecclesiis. ¹⁴Et angelo ecclesiae, quae est Laodiciae, scribe: Haec dicit Amen, testis fidelis et verus, principium creaturae Dei: ¹⁵Scio opera tua, quia neque frigidus es neque calidus. Utinam frigidus esses aut calidus! ¹⁶Sic quia tepidus es et nec calidus nec frigidus, incipiam te evomere ex ore meo. ¹⁷Quia dicis: "Dives sum et locupletatus et nullius egeo", et nescis quia tu es miser et miserabilis et pauper et caecus et nudus, ¹⁸suadeo tibi emere a me aurum igne probatum, ut locuples fias et vestimentis albis induaris, et non appareat confusio nuditatis tuae, et collyrium ad inunguendum oculos tuos ut videas. ¹⁹Ego, quos amo, arguo et castigo. Aemulare ergo et paenitentiam age. ²⁰Ecce sto ad ostium et pulso. Si quis audierit vocem meam et aperuerit ianuam, introibo ad illum et cenabo cum illo, et ipse mecum. ²¹Qui vicerit, dabo ei sedere mecum in throno meo, sicut et ego vici et sedi cum Patre meo in throno eius. ²²Qui habet aurem, audiat quid Spiritus dicat ecclesiis». [4] ¹Post haec vidi: et ecce ostium apertum in caelo, et vox prima, quam audivi, tamquam tubae loquentis mecum dicens: «Ascende huc, et ostendam tibi, quae oportet fieri post haec». ²Statim fui in spiritu: et ecce thronus positus erat in caelo; et supra thronum sedens; ³et, qui sedebat, similis erat aspectu lapidi iaspidi et sardino; et iris erat in circuitu throni, aspectu similis smaragdo. ⁴Et in circuitu throni, viginti quattuor thronos et super thronos viginti quattuor seniores sedentes circumamictos vestimentis albis et super capita eorum coronas aureas. ⁵Et de throno procedunt fulgura et voces et tonitrua; et septem lampades ignis ardentes ante thronum, quae sunt septem spiritus Dei, ⁶et in conspectu throni tamquam mare vitreum simile crystallo. Et in medio throni et in circuitu throni quattuor animalia, plena oculis ante et retro: ⁷et animal *primum* simile *leoni et secundum* animal simile *vitulo et tertium* animal habens *faciem* quasi *hominis et quartum* animal simile *aquilae* volanti. ⁸Et quattuor animalia *singula* eorum habebant *alas senas,* in circuitu et intus plenae sunt oculis; et requiem non habent die et nocte dicentia: «*Sanctus, sanctus, sanctus Dominus, Deus omnipotens,* qui erat et qui est et qui venturus est!». ⁹Et cum darent illa animalia gloriam et honorem et gratiarum actionem sedenti super thronum, viventi in saecula saeculorum, ¹⁰procidebant viginti quattuor seniores ante sedentem in throno et adorabant viventem in saecula saeculorum et mittebant coronas suas ante thronum dicentes: ¹¹«Dignus es, Domine et Deus noster, / accipere gloriam et honorem et virtutem, / quia tu creasti omnia, / et propter voluntatem tuam erant et creata sunt». [5] ¹Et vidi in dextera sedentis super thronum librum scriptum intus et foris, signatum sigillis septem. ²Et vidi angelum fortem praedicantem voce magna: «Quis est dignus aperire librum et solvere signacula eius?». ³Et nemo poterat in caelo neque in terra neque subtus terram aperire librum neque respicere illum. [4]Et ego flebam multum, quoniam nemo dignus inventus est aperire librum nec respicere eum. [5]Et unus de senioribus dicit mihi: «Ne fleveris; ecce vicit leo de tribu Iudae, radix David, aperire librum et septem signacula eius». [6]Et vidi in medio throni et quattuor animalium et in medio seniorum Agnum stantem tamquam occisum, habentem cornua septem et oculos septem, qui sunt septem spiritus Dei missi in omnem terram. [7]Et venit et accepit de dextera sedentis in throno. [8]Et cum accepisset librum, quattuor animalia et viginti quattuor seniores ceciderunt coram Agno, habentes singuli citharas et phialas aureas plenas incensorum, quae sunt orationes sanctorum. [9]Et cantant novum canticum dicentes: «Dignus es accipere librum / et aperire signacula eius, / quoniam occisus es et redemisti Deo in sanguine tuo / ex omni tribu et lingua et populo et natione / [10]et fecisti eos Deo nostro regnum et sacerdotes, / et regnabunt super terram». [11]Et vidi et audivi vocem angelorum multorum in circuitu throni et animalium et seniorum, et erat numerus eorum myriades myriadum et milia milium [12]dicentium voce magna: «Dignus est Agnus, qui occisus est, / accipere virtutem et divitias et sapientiam / et fortitudinem et honorem et gloriam et benedictionem». [13]Et omnem creaturam, quae in caelo est et super terram et sub terra et super mare et quae in eis omnia, audivi dicentes: «Sedenti super thronum et Agno benedictio et honor et gloria et potestas in saecula saeculorum». [14]Et quattuor animalia dicebant: «Amen»; et seniores ceciderunt et adoraverunt. **[6]** [1]Et vidi, cum aperuisset Agnus unum de septem sigillis, et audivi unum de quattuor animalibus dicens tamquam vox tonitrui: «Veni». [2]Et vidi: et ecce equus albus; et, qui sedebat super illum, habebat arcum, et data est ei corona, et exivit vincens et ut vinceret. [3]Et cum aperuisset sigillum secundum, audivi secundum animal dicens: «Veni». [4]Et exivit alius equus rufus; et, qui sedebat super illum, datum est ei, ut sumeret pacem de terra, et ut invicem se interficiant, et datus est illi gladius magnus. [5]Et cum aperuisset sigillum tertium, audivi tertium animal dicens: «Veni». Et vidi: et ecce equus niger; et, qui sedebat super eum, habebat stateram in manu sua. [6]Et audivi tamquam vocem in medio quattuor animalium dicentem: «Bilibris tritici denario, et tres bilibres hordei denario; et oleum et vinum ne laeseris». [7]Et cum aperuisset sigillum quartum, audivi vocem quarti animalis dicentis: «Veni». [8]Et vidi: et ecce equus pallidus; et, qui sedebat desuper, nomen illi Mors, et Infernus sequebatur eum, et data est illis potestas super quartam partem terrae, interficere gladio et fame et morte et a bestiis terrae. [9]Et cum aperuisset quintum sigillum, vidi subtus altare animas interfectorum propter verbum Dei et propter testimonium, quod habebant. [10]Et clamaverunt voce magna dicentes: «Usquequo, Domine, sanctus et verus, non iudicas et vindicas sanguinem nostrum de his, qui habitant in terra?». [11]Et datae sunt illis singulae stolae albae, et dictum est illis, ut requiescant tempus adhuc modicum, donec impleantur et conservi eorum et fratres eorum, qui interficiendi sunt sicut et illi. [12]Et vidi, cum aperuisset sigillum sextum, et terraemotus factus est magnus, et sol factus est niger tamquam saccus cilicinus, et luna tota facta est sicut sanguis, [13]et stellae caeli ceciderunt in terram, sicut ficus mittit grossos suos, cum vento magno movetur, [14]et caelum recessit sicut liber involutus, et omnis mons et insula de locis suis motae sunt. [15]Et reges terrae et magnates et tribuni et divites et fortes et omnis servus et liber absconderunt se in speluncis et in petris montium; [16]*et dicunt montibus et petris*: «Cadite super nos et *abscondite nos* a facie sedentis super thronum et ab ira Agni, [17]quoniam venit dies magnus irae ipsorum, et quis poterit stare?». **[7]** [1]Post haec vidi quattuor angelos stantes super quattuor angulos terrae tenentes quattuor ventos terrae, ne flaret ventus super terram neque super mare neque in ullam arborem. [2]Et vidi alterum angelum ascendentem ab ortu solis, habentem sigillum Dei vivi, et clamavit voce magna quattuor angelis, quibus datum est nocere terrae et mari, [3]dicens: «Nolite nocere terrae neque mari neque arboribus, quoadusque signemus servos Dei nostri in frontibus eorum». [4]Et audivi numerum signatorum, centum quadraginta quattuor milia signati ex omni tribu filiorum Israel: [5]ex tribu Iudae duodecim milia signati, ex tribu Ruben duodecim milia, ex tribu Gad duodecim milia, [6]ex tribu Aser duodecim milia, ex tribu Nephthali duodecim milia, ex tribu Manasse duodecim milia, [7]ex tribu Simeon duodecim milia, ex tribu Levi duodecim milia, ex tribu Issachar duodecim milia, [8]ex tribu Zabulon duodecim milia, ex tribu Ioseph duodecim milia, ex tribu Beniamin duodecim milia signati. [9]Post haec vidi: et ecce turba magna, quam dinumerare nemo poterat, ex omnibus gentibus et tribubus et populis et linguis stantes ante thronum et in conspectu Agni, amicti stolis albis, et palmae in manibus eorum; [10]et clamant voce magna dicentes: «Salus Deo nostro, qui sedet super thronum, et Agno». [11]Et omnes angeli stabant in circuitu throni et seniorum et quattuor animalium, et ceciderunt in conspectu throni in facies suas et adoraverunt Deum [12]dicentes: «Amen! Benedictio et gloria et sapientia et gratiarum actio et honor et virtus et fortitudo Deo nostro in saecula saeculorum. Amen». [13]Et respondit unus de senioribus dicens mihi: «Hi qui amicti sunt stolis albis, qui sunt et unde venerunt?». [14]Et dixi illi: «Domine mi, tu scis». Et dixit mihi: «Hi sunt qui veniunt de tribulatione magna et laverunt stolas suas et dealbaverunt eas in sanguine Agni. [15]Ideo sunt ante thronum Dei et serviunt ei die ac nocte in

Revelation 7:16 New Vulgate

templo eius; et, qui sedet in throno, habitabit super illos. [16]*Non esurient* amplius *neque sitient* amplius, *neque cadet super illos sol neque* ullus *aestus,* [17]quoniam Agnus, qui in medio throni est, *pascet illos et deducet eos ad vitae fontes aquarum, et absterget Deus omnem lacrimam* ex oculis eorum». **[8]** [1]Et cum aperuisset sigillum septimum, factum est silentium in caelo quasi media hora. [2]Et vidi septem angelos, qui stant in conspectu Dei, et datae sunt illis septem tubae. [3]Et alius angelus venit et stetit ante altare habens turibulum aureum, et data sunt illi incensa multa, ut daret orationibus sanctorum omnium super altare aureum, quod est ante thronum. [4]Et ascendit fumus incensorum de orationibus sanctorum de manu angeli coram Deo. [5]Et accepit angelus turibulum et implevit illud de igne altaris et misit in terram; et facta sunt tonitrua et voces et fulgura et terraemotus. [6]Et septem angeli, qui habebant septem tubas, paraverunt se, ut tuba canerent. [7]Et primus tuba cecinit. Et facta est grando et ignis mixta in sanguine, et missum est in terram: et tertia pars terrae combusta est, et tertia pars arborum combusta est, et omne fenum viride combustum est. [8]Et secundus angelus tuba cecinit. Et tamquam mons magnus igne ardens missus est in mare: et facta est tertia pars maris sanguis, [9]et mortua est tertia pars creaturarum, quae in mari sunt, quae habent animas, et tertia pars navium interiit. [10]Et tertius angelus tuba cecinit. Et cecidit de caelo stella magna ardens tamquam facula et cecidit super tertiam partem fluminum et super fontes aquarum. [11]Et nomen stellae dicitur Absinthius. Et facta est tertia pars aquarum in absinthium, et multi hominum mortui sunt de aquis, quia amarae factae sunt. [12]Et quartus angelus tuba cecinit. Et percussa est tertia pars solis et tertia pars lunae et tertia pars stellarum, ut obscuraretur tertia pars eorum, et diei non luceret pars tertia, et nox similiter. [13]Et vidi et audivi unam aquilam volantem per medium caelum dicentem voce magna: «Vae, vae, vae habitantibus in terra de ceteris vocibus tubae trium angelorum, qui tuba canituri sunt!». **[9]** [1]Et quintus angelus tuba cecinit. Et vidi stellam de caelo cecidisse in terram, et data est illi clavis putei abyssi. [2]Et aperuit puteum abyssi, et ascendit fumus ex puteo sicut fumus fornacis magnae, et obscuratus est sol et aer de fumo putei. [3]Et de fumo exierunt locustae in terram, et data est illis potestas, sicut habent potestatem scorpiones terrae. [4]Et dictum est illis, ne laederent fenum terrae neque omne viride neque omnem arborem, nisi tantum homines, qui non habent signum Dei in frontibus. [5]Et datum est illis, ne occiderent eos, sed ut cruciarentur mensibus quinque; et cruciatus eorum ut cruciatus scorpii, cum percutit hominem. [6]Et in diebus illis quaerent homines mortem et non invenient eam; et desiderabunt mori, et fugit mors ab ipsis. [7]Et similitudines locustarum similes equis paratis in proelium, et super capita earum tamquam coronae similes auro, et facies earum sicut facies hominum, [8]et habebant capillos sicut capillos mulierum, et dentes earum sicut leonum erant, [9]et habebant loricas sicut loricas ferreas, et vox alarum earum sicut vox curruum equorum multorum currentium in bellum. [10]Et habent caudas similes scorpionibus et aculeos, et in caudis earum potestas earum nocere hominibus mensibus quinque. [11]Habent super se regem angelum abyssi, cui nomen Hebraice Abaddon et Graece nomen habet Apollyon. [12]Vae unum abiit. Ecce veniunt adhuc duo vae post haec. [13]Et sextus angelus tuba cecinit. Et audivi vocem unam ex cornibus altaris aurei, quod est ante Deum, [14]dicentem sexto angelo, qui habebat tubam: «Solve quattuor angelos, qui alligati sunt super flumen magnum Euphraten». [15]Et soluti sunt quattuor angeli, qui parati erant in horam et diem et mensem et annum, ut occiderent tertiam partem hominum. [16]Et numerus equestris exercitus vicies milies dena milia; audivi numerum eorum. [17]Et ita vidi equos in visione et, qui sedebant super eos, habentes loricas igneas et hyacinthinas et sulphureas; et capita equorum erant tamquam capita leonum, et de ore ipsorum procedit ignis et fumus et sulphur. [18]Ab his tribus plagis occisa est tertia pars hominum, de igne et fumo et sulphure, qui procedebat ex ore ipsorum. [19]Potestas enim equorum in ore eorum est et in caudis eorum, nam caudae illorum similes serpentibus habentes capita, et in his nocent. [20]Et ceteri homines, qui non sunt occisi in his plagis neque paenitentiam egerunt de operibus manuum suarum, ut non adorarent daemonia et *simulacra aurea et argentea et aerea et lapidea et lignea, quae neque videre* possunt *neque audire neque ambulare,* [21]et non egerunt paenitentiam ab homicidiis suis neque a veneficiis suis neque a fornicatione sua neque a furtis suis. **[10]** [1]Et vidi alium angelum fortem descendentem de caelo amictum nube, et iris super caput, et facies eius erat ut sol, et pedes eius tamquam columnae ignis, [2]et habebat in manu sua libellum apertum. Et posuit pedem suum dexterum supra mare, sinistrum autem super terram, [3]et clamavit voce magna, quemadmodum cum leo rugit. Et cum clamasset, locuta sunt septem tonitrua voces suas. [4]Et cum locuta fuissent septem tonitrua, scripturus eram; et audivi vocem de caelo dicentem: «Signa, quae locuta sunt septem tonitrua, et noli ea scribere». [5]Et angelus, quem vidi stantem supra mare et supra terram, *levavit manum suam dexteram ad caelum* [6]*et iuravit per Viventem in saecula* saeculorum, qui creavit caelum et ea, quae in illo sunt, et terram et ea, quae in ea sunt, et mare et ea, quae in eo sunt: «Tempus amplius non erit, [7]sed in diebus vocis septimi angeli, cum coeperit tuba canere, et consummatum est mysterium Dei, sicut evangelizavit servis suis prophetis». [8]Et vox, quam audivi de caelo, iterum loquentem mecum et dicentem: «Vade, accipe librum apertum de manu angeli stantis supra mare et supra terram». [9]Et abii ad angelum dicens ei, ut daret mihi libellum. Et dicit mihi: «Accipe et devora illum; et faciet amaricare ventrem tuum, sed in ore tuo erit dulcis tamquam mel». [10]Et accepi libellum de manu angeli et devoravi eum, et erat in ore meo tamquam mel dulcis; et cum devorassem eum, amaricatus est venter meus. [11]Et dicunt mihi: «Oportet te iterum prophetare super populis et gentibus et linguis et regibus multis». [11] [1]Et datus est mihi calamus similis virgae dicens: «Surge et metire templum Dei et altare et adorantes in eo. [2]Atrium autem, quod est foris templum, eice foras et ne metiaris illud, quoniam datum est gentibus, et civitatem sanctam calcabunt mensibus quadraginta duobus. [3]Et dabo duobus testibus meis, et prophetabunt diebus mille ducentis sexaginta amicti saccis». [4]*Hi sunt duae olivae et duo candelabra in conspectu Domini terrae stantes.* [5]Et si quis eis vult nocere, ignis exit de ore illorum et devorat inimicos eorum; et si quis voluerit eos laedere, sic oportet eum occidi. [6]Hi habent potestatem claudendi caelum, ne pluat pluvia diebus prophetiae ipsorum, et potestatem habent super aquas convertendi eas in sanguinem et percutere terram omni plaga, quotienscumque voluerint. [7]Et cum finierint testimonium suum, bestia, quae ascendit de abysso, faciet adversus illos bellum et vincet eos et occidet illos. [8]Et corpus eorum in platea civitatis magnae, quae vocatur spiritaliter Sodoma et Aegyptus, ubi et Dominus eorum crucifixus est; [9]et vident de populis et tribubus et linguis et gentibus corpus eorum per tres dies et dimidium, et corpora eorum non sinunt poni in monumento. [10]Et inhabitantes terram gaudent super illis et iucundantur et munera mittent invicem, quoniam hi duo prophetae cruciaverunt eos, qui inhabitant super terram. [11]Et post dies tres et dimidium spiritus vitae a Deo intravit in eos, et steterunt super pedes suos; et timor magnus cecidit super eos, qui videbant eos. [12]Et audierunt vocem magnam de caelo dicentem illis: «Ascendite huc»; et ascenderunt in caelum in nube, et viderunt illos inimici eorum. [13]Et in illa hora factus est terraemotus magnus, et decima pars civitatis cecidit, et occisi sunt in terraemotu nomina hominum septem milia, et reliqui in timorem sunt missi et dederunt gloriam Deo caeli. [14]Vae secundum abiit; ecce vae tertium venit cito. [15]Et septimus angelus tuba cecinit, et factae sunt voces magnae in caelo dicentes: «Factum est regnum huius mundi Domini nostri et Christi eius, et regnabit in saecula saeculorum». [16]Et viginti quattuor seniores, qui in conspectu Dei sedent in thronis suis, ceciderunt super facies suas et adoraverunt Deum [17]dicentes: «Gratias agimus tibi, / Domine, Deus omnipotens, / qui es et qui eras, / quia accepisti virtutem tuam magnam et regnasti. / [18]Et iratae sunt gentes, / et advenit ira tua, et tempus mortuorum iudicari / et reddere mercedem servis tuis prophetis et sanctis / et timentibus nomen tuum, pusillis et magnis, / et exterminare eos, qui exterminant terram». [19]Et apertum est templum Dei in caelo, et visa est arca testamenti eius in templo eius; et facta sunt fulgura et voces et terraemotus et grando magna. [12] [1]Et signum magnum apparuit in caelo: mulier amicta sole, et luna sub pedibus eius, et super caput eius corona stellarum duodecim; [2]et in utero habens, et clamat parturiens et cruciatur, ut pariat. [3]Et visum est aliud signum in caelo: et ecce draco rufus magnus, habens capita septem et cornua decem, et super capita sua septem diademata; [4]et cauda eius trahit tertiam partem stellarum caeli et misit eas in terram. Et draco stetit ante mulierem, quae erat paritura, ut, cum peperisset, filium eius devoraret. [5]Et peperit filium, masculum, qui *recturus est* omnes *gentes in virga ferrea*; et raptus est filius eius ad Deum et ad thronum eius. [6]Et mulier fugit in desertum, ubi habet locum paratum a Deo, ut ibi pascant illam diebus mille ducentis sexaginta. [7]Et factum est proelium in caelo, Michael et angeli eius, ut proeliarentur cum dracone. Et draco pugnavit et angeli eius, [8]et non valuit, neque locus inventus est eorum amplius in caelo. [9]Et proiectus est draco ille magnus, serpens antiquus, qui vocatur Diabolus et Satanas, qui seducit universum orbem; proiectus est in terram, et angeli eius cum illo proiecti sunt. [10]Et audivi vocem magnam in caelo dicentem: «Nunc facta est salus et virtus et regnum Dei nostri / et potestas Christi eius, / quia proiectus est accusator fratrum nostrorum, / qui accusabat illos ante conspectum Dei nostri die ac nocte. / [11]Et ipsi vicerunt illum propter sanguinem Agni / et propter verbum testimonii sui; / et non dilexerunt animam suam / usque ad mortem. / [12]Propterea laetamini, caeli / et qui habitatis in eis. Vae terrae et mari, quia descendit Diabolus ad vos habens iram magnam, sciens quod modicum tempus habet!». [13]Et postquam vidit draco quod proiectus est in terram, persecutus est mulierem, quae peperit masculum. [14]Et datae sunt mulieri duae alae aquilae magnae, ut volaret in desertum in locum suum, ubi alitur per tempus et tempora et dimidium temporis a facie serpentis. [15]Et misit serpens ex ore suo post mulierem aquam tamquam flumen, ut eam faceret trahi a flumine. [16]Et adiuvit terra mulierem, et aperuit terra os suum et absorbuit flumen, quod misit draco de ore suo. [17]Et iratus est draco in mulierem et abiit facere proelium cum reliquis de semine eius, qui custodiunt mandata Dei et habent testimonium Iesu. [18]Et stetit super arenam maris. [13] [1]Et vidi de mari bestiam ascendentem habentem cornua decem et capita septem, et super cornua eius decem diademata, et super capita eius nomina blasphemiae. [2]Et bestia, quam vidi, similis erat pardo, et pedes eius sicut ursi, et os eius sicut os leonis. Et dedit illi draco virtutem suam et thronum suum et potestatem magnam. ³Et unum de capitibus suis quasi occisum in mortem, et plaga mortis eius curata est. Et admirata est universa terra post bestiam, ⁴et adoraverunt draconem, quia dedit potestatem bestiae, et adoraverunt bestiam dicentes: «Quis similis bestiae, et quis potest pugnare cum ea?». ⁵Et datum est ei os loquens magna et blasphemias, et data est illi potestas facere menses quadraginta duos. ⁶Et aperuit os suum in blasphemias ad Deum, blasphemare nomen eius et tabernaculum eius, eos, qui in caelo habitant. ⁷Et datum est illi bellum facere cum sanctis et vincere illos, et data est ei potestas super omnem tribum et populum et linguam et gentem. ⁸Et adorabunt eum omnes, qui inhabitant terram, cuiuscumque non est scriptum nomen in libro vitae Agni, qui occisus est, ab origine mundi. ⁹Si quis habet aurem, audiat: ¹⁰*Si quis in captivitatem, / in captivitatem* vadit; */ si quis in gladio debet occidi, /* oportet eum *in gladio* occidi. Hic est patientia et fides sanctorum. ¹¹Et vidi aliam bestiam ascendentem de terra, et habebat cornua duo similia agni, et loquebatur sicut draco. ¹²Et potestatem prioris bestiae omnem facit in conspectu eius. Et facit terram et inhabitantes in ea adorare bestiam primam, cuius curata est plaga mortis. ¹³Et facit signa magna, ut etiam ignem faciat de caelo descendere in terram in conspectu hominum. ¹⁴Et seducit habitantes terram propter signa, quae data sunt illi facere in conspectu bestiae, dicens habitantibus in terra, ut faciant imaginem bestiae, quae habet plagam gladii et vixit. ¹⁵Et datum est illi, ut daret spiritum imagini bestiae, ut et loquatur imago bestiae et faciat, ut quicumque non adoraverint imaginem bestiae, occidantur. ¹⁶Et facit omnes pusillos et magnos et divites et pauperes et liberos et servos accipere characterem in dextera manu sua aut in frontibus suis, ¹⁷et ne quis possit emere aut vendere, nisi qui habet characterem, nomen bestiae aut numerum nominis eius. ¹⁸Hic sapientia est: qui habet intellectum, computet numerum bestiae; numerus enim hominis est: et numerus eius est sescenti sexaginta sex. **[14]** ¹Et vidi: et ecce Agnus stans supra montem Sion, et cum illo centum quadraginta quattuor milia, habentes nomen eius et nomen Patris eius scriptum in frontibus suis. ²Et audivi vocem de caelo tamquam vocem aquarum multarum et tamquam vocem tonitrui magni; et vox, quam audivi, sicut cithaoedorum citharizantium in citharis suis. ³Et cantant quasi canticum novum ante thronum et ante quattuor animalia et seniores. Et nemo poterat discere canticum nisi illa centum quadraginta quattuor milia, qui empti sunt de terra. ⁴Hi sunt qui cum mulieribus non sunt coinquinati, virgines enim sunt. Hi qui sequuntur Agnum, quocumque abierit. Hi empti sunt ex hominibus primitiae Deo et Agno; ⁵et in ore ipsorum non est inventum mendacium: sine macula sunt. ⁶Et vidi alterum angelum volantem per medium caelum, habentem evangelium aeternum ut evangelizaret super sedentes in terra et super omnem gentem et tribum et linguam et populum, ⁷dicens magna voce: «Timete Deum et date illi gloriam, quia venit hora iudicii eius, et adorate eum, qui fecit caelum et terram et mare et fontes aquarum». ⁸Et alius angelus secutus est dicens: «Cecidit, cecidit Babylon illa magna, quae a vino irae fornicationis suae potionavit omnes gentes!». ⁹Et alius angelus tertius secutus est illos dicens voce magna: «Si quis adoraverit bestiam et imaginem eius et acceperit characterem in fronte sua aut in manu sua, ¹⁰et hic bibet de vino irae Dei, quod mixtum est mero in calice irae ipsius, et cruciabitur igne et sulphure in conspectu angelorum sanctorum et ante conspectum Agni. ¹¹Et fumus tormentorum eorum in saecula saeculorum ascendit, nec habent requiem die ac nocte, qui adoraverunt bestiam et imaginem eius, et si quis acceperit characterem nominis eius». ¹²Hic patientia sanctorum est, qui custodiunt mandata Dei et fidem Iesu. ¹³Et audivi vocem de caelo dicentem: «Scribe: Beati mortui, qui in Domino moriuntur amodo. Etiam, dicit Spiritus, ut requiescant a laboribus suis; opera enim illorum sequuntur illos». ¹⁴Et vidi: et ecce nubem candidam, et supra nubem sedentem quasi Filium hominis, habentem super caput suum coronam auream et in manu sua falcem acutam. ¹⁵Et alter angelus exivit de templo clamans voce magna ad sedentem super nubem: «Mitte falcem tuam et mete, quia venit hora, ut metatur, quoniam aruit messis terrae». ¹⁶Et misit, qui sedebat supra nubem, falcem suam in terram, et messa est terra. ¹⁷Et alius angelus exivit de templo, quod est in caelo, habens et ipse falcem acutam. ¹⁸Et alius angelus de altari, habens potestatem supra ignem, et clamavit voce magna ad eum, qui habebat falcem acutam, dicens: «Mitte falcem tuam acutam et vindemia botros vineae terrae, quoniam maturae sunt uvae eius». ¹⁹Et misit angelus falcem suam in terram et vindemiavit vineam terrae et misit in lacum irae Dei magnum. ²⁰Et calcatus est lacus extra civitatem, et exivit sanguis de lacu usque ad frenos equorum per stadia mille sescenta. **[15]** ¹Et vidi aliud signum in caelo magnum et mirabile: angelos septem habentes plagas septem novissimas, quoniam in illis consummata est ira Dei. ²Et vidi tamquam mare vitreum mixtum igne et eos, qui vicerunt bestiam et imaginem illius et numerum nominis eius, stantes supra mare vitreum, habentes citharas Dei. ³Et cantant canticum Moysis servi Dei et canticum Agni dicentes: «Magna et mirabilia opera tua, / Domine, Deus omnipotens; / iustae et verae viae tuae, / Rex gentium! / ⁴Quis non timebit, Domine, / et glorificabit nomen tuum? / Quia solus Sanctus, / quoniam omnes gentes venient / et adorabunt in conspectu tuo, / quoniam iudicia tua manifestata sunt». ⁵Et post haec vidi: et apertum est templum tabernaculi testimonii in caelo, [6]et exierunt septem angeli habentes septem plagas de templo, vestiti lino mundo candido et praecincti circa pectora zonis aureis. [7]Et unum ex quattuor animalibus dedit septem angelis septem phialas aureas plenas iracundiae Dei viventis in saecula saeculorum. [8]Et impletum est templum fumo de gloria Dei et de virtute eius, et nemo poterat introire in templum, donec consummarentur septem plagae septem angelorum. [16] [1]Et audivi vocem magnam de templo dicentem septem angelis: «Ite et effundite septem phialas irae Dei in terram». [2]Et abiit primus et effudit phialam suam in terram; et factum est vulnus saevum ac pessimum in homines, qui habebant characterem bestiae, et eos, qui adorabant imaginem eius. [3]Et secundus effudit phialam suam in mare; et factus est sanguis tamquam mortui, et omnis anima vivens mortua est, quae est in mari. [4]Et tertius effudit phialam suam in flumina et in fontes aquarum; et factus est sanguis. [5]Et audivi angelum aquarum dicentem: «Iustus es, qui es et qui eras, Sanctus, quia haec iudicasti, [6]quia sanguinem sanctorum et prophetarum fuderunt, et sanguinem eis dedisti bibere: digni sunt!». [7]Et audivi altare dicens: «Etiam, Domine, Deus omnipotens, vera et iusta iudicia tua!». [8]Et quartus effudit phialam suam in solem; et datum est illi aestu afficere homines in igne. [9]Et aestuaverunt homines aestu magno et blasphemaverunt nomen Dei habentis potestatem super has plagas et non egerunt paenitentiam, ut darent illi gloriam. [10]Et quintus effudit phialam suam super thronum bestiae; et factum est regnum eius tenebrosum, et commanducaverunt linguas suas prae dolore [11]et blasphemaverunt Deum caeli prae doloribus suis et vulneribus suis et non egerunt paenitentiam ex operibus suis. [12]Et sextus effudit phialam suam super flumen illud magnum Euphraten; et exsiccata est aqua eius, ut praepararetur via regibus, qui sunt ab ortu solis. [13]Et vidi de ore draconis et de ore bestiae et de ore pseudoprophetae spiritus tres immundos velut ranas: [14]sunt enim spiritus daemoniorum facientes signa, qui procedunt ad reges universi orbis congregare illos in proelium diei magni Dei omnipotentis. [15]Ecce venio sicut fur. Beatus, qui vigilat et custodit vestimenta sua, ne nudus ambulet, et videant turpitudinem eius. [16]Et congregavit illos in locum, qui vocatur Hebraice Harmagedon. [17]Et septimus effudit phialam suam in aerem; et exivit vox magna de templo a throno dicens: «Factum est!». [18]Et facta sunt fulgura et voces et tonitrua, et terraemotus factus est magnus, qualis numquam fuit, ex quo homo fuit super terram, talis terraemotus sic magnus. [19]Et facta est civitas magna in tres partes, et civitates gentium ceciderunt. Et Babylon magna venit in memoriam ante Deum dare ei calicem vini indignationis irae eius. [20]Et omnis insula fugit, et montes non sunt inventi. [21]Et grando magna sicut talentum descendit de caelo in homines; et blasphemaverunt homines Deum propter plagam grandinis, quoniam magna est plaga eius nimis. [17] [1]Et venit unus de septem angelis, qui habebant septem phialas, et locutus est mecum dicens: «Veni, ostendam tibi damnationem meretricis magnae, quae sedet super aquas multas, [2]cum qua fornicati sunt reges terrae, et inebriati sunt, qui inhabitant terram, de vino prostitutionis eius». [3]Et abstulit me in desertum in spiritu. Et vidi mulierem sedentem super bestiam coccineam, plenam nominibus blasphemiae, habentem capita septem et cornua decem. [4]Et mulier erat circumdata purpura et coccino et inaurata auro et lapide pretioso et margaritis, habens poculum aureum in manu sua plenum abominationibus et immunditiis fornicationis eius, [5]et in fronte eius nomen scriptum, mysterium: «Babylon magna, mater fornicationum et abominationum terrae». [6]Et vidi mulierem ebriam de sanguine sanctorum et de sanguine martyrum Iesu. Et miratus sum, cum vidissem illam admiratione magna. [7]Et dixit mihi angelus: «Quare miraris? Ego tibi dicam mysterium mulieris et bestiae, quae portat eam, quae habet capita septem et decem cornua: [8]bestia, quam vidisti, fuit et non est, et ascensura est de abysso et in interitum ibit. Et mirabuntur inhabitantes terram, quorum non sunt scripta nomina in libro vitae a constitutione mundi, videntes bestiam, quia erat et non est et aderit. [9]Hic est sensus, qui habet sapientiam. Septem capita septem montes sunt, super quos mulier sedet. Et reges septem sunt: [10]quinque ceciderunt, unus est, alius nondum venit et, cum venerit, oportet illum breve tempus manere. [11]Et bestia, quae erat et non est, et is octavus est et de septem est et in interitum vadit. [12]Et decem cornua, quae vidisti, decem reges sunt, qui regnum nondum acceperunt, sed potestatem tamquam reges una hora accipiunt cum bestia. [13]Hi unum consilium habent et virtutem et potestatem suam bestiae tradunt. [14]Hi cum Agno pugnabunt; et Agnus vincet illos, quoniam Dominus dominorum est et Rex regum, et qui cum illo sunt vocati et electi et fideles». [15]Et dicit mihi: «Aquae, quas vidisti, ubi meretrix sedet, populi et turbae sunt et gentes et linguae. [16]Et decem cornua, quae vidisti, et bestia, hi odient fornicariam et desolatam facient illam et nudam, et carnes eius manducabunt et ipsam igne concremabunt; [17]Deus enim dedit in corda eorum, ut faciant, quod illi placitum est, et faciant unum consilium et dent regnum suum bestiae, donec consummentur verba Dei. [18]Et mulier, quam vidisti, est civitas magna, quae habet regnum super reges terrae». [18] [1]Post haec vidi alium angelum descendentem de caelo, habentem potestatem magnam, et terra illuminata est a claritate eius. [2]Et clamavit in forti voce dicens: «Cecidit, cecidit Babylon magna et facta est habitatio daemoniorum et custodia omnis spiritus immundi et custodia omnis bestiae immundae et odibilis, ³quia de vino irae fornicationis eius biberunt omnes gentes, et reges terrae cum illa fornicati sunt, et mercatores terrae de virtute deliciarum eius divites facti sunt!». ⁴Et audivi aliam vocem de caelo dicentem: «Exite de illa, populus meus, ut ne comparticipes sitis peccatorum eius et de plagis eius non accipiatis, ⁵quoniam pervenerunt peccata eius usque ad caelum, et recordatus est Deus iniquitatum eius. ⁶Reddite illi, sicut et ipsa reddidit, et duplicate duplicia secundum opera eius; in poculo, quo miscuit, miscete illi duplum. ⁷Quantum glorificavit se et in deliciis fuit, tantum date illi tormentum et luctum. Quia in corde suo dicit: "Sedeo regina et vidua non sum et luctum non videbo", ⁸ideo in una die venient plagae eius, mors et luctus et fames, et igne comburetur, quia fortis est Dominus Deus, qui iudicavit illam». ⁹Et flebunt et plangent se super illam reges terrae, qui cum illa fornicati sunt et in deliciis vixerunt, cum viderint fumum incendii eius, ¹⁰longe stantes propter timorem tormentorum eius, dicentes: «Vae, vae, civitas illa magna, Babylon, civitas illa fortis, quoniam una hora venit iudicium tuum!». ¹¹Et negotiatores terrae flent et lugent super illam, quoniam mercem eorum nemo emit amplius: ¹²mercem auri et argenti et lapidis pretiosi et margaritarum, et byssi et purpurae et serici et cocci, et omne lignum thyinum et omnia vasa eboris et omnia vasa de ligno pretiosissimo et aeramento et ferro et marmore, ¹³et cinnamomum et amomum et odoramenta et unguenta et tus, et vinum et oleum et similam et triticum, et iumenta et oves et equorum et raedarum, et mancipiorum et animas hominum. ¹⁴Et fructus tui, desiderium animae, discesserunt a te, et omnia pinguia et clara perierunt a te, et amplius illa iam non invenient. ¹⁵Mercatores horum, qui divites facti sunt ab ea, longe stabunt propter timorem tormentorum eius flentes ac lugentes, ¹⁶dicentes: «Vae, vae, civitas illa magna, quae amicta erat byssino et purpura et cocco, et deaurata auro et lapide pretioso et margarita, ¹⁷quoniam una hora desolatae sunt tantae divitiae!». Et omnis gubernator et omnis, qui in locum navigat, et nautae et, quotquot maria operantur, longe steterunt ¹⁸et clamabant, videntes fumum incendii eius, dicentes: «Quae similis civitati huic magnae?». ¹⁹Et miserunt pulverem super capita sua et clamabant, flentes et lugentes, dicentes: «Vae, vae, civitas illa magna, in qua divites facti sunt omnes, qui habent naves in mari, de opibus eius, quoniam una hora desolata est! ²⁰Exsulta super eam, caelum, et sancti et apostoli et prophetae, quoniam iudicavit Deus iudicium vestrum de illa!». ²¹Et sustulit unus angelus fortis lapidem quasi molarem magnum et misit in mare dicens: «Impetu sic mittetur Babylon magna illa civitas et ultra iam non invenietur. ²²Et vox citharoedorum et musicorum et tibia canentium et tuba non audietur in te amplius, et omnis artifex omnis artis non invenietur in te amplius, et vox molae non audietur in te amplius, ²³et lux lucernae non lucebit tibi amplius, et vox sponsi et sponsae non audietur in te amplius, quia mercatores tui erant magnates terrae, quia in veneficiis tuis erraverunt omnes gentes, ²⁴et in ea sanguis prophetarum et sanctorum inventus est et omnium, qui interfecti sunt in terra!». **[19]** ¹Post haec audivi quasi vocem magnam turbae multae in caelo dicentium: «Alleluia! / Salus et gloria et virtus Deo nostro, / ²quia vera et iusta iudicia eius; / quia iudicavit de meretrice magna, quae corrupit terram in prostitutione sua, et vindicavit sanguinem servorum suorum de manibus eius!». ³Et iterum dixerunt: «Alleluia! Et fumus eius ascendit in saecula saeculorum!». ⁴Et ceciderunt seniores viginti quattuor et quattuor animalia et adoraverunt Deum sedentem super thronum dicentes: «Amen. Alleluia». ⁵Et vox de throno exivit dicens: «Laudem dicite Deo nostro, omnes servi eius / et qui timetis eum, pusilli et magni!». ⁶Et audivi quasi vocem turbae magnae et sicut vocem aquarum multarum et sicut vocem tonitruum magnorum dicentium: «Alleluia, / quoniam regnavit Dominus, Deus noster omnipotens. / ⁷Gaudeamus et exsultemus et demus gloriam ei, / quia venerunt nuptiae Agni, / et uxor eius praeparavit se. ⁸Et datum est illi, ut cooperiat se byssino splendenti mundo: byssinum enim iustificationes sunt sanctorum». ⁹Et dicit mihi: «Scribe: Beati, qui ad cenam nuptiarum Agni vocati sunt!». Et dicit mihi: «Haec verba Dei vera sunt». ¹⁰Et cecidi ante pedes eius, ut adorarem eum. Et dicit mihi: «Vide, ne feceris! Conservus tuus sum et fratrum tuorum habentium testimonium Iesu. Deum adora. Testimonium enim Iesu est spiritus prophetiae». ¹¹Et vidi caelum apertum: et ecce equus albus; et, qui sedebat super eum, vocabatur Fidelis et Verax, et in iustitia iudicat et pugnat. ¹²Oculi autem eius sicut flamma ignis, et in capite eius diademata multa, habens nomen scriptum, quod nemo novit nisi ipse, ¹³et vestitus veste aspersa sanguine, et vocatur nomen eius Verbum Dei. ¹⁴Et exercitus, qui sunt in caelo, sequebantur eum in equis albis, vestiti byssino albo mundo. ¹⁵Et de ore ipsius procedit gladius acutus, ut in ipso percutiat gentes, et ipse *reget eos in virga ferrea*; et ipse calcat torcular vini furoris irae Dei omnipotentis. ¹⁶Et habet super vestimentum et super femur suum nomen scriptum: Rex regum et Dominus dominorum. ¹⁷Et vidi unum angelum stantem in sole, et clamavit voce magna dicens omnibus avibus, quae volabant per medium caeli: «Venite, congregamini ad cenam magnam Dei, ¹⁸ut manducetis carnes regum et carnes tribunorum et carnes fortium et carnes equorum et sedentium in ipsis et carnes omnium liberorum ac servorum et pusillorum ac magnorum». ¹⁹Et vidi bestiam et reges terrae et exercitus eorum congregatos ad faciendum proelium cum illo, qui sedebat super equum, et cum exercitu eius. [20]Et apprehensa est bestia et cum illa pseudopropheta, qui fecit signa coram ipsa, quibus seduxit eos, qui acceperunt characterem bestiae et qui adorant imaginem eius; vivi missi sunt hi duo in stagnum ignis ardentis sulphure. [21]Et ceteri occisi sunt in gladio sedentis super equum, qui procedit de ore ipsius, et omnes aves saturatae sunt carnibus eorum. **[20]** [1]Et vidi angelum descendentem de caelo habentem clavem abyssi et catenam magnam in manu sua. [2]Et apprehendit draconem, serpentem antiquum, qui est Diabolus et Satanas, et ligavit eum per annos mille [3]et misit eum in abyssum et clausit et signavit super illum, ut non seducat amplius gentes, donec consummentur mille anni; post haec oportet illum solvi modico tempore. [4]Et vidi thronos, et sederunt super eos, et iudicium datum est illis; et animas decollatorum propter testimonium Iesu et propter verbum Dei, et qui non adoraverunt bestiam neque imaginem eius nec acceperunt characterem in frontibus et in manibus suis; et vixerunt et regnaverunt cum Christo mille annis. [5]Ceteri mortuorum non vixerunt, donec consummentur mille anni. Haec est resurrectio prima. [6]Beatus et sanctus, qui habet partem in resurrectione prima! In his secunda mors non habet potestatem, sed erunt sacerdotes Dei et Christi et regnabunt cum illo mille annis. [7]Et cum consummati fuerint mille anni, solvetur Satanas de carcere suo [8]et exibit seducere gentes, quae sunt in quattuor angulis terrae, Gog et Magog, congregare eos in proelium, quorum numerus est sicut arena maris. [9]Et ascenderunt super latitudinem terrae et circumierunt castra sanctorum et civitatem dilectam. Et descendit ignis de caelo et devoravit eos; [10]et Diabolus, qui seducebat eos, missus est in stagnum ignis et sulphuris, ubi et bestia et pseudopropheta, et cruciabuntur die ac nocte in saecula saeculorum. [11]Et vidi thronum magnum candidum et sedentem super eum, a cuius aspectu fugit terra et caelum, et locus non est inventus eis. [12]Et vidi mortuos, magnos et pusillos, stantes in conspectu throni; et libri aperti sunt. Et alius liber apertus est, qui est vitae; et iudicati sunt mortui ex his, quae scripta erant in libris secundum opera ipsorum. [13]Et dedit mare mortuos, qui in eo erant, et mors et infernus dederunt mortuos, qui in ipsis erant; et iudicati sunt singuli secundum opera ipsorum. [14]Et mors et infernus missi sunt in stagnum ignis. Haec mors secunda est, stagnum ignis. [15]Et si quis non est inventus in libro vitae scriptus, missus est in stagnum ignis. **[21]** [1]Et vidi caelum novum et terram novam; primum enim caelum et prima terra abierunt, et mare iam non est. [2]Et civitatem sanctam Ierusalem novam vidi descendentem de caelo a Deo, paratam sicut sponsam ornatam viro suo. [3]Et audivi vocem magnam de throno dicentem: «*Ecce tabernaculum* Dei cum hominibus! *Et habitabit cum eis, et ipsi populi eius erunt, et* ipse Deus cum eis erit eorum Deus, [4]*et absterget omnem lacrimam* ab oculis eorum, et mors ultra non erit, neque luctus neque clamor neque dolor erit ultra, quia prima abierunt». [5]Et dixit, qui sedebat super throno: «Ecce nova facio omnia». Et dicit: «Scribe: Haec verba fidelia sunt et vera». [6]Et dixit mihi: «Facta sunt! Ego sum Alpha et Omega, principium et finis. Ego sitienti dabo de fonte aquae vivae gratis. [7]Qui vicerit, hereditabit haec, et *ero illi Deus, et ille erit mihi filius*. [8]Timidis autem et incredulis et exsecratis et homicidis et fornicatoribus et veneficis et idololatris et omnibus mendacibus, pars illorum erit in stagno ardenti igne et sulphure, quod est mors secunda». [9]Et venit unus de septem angelis habentibus septem phialas plenas septem plagis novissimis et locutus est mecum dicens: «Veni, ostendam tibi sponsam uxorem Agni». [10]Et sustulit me in spiritu super montem magnum et altum et ostendit mihi civitatem sanctam Ierusalem descendentem de caelo a Deo, [11]habentem claritatem Dei; lumen eius simile lapidi pretiosissimo, tamquam lapidi iaspidi, in modum crystalli; [12]et habebat murum magnum et altum et habebat *portas* duodecim et super portas angelos duodecim et *nomina* inscripta, quae sunt duodecim *tribuum filiorum Israel*. [13]*Ab oriente portae tres et ab aquilone portae tres et ab austro portae tres et ab occasu portae tres*; [14]et murus civitatis habens fundamenta duodecim, et super ipsis duodecim nomina duodecim apostolorum Agni. [15]Et, qui loquebatur mecum, habebat mensuram arundinem auream, ut metiretur civitatem et portas eius et murum eius. [16]Et civitas in quadro posita est, et longitudo eius tanta est quanta et latitudo. Et mensus est civitatem arundine per stadia duodecim milia; longitudo et latitudo et altitudo eius aequales sunt. [17]Et mensus est murum eius centum quadraginta quattuor cubitorum, mensura hominis, quae est angeli. [18]Et erat structura muri eius ex iaspide, ipsa vero civitas aurum mundum simile vitro mundo. [19]Fundamenta muri civitatis omni lapide pretioso ornata: fundamentum primum iaspis, secundus sapphirus, tertius chalcedonius, quartus smaragdus, [20]quintus sardonyx, sextus sardinus, septimus chrysolithus, octavus beryllus, nonus topazius, decimus chrysoprasus, undecimus hyacinthus, duodecimus amethystus. [21]Et duodecim portae duodecim margaritae sunt, et singulae portae erant ex singulis margaritis. Et platea civitatis aurum mundum tamquam vitrum perlucidum. [22]Et templum non vidi in ea: Dominus enim, Deus omnipotens, templum illius est, et Agnus. [23]Et civitas non eget sole neque luna, ut luceant ei, nam claritas Dei illuminavit eam, et lucerna eius est Agnus. [24]Et ambulabunt gentes per lumen eius, et reges terrae afferunt gloriam suam in illam; [25]et portae eius non claudentur per diem, nox enim non erit illic; [26]et afferent gloriam et divitias gentium in illam. [27]Nec intrabit in ea aliquid coinquinatum et faciens abominationem et mendacium, nisi qui scripti sunt in libro vitae Agni. **[22]** ¹Et ostendit mihi fluvium aquae vitae splendidum tamquam crystallum, procedentem de throno Dei et Agni. ²*In medio* plateae eius et *fluminis ex utraque parte lignum vitae* afferens fructus duodecim, *per menses* singulos reddens *fructum suum, et folia* ligni *ad sanitatem* gentium. ³Et omne maledictum non erit amplius. Et thronus Dei et Agni in illa erit; et servi eius servient illi ⁴et videbunt faciem eius, et nomen eius in frontibus eorum. ⁵Et nox ultra non erit, et non egent lumine lucernae neque lumine solis, quoniam Dominus Deus illuminabit super illos, et regnabunt in saecula saeculorum. ⁶Et dixit mihi: «Haec verba fidelissima et vera sunt, et Dominus, Deus spirituum prophetarum, misit angelum suum ostendere servis suis, quae oportet fieri cito. ⁷Et ecce venio velociter. Beatus, qui servat verba prophetiae libri huius». ⁸Et ego Ioannes, qui audivi et vidi haec. Et postquam audissem et vidissem, cecidi, ut adorarem ante pedes angeli, qui mihi haec ostendebat. ⁹Et dicit mihi: «Vide, ne feceris. Conservus tuus sum et fratrum tuorum prophetarum et eorum, qui servant verba libri huius; Deum adora!». ¹⁰Et dicit mihi: «Ne signaveris verba prophetiae libri huius; tempus enim prope est! ¹¹Qui nocet, noceat adhuc, et, qui sordibus est, sordescat adhuc, et iustus iustitiam faciat adhuc, et sanctus sanctificetur adhuc. ¹²Ecce venio cito, et merces mea mecum est, reddere unicuique sicut opus eius est. ¹³Ego Alpha et Omega, primus et novissimus, principium et finis. ¹⁴Beati, qui lavant stolas suas, ut sit potestas eorum super lignum vitae, et per portas intrent in civitatem. ¹⁵Foris canes et venefici et impudici et homicidae et idolis servientes et omnis, qui amat et facit mendacium! ¹⁶Ego Iesus misi angelum meum testificari vobis haec super ecclesiis. Ego sum radix et genus David, stella splendida matutina». ¹⁷Et Spiritus et sponsa dicunt: «Veni!». Et, qui audit, dicat: «Veni!». Et, qui sitit, veniat; qui vult, accipiat aquam vitae gratis. ¹⁸Contestor ego omni audienti verba prophetiae libri huius: Si quis apposuerit ad haec, apponet Deus super illum plagas scriptas in libro isto; ¹⁹et si quis abstulerit de verbis libri prophetiae, huius, auferet Deus partem eius de ligno vitae et de civitate sancta, de his, quae scripta sunt in libro isto. ²⁰Dicit, qui testimonium perhibet istorum: «Etiam, venio cito». «Amen. Veni, Domine Iesu!». ²¹Gratia Domini Iesu cum omnibus.

EPISTOLA AD HEBRAEOS

[1] ¹ Multifariam et multis modis olim Deus locutus patribus in prophetis, ²in novissimis his diebus locutus est nobis in Filio, quem constituit heredem universorum, per quem fecit et saecula; ³qui, cum sit splendor gloriae et figura substantiae eius et portet omnia verbo virtutis suae, purgatione peccatorum facta, consedit ad dexteram maiestatis in excelsis, ⁴tanto melior angelis effectus, quanto differentius prae illis nomen hereditavit.⁵Cui enim dixit aliquando angelorum: «*Filius meus es tu; / ego hodie genui te*» et rursum: «*Ego ero illi in patrem, et ipse erit mihi in filium*»? ⁶Cum autem iterum introducit primogenitum in orbem terrae, dicit: «*Et adorent eum omnes angeli Dei*». ⁷Et ad angelos quidem dicit: «*Qui facit angelos suos spiritus / et ministros suos flammam ignis*»; ⁸ad Filium autem: «*Thronus tuus, Deus, in saeculum saeculi, / et virga aequitatis virga regni tui. / ⁹Dilexisti iustitiam et odisti iniquitatem, / propterea unxit te Deus, Deus tuus, / oleo exsultationis prae participibus tuis*» ¹⁰et: «*Tu in principio, Domine, terram fundasti; / et opera manuum tuarum sunt caeli. / ¹¹Ipsi peribunt, tu autem permanes; / et omnes ut vestimentum veterascent, / ¹²et velut amictum involves eos, / sicut vestimentum et mutabuntur. / Tu autem idem es, et anni tui non deficient*». ¹³Ad quem autem angelorum dixit aliquando: «*Sede a dextris meis, / donec ponam inimicos tuos scabellum pedum tuorum*»? ¹⁴Nonne omnes sunt administratorii spiritus, qui in ministerium mittuntur propter eos, qui hereditatem capient salutis? **[2]** ¹Propterea abundantius oportet observare nos ea, quae audivimus, ne forte praeterfluamus. ²Si enim, qui per angelos dictus est, sermo factus est firmus, et omnis praevaricatio et inoboedientia accepit iustam mercedis retributionem, ³quomodo nos effugiemus si tantam neglexerimus salutem? Quae, cum initium accepisset enarrari per Dominum, ab eis, qui audierunt, in nos confirmata est, ⁴contestante Deo signis et portentis et variis virtutibus et Spiritus Sancti distributionibus secundum suam voluntatem. ⁵Non enim angelis subiecit orbem terrae futurum, de quo loquimur. ⁶Testatus est autem in quodam loco quis dicens: «*Quid est homo, quod memor es eius, / aut filius hominis, quoniam visitas eum? / ⁷Minuisti eum paulo minus ab angelis, / gloria et honore coronasti eum, / ⁸omnia subiecisti sub pedibus eius*». In eo enim quod ei omnia subiecit, nihil dimisit non subiectibile ei. Nunc autem necdum videmus omnia subiecta ei; ⁹eum autem, qui *paulo minus ab angelis minoratus est*, videmus Iesum propter passionem mortis *gloria et honore coronatum*, ut gratia Dei pro omnibus gustaverit mortem. ¹⁰Decebat enim eum, propter quem omnia et per quem omnia, qui multos filios in gloriam adduxit, ducem salutis eorum per passiones consummare. ¹¹Qui enim sanctificat et qui sanctificantur, ex uno omnes; propter quam causam non erubescit fratres eos vocare ¹²dicens: *«Nuntiabo nomen tuum fratribus meis, / in medio ecclesiae laudabo te»*; ¹³et iterum: *«Ego ero fidens in eum»*; et iterum: *«Ecce ego et pueri, quos mihi dedit Deus»*. ¹⁴Quia ergo pueri communicaverunt sanguini et carni, et ipse similiter participavit iisdem, ut per mortem destrueret eum, qui habebat mortis imperium, id est Diabolum, ¹⁵et liberaret eos, qui timore mortis per totam vitam obnoxii erant servituti. ¹⁶Nusquam enim angelos apprehendit, sed *semen Abrahae apprehendit*. ¹⁷Unde debuit per omnia fratribus similari, ut misericors fieret et fidelis pontifex in iis, quae sunt ad Deum, ut repropitiaret delicta populi; ¹⁸in quo enim passus est ipse tentatus, potens est eis, qui tentantur, auxiliari. **[3]** ¹Unde, fratres sancti, vocationis caelestis participes, considerate apostolum et pontificem confessionis nostrae Iesum, ²qui fidelis est ei, qui fecit illum, sicut et *Moyses in tota domo illius*. ³Amplioris enim gloriae iste prae Moyse dignus est habitus, quanto ampliorem honorem habet quam domus, qui fabricavit illam. ⁴Omnis namque domus fabricatur ab aliquo; qui autem omnia fabricavit, Deus est. ⁵Et *Moyses* quidem *fidelis erat in tota domo eius* tamquam *famulus* in testimonium eorum, quae dicenda erant, ⁶Christus vero tamquam Filius super domum illius; cuius domus sumus nos, si fiduciam et gloriationem spei retineamus. ⁷Quapropter, sicut dicit Spiritus Sanctus: *«Hodie, si vocem eius audieritis, / ⁸nolite obdurare corda vestra sicut in exacerbatione, / secundum diem tentationis in deserto, / ⁹ubi tentaverunt me patres vestri in probatione / et viderunt opera mea ¹⁰quadraginta annos. / Propter quod infensus fui generationi huic / et dixi: Semper errant corde. / Ipsi autem non cognoverunt vias meas; / ¹¹sicut iuravi in ira mea: / Non introibunt in requiem meam»*. ¹²Videte, fratres, ne forte sit in aliquo vestrum cor malum incredulitatis discedendi a Deo vivo, ¹³sed adhortamini vosmetipsos per singulos dies, donec illud *«hodie»* vocatur, ut non obduretur quis ex vobis fallacia peccati; ¹⁴participes enim Christi effecti sumus, si tamen initium substantiae usque ad finem firmum retineamus, ¹⁵dum dicitur: *«Hodie, si vocem eius audieritis, / nolite obdurare corda vestra quemadmodum in illa exacerbatione»*. ¹⁶Qui sunt enim qui audientes exacerbaverunt? Nonne universi, qui profecti sunt ab Aegypto per Moysen? ¹⁷Quibus autem *infensus fuit quadraginta annos*? Nonne illis, qui peccaverunt, quorum *membra ceciderunt in deserto*? ¹⁸Quibus autem *iuravit non introire in requiem ipsius*, nisi illis, qui increduli fuerunt? ¹⁹Et videmus quia non potuerunt introire propter incredulitatem. **[4]** ¹Timeamus ergo, ne forte, relicta pollicitatione introeundi in requiem eius, existimetur aliquis ex vobis deesse; ²etenim et nobis evangelizatum est quemadmodum et illis, sed non profuit illis sermo auditus, non commixtis fide cum iis, qui audierant. ³Ingredimur enim in requiem, qui credidimus, quemadmodum dixit: *«Sicut iuravi in ira mea: / Non introibunt in requiem meam»*, et quidem operibus ab institutione mundi factis. ⁴Dixit enim quodam loco de die septima sic: *«Et requievit Deus die septima ab omnibus operibus suis»*; ⁵et in isto rursum: *«Non introibunt in requiem meam»*. ⁶Quoniam ergo superest quosdam introire in illam, et hi, quibus prioribus evangelizatum est, non introierunt propter inoboedientiam, ⁷iterum terminat diem quendam, "Hodie", in David dicendo post tantum temporis, sicut supra dictum est: *«Hodie, si vocem eius audieritis, / nolite obdurare corda vestra»*. ⁸Nam si eis Iesus requiem praestitisset, non de alio loqueretur posthac die. ⁹Itaque relinquitur sabbatismus populo Dei; ¹⁰qui enim ingressus est in requiem eius, etiam ipse requievit ab operibus suis, sicut a suis Deus. ¹¹Festinemus ergo ingredi in illam requiem, ut ne in idipsum quis incidat inoboedientiae exemplum. ¹²Vivus est enim Dei sermo et efficax et penetrabilior omni gladio ancipiti et pertingens usque ad divisionem animae ac spiritus, compagum quoque et medullarum, et discretor cogitationum et intentionum cordis; ¹³et non est creatura invisibilis in conspectu eius, omnia autem nuda et aperta sunt oculis eius, ad quem nobis sermo. ¹⁴Habentes ergo pontificem magnum, qui penetravit caelos, Iesum Filium Dei, teneamus confessionem. ¹⁵Non enim habemus pontificem, qui non possit compati infirmitatibus nostris, tentatum autem per omnia secundum similitudinem absque peccato; ¹⁶adeamus ergo cum fiducia ad thronum gratiae, ut misericordiam consequamur et gratiam inveniamus in auxilium opportunum. **[5]** ¹Omnis namque pontifex ex hominibus assumptus pro hominibus constituitur in his, quae sunt ad Deum, ut offerat dona et sacrificia pro peccatis, ²qui aeque condolere possit his, qui ignorant et errant, quoniam et ipse circumdatus est infirmitate ³et propter eam debet, quemadmodum et pro populo, ita etiam pro semetipso offerre pro peccatis. ⁴Nec quisquam sumit sibi illum honorem, sed qui vocatur a Deo tamquam et Aaron. ⁵Sic et Christus non semetipsum glorificavit, ut pontifex fieret, sed qui locutus est ad eum: *«Filius meus es tu; / ego hodie genui te»*; ⁶quemadmodum et in alio dicit: *«Tu es sacerdos in aeternum secundum ordinem Melchisedech»*. ⁷Qui in diebus carnis suae, preces supplicationesque ad eum, qui possit salvum illum a morte facere, cum clamore valido et lacrimis offerens et exauditus pro sua reverentia, ⁸et quidem cum esset Filius, didicit ex his, quae passus est, oboedientiam; ⁹et, consummatus, factus est omnibus oboedientibus sibi auctor salutis aeternae, ¹⁰appellatus a Deo pontifex *iuxta ordinem Melchisedech*. ¹¹De quo grandis nobis sermo et ininterpretabilis ad dicendum, quoniam segnes facti estis ad audiendum.

Hebrews 5:12 New Vulgate

¹²Etenim cum deberetis magistri esse propter tempus, rursum indigetis, ut vos doceat aliquis elementa exordii sermonum Dei, et facti estis, quibus lacte opus sit, non solido cibo. ¹³Omnis enim, qui lactis est particeps, expers est sermonis iustitiae, parvulus enim est; ¹⁴perfectorum autem est solidus cibus, eorum, qui pro consuetudine exercitatos habent sensus ad discretionem boni ac mali. [6] ¹Quapropter praetermittentes inchoationis Christi sermonem ad perfectionem feramur, non rursum iacientes fundamentum paenitentiae ab operibus mortuis et fidei ad Deum, ²baptismatum doctrinae, impositionis quoque manuum, ac resurrectionis mortuorum et iudicii aeterni. ³Et hoc faciemus siquidem permiserit Deus. ⁴Impossibile est enim eos, qui semel sunt illuminati, gustaverunt etiam donum caeleste et participes sunt facti Spiritus Sancti ⁵et bonum gustaverunt Dei verbum virtutesque saeculi venturi ⁶et prolapsi sunt, rursus renovari ad paenitentiam rursum crucifigentes sibimetipsis Filium Dei et ostentui habentes. ⁷Terra enim saepe venientem super se bibens imbrem et generans herbam opportunam illis propter quos et colitur, accipit benedictionem a Deo; ⁸*proferens* autem *spinas ac tribulos* reproba est et *maledicto* proxima, cuius finis in combustionem. ⁹Confidimus autem de vobis, dilectissimi, meliora et viciniora saluti, tametsi ita loquimur; ¹⁰non enim iniustus Deus, ut obliviscatur operis vestri et dilectionis, quam ostendistis nomini ipsius, qui ministrastis sanctis et ministratis. ¹¹Cupimus autem unumquemque vestrum eandem ostentare sollicitudinem ad expletionem spei usque in finem, ¹² ut non segnes efficiamini, verum imitatores eorum, qui fide et patientia hereditant promissiones. ¹³Abrahae namque promittens Deus, quoniam neminem habuit, per quem iuraret maiorem, *iuravit per semetipsum* ¹⁴dicens: «*Utique benedicens benedicam te et multiplicans multiplicabo te*»; ¹⁵et sic longanimiter ferens adeptus est repromissionem. ¹⁶Homines enim per maiorem sui iurant, et omnis controversiae eorum finis ad confirmationem est iuramentum; ¹⁷in quo abundantius volens Deus ostendere pollicitationis heredibus immobilitatem consilii sui, se interposuit iure iurando, ¹⁸ut per duas res immobiles, in quibus impossibile est mentiri Deum, fortissimum solacium habeamus, qui confugimus ad tenendam propositam spem, ¹⁹quam sicut ancoram habemus animae, tutam ac firmam et incedentem usque in interiora velaminis, ²⁰ubi praecursor pro nobis introivit Iesus, *secundum ordinem Melchisedech* pontifex factus *in aeternum*. [7] ¹Hic enim *Melchisedech, rex Salem, sacerdos Dei summi*, qui *obviavit Abrahae regresso a caede regum et benedixit ei*, ²cui et *decimam omnium* divisit *Abraham*, primum quidem, qui interpretatur rex iustitiae, deinde autem et *rex Salem*, quod est rex Pacis, ³sine patre, sine matre, sine genealogia, neque initium dierum neque finem vitae habens, assimilatus autem Filio Dei, manet sacerdos in perpetuum. ⁴Intuemini autem quantus sit hic, cui et decimam dedit de praecipuis Abraham patriarcha. ⁵Et illi quidem, qui de filiis Levi sacerdotium accipiunt, mandatum habent decimas sumere a populo secundum legem, id est a fratribus suis, quamquam et ipsi exierunt de lumbis Abrahae; ⁶hic autem, cuius generatio non annumeratur in eis, decimam sumpsit ab Abraham, et eum, qui habebat repromissiones, benedixit. ⁷Sine ulla autem contradictione, quod minus est, a meliore benedicitur. ⁸Et hic quidem decimas morientes homines sumunt, ibi autem testimonium accipiens, quia vivit. ⁹Et ut ita dictum sit, per Abraham et Levi, qui decimas accipit, decimatus est, ¹⁰adhuc enim in lumbis patris erat, quando *obviavit ei Melchisedech*. ¹¹Si ergo consummatio per sacerdotium leviticum erat, populus enim sub ipso legem accepit, quid adhuc necessarium *secundum ordinem Melchisedech* alium surgere *sacerdotem* et non *secundum ordinem* Aaron dici? ¹²Translato enim sacerdotio, necesse est, ut et legis translatio fiat. ¹³De quo enim haec dicuntur, ex alia tribu est, ex qua nullus altari praesto fuit; ¹⁴manifestum enim quod ex Iuda ortus sit Dominus noster, in quam tribum nihil de sacerdotibus Moyses locutus est. ¹⁵Et amplius adhuc manifestum est, si *secundum* similitudinem *Melchisedech* exsurgit alius *sacerdos*, ¹⁶qui non secundum legem mandati carnalis factus est sed secundum virtutem vitae insolubilis, ¹⁷testimonium enim accipit: «*Tu es sacerdos in aeternum secundum ordinem Melchisedech*». ¹⁸Reprobatio quidem fit praecedentis mandati propter infirmitatem eius et inutilitatem, ¹⁹nihil enim ad perfectum adduxit lex, introductio vero melioris spei, per quam proximamus ad Deum. ²⁰Et quantum non est sine iure iurando, illi quidem sine iure iurando sacerdotes facti sunt, ²¹hic autem cum iure iurando per eum, qui dicit ad illum: «*Iuravit Dominus et non paenitebit eum: / Tu es sacerdos in aeternum*», ²²in tantum et melioris testamenti sponsor factus est Iesus. ²³Et illi quidem plures facti sunt sacerdotes, idcirco quod morte prohibebantur permanere; ²⁴hic autem eo quod manet in aeternum, intransgressibile habet sacerdotium, ²⁵unde et salvare in perpetuum potest accedentes per semetipsum ad Deum, semper vivens ad interpellandum pro eis. ²⁶Talis enim et decebat, ut nobis esset pontifex, sanctus, innocens, impollutus, segregatus a peccatoribus et excelsior caelis factus, ²⁷qui non habet necessitatem cotidie, quemadmodum pontifices, prius pro suis delictis hostias offerre, deinde pro populi; hoc enim fecit semel semetipsum offerendo. ²⁸Lex enim homines constituit pontifices infirmitatem habentes, sermo autem iuris iurandi, quod post legem est, Filium in aeternum consummatum. [8] ¹Caput autem super ea, quae dicuntur: talem habemus pontificem, qui consedit in dextera throni

Maiestatis in caelis, ²sanctorum minister et tabernaculi veri, quod fixit Dominus, non homo. ³Omnis enim pontifex ad offerenda munera et hostias constituitur; unde necesse erat et hunc habere aliquid, quod offerret. ⁴Si ergo esset super terram, nec esset sacerdos, cum sint qui offerant secundum legem munera; ⁵qui figurae et umbrae deserviunt caelestium, sicut responsum est Moysi, cum consummaturus esset tabernaculum: «*Vide* enim, inquit, *omnia facies secundum exemplar, quod tibi ostensum est in monte*». ⁶Nunc autem differentius sortitus est ministerium, quanto et melioris testamenti mediator est, quod in melioribus repromissionibus sancitum est. ⁷Nam si illud prius culpa vacasset, non secundi locus inquireretur; ⁸vituperans enim eos dicit: «*Ecce dies veniunt, dicit Dominus, et consummabo super domum Israel et super domum Iudae testamentum novum*; ⁹*non secundum testamentum, quod feci patribus eorum, in die, qua apprehendi manum illorum, ut educerem illos de terra Aegypti; quoniam ipsi non permanserunt in testamento meo, et ego neglexi eos, dicit Dominus.* ¹⁰*Quia hoc est testamentum, quod testabor domui Israel post dies illos, dicit Dominus, dando leges meas in mentem eorum, et in corde eorum superscribam eas; et ero eis in Deum, et ipsi erunt mihi in populum.* ¹¹*Et non docebit unusquisque civem suum, et unusquisque fratrem suum dicens*: "*Cognosce Dominum*"; *quoniam omnes scient me, a minore usque ad maiorem eorum,* ¹²*quia propitius ero iniquitatibus eorum et peccatorum illorum iam non memorabor*». ¹³Dicendo «*novum*» veteravit prius; quod autem antiquatur et senescit, prope interitum est.   **[9]** ¹Habuit ergo et prius praecepta cultus et Sanctum huius saeculi. ²Tabernaculum enim praeparatum est primum, in quo inerat candelabrum et mensa et propositio panum, quod dicitur Sancta; ³post secundum autem velamentum, tabernaculum, quod dicitur Sancta Sanctorum, ⁴aureum habens turibulum et arcam testamenti circumtectam ex omni parte auro, in qua urna aurea habens manna et virga Aaron, quae fronduerat, et tabulae testamenti, ⁵superque eam cherubim gloriae obumbrantia propitiatorium; de quibus non est modo dicendum per singula. ⁶His vero ita praeparatis, in prius quidem tabernaculum semper intrant sacerdotes sacrorum officia consummantes, ⁷in secundum autem semel in anno solus pontifex, non sine sanguine, quem offert pro suis et populi ignorantiis, ⁸hoc significante Spiritu Sancto, nondum propalatam esse sanctorum viam, adhuc priore tabernaculo habente statum; ⁹quae parabola est temporis instantis, iuxta quam munera et hostiae offeruntur, quae non possunt iuxta conscientiam perfectum facere servientem, ¹⁰solummodo in cibis et in potibus et variis baptismis, quae sunt praecepta carnis usque ad tempus correctionis imposita. ¹¹Christus autem cum advenit pontifex futurorum bonorum, per amplius et perfectius tabernaculum, non manufactum, id est non huius creationis, ¹²neque per sanguinem hircorum et vitulorum sed per proprium sanguinem introivit semel in Sancta, aeterna redemptione inventa. ¹³Si enim sanguis hircorum et taurorum et cinis vitulae aspersus inquinatos sanctificat ad emundationem carnis, ¹⁴quanto magis sanguis Christi, qui per Spiritum aeternum semetipsum obtulit immaculatum Deo, emundabit conscientiam nostram ab operibus mortuis ad serviendum Deo viventi. ¹⁵Et ideo novi testamenti mediator est, ut, morte intercedente, in redemptionem earum praevaricationum, quae erant sub priore testamento, repromissionem accipiant, qui vocati sunt aeternae hereditatis. ¹⁶Ubi enim testamentum, mors necesse est afferatur testatoris; ¹⁷testamentum autem in mortuis est confirmatum, nondum enim valet, dum vivit, qui testatus est. ¹⁸Unde ne prius quidem sine sanguine dedicatum est; ¹⁹enuntiato enim omni mandato secundum legem a Moyse universo populo, accipiens sanguinem vitulorum et hircorum cum aqua et lana coccinea et hyssopo, ipsum librum et omnem populum aspersit ²⁰dicens: «*Hic sanguis testamenti, quod mandavit ad vos Deus*»; ²¹etiam tabernaculum et omnia vasa ministerii sanguine similiter aspersit. ²²Et omnia paene in sanguine mundantur secundum legem, et sine sanguinis effusione non fit remissio. ²³Necesse erat ergo figuras quidem caelestium his mundari, ipsa autem caelestia melioribus hostiis quam istis. ²⁴Non enim in manufacta Sancta Christus introivit, quae sunt similitudo verorum, sed in ipsum caelum, ut appareat nunc vultui Dei pro nobis; ²⁵neque ut saepe offerat semetipsum, quemadmodum pontifex intrat in Sancta per singulos annos in sanguine alieno. ²⁶Alioquin oportebat eum frequenter pati ab origine mundi; nunc autem semel in consummatione saeculorum ad destitutionem peccati per sacrificium sui manifestatus est. ²⁷Et quemadmodum statutum est hominibus semel mori, post hoc autem iudicium, ²⁸sic et Christus, qui semel oblatus ad multorum auferenda peccata, secundo sine peccato apparebit exspectantibus se in salutem.   **[10]** ¹Umbram enim habens lex bonorum futurorum, non ipsam imaginem rerum, per singulos annos iisdem ipsis hostiis, quas offerunt indesinenter, numquam potest accedentes perfectos facere. ²Alioquin nonne cessassent offerri, ideo quod nullam haberent ultra conscientiam peccatorum cultores semel mundati? ³Sed in ipsis commemoratio peccatorum per singulos annos fit. ⁴Impossibile enim est sanguinem taurorum et hircorum auferre peccata. ⁵Ideo ingrediens mundum dicit: «*Hostiam et oblationem noluisti, / corpus autem aptasti mihi; / ⁶holocautomata et sacrificia pro peccato / non tibi placuerunt. / ⁷Tunc dixi: Ecce venio, / in capitulo libri scriptum est de me, / ut faciam, Deus, voluntatem tuam*». ⁸Superius dicens:

«*Hostias et oblationes et holocautomata et sacrificia pro peccato noluisti, nec placuerunt* tibi», quae secundum legem offeruntur, ⁹*tunc* dixit: «*Ecce venio, ut faciam voluntatem tuam*». Aufert primum, ut secundum statuat; ¹⁰in qua voluntate sanctificati sumus per oblationem corporis Christi Iesu in semel. ¹¹Et omnis quidem sacerdos stat cotidie ministrans et easdem saepe offerens hostias, quae numquam possunt auferre peccata. ¹²Hic autem, una pro peccatis oblata hostia, in sempiternum *consedit in dextera Dei,* ¹³de cetero exspectans, *donec ponantur inimici eius scabellum pedum eius;* ¹⁴una enim oblatione consummavit in sempiternum eos, qui sanctificantur. ¹⁵Testificatur autem nobis et Spiritus Sanctus; postquam enim dixit: ¹⁶«*Hoc est testamentum, quod testabor ad illos post dies illos, dicit Dominus, dando leges meas in cordibus eorum et in mente eorum superscribam eas;* ¹⁷*et peccatorum eorum et iniquitatum eorum iam non recordabor amplius*». ¹⁸Ubi autem horum remissio, iam non oblatio pro peccato. ¹⁹Habentes itaque, fratres, fiduciam in introitum Sanctorum in sanguine Iesu, ²⁰quam initiavit nobis viam novam et viventem per velamen, id est carnem suam, ²¹et sacerdotem magnum super domum Dei, ²²accedamus cum vero corde in plenitudine fidei, aspersi corda a conscientia mala et abluti corpus aqua munda; ²³teneamus spei confessionem indeclinabilem, fidelis enim est, qui repromisit; ²⁴et consideremus invicem in provocationem caritatis et bonorum operum, ²⁵non deserentes congregationem nostram, sicut est consuetudinis quibusdam, sed exhortantes, et tanto magis quanto videtis appropinquantem diem. ²⁶Voluntarie enim peccantibus nobis, post acceptam notitiam veritatis, iam non relinquitur pro peccatis hostia, ²⁷terribilis autem quaedam exspectatio iudicii et ignis aemulatio, quae consumptura est adversarios. ²⁸Irritam quis faciens legem Moysis sine ulla miseratione *duobus vel tribus testibus moritur;* ²⁹quanto deteriora putatis merebitur supplicia, qui Filium Dei conculcaverit et sanguinem testamenti communem duxerit, in quo sanctificatus est, et Spiritui gratiae contumeliam fecerit? ³⁰Scimus enim eum, qui dixit: «*Mihi vindicta, ego retribuam*» et iterum: «*Iudicabit Dominus populum suum*». ³¹Horrendum est incidere in manus Dei viventis. ³²Rememoramini autem pristinos dies, in quibus illuminati magnum certamen sustinuistis passionum; ³³in altero quidem opprobriis et tribulationibus spectaculum facti, in altero autem socii taliter conversantium effecti; ³⁴nam et vinctis compassi estis et rapinam bonorum vestrorum cum gaudio suscepistis, cognoscentes vos habere meliorem substantiam et manentem. ³⁵Nolite itaque abicere confidentiam vestram, quae magnam habet remunerationem; ³⁶patientia enim vobis necessaria est, ut voluntatem Dei facientes reportetis promissionem. ³⁷Adhuc enim *modicum quantulum,* / qui *venturus est, veniet et non tardabit.* / ³⁸*Iustus autem meus ex fide vivet*; / quod *si subtraxerit se,* / *non sibi complacet in eo anima mea.* ³⁹Nos autem non sumus subtractionis in perditionem, sed fidei in acquisitionem animae. **[11]** ¹Est autem fides sperandorum substantia, rerum argumentum non apparentium. ²In hac enim testimonium consecuti sunt seniores. ³Fide intellegimus aptata esse saecula verbo Dei, ut ex invisibilibus visibilia facta sint. ⁴Fide ampliorem hostiam Abel quam Cain obtulit Deo, per quam testimonium consecutus est esse iustus, testimonium perhibente muneribus eius Deo, et per illam defunctus adhuc loquitur. ⁵Fide Henoch translatus est ne videret mortem, et *non inveniebatur, quia transtulit illum Deus*; ante translationem enim testimonium accepit *placuisse Deo.* ⁶Sine fide autem impossibile placere; credere enim oportet accedentem ad Deum quia est et inquirentibus se remunerator fit. ⁷Fide Noe responso accepto de his, quae adhuc non videbantur, reveritus aptavit arcam in salutem domus suae; per quam damnavit mundum, et iustitiae, quae secundum fidem est, heres est institutus. ⁸Fide vocatus Abraham oboedivit in locum exire, quem accepturus erat in hereditatem, et exivit nesciens quo iret. ⁹Fide peregrinatus est in terra promissionis tamquam in aliena in casulis habitando cum Isaac et Iacob, coheredibus promissionis eiusdem; ¹⁰exspectabat enim fundamenta habentem civitatem, cuius artifex et conditor Deus. ¹¹Fide —et ipsa Sara sterilis— virtutem in conceptionem seminis accepit etiam praeter tempus aetatis, quoniam fidelem credidit esse, qui promiserat; ¹²propter quod et ab uno orti sunt, et hoc emortuo, *tamquam sidera caeli* in multitudine *et sicut arena, quae est ad oram maris innumerabilis.* ¹³Iuxta fidem defuncti sunt omnes isti, non acceptis promissionibus, sed a longe eas aspicientes et salutantes, et confitentes quia peregrini et hospites sunt supra terram; ¹⁴qui enim haec dicunt, significant se patriam inquirere. ¹⁵Et si quidem illius meminissent, de qua exierant, habebant utique tempus revertendi; ¹⁶nunc autem meliorem appetunt, id est caelestem. Ideo non confunditur Deus vocari Deus eorum, paravit enim illis civitatem. ¹⁷Fide obtulit Abraham Isaac, cum tentaretur, et unigenitum offerebat ille, qui susceperat promissiones, ¹⁸ad quem dictum erat: «*In Isaac vocabitur tibi semen*», ¹⁹arbitratus quia et a mortuis suscitare potens est Deus; unde eum et in parabola reportavit. ²⁰Fide et de futuris benedixit Isaac Iacob et Esau. ²¹Fide Iacob moriens singulis filiorum Ioseph benedixit et *adoravit super fastigium virgae suae.* ²²Fide Ioseph moriens de profectione filiorum Israel memoratus est et de ossibus suis mandavit. ²³Fide Moyses natus occultatus est mensibus tribus a parentibus suis, eo quod vidissent formosum infantem et non timuerunt regis edictum. ²⁴Fide Moyses grandis factus negavit se dici filium filiae pharaonis, ²⁵magis eligens affligi cum populo Dei quam temporalem peccati habere iucunditatem, ²⁶maiores divitias aestimans thesauris Aegypti improperium Christi; aspiciebat enim in remunerationem. ²⁷Fide reliquit Aegyptum non veritus animositatem regis, invisibilem enim tamquam videns sustinuit. ²⁸Fide celebravit Pascha et sanguinis effusionem, ne, qui vastabat primogenita, tangeret ea. ²⁹Fide transierunt mare Rubrum tamquam per aridam terram, quod experti Aegyptii devorati sunt. ³⁰Fide muri Iericho ruerunt circuiti diebus septem. ³¹Fide Rahab meretrix non periit cum incredulis, quia exceperat exploratores cum pace. ³²Et quid adhuc dicam? Deficiet enim me tempus enarrantem de Gedeon, Barac, Samson, Iephte, David et Samuel atque prophetis, ³³qui per fidem devicerunt regna, operati sunt iustitiam, adepti sunt repromissiones, obturaverunt ora leonum, ³⁴exstinxerunt impetum ignis, effugerunt aciem gladii, convaluerunt de infirmitate, fortes facti sunt in bello, castra verterunt exterorum; ³⁵acceperunt mulieres de resurrectione mortuos suos; alii autem distenti sunt, non suscipientes redemptionem, ut meliorem invenirent resurrectionem; ³⁶alii vero ludibria et verbera experti sunt, insuper et vincula et carcerem; ³⁷lapidati sunt, secti sunt, in occisione gladii mortui sunt, circumierunt in melotis, in pellibus caprinis, egentes, angustiati, afflicti, ³⁸quibus dignus non erat mundus, in solitudinibus errantes et montibus et speluncis et in cavernis terrae. ³⁹Et hi omnes testimonium per fidem consecuti non reportaverunt promissionem, ⁴⁰Deo pro nobis melius aliquid providente, ut ne sine nobis consummarentur. **[12]** ¹Ideoque et nos tantam habentes circumpositam nobis nubem testium, deponentes omne pondus et circumstans nos peccatum, per patientiam curramus propositum nobis certamen, ²aspicientes in ducem fidei et consummatorem Iesum, qui pro gaudio sibi proposito sustinuit crucem, confusione contempta, atque in dextera throni Dei sedet. ³Recogitate enim eum, qui talem sustinuit a peccatoribus adversum semetipsum contradictionem, ut ne fatigemini animis vestris deficientes. ⁴Nondum usque ad sanguinem restitistis adversus peccatum repugnantes ⁵et obliti estis exhortationis, quae vobis tamquam filiis loquitur: «*Fili mi, noli neglegere disciplinam Domini, / neque deficias, dum ab eo argueris: /* ⁶*quem enim diligit, Dominus castigat, / flagellat autem omnem filium, quem recipit*». ⁷Ad disciplinam suffertis; tamquam filios vos tractat Deus. Quis enim filius, quem non corripit pater? ⁸Quod si extra disciplinam estis, cuius participes facti sunt omnes, ergo adulterini et non filii estis! ⁹Deinde patres quidem carnis nostrae habebamus eruditores et reverebamur; non multo magis obtemperabimus Patri spirituum et vivemus? ¹⁰Et illi quidem ad tempus paucorum dierum, secundum quod videbatur illis, castigabant, hic autem ad id, quod utile est ad participandam sanctitatem eius. ¹¹Omnis autem disciplina in praesenti quidem videtur non esse gaudii sed maeroris, postea autem fructum pacificum exercitatis per eam reddit iustitiae. ¹²Propter quod *remissas manus et soluta genua erigite* ¹³*et gressus rectos facite pedibus* vestris, ut, quod claudum est, non extorqueatur, magis autem sanetur. ¹⁴Pacem sectamini cum omnibus et sanctificationem, sine qua nemo videbit Dominum, ¹⁵providentes, ne quis desit gratiae Dei, ne qua radix amaritudinis sursum germinans perturbet et per illam inquinentur multi, ¹⁶ne quis fornicator aut profanus ut Esau, qui propter unam escam vendidit primogenita sua. ¹⁷Scitis enim quoniam et postea cupiens hereditare benedictionem reprobatus est, non enim invenit paenitentiae locum, quamquam cum lacrimis inquisisset eam. ¹⁸Non enim accessistis ad tractabilem et ardentem ignem et turbinem et caliginem et procellam ¹⁹et tubae sonum et vocem verborum, quam qui audierunt, recusaverunt, ne ultra eis fieret verbum; ²⁰non enim portabant mandatum: «*Et si bestia tetigerit montem, lapidabitur*»; ²¹et ita terribile erat, quod videbatur, Moyses dixit: «*Exterritus sum* et tremebundus». ²²Sed accessistis ad Sion montem et civitatem Dei viventis, Ierusalem caelestem, et multa milia angelorum, frequentiam ²³et ecclesiam primogenitorum, qui conscripti sunt in caelis, et iudicem Deum omnium et spiritus iustorum, qui consummati sunt, ²⁴et testamenti novi mediatorem Iesum et sanguinem aspersionis, melius loquentem quam Abel. ²⁵Videte, ne recusetis loquentem; si enim illi non effugerunt recusantes eum, qui super terram loquebatur, multo magis nos, qui de caelis loquentem avertimus; ²⁶cuius vox movit terram tunc, modo autem pronuntiavit dicens: «*Adhuc semel ego movebo* non solum *terram* sed et *caelum*». ²⁷Hoc autem «*adhuc semel*» declarat mobilium translationem tamquam factorum, ut maneant ea, quae sunt immobilia. ²⁸Itaque, regnum immobile suscipientes, habeamus gratiam, per quam serviamus placentes Deo cum reverentia et metu; ²⁹etenim *Deus* noster *ignis consumens* est. **[13]** ¹Caritas fraternitatis maneat. ²Hospitalitatem nolite oblivisci, per hanc enim quidam nescientes hospitio receperunt angelos. ³Mementote vinctorum tamquam simul vincti, laborantium tamquam et ipsi in corpore morantes. ⁴Honorabile conubium in omnibus et torus immaculatus, fornicatores enim et adulteros iudicabit Deus. ⁵Sint mores sine avaritia; contenti praesentibus. Ipse enim dixit: «*Non te deseram, neque derelinquam*», ⁶ita ut confidenter dicamus: «*Dominus mihi adiutor est, non timebo; / quid faciet mihi homo?*». ⁷Mementote praepositorum vestrorum, qui vobis locuti sunt verbum Dei, quorum intuentes exitum conversationis imitamini fidem. ⁸Iesus Christus heri et hodie idem, et in saecula! ⁹Doctrinis variis et peregrinis nolite abduci; optimum enim est gratia stabiliri cor, non escis, quae non profuerunt ambulantibus in eis. ¹⁰Habemus altare, de quo edere non habent potestatem, qui tabernaculo deserviunt. ¹¹Quorum enim animalium infertur sanguis pro peccato in Sancta per pontificem, horum corpora cremantur extra castra. ¹²Propter quod et Iesus, ut sanctificaret per suum sanguinem populum, extra portam passus est. ¹³Exeamus igitur ad eum extra castra, improperium eius portantes; ¹⁴non enim habemus hic manentem civitatem, sed futuram inquirimus. ¹⁵Per ipsum ergo offeramus hostiam laudis semper Deo, id est fructum labiorum confitentium nomini eius. ¹⁶Beneficientiae autem et communionis nolite oblivisci, talibus enim hostiis oblectatur Deus. ¹⁷Oboedite praepositis vestris et subiacete eis, ipsi enim pervigilant pro animabus vestris quasi rationem redditouri, ut cum gaudio hoc faciant et non gementes, hoc enim non expedit vobis. ¹⁸Orate pro nobis; confidimus enim quia bonam conscientiam habemus, in omnibus bene volentes conversari. ¹⁹Amplius autem deprecor vos hoc facere, ut quo celerius restituar vobis. ²⁰Deus autem pacis, qui eduxit de mortuis pastorem magnum ovium in sanguine testamenti aeterni, Dominum nostrum Iesum, ²¹aptet vos in omni bono, ut faciatis voluntatem eius, faciens in nobis, quod placeat coram se per Iesum Christum, cui gloria in saecula saeculorum. Amen. ²²Rogo autem vos, fratres, sufferte sermonem exhortationis, etenim perpaucis scripsi vobis. ²³Cognoscite fratrem nostrum Timotheum dimissum esse, cum quo si celerius venerit, videbo vos. ²⁴Salutate omnes praepositos vestros et omnes sanctos. Salutant vos, qui de Italia sunt. ²⁵Gratia cum omnibus vobis.

EPISTOLA IACOBI

[1] ¹Iacobus, Dei et Domini Iesu Christi servus, duodecim tribubus, quae sunt in dispersione, salutem. ²Omne gaudium existimate, fratres mei, cum in tentationibus variis incideritis, ³scientes quod probatio fidei vestrae patientiam operatur; ⁴patientia autem opus perfectum habeat, ut sitis perfecti et integri, in nullo deficientes. ⁵Si quis autem vestrum indiget sapientia, postulet a Deo, qui dat omnibus affluenter et non improperat, et dabitur ei. ⁶Postulet autem in fide nihil haesitans; qui enim haesitat, similis est fluctui maris, qui a vento movetur et circumfertur. ⁷Non ergo aestimet homo ille quod accipiat aliquid a Domino, ⁸vir duplex animo, inconstans in omnibus viis suis. ⁹Glorietur autem frater humilis in exaltatione sua, ¹⁰dives autem in humilitate sua, quoniam sicut flos feni transibit. ¹¹Exortus est enim sol cum ardore et arefecit fenum, et flos eius decidit, et decor vultus eius deperiit; ita et dives in itineribus suis marcescet. ¹²Beatus vir, qui suffert tentationem, quia, cum probatus fuerit, accipiet coronam vitae, quam repromisit Deus diligentibus se. ¹³Nemo, cum tentatur, dicat: «A Deo tentor»; Deus enim non tentatur malis, ipse autem neminem tentat. ¹⁴Unusquisque vero tentatur a concupiscentia sua abstractus et illectus; ¹⁵dein concupiscentia, cum conceperit, parit peccatum, peccatum vero, cum consummatum fuerit, generat mortem. ¹⁶Nolite errare, fratres mei dilectissimi. ¹⁷Omne datum optimum et omne donum perfectum de sursum est, descendens a Patre luminum, apud quem non est transmutatio nec vicissitudinis obumbratio. ¹⁸Voluntarie genuit nos verbo veritatis, ut simus primitiae quaedam creaturae eius. ¹⁹Scitis, fratres mei dilecti. Sit autem omnis homo velox ad audiendum, tardus autem ad loquendum et tardus ad iram; ²⁰ira enim viri iustitiam Dei non operatur. ²¹Propter quod abicientes omnem immunditiam et abundantiam malitiae in mansuetudine suscipite insitum verbum, quod potest salvare animas vestras. ²²Estote autem factores verbi et non auditores tantum fallentes vosmetipsos. ²³Quia si quis auditor est verbi et non factor, hic comparabitur viro consideranti vultum nativitatis suae in speculo; ²⁴consideravit enim se et abiit, et statim oblitus est qualis fuerit. ²⁵Qui autem perspexerit in lege perfecta libertatis et permanserit, non auditor obliviosus factus sed factor operis, hic beatus in facto suo erit. ²⁶Si quis putat se religiosum esse non freno circumducens linguam suam sed seducens cor suum, huius vana est religio. ²⁷Religio munda et immaculata apud Deum et Patrem haec est: visitare pupillos et viduas in tribulatione eorum, immaculatum se custodire ab hoc saeculo.   [2] ¹Fratres mei, nolite in personarum acceptione habere fidem Domini nostri Iesu Christi gloriae. ²Etenim si introierit in synagogam vestram vir aureum anulum habens in veste candida, introierit autem et pauper in sordido habitu, ³et intendatis in eum, qui indutus est veste praeclara, et dixeritis: «Tu sede hic bene», pauperi autem dicatis: «Tu sta illic aut sede sub scabello meo», ⁴nonne iudicatis apud vosmetipsos et facti estis iudices cogitationum iniquarum? ⁵Audite, fratres mei dilectissimi. Nonne Deus elegit, qui pauperes sunt mundo, divites in fide et heredes regni, quod repromisit diligentibus se? ⁶Vos autem exhonorastis pauperem. Nonne divites opprimunt vos et ipsi trahunt vos ad iudicia? ⁷Nonne ipsi blasphemant bonum nomen, quod invocatum est super vos? ⁸Si tamen legem perficitis regalem secundum Scripturam: «*Diliges proximum tuum sicut teipsum*», bene facitis; ⁹si autem personas accipitis, peccatum operamini,

redarguti a lege quasi transgressores. ¹⁰Quicumque autem totam legem servaverit, offendat autem in uno, factus est omnium reus. ¹¹Qui enim dixit: «*Non moechaberis*», dixit et: «*Non occides*»; quod si non moecharis, occidis autem, factus es transgressor legis. ¹²Sic loquimini et sic facite sicut per legem libertatis iudicandi. ¹³Iudicium enim sine misericordia illi, qui non fecit misericordiam; superexsultat misericordia iudicio. ¹⁴Quid proderit, fratres mei, si fidem quis dicat se habere, opera autem non habeat? Numquid poterit fides salvare eum? ¹⁵Si frater aut soror nudi sunt et indigent victu cotidiano, ¹⁶dicat autem aliquis de vobis illis: «Ite in pace, calefacimini et saturamini», non dederitis autem eis, quae necessaria sunt corporis, quid proderit? ¹⁷Sic et fides, si non habeat opera, mortua est in semetipsa. ¹⁸Sed dicet quis: «Tu fidem habes, et ego opera habeo». Ostende mihi fidem tuam sine operibus, et ego tibi ostendam ex operibus meis fidem. ¹⁹Tu credis quoniam unus est Deus? Bene facis; et daemones credunt et contremiscunt! ²⁰Vis autem scire, o homo inanis, quoniam fides sine operibus otiosa est? ²¹Abraham pater noster nonne ex operibus iustificatus est offerens Isaac filium suum super altare? ²²Vides quoniam fides cooperabatur operibus illius, et ex operibus fides consummata est, ²³et suppleta est Scriptura dicens: «*Credidit Abraham Deo, et reputatum est illi ad iustitiam*», et amicus Dei appellatus est. ²⁴Videtis quoniam ex operibus iustificatur homo et non ex fide tantum. ²⁵Similiter autem et Rahab meretrix nonne ex operibus iustificata est suscipiens nuntios et alia via eiciens? ²⁶Sicut enim corpus sine spiritu emortuum est, ita et fides sine operibus mortua est. **[3]** ¹Nolite plures magistri fieri, fratres mei, scientes quoniam maius iudicium accipiemus. ²In multis enim offendimus omnes. Si quis in verbo non offendit, hic perfectus est vir, potens etiam freno circumducere totum corpus. ³Si autem equorum frenos in ora mittimus ad oboediendum nobis, et omne corpus illorum circumfermus. ⁴Ecce et naves, cum tam magnae sint et a ventis validis minentur, circumferuntur a minimo gubernaculo, ubi impetus dirigentis voluerit; ⁵ita et lingua modicum quidem membrum est et magna exsultat. Ecce quantus ignis quam magnam silvam incendit! ⁶Et lingua ignis est, universitas iniquitatis; lingua constituitur in membris nostris, quae maculat totum corpus et inflammat rotam nativitatis et inflammatur a gehenna. ⁷Omnis enim natura et bestiarum et volucrum et serpentium et etiam cetorum domatur et domita est a natura humana; ⁸linguam autem nullus hominum domare potest, inquietum malum, plena veneno mortifero. ⁹In ipsa benedicimus Dominum et Patrem et in ipsa maledicimus homines, qui ad similitudinem Dei facti sunt; ¹⁰ex ipso ore procedit benedictio et maledictio. Non oportet, fratres mei, haec ita fieri. ¹¹Numquid fons de eodem foramine emanat dulcem et amaram aquam? ¹²Numquid potest, fratres mei, ficus olivas facere aut vitis ficus? Neque salsa dulcem potest facere aquam. ¹³Quis sapiens et disciplinatus inter vos? Ostendat ex bona conversatione operationem suam in mansuetudine sapientiae. ¹⁴Quod si zelum amarum habetis et contentiones in cordibus vestris, nolite gloriari et mendaces esse adversus veritatem. ¹⁵Non est ista sapientia desursum descendens, sed terrena, animalis, diabolica; ¹⁶ubi enim zelus et contentio, ibi inconstantia et omne opus pravum. ¹⁷Quae autem desursum est sapientia primum quidem pudica est, deinde pacifica, modesta, suadibilis, plena misericordia et fructibus bonis, non iudicans, sine simulatione; ¹⁸fructus autem iustitiae in pace seminatur facientibus pacem. **[4]** ¹Unde bella et unde lites in vobis? Nonne hinc, ex concupiscentiis vestris, quae militant in membris vestris? ²Concupiscitis et non habetis; occiditis et zelatis et non potestis adipisci; litigatis et belligeratis. Non habetis, propter quod non postulatis; ³petitis et non accipitis, eo quod male petitis, ut in concupiscentiis vestris insumatis. ⁴Adulteri, nescitis quia amicitia huius mundi inimica est Dei? Quicumque ergo voluerit amicus esse saeculi huius, inimicus Dei constituitur. ⁵Aut putatis quia inaniter Scriptura dicat: «Ad invidiam concupiscit Spiritus, qui inhabitat in nobis?». ⁶Maiorem autem dat gratiam; propter quod dicit: «*Deus superbis resistit, / humilibus autem dat gratiam*». ⁷Subicimini igitur Deo; resistite autem Diabolo, et fugiet a vobis. ⁸Appropiate Deo, et appropinquabit vobis. Emundate manus, peccatores, et purificate corda, duplices animo. ⁹Miseri estote et lugete et plorate; risus vester in luctum convertatur et gaudium in maerorem. ¹⁰Humiliamini in conspectu Domini, et exaltabit vos. ¹¹Nolite detrahere alterutrum, fratres; qui detrahit fratri aut qui iudicat fratrem suum, detrahit legi et iudicat legem; si autem iudicas legem, non es factor legis sed iudex. ¹²Unus est legislator et iudex, qui potest salvare et perdere; tu autem quis es, qui iudicas proximum? ¹³Age nunc, qui dicitis: «Hodie aut crastino ibimus in illam civitatem et faciemus quidem ibi annum et mercabimur et lucrum faciemus», ¹⁴qui ignoratis, quae erit in crastinum vita vestra! Vapor enim estis ad modicum parens, deinceps exterminatur; ¹⁵pro eo ut dicatis: «Si Dominus voluerit, et vivemus et faciemus hoc aut illud». ¹⁶Nunc autem gloriamini in superbiis vestris; omnis gloriatio talis maligna est. ¹⁷Scienti igitur bonum facere et non facienti, peccatum est illi! **[5]** ¹Age nunc, divites, plorate ululantes in miseriis, quae advenient vobis. ²Divitiae vestrae putrefactae sunt, et vestimenta vestra a tineis comesta sunt, ³aurum et argentum vestrum aeruginavit, et aerugo eorum in testimonium vobis erit et manducabit carnes vestras sicut ignis: thesaurizastis in novissimis diebus. ⁴Ecce merces operariorum, qui messuerunt regiones vestras, quae fraudata est a vobis, clamat, et clamores eorum, qui messuerunt, in aures Domini Sabaoth introierunt. ⁵Epulati estis super terram et in luxuriis fuistis, enutristis corda vestra in die occisionis. ⁶Addixistis, occidistis iustum. Non resistit vobis. ⁷Patientes igitur estote, fratres, usque ad adventum Domini. Ecce agricola exspectat pretiosum fructum terrae, patienter ferens, donec accipiat *imbrem temporaneum et serotinum.* ⁸Patientes estote et vos, confirmate corda vestra, quoniam adventus Domini appropinquavit. ⁹Nolite ingemiscere, fratres, in alterutrum, ut non iudicemini; ecce iudex ante ianuam assistit. ¹⁰Exemplum accipite, fratres, laboris et patientiae prophetas, qui locuti sunt in nomine Domini. ¹¹Ecce beatificamus eos, qui sustinuerunt; sufferentiam Iob audistis et finem Domini vidistis, quoniam *misericors est Dominus et miserator.* ¹²Ante omnia autem, fratres mei, nolite iurare, neque per caelum neque per terram, neque aliud quodcumque iuramentum; sit autem vestrum «Est» est, et «Non» non, uti non sub iudicio decidatis. ¹³Tristatur aliquis vestrum? Oret. Aequo animo est? Psallat. ¹⁴Infirmatur quis in vobis? Advocet presbyteros ecclesiae, et orent super eum, unguentes eum oleo in nomine Domini. ¹⁵Et oratio fidei salvabit infirmum, et allevabit eum Dominus; et si peccata operatus fuerit, dimittentur ei. ¹⁶Confitemini ergo alterutrum peccata et orate pro invicem, ut sanemini. Multum enim valet deprecatio iusti operans. ¹⁷Elias homo erat similis nobis passibilis et oratione oravit, ut non plueret, et non pluit super terram annos tres et menses sex; ¹⁸et rursum oravit, et caelum dedit pluviam, et terra germinavit fructum suum. ¹⁹Fratres mei, si quis ex vobis erraverit a veritate et converterit quis eum, ²⁰scire debet quoniam, qui converti fecerit peccatorem ab errore viae eius, salvabit animam suam a morte et operiet multitudinem peccatorum.

EPISTOLA PRIMA PETRI

[1] ¹Petrus apostolus Iesu Christi electis advenis dispersionis Ponti, Galatiae, Cappadociae, Asiae et Bithyniae, ²secundum praescientiam Dei Patris, in sanctificatione Spiritus, in oboedientiam et aspersionem sanguinis Iesu Christi: gratia vobis et pax multiplicetur. ³Benedictus Deus et Pater Domini nostri Iesu Christi, qui secundum magnam misericordiam suam regeneravit nos in spem vivam per resurrectionem Iesu Christi ex mortuis, ⁴in hereditatem incorruptibilem et incontaminatam et immarcescibilem, conservatam in caelis propter vos, ⁵qui in virtute Dei custodimini per fidem in salutem paratam revelari in tempore novissimo. ⁶In quo exsultatis, modicum nunc si oportet contristati in variis tentationibus, ⁷ut probatio vestrae fidei multo pretiosior auro, quod perit, per ignem quidem probato, inveniatur in laudem et gloriam et honorem in revelatione Iesu Christi. ⁸Quem cum non videritis, diligitis; in quem nunc non videntes, credentes autem, exsultatis laetitia inenarrabili et glorificata, ⁹reportantes finem fidei vestrae salutem animarum. ¹⁰De qua salute exquisierunt atque scrutati sunt prophetae, qui de futura in vos gratia prophetaverunt, ¹¹scrutantes in quod vel quale tempus significaret, qui erat in eis Spiritus Christi, praenuntians eas, quae in Christo sunt, passiones et posteriores glorias; ¹²quibus revelatum est quia non sibi ipsis, vobis autem ministrabant ea, quae nunc nuntiata sunt vobis per eos, qui evangelizaverunt vos, Spiritu Sancto misso de caelo, in quae desiderant angeli prospicere. ¹³Propter quod succincti lumbos mentis vestrae, sobrii, perfecte sperate in eam, quae offertur vobis, gratiam in revelatione Iesu Christi. ¹⁴Quasi filii oboedientiae, non configurati prioribus in ignorantia vestra desideriis, ¹⁵sed secundum eum, qui vocavit vos, sanctum, et ipsi sancti in omni conversatione sitis, ¹⁶quoniam scriptum est: «Sancti eritis, quia ego sanctus sum». ¹⁷Et si Patrem invocatis eum, qui sine acceptione personarum iudicat secundum uniuscuiusque opus, in timore incolatus vestri tempore conversamini, ¹⁸scientes quod non corruptibilibus argento vel auro redempti estis de vana vestra conversatione a patribus tradita, ¹⁹sed pretioso sanguine quasi Agni incontaminati et immaculati Christi, ²⁰praecogniti quidem ante constitutionem mundi, manifestati autem novissimis temporibus propter vos, ²¹qui per ipsum fideles estis in Deum, qui suscitavit eum a mortuis et dedit ei gloriam, ut fides vestra et spes esset in Deum. ²²Animas vestras castificantes in oboeditione veritatis ad fraternitatis amorem non fictum, ex corde invicem diligite attentius, ²³renati non ex semine corruptibili sed incorruptibili per verbum Dei vivum et permanens; ²⁴quia *omnis caro ut fenum, / et omnis gloria eius tamquam flos feni. / Exaruit fenum, et flos decidit; /* ²⁵*verbum autem Domini manet in aeternum.* Hoc est autem verbum, quod evangelizatum est in vos. **[2]**¹Deponentes igitur omnem malitiam et omnem dolum et simulationes et invidias et omnes detractiones, ²sicut modo geniti infantes, rationale sine dolo lac concupiscite, ut in eo crescatis in salutem, ³si *gustastis quoniam dulcis Dominus.* ⁴Ad quem accedentes, lapidem vivum, ab hominibus quidem reprobatum, coram Deo autem electum, pretiosum, ⁵et ipsi tamquam lapides vivi aedificamini domus spiritalis in sacerdotium sanctum offerre spiritales hostias acceptabiles Deo per Iesum Christum. ⁶Propter quod continet Scriptura: *«Ecce pono in Sion lapidem angularem, electum, pretiosum; / et, qui credit in eo, non confundetur».* ⁷Vobis igitur honor credentibus; non credentibus autem *«Lapis, quem reprobaverunt aedificantes, / hic factus est in caput anguli»* ⁸et *«lapis offensionis et petra scandali»*; qui offendunt verbo non credentes, in quod et positi sunt. / ⁹Vos autem *genus electum, regale sacerdotium, gens sancta, populus in acquisitionem, ut virtutes annuntietis* eius, qui de tenebris vos vocavit in admirabile lumen suum; ¹⁰qui aliquando *non populus,* nunc autem *populus Dei; qui non consecuti misericordiam,* nunc autem *misericordiam consecuti.* ¹¹Carissimi, obsecro tamquam advenas et peregrinos abstinere vos a carnalibus desideriis, quae militant adversus animam; ¹²conversationem vestram inter gentes habentes bonam, ut in eo, quod detrectant de vobis tamquam de malefactoribus, ex bonis operibus considerantes glorificent Deum in die visitationis. ¹³Subiecti estote omni humanae creaturae propter Dominum: sive regi quasi praecellenti ¹⁴sive ducibus tamquam ab eo missis ad vindictam malefactorum, laudem vero bonorum; ¹⁵quia sic est voluntas Dei, ut benefacientes obmutescere faciatis imprudentium hominum ignorantiam, ¹⁶quasi liberi, et non quasi velamen habentes malitiae libertatem, sed sicut servi Dei. ¹⁷Omnes honorate, fraternitatem diligite, Deum timete, regem honorificate. ¹⁸Servi, subditi estote in omni timore dominis, non tantum bonis et modestis sed etiam pravis. ¹⁹Haec est enim gratia, si propter conscientiam Dei sustinet quis tristitias, patiens iniuste. ²⁰Quae enim gloria est, si peccantes et colaphizati sustinetis? Sed si benefacientes et patientes sustinetis, haec est gratia apud Deum. ²¹In hoc enim vocati estis, quia / et Christus passus est pro vobis, / vobis relinquens exemplum, / ut sequamini vestigia eius: / ²²qui *peccatum non fecit, / nec inventus est dolus in ore ipsius;* / ²³qui cum malediceretur, non remaledicebat; / cum pateretur, non comminabatur, / commendabat autem iuste iudicanti; / ²⁴qui *peccata* nostra *ipse pertulit /* in corpore suo super lignum, / ut peccatis mortui iustitiae viveremus; / cuius *livore sanati estis.* / ²⁵Eratis enim *sicut oves errantes,* sed conversi estis nunc ad pastorem et episcopum animarum vestrarum. **[3]** ¹Similiter mulieres subditae sint suis viris, ut et si qui non credunt verbo, per mulierum conversationem sine verbo lucrifiant, ²considerantes castam in timore conversationem vestram; ³quarum sit non extrinsecus capillaturae aut circumdationis auri aut indumenti vestimentorum cultus, ⁴sed qui absconditus cordis est homo in incorruptibilitate mitis et quieti spiritus, qui est in conspectu Dei locuples. ⁵Sic enim aliquando et sanctae mulieres sperantes in Deo ornabant se subiectae propriis viris, ⁶sicut Sara oboediebat Abrahae dominum eum vocans; cuius estis filiae benefacientes et non timentes ullam perturbationem. ⁷Viri similiter cohabitantes secundum scientiam quasi infirmiori vaso muliebri impertientes honorem, tamquam et coheredibus gratiae vitae, uti ne impediantur orationes vestrae. ⁸In fine autem omnes unanimes, compatientes, fraternitatis amatores, misericordes, humiles, ⁹non reddentes malum pro malo vel maledictum pro maledicto, sed e contrario benedicentes, quia in hoc vocati estis, ut benedictionem hereditate accipiatis. ¹⁰*«Qui enim vult vitam diligere / et videre dies bonos, / coerceat linguam suam a malo, / et labia eius ne loquantur dolum;* / ¹¹*declinet autem a malo et faciat bonum, / inquirat pacem et persequatur eam. /* ¹²Quia *oculi Domini super iustos, / et aures eius in preces eorum; / vultus autem Domini super facientes mala».* ¹³Et quis est qui vobis noceat, si boni aemulatores fueritis? ¹⁴Sed et si patimini propter iustitiam, beati! *Timorem autem eorum ne timueritis et non conturbemini,* ¹⁵*Dominum* autem Christum *sanctificate* in cordibus vestris, parati semper ad defensionem omni poscenti vos rationem de ea, quae in vobis est spe, ¹⁶sed cum mansuetudine et timore, conscientiam habentes bonam, ut in quo de vobis detrectatur, confundantur, qui calumniantur vestram bonam in Christo conversationem. ¹⁷Melius est enim benefacientes, si velit voluntas Dei, pati quam malefacientes. ¹⁸Quia et Christus semel pro peccatis passus est, iustus pro iniustis, ut vos adduceret ad Deum, mortificatus quidem carne, vivificatus autem Spiritu; ¹⁹in quo et his, qui in carcere erant, spiritibus adveniens praedicavit, ²⁰qui increduli fuerant aliquando, quando exspectabat Dei patientia in diebus Noe, cum fabricaretur arca, in qua pauci, id est octo animae, salvae factae sunt per aquam. ²¹Cuius antitypum, baptisma, et vos nunc salvos facit, non carnis depositio sordium sed conscientiae bonae rogatio in Deum, per resurrectionem Iesu Christi, ²²qui est in dextera Dei, profectus in caelum, subiectis sibi angelis et potestatibus et virtutibus. **[4]** ¹Christo igitur passo in carne, et vos eadem cogitatione armamini, quia, qui passus est carne, desiit a peccato, ²ut iam non hominum concupiscentiis sed voluntate Dei quod reliquum est in carne vivat temporis. ³Sufficit enim praeteritum tempus ad voluntatem gentium consummandam, vobis, qui ambulastis in luxuriis, concupiscentiis, vinolentiis, comissationibus, potationibus et illicitis idolorum cultibus. ⁴In quo mirantur non concurrentibus vobis in eandem luxuriae effusionem, blasphemantes; ⁵qui reddent rationem ei, qui paratus est iudicare vivos et mortuos. ⁶Propter hoc enim et mortuis evangelizatum est, ut iudicentur quidem secundum homines carne, vivant autem secundum Deum Spiritu. ⁷Omnium autem finis appropinquavit. Estote itaque prudentes et vigilate in orationibus. ⁸Ante omnia mutuam in vosmetipsos caritatem continuam habentes, quia caritas operit multitudinem peccatorum; ⁹hospitales invicem sine murmuratione; ¹⁰unusquisque, sicut accepit donationem, in alterutrum illam administrantes sicut boni dispensatores multiformis gratiae Dei. ¹¹Si quis loquitur, quasi sermones Dei; si quis ministrat, tamquam ex virtute, quam largitur Deus, ut in omnibus glorificetur Deus per Iesum Christum: cui est gloria et imperium in saecula saeculorum. Amen. ¹²Carissimi, nolite mirari in fervore, qui ad tentationem vobis fit, quasi novi aliquid vobis contingat, ¹³sed, quemadmodum communicatis Christi passionibus, gaudete, ut et in revelatione gloriae eius gaudeatis exsultantes. ¹⁴Si exprobramini in nomine Christi, beati, quoniam Spiritus gloriae et Dei super vos requiescit. ¹⁵Nemo enim vestrum patiatur quasi homicida aut fur aut maleficus aut alienorum speculator; ¹⁶si autem ut christianus, non erubescat, glorificet autem Deum in isto nomine. ¹⁷Quoniam tempus est, ut incipiat iudicium a domo Dei; si autem primum a nobis, qui finis eorum, qui non credunt Dei evangelio? ¹⁸«Et si *iustus vix salvatur, / impius et peccator ubi parebit?*». ¹⁹Itaque et hi, qui patiuntur secundum voluntatem Dei, fideli Creatori commendent animas suas in benefacto. **[5]** ¹Seniores ergo, qui in vobis sunt, obsecro, consenior et testis Christi passionum, qui et eius, quae in futuro revelanda est, gloriae communicator: ²Pascite, qui est in vobis, gregem Dei, providentes non coacto sed spontane secundum Deum, neque turpis lucri gratia sed voluntarie, ³neque ut dominantes in cleris sed formae facti gregis. ⁴Et cum apparuerit Princeps pastorum, percipietis immarcescibilem gloriae coronam. ⁵Similiter, adulescentes, subditi estote senioribus. Omnes autem invicem humilitatem induite, quia *Deus superbis resistit, / humilibus autem dat gratiam.* ⁶Humiliamini igitur sub potenti manu Dei, ut vos exaltet in tempore, ⁷omnem sollicitudinem vestram proicientes in eum, quoniam ipsi cura est de vobis. ⁸Sobrii estote, vigilate. Adversarius vester Diabolus tamquam leo rugiens circuit quaerens quem devoret. ⁹Cui resistite fortes fide, scientes eadem passionum ei, quae in mundo est, vestrae fraternitati fieri. ¹⁰Deus autem omnis gratiae, qui vocavit vos in aeternam suam gloriam in Christo Iesu, modicum passos ipse perficiet, confirmabit, solidabit, fundabit. ¹¹Ipsi imperium in saecula saeculorum. Amen. ¹²Per Silvanum vobis fidelem fratrem, ut arbitror, breviter scripsi, obsecrans et contestans hanc esse veram gratiam Dei; in qua state. ¹³Salutat vos, quae est in Babylone, coelecta et Marcus filius meus. ¹⁴Salutate invicem in osculo caritatis. Pax vobis omnibus, qui estis in Christo.

EPISTOLA SECUNDA PETRI

[1] ¹Simon Petrus servus et apostolus Iesu Christi his, qui coaequalem nobis sortiti sunt fidem in iustitia Dei nostri et salvatoris Iesus Christi: ²gratia vobis et pax multiplicetur in cognitione Dei et Iesu Domini nostri. ³Quomodo omnia nobis divinae virtutis suae ad vitam et pietatem donatae per cognitionem eius, qui vocavit nos propria gloria et virtute, ⁴per quae pretiosa et maxima nobis promissa donata sunt, ut per haec efficiamini divinae consortes naturae, fugientes eam, quae in mundo est in concupiscentia, corruptionem; ⁵et propter hoc ipsum curam omnem subinferentes ministrate in fide vestra virtutem, in virtute autem scientiam, ⁶in scientia autem continentiam, in continentia autem patientiam, in patientia autem pietatem, ⁷in pietate autem amorem fraternitatis, in amore autem fraternitatis caritatem. ⁸Haec enim vobis, cum adsint et abundent, non vacuos nec sine fructu vos constituunt in Domini nostri Iesu Christi cognitionem; ⁹cui enim non praesto sunt haec, caecus est et nihil procul cernens, oblivionem accipiens purgationis veterum suorum delictorum. ¹⁰Quapropter, fratres, magis satagite, ut firmam vestram vocationem et electionem faciatis. Haec enim facientes non offendetis aliquando; ¹¹sic enim abundanter ministrabitur vobis introitus in aeternum regnum Domini nostri et salvatoris Iesu Christi. ¹²Propter quod incipiam vos semper commonere de his, et quidem scientes et confirmatos in praesenti veritate. ¹³Iustum autem arbitror, quamdiu sum in hoc tabernaculo, suscitare vos in commonitione, ¹⁴certus quod velox est depositio tabernaculi mei, secundum quod et Dominus noster Iesus Christus significavit mihi; ¹⁵dabo autem operam et frequenter habere vos post obitum meum, ut horum memoriam faciatis. ¹⁶Non enim captiosas fabulas secuti notam fecimus vobis Domini nostri Iesu Christi virtutem et adventum, sed speculatores facti illius magnitudinis. ¹⁷Accipiens enim a Deo Patre honorem et gloriam, voce prolata ad eum huiuscemodi a magnifica gloria: «Filius meus, dilectus meus hic est, in quo ego mihi complacui»; ¹⁸et hanc vocem nos audivimus de caelo prolatam, cum essemus cum ipso in monte sancto. ¹⁹Et habemus firmiorem propheticum sermonem, cui bene facitis attendentes quasi lucernae lucenti in caliginoso loco, donec dies illucescat, et lucifer oriatur in cordibus vestris, ²⁰hoc primum intellegentes quod omnis prophetia Scripturae propria interpretatione non fit; ²¹non enim voluntate humana prolata est prophetia aliquando, sed a Spiritu Sancto ducti locuti sunt a Deo homines.

[2] ¹Fuerunt vero et pseudoprophetae in populo, sicut et in vobis erunt magistri mendaces, qui introducent sectas perditionis et eum, qui emit eos, Dominatorem negantes superducent sibi celerem perditionem. ²Et multi sequentur eorum luxurias, propter quos via veritatis blasphemabitur; ³et in avaritia fictis verbis de vobis negotiabuntur. Quibus iudicium iam olim non cessat, et perditio eorum non dormitat. ⁴Si enim Deus angelis peccantibus non pepercit, sed rudentibus inferni detractos in tartarum tradidit in iudicium reservatos; ⁵et originali mundo non pepercit, sed octavum Noe iustitiae praeconem custodivit diluvium mundo impiorum inducens; ⁶et civitates Sodomae et Gomorrae in cinerem redigens eversione damnavit, exemplum ponens eorum, quae sunt impiis futura; ⁷et iustum Lot oppressum a nefandorum luxuria conversationis eruit: ⁸aspectu enim et auditu iustus habitans apud eos, de die in diem animam iustam iniquis operibus cruciabat. ⁹Novit Dominus pios de tentatione eripere, iniquos vero in diem iudicii puniendos reservare, ¹⁰maxime autem eos, qui post carnem in concupiscentia immunditiae ambulant dominationemque contemnunt. Audaces, superbi, glorias non metuunt blasphemantes, ¹¹ubi angeli fortitudine et virtute cum sint maiores, non portant adversum illas coram Domino iudicium blasphemiae. ¹²Hi vero velut irrationabilia animalia naturaliter genita in captionem et in corruptionem, in his, quae ignorant, blasphemantes, in corruptione sua et corrumpentur ¹³inviti percipientes mercedem iniustitiae; voluptatem existimantes diei delicias, coinquinationes et maculae deliciis affluentes, in voluptatibus suis luxuriantes vobiscum, ¹⁴oculos habentes plenos adulterae et incessabiles delicti, pellicientes animas instabiles, cor exercitatum avaritiae habentes, maledictionis filii, ¹⁵derelinquentes rectam viam erraverunt, secuti viam Balaam ex Bosor, qui mercedem iniquitatis amavit, ¹⁶correptionem vero habuit suae praevaricationis; subiugale mutum in hominis voce loquens prohibuit prophetae insipientiam. ¹⁷Hi sunt fontes sine aqua et nebulae turbine exagitatae, quibus caligo tenebrarum reservatur. ¹⁸Superba enim vanitatis loquentes pelliciunt in concupiscentiis carnis luxuriis illos, qui paululum effugiunt eos, qui in errore conversantur, ¹⁹libertatem illis promittentes, cum ipsi servi sint corruptionis; a quo enim quis superatus est, huius servus est. ²⁰Si enim refugientes coinquinationes mundi in cognitione Domini nostri et Salvatoris Iesu Christi his rursus implicati superantur, facta sunt eis posteriora deteriora prioribus. ²¹Melius enim erat illis non cognoscere viam iustitiae quam post agnitionem retrorsum converti ab eo, quod illis traditum est, sancto mandato. ²²Contigit enim eis illud veri proverbii: «*Canis reversus ad suum vomitum,* / et sus lota in volutabro luti». [3] ¹Hanc vobis, carissimi, iam secundam scribo epistulam, in quibus excito vestram in commonitione sinceram mentem, ²ut memores sitis eorum, quae praedicta sunt verborum a sanctis prophetis, et ab apostolis traditi vobis praecepti Domini et Salvatoris; ³hoc primum scientes quod venient in novissimis diebus in illusione illudentes, iuxta proprias concupiscentias suas ambulantes, ⁴dicentes: «Ubi est promissio adventus eius?». Ex quo enim patres dormierunt, omnia sic perseverant ab initio creaturae. ⁵Latet enim eos hoc volentes quod caeli erant prius et terra de aqua et per aquam consistens Dei verbo, ⁶per quae ille tunc mundus aqua inundatus periit; ⁷caeli autem, qui nunc sunt, et terra eodem verbo repositi sunt igni, servati in diem iudicii et perditionis impiorum hominum. ⁸Unum vero hoc non lateat vos, carissimi, quia unus dies apud Dominum sicut mille anni, et mille anni sicut dies unus. ⁹Non tardat Dominus promissionem, sicut quidam tarditatem existimant, sed patienter agit in vos nolens aliquos perire, sed omnes ad paenitentiam reverti. ¹⁰Adveniet autem dies Domini ut fur, in qua caeli magno impetu transient, elementa vero calore solventur, et terra et opera, quae in ea invenientur. ¹¹Cum haec omnia ita dissolvenda sint, quales oportet esse vos in sanctis conversationibus et pietatibus ¹²exspectantes et properantes adventum diei Dei, propter quam caeli ardentes solventur, et elementa ignis ardore tabescent. ¹³*Novos* vero *caelos et terram novam* secundum promissum ipsius exspectamus, in quibus iustitia habitat. ¹⁴Propter quod, carissimi, haec exspectantes satagite immaculati et inviolati ei inveniri in pace ¹⁵et Domini nostri longanimitatem salutem arbitramini, sicut et carissimus frater noster Paulus secundum datam sibi sapientiam scripsit vobis, ¹⁶sicut et in omnibus epistulis loquens in eis de his, in quibus sunt quaedam difficilia intellectu, quae indocti et instabiles depravant sicut et ceteras Scripturas ad suam ipsorum perditionem. ¹⁷Vos igitur, dilecti, praescientes custodite, ne iniquorum errore simul abducti excidatis a propria firmitate; ¹⁸crescite vero in gratia et in cognitione Domini nostri et Salvatoris Iesu Christi. Ipsi gloria et nunc et in diem aeternitatis. Amen.

EPISTOLA PRIMA IOANNIS

[1] ¹Quod fuit ab initio, quod audivimus, quod vidimus oculis nostris, quod perspeximus, et manus nostrae contrectaverunt de verbo vitae ²—et vita apparuit, et vidimus et testamur et annuntiamus vobis

vitam aeternam, quae erat coram Patre et apparuit nobis—³quod vidimus et audivimus, annuntiamus et vobis, ut et vos communionem habeatis nobiscum. Communio autem nostra est cum Patre et cum Filio eius Iesu Christo. ⁴Et haec scribimus nos, ut gaudium nostrum sit plenum. ⁵Et haec est annuntiatio, quam audivimus ab eo et annuntiamus vobis, quoniam Deus lux est, et tenebrae in eo non sunt ullae. ⁶Si dixerimus quoniam communionem habemus cum eo et in tenebris ambulamus, mentimur et non facimus veritatem; ⁷si autem in luce ambulemus, sicut ipse est in luce, communionem habemus ad invicem, et sanguis Iesu Filii eius mundat nos ab omni peccato. ⁸Si dixerimus quoniam peccatum non habemus, nosmetipsos seducimus, et veritas in nobis non est. ⁹Si confiteamur peccata nostra, fidelis est et iustus, ut remittat nobis peccata et emundet nos ab omni iniustitia. ¹⁰Si dixerimus quoniam non peccavimus, mendacem facimus eum, et verbum eius non est in nobis. [2] ¹Filioli mei, haec scribo vobis, ut non peccetis. Sed si quis peccaverit, advocatum habemus ad Patrem, Iesum Christum iustum; ²et ipse est propitiatio pro peccatis nostris, non pro nostris autem tantum sed etiam pro totius mundi. ³Et in hoc cognoscimus quoniam novimus eum: si mandata eius servemus. ⁴Qui dicit: «Novi eum», et mandata eius non servat, mendax est, et in isto veritas non est; ⁵qui autem servat verbum eius, vere in hoc caritas Dei consummata est. In hoc cognoscimus quoniam in ipso sumus. ⁶Qui dicit se in ipso manere, debet, sicut ille ambulavit, et ipse ambulare. ⁷Carissimi, non mandatum novum scribo vobis, sed mandatum vetus, quod habuistis ab initio: mandatum vetus est verbum, quod audistis. ⁸Verumtamen mandatum novum scribo vobis, quod est verum in ipso et in vobis, quoniam tenebrae transeunt, et lumen verum iam lucet. ⁹Qui dicit se in luce esse et fratrem suum odit, in tenebris est usque adhuc. ¹⁰Qui diligit fratrem suum, in lumine manet, et scandalum ei non est; ¹¹qui autem odit fratrem suum, in tenebris est et in tenebris ambulat et nescit quo vadat, quoniam tenebrae obcaecaverunt oculos eius. ¹²Scribo vobis, filioli: Remissa sunt vobis peccata propter nomen eius. ¹³Scribo vobis, patres: Nostis eum, qui ab initio est. Scribo vobis, adulescentes: Vicistis Malignum. ¹⁴Scripsi vobis, parvuli: Nostis Patrem. Scripsi vobis, patres: Nostis eum, qui ab initio est. Scripsi vobis, adulescentes: Fortes estis, et verbum Dei in vobis manet, et vicistis Malignum. ¹⁵Nolite diligere mundum neque ea, quae in mundo sunt. Si quis diligit mundum, non est caritas Patris in eo; ¹⁶quoniam omne, quod est in mundo, concupiscentia carnis et concupiscentia oculorum et iactantia divitiarum, non est ex Patre, sed ex mundo est. ¹⁷Et mundus transit et concupiscentia eius; qui autem facit voluntatem Dei, manet in aeternum. ¹⁸Filioli, novissima hora est; et sicut audistis quia antichristus venit, ita nunc antichristi multi adsunt, unde cognoscimus quoniam novissima hora est. ¹⁹Ex nobis prodierunt, sed non erant ex nobis, nam si fuissent ex nobis, permansissent nobiscum; sed ut manifestaretur quoniam illi omnes non sunt ex nobis. ²⁰Sed vos unctionem habetis a Sancto et scitis omnes. ²¹Non scripsi vobis quasi nescientibus veritatem sed quasi scientibus eam, et quoniam omne mendacium ex veritate non est. ²²Quis est mendax, nisi is qui negat quoniam Iesus est Christus? Hic est antichristus, qui negat Patrem et Filium. ²³Omnis, qui negat Filium, nec Patrem habet; qui confitetur Filium, et Patrem habet. ²⁴Vos, quod audistis ab initio, in vobis permaneat; si in vobis permanserit, quod ab initio audistis, et vos in Filio et in Patre manebitis. ²⁵Et haec est repromissio, quam ipse pollicitus est nobis: vitam aeternam. ²⁶Haec scripsi vobis de eis, qui seducunt vos. ²⁷Et vos unctionem, quam accepistis ab eo, manet in vobis, et non necesse habetis, ut aliquis doceat vos; sed sicut unctio ipsius docet vos de omnibus, et verum est et non est mendacium, et, sicut docuit vos, manetis in eo. ²⁸Et nunc, filioli, manete in eo, ut, cum apparuerit, habeamus fiduciam et non confundamur ab eo in adventu eius. ²⁹Si scitis quoniam iustus est, scitote quoniam et omnis, qui facit iustitiam, ex ipso natus est. [3] ¹Videte qualem caritatem dedit nobis Pater, ut filii Dei nominemur, et sumus! Propter hoc mundus non cognoscit nos, quia non cognovit eum. ²Carissimi, nunc filii Dei sumus, et nondum manifestatum est quid erimus; scimus quoniam, cum ipse apparuerit, similes ei erimus, quoniam videbimus eum, sicuti est. ³Et omnis, qui habet spem hanc in eo, purificat se, sicut ille purus est. ⁴Omnis, qui facit peccatum, et iniquitatem facit, quia peccatum est iniquitas. ⁵Et scitis quoniam ille apparuit, ut peccata tolleret, et peccatum in eo non est. ⁶Omnis, qui in eo manet, non peccat; omnis, qui peccat, non vidit eum nec novit eum. ⁷Filioli, nemo vos seducat. Qui facit iustitiam, iustus est, sicut ille iustus est; ⁸qui facit peccatum, ex Diabolo est, quoniam a principio Diabolus peccat. Propter hoc apparuit Filius Dei, ut dissolvat opera Diaboli. ⁹Omnis, qui natus est ex Deo, peccatum non facit, quoniam semen ipsius in eo manet; et non potest peccare, quoniam ex Deo natus est. ¹⁰In hoc manifesti sunt filii Dei et filii Diaboli: omnis, qui non facit iustitiam, non est ex Deo, et qui non diligit fratrem suum. ¹¹Quoniam haec est annuntiatio, quam audistis ab initio, ut diligamus alterutrum. ¹²Non sicut Cain: ex Maligno erat et occidit fratrem suum. Et propter quid occidit eum? Quoniam opera eius maligna erant, fratris autem eius iusta. ¹³Nolite mirari, fratres, si odit vos mundus. ¹⁴Nos scimus quoniam transivimus de morte in vitam, quoniam diligimus fratres; qui non diligit, manet in morte. ¹⁵Omnis, qui odit fratrem suum, homicida est, et scitis quoniam omnis homicida non habet vitam aeternam in semetipso manentem. ¹⁶In hoc novimus caritatem quoniam ille pro nobis animam suam posuit; et nos debemus pro fratribus animas ponere. ¹⁷Qui habuerit substantiam mundi et viderit fratrem suum necesse habere et clauserit viscera sua ab eo, quomodo caritas Dei manet in eo? ¹⁸Filioli, non diligamus verbo nec lingua sed in opere et veritate. ¹⁹In hoc cognoscemus quoniam ex veritate sumus, et in conspectu eius placabimus corda nostra, ²⁰quoniam si reprehenderit nos cor, maior est Deus corde nostro et cognoscit omnia. ²¹Carissimi, si cor nostrum non reprehenderit nos, fiduciam habemus ad Deum ²²et, quodcumque petierimus, accipimus ab eo, quoniam mandata eius custodimus et ea, quae sunt placita coram eo, facimus. ²³Et hoc est mandatum eius, ut credamus nomini Filii eius Iesu Christi et diligamus alterutrum, sicut dedit mandatum nobis. ²⁴Et, qui servat mandata eius, in ipso manet, et ipse in eo; et in hoc cognoscimus quoniam manet in nobis, ex Spiritu, quem nobis dedit. **[4]** ¹Carissimi, nolite omni spiritui credere, sed probate spiritus si ex Deo sint, quoniam multi pseudoprophetae prodierunt in mundum. ²In hoc cognoscitis Spiritum Dei: omnis spiritus, qui confitetur Iesum Christum in carne venisse, ex Deo est. ³Et omnis spiritus, qui non confitetur Iesum, ex Deo non est; et hoc est antichristi, quod audistis quoniam venit, et nunc iam in mundo est. ⁴Vos ex Deo estis, filioli, et vicistis eos, quoniam maior est, qui in vobis est quam qui in mundo. ⁵Ipsi ex mundo sunt; ideo ex mundo loquuntur, et mundus eos audit. ⁶Nos ex Deo sumus. Qui cognoscit Deum, audit nos; qui non est ex Deo, non audit nos. Ex hoc cognoscimus Spiritum veritatis et spiritum erroris. ⁷Carissimi, diligamus invicem, quoniam caritas ex Deo est, et omnis, qui diligit, ex Deo natus est et cognoscit Deum. ⁸Qui non diligit, non cognovit Deum, quoniam Deus caritas est. ⁹In hoc apparuit caritas Dei in nobis, quoniam Filium suum unigenitum misit Deus in mundum, ut vivamus per eum. ¹⁰In hoc est caritas, non quasi nos dilexerimus Deum, sed quoniam ipse dilexit nos et misit Filium suum propitiationem pro peccatis nostris. ¹¹Carissimi, si sic Deus dilexit nos, et nos debemus alterutrum diligere. ¹²Deum nemo vidit umquam; si diligamus invicem, Deus in nobis manet, et caritas eius in nobis consummata est. ¹³In hoc cognoscimus quoniam in ipso manemus, et ipse in nobis, quoniam de Spiritu suo dedit nobis. ¹⁴Et nos vidimus et testificamur quoniam Pater misit Filium salvatorem mundi. ¹⁵Quisque confessus fuerit: «Iesus est Filius Dei», Deus in ipso manet, et ipse in Deo. ¹⁶Et nos, qui credidimus, novimus caritatem, quam habet Deus in nobis. Deus caritas est, et, qui manet in caritate, in Deo manet, et Deus in eo manet. ¹⁷In hoc consummata est caritas nobiscum, ut fiduciam habeamus in die iudicii, quia sicut ille est, et nos sumus in hoc mundo. ¹⁸Timor non est in caritate, sed perfecta caritas foras mittit timorem, quoniam timor poenam habet; qui autem timet, non est consummatus in caritate. ¹⁹Nos diligimus, quoniam ipse prior dilexit nos. ²⁰Si quis dixerit: «Diligo Deum», et fratrem suum oderit, mendax est; qui enim non diligit fratrem suum, quem videt, Deum, quem non videt, non potest diligere. ²¹Et hoc mandatum habemus ab eo, ut, qui diligit Deum, diligat et fratrem suum. **[5]** ¹Omnis, qui credit quoniam Iesus est Christus, ex Deo natus est; et omnis, qui diligit Deum qui genuit, diligit et eum qui natus est ex eo. ²In hoc cognoscimus quoniam diligimus natos Dei, cum Deum diligamus et mandata eius faciamus. ³Haec est enim caritas Dei, ut mandata eius servemus; et mandata eius gravia non sunt, ⁴quoniam omne, quod natum est ex Deo, vincit mundum; et haec est victoria, quae vicit mundum: fides nostra. ⁵Quis est qui vincit mundum, nisi qui credit quoniam Iesus est Filius Dei? ⁶Hic est qui venit per aquam et sanguinem, Iesus Christus; non in aqua solum sed in aqua et in sanguine. Et Spiritus est, qui testificatur, quoniam Spiritus est veritas. ⁷Quia tres sunt qui testificantur: ⁸Spiritus et aqua et sanguis; et hi tres in unum sunt. ⁹Si testimonium hominum accipimus, testimonium Dei maius est, quoniam hoc est testimonium Dei, quia testificatus est de Filio suo. ¹⁰Qui credit in Filium Dei, habet testimonium in se. Qui non credit Deo, mendacem facit eum, quoniam non credidit in testimonium, quod testificatus est Deus de Filio suo. ¹¹Et hoc est testimonium, quoniam vitam aeternam dedit nobis Deus, et haec vita in Filio eius est. ¹²Qui habet Filium, habet vitam; qui non habet Filium Dei, vitam non habet. ¹³Haec scripsi vobis, ut sciatis quoniam vitam habetis aeternam, qui creditis in nomen Filii Dei. ¹⁴Et haec est fiducia, quam habemus ad eum, quia si quid petierimus secundum voluntatem eius, audit nos. ¹⁵Et si scimus quoniam audit nos, quidquid petierimus, scimus quoniam habemus petitiones, quas postulavimus ab eo. ¹⁶Si quis videt fratrem suum peccare peccatum non ad mortem, petet, et dabit ei Deus vitam, peccantibus non ad mortem. Est peccatum ad mortem; non pro illo dico, ut roget. ¹⁷Omnis iniustitia peccatum est, et est peccatum non ad mortem. ¹⁸Scimus quoniam omnis, qui natus est ex Deo, non peccat, sed ille qui genitus est ex Deo, conservat eum, et Malignus non tangit eum. ¹⁹Scimus quoniam ex Deo sumus, et mundus totus in Maligno positus est. ²⁰Et scimus quoniam Filius Dei venit et dedit nobis sensum, ut cognoscamus eum, qui verus est; et sumus in eo, qui verus est, in Filio eius Iesu Christo. Hic est qui verus est, Deus et vita aeterna. ²¹Filioli, custodite vos a simulacris!

EPISTOLA SECUNDA IOANNIS

¹Presbyter electae dominae et filiis eius, quos ego diligo in veritate, et non ego solus, sed et omnes, qui noverunt veritatem, ²propter veritatem, quae permanet in nobis et nobiscum erit in sempiternum. ³Erit nobiscum gratia, misericordia, pax a Deo Patre et a Iesu Christo, Filio Patris, in veritate et caritate. ⁴Gavisus sum valde quoniam inveni de filiis tuis ambulantes in veritate, sicut mandatum accepimus a Patre. ⁵Et nunc rogo te, domina, non tamquam mandatum novum scribens tibi, sed quod habuimus ab initio, ut diligamus alterutrum. ⁶Et haec est caritas, ut ambulemus secundum mandata eius; hoc mandatum est, quemadmodum audistis ab initio, ut in eo ambuletis. ⁷Quoniam multi seductores prodierunt in mundum, qui non confitentur Iesum Christum venientem in carne; hic est seductor et antichristus. ⁸Videte vosmetipsos, ne perdatis, quae operati estis, sed ut mercedem plenam accipiatis. ⁹Omnis, qui ultra procedit et non manet in doctrina Christi, Deum non habet; qui permanet in doctrina, hic et Patrem et Filium habet. ¹⁰Si quis venit ad vos et hanc doctrinam non affert, nolite accipere eum in domum nec «Ave» ei dixeritis; ¹¹qui enim dicit illi: «Ave», communicat operibus illius malignis. ¹²Plura habens vobis scribere nolui per chartam et atramentum, spero enim me futurum apud vos et os ad os loqui, ut gaudium nostrum plenum sit. ¹³Salutant te filii sororis tuae electae.

EPISTOLA TERTIA IOANNIS

¹Presbyter Gaio carissimo, quem ego diligo in veritate. ²Carissime, in omnibus exopto prospere te agere et valere, sicut prospere agit anima tua. ³Nam gavisus sum valde venientibus fratribus et testimonium perhibentibus veritati tuae, quomodo tu in veritate ambules. ⁴Maius horum non habeo gaudium, quam ut audiam filios meos in veritate ambulare. ⁵Carissime, fideliter facis, quidquid operaris in fratres et hoc in peregrinos, ⁶qui testimonium reddiderunt caritati tuae in conspectu ecclesiae. Bene facies subveniens illis in via digne Deo; ⁷pro nomine enim profecti sunt, nihil accipientes a gentilibus. ⁸Nos ergo debemus sublevare huiusmodi, ut cooperatores simus veritatis. ⁹Scripsi aliquid ecclesiae; sed is qui amat primatum gerere in eis, Diotrephes, non recipit nos. ¹⁰Propter hoc, si venero, commonebo eius opera, quae facit verbis malignis garriens in nos; et quasi non ei ista sufficiant, nec ipse suscipit fratres et eos, qui cupiunt, prohibet et de ecclesia eicit. ¹¹Carissime, noli imitari malum, sed quod bonum est. Qui benefacit, ex Deo est; qui malefacit, non vidit Deum. ¹²Demetrio testimonium redditur ab omnibus et ab ipsa veritate; sed et nos testimonium perhibemus, et scis quoniam testimonium nostrum verum est. ¹³Multa habui scribere tibi, sed nolo per atramentum et calamum scribere tibi; ¹⁴spero autem protinus te videre, et os ad os loquemur. ¹⁵Pax tibi. Salutant te amici. Saluta amicos nominatim.

EPISTOLA IUDAE

¹Iudas Iesu Christi servus, frater autem Iacobi, his qui sunt vocati, in Deo Patre dilecti et Christo Iesu conservati: ²misericordia vobis et pax et caritas adimpleatur. ³Carissimi, omnem sollicitudinem faciens scribendi vobis de communi nostra salute necesse habui scribere vobis, deprecans certare pro semel tradita sanctis fide. ⁴Subintroierunt enim quidam homines, qui olim praescripti sunt in hoc iudicium, impii, Dei nostri gratiam transferentes in luxuriam et solum Dominatorem et Dominum nostrum Iesum Christum negantes. ⁵Commonere autem vos volo, scientes vos omnia, quoniam Dominus semel populum de terra Aegypti salvans, secundo eos, qui non crediderunt, perdidit; ⁶angelos vero, qui non servaverunt suum principatum, sed dereliquerunt suum domicilium, in iudicium magni diei vinculis aeternis sub caligine reservavit. ⁷Sicut Sodoma et Gomorra et finitimae civitates, simili modo exfornicatae et abeuntes post carnem alteram, factae sunt exemplum, ignis aeterni poenam sustinentes. ⁸Similiter vero et hi somniantes carnem quidem maculant, dominationem autem spernunt, glorias autem blasphemant. ⁹Cum Michael archangelus cum Diabolo disputans altercaretur de Moysis corpore, non est ausus iudicium inferre blasphemiae, sed dixit: «*Increpet te Dominus!*». ¹⁰Hi autem, quaecumque quidem ignorant, blasphemant, quaecumque autem naturaliter tamquam muta animalia norunt, in his corrumpuntur. ¹¹Vae illis, quia via Cain abierunt et errore Balaam mercede effusi sunt et contradictione Core perierunt! ¹²Hi sunt in agapis vestris maculae convivantes sine timore, semetipsos pascentes, nubes

sine aqua, quae a ventis circumferuntur, arbores autumnales infructuosae bis mortuae, eradicatae, ¹³fluctus feri maris despumantes suas confusiones, sidera errantia, quibus procella tenebrarum in aeternum servata est. ¹⁴Prophetavit autem et his septimus ab Adam Henoch dicens: «Ecce venit Dominus in sanctis milibus suis ¹⁵facere iudicium contra omnes et arguere omnem animam de omnibus operibus impietatis eorum, quibus impie egerunt, et de omnibus duris, quae locuti sunt contra eum peccatores impii». ¹⁶Hi sunt murmuratores, querelosi, secundum concupiscentias suas ambulantes, et os illorum loquitur superba, mirantes personas quaestus causa. ¹⁷Vos autem, carissimi, memores estote verborum, quae praedicta sunt ab apostolis Domini nostri Iesu Christi, ¹⁸quoniam dicebant vobis: «In novissimo tempore venient illusores, secundum suas concupiscentias ambulantes impietatum». ¹⁹Hi sunt qui segregant, animales, Spiritum non habentes. ²⁰Vos autem, carissimi, superaedificantes vosmetipsos sanctissimae vestrae fidei, in Spiritu Sancto orantes, ²¹ipsos vos in dilectione Dei servate, exspectantes misericordiam Domini nostri Iesu Christi in vitam aeternam. ²²Et his quidem miseremini disputantibus, ²³illos vero salvate de igne, rapientes, aliis autem miseremini in timore, odientes et eam, quae carnalis est, maculatam tunicam. ²⁴Ei autem, qui potest vos conservare sine peccato et constituere ante conspectum gloriae suae immaculatos in exsultatione, ²⁵soli Deo salvatori nostro per Iesum Christum Dominum nostrum gloria, magnificentia, imperium et potestas ante omne saeculum et nunc et in omnia saecula. Amen.

Explanatory Notes
Asterisks in the text of the New Testament refer to these "Explanatory Notes" in the RSVCE.

THE REVELATION TO JOHN

1:4–8: Describes the glorious coming and reign of the Messiah.

1:13, *son of man* refers to Dan 7:13. The Messiah is described in symbolic terms.

2:10, *ten days*: Not literally. It means the persecution will be short.

2:20–21, *immorality* here seems to mean idolatry rather than sexual excess.

2:24, *deep things of Satan*: The doctrine of the Nicolaitans. *They* called them the "deep things of God".

2:28, *morning star*: Probably Christ himself.

3:12, *new name*: cf. Is 62:2. Perhaps it was "the Word", or perhaps it is not to be revealed till the last day.

4:3: John describes God in symbolic terms.

4:4, *elders*: They perform a priestly and royal task, since they praise God and share in the government of the world.

4:6, *four living creatures*: cf. Ezek 1:4–25: the four angels who preside over the government of the world. But in Christian tradition these symbols are used for the four evangelists.

4:8, *Holy, holy, holy*: Quoted in the *Sanctus* at Mass.

5:1, *a scroll*: This contained God's designs, kept secret till now; being written on both sides, nothing could be added.

5:6: The seven horns and seven eyes symbolize Christ's full power and knowledge.

6:1: Begins the account of the destruction of the Roman Empire, chapters 6–9.

6:5, *balance*: Symbol of famine. The balance was to measure rations.

7:4, *a hundred and forty-four thousand*: A symbolic number, i.e., 12 (the sacred number) squared and multiplied by 1,000 to denote a multitude. It is the church, the spiritual Israel, that is meant.

7:14, *the great tribulation*: The Neronian persecution?

8:5: Coals from the altar of burnt offering were brought to the altar of incense.

9:1, *star*: A fallen angel.

9:14, *Euphrates*: The region of the Parthians.

9:21, *immorality*: See note on 2:20–21.

10:7, *mystery of God*: i.e., the establishment of the kingdom of God following on the destruction of Israel's enemies.

10:9, *bitter ... sweet*: The scroll related both the sufferings and the victories of Christ's church.

11:1–19: The Jerusalem here described stands for the church, which is to be persecuted by the Romans.

11:2: The three and a half years' persecution of the Jews by Antiochus Epiphanes, 168–165 BC, had become the standard time of a persecution. Three and a half years = 42 months = 1,260 days (verse 3).

11:3, *two witnesses*: As they have yet to die, possibly they are Elijah and Enoch.

11:8, *the great city*: i.e., Rome.

12:1–6: The *child* brought forth is the Messiah; the *dragon* is the devil; the *woman* who gave birth to the Messiah is Israel, and then becomes the Christian church, which continually gives birth to the faithful.

12:14, *a time, and times, and half a time*: This is the three and a half years of 11:2.

12:17: Mary; the mother of the Messiah, must also be included in the meaning.

13:1, *a beast*: This symbolizes the material forces of evil, arrayed against the church.

13:11, *another beast*: i.e., the false prophets.

13:18, *six hundred and sixty-six*: The letters of Nero's name plus the title of Caesar, given their numerical meaning in Hebrew and added together, make 666.

14:4: Although tradition tends to take this literally, the context and Old Testament metaphor suggest that it means they have kept free from idolatry.

Explanatory Notes

14:8, *Babylon*: i.e., Rome.

15:3–4: The song of Moses in Ex 15:1–18 celebrated victory over Pharaoh. This is seen as foreshadowing the triumph of the Lamb.

16:14, *the great day*: On which all the Gentile armies shall be gathered to give battle.

16:16, *Armageddon*: i.e., Megiddo, where Josiah was defeated by the king of Egypt; cf. 2 Kings 23:29.

17:1, *great harlot*: i.e., Rome.

17:2, *fornication*: i.e., idolatry.

18:11–20: The description abruptly assumes the language of Ezekiel's prophecy of the destruction of Tyre, another city notorious for its sins (Ezek 27:1—28:19).

19:7, *marriage of the Lamb*: i.e., final establishment of the kingdom of God. The spouse is the church.

20:3: The destruction of the dragon must coincide in time with that of the beast (19:20), so that the first resurrection with the reign of the martyrs refers to the revival and expansion of the church after the years of persecution.

21:1: Creation will be renewed one day, freed from corruption and illumined by God's glory.

21:8, *second death*: i.e., eternal damnation.

Changes in the RSV for the Catholic Edition

	TEXT		FOOTNOTES	
	RSV	RSVCE	RSV	RSVCE
Rev (Title)	THE REVELATION TO JOHN	THE REVELATION TO JOHN (THE APOCALYPSE)		
Rev 6:6			ªDelete existing note and substitute:	ªThe denarius was a day's wage for a labourer

THE LETTER TO THE HEBREWS

1:1–4: A contrast between the progressive and piecemeal revelation of the old dispensation and the complete revelation of the new given by a single representative—no mere prophet but the Son of God himself.

2:2, *angels*: The Covenant of Sinai was thought to have been given through the angels.

2:10, *suffering*: The divinely appointed means of progress towards God; cf. verse 18.

3:11: Those who murmured against God in the desert were excluded from the promised land (the "rest"). Christians should be aware lest, by offending God, they be excluded from heaven, the true rest, of which the promised land was a type.

5:1–5: If Jesus was to be mediator, he had to have a human nature like ours and, moreover, he could not appoint himself, but had to be appointed by God.

6:4, *impossible*: The apostasy referred to in verse 6 is clearly thought of as so deliberate as to preclude any real possibility of repentance; or there may be a reference here to the impossibility of being baptized a second time.

7:3, *without father*: i.e., the father is not mentioned in scripture.
neither beginning of days nor end of life: So too here, they are not mentioned in scripture either. Thus his priesthood can be taken to foreshadow or symbolize the Christian priesthood. "You are a priest for ever after the order of Melchizedek" (Ps 110:4; cf. Heb 7:17).

8:11: This verse merely means that knowledge of God will be commonly shared, and is not literally intended to exclude the ministry of teaching in the Messianic times.

10:1ff.: The sacrifices of the old law, being imperfect, were repeated, and did at least keep alive a sense of sin. Contrast with Christ's sacrifice (verse 14).

Explanatory Notes

11:6: Here is stated the minimum necessary for salvation.
12:1ff: After explaining in the preceding chapters how we are redeemed through faith in Jesus Christ, the author now exhorts his readers to run the race with perseverance.
13:1ff: Moral exhortation.
13:9: Again the warning against false doctrine, especially the Judaizers' teachings; cf. Phil 3:19; 1 Tim 1:4; 4:3.
13:13: i.e., "Let us leave the observances of Judaism behind us."

Changes in the RSV for the Catholic Edition

	RSV	RSVCE
Heb 11:19	hence, figuratively speaking, he did receive him back	hence he did receive him back, and this was a symbol

THE LETTER OF JAMES

1:1, *twelve tribes*: i.e., Jewish Christians outside Palestine.
1:22: This is the main theme of the letter.
2:1–7: These are hard words, but no harder than those of Jesus.
2:10: In keeping the Law, we must keep *the whole Law*. We cannot pick and choose.
2:14: Good works are necessary besides faith.
5:3: The "treasure" they have laid up is described in the following verses.
5:13–15: This passage is the scriptural basis for the sacrament of Anointing of the Sick.

THE FIRST LETTER OF PETER

1:1: See note on Jas 1:1. Baptism is the main theme of this letter, which may in fact, have been a baptismal address.
1:11, *Spirit of Christ*: Christ, as the eternally existing Word, is envisaged as inspiring the prophets of old.
3:1–6: Peter's teaching on the behaviour and status of women corresponds to that of Paul, though without Paul's forthrightness.
4:1, *ceased from sin*: Peter means that a continual acceptance of suffering is incompatible with a proneness to sin.
5:13, *Babylon*: Rome was as full of iniquity as ancient Babylon; cf. Rev 17:9.

THE SECOND LETTER OF PETER

1:4, *partakers of the divine nature*: A strong expression to describe the transformation of human nature by divine grace.
1:16–18: A reference to the transfiguration.
2:3: Much of the material of this chapter appears to be from the Letter of Jude.
3:16: *this* seems to refer to the theme of the end of the world and the Second Coming of Christ, about which Paul had written in his letters to the Thessalonians.

Explanatory Notes

THE FIRST LETTER OF JOHN

1:1–7: Note the likeness with John's Gospel 1:1–18.
1:3, *fellowship*: A Johannine theme.
1:5, *light . . . darkness*: Another familiar theme in John's Gospel.
2:3: cf. the words of Jesus, "If you love me, you will keep my commandments" (Jn 14:15).
2:18, *the last hour*: John exhorts his readers to hold fast, as though the end were at hand.
3:6, *sins*: i.e., remains in sin, or has a habit of sin.
4:1, *test the spirits*: i.e., examine those who claim to have special gifts from the Holy Spirit; cf.1 Cor 14:32.
5:8, *There are three witnesses*: After these words, the Vulgate adds the following: "in heaven, the Father, the Word, and the Holy Ghost. And these three are one. And these are three that give testimony on earth." This passage, known as the Comma Johanneum or "The Three Heavenly Witnesses," is first found in the Latin (fourth century), and does not appear in any Greek New Testament manuscript before the sixteenth century. It is probably a marginal gloss which found its way into the text.

THE SECOND LETTER OF JOHN

1, *The elder*: Perhaps the head of the group or "college" of elders that presided over each Christian community. John was head not only of the Ephesus community but of all the communities in the province of Asia.
  the elect lady: Probably not an individual lady but a particular church or community in Asia.
13, *children*: i.e., the Christians of Ephesus.

THE THIRD LETTER OF JOHN

12, *Demetrius*: Evidently a leading Christian, recommended to Gaius.

THE LETTER OF JUDE

6: It is not clear to what Jude refers. Perhaps Gen 6:2 or the apocryphal Enoch, chapters 6–15.
9: Apparently a reference to another apocryphal work, the Assumption of Moses.

Headings added to the Biblical Text

REVELATION

Prologue 1:1

Part One: Letters to the seven churches

Address and greeting 1:4
Reason for writing 1:9
Letter to the church of Ephesus 2:1
Letter to the church of Smyrna 2:8
Letter to the church of Pergamum 2:12
Letter to the church of Thyatira 2:18
Letter to the church of Sardis 3:1
Letter to the church of Philadelphia 3:7
Letter to the church of Laodicea 3:14

Part Two: Eschatological visions

1. INTRODUCTORY VISION
God in majesty 4:1
The sealed scroll and the Lamb 5:1

2. EVENTS PRIOR TO THE FINAL OUTCOME
Christ opens the first six seals. Vision of the four horsemen 6:1
The great multitude of the saved 7:1
The opening of the seventh seal 8:1
The first six trumpet calls. The three woes 8:7
The seer is given a little scroll to eat 10:1
Death and resurrection of the two witnesses 11:1

3. CHRIST'S VICTORY OVER THE POWERS OF EVIL. THE CHURCH IN GLORY
The seventh trumpet call 11:15
The woman pursued by the dragon 12:1
The beasts given authority by the dragon 13:1
The beast rising from out of the earth 13:11
The Lamb and his entourage 14:1
Proclamation and symbols of the Judgment 14:6
The harvest and the vintage 14:14
The hymn of the saved 15:1
The seven bowls of plagues 15:5
The great harlot and the beast 17:1
The fall of Babylon announced 18:1
Songs of victory in heaven 19:1
The first battle—the beast is destroyed 19:11
The thousand-year reign of Christ and his people 20:1
The second battle—Satan is overthrown 20:7
The Last Judgment of the living and the dead 20:11
A new world comes into being. The new Jerusalem 21:1
The visions come to an end 22:6

4. EPILOGUE
Prayer of the Spirit and the Bride. Words of warning and farewell 22:17

HEBREWS

The greatness of the incarnate Son of God 1:1

Part One: Excellence of the religion revealed by Christ

1. CHRIST IS GREATER THAN THE ANGELS
Proof from Holy Scripture 1:5
An appeal for faith 2:1
Jesus, man's brother, was crowned with glory and honour above the angels 2:5

2. CHRIST IS GREATER THAN MOSES
Moses' ministry and that of Christ compared 3:1
The need for faith. The bad example given by the Chosen People 3:8
Through faith we can attain God's "rest" 4:1
The power of God's word 4:12

3. CHRIST, OUR HIGH PRIEST, IS GREATER THAN THE PRIESTS OF THE MOSAIC LAW
Our confidence is based on Christ's priesthood 4:14
Christ has been made high priest by God the Father 5:1
The need for religious instruction 5:11
The danger of apostasy and the need for perseverance 6:4
The promises made to Abraham were confirmed by oath and cannot be broken 6:13
Jesus Christ is a priest after the order of Melchizedek 7:1
Melchizedek's priesthood is greater than that of Abraham's line 7:4
Christ is perfect high priest, and his priesthood endures forever 7:20

Headings added to the Biblical Text

4. CHRIST'S SACRIFICE IS MORE EXCELLENT THAN ALL THE SACRIFICES OF THE OLD LAW
Christ is high priest of a New Covenant, which replaces the Old 8:1
The rites of the Old Covenant prefigure those of the New 9:1
Christ sealed the New Covenant with his blood once and for all 9:11
The sacrifices of the Old Covenant could not take away sins 10:1
Christ's offering of himself has infinite value 10:5

Part Two: Faith and perseverance in faith

5. A CALL FOR LOYALTY
Motives for staying loyal to Christ 10:19
The good example of the patriarchs 11:1
The faith of Moses, the judges and the prophets 11:23

6. THE EXAMPLE OF CHRIST AND THE DUTIES OF CHRISTIANS
The example of Christ 12:1

Perseverance in the midst of trials 12:4
Striving for peace. Purity. Reverent worship 12:14
Duties towards others—charity, hospitality, fidelity in marriage 13:1
Religious duties—obeying lawful pastors; religious worship 13:7
Words of farewell 13:20

CATHOLIC LETTERS

JAMES

Greeting 1:1

1. OPENING INSTRUCTIONS
The value of suffering 1:2
The source of temptation 1:13
Doers of the word, not hearers only 1:19
Impartiality 2:1

2. FAITH AND GOOD WORKS
Faith without good works is dead 2:14
Examples from the Bible 2:20

3. PRACTICAL APPLICATIONS
Controlling one's tongue 3:1
True and false wisdom 3:13
The source of discord 4:1
Trust in divine providence 4:13
A warning to the rich 5:1

4. FINAL COUNSELS
A call for constancy 5:7
On oath-taking 5:12
The value of prayer. The sacrament of the Anointing of the Sick 5:13
Concern for one another 5:19

1 PETER

Greeting 1:1
Praise and thanksgiving to God 1:3

1. A CALL TO HOLINESS
Christians are called to be saints 1:13
The blood of Christ has ransomed us 1:17
Brotherly love 1:22
Like newborn babies 2:1
The priesthood that all believers share 2:4

2. THE OBLIGATIONS OF CHRISTIANS
Setting an example for pagans 2:11
Obedience to civil authority 2:13
Duties towards masters. Christ's example 2:18

Exemplary family life 3:1
Love of the brethren 3:8

3. THE CHRISTIAN'S ATTITUDE TO SUFFERING
Undeserved suffering is a blessing 3:13
Christ's suffering and glorification 3:18
The Christian has broken with sin 4:1
A call for charity 4:7
The Christian meaning of suffering 4:12

4. FINAL EXHORTATIONS
To priests 5:1
To all the faithful 5:5
Words of farewell 5:12

2 PETER

Greeting 1:1

1. A CALL TO FIDELITY
Divine largesse 1:3
Christian virtues 1:5
Spiritual testimony 1:12

The Transfiguration, an earnest of the Second Coming 1:16
Prophecy and the Second Coming 1:19

2. FALSE TEACHERS DENOUNCED
The harm done by false teachers 2:1
The punishment that awaits them 2:4

Headings added to the Biblical Text

Their arrogance and immorality 2:10
Apostasy, a grave sin 2:20

3. THE SECOND COMING OF CHRIST
The teaching of Tradition 3:1

Mistaken notions 3:3
True teaching about the End 3:5
Moral lessons to be drawn 3:11
Final exhortation and doxology 3:17

1 JOHN

Prologue 1:1

1. UNION WITH GOD
God is light 1:5
Walking in the light. Rejecting sin 1:6
Keeping the commandments 2:3
The apostle's confidence in the faithful 2:12
Detachment from the world 2:15
Not listening to heretics 2:18

2. LIVING AS GOD'S CHILDREN
We are children of God 3:1

A child of God does not sin 3:3
Loving one another 3:11

3. FAITH IN CHRIST. BROTHERLY LOVE
Faith in Christ, not in false prophets 4:1
God is love. Brotherly love, the mark of Christians 4:7
Everyone who believes in Jesus overcomes the world 5:1
Testimony borne to Christ 5:6

4. CONCLUSION
Prayer for sinners 5:14
The Christian's confidence as a child of God 5:18

2 JOHN

Greeting 1
The law of love 4

Precautions against heretics 7
Conclusion and greetings 12

3 JOHN

Greeting 1
Praise of Gaius 3
Diotrephes' misconduct 9

Commendation of Demetrius 11
Conclusion and farewell 13

JUDE

Greeting and blessing 1
His reason for writing 3

1. FALSE TEACHERS DENOUNCED
The punishment that awaits them 5
Their immorality 8
The judgment of God 14

2. EXHORTATION
False teachers were predicted 17
Faith, hope and charity 20
Attitude towards waverers 22
Final doxology 24

Sources quoted in the Navarre Bible New Testament Commentary

1. DOCUMENTS OF THE CHURCH AND OF POPES

Benedict XII
Const. *Benedictus Deus*, 29 January 1336
Benedict XV
Enc. *Humani generis redemptionem*, 15 June 1917
Enc. *Spiritus Paraclitus*, 1 September 1920
Clement of Rome, St
Letter to the Corinthians
Constantinople, First Council of
Nicene-Constantinopolitan Creed
Constantinople, Third Council of
Definitio de duabus
    in Christo voluntatibus et operationibus
Florence, Council of
Decree *Pro Jacobitis*
Laetentur coeli
Decree *Pro Armeniis*
John Paul II
Addresses and homilies
Apos. Exhort. *Catechesi tradendae*, 16 October 1979
Apos. Exhort. *Familiaris consortio*, 22 November 1981
Apos. Exhort. *Reconciliatio et paenitentia*, 2 December 1984
Apos. Letter. *Salvifici doloris*, 11 February 1984
Bull, *Aperite portas*, 6 January 1983
Enc. *Redemptor hominis*, 4 March 1979
Enc. *Dives in misericordia*, 30 November 1980
Enc. *Dominum et Vivificantem*, 30 May 1986
Enc. *Laborem exercens*, 14 September 1981
Letter to all priests, 8 April 1979
Letter to all bishops, 24 February 1980
Gelasius I
Ne forte
Gregory the Great, St
Epistula ad Theodorum medicum contra Fabianum
Exposition on the Seven Penitential
Ne forte
In Evangelia homiliae
In Ezechielem homiliae
Moralia in Job

Regulae pastoralis liber
Innocent III
Letter *Eius exemplo*, 18 December 1208
John XXIII
Pacem in terris, 11 April 1963
Enc. *Ad Petri cathedram*, 29 June 1959
Lateran Council (649)
Canons
Leo the Great, St
Homilies and sermons
Licet per nostros
Promisisse mememeni
Leo IX
Creed
Leo XIII
Enc. *Aeterni Patris*, 4 August 1879
Enc. *Immortale Dei*, 1 November 1885
Enc. *Libertas praestantissimum*, 20 June 1888
Enc. *Sapientiae christianae*, 18 January 1890
Enc. *Rerum novarum*, 15 May 1891
Enc. *Providentissimus Deus*, 18 November 1893
Enc. *Divinum illud munus*, 9 May 1897
Lateran, Fourth Council of (1215)
De fide catholica
Lyons, Second Council of (1274)
Doctrina de gratia
Profession of faith of Michael Palaeologue
Orange, Second Council of (529)
De gratia
Paul IV
Const. *Cum quorumdam*, 7 August 1555
Paul VI
Enc. *Ecclesiam suam*, 6 August 1964
Enc. *Mysterium fidei*, 9 September 1965
Apos. Exhort. *Marialis cultus*, 2 February 1974
Apos. Letter *Petrum et Paulum*, 27 February 1967
Enc. *Populorum progressio*, 26 March 1967
Enc. *Sacerdotalis coelibatus*, 24 June 1967
Creed of the People of God: Solemn Profession of Faith, 30 June 1968
Apos. Letter *Octagesima adveniens*, 14 June 1971

Sources quoted in the Commentary

Apos. Exhort. *Gaudete in Domino*, 9 May 1975
Apos. Exhort. *Evangelii nuntiandi*, 8 Dec. 1975
Homilies and addresses
Pius V, St
Catechism of the Council of Trent for Parish Priests or *Pius V Catechism*
Pius IX, Bl.
Bull *Ineffabilis Deus*, 8 December 1854
Syllabus of Errors
Pius X, St
Enc. *E supreme apostolatus*, 4 October 1903
Enc. *Ad Diem illum*, 2 February 1904
Enc. *Acerbo nimis*, 15 April 1905
Catechism of Christian Doctrine, 15 July 1905
Decree *Lamentabili*, 3 July 1907
Enc. *Haerent animo*, 4 August 1908
Pius XI
Enc. *Quas primas*, 11 December 1925
Enc. *Divini illius magistri*, 31 December 1929
Enc. *Mens nostra*, 20 December 1929
Enc. *Casti connubii*, 31 December 1930
Enc. *Quadragesimo anno*, 15 May 1931
Enc. *Ad catholici sacerdotii*, 20 December 1935
Pius XII
Enc. *Mystici Corporis*, 29 June 1943
Enc. *Mediator Dei*, 20 November 1947
Enc. *Divino afflante Spiritu*, 30 September 1943
Enc. *Humani generis*, 12 August 1950
Apost. Const. *Menti nostrae*, 23 September 1950
Enc. *Sacra virginitas*, 25 March 1954
Enc. *Ad caeli Reginam*, 11 October 1954
Homilies and addresses
Quierzy, Council of (833)
Doctrina de libero arbitrio hominis et de praedestinatione
Trent, Council of (1545–1563)
De sacris imaginibus
De Purgatorio
De reformatione
De sacramento ordinis
De libris sacris
De peccato originale
De SS. Eucharistia
De iustificatione
De SS. Missae sacrificio
De sacramento matrimonio
Doctrina de peccato originali
Doctrina de sacramento extremae unctionis
Doctrina de sacramento paenitentiae
Toledo, Ninth Council of (655)
De Redemptione
Toledo, Eleventh Council of (675)
De Trinitate Creed
Valence, Third Council of (855)
De praedestinatione
Vatican, First Council of the (1869–1870)
Dogm. Const. *Dei Filius*
Dogm. Const. *Pastor aeternus*
Vatican, Second Council of the (1963–1965)
Const. *Sacrosanctum Concilium*
Decree *Christus Dominus*
Decl. *Dignitatis humanae*
Decl. *Gravissimum educationis*
Decl. *Nostrae aetate*
Decree *Optatam totius*
Decree *Ad gentes*
Decree *Apostolicam actuositatem*
Decree *Perfectae caritatis*
Decree *Presbyterorum ordinis*
Decree *Unitatis redintegratio*
Dogm. Const. *Dei Verbum*
Dogm. Const. *Lumen gentium*
Past. Const. *Gaudium et spes*

Liturgical Texts

Roman Missal: Missale Romanum, editio typica altera (Vatican City, 1975)
The Divine Office (London, Sydney, Dublin, 1974)

Other Church Documents

Code of Canon Law
Codex Iuris Canonici (Vatican City, 1983)
Congregation for the Doctrine of the Faith
Declaration concerning Sexual Ethics, December 1975
Instruction on Infant Baptism, 20 October 1980
Inter insigniores, 15 October 1976
Letter on certain questions concerning Eschatology, 17 May 1979
Libertatis conscientia, 22 March 1986
Sacerdotium ministeriale, 6 August 1983
Libertatis nuntius, 6 August 1984
Mysterium Filii Dei, 21 February 1972
Pontifical Biblical Commission
Replies
New Vulgate
Nova Vulgata Bibliorum Sacrorum editio typica altera (Vatican City, 1986)

Sources quoted in the Commentary

2. THE FATHERS, ECCLESIASTICAL WRITERS AND OTHER AUTHORS

Alphonsus Mary Liguori, St
Christmas Novena
The Love of Our Lord Jesus Christ reduced to practice
Meditations for Advent
Thoughts on the Passion
Shorter Sermons
Sunday Sermons
Treasury of Teaching Material
Ambrose, St
De sacramentis
De mysteriis
De officiis ministrorum
Exameron
Expositio Evangelii secundum Lucam
Expositio in Ps 118
Treatise on the Mysteries
Anastasius of Sinai, St
Sermon on the Holy Synaxis
Anon.
Apostolic Constitutions
Didache, or *Teaching of the Twelve Apostles*
Letter to Diognetus
Shepherd of Hermas
Anselm, St
Prayers and Meditations
Aphraates
Demonstratio
Athanasius, St
Adversus Antigonum
De decretis nicaenae synodi
De Incarnatio contra arianos
Historia arianorum
Oratio I contra arianos
Oratio II contra arianos
Oratio contra gentes
Augustine, St
The City of God
Confessions
Contra Adimantum Manichaei discipulum
De Actis cum Felice Manicheo
De agone christiano
De bono matrimonii
De bono viduitatis
De catechizandis rudibus
De civitate Dei
De coniugiis adulterinis
De consensu Evangelistarum
De correptione et gratia
De doctrina christiana
De dono perseverantiae
De fide et operibus
De fide et symbolo
De Genesi ad litteram
De gratia et libero arbitrio
De natura et gratia
De praedestinatione sanctorum
De sermo Domini in monte
De spiritu et littera
De Trinitate
De verbis Domini sermones
Enarrationes in Psalmos
Enchiridion
Expositio epistulae ad Galatas
In I Epist. Ioann. ad Parthos
In Ioannis Evangelium tractatus
Letters
Quaestiones in Heptateuchum
Sermo ad Caesariensis Ecclesiae plebem
Sermo de Nativitate Domini
Sermons
Basil, St
De Spiritu Sancto
Homilia in Julittam martyrem
In Psalmos homiliae
Bede, St
Explanatio Apocalypsis
In Ioannis Evangelium expositio
In Lucae Evangelium expositio
In Marci Evangelium expositio
In primam Epistolam Petri
In primam Epistolam S. Ioanis
Sermo super Qui audientes gavisi sunt
Super Acta Apostolorum expositio
Super divi Iacobi Epistolam
Bernal, Salvador
Monsignor Josemaría Escrivá de Balaguer, Dublin, 1977
Bernard, St
Book of Consideration
De Beata Virgine
De fallacia et brevitate vitae
De laudibus novae militiae
Divine amoris
Meditationes piissimae de cognitionis humanae conditionis
Sermons on Psalm 90
Sermon on Song of Songs
Sermons
Bonaventure, St
In IV Libri sententiarum
Speculum Beatae Virgine
Borromeo, St Charles
Homilies

Sources quoted in the Commentary

Catherine of Siena, St
Dialogue
Cano, Melchor
De locis
Cassian, John
Collationes
De institutis coenobiorum
Clement of Alexandria
Catechesis III, De Baptismo
Commentary on Luke
Quis dives salvetur?
Stromata
Cyprian, St
De bono patientiae
De dominica oratione
De mortalitate
De opere et eleemosynis
De unitate Ecclesiae
De zelo et livore
Epist. ad Fortunatum
Quod idola dii non sint
Cyril of Alexandria, St
Commentarium in Lucam
Explanation of Hebrews
Homilia XXVIII in Mattheum
Cyril of Jerusalem, St
Catecheses
Mystagogical Catechesis
Diadochus of Photike
Chapters on Spiritual Perfection
Ephrem, St
Armenian Commentary on Acts
Commentarium in Epistolam ad Haebreos
Eusebius of Caesarea
Ecclesiastical History
Francis de Sales, St
Introduction to the Devout Life
Treatise on the Love of God
Francis of Assisi, St
Little Flowers
Reflections on Christ's Wounds
Fulgentius of Ruspe
Contra Fabianum libri decem
De fide ad Petrum
Gregory Nazianzen, St
Orationes theologicae
Sermons
Gregory of Nyssa, St
De instituto christiano
De perfecta christiana forma
On the Life of Moses
Oratio catechetica magna
Oratio I in beatitudinibus
Oratio I in Christi resurrectionem

Hippolytus, St
De consummatione saeculi
Ignatius of Antioch, St
Letter to Polycarp
Letters to various churches
Ignatius, Loyola, St
Spiritual Exercises
Irenaeus, St
Against Heresies
Proof of Apostolic Preaching
Jerome, St
Ad Nepotianum
Adversus Helvidium
Comm. in Ionam
Commentary on Galatians
Commentary on St Mark's Gospel
Contra Luciferianos
Dialogus contra pelagianos
Expositio in Evangelium secundum Lucam
Homilies to neophytes on Psalm 41
Letters
On Famous Men
John of Avila, St
Audi, filia
Lecciones sobre Gálatas
Sermons
John Chrysostom, St
Ante exilium homilia
Adversus Iudaeos
Baptismal Catechesis
De coemeterio et de cruce
De incomprehensibile Dei natura
De sacerdotio
De virginitate
Fifth homily on Anna
Hom. De Cruce et latrone
*Homilies on St Matthew's Gospel, St John's
    Gospel, Acts of the Apostles, Romans,
    Ephesians, 1 and 2 Corinthians, Colossians,
    1 and 2 Timothy, 1 and 2 Thessalonians,
    Philippians, Philemon, Hebrews*
II Hom. De proditione Iudae
Paraeneses ad Theodorum lapsum
Second homily in praise of St Paul
Sermon recorded by Metaphrastus
John of the Cross, St
A Prayer of the Soul enkindled by Love
Ascent of Mount Carmel
Dark Night of the Soul
Spiritual Canticle
John Damascene, St
De fide orthodoxa
John Mary Vianney, St
Sermons

Sources quoted in the Commentary

Josemaría Escrivá, St
Christ Is Passing By
Conversations
The Forge
Friends of God
Furrow
Holy Rosary
In Love with the Church
The Way
The Way of the Cross
Josephus, Flavius
Against Apion
Jewish Antiquities
The Jewish War
Justin Martyr, St
Dialogue with Tryphon
First and Second Apologies
à Kempis, Thomas
The Imitation of Christ
Luis de Granada, Fray
Book of Prayer and Meditation
Guide for Sinners
Introduccíon al símbolo de la fe
Life of Jesus Christ
Sermon on Public Sins
Suma de la vida cristiana
Luis de Léon, Fray
Exposición del Libro de Job
Minucius Felix
Octavius
Newman, J.H.
Biglietto Speech
Discourses to Mixed Congregations
Historical Sketches
Origen
Contra Celsum
Homilies on Genesis
Homilies on St John
In Exodum homiliae
Homiliae in Iesu nave
In Leviticum homiliae
In Matth. comm.
In Rom. comm.
Philo of Alexandria
De sacrificio Abel
Photius
Ad Amphilochium
Polycarp, St
Letter to the Philippians
del Portillo, A.
On Priesthood, Chicago, 1974
Primasius
Commentariorum super Apocalypsim B. Ioannis libri quinque
Prosper of Aquitaine, St
De vita contemplativa

Pseudo-Dionysius
De divinis nominibus
Pseudo-Macarius
Homilies
Severian of Gabala
Commentary on 1 Thessalonians
Teresa of Avila, St
Book of Foundations
Exclamations of the Soul to God
Interior Castle
Life
Poems
Way of Perfection
Tertullian
Against Marcion
Apologeticum
De baptismo
De oratione
Theodore the Studite, St
Oratio in adorationis crucis
Theodoret of Cyrrhus
Interpretatio Ep. ad Haebreos
Theophylact
Enarratio in Evangelium Marci
Thérèse de Lisieux, St
The Autobiography of a Saint
Thomas Aquinas, St
Adoro te devote
Commentary on St John = *Super Evangelium S. Ioannis lectura*
Commentaries on St Matthew's Gospel, Romans, 1 and 2 Corinthians, Galatians, Ephesians, Colossians, Philippians, 1 and 2 Timothy, 1 and 2 Thessalonians, Titus, Hebrews
De veritate
Expositio quorumdam propositionum ex Epistola ad Romanos
On the Lord's Prayer
On the two commandments of Love and the ten commandments of the Law
Summa contra gentiles
Summa theologiae
Super Symbolum Apostolorum
Thomas More, St
De tristitia Christi
Victorinus of Pettau
Commentary on the Apocalypse
Vincent Ferrer, St
Treatise on the Spiritual Life
Vincent of Lerins, St
Commonitorium
Zosimus, St
Epist. Enc. "Tractoria" ad Ecclesias Orientales

Subject Index to the New Testament

abandonment in God's hands: Lk 12:22–34.
Abraham: made righteous by faith: Rom 4:1–25; Gal 3:6–9; the promises made to him cannot be withdrawn: Heb 6:13–20; 11:8–19.
adoration: by the Magi: Mt 2:3–11; by the Shepherds: Lk 2:8–20; of God: Jn 4:1–45.
adultery: Mt 5:27–30; the woman taken in adultery: Jn 8:1–11.
almsgiving: the right intention: Mt 6:24; generous: 2 Cor 9:6–15; joyful: Phil 4:10–20; by the widow in the temple: Mk 12:12–44; Lk 21:1–3.
Ananias: a Christian who baptizes Saul: Acts 9:10–19; the high priest who strikes Paul: Acts 23:1–11; Ananias and Sapphira: Acts 5:1–11.
Andrew, St: his calling: Mt 4:18–25; Mk 1:16–20; Lk 5:1–11; Jn 1:35–51; one of the Twelve: Mt 10:1–4; Mk 3:13–19; Lk 6:12–16; Acts 1:12–14; accompanies Jesus: Jn 6:8; 12:22.
angels: Christ's ministers: Mt 4:1–11; Mk 1:12–13; Lk 4:1–13; 22:39–46; are inferior to Christ: Heb 1:5–14; 2:5–18; their mission to men: Mt 18:10; Acts 12:1–19. *See* St Gabriel; St Michael.
annunciation: to Joseph: Mt 1:18–25; to Zechariah: Lk 1:5–25; to Mary: Lk 1:26–38. *See also* prophecy.
anointing of the sick: Mt 6:6–13; Jas 5:13–18.
Antioch (church of): beginnings: Acts 11:19–26; helps the church of Jerusalem: Acts 11:27–30; strife with Judaizers at: Acts 15:1–2; Gal 1:11–21.
apostasy: its gravity: 2 Pet 2:20–22; the danger of: Heb 6:4–12.
apostolate: Jas 5:19–20; 3 Jn 3–8. *See* apostles, evangelization.
apostles: their election and personal traits: Mt 10:1–4; Lk 6:12–16; Mk 3:13–19; their mission and preaching: Mt 10:5–15; Mk 6:6–13; Lk 9:1–6; they are sent to the whole world: Mt 28:16–20; Mk 16:14–18; 16:20; the apostolic college: Acts 1:12–26; their spirit of self-denial: 1 Cor 1:8–13; their upkeep: 1 Cor 9:1–14.

appearances (of Jesus): to the women: Mt 28:1–10; to Mary Magdalene: Mt 16:9–11; Jn 20:11–18; in Galilee: Mt 28:6–20; Mk 16:14–18; to the disciples of Emmaus: Lk 24:13–35; in the upper room: Lk 24:36–49; Jn 20:19–31; by the Sea of Tiberias: Jn 21:1–14; to many: 1 Cor 15:1–11.
Aquila and Priscilla: Acts 18:1–4.
ascension of Christ: Mt 16:19; Lk 24:50–53; Acts 1:6–11.
authorities: obedience towards and respect for: Mt 12:13–17; Rom 13:1–7; 1 Pet 2:13–17; Tit 3:1–2.
authority of Christ's teaching: Mt 7:28–29.
Baptism: of Jesus by John: Mt 3:13–17; Mk 1:9–11; Lk 3:21–22; of many at Pentecost: Acts 2:37–41; of the Ethiopian eunuch: Acts 8:26–40; of Paul: Acts 9:16–18; of Cornelius and his family: Acts 10:44–48; of Paul's jailer, of children: Acts 16:25–34; being born again: Jn 3:1–21; 1 Pet 2:1–10; it links one to Christ's death and resurrection: Rom 6:1–11.
Barnabas, St: Acts 4:32–37; 9:26–30; 11:19–30; 12:24–25; 13:1—15:41.
Bartholomew, St: Mt 10:1–4; Mk 3:13–19; Lk 6:12–16; Jn 1:35–51; 21:2; Acts 1:12–14.
beatitudes, the: Mt 5:1–12; Lk 6:20–26.
Bethany: Mt 26:6–13; Mk 14:3–11; Jn 11:1–44.
Bethlehem: Mt 2:1–18; Lk 2:1–20; Jn 7:42.
bishops: qualities: 1 Tim 3:1–7.
body, the human: its dignity: 1 Cor 6:12–20. *See* purity.
burial of Jesus: Mt 27:57–66; Mk 15:42–47; Lk 23:50–56.
Caesar: tribute to: Mt 22:15–22; Mk 12:13–17; Lk 20:20–26. *See* authorities.
Caiaphas: Mt 26:3, 57–58; Lk 3:2; Jn 11:45–57; 18:13–27; Acts 2:6.
calling: of the first disciples: Mt 4:18–25; Mk 1:16–20; Lk 5:1–11; Jn 1:35–51; of Matthew: Mt 9:9–13; Mk 2:13–17; Lk 5:27–32; rejected by the rich young man: Mt 19:16–30; Mk 10:17–29; Lk 18:18–30; of St Paul: Acts 9:1–19; 22:1–21; 26:9–18; Gal 1:11–12; 1 Tim 1:12–13; fidelity to: 1 Cor 7:17–24; Col 1:24–29. *See* discipleship.

Subject Index to New Testament

Cana: Jn 2:1–12; 4:46–54.
celibacy: *see* virginity.
charisms: Rom 12:1–8; 1 Cor 12:1–31; 14:1–40.
charity: its excellence: 1 Cor 13:13; the fullness of the Law: Rom 13:8–14; fraternal: Gal 6:1–10; 1 Thess 4:9–12; 1 Pet 1:22–25; 1 Jn 3:11–24; 1 Jn 4:7–21; 1 Pet 4:7–11; towards one's neighbour: Rom 12:9–21; must include all: Jas 2:1–13; discord originates in the passions: Jas 4:1–12. *See* love.
childhood, spiritual: Mt 18:1–14; 19:13–15; Mk 10:13–16; Lk 9:46–50; 10:21–24; 18:15–17.
children: their duties: Eph 6:1–4.
Christian, the: is free of the Law: Rom 7:1–6; is a child of God: 8:14–30; is called to be holy: 1 Pet 1:13–16; is ransomed by Christ's blood: 1 Pet 1:17–21; is the light of the world: Phil 2:12–18; his/her duties: Tit 2:1–10.
Christians, the early: everyday life: Acts 2:42–47; Acts 4:32–37; Rom 16:1–24; at prayer: 4:23–31; their fraternity: Acts 28:11–16. Their behaviour towards sinners: 1 Cor 5:9–13; towards their fellow Christians as regards pagan courts: 1 Col 6:1–11; towards waverers: Jude 22–23.
Church: founded by Jesus: Mt 16:13–20; new People of God: Mt 2:13–18; 21:28–46; Rev 7:1–17; God's household: 1 Tim 3:14–15; 2 Tim 2:14–21; Christ's Body: Eph 1:15–23; 4:1–16. Its unity: that of a body: 1 Cor 12:12–31; of a vine and branches: Jn 15:1–8. Its struggle and victory: Rev 12:1–18; 22:17–21; protected by Jesus: Mt 8:23–27; Mt 4:35–41; Mk 6:45–52; Jn 6:16–21.
circumcision; *of the heart*: Rom 2:25—3:8.
commandments: of love of God and neighbour: Mt 22:34–40; Mk 12:28–34; Lk 10:25–37; keeping them: 1 Jn 2:3–11. *See* love.
coming, second coming of Christ: 1 Thess 4:13; 5:5; 2 Thess 2:1–12; 2 Pet 1:19–21; errors about: 2 Pet 3:5–10. *See* last judgment, end of the world.
Communion of saints: 1 Cor 12:12–31.
concupiscence: and the Law: Rom 7:7–13.
Confirmation, sacrament of: Acts 8:14–25.
constancy: Jas 5:7–11; in the faith: 2 Thess 2:13–17; in work and in doing good: 2 Thess 3:6–15.
conversion: Lk 13:1–5; 15:11–32; 19:1–10; Eph 4:17–24.
Cornelius (centurion): Acts 10:1—11:18.
correction, fraternal: Mt 18:15–17; given by St Paul to the Corinthians: 1 Cor 4:14–21; 2 Cor 7:2–16; to the Galatians: Gal 4:12–20

covenant: sealed with Christ's blood: Mt 26:26–29; Mk 14:22–25; Lk 22:14–20; Old and New: 2 Cor 4:21–3l; New: Heb 8:1–13; 9:11–28.
creation: Christ's primary role in: Col 1:15–20; new creation: 2 Pet 3:11–13; Rev 21:1–27.
cross: bearing the cross: Mt 16:21–28; Mk 8:31—9:1; Lk 9:22–27; 2 Cor 11:21–33; Phil 1:27–30; Church's cross means salvation and wisdom: Jn 12:20–36; 1 Cor 1:18–31; Gal 6:11–18.
deacons: the Seven: Acts 6:1–7; qualities of: 1 Tim 3:8–13.
death: of Jesus on the cross: Mt 27:32–56; Mk 15:21–41; Lk 23:26–49; Jn 19:17–30; the resurrection of the dead: Mt 22:23–33; Mk 12:18–27; Lk 20:27–40. *See* resurrection.
deception: the instance of Ananias and Sapphira: Acts 5:1–11.
desertion of Christ by his disciples: Mt 26:30–35; Mk 14:26–31; Lk 22:31–33; Jn 13:36–38.
devil: his expulsion is a sign of the Kingdom of God: Lk 10:14–26; the father of lies: Jn 8:21–59; his opposition to the Church: Rev 12:1–18.
disciples: the calling of the first: Mt 4:18–25; Mk 1:16–20; Lk 5:1–11; Jn 1:35–51; the salt of the earth and the light of the world: Mt 5:13–16; will be hated by the world: Jn 15:18–26. *See* apostles, discipleship.
discipleship: Mt 13:53—16:20; what it involves: Mt 8:18–22; Lk 9:57–62; 14:25–35. *See* calling.
discord: its origin lies in the passions: Jas 4:1–12.
discourses (sermons): *of Jesus*: on the mount: Mt 5:1—7:29; on the plain: Lk 6:17–49; missionary: Mt 10:42; "parabolic": Mt 13:1–52; "of the Church" ("ecclesiastical"): Mt 18:1–35; eschatological: Mt 24:1—25:46; of the Bread of Life: Jn 6:26–59; of the Resurrection and the Life: Jn 11:1–44; at the Last Supper: Jn 14:1—16:31; *of Peter*: Acts 2:14–36; 3:11–26; 4:5–22; 10:24–43; 11:4–17; 15:7–11; *of Paul*: Acts 13:16–41; 17:22–31; 22:17–35; 22:1–21; 24:10–21; 26:2–23.
divorce: Mt 5:31–32; 19:1–12. *See* marriage.
doctrine: *see* teaching
Eucharist: institution of: Mt 26:26–29; Mk 14:22–25; Lk 22:14–20; 1 Cor 11:23–34; incompatible with idolatry: 1 Cor 10:14–22; abuses in celebration of: 1 Cor 11:17–22; to

Subject Index to New Testament

be received worthily: 1 Cor 11: 23–34; effects: Lk 9:10–17; Jesus, the Bread of Life: Jn 6:1–15, 26–59.

evangelization Rom 10:1–21; Col 4:2–6; 1 Thess 1:2–10.

examination, spirit of: *see* watchfulness.

example: Jesus': Jn 13:1–20; good example in general: 2 Cor 3:1–3; 1 Pet 2:11–12.

faith: of the Blessed Virgin: Lk 1:26–28, 39–56. *Examples of faith:* the patriarchs: Heb 11:1–22; Moses, the judges and the prophets: Heb 11:23–40; Abraham and Rahab: Jas 2:20–24. *Faith in Jesus Christ:* overcomes the world: 1 Jn 4:1–6; 1 Jn 5:1–5; leads to justification: Rom 3:21–31; of a centurion: Mt 8:5–13; Lk 7:1–10; of the paralytic's friends: Mt 9:1–7; 9:18–26; of Peter: Mt 14:22–33; of a Canaanite woman: Mt 15:21–28; Mk 7:24–30; of a leper: Mk 1:40–45; of Jairus and the woman with a hemorrhage: Mk 5:21–43; Lk 8:40–56; of Bartimeus: Mt 10:46–52. *Features of faith:* strength: Lk 17:5–6; Mt 17:14–20; it can grow: Mk 8:27–30; 9:14–29; constancy and protecting one's faith: Heb 2:1–4; 2 Thess 2:13–17; 1 Tim 2:18–21; 6:11–16; need for faith: Heb 3:7–4:11; faith and works: Jas 2:14–19; Mt 25:1–13; *Deposit of faith:* 1 Tim 6:20–21. *See* unbelief.

faithfulness: of God: Rom 9:1–13; 11:25–36; to the ministry: 2 Tim 2:1–17; the reward for: 2 Tim 4:6–8; motives for: Heb 10:19–39.

family: *see* marriage.

fasting: by Jesus: Mt 4:1–11; Mk 1:14–15; Lk 4:1–13; by the disciples: Mt 9:14–17; Mk 2:18–21; Lk 5:33–39; with the right intention: Mt 6:16–18.

filiation, divine: Rom 8:14–30; Gal 4:1–11; 1 Jn 3:1–2; 3:3–10; 5:18–21.

flesh: its works: Rom 7:14–24; 8:1–13; Gal 5:13–26.

forgiveness: of man by God: Mt 6:9,15; of sins: Mt 18:21–35; Lk 17:1–10; Jesus, the model of: Lk 23:26–49; of the sinful woman: Lk 7:36–50; of the adulterous woman: Jn: 8:1–11; of those who offend him, by St Paul: 2 Cor 2:5–11.

fraternity: *see* love; charity.

freedom: Christian: Gal 5:1–14; false: 1 Cor 6:12–14; and truth: Jn 8:21–59; Jude 3–4; liberation from sin: Rom 6:12–23.

Gabriel, St: Lk 1:5–38.

Gamaliel: Acts 5:34–42; 22:3.

generosity: Mt 12:41–44; 14:1–11; Lk 21:1–4; Jn 12:1–11; 2 Cor 8:7–17; 9:6–15; Phil 4:10–20. *See* self-surrender.

Gentiles: as guilty of sin as the Jews: Rom 1:18–32; 3:9–20; new People of God: Rom 11:13–24; reconciled in Christ: Eph 2:11–22.

gifts from God: 2 Pet 1:34. *See* charisms.

Gospel: preached by Jesus: Mk 1:14–15; will be a cause of persecution: Mt 24:1–13; proclaimed in the Church: 1 Cor 15:1–11.

heart: Jesus': Mt 9:35–38; sincerity of heart: Lk 6:39–49; circumcision of the heart: Rom 2:25–3:8.

heaven: where God dwells: Mt 6:9–13; men's destiny: Mt 7:21–23; Lk 13:25–30; Jn 14:1–14; is where Christ is: Mk 16:19; Lk 24:50–53; Acts 1:6–11; 1 Thess 1:6–10.

Herod Agrippa I: puts James to death and imprisons Peter: Acts 12:1–23.

Herod Agrippa II: hears Paul: Acts 25:13–27.

Herod Antipas: does not know who Jesus is: Mt 14:1–2; Mk 6:14–16; Lk 9:7–9; puts the Baptist to death: Mt 14:1–12; Mk 6:17–29; is criticized by Jesus: Lk 13:31–33; makes fun of Jesus: Lk 23:6–12.

Herod the Great: persecutes Jesus and kills the Innocents: Mt 2:1–18.

holiness: Mt 5:48; Rom 6:12–23; 1 Thess 4:1–8; 1 Pet 1:13–16.

hope: Lk 21:25–28; Heb 6:13–20; 2 Pet 3:11–16; based on Christ: Rom 5:1–11; and on God's promises: Heb 6:13–20; it sustains us in trials: 2 Cor 4:13–5:10; Judas' despair: 27:3–10.

humility: taught by Jesus: Mt 18:1–14; Mk 9:33–50; Lk 9:46–50; 14:7–11; of the Baptist: Lk 3:1–20; hymn to Christ's self-emptying: Phil 2:5–11.

hypocrisy: Lk 11:37–54.

idolatry: 1 Cor 8:1–6; Rev 2:1–7, 12–29.

Incarnation of Christ: Lk 1:26–38; the basis of Christian devotion and behaviour: Tit 2:11–15.

Israel: privileges and calling: Rom 9:1–33; unfaithfulness and salvation: Rom 10:1–11:12; its conversion: Rom 11:25–36; its rejection of Jesus: Mt 27:11–26; Mk 12:1–12.

James the Greater, St: his calling: Mt 4:18–25; Mk 1:16–20; Lk 5:1–11; one of the Twelve: Mt 10:1–4; Mk 3:13–19; Lk 6:12–16; Acts 1:12–14; in the Transfiguration: Mt 17:1–13; Mk 9:2–13; Lk 9:28–36; his request to Jesus: Mt 20:20–28; Mk 10:35–45; prayer in the garden: Mt 26:36–46; Mk 14:32–42; Lk 22:39–46; with the risen Jesus: Jn 21:2–14; martyrdom: Acts 12:2.

Subject Index to New Testament

James, the Less, St: one of the Twelve: Mt 10:1–4; Mk 3:13–19; Lk 6:12–16; Acts 1:12–14; a relative of Jesus and bishop of Jerusalem: Mt 13:55; Mk 6:3; Acts 12:17; 15:12–21; 21:18; 1 Cor 15:7; Gal 1:19; 2:9–12; Jude 1. *See* Introduction to the Letter of St James.

Jerusalem: Jesus' complaint and lamentation: Mt 23:37–39; Lk 19:41–44; its time of tribulation: Lk 21:20–24; council of: Acts 15:3–35.

Jesus Christ: genealogy: Mt 1:1–17; Lk 3:23–38; born of a virgin: Mt 1:1–17; 18–25; Lk 1:26–38; 2:1–27; adored by Magi: Mt 2:1–12; and by shepherds: Lk 2:8–20; circumcised on the eight day: Lk 2:21; presented in the temple: Lk 2:22–24; flees to Egypt: Mt 2:13–18; found by his parents in the temple: Lk 2:41–50. *Hidden life in Nazareth*: Mt 2:19–23; 13:53–58; Mk 6:1–6; Lk 2:39–40; 2:51–52. *Public life*: see fasting; Baptism; discourses; miracles; parables; preaching; Kingdom of God, etc. *His passion brings salvation*: announcement of his passion and glorification: Mt 16:21–28; 17:22–27; 20:17–19; 26:1–5; Mk 8:31—9:1; 8:30–32; 10:32–34; Lk 9:22–27; 43–45; 18:31–34; Jn 12:20–36; entry into Jerusalem: Mt 21:1–11; Mark 11:1–11; Lk 19:28–40; Jn 12:12–19; purification of temple: Mt 21:12–17; Mk 11:12–23; Lk 19:45–48; anointing at Bethany: Mt 26:6–16; Mk 14:2–11; Jn 12:1–11; cleans his disciples' feet: Jn 13:1–20; institution of the Eucharist: Mt 26:26–29; Mk 14:22–25; Lk 22:14–20; prayer and agony in the garden: Mt 26:36–46; Mk 14:32–42; Lk 22:39–46; his arrest: Mt 26:47–56; Mk 14:43–52; Lk 22:47–53; Jn 18:1–12; is interrogated by the chief priests: Mt 26:57–68; Mk 14:53–65; Lk 22:66–71; Jn 12:13–27; judged by Pilate: Mt 27:11–26; Mk 15:1–15; Lk 23:1–5; 13–25; Jn 18:28—19:16; insults done him: Mt 27:27–31; Mk 15:16–20; Lk 22:63–65; Jn 19:1–5. *Death and resurrection:* was crucified and died on the cross: Mt 27:32–55; Mk 15:21–40; Lk 23:26–49; Jn 19:17–30; buried: Mt 27:57–66; Mk 15:42–47; Lk 23:50–66; his side lanced; burial: Jn 19:31–42; resurrection: Mt 28:1–10; Mk 16:1–8; Lk 24:1–12; Jn 20:1–10. *See* appearances. *Titles:* servant of God: Mt 12:15–21; Messiah, King, Son of David: Mt 21:1–11; Mk 11:1–11; Lk 19:28–40; Jn 12:12–19; Lord: Mt 22:41–46; Mk 12:35–37; Lk 20:41–44; Son of man in glory: Mt 24:29–31; Mk 13:24–27; Lk 21:25–28; Word: Jn 1:1–18; Lamb of God, Teacher, Son of God, King of Israel, Christ, Son of Man: Jn 1:35–51; Son of God: Rom 1:1–15; first-born of creation: Col 1:15–20; high priest and mediator: Heb 9:11–28. *See* Revelation; salvation; etc.

Jews: chosen people: Jn 4:1–43; opposed to Jesus: Jn 9:1–40; as guilty of sin as the gentiles are: Rom 2:1–24; 3:9–20. *See* Israel.

John the Baptist, St: annunciation: Lk 1:5–25; birth and circumcision: Lk 1:57–66; mission and preaching: Mt 3:1–12; Mk 1:1–8; Lk 3:1–20; bears witness about Jesus: Jn 1:19–34; disciples: Acts 19:1–7; his greatness: Mt 11:1–15; Lk 7:18–30; imprisonment and death: Mt 14:1–12; Mk 6:17–29; Lk 3:19–20.

John the Evangelist: his calling: Mt 4:18–25; Mt 1:16–20; Lk 5:1–11; one of the Twelve: Mt 10:1–4; Mk 3:13–19; Lk 6:12–16; Acts 1:12–14; at the Transfiguration: Mt 17:1–13; Mk 9:2–13; Lk 9:28–36; his request to Jesus: Mt 20:20–28; Mk 10:35–45; in the garden of olives: Mt 26:36–46; Mk 14:32–42; Lk 22:39–46; the beloved disciple: Jn 13:23; 19:17–30; 20:1–9; 21:1–25; in the early Church: Acts 3:1–4:22. *See* Introduction to the Gospels; Introduction to the Letters of St John.

Joseph of Arimathea: Mt 27:57–66; Mk 15:42–47; Lk 23:50–56; Jn 19:31–42.

Joseph, St: Mt 1:1—2:23; 13:55; Mk 6:3; Lk 1:27; 2:4, 16; 3:23; 4:22; Jn 1:45; 6:42.

joy: Mary's: Lk 1:46–56; Zechariah's: Lk 1:67–80; at the coming of Jesus: Mk 2:18–22; the fullness of joy: Jn 16:1–31; rejoice always: Phil 4:1–19.

Judas Iscariot: Jesus predicts his treachery: Lk 22:21–23; Jn 13:21–32; his betrayal of Jesus: Mt 26:6–16; Mk 14:3–11; Lk 21:1–6; despair and death: Mt 27:3–10.

judging: it is for God to judge: Jn 5:19–46; on not judging one's neighbour: Mt 7:1–5. *See* judgment.

judgment: last judgment: Mt 7:21–23; 13:24–52; 25:31–46; Rev 14:14–20; 20:11–15; and punishment: 2 Thess 1:6–10; particular judgment and last judgment: Heb 9:11–28.

justification: a free gift through faith in Christ: Rom 3:21–31; Gal 3:1–14; Phil 3:7–11.

Subject Index to New Testament

Kingdom of God: preached by Jesus: Mt 4:12–25; taught in parables and explained to his disciples: Mk 4:1–34; Jesus' actions and miracles are signs that the K. has come: Mt 8:14–17; Lk 10:14–26; its coming: Lk 17:20–37; its establishment: Rev 21:1—22:5.

law: Jesus and his teaching mark the fullness of the Law: Mt 5:17–48; Jesus is the Law's interpreter: Mt 12:1–14; the Law and the Gospel: Lk 16:16–18; charity, the fullness of the Law: Rom 13:8–14; the Christian is free of the Law: Rom 7:1–6; the Law and man's passions: Rom 7:7–13; the Law and the promise: Gal 3:15–29; the purpose of the Law: Acts 7:1–53; 1 Tim 1:8–11.

Lazarus: Jn 11:1–44; 12:1–11.

life, Christian: ordinary life: Mk 6:1–6; Lk 2:51–52; 1 Thess 4:12–22; Heb 13:1–6; 1 Pet 5:5–11; 2 Pet 3:11–16; renewed in the Spirit: Rom 8:1–13; Tit 3:3–8; supernatural: Col 3:1–4; progress in: Col 3:12–17.

life, eternal: the narrow gate, the hard way: Mt 7:13–14; Lk 13:22–30.

light: God's light: 1 Jn 1:5; Jesus, the light of the world: Jn 1:12–20; Christianity the light of the world: Mt 5:14–16; Phil 2:12–18; 1 Jn 1:6–22.

love: God is Love: 1 Jn 4:7–21; the twofold commandment of love: Mt 22:34–40; Mk 12:28–34; Lk 10:25–37; the new commandment: Jn 13:33–38; 15:9–17; 2 Jn 2–6; of one's neighbour: Mt 5:17–43; Mt 25:31–46; brotherly: 1 Pet 3:8–12; of one's enemies: Lk 6:27–38; the golden rule: Mt 7:12. *See* charity.

Luke, St: Col 4:14; 2 Tim 4:11; Philem 24. *See* Introduction to the Gospel of St Luke; Introduction to the Acts of the Apostles.

lukewarmness: Rev 3:14–22.

Mark St: Acts 12:12, 25; 13:4–14; 11:36–41; Col 4:10; 2 Tim 4:11; Philem 24; 1 Pet 5:13. *See* Introduction to the Gospel of St Mark.

marriage: Mt 19:1–12; indissoluble: Mk 10:1–12; 1 Cor 1:10–11; blessed by Jesus at Cana: Jn 12:1–12; Pauline privilege: 1 Cor 1:12–16; relations between husband and wife: 1 Cor 7:1–9; Eph 5:21–33; family life: Col 3:18—4:1; 1 Pet 3:1–7; evangelical zeal of Christian married couples: Acts 18:24–28.

Martha, sister of Mary and Lazarus: welcomes Jesus: Lk 10:38–42; at the raising of Lazarus: Jn 11:1–44.

martyrdom: of the Innocents: Mt 2:13–18; of John the Baptist: Mt 14:1–12; Mk 6:17–29; of St Stephen: Acts 7:54–60.

Mary Magdalen: Mk 16:9–11; Jn 20:11–18.

Mary, Mother of Jesus: conception of Jesus, and his infancy: Lk 1:26–56; 2:1–52; in Jesus' public life: Mt 12:46–50; Mk 3:31–35; Lk 8:19–21; 11:27–28; Jn 2:1–12; 19:16–30; in the early Church: Acts 1:12–14. *Virtues:* doing God's will: Mk 3:31–35; virginity: Mt 12:46–50; Lk 1:26–38; faith and obedience: Lk 1:26–38; 39–56; 8:19–21; faithfulness: Lk 11:27–28; her solicitude: Jn 2:12; 19:16–30; Mother of the Church: Acts 1:12–14; the woman of the Apocalypse: Rev 12:1–18.

Mary, the sister of Martha: is attentive to Jesus: Lk 10:38–42; at the raising of Lazarus: Jn 11:1–44; anoints Jesus' feet: Jn 12:1–11.

Mass, the: Heb 10:1–18. *See* Eucharist.

masters: duties of: Eph 6:5–9.

Matthew, St: his calling: Mt 9:1–13; Mk 2:13–17; Lk 5:27–32; one of the Twelve: Mt 10:1–4; Mk 3:13–19; Lk 6:12–16; Acts 1:12–14. *See* Introduction to the Gospel of St Matthew

Matthias, St: Acts 1:15–26.

mercy: Mt 20:1–16; Lk 15:1–32; Jn 8:1–11; shown by Jesus: Mt 20:29–34; Lk 7:11–17.

Michael, St: Jude 9; Rev 12:7.

ministry: ministers of God: 2 Cor 11:1–6; their lifestyle: 1 Tim 4:12—5:2. *Apostolic ministry:* its nature: 1 Cor 3:4–23; 1 Cor 4:1–7; 2 Cor 5:11–21; superior to that of the Old Covenant: 2 Cor 3:4–18.

miracles: a) worked by Jesus. *Raising people to life*: Lazarus: Jn 11:1–44; the daughter of Jairus: Mt 9:18–24; Mk 5:21–42; Lk 8:40–55; the son of the widow of Nain: Lk 7:11–17. *Cures:* two blind men: Mt 9:27–31; the blind man of Bethsaida: Mk 8:22–26; the man blind from birth: Jn 9:1–13; the blind man (Bartimeus) of Jericho: Mk 10:46–52; Lk 18:35–43; the possessed man/men of Gadara: Mt 8:28–34; Mk 5:1–20; Lk 8:26–39; a dumb man: Mt 9:32–34; the woman with a hemorrhage: Mt 9:18–24; Mk 21–42; Lk 8:40–55; a man with dropsy: Lk 14:1–6; the daughter of the Cyro-Phoenician woman: Mt 15:21–28; Mk 7:24–30; the son of the royal official: Jn 4:46–54; the man with the withered hand: Mt 12:9–14; Mk 3:1–6; Lk 6:6–11; the ten lepers: Lk 17:11–19; a leper: Mt 12:9–14; Mk 3:1–6; Lk 5:12–16; the lunatic boy: Mt 17:14–20; Mk 8:14–29; Lk 9:37–43; a woman on the sabbath: Lk 13:10–17; a paralyzed man: Mt

Subject Index to New Testament

miracles: a) *(cont.)* 9:1–7; Mk 2:1–12; Lk 5:17–26; the paralyzed man at the pool: Jn 51–18; a centurion's servant: Mt 8:5–13; Lk 7:1–10; Peter's sister-in-law; Mt 8:14–15; Mk 1:29–31; Lk 4:38–39; a deaf man: Mk 7:31–36; many people near the Sea of Galilee: Mk 3:7–12; many infirm and possessed: Mt 8:16–17; Mk 1:32–34; Lk 4:40–41; Mk 1:32–34; many at Gennesaret: Mt 14:34–36; Mk 6:53–56; many sick people: Mt 15:29–31. *Over elements of nature*: walking on water: Mt 14:22–32; Mk 6:45–52; Jn 6:16–21; multiplication of loaves: Mt 14:13–21; 15:32–39; Mk 6:30–44; 8:1–10; Lk 9:10–17; Jn 6:1–15; miraculous draught of fish: Lk 5:1–11; Jn 21:1–14; the calming of the storm: Mt 8:23–27; Mk 4:35–41; Lk 8:22–25. *Their meaning as signs of other things*: Mt 8:14–17; Mt 15:29—16:12; Mk 2:1–12; Jn 2:1–12; 11:1–44; Acts 5:12–16.

b) *worked by Apostles:* Peter and John cure a man lame from birth: Acts 3:1–11; Peter cures a lame man at Lydda: Acts 9:32–35; Peter raises Tabitha in Joppa: Acts 9:36–43; Peter cures a lame man at Lystra: Acts 14:8–18; Paul raises Eutychus at Troas: Acts 20:7–11.

mission, apostolic: Christ's instructions to the Twelve: Mt 10:16–42; Mk 6:6–13; to the seventy: Lk 10:1–12; St Paul's: Eph 3:1–13.

Moses: his ministry and that of Christ: Heb 3:1–6; the yoke of the Law of Moses and that of Jesus: Mt 11:25–30; Jesus, the new Moses: Mt 2:13–18; 4:1–11; 5:17–48.

neighbour: love for: Mt 5:17–42; 22:34–40; 25:31–46; Mk 12:28–34; Lk 10:25–37; Rom 12:9–21; not judging him/her: Mt 7:1–5; being understanding towards: Rom 14:1–12.

Nicodemus: Jn 3:1–36; 7:50; 19:31–42.

obedience: Christ's example: Phil 2:5–11; to civil authorities: Rom 13:1–7; 1 Pet 13–17; to pastors: Heb 13:7–19.

Our Father prayer: Mt 6:5–15; Lk 11:1–4.

parables: the faithful and prudent steward: Lk 12:35–48; the unfaithful steward: Lk 16:1–15; the Good Samaritan: Lk 10:25–37; the Pharisee and the tax collector: Lk 18:9–14; the grain of mustard seed: Mt 13:31–32; Lk 13:18–19; Mk 4:30–32; the prodigal son: Lk 15:1–32; the unjust judge: Lk 15:11–32; the rich man and the poor man: Lk 16:19–31; the foolish rich man: Lk 12:13–21; the sower: Mt 13:1–23; Mk 4:1–20; Lk 8:1–15; the merciless servant: Mt 18:21–35; the faithful servant: Mt 24:45–51; the hidden treasure: Mt 13:44; the weeds: Mt 13:24–30, 36–43; the lost coin: Lk 15:8–10; the barren fig-tree: Lk 13:6–9; the lamp: Mk 4:21–23; Lk 8:16–18; the leaven: Mt 13:33; Lk 13:20–21; the measure: Mk 4:24–25; the lost sheep: Mt 18:12–14; Lk 15:1–7; the pearl: Mt 13:45; the net: Mt 13:44–50; the seed: Mk 4:26–29; the sheep and the goats: Mt 25:31–46; the wise and foolish maidens: Mt 25:1–13; the two sons: Mt 21:28–32; those invited to a banquet: Lk 14:7–11; the workers in the vineyard: Mt 22:1–14; Lk 14:15–24; those invited to a wedding: Mt 22:1–14; Lk 14:7–11; the workers in the vineyard: Mt 20:1–16; the talents: Mt 25:14–30; Lk 19:11–27; the murderous tenants: Mt 21:33–46; Mk 12:1–12; Lk 20:9–19; the meaning of the parables: Mt 13:1–23; Mk 4:1–20; Lk 8:1–15.

parents: duties of: Eph 6:1–4.

patience: God's: Mt 11:21–35; Lk 13:6–9; the Christian's: Lk 21:7–19; towards those who sin: 2 Rom 2:22–26.

Paul, St: *life*: his calling: Acts 9:1–9; 22:1–21; 26:9–18; Gal 1:11–12; 1 Tim 1:12–13; baptism and start of his work of evangelization: Acts 9:10–30; apostolic journeys: Acts 13:1—14:28; 15:35—18:22; 18:23—21:16; 27:1—28:16. *Discourses*: Acts 13:16–41; 17:22–31; 20:17–35; 22:1–21; 24:10–21; 26:2–23. *Apostolic ministry*: he glories in Christ: Rom 15:22–33; 1 Cor 2:1–5; reasons for boasting: 2 Cor 11:16—12:18; visions and revelations: 2 Cor 12:1–10; the hard life of an apostle: 1 Cor 4:8–13; he gives up everything for the sake of the apostolate: 1 Cor 9:15–23; tribulation: 2 Cor 4:7–12; 11:21–33; his response to his calling: Col 1:4–29; is sincere in his actions: 2 Cor 4:1–6; his solicitude for all: Col 2:1–3; 1 Thess 2:17–20; apostolic zeal: Acts 26:24–32. *See* Introduction to the Letters of St Paul.

peace: a gift from Jesus: Lk 24:36; Jn 14:27; 20:19–31; seeking it: Heb 12:14–29; not letting difficulties undermine it: Phil 4:10–20.

penance, sacrament of: Jn 20:19–31. *See* fasting, conversions, power of binding and loosing.

Subject Index to New Testament

persecution on account of the Gospel: Mt 24:3–13; to be faced up to bravely: Lk 12:1–12; with Jesus' help: Acts 4:1–22; benefits of: Acts 8:1–8; 14:19–28.

perseverance: in the Christian life: Lk 8:15; 21:7–19; in prayer: Lk 18:1–7; in faith: Heb 6:4–12; 10:19–39; 1 Jn 2:18–29; with one's eyes on Christ: Heb 12:1–3; in the face of trials: Heb 12:4–13; reasons for: 1 Pet 1:3–12; in preaching: 2 Tim 4:1–5. *See* constancy.

Peter, St: his life with Jesus: his calling: Mt 4:18–25; Mk 1:16–20; Lk 5:1–11; Jn 1:35–51; he sinks in the lake due to lack of faith: Mt 14:22–32; he professes Jesus to be the Messiah: Mt 16:13–20; Mk 8:27–30; Lk 9:18–21; he is made first among the apostles: Mt 16:13–20; Jn 21:15–23; Jesus associates him with his payment of temple tax: Mt 17:22–26; he denies Jesus: Mt 26:69–75; Mk 14:66–72; Lk 22:54–61; Jn 18:13–27; Jesus predicts his denials and tells him to encourage his brethren: Lk 22:31–34. His apostolic activity in the early Church: Acts 1–6; 8:1–25; 9:32—12:19; 15:1–35. Discourses: Acts 2:14–36; 3:11–26; 4:5–22; 10:34–43; 11:4–17; 15:7–11. *See* Introduction to the Letters of St Peter.

Pharisees: misrepresent Jesus: Mt 12:22–37; they try to trick him: Mt 16:1–12; Mk 8:11–21; Jesus censures them: Mt 23:1–36; Lk 11:37–54.

Philip, St: Mt 10:1–4; Mk 3:13–19; Lk 6:12–16; Jn 1:35–51; 6:5–7; 12:21–22; 14:8–9; Acts 1:12–14.

Philip the Deacon: Acts 6:5; 8:5–8, 26–40.

Pilate: Mt 27:11–26; Mk 15:1–15; Lk 23:1–5, 13–25; Jn 18:28—19:16.

poverty: Jesus': Lk 2:1–21; detachment needed to follow Jesus: Mt 19:16–30; Mk 10:17–31; Lk 18:18–30; Acts 4:32–37; 1 Tim 6:3–10; attitude towards the poor: Lk 14:12–14. *See* riches.

power(s): Jesus': Mt 8:28–34; 9:1–18; Mt 21:23–27; Mk 11:27–33; Lk 20:1–8; Jn 5:19–47; of Jesus' word: Mk 1:21–28; Lk 4:31–37; of binding and losing: Mt 16:13–20; 18:15–20.

praise: Eph 3:20–21; 1 Pet 1:3–12; in the liturgy: Rev 4:1–11; in prayer: Rev 15:1–4. *See* thanksgiving.

prayer: *of Jesus*: in the Garden of Olives: Mt 26:36–46; Mk 12:32–42; Lk 22:39–46; early, in a place apart: Mk 1:35–39; prior to important events: Lk 6:12–16; his priestly prayer: Jn 17:1–26; *of St Paul*: for the Ephesians: Eph 3:14–19; for the Colossians: Col 1:9–14; for the Thessalonians: 2 Thess 1:11–12; *of the first Christians*: Acts 4:23–31. *Qualities:* with the right intention: Mt 6:5–14; perseverance and faith: Mt 15:21–28; constant: 1 Thess 5:12–22; effective: Mt 7:7–11; Lk 10:5–13; Jas 5:13–18; in common: Mt 18:19–20; of praise: Rev 15:1–4.

preaching: the start of Jesus' preaching in Galilee: Mt 1:14–15; in Nazareth: Lk 4:16–30; perseverance in preaching: 2 Tim 4:1–5. *See* discourses; teaching; mission, apostolic.

presbyters/priests: selection and qualities: 1 Tim 5:17–25; Tit 1:5–9; duties: 1 Pet 5:1–4.

priesthood: of Christ, and Christian priesthood: Heb 4:14–16; established by God: Heb 5:1–10; according to the order of Melchizedek: Heb 7:1–3; Christ's superior to that of descendants of Abraham: Heb 7:4–19, and is perfect: Heb 7:20–28; 8:1–13; common priesthood of the Christian faithful: 1 Pet 2:4–10; priestly prayer of Jesus: Jn 17:1–26.

primacy of Peter: Mt 16:13–20; Lk 22:31–34; Jn 21:15–23.

prophecy by Jesus: of his passion and resurrection: Mt 16:21–28; 17:22–27; 20:17–19; 26:1–5; Mk 8:31—9:1; 8:30–32; 10:32–34; Lk 9:22–27; 9:43–45; 18:31–34; Jn 12:20–36; of Judas' treachery: Lk 22:21–23; Jn 13:21–32; of Peter's denials: Lk 23:31–34; Jn 13:33–38; of the destruction of the temple: Mt 25:1–2; Mk 13:1–2; Lk 21:5–6; of his second coming: Mt 24:29–31; Mk 13:24–27; Lk 21:25–28.

prophets: Simeon and Anna: Lk 2:25–38; John the Baptist, Jesus' prophet: Mt 3:1–17; Mk 1:1–11; Lk 3:1–18; Jn 1:19–34. *False prophets*: description: 1 Tim 6:3–10; their behaviour: 2 Pet 2:10–19; Jude 8–13; the harm they do: 2 Pet 2:1–3; the punishment that awaits them: 2 Pet 2:4–10; Jude 5–7; keeping away from them: Mt 7:15–20; 1 Tim 1:3–7; 4:1–10; Tit 1:10–16; 2 Jn 7–11; 2 Tim 3:1–10; faith in Jesus defeats them: 1 Jn 4:1–11.

providence of God: Mt 6:19–33; towards the apostles: Mt 10:16–42; trust in providence: Jas 4:13–17.

prudence: prudent maidens: Mt 25:1–13.

purity: true purity: Mt 15:1–20; Mk 7:1–23; gravity of fornication and the dignity of the human body: 1 Cor 6:12–20; 2 Pet 2:4–10; and Christian living: Eph 5:1–17; Thess 4:1–8; Heb 12:14–29.

Subject Index to New Testament

rectitude of intention: Mt 6:1–34; Lk 6:39–49; 11:33–36; necessary in order to recognize Christ: Jn 7:1–30.

relationships: true relationship with Jesus: Mt 12:46–50; Mk 3:31–35; Lk 8:19–21; Jesus' relatives are uneasy: Mk 3:20–21.

religion, piety: 1 Tim 4:1–11; the mystery of our religion: 1 Tim 3:16; the rewards of piety: Acts 9:36–43.

renunciation, Christian: Mt: 16:21–28; Mk 8:31—9:1; Lk 9:22–27.

resoluteness: 2 Tim 2:1–7.

resurrection: of Jesus: Mt 28:1–10; Mk 16:1–8; Lk 24:1–12; Jn 20:1–10; 1 Cor 15:1–11; the basis of our faith: 1 Cor 15:12–19; the cause of our resurrection:1 Cor 15:20–34; of the dead: Mt 22:23–33; Mk 12:18–27; Lk 20:27–40; the manner of resurrection: 1 Cor 15:35–58; Jesus is the Resurrection and the Life: Jn 11:1–44. *See also* miracles.

revelation: Jesus reveals the Father: Mt 17:1–13; Jn 14:1–14; Heb 1:1–4; Rev 5:1–14; to St Paul, of his ministry: Eph 3:1–13.

riches: Mt 19:16–30; Mk 10:23–31; Lk 12:13–34; 16:1–15, 19–31; 18:18–30; Jas 5:1–6; 1 Tim 6:17–19; Rev 18:1–24.

sabbath: Jesus, lord of the sabbath: Mt 12:1–8; Mk 2:23–28; Lk 6:1–5; Jesus cures on the s.: Mt 12:9–14; Mk 3:1–16; Lk 6:6–11; 13:10–17; 14:1–6; Jn 5:1–18.

sacrifice(s): the Sacrifice of Christ and its power: Rom 5:1–11; Heb 10:5–18; of Old and New Law, compared: Heb 10:1–4.

Sadducees: try to trick Jesus: Mt 16:1–12; 22:23–33; Lk 20:27–40.

sadness: combatted by prayer: Jas 5:13–18.

salt: the disciples, the salt of the earth: Mt 5:13.

salvation: plan of salvation; Eph 1:3–14; a gratuitous gift from God: Eph 2:1–10; extends to all: Mt 2:1–12; Mk 2:13–17; 7:24–30; 8:1–10; Lk 13:20–30.

sanhedrin (council): decrees the death of Jesus: Jn 11:45–57; interrogates Peter and John: Acts 4:5–22; interrogates the apostles: Acts 5:26–33.

scandal: Mt 18:1–18; Mk 8:33–50; Lk 17:1–10; Rom 14:13–23; 1 Cor 8:7–13.

scribes: misrepresent Jesus: Mk 3:22–30; seek his arrest: Mk 14:1–2; censured by Jesus: Mk 12:38–40; Lk 11:37–54; 20:45–47.

Scripture, Holy: bears witness to Christ: Jn 5:19–47; 10:31–42; 1 Cor 15:1–11; nature and benefit of: 2 Tim 3:14–17; 2 Pet 1:19–21; its importance in evangelization: Acts 8:26–40; is fulfilled in Jesus: Introduction to St Matthew's Gospel: cf. also: Mt 26:1–16, 47–56; 27:3–10.

self-surrender: of Jesus to the Father: Mt 26:36–46; Mk 14:32–42; Lk 22:39–46; in following Jesus: Lk 14:25–35; its reward: Mt 13:44–46; 19:16–30; Mk 10:17–31; Lk 18:18–30.

servants: Eph 6:5–9; 1 Tim 6:1–2; Philem 1–21; 1 Pet 2:18–25.

service, spirit of: a feature of Jesus and of his followers: Mt 20:28; 24:1–51; Mk 9:33–50; 10:32–45; Jn 13:1–20; service in the ministry: 1 Cor 9:15–23.

shepherd, good: Jesus, the Good Shepherd: Lk 15:1–10; Jn 10:1–21; the need to pray for: Mt 9:35–38.

Simon Peter: See Peter, St.

Simon the Apostle, St: Mt 10:1–4; Mk 3:13–19; Lk 6:12–16; Acts 1:12–14.

sin: cannot be erased by the sacrifices of the Old Covenant: Heb 10:1–4; grace sets us free: Rom 6:12–33. Original sin: Rom 5:17. Sin against the Holy Spirit: Mt 12:22–37; Mt 3:22–30; Heb 6:4–12; of simony: Acts 8:18–25. The Christian has broken with sin: Col 3:5–11; and rejected it: 1 Jn 1:6—2:2; sinners should be prayed for: 1 Jn 5:4–17; but not associated with: 1 Cor 5:9–13.

Spirit, Holy and the conception of Jesus: Mt 1:18–25; Lk 1:26–38; in Jesus' life and mission: Mt 4:1; Mk 1:12; Lk 4:1,13–40; is promised by Jesus: Lk 11:5–13; Jn 14:15–31. *His action*: Jn 16:1–15; at Pentecost: Acts 2:1–13; and the calling of the Gentiles: Acts 10:1–48; his help to the Apostles: Acts 15:22–29; in the early Church: Acts 16:1–10. *Life in the Spirit*: Rom 8:1–12; fruits: Gal 5:13–26; presence in the Church: 2 Tim 1:8–14; sin against the Holy Spirit: Mt 12:22–37; Mk 3:22–30; Heb 6:4–12.

Stephen, St: Acts 6:8—7:60.

struggle, ascetical: Rom 7:14–24; 1 Cor 9:24–27; Eph 5:8–20; 6:10–20; Phil 1:27–30; 3:12–16; 1 Pet 15:5–11; Rev 19:11–21.

suffering: value of Jesus': Mt 27:27–35; value of suffering: Phil 2:25–30; Col 1:24–29; 2 Thess 1:3–5; Jas 1:2–13; 1 Pet 3:13–17. *See* cross, trials.

Supper, Last: Mt 26:17–25; Mk 14:12–21; Lk 22:7–20.

Subject Index to New Testament

teaching: Jesus' teaching is the fullness of the Law: Mt 5:17–48; authority of Jesus': Mt 7:28–29; teaching is handed down: 2 Pet 3:1–2; the need for instruction in the faith: Heb 5:11—6:3; empty philosophy and vain disputes: Col 2:9–15; 2 Tim 2:14–21; primitive kerygma: Acts 2:14–41; 13:15–43. *See* discourses; preaching.

temple: Jesus pays the temple tax: Mt 17:22–26; Jesus cleanses the temple: Mt 21:12–17; Mk 11:12–25; Lk 19:45–48; Jn 2:13–25; its destruction foretold: Mt 24:1–2; Mk 13:1–2; Lk 21:5–6; the widow's penny: Mt 12:41–44; Lk 21:1–4; its transitory role: Acts 7:1–53.

temptations: of Jesus: Mt 4:1–11; Mk 1:12–13; Lk 4:1–13; history carries lessons to help us deal with temptation: 1 Cor 10:1–13; source of: Jas 1:13–18.

thanksgiving: by Jesus to the Father: Mt 11:25–30; Lk 10:21–24; by a Samaritan to Jesus: Lk 17:11–19; to God for his doings: 1 Pet 1:3–12; by St Paul; 1 Cor 1:4–9; 2 Cor 1:3–11; Eph 1:15–23; Phil 1:3–11; 4:10–20; Col 1:3–8; 1 Thess 1:2–10; 2 Thess 1:3–5.

Thomas the Apostle, St: Jn 11:16; 14:5; 20:24–29; one of the Twelve: Mt 10:1–14; Mk 3:13–19; Lk 6:12–16; Acts 1:12–14.

tolerance: Mk 9:33–50; Lk 9:46–50.

tradition(s): of the ancients: Mt 15:1–20; Mk 7:1–23; the teaching of tradition: 2 Pet 3:1–2.

Transfiguration, the: Mt 17:1–13; Mk 9:2–13; Lk 9:28–36; 2 Pet 1:16–18.

trials and tribulations: Mt 24:3–28; Mk 13:3–23; Lk 21:7–19; Rev 6:1–17; 11:1–14; persevering when they occur: Heb 12:4–13; the Christian meaning of: 1 Pet 4:12–19; in St Paul's life: 2 Cor 12:21–33; 1 Thess 3:1–5. *See* persecution

tribute tax: Jesus pays the temple tax: Mt 17:22–26; tribute to Caesar: Mt 22:15–22; Mk 12:13–17; Lk 20:20–26.

Trinity, Blessed: Jn 16: 1–15; Eph 2:11–22; 2 Cor 1:15—2:4; Jesus' Baptism: Mt 1:9–13; at the Transfiguration: Lk 9:28–36.

trust: in Providence: Mt 6:19–33; Rom 8:31–39; Jas 4:13–17; in Church's priesthood: Heb 4:14–16.

truth: knowing it by being disciples of Jesus: Jn 8:21–59; Jesus is the Truth; Jn 14:1–4; abiding in the truth; 1 Jn 2:18–29.

unbelief: Mt 11:16–19; 11:20–24; Lk 7:31–35; 10:13–16; Jn 8:21–59; 12:37–50.

understanding: putting oneself in another's shoes: Rom 14:1–12; Christ's example: Rom 15:1–13.

unity, solidarity: like vine and branches: Jn 15:1–18; like a body: Rom 12:1–8; 1 Cor 12:12–31; Eph 4:1–16; recommended: 1 Cor 1:10–17; Phil 2:1–4.

universality: the Gospel is revealed to all: Mt 8:5–13; Mk 5:1–20; Lk 6:17–19; 10:1–12; universality of salvation: Mk 2:13–17; 7:24–30; 8:1–10; Lk 13:22–30.

virginity: Mt 19:1–12; its excellence: 1 Cor 7:25–38.

watchfulness: Mt 22:1–14; 24:42–51; Lk 12:35–48; 21:5–36; 2 Pet 3:5–10.

way: Jesus is the Way: Jn 14:1–14; the nascent Church is called the 'Way': Acts 9:2; 19:23; 22:4; 24:14, 22.

will of God: John the Baptist and Jesus obey it: Mt 3:13–17; doing it really: Mt 7:21ff; by doing it one is truly a relation of Jesus: Mt 12:46–50; Mk 3:31–35; discovering it through prayer: Mt 26:31–46; accepting it brings peace: Acts 21:1–14; God wants all to be saved: 1 Tim 2:1–7.

wisdom: Jesus, the wisdom of God: Mt 11:16–19; 12:38–42; Lk 7:31–35; 11:29–32; of the cross: 1 Cor 1:18–31; 2:1–5; hidden in Christ: Col 2:1–8; revealed by God: 1 Cor 2:6–16; true and false w.: Jas 3:13–18; must be accompanied by charity: 1 Cor 8:1–6.

witness, bearing of: by God about the Son: 1 Jn 5:6–12; by the Baptist about Jesus: Jn 1:12–34; 3:22–36.

women: the sinner pardoned by Jesus: Lk 7:36–50; Jn 8:1–11; those who follow Jesus: Lk 8:1–3; Jesus' appearance to the women: Mt 28:1–10; women in the Church: 1 Cor 11:1–16; their prayer: 2 Tim 2:11–14; the woman of the Apocalypse: Rev 12:1–18.

word of God: its power: Heb 4:12–13; guarding it is a sign of happiness and solidarity with Jesus: Lk 8:19–21; 10:38–42; 11:27–28; putting it into practice: Jas 1:19–27.

work: 1 Thess 4:9–12; 2 Thess 3:6–15.

world: God's love for: Jn 3:1–21; keeping pure from: Jn 15:18–27; 2 Pet 2:15–17; 1 Jn 2:15–17

world, end of: will come: Mt 24:32–35; Rom 13:28–31; Lk 21:29–33; when it will be: Mt 24:36–41; Mk 13:32–37; Lk 17:22–37.